THE COMIC BOOK HEROES

THE COMIC BOOK HEROES

GERARD JONES AND WILL JACOBS

PRIMA PUBLISHING

ISBN: 0-7615-0393-5
Library of Congress Catalog Card Number: 95-70968
96 97 98 99 GG 10 9 8 7 6 5 4 3 2 1
Printed in the United States of America

How to Order

Single copies may be ordered from Prima Publishing, P.O. Box 1260BK, Rocklin, CA 95677; telephone (916) 632-4400. Quantity discounts are also available. On your letterhead, include information concerning the intended use of the books and the number of books you wish to purchase.

Visit us online at http://www.primapublishing.com

For Russell and Leslie Jones and Ian and Mary Jacobs,
who waited around in drugstores and drove us to dingy shops in the armpits of cities
and let us blow our allowances to satisfy our hunger
for all this glorious garbage.

CONTENTS

PART TWO: **THE AWKWARD AGE**

PART THREE: **THE GILDED AGE**

A Tip of the Cowl

Edith Wharton, amid the agonies of creating her masterwork, *The Age of Innocence*, once remarked to her friend and mentor Henry James, "Hey, Hank, next time I have an idea for a novel, remind me how much this writing jive *sucks!*"

Well, okay, so Mrs. Wharton said nothing of the kind. But I really wish she had, because it wasn't until I was too deep into this project to extract myself that I remembered just what hell writing a book can be. And no such hell can be endured alone. No two people suffered more for this project and stood to get less out of it than Jennie Kajiko and Nick Jones, and for their patience and only-occasionally-wavering support (along with so much else) I will be eternally grateful. Nearly equal patience and support, not to mention a whole lot of typing, was displayed by my editor, Dallas Middaugh, who had far more hair when this project began. I will also be forever in the debt of Joseph P. Filice, Ph.D. (which must stand for Phunnybook Documenter), who lent his time, critical skills, and comic books to the cause; and of Maura Healy, my lovely attorney, who not only made possible the appearance of many of the illustrations herein but held my hand during the most stressful of times.

My thanks also go to all those who aided the research of this and the previous edition: Brian Augustyn, Murray Boltinoff, E. Nelson Bridwell, John Broome, John Clemons, Mark Evanier, Gardner Fox, Mike Friedrich, Dick Giordano, Archie Goodwin, Mike Grell, Tom Kee, Roz Kirby, Joe Kubert, Paul Levitz, Teresa Marovich, Scott McAdam, Doug Moench, Denny O'Neil, Bud Plant, Peter Sanderson, Jack Schiff, Julius Schwartz, Jim Shooter, Kim Thompson, Mark Waid, and others. I could never have pulled off the last few chapters, in which I had to organize into a few dozen pages what it took me a decade to live (and a year to repress), without the exhaustive research of the Internet Gang: Rodrigo Baeza, Seth Biederman, Scott Cederlund, Johanna Draper, Michael Grabois, Kevin Maroney, Bill May, Sean Medlock, Dave Oakes, Elayne Wechsler-Chaput, Dwight Williams, and others who offered what help they could. Some of them, especially the indefatigable Messrs. Baeza and May, gave me far more information than I was able to use, but all of it was useful in forming an overview of the very strange world of '80s and '90s comics. Thanks also to Frank McGinn of Comics & Comix on Irving Street in San Francisco for loaning us comics for reproduction purposes. Thanks and an apology to Hal Schuster, formerly of *Comics Feature*, and Dave Olbrich, formerly of *Amazing Heroes*, who were inadvertently cheated of a plug for publishing chapters from the first edition. To Greg Aaron, Peter Cannon, Carol Mann, Martha Millard, Roger Stewart, and other editors and agents, past and present, I offer the cliché but heartfelt, "It couldn't have happened without you." Grudging thanks to Sam Hamm, who wouldn't stop at providing amusing quotes but checked my prose the way a tailor checks a suit, always letting me know which sentence was a perfect fit and which was a *shmatte*. And I owe a special debt to Jack Kirby, who not only did more than anyone to make me a comic book fan in the first place, who not only helped with the research on the first edition, who not only raised the historical awareness and political consciousness of everyone in this business with his struggles against Marvel Comics, but who said the words that jumped out at me from the first edition and guided every sentence of this rewrite: "I felt there was a time that a man had to tell a story in which he felt there was no bullshit." I've done my best to make this such a time for me.

I also owe a debt to many comic book historians and interviewers before me for some of the facts and quotes herein. Many of them did their work in the obscurity of fanzines and comics-industry publications, but some have written books that are still more-or-less available, and may be of interest to readers made curious by this book to learn more. I offer authors and titles here, not as a comprehensive list of sources, but as a combined "thank you" and "recommended for further reading:" *Marvel* and *DC Comics* by Les Daniels; *Comic Book Rebels* by Stanley Wiater and Stephen R. Bissette; *Masters of Imagination, Superhero Comics of the Silver Age, Science Fiction Comics,* and other books by Mike Benton; *The Art of Jack Kirby* by Ray Wyman, Jr. and Catherine Hohlfeld; *The Art of the Comic Book* by R.C. Harvey; *Canuck Comics* and *Guardians of the North* by John Bell, for those interested in the Canadian comics which we've had to neglect here; *The New Comics* by Gary Groth and Robert Fiore; *Women and the Comics* by Trina Robbins and Cat Yronwode; *A Century of Women Cartoonists* by Robbins alone; and *The Golden Age of Comics Fandom* by Bill Schelly. There are more, but that's a start. For the "prehistory" to this book, look for *The Steranko History of Comics*, Vol. 1 and 2, by Jim Steranko; *The Great Comic Book Heroes* by Jules Feiffer; and *All in Color for a Dime* and *The Comic-Book Book* by Richard Lupoff and the late Don Thompson. Robert M. Overstreet's *Overstreet Comic Book Price Guide* is the best general reference in the field on publication dates, publishers, and other hard data, although it's still riddled with errors, particularly in regard to artist credits. Other helpful reference works are *The World Encyclopedia of Comics* and other books by Maurice Horn, and *The Encyclopedia of American Comics* and others by Ron Goulart. The first edition of Will Jacobs and Gerard Jones's *The Comic Book Heroes* is still a good reference on superhero comics from 1956 to 1980, with some information no longer included in this edition. For an understanding of comics as a medium, no one should skip *Understanding Comics* by Scott McCloud and *Comics and Sequential Art* by Will Eisner. Keep an eye out for Mark Evanier's coming tribute book on Jack Kirby and the revised edition of Jerry Bails's monumental *Who's Who in American Comic Books.*

There are, of course, more ways to help a writer than editing and research help, and I would hate to ignore those who provided less tangible support. We dedicated our first edition to our friends and fellow fans Joe Filice, Mike Forrester, and Mike Jensen, and although we've supplanted them this time with our parents—the difference, I suppose, between writers in their twenties and writers at mid-life—we remain grateful to them, and to all those who've helped us come to love and understand the bizarre medium that has taken up so many hours and years of our lives. Jack Baty got me into comic books in the first place, with help from Tim Burdick, curse them both. And Ray Jones, as good a mentor and protector as any Boy Wonder ever had, helped me feel that comics were somehow worth reading and thinking about. Lisa Yaszek, soon to be Ph.D., has helped me enormously in understanding the relationship of junk culture and serious thought, and my own awkward place between them. That other good Catholic girl, Lia Pelosi, has been an inspiration in making the transition from commercial comic-book writing back to my "true path." My thanks to Phyllis Shulman, also soon to be Ph.D., for helping me to sort out the importance of superheroes in my own development as a boy and as a man. Dr. Valerie Hearn has been invaluable in my quest to learn tools for making the life of the writer more sane and productive. Thanks to Carrie, Liz, Karen, Anna 1, Anna 2, Michelle, Celeste, Jillian, Tiffany, and all the other beautiful Spinellettes of Spinelli on 24th

Street, whose coffee, tea, and sympathy made my long hours chained to a laptop nearly blissful. And thanks to those Precolumbian horticulturists of the Central American highlands who first discovered the magic of coffee.

In many ways this book has grown less from research than from experience. Everyone with whom I've worked in the comic book industry has played an important part in my understanding the medium and the community well enough to venture to write 200,000 words about it. My editors and fellow writers have been particularly close companions, but it's been from the artists that I've really learned the essence of the comic book, its strange codes of storytelling and its hypnotic sensuality. The comic book world belongs to the artists—they just let us writers live in it. I've been privileged to work with some of the "old masters" of the field: Carmine Infantino, Curt Swan, Kurt Schaffenberger, Dan Spiegle, Martin Nodell. But I've learned even more from artists of my own generation and younger, some of whom I feel I've grown up with: Chuck Austen, Eduardo Barreto, Bret Blevins, Norm Breyfogle, M.D. Bright, Pat Broderick, Bryan Carson, Malcolm Davis, Keith Giffen, Paul Gulacy, Gene Ha, Cully Hamner, Ben Herrera, Jeff Johnson, Steve Jones, Scott Kolins, Marv Mann, Jeff Parker, George Pérez, Ron Randall, Darick Robertson, Joe Staton, David Antoine

Williams, Chuck Wojtkiewicz, Gary Yap, and many others, with special mention of the first, Tim Hamilton, and the one that just won't go away, Mark Badger. I wish I could be just a few months earlier in expressing my gratitude to Mike Parobeck, my collaborator on my first regular mainstream assignment and the one artist with whom I most wanted to work again. The world was far too brutal to Mike, but in his short life he gave it as much joy and brightness as he could. For all the sadness that his death has brought, his art in *El Diablo*, *The Fly*, *The Elongated Man*, *The Justice Society of America*, and *Batman Adventures* can still make me smile.

Above everyone, I must thank my friend and collaborator Will Jacobs. Not only did he introduce me to the glories of '60s DC, not only did he force me into becoming a better writer through his criticism and collaboration, not only did he help me form my comic book aesthetic through years of seemingly endless conversation about the nuances of Carmine Infantino and Gil Kane, not only did he cowrite the first edition of this book, but after all that he stepped graciously aside to let me desecrate that monument to our innocent youth with this sadder, wiser, and far more personal work. *Viva Turlock.*

Gerard Jones
September 1996

X

INTRODUCTION

A funny thing happened on the way to this second edition: we became comic book writers. When we wrote the first edition of this book eleven years ago we were only interested observers of the comics world, but one thing led to another and in 1987 our comic book *The Trouble with Girls* premiered. A great deal more work followed—one of us, for a time, was the most prolific writer in the field—until we moved on, in just this past year. This has, of course, affected our views. We now have an intimate understanding of the commercial forces and personalities that shape comics, but less ability to read the comics themselves dispassionately. And because one of us has been so much more involved than the other in the industry, this has become a more personal statement, mainly a reflection of one voice and one viewpoint—although that viewpoint could never have been formed without all those years of funnybook conversations between us both.

Readers who wish to compare this edition to the first (and isn't that the sort of thing comic book fans do, after all?) will find that it is essentially a whole new book, starting from page one. The latter part, of course, covers comics undreamed of when we wrote the first edition, and we cover them differently from the comics of the preceding twenty-five years. From about 1980 to 1993, the number of comics published each month soared from fewer than a hundred to more than nine hundred. The number of publishers producing superheroes rose from two to, at the market's peak, more than a dozen. A once steady but constricted market controlled by a few giant distributors and limited by the small capacities of newsstands has become a volatile, speculation-driven arena propelled by specialty stores and encouraging to small publishers. The uniform newsprint comic book has been supplanted by comics, magazines, and "graphic novels" in an endless range of sizes, formats, paper stocks, and publishing frequencies. Movies, TV, video games, trading cards, and toys have become a bigger part of the business than ever before. Yet, although the last fifteen years have seen the full flowering of that revolution, all its seeds were planted by the early 1980s. The quarter-century from 1956 to 1981 was the crucible that transformed comics from anonymously produced diversions for grade schoolers into the *oeuvres* of a would-be art form with its own subculture, business infrastructure, and nearly religious adherents. We hope we're forgiven, then, for flying quickly over the mountains of '80s and '90s comics, seeking the relatively few significant ones.

A better understanding of how comics connect with American culture has led us to deepen the social and biographical explorations of the book. This has meant cutting some of our historical criticism and bibliography, which may disappoint those readers who told us they valued the first edition as a "collectors' guide." We hope we've given them, in compensation, a much more compelling and streamlined story.

This is the story of a genre. Superheroes were born in the late 1930s in a low-priced and low-quality medium, aimed at an audience of kids, semiliterate workers, and later, GIs. Their creators were young cartoonists, working quickly and in a vast range of genres, with little financial stake in their creations, and their work was raw and energetic, violent and clamorous with the storm and stress of class conflict and war. When the heroes were supplanted after World War II by romance, crime, horror, and other genres, most of those cartoonists just shifted gears and kept going, their creations more subtle and human but still noisome and violent. Then came a do-gooders' crusade that branded comics as a cause of juvenile delinquency. The industry was nearly destroyed, and a Comics Code instituted to ensure that any surviving comics would be so squeaky clean and wholesome as to bore any red-blooded kid into turning back to his homework. Fistfights, explosions, and death—the very stuff of the early superheroes—were virtually forbidden by terrified publishers. And yet in that environment the superheroes were reborn, and while other genres have cycled through and disappeared, the heroes have gone on without a break for forty years. The mid-1960s—as different a cultural moment from World War II as could be imagined—proved to be a second peak for those odd icons, and by the early 1990s, in a pop culture that placed a higher premium on violence and cynicism than ever before, they reached new heights of commercial success.

This is the story of how clever and occasionally inspired artists, writers, and editors, often battling desperately to save their chosen field from extinction—once just to keep food on the table, more recently to keep alive the beloved heroes of their childhoods—have constantly reinvented the same concepts, making them speak again and again to new waves of kids. How a few creators who cared about the quality of what they were doing strained against publishers interested only in the bottom line, and slowly forced those publishers to change their ways. They, not the guys in the tights, are the comic book heroes. It's a small part of the American story, but it is a part.

The fact that this book is about superhero

© 1986 Will Eisner

The sweatshops that gave birth to superheroic fantasies, as remembered by Will Eisner, one of the first and best of the comic book men. Here he caricatures Bob Powell (Stanley Pulowski), Lou Fine, and the great Jack "King" Kirby. (*The Dreamer*, Kitchen Sink Press, 1986.)

comics shouldn't be taken as a statement that superheroes are the whole or even the best of the medium. From the mid-1940s to the early 1970s, the capes-and-masks genre never once exceeded twenty per cent of the total number of comics titles published in a single year. Readers interested in comics as a whole will find mountains of work in humor, crime, satire, history, and other comics of an artistry and richness to which superhero creators rarely even aspire. We touch on much of that work here, because the story of a genre can't be separated from that of the industry that produced it. We hope that will make this story interesting even to readers who aren't particularly devoted to superpowered musclemen.

We've chosen to begin in 1956, when that first comeback of the heroes began, with only a glance back to 1938 when they were created. This is in part because the first wave, what fans call the "golden age" of superheroes has been treated extensively in other books. But the last forty years are also where our passions lie. As children of the '60s, we find that the superheroes of the "silver age" are vivid parts of our own lives. The heroes of the '30s and '40s, though intriguing, strike us as an antediluvian race. We try to be informative—and we'll convey enough about the old heroes to make clear what's happened since—but we never hesitate to be biased.

Our first edition opened with the words, "The comic book business is exploding." In sheer volume that explosion turned out to be bigger than we expected. At the same time the explosion failed to blast out in as many directions as we hoped. Comics have attained a mass media visibility, a profitability, and a presence in bookstores and other venues that would have been inconceivable to past generations of publishers and creators. Yet, paradoxically, they are increasingly dependent on an in-grown subculture of limited taste. And now, in keeping with the suck-and-run philosophy of modern American business, the publishers are alienating those fans. Comics may be facing as big a crisis as that of forty years ago, when this story began. Like all crises, it may be a time of tremendous opportunity or of self-destruction. This is the story of how this oddest of American entertainment genres came to this point. Maybe by the end of it we'll have some idea of what's next.

PART ONE

THE SILVER AGE

CHAPTER 1

PRESENTING THE SILVER AGE

A kid looking for exciting comic books in 1956 would have had a rough time. The great horror and crime comics that had haunted the newsstands just a couple of years before were gone, slaughtered by headlines in the newspaper and senators on TV. There were romances, but now all safe and bland. There were a lot of humor comics, about intelligent ducks and stupid teenagers, some of them very good. But if a kid wanted adventure, he'd have to lay down his dime for some pretty good science fiction or a decent western or something else aping the current Saturday matinee fashions. If he wanted *heroes*—if he wanted symbolic, bigger-than-big action of the kind that made the American comic book what it was—then it was a bleak time indeed.

He might have dimly remembered the great days of the superheroes, when their costumes blazed from the newsstands with lurid color and insane variety— Flash, Captain Marvel, Green Lantern, the Human Torch, Plastic Man, dozens more—but they were gone, as suddenly and completely as the dinosaurs. Even the Justice Society of America, in which the greatest heroes had banded together to fight world-threatening foes, had vanished a few years before. Without them, adventure comics weren't much more than short stories with pictures, movies without movement. Oh, there were still nine superhero comics, but six of them starred Superman, or his junior self, Superboy, and they got old fast. It seemed like every story was just like the TV show: a hero capable of moving worlds wasting his talents trying to outwit petty crooks full of tiresome schemes and chunks of kryptonite, losers with names like Bullets Barton and Mr. Wheels. His old friend Batman hadn't sunk quite

so low, but most of the stories in the Caped Crusader's two comics were coarsely drawn, full of tired gimmicks, with sometimes a tantalizing echo of something older, better, more atmospheric. And then there was Wonder Woman, whose adventures weren't just dull, but usually didn't even make sense.

All those comics bore the "DC" symbol in the upper left corner. There'd been well over a dozen publishers just a few years before, every one with a full line of comics, but now there were just DC and Dell and Archie and Harvey, plus some no-names cranking out cheap-looking comics that hardly any kid would buy. Comics were smaller, too. Once they'd been "64 Pages for a Dime," but the publishers, with aspirations apparently as small and cheap as their medium, had fought inflation by keeping the price the same but cutting the page count in half. Just finding comics was harder now. The new suburbs didn't have newsstands like the cities, and the chain supermarkets and drugstores would give only a little room to something that took up so much display space but sold for just a dime. The "pulp magazines" that the kid's dad remembered were already extinct. It looked like the comics might follow them soon.

Spinning the squeaky comics rack in the late summer of that year, a kid might have felt that the death of comic books wouldn't be such a great loss. Without the superheroes who had made comic books unique, who had virtually created comic books in the first place, what was there to lose? There was no comic to satisfy his hunger for superhuman feats and high adventure, no comic to make thrilling those last days before school started again, no comic that drew his hand irresistibly to the rack.

Except one.

There was one that begged to be bought. Across its cover undulated a strip of movie film. From frame to frame in the film, a red-garbed figure was running, running fast, running so fast that his speed hurled him out of the film and right off the stands. "Presenting the Flash!" read the copy. "Whirlwind Adventures of the Fastest Man Alive!"

Whirlwind they were. A flip through the pages showed this new hero, this Flash, outracing a bullet, zipping up and down the sides of skyscrapers, battling a super-slow villain called the Turtle, thwarting a scientific thief from the future, and then—as a coup de grâce—breaking the time barrier by his sheer velocity.

There was no question about this one. Any kid who had ever dreamed of running fast—and was there ever a kid who hadn't?—would have dashed for the cash register like the Fastest Kid Alive, dime in one hand and Flash in the other.

If the kid had looked up a couple of feet, he might have noticed someone else buying the very same comic: a teenage egghead who liked science fiction, even a college student who'd loved comics too much in the "golden age of superheroes" ever to outgrow them completely. They might have seen this Flash in a different light: the art carried the action with dynamic clarity and fluidity, the stories were fast and complex but remarkably well-developed. Not only had DC revived, in a new version, one of its best heroes of the 1940s, but it had done so with a tautness and refinement rare in comics. It had laid the foundation for a whole new approach—and a whole new audience—for superheroes.

In his origin story, the new Flash tipped his hat to any older readers who might be out there. Barry Allen is a police scientist always ridiculed for his slowness—which may be why we first find him reading an old comic book about his boyhood hero, the Flash. When lightning strikes a cabinet of chemicals beside which he's standing, transfiguring every cell in his body in an electrochemical blast, he's endowed with "supersonic speed, undreamed-of speed." He immediately dedicates his life to fighting crime, tak-

ing the name of his hero, and streamlining the lightning-bolt symbol and red-and-yellow jersey of the original Flash into the look of a scarlet bullet.

Here was a hero who suggested a return to the "golden age," but who also, with a sleek style and science fictional milieu, was purely of the new decade. These were the years of monsters in the matinees and saucers in the skies, and the mounting science fiction fad was only one year shy of exploding into a craze. Yet, here science wasn't demonized or cloaked in clouds of mystery and horror, as it usually was in comics. In the real world the Cold War was thawing, incomes were rising, and the American home was becoming a shrine to Hotpoint, Amana, and Frigidaire. For most American kids the future looked like a sunny place, and Flash's awesome pow-

The one that begged to be bought. Our lack of color prevents us from conveying its vibrancy, but even in black-and-white there's no missing the sleekness and innovative design that made *Showcase #4* relevant to a high-tech age. Pencils by Carmine Infantino, inks by Joe Kubert. (Oct. 1956.)

ers were just a ticket to convenience and excitement. Whoever was behind this new hero obviously liked comics, understood kids, and felt the beat of his times. A man like that could be the one, if anyone could, to give superheroes a second chance at life.

He grew up in the '20s in the middle-class Bronx with two consuming passions: the New York Yankees, with their superhero Babe Ruth, and the broadly ridiculed new world of science fiction. Young Julius Schwartz faced life with a bucktoothed grin and a wiseacre wit, apparently happy to follow wherever his enthusiasms and his considerable nose led him. As teenagers, he and a friend named Mort Weisinger launched the first true science fiction fan magazine—or "fanzine"—*The Time Traveler,* and with it helped lay the foundations of the zealous, noisy world of SF fandom. Weisinger, ever driven by ambition, then suggested supporting their habit by acting as literary agents for the many writers they'd met. When Mort hit the career track as an editor, Julie found himself almost accidentally, while still in his early twenties, the premier agent in his field. He earned a reputation for working with his clients, making demands of them, and nursing them until he felt they were doing their best work. Acting more like a big brother than an agent, he helped a young Ray Bradbury find his voice and taught Alfred Bester to play pinochle and bridge when he wasn't marketing his stories. When he and Edmond Hamilton roomed together in California, Schwartz would doze on a couch as Hamilton typed up his *Captain Future* space operas for penny-a-word rates. Whenever the typewriter bell would ring, announcing that Hamilton had typed about another ten words, Schwartz would tally his commission with a cry of, "Another penny!"

The Depression was hurting the cheap "pulps," where nearly all science fiction was published, but it was giving birth to another business, one even lower on the cultural ladder. It started when a printing company salesman, Max Gaines, slapped together cheap collections of newspaper comics to fill the gaps in Depression-blasted newsstands. A horde of hustlers followed him, including a pulp writer and master liar

calling himself Major Malcolm Wheeler-Nicholson (he may or may not have been kicked out of the Cavalry). The Major didn't have enough money to buy newspaper strips, so he gobbled up new stuff from starving young cartoonists and vanished into the night when they came for their pay. His comics were picked up in bankruptcy court by "National Periodical Publications," consisting of Harry Donenfeld, a pulp magazine publisher who bucked the Depression by flirting with pornography in *Spicy Detective* and *Spicy Romance*, and Jack Liebowitz, a cunning young accountant then helping Donenfeld create Independent News, a distribution service for the cheap magazines emerging from those cash-strapped times.

It was a risky business: publishers allowed retailers to return whatever they didn't sell for credit, so the publisher/distributor's trick was to guess at a reasonable print run and pray for a sell-through of more than half. A too-pessimistic print run meant a failure to maximize profits, but a too-optimistic one could mean a huge loss of money. The result was publishers who thought conservatively and imitatively, and retailers with hardly any incentive to sell the product—almost the ideal recipe for a business destined to shrink steadily away.

It was also a tough business. "Independent distributors" like Liebowitz and Donenfeld's were fighting a decades-long war against the would-be monopoly of the American News Company. With its outright ownership of nearly every newsstand in the train stations, bus depots, and other key locations of America's cities, American News had a stranglehold on the circulation of every major newspaper and magazine in the country. Then came William Randolph Hearst, whose combination of comic strips and sensationalistic news ("yellow journalism," they called it, after Hearst's first comic strip star, the Yellow Kid) had made him rich and cocky. He'd shattered the Spanish Empire, with an assist from the U.S. government, and in 1910 he dared to take on American News, handling his own distribution for the Chicago *Evening American*. The Chicago street corners and small shops where the paper was sold

weren't run on *laissez-faire* economics, however. In a two-year period, twenty-seven news vendors were murdered in a Chicago "circulation war," and it was only through an alliance with a local enforcer named Max Annenberg that Hearst won the battle. Max's brother Moe, the big *macher* of *The Racing Form* and the national betting wire, then became the locus of a spreading network: pulp magazines and proletarian newspapers sold through candy stores, cigar stores, and independent newsstands, a lot of which were fronts for bookie joints and numbers rackets. It was a network made possible by comic strips, and it made possible the comic book.

This was the world that gave America's kiddies the funnybook. The owners of the "IDs," the independent distributors, were young and aggressive, mostly urban and Jewish guys, who could gladhand the local leg-breakers and the *goombahs* who were organizing the trucking unions as well as Mom and Pop at the candy store. To be a publisher also meant working with mob-run printers' unions. Payola would become so endemic to comics that eventually some artists would provide hookers to art directors in exchange for work, and writers would conspire with editors to cheat their companies with phony script scams. A tough business indeed, but Jack and Harry must have been tough cookies, because Independent News would eventually be the biggest distributor in the country, and National the biggest comic book publisher.

To fill pages for *Detective*, *Adventure*, and *More Fun Comics*, Liebowitz relied on young guys like Jerry Siegel and Joe Shuster, whose career plans revolved around newspaper comic strips but, until they were good enough for the big time, were willing to crank out fodder in any genre. They sold all their rights without thinking about it—and why not? Even the biggest newspaper cartoonists didn't own their own creations, and not even the publishers saw a future in

'The Block': in his later years, Jack Kirby evoked the hustling, crowded, immigrant world from which he—and the comic book—emerged. In Kirby's hands, even the daily business of the Lower East Side becomes superheroic. (From Street Code, drawn in 1983, published in Argosy Magazine Vol. 3 No. 2, 1990.)

these "comic books." After three years, and sales of five separate series, Siegel and Shuster were finally able to unload a piece of juvenilia that *everyone* had rejected. It had no genre and no precedent, this hunk of raw, teenage wish-fulfillment that had excited Jerry and Joe when they were just painfully shy little science fiction addicts in a Cleveland high school. Back then they lived in the fever dreams of the pulps, blissfully unaware of moneymen like Jack Liebowitz. They retreated into stories of their own that they advertised in Schwartz and Weisinger's *Time Traveler*, yearning for connection with their fellow social rejects in fandom, pining hopelessly for the pretty girls who wouldn't give the time of day to a couple of myopic nebbishes on the school newspaper. The antidote for their agony was a timid little reporter with glasses who was secretly a Man of Steel, beating up tough guys and winning the adoration—but never returning it—of the beautiful girl who scorned him during the day (that'll teach her!). No wonder that for four years no adult publisher could bring himself to buy it: "A rather immature work," read United Features's rejection. It took a cartoonist barely past his twentieth birthday, Max Gaines' assistant, Sheldon Mayer, to key into that adolescent fantasy. He showed it to another young cartoonist, Vin Sullivan, who happened to be slapping together a new project for Jack Liebowitz called *Action Comics*. Sullivan and Liebowitz were up against the deadline, desperate to buy anything. When this "Superman" finally hit the stands in 1938, it turned out that a few hundred thousand comic-reading kids shared Siegel and Shuster's embarrassing yearnings. So was born the superhero, god of the disenfranchised, consolation of the powerless, revenge of the nerd and companion of the lonely American boy.

Liebowitz's own bookkeeper, Victor Fox, took one look at the sales figures on that first *Action*, closed his ledger, took a lunch break, rented an office nearby, and started publishing his own cheap knock-offs. Fawcett Publications, with a fortune built on the vaguely disreputable *Captain Billy's Whiz-Bang*, followed with a Superman imitation named *Captain Marvel*. Then Martin Goodman, a whiz-kid pulp pub-

lisher already imitating Donenfeld's sleaze-and-tease ("New Girls for Satan's Blood Ballet," for example), whipped out *Marvel Comics* , and the gold rush was on. Liebowitz himself, unable to persuade Donenfeld that this was more than a fad, teamed up with Max Gaines to create a second company, All-American Comics. Liebowitz actually saw a future in this junk, so he retained smart young cartoonists—Whitney Ellsworth, Sheldon Mayer—as editors. When more bodies were needed, he let Ellsworth pay for the best young editors of the pulps, like Mort Weisinger.

Now the pulps were reeling, thanks to both comics and the new "paperbacks," and when the war came, with its paper shortages, they were doomed. All of a sudden Julie Schwartz found himself without an income. It was his friend Alfred Bester who told him in 1944 that All-American Comics was outgrowing its staff and needed a story editor. Comics were a schlock business, even to a pulp writer, all about speed and volume and staying attuned to the latest fads. Bester wasn't planning a career writing stuff like *Green Lantern*—who would?—but it only took about half his brain and it paid the bills. So Julie went to see Sheldon Mayer, now described as one of the seminal editors of the golden age but then just a cartoonist with an office job, trying to learn to be an editor while battling ever-mounting deadlines. He was an artist whose hand hadn't caught up to his eye or his imagination, unable yet to make a living drawing, but able to see the promise of other people and of the comic book medium. Most editors and publishers of the time liked their art clean and simple, instantly accessible to kids, as Joe Shuster's was, but he worked with raw but vigorous teenagers like Joe Kubert and Gil Kane, the latter a former assistant to the great action-artist Jack Kirby. Meyer's prize student was Alex Toth, a follower of *Terry and the Pirates*'s Milton Caniff and Noel Sickles. Mayer helped Toth turn his cantankerous snobbishness toward the world into a flamboyant elevation of his art, a gauntlet tossed in front of every artist of his generation to make comics not just boyishly vigorous but *elegant*.

© 1958 Walt Disney Publications

Mayer saw potential, too, in Schwartz, this friend of Bester who reminded him of a "chipmunk," this overgrown fan who never did anything that didn't excite him. "Though I liked him at once, I remember feeling that background-wise, Julie didn't have too much going for him," Mayer later said. "I don't think he had ever read a comic book before he had bought a few of ours and read them in the subway on the way to the interview." But Mayer saw in Schwartz and his agenting style the kind of editor he wanted, "the kind of guy who would be sympathetic to the needs of writers and artists . . . and yet be able to cajole, coerce, and/or inspire them to do their best work."

Just a few months after Schwartz started his new job, Liebowitz orchestrated an absorption of All-American into National Periodicals, all under the DC (for *Detective Comics*) slug. Suddenly National found itself the giant of the industry, and Julie Schwartz found himself working again with Mort Weisinger, already a powerhouse of an editor on Siegel and Shuster's *Superman*. The comics world was a small one from the beginning, part family business, part boys' club, part mafia, and part ghetto.

Superheroes had been conceived in the Depression and raised under the darkening clouds of war. Their creators were young cartoonists, many still in their teens, many the children of immigrants, working with no ownership of their creations, no job security, no royalties or employee benefits—not even the right to get their original art back— and always with an eye on the next project. Through their heroes they reflected in broad strokes the turmoil of the times and their own lives, making their themes the war against fascism, the little man against science and the machine, the poor against the corrupt rich. By 1944, when Schwartz started teaching himself the job of editing on *Flash, Green Lantern, Justice Society of America*, they'd changed. Under corporate control and the culture of war, the heroes had become flattened-out good guys, their adventures exercises in genre formula, and that's where Schwartz's cleverness and humor served him well.

Then came the end of the war, an American mood less fanciful and optimistic, a fading of heroes, and an explosion in comics about tortured young love, brutal crime, domestic comedy, and the horror that lurks beneath the veneer of normality. Liebowitz and Donenfeld were in a bind: they had writers and artists who could have made gangland wars and bloody ax murders work for them, like *Spicy Detective* had worked before, but now their status as custodians of the quasi-institutional Superman made them acutely conscious of respectability and parental approval. Liebowitz had even created a nominal "advisory committee" for his comics, headed by Pearl S. Buck, of all people. He decided to tough it out with the whole-

Escape from 'the Block.' Through the '50s, Alex Toth inspired his comic book peers to strive for elegance and grace in their fantasies. Here he breathes life into one of the principal inspirations for all comic book superheroes—Zorro. (*Four Color* #882, Dell Publishing, Feb. 1958.)

The crewcut, the cinematic storytelling. . .

some approach and high standards of art and writing that Mayer and Ellsworth had instituted. Donenfeld found a way partly around the problem by creating another publisher, the American Comics Group, that could jump on the horror trend with gory indifference. And Independent News put cash in both partners' pockets by handling some of their own competitors. But it was still ugly to be looking way up all of a sudden at Dell Comics, distributed by the hated American News Company, and now the king of the industry with its Disney and other franchises. It was even uglier to be looking up at Martin Goodman, the knockoff champion of a knockoff business, making a climb for the top of the sales heap by sheer volume of schlock.

So here was Julie Schwartz, superheroless, doing animal adventures, with the strange and charming *Adventures of Rex the Wonder Dog*, and

westerns, a genre he admits he "didn't get at all," handled in a strangely superheroic way (Nighthawk in *Western Comics* and Johnny Thunder in *All Star Western* were always protecting their secret identities; then there was Super-Chief, later in *All Star*, an Iroquois warrior granted superpowers and a mask by the Great Spirit). Luckily for Schwartz's sanity, science fiction caught on briefly, and in 1950 and '51 he launched *Strange Adventures* and *Mystery in Space*. The genre died quickly for everybody else, but Schwartz kept his two entries sailing right through the decade, making him about the only man who could ever sell SF in comics. He was everything Shelly Mayer had hoped, as patient and demanding an editor as he'd been as an agent, strict about keeping the same writer and artist together on every episode of a series, developing a sharp sense for matching the right men to the right material, slowly building a stable of dependable freelancers who could make comics the way he liked them: classy but playful.

What he didn't know at first was art. An art student named Frank Giacoia, more affable and competent than artistically ambitious, went to National's offices with a friend one day in 1947 to show his work. He became a DC mainstay almost immediately, but his friend, Carmine Infantino, remembers that, "My work had a lukewarm reception by most editors and was disliked by one in particular." That one, of course, was Schwartz. Infantino was another "Caniffty," like Toth. He had Caniff's angularity and a good sense of movement, but the stuff went wild occasionally. Under the gruff mask of a working class Italian kid, Carmine hid a visual intellectuality that his unskilled hand betrayed—but couldn't keep up with. Shelly Mayer, thankfully, could see it, could see that here was a kid willing to pick up the gauntlet thrown down by Toth, and hired him. Then Mayer promptly quit his job in favor of freelance cartooning and left Schwartz and Infantino to educate each other. Slowly, over more than a decade, Infantino would develop into one of the finest visual storytellers ever to work in his field, the only layout man who could almost stand with Toth. For giving him that chance to grow, Infantino would remain fiercely loyal to DC.

Schwartz was having similar luck, meanwhile, with his best friend and former client, John Broome, a gentle young writer with an intellectual bent, drawn to Asian art and travel and Dixieland jazz (which was then quite a passion among creative, young white folk, and one he passed on to Schwartz). He avoided the DC offices, preferring his house upstate where, according to Schwartz and Gil Kane, he grew copious quantities of the forbidden vegetation that made so many jazzbos hear a little deeper and play a little lighter. Yet somehow, working with Julie through years of plot conferences, year after year, Broome became the master of the miniature narrative. His were intricate short stories that held everything a genre story had to have, all in graceful balance: character, setting, mystery, suspense, humor, action, the inevitable showdown, and the happy resolution. By mid-decade, Schwartz was the leader of the smartest little stable in comics. Suddenly in his forties, the chipmunk had become downright avuncular.

Of course, by mid-decade there weren't many stables left in comics. TV was competing, supermarkets were replacing mom-and-pop groceries (and mob candy stores), and a campaign to keep kids "active" and "fit"—scouting, Little League, dance lessons, swimming—was sweeping the country like a religion, ostensibly heading off delinquency and definitely cutting into reading time.

... the rail car diner: in 1956, Carmine Infantino shaped the first modern superhero. Inks by Joe Kubert, script by Robert Kanigher. (*Showcase 4*, Oct. 1956).

[1] DC was an enthusiastic supporter of the code, as was Archie Comics, which had never led the pack as a superhero or crime peddler but was having huge success with its "wholesome" Archie Andrews. The Code Authority, initially ramrodded by Archie's John Goldwater, specifically gimmicked the rules to wipe out EC, the one publisher that fought censorship. "Horror" and "Terror" were forbidden in comics titles, destroying EC's bestsellers, *Vault of Horror* and *Crypt of Terror*, while "Crime," the principal concern of the anticomics crusade but also the key word in the titles of Lev Gleason's comics, *Crime Does Not Pay* et al, was permitted, for Gleason was a Code signee. Gleason was destroyed anyway when the New York State Legislature did what the Code wouldn't and forbade the selling of comics with "Crime" in the title to minors.

Then came Dr. Fredric Wertham, a left-wing academic with a belief in enlightened institutions, a terror of the working classes, and an almost paranoid hatred of capitalist junk-culture. His hysterical *Seduction of the Innocent* blamed comics for juvenile delinquency and homosexuality. He gave the press a profitable uproar to sell to apocalyptically minded Americans, and legislators an easy way to score points with parents by attacking an industry geared at kids who couldn't vote. Retailers and distributors started returning comics *en masse* that were even vaguely suspect, and publishers responded with a Comics Code that proved to be more effective for cutting each other's throats than winning back the approval of parents.[1] The comics got duller, kids lost interest, sales dropped, writers and artists left, quality slipped, kids lost more interest, and sales dropped further. By 1956 companies were folding, artists were racing each other to advertising agencies, and the business was in a panic. There had been nearly 650 comic book titles in 1952; by 1956 there were barely 400, and a few years later there would be scarcely 250. Max Gaines's impish son Bill had set the industry on fire in 1950 with his smart, gory EC horror comics, and now all he had was *Mad* magazine. Martin Goodman's tower of schlock was collapsing faster than Babel.

Only Dell prospered, because even Wertham couldn't make Americans doubt Donald Duck. National—with some well-known characters, slick art, a *Superman* TV show in syndication, and cashflow wizardry from Jack Liebowitz—was still staying afloat, but it needed a hit. Everybody needed a hit, but the usual way of finding one—the scattershot publication of new titles—had become too big a financial gamble. It took six months to get definitive "return" statements from the distributors, by which time a ton of money might have been invested in a series that was bombing. Publishers did everything they could to avoid printing the words "Number 1" on a cover, even transiting from genre to genre with titles like *Space Western* (with stories like "Spurs Jackson vs. the Flying Saucers"). It was Liebowitz and Irwin Donenfeld (replacing his retired father

Harry) who found a way to streamline the process in early 1956: *Showcase*, an ongoing series that auditioned concepts in one-issue installments. At first they steered clear of superheroes. Maybe frogmen would be the next big thing, or firemen. But then, at an editorial meeting, "someone, some unknown inspirational genius, suggested that we bring back the Flash," Schwartz recalled. "Irwin asked who would be the editor, and they all looked at me. I said I didn't want to do the Flash. Everything was wrong about it. I didn't even like his uniform." He finally agreed, as long as he could change whatever he wanted.

Schwartz gave the new Flash's "origin" story to Robert Kanigher, an editor/writer who shared a two-desk, too-small office with him for years. Kanigher cranked out scripts faster than the Flash could run, but he did a good enough job with an origin that was largely Schwartz's conception. The bit with Barry Allen reading the old *Flash* comic surely must have been Julie's. As a science fiction fan, he knew how a grown man could become attached to a piece of pop-culture junk from his childhood, and he knew that a few adult SF fans paid attention to comics (after all, his old buddy Bradbury had let EC adapt his stories, and the new generation of fans, like Harlan Ellison, had plugged EC in their fanzines). If there were grown-ups out there engaged in the solitary hunt for the old comics that mom had thrown away, glancing at newsstands to see if their heroes had ever come back, Schwartz would want to make them happy.

He made everybody happy when he assigned the back-up story to John Broome. For the art he turned to Carmine Infantino, then just beginning to come into his own. Another Mayer alumnus, Joe Kubert, finished the art in ink. The DC production department worked its magic.

And *that*, in short, was how the small miracle of Showcase 4, "Presenting the Flash," found its way to the stands in August, 1956.[2]

The kids rushed to the cashiers with their dimes, gobbled their *Flashes*, and waited for more. They waited for a long time because Irwin Donenfeld was waiting for return figures. Life, westerns, and science fiction went on for Julie Schwartz. Even when the numbers on *Showcase* 4 were good, Donenfeld couldn't quite believe superheroes were coming back. A second Flash tryout sold well (*Showcase* 8, June 1957), but the next project he gave Schwartz was *The New Adventures of Charlie Chan*. Nearly a year later—a year in which Sputnik went up, cars started to grow fins, *Chan* bombed, and American culture moved closer to Schwartz's futurism—two more Flash tryouts outsold the first two (*Showcase* 13–14, Apr.–June 1958). At long last the scarlet speedster was allowed to take off in his own title, picking up where his namesake had left off nearly a decade before (*The Flash* 105, Mar. 1959). He proved that kids would still buy superheroes if the superheroes could speak to the kids. He also proved that older readers were, indeed, out there. A mathematics grad student named Jerry Bails started writing to Schwartz, campaigning for the return of his beloved *Justice Society of America*. Larry Ivie, artist and fanzine publisher, pitched National a *JSA* revival called *Justice Legion of the World*.

Over the Flash's first few years Infantino refined a style of sparse backgrounds, novel page layouts, and relaxed lines that gave his stories an open, fluid feeling never before seen in comics. He owed a debt to Alex Toth, but even Toth couldn't do superheroes like this—this wealth of poised, energetic characters and visual speed-gimmicks propelling the story from panel to panel to its climax. To all this Infantino added a subtle skill for characterization and a sophisticated eye for the settings and situations of American life. His design of Barry Allen, with the sly intelligence of a scientist but the crewcut of an Organization Man, would have been a hero for his time even without his superspeed. Infantino won over young readers and won a National Cartoonists Society award, cementing DC's reputation as the Tiffany of comic book publishers.

He had the perfect partner in Broome. Like the Dixieland musicians he loved—those White New Yorkers and Chicagoans who took the visceral sounds of black New Orleans and turned them into a complex play of humor and virtuosity—Broome took the stuff

of superheroes, the crude violence of the hungry teenage cartoonists of the Depression, and made it something consciously modern, self-amused, and expertly fun. He could weave a major conflict between Flash and a villain into fourteen pages, a clever human-interest story into eight. Although he stuck to formula as religiously as Eddie Condon playing a two-beat stomp (colorful villain commits gimmicky robberies, Flash hunts villain down, villain traps Flash in a diabolical device, Flash ingeniously escapes and hauls villain off to jail), Broome had a genius for the little improvisation that would make an old plot feel fresh. In those Code-skittish days, DC (as inconceivable as it must seem to anyone who's only seen comics of the last thirty years) avoided violence, even fistfights, almost completely. Yet Broome's ever-growing repertoire of speed tricks for Flash—running on water, turning invisible, passing through walls, whipping up tornadoes—kept kids spellbound for years.

At the time, the norm of superhero writing was to leave no room for character development, but Broome had a wry sensitivity to the little strokes of humanity that gave substance to even his most absurd creations. The villains he invented for Flash were a rogues' gallery of absurd eccentrics, the likes of Captain Boomerang, the Weather Wizard, Grodd the gorilla genius, and the magical Abra Kadabra. Yet when the fiendish Mirror Master sits in jail, fretting because the Trickster and Captain Cold have edged him out in the prison newspaper's "Most Successful Criminal Poll," we have no choice but to believe it (*Flash* 136, May 1963). Broome gave even more character to Flash's friends. Ralph Dibny, the Elongated Man, a stretchable sleuth with a love of attention, became the only DC hero to announce his true identity to the world (*Flash* 112, May 1960). The Elongated Man was an incorrigible seeker of mysteries, who could find himself shrunk by aliens while vacationing in the Yucatan (*Flash* 115, Sept. 1960) or hypnotized by undersea conquerors during his honeymoon in the Caribbean (*Flash* 119, Mar. 1961). Whatever happened, he always came up smiling, for the world of *Flash* was a simply joyous one. Broome's affectionate handling of

[2] Published in August, 1956. From early in their history comics publishers have "postdated" their covers in a bald-faced attempt to manipulate retailers into displaying them longer. We cite only cover dates in this book; in general it's safe to assume that the comics were actually on sale two months before that date, and, over the last twenty years, were on sale in the "direct market" *three* months before.

The mature Infantino united design, action, and cartooning as no comic book artist ever had—or ever has. Inks by Murphy Anderson, script by John Broome. (*The Flash* 126, Feb. 1962.)

the camaraderie between Barry and Ralph made their team-ups some of the most appealing episodes in the annals of superheroes.

It was in this human dimension that Broome most needed Infantino. The mature Infantino drew everything—a hidden city of scientific gorillas, a harlequin committing crimes with toys, Flash strapped to a giant boomerang—as if he believed absolutely in its existence. His witty drawings and ability to stretch reality without breaking it pulled readers magnetically into his world. Infantino even made Kid Flash believable. When Iris's nephew, Wally West, gained speed identical to Flash's through a convenient fluke of nature (*Flash* 110, Jan. 1960), many readers reacted with outrage. After all, junior sidekicks were certifiable baby stuff. But Infantino's art could so fully evoke the quiet of a small-town afternoon or the cool of a shaded lawn that readers could forgive even the plots full of beatniks, schoolteachers, and singing idols. Even those of us who resented, as kids, finding Kid Flash stories in the backs of so many *Flash* comics now find them hypnotically nostalgic.

It's in that nostalgia that we can see why the early '60s *Flash* was so successful in its day and is still the most charming of all superhero series. America was enjoying a suburban boom, a baby boom, and an economic boom, creating an illusion of unprecedented political calm and social satisfaction. There were rumblings—the civil rights movement, for one—but most of the terrors of the previous quarter-century—the Depression, the war, the postwar shortages, McCarthyism, the juvenile delinquency panic—were vanishing like an urban skyline in the rearview mirror of a Nomad station wagon. If you were young enough, it was almost possible to believe in a world where order and neatness were fundamental, where villainy was the work of amusing goofballs, all part of an afternoon's amusement. Infantino echoed that in his visual style, with his flat, open fields of action, often reducing the urban setting to a geometric, nearly abstract skyline in the deep background. This was a new visual metaphor for entertainment. Gone from pop culture were the lurid exoticism of Coney Island and the portentous towers of the New York World's Fair's "World of Tomorrow." Disneyland, opened just a year before the new Flash appeared, was the symbol of the day.

Scarcely anything about this Flash was altogether new—Julie Schwartz and his group didn't experiment any more than Bobby Hackett playing old Louis Armstrong tunes—but superheroes had never before been handled with such sophistication, with art that was at once so dynamic and so pristine, and stories so entertaining to children and so satisfying to adults. If the heroes were to return, it could never be with the innocent abandon and crude vitality that made the "golden age" seem so golden in retrospect. Nothing is ever new twice. The Schwartz stable showed an alternative: high standards of craftsmanship and a self-conscious modernity, bringing such high polish and increased complexity to the genre that the coming years would have to be, at the very least, a "silver age of comics."

CHAPTER 2

THE SUPERMAN MYTHOS

"We were hiking in New Jersey's Palisades Park, Julie, Otto Binder, myself, and some of the other Scienceers," said Mort Weisinger of a day with Julius Schwartz and their science fiction club, "when suddenly we woke up in the hospital! A car had hit us and knocked us over like a row of clay pigeons. We could have all been wiped out, but we were very fortunate. I often wonder, immodestly, what would have happened to science fiction and comics if we'd all been obliterated there."

What indeed? Schwartz denies the incident ever happened, but it's a typical Weisinger tale, full of coincidence and irony and all-encompassing cataclysm. And, in truth, the comic book world would have been no less poor for the loss of Weisinger and Binder than of Schwartz. Their paths crossed off and on for thirty-five years, but in two of those years, two conflictive and frustrating years, they made possible the second step in the making of the silver age: the revitalization of Superman.

His friend Julie may have let whim and chance choose his path, but Mort was a driven young man. He had a harsh father, a self-made footwear manufacturer who would accept nothing less than his son becoming a doctor, but Mort preferred the control and power that comes only from mastering fictional worlds. He defied his father, then spent the rest of his life proving that he'd done the right thing, with an ambition that grew with his girth and his anger. He was the force behind *Science Fiction Digest*, a "fanzine" of near professional quality, and that won him an editorial job by the age of twenty. His specialties as both writer and editor were the startling "angle" and the tight control that comes with brevity:

he impressed his first boss by crafting a 500-word whodunit. He made a name for himself by redirecting *Thrilling Wonder Stories* at the teenage market when most SF writers and fans were pushing the genre toward more adult material. Whatever his own tastes, Mort knew from the start that success is measured in dollars. In 1941 Whitney Ellsworth hired him to bring his fierce commercial skills to the hottest property in American publishing, the source material for an empire of cartoons, movie serials, comic strips, kids' books, toys, radio adventures, and product endorsements: *Superman*.

When launched by Siegel and Shuster at the weary end of the Depression, Superman was an all-action, all-business defender of the oppressed. Weisinger kept the tone, tightened the structure, and shifted the politics to the defense of the status quo. Although he allowed a little comic relief, his Superman was almost a god: he had no private life, except in his self-invented guise as meek Clark Kent, no personal quirks, no failings, only that arsenal of powers to which Weisinger and his crew added almost compulsively, until even his breath and voice and eyes and memory were superpowered. Weisinger's writers had occasional flights of colorful fancy, but even their flights were constrained by the brevity and plotting precision their editor demanded. And they were, increasingly, "his" writers. Although he was technically coediting with Jack Schiff and under Ellsworth, it's been said that no one ever won a policy argument with Mort Weisinger.

Otto Binder, meanwhile, had become one of the most prolific science fiction writers of the pulp magazines. For him, fantastic stories were the only escape, both emotionally and financially, from the grinding jobs the Depression had forced him into, and he produced them with an almost desperate velocity. He was less than a visionary, but his stories had a tender touch, especially those about an appealingly human robot named Adam Link. For a while his agents were Weisinger and Schwartz, and later one of his biggest markets was Mort's *Thrilling Wonder*. But the pulps were fading, and Binder, with visions of office drudgery dancing in his head, cast around for something more secure. His brother Jack, a cartoonist, told him about the explosion in the comics market. Through him, Otto became a writer for Fawcett, and from 1941 on he was the principal writer for its big star, Captain Marvel. "Comics were like a drug, or a hypnotic spell, to me," Binder once said. "The moment I began writing them . . . I was a captive of this new and colorful way of writing stories." During his comic book career alone, Binder would write more than two thousand stories for twenty publishers, including well over half the Captain Marvel canon. For twelve years he and Weisinger were competitors, and in the process they helped make their characters the two most popular heroes of the golden age.

Of all the heroes who sprang up in the wake of Superman's success, none paralleled his look and powers more than Captain Marvel. National sued Fawcett for copyright infringement, and a battle began—of lawyers, of sales figures, and of loyal young readers—that would rage through the 1940s and into the 1950s. Yet, the Captain had a different personality, a humor and cuteness, as if he were more an affectionate parody than an imitation. Fawcett was a Minnesota company recently relocated to New York; the Captain's creators were Bill Parker and C.C. Beck, the latter the son of a Lutheran minister from rural Minnesota, and his early editors France Herron and Bill Woolfolk. He was a more gentle, genteel, and gentile hero from the start. Otto Binder's treatment of him was amused and light: the "Big Red Cheese" was a powerful but amiable, sometimes bumbling, fellow who often depended on the wits of his boy alter ego, Billy Batson, to save his skin. He was the World's Mightiest Mortal, not the Man of Steel. Binder let his stories flow leisurely, allowing his imagination to pour forth an unending stream of wonders: a world-conquering worm, a gentlemanly talking tiger, a bickering family of mad scientists. He and his cohorts fleshed out a whole "Marvel Family," complete with Captain Marvel Jr., Mary Marvel, a charlatan "Uncle Marvel," and Hoppy, the Marvel Bunny. If Weisinger fascinated his readers by exploring the very concept of an all-powerful hero, Binder charmed his with his all-too-human characters. Unfortunately, even the mightiest heroes were vulnerable to the hard times that beset costumed characters in the 1950s. Falling sales and National's lawsuit forced Fawcett to abandon its comics in 1953.

By then money was tight at National as well, and Weisinger had lost some of his best writers. Superman's popularity continued largely because of the George Reeves TV show that had premiered in 1952, but the show only made the quality of the comics worse. Low-budget TV allowed only a limited range of challenges for Superman, and the comics were made to follow suit. It didn't help that Ellsworth and Weisinger spent months in Hollywood serving, respectively, as the show's producer and story editor. Jack Schiff was left drowning in work, and the Man of Steel was left to rust.

In November 1957 the TV *Superman* ceased production, and Weisinger came home to the comics. He came without Ellsworth, who stayed out West to try (vainly) to make some more TV projects happen, permanently surrendering his duties as editorial director. Jack Liebowitz, trying to stay afloat, decided the DC line could survive without a chief editor, and duties were reshuffled: Weisinger took sole editorship of the whole "Superman family," giving Jack Schiff full control of *Batman* and other comics that they had coedited. Weisinger took a hard look at his new fiefdom—*Action Comics, Adventure Comics, Superman, Superboy, Superman's Pal Jimmy Olsen,* and *Superman's Girlfriend Lois Lane*—and found his hero sadly lacking in vitality, especially compared with the new Flash who was evolving just a few offices away. Something had to be done with DC's premier hero, and the times said that science fiction should be part of it. But the regular writers seemed virtually drained of ideas, and even Weisinger himself, always an idea man, appeared to have little notion where to turn for Superman's new direction. He needed a new element on his staff, one not conditioned by sixteen years of Weisinger training. He found it in Otto Binder.

He'd been buying stories from Binder since Fawcett's demise in 1953, along with art from two of the main Captain Marvel artists, Kurt Schaffenberger and Pete Constanza. (Soon after, he also rehired Jerry Siegel, who had just lost a decade-long legal battle with National, trying to get back some of his rights to Superman; Mort liked having defeated opponents in his ranks.) It was a few years, however, before Weisinger began drawing on Binder's talent and science fiction background to remake Superman's world. Their relationship would be a tense one. Their basic approaches to superheroes were opposite: Binder had always given Captain Marvel room to stretch out and show off his powers, but Weisinger wanted Superman's stunts boiled down to a single panel, with no "action sequences" that would delay the plot. And no one had ever called Mort Weisinger a pleasant man to work for. In fact, most of what his former associates have called him is unprintable in a book that young people may be reading. Yet somehow theirs was a productive union, and in 1958, 1959, and 1960 they introduced a constellation of changes that turned Superman from a concept into a character and gave him as delightful a universe as any Captain Marvel had ever inhabited. There's no point in trying to determine which ideas were Binder's and which were Weisinger's. Most of them were probably born in conference, and Mort always obfuscated the issue of credit anyway, never wanting to seem dependent on his writers. Other writers, especially Siegel, also augmented many of the ideas. Let's just say that probably none of them could have existed without the marriage of Binder's imagination and Weisinger's sharp editorial eye. It was as if the spirit of Captain Marvel had entered the body of Superman.

Conveniently, the twentieth anniversary of Superman's publication provided a launching point. In an understated anniversary celebration, *Action* 241 (June 1958) introduced us to Superman's Fortress of Solitude in the Arctic, and gave the hero his first opportunity to appear not merely as a hero but as a character: putting his feet up, playing a little high-speed chess with a robot, painting a Martian landscape with the aid of his telescopic vision, joking with his old pal Batman. The very next issue built impressively on that one. Weisinger had long been fascinated with Superman's origin: his birth on the superscientific planet Krypton, the planet's destruction, and baby Kal-El's Moses-like exodus to Earth. Now, in the shadow of Sputnik, the space-travel theme seemed especially vital. Somehow, though, he had never been able to wring a really good story out of the Krypton idea until he and Binder, in 1958, pitted Superman against an alien villain called Brainiac. As Superman's first worthy extraterrestrial foe, Brainiac was interesting enough. But he paled beside what Superman discovered aboard his spaceship, for Brainiac's hobby was shrinking cities from many worlds and imprisoning them in bottles, and one of those cities was Kandor, from the planet Krypton (*Action* 242, July 1958).

Kandor was like a kid's most private fantasies made real. It was all of childhood's dollhouses, ant farms, secret hiding places, and imaginary playmates rolled into one. When Superman turned a shrinking ray on himself and entered the Bottle City, he plunged into a tiny world in which the ancient ways of Krypton had never died. There the people welcomed him as one of their own. Some of them had even been friends of his mother and father. There, among brilliant-colored skyscrapers, wizened men in togas performed miracles of science. There, strange animals labored in farms beneath an artificial sun. No one on Earth dreamed of Kandor's existence, for Superman hid it in his Arctic Fortress. The Kandorians there were his secret friends, putting their scientific wizardry always at his disposal. And when he tired of his lonely life as the Superman of Earth, he could always shrink into that sheltered world and walk among his own people as Kal-El of Krypton.

As thrilled as the kids were by Kandor, none of them could have been more so than Mort Weisinger

PART II
SUPERMAN'S KRYPTONIAN ROMANCE

Wayne Boring's art was like no one else's, blending operatic grandeur, golden-age goofiness, and an almost dreamlike oddity. He gave power to Superman's new emotionality, but he couldn't keep up with the new intimacy. Script by Otto Binder or Jerry Siegel. (*Superman* 141, Nov. 1960.)

himself. He saw immediately that the focal point of Superman's new direction would have to be his Kryptonian background. For one thing, whenever Superman entered the Kryptonian conditions of Kandor, he lost his superpowers, opening up countless plot avenues that had been closed by the hero's near-omnipotence. For another, Kandor and the Fortress ended Superman's days as an impersonal symbol of justice. Suddenly he was an individual, with a people and a past, with hobbies and friends, an object of interest in and of himself.

The logical encore to Kandor was Krypton itself. Through the device of time travel, Binder took us there, first with Jimmy Olsen (*SPJO* 36, Apr. 1959) and soon with Superman himself (*Superman* 133, Nov. 1959). Though other writers would set stories

on that planet, Binder was its protean geographer. He and his successors gave us a wonderland of robot factories, jewel mountains, sky palaces, fire-falls, scarlet jungles, interplanetary zoos, jet taxis, fire-breathing dogs, scientific tribunals, even antigravity swimming pools. This was the setting for one of the finest of the Weisinger stories, variously attributed both to Binder and Jerry Siegel, which marked the first of a type of epic, emotional adventure that would come to distinguish the Superman line: "Superman's Return to Krypton" (*Superman* 141, Nov. 1960). This full-issue story—three times the length of the usual Weisinger tale—tells of Superman's struggle, bereft of his powers and acting as his father's laboratory assistant before his own birth, to prevent the approaching doom of Krypton. The struggle becomes desperate when he falls in love with a mysterious beauty, Krypton's leading actress. But destiny cannot be changed, and in the end Kal-El returns to the Earth of the present, orphaned and homeless.

This introduction of pathos to Superman, the realization that not even all his powers could give him back what he loved most in life, elevated him from a mere costumed crime fighter to something close to a tragic figure. This was a dark element alien to Julius Schwartz's aesthetic, an almost Greek sense of fatalism. Weisinger's hero was as rational as Schwartz's, and his cosmos nearly as materialistic, but in Weisinger's world there was Something Bigger than mechanistic cause and effect: fate presented almost as a physical law. Although Superman would try repeatedly to use his reason and powers to change the past, he would be slapped down again and again, punished for his superhubris, reminded like a classical hero that the ultimate function of reason is to help us accept what must be. Yet there is also a profoundly Jewish sense to Superman's tragedy, planted there since Siegel's origin story with its references to Moses, amplified in the hero's obsessive returns to the holocaust of his home world now that Weisinger was giving his heart to the hero. He may accept fate, but still this survivor guards his "bottle city," his private, living grief, to ensure that he never forgets. This depth and darkness was something new, not only to

Weisinger and Binder, but to comics in general. It opened an emotional range that even modern superhero comics, for all their overheated passion, have never reached. It also struck chords in young readers—younger than Schwartz's core audience of smart, optimistic preteens—for whom the world is often terrifying and run by incomprehensible laws. Weisinger and Binder had discovered that the hero grew more heroic as he grew less powerful.

The next step in the development of this Krypton past was sparked by the letters of inquisitive young fans. For most of his history, Superman's great prowess had been attributed to Earth having less of a gravitational pull than Krypton. That explanation had worked well when his only real power had been unusual strength, but it fell apart under the gaze of the science-minded kids of the Sputnik era: how could lesser gravity give Superman the powers of flight, X-ray vision, total recall, or super ventriloquism? Now Weisinger answered that Krypton had orbited a red sun, and that somehow, under Earth's yellow sun, Kryptonians are granted remarkable powers. More than a convenient explanation, this provided the springboard for a number of adventures in which Superman found himself powerless and stranded on savage planets orbiting red suns. The first, by Binder, was little more than an exercise in cleverness, as Superman slipped out of danger after danger by his wits (*Action* 262, Mar. 1960), but Weisinger saw the potential for a newly imaginative and suspenseful body of stories.

The genesis of the "red sun" stories shows the new Weisinger method of developing his mythos. He pushed his writers to try whatever they could imagine, threw in twists of his own—and then listened to the fans. After all, he'd been a fan himself, and although he allowed himself no sentimentality for his youth, he knew that fans were buyers, and they knew what they wanted. As a pulp editor he'd promoted fanzines and attended early science fiction conventions. Now, in 1958, one of his first acts was to add letters pages to his comics. Such things weren't unknown in horror and romance comics aimed at older readers—EC had had great letters

pages—but after twenty years of superheroes, it was the first time anyone had asked the kids who bought them what they wanted to read.

A lot of the letters to the "Metropolis Mailbag" were devoted to pointing out gleefully what the kids considered "goofs" or "boo-boos" ("In your story, 'When the World Forgot Superman'. . . the sun is out, and everything is bright. But the calendar reads 'Dec. 11'!") and challenging the editor to squirm his way out of them. Some changed the texture of the comics. After enough readers asked why *Superboy,* supposedly set in the past, featured television and atomic bombs, Weisinger has his artists switch to drawing prewar cars and propeller airliners.

Most important, the letters told the editor what his readers wanted to see more of. When one story featured a superpowered woman (*Superman* 123, Aug. 1958), hundreds of girls wrote to demand a female counterpart for Superman. Weisinger's letter pages revealed a higher proportion of female readers than was typical of superhero comics, and he steadily strengthened his distaff readership base with an attention to female characters and an increasing number of "tales of the heart" that helped keep Superman the best-selling superhero in America through the '60s, long after his TV show was gone. Weisinger and Binder met the girls' demand with Supergirl, a teenage Kryptonian with powers nearly equal to her cousin Superman's. She was promptly awarded a series of her own in the back of *Action Comics* (252, May 1959). Apart from Krypto the Super-Dog, Supergirl was the first Kryptonian to join Superman in his life on Earth. Although Binder's Supergirl stories tended toward condescension and contrivance, Kal-El's cousin Kara did bring another element to his life—a sense of family akin to Captain Marvel's—around which new kinds of stories could be woven. Writers wouldn't be restricted to formula hero-verses-crook plots anymore, but could give the Man of Steel adventures alone or with Supergirl, with his powers or without, on Earth or in Kandor.

In trying to broaden the range of plots still further, Weisinger and Binder introduced a pair of concepts unlike anything comics had ever seen. The first was red kryptonite. This aberration of the notorious green kryptonite, the only substance in the universe capable of weakening Superman, worked weird transformations in Kryptonian minds and bodies for up to forty-eight hours. This gave Superman's writers an open field for bizarre story angles, turning him into a fire-breathing dragon, making him a giant or a midget, giving him a third eye in the back of his head, even splitting him into two beings, one good and one evil. In the glorious "Orphans of Space," Superman and Supergirl accidentally destroy the earth—then find it was all a red K hallucination (*Superman* 144, Apr. 1961).

The use of dreams to tell "impossible" stories intrigued both writer and editor. After all, why should a character as fanciful as Superman be bound by a single invented reality? The "Imaginary Stories" started small, as a series in *Superman's Girlfriend Lois Lane* in 1960, speculating on what Lois's life might be like if she ever succeeded in marrying Superman. Binder wrote the earliest of them, but he quit before Weisinger saw their full potential and spread them throughout the Superman line. As with so much of Binder's work for the Man of Steel, these stories would blossom only later, under other writers. Binder never plotted with the cleverness of Weisinger's veterans, Jerry Siegel and Edmond Hamilton, and some time would pass before those other writers wove the new ideas into their intricate stories.

The art wasn't up to the challenge of the new ideas, either. It had been dominated since the 1940s by Wayne Boring, a forceful draftsman with a grand imagination for fantastic landscapes, which helped stories like "Superman's Return to Krypton." But his style was baroque, almost grotesque, looking back to prewar ornamentalism, and clashed with the new, intimate treatment of Superman. Overall, the craftsmanship fell far below that of the Schwartz stable in both writing and art. Superman's best years still lay ahead. But by the summer of 1960, Superman and his world were already infinitely more interesting than they had been a mere three years before.

The interest was showing up in sales, too. Dell had been doing well for years with its "Giants" and "Annuals," double or triple the usual pages and selling for a whole quarter (when regular comics were a dime). Hardly anyone else, however, dared gamble that kids would pay so much for their product. In 1960, encouraged by reader response to *Superman*, National dared to publish its first annual, eighty pages reprinting Superman stories that fans had asked to see again. It sold stunningly well, and soon not only did Batman have an annual too, but *80 Page Giants* became a regular series. National was firmly back in the number-two spot in the business, and closing the gap.

Otto Binder kept inventing. He helped give Jimmy Olsen a stretchable alter ego called Elastic Lad and invented such menaces as a giant gorilla with kryptonite eyes named Titano. With Siegel and Weisinger he introduced a breed of moronic pseudo-Supermen called Bizarros, who lived on a square planet and did everything backwards. One of his then least-noticed creations was a trio of teenage super heroes who came from the future to meet Superboy (*Adventure* 247, Apr. 1958). It was an undistinguished story and lay forgotten for a year and a half. A few fans, however, thought this Legion of Superheroes showed promise, and beginning in late 1959, it would play an ever-greater role in Superboy's life. Not in Binder's life, though. In 1960, he left DC to write science articles, saying that Weisinger had put him through so many rewrites he couldn't finish enough scripts to make a living.

He'd done his job. He'd given Superman a new lease on life, given him greater fictional freedom than any superhero before or since, and helped his editor lay the foundation of a dazzling and endearing new universe. He'd helped give the comics' greatest hero, at last, a world worthy of him.

Now it would be up to Mort Weisinger and his staff to make Superman a figure as fascinating as any in his world. Already the seeds had been planted for a new Man of Steel, one who would be less steel and more man.

CHAPTER 3

STRANGE ADVENTURES IN SPACE

While Irwin Donenfeld was still waiting for figures on the new Flash's second appearance, the growing American interest in science, outer space and the future exploded into a mania. The launching of that Russian satellite in October 1957 started a space race that sent America's politicians and educators hustling to bring the country up to speed in knowledge and awareness of science and technology. Almost immediately, the center of National's editorial conferences became the creation of two space-faring heroes, one to be set in the far future, in the Buck Rogers tradition, the other in the present, à la Flash Gordon. Editor Jack Schiff "opted for the one from the future," said Schwartz. "I opted for the one from today because I think it's more dramatic having something strange and imaginary happening today than in the far future which is *already* imaginary."

By the end of the '50s, things were looking stable on the DC line. Except for Dell, the competition was basically gone. National bought the Quality Comics properties in 1956. Martin Goodman's distribution operation collapsed the next year, and to stay afloat he'd have to sign with Independent News, becoming a vassal to Jack Liebowitz. Liebowitz was happy to take Goodman's money, and his pride, but he wasn't going to let him flood the market again—he'd sell a pathetic eight Goodman titles a month, no more. The Goodman comics line didn't even have a name anymore, and was almost certainly moribund. Marty himself was making more money off non-comics publishing, and some insiders figured he only kept the comics alive so he could delay having to fire his comics editor, Stanley Lieber—who happened to be related to Marty's wife.

Most of the comic book part-timers—the likes of Alfred Bester, Frank Frazetta, David V. Reed and Virgil Finlay, who'd shuttled back and forth between comics and more "legit" media—were now gone from the business. Those who stayed clung to any steady gig they could get. Julie Schwartz now pared his core stable down to seven freelancers who could steadily deliver the kind of intricate but clear, gimmick-filled stories that he wanted: writers John Broome and Gardner Fox, and artists Carmine Infantino, Murphy Anderson, Mike Sekowsky, Sid Greene, and Gil Kane. In *Mystery in Space* and *Strange Adventures* they were building well-crafted stories on devilishly inventive premises, but the plots were gruelingly repetitive: a screwy event proves to be part of an alien invasion of earth, cleverly repelled by a lone hero through a quasiscientific gimmick. The only relief was the occasional cute little series like *Space Cabbie* or *Interplanetary Insurance*. Schwartz's new science fiction hero, Adam Strange, came as a shot in the arm to the whole stable.

The first problem presented by the notion of a present-day spaceman was transportation: the American rockets of those days could barely clear the Florida rooftops without ignominiously exploding,

ONLY A MOMENT LEFT TO AVERT A COLLISION BETWEEN *EARTH* AND MY ADOPTED PLANET *RANN!*

ADAM STRANGE *and* HAWKMAN IN A DUAL ADVENTURE... "PLANETS *in* PERIL!"

Sleek, optimistic, cool but masculine: the Schwartz weltanschauung in one image. Infantino at his peak, inked by Murphy Anderson. (*Mystery in Space* #90, Apr. 1964.)

ment of reality. And poor Adam has fallen in love with Alanna, beautiful daughter of the chief scientist of Rann. His enforced separation from her is an agony; his only solace lies in waiting for the next zeta-beam. Fortunately, a long series of them had been fired toward Earth, and Adam is able to calculate when and where each will strike. And so he waits, gazing at the indifferent stars, for his next fabulous adventure.

The first Adam stories, in *Showcase* (17–19, Dec. 1958–Apr. 1959), were standard Flash Gordon fare, in which the swashbuckling off-worlder turned back would-be tyrants on his adopted planet. But after beginning his regular appearances in *Mystery in Space* (*MIS* 53, Aug. 1959) Adam's life took a decided turn for the peculiar. No sooner would he materialize on Rann than he would find himself facing a man-eating vacuum cleaner, a giant sentient atom, a huge magnifying glass that floated in the sky and burned the cities below it with sunlight, or even a giant duplicate of himself. Soon even Adam was wondering wryly why some impossible menace always seemed to strike Rann when he arrived. He wouldn't have had to wonder if he'd known his adventures were being written by Gardner F. Fox.

Fox was an indefatigable producer of comics and paperback potboilers, with an output he described as "a comic book a week, four or five novels a year." Under at least six pseudonyms he tossed off science fiction, horror, mystery, gothic, romance and historical novels, none of them artful but most displaying a free imagination and a sweeping sense of romance. Most of his early comic book work had been on superheroes, but now, on SF, he was able to combine his imagination with a remarkably varied store of knowledge. Fox held a law degree and was fascinated with magic and science, and he filled thousands of index cards with odd facts. His Adam Strange stories always revolved around some peculiarity of chemistry or physics, often turning some commonplace item into a menace, and it was usually through a combination of Yankee know-how and scientific knowledge that

and could hardly have carried a man to exciting adventures in space. The ingenious solution was a flash of light, the zeta-beam, a teleportation ray fired at Earth years before by the scientists of Rann, a planet orbiting Alpha Centauri. When it strikes archaeologist Adam Strange while he is on a dig in South America, it hurtles him instantaneously twenty-five trillion miles across the gulf of space. Just as a flashlight cast on the pages of a comic book hidden under the covers at night transports a kid to a world of wonder, so the zeta-beam takes Adam Strange to the beautiful, perilous, superscientific planet Rann. But there's a catch: the beam wears off at unpredictable times, throwing him back to Earth and the imprison-

Adam triumphed. How do you defeat a gang of villainously intelligent dust devils? Well, if you're able, as Adam was, to deduce that they are a sodium-based life-form—which would have to be animated by high internal temperatures—then you simply throw sand on them. "I added the silicate," our hero says, "needed to transform the sodiums and calciums in their bodies . . . to glass!" (*MIS* 68, June 1961). An unspoken challenge to the reader was always to spot the nemesis's scientific Achilles' heel before Adam could. We rarely succeeded.

Schwartz played off this quasiscientific tone with "editor's notes" full of relevant facts, flashing back to the early days of the pulps, when science fiction and science fact were often married in a single magazine. The notes even found their way into his superhero stories, explaining how Flash could zoom through a wall or run on water. When Schwartz followed Mort Weisinger's lead and added letters pages, they immediately took on a brainy tone, as young SF readers like Paul Seydor and Richard C. West subjected Schwartz's works to the same standards as books and short stories. Suddenly the kids were becoming the critics, and Schwartz knew from his experience in the '30s where that could lead: older and more educated readers would allow for smarter and more sophisticated stories.

Only one artist could hope to keep Fox's plots looking sophisticated, to render his parade of outlandish creations amazing and not laughable: Carmine Infantino. With the master of the magically plausible to make his ideas real, Fox was truly able to flex his creative muscles, and under the writer's pressure, Infantino produced some of the most inventive and beautiful art of his career. He brought to life the exhilaration of Adam soaring skyward with his rocket-pack, the passion between him and the exotic Alanna, the breathtaking futuristic cityscapes of Rann, full of sweeping curves, delicate spires and swirling aerial pathways. Earlier comic book artists had based their alien settings on the vertical thrust of industrial modernism or a sort of Oriental exoticism, but Infantino's was a fantasy on LeCorbusier: horizontal, weightless and postindustrial. *Adam Strange* was a modernist high romance.

Turning these exquisite designs into a lush and solid world was inker Murphy Anderson.[2] On *Flash*, Schwartz generally had Infantino inked by Joe Giella, whose work was scratchy but always serviceable. Infantino and Anderson, though, were Schwartz's dream team, which shows where SF ranked in his priorities. Schwartz admitted he knew little about art, but he had a safe fallback position: "If it's not clear, it's worthless. So I look at the artwork from my point of view, an ordinary, average Mr. Joe." His was an ascendant aesthetic in the Frigidaire age. Sheldon Mayer may have liked Caniff-influenced artists, but Sol Harrison, who as head of National's production department had come to dominate DC's look since the early '50s, preferred those who followed that other seminal adventure-cartoonist, Alex Raymond. On *Flash Gordon* Raymond had perfected a fluid elegance as smooth as Caniff's expressionism was angular and loose. Harrison liked artists who could simplify Raymond's style into clean lines that printed sharply, especially Raymond's successor on *Flash Gordon*, a pristinely polished but passionless cartoonist named Dan Barry. There were other big influences, including Warren Tufts, but "the DC house style in the '50s," said Gil Kane, "was watered-down Dan Barry." Schwartz even employed Barry's brother Sy to bring the new *Gordon* look direct to DC science fiction.

"House styles" can be fatal for artists, but for Infantino this one was a valuable education. He'd come in bristling with raw Canifftiness, then passed through a duller but more assured Barryesque chrysalis before breaking through into maturity. Murphy Anderson, meanwhile, had been bringing a Raymond sleekness to various SF comics and to *Flash Gordon*'s competitor, the *Buck Rogers* strip. He and Infantino were the most unlikely of artistic partners. Infantino distorted perspective and anatomy to create effect, while Anderson believed in strict naturalism and classic balance, finding it maddening to wrestle with Infantino's "impossible" character poses. Schwartz, however, proved that the "average Mr. Joe"

[2] Standard comic book production resembles an assembly line, the better to exploit each worker's time and ability: one artist turns in only a pencil drawing of each story, usually sparse in detail, which another artist then finishes in ink, to have letters added by a third and colors by a fourth.

had learned a few things about art. "Carmine and Anderson," he said, "were both just at the point in their artistic development when they could balance each other and be a great team." They combined to give Adam Strange's adventures a polished dynamism nearly unparalleled in comics history.

The wild stories in the Schwartz science fiction comics challenged the skills of the artists, but the artists were able to respond with a challenge of their own. Throughout the '50s and '60s, in a system devised for the pulp magazines by his old friend Weisinger, Schwartz worked out the cover design for each issue with an artist and had it drawn *before* the story was written, thus ensuring that every comic would have an eye-catching, kid-thrilling cover. Often Schwartz would have a plot idea to go with the cover, but sometimes he and the writer would have to make up a story from scratch to go with some outlandish picture conceived solely for its visual appeal: say, a man with a miniature planet Saturn in place of his head, or a fisherman in a flying boat reeling in a green alien from a "fishing hole in the sky." The result was a stable of comics that united visual imagination and story more completely than any of their contemporaries. That was to be one of the great appeals of Schwartz's superhero comics in the next few years.

In *Strange Adventures*, especially from 1959 on, Schwartz's staff played with characters and stories that weren't quite superheroic, but that set standards for the coming heroic revival. Most science fiction in comics had tended to the horrific or cautionary, the vision of an industrial working class gaping up at the monstrous machines that both provided and mastered, of a provincial America recently thrust into the horror of a global technological slaughterhouse. Schwartz, an optimist and a technophile in an America becoming briefly more optimistic and technophilic, saw that a lighter approach could be better suited to his medium and his moment. He, Fox, and Broome displayed a remarkable sensitivity to the imaginations of their young readers, for the themes of their stories seemed to spring straight from the fantasies of ten-year-olds.

The plots were still repetitive, but now they drew a special enchantment from the details around which they were woven, images that held magical significance for kids at the beginning of the 1960s: astronauts, aliens, pets, dinosaurs, cavemen, toys, ray guns, apes, contests, scientists, lost civilizations, and heroic fathers. They were details both fantastic and comfortingly familiar, skillfully blended into nifty little mysteries. Schwartz's own boyhood love of athletics bubbled up in stories of sports in the future and on other worlds; such stories nearly received their own title when five issues of *The Brave and the Bold* (45–49, Jan.–Sep. 1963) were turned over to *Strange Sports Stories,* with imaginative Fox and Broome stories and Infantino art. Many stories even featured children as protagonists, like "Earth Boy Meets Spaceboy," a futuristic twist on *The Prince and the Pauper* (*SA* 123, Dec. 1960).

As heroes started generating more interest, Schwartz introduced regular, alternating series into *Strange Adventures*. The first, and best realized, was *Space Museum* (from issue 104, May 1959). Its only recurring characters were the narrator, Howard Parker, and his son Tommy, who once a month visit the Space Museum, one of the wonders of the 25th century, where, behind every fabulous object on display, ". . . there's a story of heroism, daring, and self-sacrifice." Astronaut Mike Dillon, for instance, was cursed to finish in second place in every contest he undertook, until the day he discovered that only silver could power the device needed to repel an alien invasion, and so saved the world with his silver medals (*SA* 136, Jan. 1962). Here was the unvarying Schwartz hero, just like Adam Strange and the Flash: a positivist in a positivistic world, using reason and knowledge to master an ultimately knowable universe and thus restore our unquestioned status quo to proper order.

All twenty *Space Museum* stories were written by Fox and all but the first drawn by Infantino. But this wasn't the pristine Infantino of *The Flash* and *Adam Strange*, this was an Infantino with a loose and exuberant line that suggested rather than delineated, a line sometimes rough and scratchy, sometimes delicate and wistful, but never merely illustrative. This was Infantino inking his own pencils. Schwartz was always uneasy about Infantino's self-inking jobs, calling them "too impressionistic" for the readers—and perhaps too subjective for his own worldview—and it was only through stubbornness that Carmine won the right to ink the *Detective Chimp* stories in *Rex the Wonder Dog* (*ARWD* 15-46, June 1954-Oct. 1959). In the process he turned a series of lightweight tales about a mischievous ape into some of the loveliest showpieces in comics history, pen-and-brush meditations on the palm trees, swamps and *moderne* hotels of a Florida resort. From that point on, Infantino always had one or two low-profile venues for his inks—the delightful *Pow Wow Smith, Indian Lawman* (*WC* 57–85, June 1956–Feb. 1961), *Super-Chief* with its evocative woodlands (*ASW* 117–119, Mar.–July, 1961), *Space Museum* and, later, *The Elongated Man* —though Schwartz would never let him foist his "impressionism" on a front-line hero. It is work that still stands out for its elegance and individuality, its effort to elevate trivial material into art by brushstroke alone, and it provides a glimpse of Infantino's true artistic sensibility—a sensibility that would slowly reshape him, and then the DC comics themselves.

Less than a year after *Space Museum*, Schwartz added *Star Hawkins*, the adventures of the ace private detective of the twenty-first century and his "amazing robot secretary," Ilda (*SA* 114, Mar. 1960). Nearly every story revolved around one of them getting into some wacky jam, to be bailed out by the other in a mock-heroic feat of physical prowess or cleverness. It was a charming and boisterous entry in the Schwartz stable, even if the plots were predictable and the humor pretty cornball (and it *was* funny when Star couldn't pay the rent and dumped Ilda in a pawn shop). The artist was Mike Sekowsky, about the same age as Infantino and Anderson, but with a background mainly in humor comics. Often maligned for his strange interpretation of human anatomy and his blocky lines, Sekowsky had an intelligent sense of

The other side of Carmine Infantino. Gardner Fox's script obviously called for a spaceman zapping aliens with a ray gun, but in the course of inking it, Infantino made it a study in texture, depth, and boldly spotted blacks. (*Strange Adventures* 161, Mar. 1964.)

storytelling that was fluid and dynamic, and that would soon serve him and DC very well.

There was one turkey on the Schwartz ranch, one that serves as a negative demonstration of the delicate balance of elements that made Schwartz's good comics good. Gardner Fox built *The Star Rovers* around one plot trick: three space-faring adventurers experience three almost identical action-packed mysteries, retell them later to each other and discover a single explanation for all. Since the mysteries were as dull as they were similar, sitting through each one three times became a test of patience. They weren't helped by the art of Sid Greene, who, despite delivering attractive cartoony pencils and some of the best inking in the business, lacked that gift of Infantino's to make the absurd palpable. It was best for everyone that the series only lasted for a few issues of *Mystery in Space* and *Strange Adventures*.

The readers' favorite of the new series was *The Atomic Knights*, the closest to superherodom in structure but the farthest in tone—at least when it began. Written by Broome, it was set in the wake of World War III, when plant and animal life was nearly extinct and man barely lingered on. The Atomic Knights, who wear ancient suits of armor that shield them from nuclear radiation, comprised a small "organization determined to represent law and order and the forces of justice and to help right wrong and prevent evil." They were reason and order personified: an ex-schoolteacher, a scientist, two ex-soldiers, a pretty girl and Gardner Grayle, their levelheaded leader. Yet here, alone among Schwartz's comics, science was shown not benefiting mankind but bringing terrible destruction. Broome's work often hinted at a darker imagination than those of his editor or the index-card-collecting Fox, and his focus was always more on the human dilemma than physical fact. The series started with the Knights forming to depose the Black Baron, an evil despot hoarding a badly needed food supply (*SA* 117, June 1960). Next they settle in the first postwar pioneer village, where they manage to grow food, start a school and form a political structure to govern the town, beginning the long, hard climb back to civilization. Their best stories follow the pattern, especially when Broome takes us on tours of ruined American cities. In "Cavemen of New York" (123, Dec. 1960), the Knights help New

Yorkers who've devolved to savagery regain their humanity (one can imagine Broome riding the subway and dreaming of his weed-mantled home upstate when he thought of it). In "The King of New Orleans" (147, Dec. 1962) they defeat a ruthless monarch with, yes, Dixieland jazz, and in "Danger in Detroit" (153, June 1963) they're given the first postwar automobile for overthrowing a futuristic Gestapo (and in 1963 it must have seemed as though not even a holocaust could slow down America's greatest industry). Murphy Anderson carved it all in pencil and ink, making lovely pastoral scenes and stark ruins real with sculptural solidity and precise detail.

But as early as the Knights' fifth appearance something strange was happening: in "World Out of Time," they found themselves in Atlantis, of all places (*SA* 129, June 1961). More departures from the established milieu followed—Knights fight Atlanteans twice again, Knights domesticate giant dalmatians, Knights fight aliens—until the departures became the norm. Then came "When the Earth Blacked Out," in which they tangled with a race of subterranean mole creatures who turn out to be the real perpetrators of World War III (144, Sept. 1962). In one stroke, the plausibility and daring on which the strip had been based was undermined.

It just went to show how ingrained was Julius Schwartz's sunny rationalism and how thoroughly he pressed down the darker sides of the modern world. It made his comics popular, but it would also ultimately, inevitably, make them something to rebel against.

CHAPTER 4

BIZARRE CHARACTERS AND FANTASTIC WEAPONS

The comic book field was a tragic one. Its readers would always grow up and leave it behind. The few who stayed with it into adulthood usually did so because of unresolved feelings that kept them spinning through old fantasies. Nearly all the writers, artists, and editors who started in comics originally aspired to bigger things. Those with the talent and boldness to move on to those bigger things never revisited the ghetto from which they'd escaped. Those who stayed felt trapped, and few continued to grow artistically once they'd attained a mastery of their craft. There was no Tolstoy or Rembrandt of comics, hardly even a Hitchcock or Billy Wilder, using the second half of life to delve deeper into his art and self with the facility learned in the first half. There were few seconds acts in comic book lives, only short plateaus and long declines. Bob Kane said he once met his fellow Batman creator, Bill Finger, late in life, and found him "disheartened by the lack of major accomplishments in his career. . . . I had to agree, for I realized that Bill could have become a great screen writer or perhaps the author of a best-seller instead of hacking out comic book stories anonymously. How sad—a great talent wasted." Kane himself dropped comic book art as soon as he could afford to. Julius Schwartz called Finger "a haunted man," and the description could have applied

to many others. Schwartz was one of the lucky few with a gift for adjusting to changing times. Most spent decades swimming upstream with ever-diminishing energy and ever-growing bitterness.

Science fiction was doing wonders for Schwartz and Weisinger in the late 1950s, but for them it was a labor of love. For Jack Schiff it was only a labor, and when it was forced on him it virtually destroyed him—the end of the Eisenhower age separated the men of the past from the boys of the future. Schiff had begun as a pulp editor at Standard Magazines in the 1930s, but his beats were mystery and horror, not SF. He had, in fact, helped hire Mort Weisinger to take over the SF line in 1938. When Weisinger entered the military during World War II, he completed the circle by having Schiff hired to take his place at National. By the time Weisinger returned, Schiff had made himself an indispensable part of the company. As *de facto* managing editor, he coordinated production schedules, issued writing and art assignments, and acted as liaison between freelancers and the front office. He made himself valuable to Jack Liebowitz when National was courting respectability, working as a contact with the Comics Code Authority and the U.S. government for various educational and international projects. He was a man with a social conscience almost freakish in the quick-buck business of comics, a prewar left-winger who managed to function in the most vulgar enclaves of capitalism, with a stubborn belief in the power of comics to educate children. He was proud of the stacks of crayoned letters he got from little kids, never courting the preteen readers Schwartz attracted. His most prized creation was a comic called *Real Fact*, which was exactly what it sounds like, and he pushed for years for a DC "educational office." Liebowitz never cut loose the money for that, but he did let Schiff spend thousands on his "institutional pages," one-page messages about issues ranging from racial tolerance to consideration for neighbors to the joys of public libraries. They were coordinated with the National Social Welfare Assembly and appeared in every DC comic from 1950 to 1967. Today they're a unique time capsule of well-meaning liberalism from that optimistic age between the fall of fascism and the fall of Americanism.

They called him "Schiff on Skates," because on top of all his "institutional" jobs, he was also scrambling to edit a wide range of comics, including the three titles featuring DC's second most popular hero: *Batman, Detective Comics,* and *World's Finest Comics.* During the 1950s he also launched the western *Tomahawk* and a quartet of supernatural titles in what he called "the Ambrose Bierce tradition": *House of Mystery, House of Secrets, My Greatest Adventure,* and *Tales of the Unexpected.* Like Weisinger, Schiff got involved in the plotting, but unlike Weisinger he was never heard to tell a writer that his script wasn't good enough to be used for toilet paper. "I insisted on good, tight plots with characterization and gimmicks," he said, "but pictures with colorful locale and sweeping action." His were the best crafted and most colorful comics of DC's golden age.

When Weisinger and Whit Ellsworth went to work on the *Superman* TV show, still more responsibilities fell onto Schiff's shoulders. He got help from a "team editing" system with art director Murray Boltinoff and copy editor George Kashdan, with assistance from writer/staffer Jack Miller, but it was still too much. Between that and the mid-'50s

malaise, the pizzazz of his stable's work was dropping. The stories—mainly by Jack Miller, Dave and Dick Wood, France "Eddie" Herron and Bill Finger—were getting more and more repetitive. The art was looking hacked out, and artists who had made great names for themselves—Mort Meskin, Howard Sherman, even the artist's artist, Alex Toth—turned in work that was a shadow of what they'd done before. A sameness set in that took away even from the reliably attractive art of Ruben Moreira, Lee Elias and Nick Cardy. Inkers were in short supply. Charlie Paris, the stable's best, handled as much as he could. But the smooth Stan Kaye was busy with a lot of work for Weisinger, and Schiff's mainstay, George Roussos, was kept too busy to produce good work.

With Ellsworth gone, most of his duties were picked up by Irwin Donenfeld. Usually the younger Donenfeld contented himself with refereeing editorial meetings, saying "Let's go" to new projects and dealing with freelancers (which involved all the standard cost-saving methods of comics publishing: fighting over raises, threatening dismissal, intimidating artists and writers into keeping their page rates secret, hiding sales figures, and watching for any signs of unionism). When it became clear that there weren't going to be any more editorial directors, however, he must have figured it was time to show the editors that he knew best. In 1957 he told Jack Schiff to revamp all his comics with space travel and aliens. He was never so doctrinaire with Weisinger—was it just because *Superman* sold better than *Batman,* or did it help that Donenfeld and Liebowitz were chummy with Weisinger, the consummate company man, but looked at Schiff as (in writer Arnold Drake's words) the "house radical"? Schiff had always had an ally in Ellsworth, who'd seen comics through the eyes of an artist, not a publisher's son, but now he was at the mercy of the owners. He wasn't a science man like Schwartz and Weisinger—he was the one DC editor whose worldview allowed him to do outright supernatural stories with conviction—and for him "science fiction" translated into "monsters," like in the Saturday matinees. Maybe it was because of his resentment, but instead of integrating SF elements into his own aesthetic he lost sight of everything that had made his comics good. He and his writers were suddenly going for the utterly fantastic, with stories hurtling mindlessly from battle to chase to battle again, starring a ceaseless parade of dinosaurs, monsters and aliens who allowed none of the characterization Schiff once demanded. Again and again came lines like, "The Shrawthca is senselessly destroying everything in its path!" (*TU* 54, Oct. 1960). Such stuff could briefly thrill the little kids of the late '50s—for Schiff's artists produced the most toothsome and colorful monsters ever in comics—but it got old quickly.

Schiff and his writers—or one writer, at least—handled science fiction better when it was the basis of a series rather than a reluctant add-on. *Space Ranger,* born of the same editorial conference that created *Adam Strange* in 1957, epitomized Schiff's colorful, juvenile slant. Through the ingenious imagination of writer Arnold Drake, it told of the adventures of futuristic policeman Rick Starr as he patrolled our solar system from his asteroid headquarters, with the aid of his girlfriend Myra and a scrappy little alien shape-changer named Cryll. There were plenty of aliens here, but made charmingly exotic by artist Bob Brown (*Showcase* 15–16, Aug.–Oct. 1958, *TU* 40–82, 1959–1964). Less colorful was *Tommy Tomorrow,* created by Schiff and Weisinger for *Real Fact* in 1947. It was intended for actual scientific speculation, but the '50s saw it transformed into a backup strip about an interstellar police force, running in *Action* and *World's Finest*, with uninspired Jack Miller scripts and muddy Jim Mooney art. Some tryouts in *Showcase* in 1962 and 1963 with Lee Elias art were fun, but came to naught. Miller had better luck working with artist Joe Certa on the Martian Manhunter, a character that writer Joe Samachson had developed with Weisinger in 1955, when they were trying to find contemporary twists on mystery stories for *Detective Comics*. In his early adventures the shape-shifting alien cop had fought crime on Earth by adopting different appearances, but now he made more use of an array of Superman-like powers:

Martian Strength, Martian Breath, and Martian Vision, plus a weird ability to elongate his body. As things got wackier he was joined by an interdimensional pet named Zook (*Detective* 311, Jan. 1963). With his cartoony face, pliable orange body, antennae, and baby talk, Zook brought a goofball quality to the stories that made them charming to kids.

The real problem with the "monster craze," as Schiff called it, wasn't with the mystery or science fiction series. The problem was what that craze did to Schiff's one major hero.

When created by Kane and Finger in 1939, Batman was a dark-night avenger of crime in the pulp tradition of the Shadow and the Spider. Soon he picked up the comics' original kid sidekick, Robin the Boy Wonder, along with a butler named Alfred, a utility belt full of remarkable gadgets, and a subterranean Batcave housing scientific criminological devices and such sleek vehicles as the Batmobile and the Batplane. By the early 1950s, Batman and Robin were spending more and more time traveling the world and donning exotic disguises, yet still Schiff and his staff kept their adventures squarely in the realm of what was plausible for a costumed master sleuth without superpowers. Then, in the jittery wake of the Comics Code, the Bat-tales were dulled down a bit as DC editors feared to show people getting shot or punching each other. In 1957, science fiction came to Gotham City, and during the next few years the Dynamic Duo went haywire. No longer would Batman match wits with such colorful psychotics of urban gangland as the Joker, the Catwoman, and the Penguin. First he faced against a thug armed with an "energy radiator" from the planet Skar (*Detective* 250, Dec. 1957), then the winged bat-people from another dimension (*Batman* 116, June 1958), next Garr of Planetoid X (*Batman* 117, Aug. 1958). Within three years Batman found himself embroiled with so many aliens and weird creatures that on one cover he was driven to remark, "Great Scott! Another bizarre character with a fantastic weapon!" (*Detective* 287, Jan. 1961).

Some new villains were created for him, but they

[1] In any given month we were bound to find either Flash's enemy Grodd, Superman's foe Titano, Superboy's pet Super-Monkey, the backup feature Congorilla, Bobo the Detective Chimp or one of the dozens of gorillas who swung through the science fiction comics—all apparently because one "gorilla cover" on a Strange Adventures in 1951 sold unusually well and Irwin Donenfeld said, "Let's do more apes." Time proved that the "gorilla boost" was a one-time occurrence, but such was the desperation of the mid-'50s.

were nearly all in the pattern of the Fox, the Shark and the Vulture, a trio of renegade inventors who used wild devices and animal-like getups in place of the personal lunacies that had made the old villains so intriguing (*Detective* 253, Mar. 1958). Suddenly Batman and Robin were wrenched from their world of dark alleys and rooftops and hurled to other dimensions and distant solar systems. As the distortions of his milieu accelerated, Batman found that he himself was subject to weird transformations. Beginning with "The Merman Batman" (*Batman* 118, Sep. 1958), in rapid order he became an invisible man, a zebra Batman, a robot, a negative Batman, an alien, a baby, a "colossus," a mummy, and the "bizarre Batman genie."

To add to the confusion, Schiff had begun populating the comics with a burgeoning "Batman family" in emulation of the growing supporting cast of Superman. The first, from 1955, was Ace the Bat-Hound. He was inspired by Superboy's dog, Krypto, but was a generic-looking dog who battled criminals wearing a black mask over his eyes (evidently to prevent thugs from recognizing him and striking at him through his loved ones). A year later came Batwoman, a slightly more original creation since Supergirl's debut still lay three years ahead. Bat-Girl appeared in 1961, with the primary role of kissing Robin on the cheek and making him blush, and briefly in 1958 there was even a Bat-Ape, testament to National's all-pervasive love of simians.[1] In 1959 came Bat-Mite—an "interdimensional imp" modeled after Superman's pesky Mr. Mxyzptlk—who dressed like a sloppy midget version of Batman and kicked off wacky adventures under the guise of trying to help his crime-fighting idol. Instead of keeping company only with the night, Batman and Robin found themselves plunked down in the middle of a peculiarly tasteless costume party.

While the stories grew more harebrained, the art became steadily more crude and repetitive. The bulk of the stories were produced by the studio—and in the manner—of Bob Kane, Batman's original artist. The amount of work actually done by Kane during

these years is difficult to determine. He claims to have done almost all of it, while nearly everyone else involved claims he did none. Kane had a venerable reputation for downplaying the contributions of his collaborators—including Bill Finger's—and until 1964 his contract reportedly stipulated that all Batman comics bear his signature, even when drawn by the distinct and vastly superior Jerry Robinson and Dick Sprang. (Kane was the lucky beneficiary of Jerry Siegel and Joe Shuster's 1948 lawsuit over the rights to Superman. Siegel and Shuster wanted Kane to join them, but National bought him off with a contract that gave him a legal and financial piece of his creations. He was one of the very few comics creators who got more than a per-page work fee.) Official DC reprint records now list veteran Sheldon Moldoff—who had first made his mark in comics with his "swipes" of Alex Raymond's *Flash Gordon* for *Hawkman*—as the artist behind most of the issues, although Schiff says other ghost artists, including Phil Kelsey, were involved. Whoever was doing the work, it wasn't much to look at. Kane's work had always been a little stiff, but after twenty years of repetition his studio had reduced the characters to ciphers, and did the storytelling by rote. Nonetheless, the Kane ghosts' work often showed a sort of juvenile vitality, and their aliens could be genuinely amusing. Now and then, when Schiff and his freelancers put no fetters on their flights of imagination, they created tales so inventive and exotic that even their rough execution was made charming.

Those virtues shone brightest in the title Schiff called his "pet baby," *World's Finest Comics*. There Batman teamed up with Superman, whose fantastic nature made their outlandish adventures believable, and there he benefited from scripts by a master of space adventure, Edmond Hamilton. Best of all, though, *World's Finest* was drawn from 1955 to 1961 by one of the last giants of the golden age, Dick Sprang. Although he worked in the same small-figured, childlike style as Kane and his ghosts, Sprang brought into his panels a unique wit and dynamism capable of breathing life into the most farfetched story. To that he added a caricaturist's talent for giving all his miniature figures character and charm, and a miniaturist's touch for the exquisitely detailed background. His page layouts were as intelligent as Infantino's, although in a voluptuous, premodern way, and his storytelling rhythms were propulsive. In one intricate, colorful gem of a tale, a beast of living fire terrorizes the picturesque Mediterranean. As Batman, Robin, and Superman search for the key to defeating it, they travel from a distant planet of odd geometric forms, through the bustling streets of ancient Greece, to exquisite miniature landscapes in the Egypt of the pharaohs (*WF* 107, Feb. 1960). Another story finds a charming little alien movie producer unleashing three of the most peculiar creatures ever conceived by a comic book artist. One looks like a giant smirking golf tee, issuing from its head a floating roadway along which scurry an army of tiny robots. The scaly green mogul films our heroes' battle with them for his next extravaganza (*WF* 108, Mar. 1960). For that wonderful run of comics we can forgive the entire Schiff "monster craze." Sprang may have been too true an artist for that tragic field, however. The other great Batman artist, Jerry Robinson, had already escaped into teaching and newspaper cartooning; in 1961, after twenty years of drawing the Dynamic Duo, Sprang left to take up Western landscape painting. His successor, Jim Mooney, was unable to sustain the charm.

In 1962 and 1963 Schiff brought the Penguin, Joker, Mirror Man and some other old villains back to the Bat-world. He also pointed to the booming sales of his *Batman Annuals,* full of reprints from the early '50s, as proof that kids didn't demand an exclusive diet of monsters, despite what the Saturday matinees suggested. "I believe that there is such a thing as developing tastes in children," he said, "instead of just succumbing to them." Dropping sales proved his point about the monsters, and he may have privately welcomed those sales reports, because in 1963 he

WORLD'S FINEST COMICS

was allowed to abandon the monsters and go back to what he did best. It was an illusion, though: his bosses had lost faith in him and would soon be planning some unpleasant moves.

While Batman struggled along, some other old crimefighters were afflicted with problems not quite so outrageous but also, unfortunately, not as interesting. *Blackhawk*, originally with Quality Comics, had originally been about a team of World War II aviators. Where the once-proud defenders of freedom had let sound their battle cry, "Hawk-a-a-a!" now, under Schiff, they could only paraphrase their fellow unfortunate, Batman: "Great Scott! The eight-limbed Octi-Ape has escaped from the spaceship and has grabbed Chop-Chop!" The artists, Dick Dillin and Chuck Cuidera, had peaked in the '40s and were now sliding slowly down. *Green Arrow* and *Aquaman* had been Mort Weisinger's first comic book creations, back in 1941, but now they were just routine backup strips in *Adventure, World's Finest* and *Detective*. Aquaman's gimmick, fighting crime under and on the sea with the aid of

When comics art was meant to enchant, not to advertise virtuosity: Dick Sprang's technique was exacting, his hand masterful, and his layouts ingenious, but all we see are charm, adventure, and magic. The work was uncredited, but we believe the inks to be by Charlie Paris and the script by Edmond Hamilton (*World's Finest* #107, Feb. 1960.)

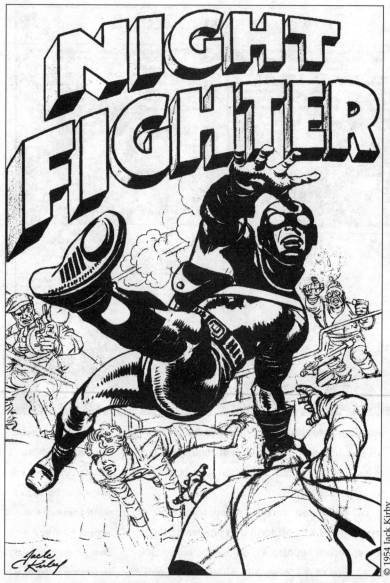

© 1954 Jack Kirby

No one drew the human figure in action like Jack Kirby—but that wasn't enough during the hard times of the mid-'50s. He turned an unpublished Fighting American cover from 1954 into this showpiece for a new idea, but he never found a buyer.

an octopus and other aquatic pals, was a little more interesting than Green Arrow's—fighting crime with superarchery—and he was granted his own title in 1962. The Sea King was also blessed by the art of Ramona Fradon, one of the few women in the business and a cartoonist with a wonderfully decorative, humorous line who never got her due. Green Arrow never had much art to brag about, except for a few fill-ins by Jack Kirby.

Kirby was the man behind one other Schiff title, a title unique among the DC comics of the time, for it was created, drawn and partly written by a single man. It fit the basic mold of monster-filled science fiction, but Kirby's powerful drawings, relentless sto-

rytelling and grand imagination raised *Challengers of the Unknown* well above the usual and raised it high above the rest.

Jack Kirby, born Jacob Kurtzberg, stands as one of the great independent spirits of comic book history. Since the birth of the medium, he'd been its most seminal and productive action artist. He and his partner Joe Simon had created Captain America for Martin Goodman in 1941, started a number of wartime features for DC, then formed their own firm for the production of comics to be sold to a variety of publishers. They created the entire romance comics genre—which for years accounted for more sales than any other—and handled it with more power and integrity than anyone since. They virtually owned the "boy gang" adventure genre, with *Newsboy Legion*, *Boy Commandoes*, and *Boys' Ranch*. They did crime, horror, westerns, humor, superheroes, even humorous superheroes, with the best of them. Kirby was another Caniff man (he called *Terry and the Pirates* "my art school") but by the age of twenty-three he had a style like no one else's. He had to pursue his dream against the resistance of his parents, like Mort Weisinger, but he was no affluent college boy like Mort. He fought his way up from the tough streets of the Lower East Side, and all his life he would push himself twelve to sixteen hours a day, seven days a week, to support his wife and children. He was a short man, and defensively conscious of it, and maybe because of that was better at capturing superhuman "bigness" than anyone else. He changed the way every artist in the business viewed action scenes, with his superhumanly dynamic figures, heroic musculature, and acrobatics that nearly flew off the page. Sensitive and intensely emotional, but with a tough veneer, he could stew with resentment for long periods—but his only violence exploded onto the page.

Kirby was an artist who cared deeply about his material and rebelled against doing stories other people's way, though he never risked his livelihood by rebelling against the wage-slave conditions of the industry. His commitment and creative generosity were astounding in a man who, until his final years, owned little of his own work, rarely seeing a royalty or even a reprint fee. He seldom stayed long with any publisher, but he worked with Simon for over fifteen years—until the crash of the mid-'50s made Simon think they'd do better peddling their creations separately. They divided up their unpublished ideas, and Kirby got the prototype issue of *Challengers*, an idea only he could have done right. It was he who brought a love of manly camaraderie and the rough-and-tumble action of street fights into the Simon-Kirby comics, and he brought it from his own youth, especially from his involvement in the radical Depression-era club called the Boys' Brotherhood Republic. It was Kirby, too, who brought in the science-fictional and grandiose, and now, on his own, his imagination would only get bigger.

The Challengers were four rugged adventurers who miraculously survive a plane crash. "We should be dead," says Red, "but we're not!" "We're living on borrowed time," says Ace, and the four of them throw in together to tackle greater dangers than they've ever dared before, dangers from "Out there— places we cannot see! Things we fear to touch! Sounds that do not belong to this world! Riddles of the ages lurking beyond the bridge without a name!" (*Showcase* 6, Feb. 1957). The first issue was probably scripted by Simon, all the subsequent ones by Dave and Dick Wood, under Schiff's editorship. The plots, however, have "Kirby" written all over them. He gave true menace to strange threats like a sorcerous descendent of Merlin and an outer-space child who wants to keep the Challengers as pets. Even when relying on the old alien-invasion cliché, he gave us not the usual monster but a vast army of trained technological conquerors with a complex plan of attack (*Showcase* 11, Dec. 1957). His art, tight and pugnacious in action sequences, inventive in alien landscapes and machinery, gave punch to his suspenseful plots. Some issues were made more gorgeous by Wally Wood, the master of science fiction art for the late EC, now reduced by the hard times to cadging inking assignments. Kirby's faults, or what

DC editors of the time to be considered his faults— rough-hewn drawings and a linear simplicity to his plots—were overshadowed by his vitality. He also took a liberty nearly unknown in those days of two-, three- and four-story comic books: he allowed some of his stories to fill the full twenty-four or twenty-five pages of the magazine. It was a liberty he would take again later, to great effect.

Once again, though, Kirby's tenure would be short. Trying to get out of comic books before he went down with them, he had cocreated a newspaper comic strip, *Sky Masters*, with the Wood brothers,

A darker and more violent science fiction vision, a portent of the decade to come. Every explosive line and anguished figure announces Kirby's need to break the bonds of the '50s and find an open space to flex his muscles. Inks by Wally Wood. (*Showcase #12*, Feb. 1958.)

and with assists from Wally Wood and Jack Schiff. A dispute over payments led Schiff to sue Kirby, and after that, justifiably or not, Kirby felt unwelcome at National. After *Challengers of the Unknown* 8 (May 1959), he departed for less acrimonious pastures.

Challengers plugged along decently under Schiff and his writers, with the ever-adaptable Bob Brown trying to preserve the excitement as penciler, but Kirby's verve and vision would never be replaced. Two similar adventure-team comics followed it in 1959 and 1960. *Rip Hunter, Time Master*, with brisk scripts by Jack Miller and superb art by the likes of Joe Kubert, Mike Sekowsky, and Nick Cardy, concerned a gang of time-travelers and their well-researched adventures in different eras. It graduated from tryouts in *Showcase* to its own title (Apr. 1961), but lost much of its early beauty when Bill Ely became the regular artist. Less successful was *Cave Carson: Adventures Beneath the Earth,* which also boasted some Kubert artwork, but never got beyond *Showcase* and *The Brave and the Bold* (a former adventure series converted to a second *Showcase*).

Rip Hunter may have mastered time, but time, it seemed, would master the likes of Schiff and Kirby. With no editorial director, the various DC stables functioned almost like separate companies, even to the use of exclusive freelancer pools, and of all of them only Schiff's had taken a major hit in quality and sales. The pressure was on him to produce a hit soon. And Kirby? He'd been king of the hill once, but that hill had vanished like a mirage. Compared with the slick Infantino, he suddenly looked old-fashioned. Nobody at National seemed to mind his leaving, and in just the short time he'd been there his career options had narrowed even more. He'd been working for Harvey Comics, but it was dropping its adventure line as Casper the Ghost and Little Dot turned out to be richer veins. He was picking up some work from Martin Goodman's company, but everybody knew the Goodman line was doomed. Page rates were down, so he needed a publisher who could toss him a ton of work, ideally with an editor who'd stay out of his way. Where to find that in a dying business? The prospects were bleak.

But Jack Kirby had fought his way up from bleaker places.

CHAPTER 5

THE RETURN OF THE HEROES

No sooner had the new *Flash* hit the ground running than comics publishers were asking themselves: could superheroes be coming back? Only Archie Comics would risk testing the waters, hiring Joe Simon to develop a couple of new heroes. Everyone else seemed willing to watch DC and wait.

Julius Schwartz now became the modernization man. His new Green Lantern, like the hero's golden-age namesake, was a man armed with a "power ring" capable of performing miracles, driven by the wearer's own willpower and energized by a sort of green railroad lantern. The "GL" of 1959 even recited a nifty oath based on Alfred Bester's original: "In brightest day, in blackest night, no evil shall escape my sight— let those who worship evil's might beware my power, Green Lantern's light!" But whereas the old Green Lantern was a semimystical character with an ancient magic lantern, this one drew his powers from a lantern-shaped "power battery" entrusted to him by a dying crime fighter from another world (*Showcase* 22, Oct. 1959). The very nature of his power would draw him to far planets, the future and parallel dimensions, leaving the world of Flash and his rogues far behind. Here John Broome added weight to his lighthearted *Flash* style, dipping into the mysteries of science, space and time to create menaces to stretch and challenge his hero's powers. In his second issue, the repressed, destructive side of a scientist's imagination springs to independent life as a faceless man, wreaking destruction with atomic weapons, until Green Lantern can exorcise and destroy it. Broome never lost his humor or humanity, though: a little later, GL lost his ring through a hole in his pocket, and a kid picked it up, to wreak some lighter-hearted destruction of his own.

GL promptly got his own magazine, and Broome launched it with what remains one of the most impressive multiple-issue sequences in the annals of superheroes. He revealed that our hero is only one of thousands of members of a Green Lantern Corps— replete with intelligent insects, plant-beings, living crystals, and bipedal fish—under the command of the godlike Guardians of the Universe. He unveiled the dimension of Qward, where crime is the social norm and those who are "unlawfully honest" are punished, and where the "renegade Green Lantern" Sinestro conceals himself. When Sinestro and the Qwardians were finally defeated, Broome had dozens of GLs charge their rings together on the mammoth "power battery of Oa," in a monumental full-page drawing that could send chills up the spine of a devoted reader (*GL* 1–9, Aug. 1960–Dec. 1961).

These cosmic spectacles were brought to life by the art of Gil Kane, née Eli Katz. He was another veteran of the generation of Infantino, Toth, Anderson, Kubert, and Sekowsky—there'd been a huge influx of young artists in the late '40s and very early '50s, until suddenly the crash hit and *no one* new was getting in—but he was only now coming into his own. He was smart and opinionated, with artistic ambitions, the way Schwartz always liked his coworkers. Apart from being a former assistant to Jack Kirby, he was an admirer of *Tarzan* cartoonist Burne Hogarth, who helped found New York's School of Visual Arts and wrote a seminal series of books on "dynamic anatomy." Not surprisingly, Kane was singularly devoted to capturing the human figure in athletic grace: "a balance between power and lyricism," he said of his Green Lantern design. When allowed to

GREEN LANTERN

A lesson in visual storytelling from Professor Kane. No one could put as much impact in a face, in a flying figure, or in the rhythms of "camera angles" like Gil. Inks by Murphy Anderson, script by John Broome.
(*Green Lantern* 1, Aug. 1960).

their broad, bold layouts, always from the point of view that would give each scene its greatest dramatic force, his figures flying, leaping and staggering right into the reader's lap. They alone could keep bringing readers back, in the hope of being there when Kane finally fulfilled his potential.

Broome lifted the idea of the Guardians from his own earlier science fiction work, the *Captain Comet* series in *Strange Adventures* in the early '50s, but it was better suited to 1960. The American mainstream then seemed comfortable with authority, and Green Lantern as a cosmic cop serving a brain trust of self-appointed leaders suited America's kids well. In the Green Lantern Corps we can see a foreshadowing of the coming Kennedy administration, with its unelected Ivy League decision-making team and its Green Berets and Peace Corps. In the dark, fearsome aesthetic of the '40s, superheroes had blazed like beacons of justice in a world black with chaos; in the aesthetic of the new DC, rapidly establishing itself as the mainstream of comic books, the heroes were reflections of a well-lit and benevolent world order, the villains eccentrics or products of an alien system like Qward. Happily for us, Broome sailed over that world on a cloud of jazz and sweet-smelling smoke, swinging with the times with a knowing, even chuckling, detachment. When he and Schwartz gave GL a smaller, nonwhite confidant (that inescapably colonialist cliché of heroic adventure), they made him an Eskimo jet-engine mechanic, which made the whole thing seem rather arch. And, apart from giving him the nickname "Pieface," Broome handled the character himself with dignity. Later, he and Schwartz devised a subset of stories in which the hero is snatched by a group of scientists from the future to serve as the Green Lantern of 5700 AD. Along the way he's robbed of his memory and given a false one, complete with secret identity and love interest, to keep him motivated. It raised some eerie questions about the nature of reality and the self, even left us wondering if this whole "hero" business is a matter of individual virtue or societal manipulation. Broome played on his authoritarian themes with a wit and fan-

ink his own pencils in some of Schwartz's '50s Westerns, he could turn out powerful and fluid action that combined the virtues of Infantino and Kirby. His early *Green Lantern* work, unfortunately, was too often rushed and undeveloped, a problem compounded by the flattening inks of Joe Giella, a rare but egregious case of Schwartz putting the wrong inker on a penciler (indeed, Kane's uninspired art had a lot to do with his resentment of Giella's treatment of it). But Kane's visual storytelling was always compelling. He was passionate about Hollywood movies, and adapted their use of camera angles and dramatic close-ups with a rhythmic force unique in comics. And his covers showed his potential as a superhero artist, with

tasy that made his the most sophisticated superhero scripts of his time—or any time.

GL's alter ego, like police scientist Barry "Flash" Allen, was an intellectual explorer with a vested place in the political establishment. But Hal Jordan's "explorations" were acts of physical daring, for he was a dashing, handsome test pilot whose fearlessness had earned him his career as a superhero. Kane modeled his likeness on Paul Newman, who'd been Kane's neighbor in his struggling days. Hal drove British sports cars, dated debutantes, and had a wild lock of hair always falling over his forehead, a prototype of the early '60s man, the John Kennedy or James Bond man. Nonetheless, since Schwartz always wanted an ongoing romantic tension, Hal's greatest efforts were spent on wooing his curvaceous boss, Carol Ferris of the Ferris Aircraft Company. Carol was a typical Schwartz heroine, emotional but hardheaded, wanting both an ideal man and a successful career. Broome handled it all with an easy charm and a simple surface, but occasionally he gave us a sly glance at the social stresses boiling beneath—especially after 1962, when a group of interdimensional amazons transformed Carol into the villainess Star Sapphire, committed to humiliating Green Lantern and then forcing him to marry her. "I seem to be two people," she said. "The dominant part of me wants to defeat Green Lantern! The other part wants him to defeat me!" Only Broome would have slipped such a perverse insight into the mouth of a supervillainess (GL 16, Oct. 1962).

Schwartz had taken to calling himself "B.O. Schwartz"—for "Be Original"—demanding a fresh twist in every story, but Broome gave him more than originality. Broome was pulling superheroes far from the "florid pre-literacy" of the golden age, as Jules Feiffer called it. His comics were so "literate" in their self-conscious reliance upon old conventions that they almost seemed created for older readers who had already read too many superhero stories. Indeed, Green Lantern was an instant hit among readers old enough and concerned enough to send in responses to a straw poll, published in Green Lantern 3: he was

their favorite hero, with 888 votes to Superman's 600, Flash's 521 and Batman's 512. Now it was time to revive the series the older fans had been pushing for, the one they considered the greatest golden age comic of all.

"Just imagine!" read the ads. "The mightiest heroes of our time have banded together as the Justice League of America to stamp out the forces of evil wherever and whenever they appear! America resounds to the trumpetlike blast of their names . . . Superman! Batman! Flash! Green Lantern! Wonder Woman! Aquaman! Manhunter from Mars!" This was Schwartz's most ambitious project yet. Here he was entrusted not only with his own two heroes but with five from other stables, to become six in issue 4 (May 1961) when joined by Green Arrow. Only one writer could have been assigned to such a comic: Gardner F. Fox.

When Fox was young and inspired he gave comics a whole constellation of characters for nothing but page rates: the original Flash, Hawkman, Sandman, Dr. Fate, and Starman, the core of Sheldon Mayer's stable. Through the 1940s he poured out story after story about his colorful crimefighters, but the best of them were his fifty-eight pagers about the heroes' combined adventures in All-Star Comics, starring the Justice Society of America. Fox invented the idea of a hero team, and although the JSA was often copied during the 1940s, it was never equaled. When Schwartz picked him to write the new Justice League, he affirmed the continuity of superhero comics. This is the one Jerry Bails and Larry Ivie had been pushing for—and Ivie believed his "Justice Legion" had an influence on it. When a college kid from Missouri named Roy Thomas wrote to National in 1960, desperate to complete his JSA collection, Fox put him and Bails in touch. "I can't tell you how happy I am," Bails wrote Thomas, "to find another All-Star enthusiast after all these years." Separately, in isolation, these young men had sought to fill holes in their lives with the heroes of their childhoods. Bails openly ascribed an almost paternal role to Fox, calling him "a most generous and compassionate man [who] influenced my basic values through the vehicle of the Justice Society." Now those comics would be the basis of a community.

Schwartz not only gave those fans their heroes back but held their attention with his intelligent sense of fun. In the process he was hooking another group of readers, one that DC had never considered worth pursuing: preteens hitting the age at which kids normally gave up comics, now finding that the Schwartz creations were just slightly too satisfying to surrender.

Gardner Fox had to refine his plotting style for the modern team. Economics had shrunk comic stories from fifty-eight pages to twenty-five; and this new generation of readers was being taught to expect more than '40s kids had, when the novelty of odd hero battling odd villain had been nearly enough. Fox fell short in the JLA's first ten adventures (*BB* 28–30, *JLA* 1–7, Mar. 1960–Nov. 1961), but then he broke the bonds of habit and turned his imagination to charting unique and devious plots that played endless variations on a single theme: that heroes triumph by brain, not brawn. When a trio of sorcerers develops a set of spells to nullify each hero's power, Green Lantern uses his power ring to make the Leaguers look like one another, and the heroes ingeniously fake each other's powers—Aquaman, disguised as Superman, destroys a ship with the aid of hidden whales and octopuses (*JLA* 11, May 1962). Fox's plots always walked an odd line between predictability and incoherent anarchy. Perhaps no comic has ever posed as many difficulties to its writer as *JLA*; editorial policy required, after all, that every story be contained in a single issue and that every hero be featured roughly equally. Fox sacrificed characterization almost completely to fit his complex plots into one comic, to the point that the liveliest personality on the team was its cornball teen mascot, Snapper Carr. Sometimes the plot convolutions seemed arbitrary and the extraordinarily wordy storytelling became cumbersome. But in his best moments, and there were many, Fox made *Justice League* the exemplar of how well a comic book can be plotted.

It was also an irresistible title to younger kids. Not only did it have all our favorite heroes under one cover, but Fox gave his stories so many ingeniously ludicrous quirks that we would gasp and laugh simultaneously. If Broome was the goateed hipster playing the square to cover his mortgage, then Fox was the pixie transforming everything he touched into wonderful toys, a warm and unpretentious man always trying to startle a smile out of his readers. In his mind, a carnival fun house could be the gateway to another world, its concave and convex mirrors actually transforming our heroes into the ridiculous shapes they reflected (*JLA* 7, Nov. 1961). An ordinary automobile from our science-based universe could be an unstoppable weapon in a universe that ran on the principles of magic, just as a magic spell would be in ours (*JLA* 2, Jan. 1961). This last story contains a scene that shows artist Mike Sekowsky's eye for humor: A group of interdimensional thieves are shown loading the goose that lays the golden eggs, the fairy gold that vanishes each dawn, and the sword Excalibur into the trunk of a big yellow Pontiac. Sekowsky's peculiar figures, comical touch and mastery of tough layout problems served him well in the strange world of the JLA (and it helped that Bernard Sachs, though not a dynamic inker, had a nice touch for detail). It became a cliché among fans who defended "Big Mike" to praise his skill at cramming a horde of heroes and villains into a single panel, but it was true, and giving graphic sense to what Fox threw at him was no easy task. Sekowsky may never have been pretty, but he always told one hell of a story.

Justice League flew off the stands from the start, becoming comics' first bona fide big hit in years, the hit National had been hunting for. Jack Liebowitz felt so cocky, one story has it, that he bragged about it on the golf course to Martin Goodman. Liebowitz later denied the whole thing, but even if it were true— even if he saw the light go on in Goodman's eyes and knew he was going to rush straight from the clubhouse showers to that cousin of his wife's, his editor, and tell him to whip up a *JLA* imitation—so what? DC comics had real writers, real artists, real editors, just about every adventure and superhero guy worth hiring who was still left in the business. Nobody could touch them. National even made a public stock offering in 1961, after Harry Donenfeld's death, quite a big-time move in a field built on bad checks and family businesses.

In the next year and a half, Julie Schwartz and Gardner Fox took on three more revivals. The Hawkman of 1939 was a flying hero who talked with birds and fought modern crime with weapons of the past, including maces, crossbows and whatever else Fox's research could turn up. The Hawkman of 1961 was about the same, although now cast as a superscientific policeman from the planet Thanagar, visiting Earth to study our law enforcement methods. He masqueraded as museum curator Carter Hall, a human identity that often led him into cases involving ancient artifacts and lost civilizations (and a perfect fantasy-projection for the fact-obsessed Fox). This dual role enabled him to battle crime with the weapons of the past, the detective procedures of the present and the science of the future. His role as an Earthling was made easier by the ultimate Fox fantasy, a device called the Absorbascon that transmitted all Earthly knowledge on any given subject telepathically to its user. As always in the Schwartz world, knowledge was the greatest power.

Hawkman's most interesting feature, however, was Hawkgirl. His wife, fellow police officer and associate curator, she was his equal partner in the battle with crime. Schwartz and his cohorts obviously liked women (indeed, Schwartz's long, loving marriage would become a legend in the business) and stayed at the forward edge of the pop culture curve in their glorification of women with lives of their own. Fox never seemed to consider keeping Hawkgirl in the background, as she fought beside her husband with wits and wings and fists; sometimes, when Hawkman was incapacitated, the final victory was hers alone. In her guise as Shiera Hall, she joined willful Carol Ferris and the Flash's level-headed Iris West in the ranks of Schwartz's gutsy professional women. She and Hawkman—along with Schwartz's Elongated Man, who tied the knot the same month

the Hawk couple premiered—were the first married superheroes in comics.

Now Schwartz was aiming straight at his older readers, not just through this depiction of marital bliss, but through the letters pages. Hawkman's first issue (*BB* 34, Mar. 1961) featured a reminiscence of the golden age by Gardner Fox and letters from Roy Thomas and other fans ecstatic over rumors of the Winged Wonder's return. Schwartz mailed photostats of that first issue to Jerry Bails and other adult *JLA* fans so their words of praise could appear in the second issue. Unfortunately, Hawkman failed to enthrall the kids who comprised the bulk of DC's readership. After a three-issue run in *The Brave and the Bold*, his sales weren't enough to justify his own comic. Once

How could a kid *not* buy this? A vivid reminder that superheroes were once about fun, not the support of fragile adolescent pretensions—and that a cartoonist like Mike Sekowsky, who started in teen humor comics, could turn a super-team into a best-seller. Inks by Bernard Sachs, script by Gardner Fox. (*Justice League of America 7*, Oct. 1961.)

37

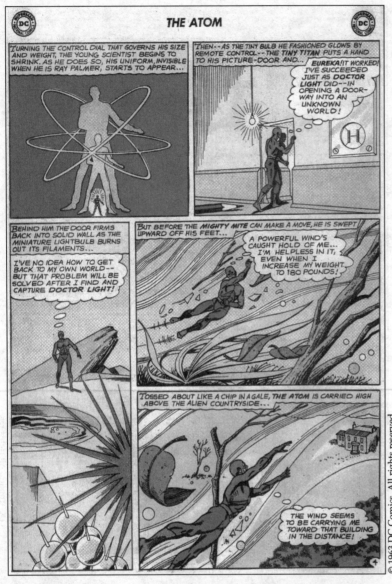

THE ATOM

TURNING THE CONTROL DIAL THAT GOVERNS HIS SIZE AND WEIGHT, THE YOUNG SCIENTIST BEGINS TO SHRINK. AS HE DOES SO, HIS UNIFORM, INVISIBLE WHEN HE IS RAY PALMER, STARTS TO APPEAR...

THEN--AS THE TINY BULB HE FASHIONED GLOWS BY REMOTE CONTROL--THE TINY TITAN PUTS A HAND TO HIS PICTURE-DOOR AND...

EUREKA! IT WORKED! I'VE SUCCEEDED JUST AS DOCTOR LIGHT DID--IN OPENING A DOORWAY INTO AN UNKNOWN WORLD!

BEHIND HIM THE DOOR FIRMS BACK INTO SOLID WALL AS THE MINIATURE LIGHTBULB BURNS OUT ITS FILAMENTS...

I'VE NO IDEA HOW TO GET BACK TO MY OWN WORLD-- BUT THAT PROBLEM WILL BE SOLVED AFTER I FIND AND CAPTURE DOCTOR LIGHT!

BUT BEFORE THE MIGHTY MITE CAN MAKE A MOVE, HE IS SWEPT UPWARD OFF HIS FEET...

A POWERFUL WIND'S CAUGHT HOLD OF ME... I'M HELPLESS IN IT, EVEN WHEN I INCREASE MY WEIGHT, TO 180 POUNDS!

TOSSED ABOUT LIKE A CHIP IN A GALE, THE ATOM IS CARRIED HIGH ABOVE THE ALIEN COUNTRYSIDE...

THE WIND SEEMS TO BE CARRYING ME TOWARD THAT BUILDING IN THE DISTANCE!

Clear, quaint, forceful, infernally intelligent—the picture language of "silver age" DC reaches its apex. Gil Kane pencils, Murphy Anderson inks, Gardner Fox script. (*Atom* 8, Sept. 1963.)

ery linework, evocative of prewar illustrators, baffled many of Schwartz's readers. The question of whether Kubert was right for Hawkman was the first serious issue to rise in DC's letters pages. Most of the older fans said yes, many younger ones said no, and a few made a finer distinction: Kubert was a superb artist whose style simply wasn't right for the kinds of stories Gardner Fox was telling. Whatever Schwartz's opinions, when he tried yet again, giving Hawkman and Hawkgirl the slot backing up Adam Strange in *Mystery in Space* (*MIS* 87, Nov. 1963), he turned to the smoother, "cleaner" Anderson. This time the series took: a hero brought back by an editor determined to please older fans, against commercial logic. It was the first little sign of a very big change.

Six months after Hawkman's debut, DC's older fans got another treat when Jay Garrick, the Flash of the 1940s—whose yellowing adventures the new Flash, Barry Allen, had been reading in his origin story—returned in the flesh. *Flash* was Broome's turf, but for this issue Schwartz brought in Fox, the character's creator. Julie suggested bringing the long-lost hero back with the old "parallel universe" idea from pulp science fiction: a second Earth, existing in the same space as our own but "vibrating at a different speed," with a history closely paralleling ours, except for the year in which superheroes first appeared. There that year had been 1938, not 1956, and the heroes were those of the golden age. When Barry Allen accidentally "vibrated" to this Earth-2, he found his boyhood comic book hero still living— older, gray at the temples, a little short on stamina, but still living—and still running fast (*Flash* 123, Sept. 1961). For adult fans, it was a validation. For the younger ones, it was a whole new world, potentially full of new heroes. And by now it was growing clear that that was what they wanted.

Schwartz and Fox's last successful revival owed less to its namesake than any of its predecessors. "Big—big—big news," read the ads, "about a small—small—small super hero . . . the ATOM." In the 1940s, the Atom had been a minor hero with no super powers, just a tough scrapper of small stature who

that might have been the end of the story, but now Schwartz had fans to keep happy, so he tried again a year later (*BB* 42–44, July–Nov. 1962). Again sales fell short. Maybe the concept of a birdman wasn't exciting enough in an increasingly technological age, as Murphy Anderson opined. Or maybe the art of Joe Kubert was both a blessing and a curse.

Kubert was the natural choice, having drawn Hawkman in the late 1940s, but in the intervening decade he had turned his art away from superheroes to become DC's premier artist of war and adventure. He wasn't a regular member of the Schwartz stable, and didn't share the dynamic simplicity of Infantino and Kane. His moody shadows and suggestive, feath-

seemed to stand for everyman in the DC pantheon. In the science-minded atmosphere of 1961, however, the name suggested a completely different type of hero, a research scientist who could actually reduce himself in size from six feet to six inches and all the way down to the subatomic level. Here the fans who'd been supporting the heroic revival became part of the process: Roy Thomas and Jerry Bails, now a Michigan science professor, had been sending ideas for an Atom revival to Schwartz and Fox for months, suggesting the research scientist and six-inch-size angles. (Schwartz said he'd conceived the ideas himself "by a fantastic coincidence," but Bails and Thomas were certain their letters had at least helped things along.)

Being a DC hero, scientist Ray Palmer no sooner bathes himself in the radiation of a white dwarf star and starts to shrink than he knows that he'll use his powers to fight crime (*Showcase* 34, Oct. 1961). Thanks to the fact that his girlfriend is a lawyer, he finds plenty of thieves, hoodlums and spies to fight right off the bat. The hero's tininess forced both him and Gardner Fox to rely heavily on their wits, and the early issues of *The Atom* set a standard for ceaseless invention and variation on the theme of smallness that made them gems of kids' entertainment. Fox came up with a rogues' gallery of his own for the series, including such gimmick-foes as Dr. Light and Chronos, the Time-Wise Guy. But his best stories were little mysteries, neat as clockwork and surprising as a jack-in-the-box, about offbeat court cases (for which Fox's law degree came in very handy) or "impossible" burglaries. He also gave us another

tough, charming Schwartz heroine in the person of "lady lawyer" Jean Loring, and a twist on the usual comic book romance: in this case it's Ray who proposes marriage every issue and Jean who puts him off for the sake of her career.

When the Atom discovered that he could retain his full 180 pounds even at peewee size, he also became an impressive action-hero, bouncing off rubber erasers and wafting on breezes, then increasing his weight and driving his tiny fist into a crook's jaw. That was a God-send to Gil Kane: after years of DC pussy-footing with physical combat, editors were finally getting bold enough to let him strut his gift for action. Murphy Anderson's inking, though, gave even the violence a tidy, everyday flavor that accented the charm of the Tiny Titan. The Atom quickly won his own title, and the question raised by the Flash was answered. All across America, in drugstores, supermarkets, candy stores, and newsstands, kids were casting their votes with the dimes they dug up from their pockets. They voted yes on superheroes. *Rex the Wonder Dog*, *All Star Western* and *Western Comics* were canceled so that Schwartz could make room on his plate for *Green Lantern*, *JLA*, and *The Atom*, and *Mystery in Space* was given wholly to Adam Strange and Hawkman. Now there could be no doubt that the best of the heroes would live again, and National was the company that knew how to bring them back. But when there was money in the air, other publishers were bound to come sniffing. Just across town, a whole new kind of hero was slouching toward the printing presses, waiting to be born.

CHAPTER 6

THE OTHER GUYS

"**S**uperheroes are dead," said Leon Harvey of Harvey Comics in early 1959, or at least so Joe Simon told it. "Of course, that's today. Tomorrow everything may change. Of course, I'm only talking out loud."

The occasion for Harvey's audible vocalization was the Silver Spider, originally called "Spiderman," a concept Simon, Kirby and others had worked up in 1953 when several publishers took one last, vain stab at superheroes as possible replacements for the crime and horror comics then attracting storm clouds. Nothing had come of it, and for six years the Spider had gathered cobwebs in Harvey's storeroom, the forgotten product of an instantly forgotten genre. Now John Goldwater of Archie Comics had a hunch—or, more likely, heard some buzz from a distributor about DC's decision to give the Flash his own title again—that the superheroes were coming back. Simon remembered the Silver Spider, dug it out of Harvey's stacks, nodded noncommittally at his requiem for the heroes, and hustled over to Archie.

In the 1940s the Big Companies—with real offices, carpeted lobbies, pretty receptionists, "respectable" product, parental advisory committees, Hollywood licensing deals and deep-pocketed owners—were National/DC, Fawcett and Dell/Western. Below those three snow-capped peaks stretched a bloody battleground of independents, hustlers, speculators, trend-watchers, pretenders, fly-by-nighters, check-bouncers, soft-porn peddlers, and moonlighting pulp publishers. By the end of the 1950s, Fawcett was out of the comics business, except for *Dennis the Menace*, and only a few of the second stringers were left: Archie, formerly MLJ, which Archie Andrews had turned from a minor to a major; Harvey, with *Casper* and other little-kid comics; the American Comics Group, the bastard son of National, reduced by the Code to a minimal "mystery" (euphemistic for watered-down horror) line; Charlton, a Sicilian *famiglia* business way off in the immigrant industrial hinterlands of Derby, Connecticut and famous for paying the lowest rates in the business; Gilberton,

Joe Simon and Jack Kirby tried to seize the Cinerama spirit of the times, but Kirby's art was just too potent, too creepy, too alive for a cautious publisher. (*The Adventures of the Fly* #1, Aug. 1959.)

© 1959 Jack Kirby

with its own little niche in *Classics Illustrated;* and Martin Goodman's company, a line of comics so lacking in identity that for most of its history it hardly even had a name, clinging to life by the graces of Jack Liebowitz.

Archie Comics was on a roll. Teenagers were big business in the '50s, and in 1956 the company had launched one of the boldest kids' comics ever, Bob Bolling's *Little Archie*. John Goldwater and company had the money and confidence to take a chance, and were the first of many to imitate DC's venture back into superheroes. Simon, as if unwilling to commit too much new work to a genre thought dead, reworked his dusty old Spider into *The Adventures of the Fly* (Aug. 1959), and varied the concept of his and Kirby's Captain America into *The Double Life of Private Strong* (June 1959), about a meek enlisted man who turns into a powerhouse called the Shield. Kirby contributed some work, along with Jack Davis, Al Williamson, and some other old friends, to give both series some visual panache, although the lack of new ideas made them feel like golden age retreads. Then National's lawyers got a look at Private Strong and sent a letter claiming that the Shield too closely duplicated Superman's powers. The series was instantly canceled—evidence of National's power and reputation in those years. That reputation was further reinforced when, after only four issues of *The Adventures of the Fly* were completed, John Goldwater's son (and managing editor) Richard said he didn't like the art. He wanted a cleaner, slicker look, "like the DC artists." Less than a decade before, Simon and Kirby had been the hottest tickets in the business, their names sometimes emblazoned on the covers as a selling point. Now Simon got out of color comic books completely, devoting himself to the editorship of *Sick*, one of many *Mad* magazine imitators. Kirby was left with no source of income but Marty Goodman. He had to be fearing for his livelihood—but at the same time dreaming, as Kirby always seemed to be, of resurrecting himself and the comic book business with him.

The new *Fly* crew—John Giunta and John Rosenberger, a couple of DC backbenchers—did indeed have DC's Frigidaire gloss, but their work was as dead as an empty refrigerator, and the hero buzzed along listlessly only until 1964. An equally dull superhero called the Jaguar joined him (Sep. 1961), also blandly drawn by Rosenberger, but didn't make it out of 1963. Archie would take a couple more stabs at heroic adventure in 1964 with *The Adventures of Young Dr. Masters* (Rosenberger again) and *The Shadow*, loosely adapted from the old pulp character and featuring a few scripts by Jerry Siegel, but neither lasted. It seemed that Archie Comics' emphases would have to remain on malt shops and jalopies.

Charlton Comics, the company that brought us *Space Western*, took a characteristically cheaper and more tentative shot at superheroes when it turned over one out of three stories in its *Space Adventures* to a new hero, Captain Atom (*SA* 33, Mar. 1960). *Space Adventures* was devoted to dark and apocalyptic SF in the pre-Schwartz mold, mostly written by workhorse Joe Gill and editor Pat Masulli, and would have been of no note at all but for the rise of a young artist named Steve Ditko. He was one of the last artists to get into comics before the business collapsed in the mid-'50s, and doors were hardly flying open for him. He was a powerful draftsman, but he had an independent mind and a strange, almost baroque style—simultaneously looking back to the golden age and forward to some world no one had imagined yet—that was nowhere near the slick clarity that DC (and now Archie) demanded. He picked up a few jobs from the low-paying Martin Goodman line but mainly had to subsist on even lower pay from Charlton. The good side to all this was that no one was trying to make him draw the "right" way. There's a definitive Ditko moment on Captain Atom's very first page. It's a six-panel page plunging us straight into the story, not the full-page "symbolic splash" excerpting a highlight of the story to follow, customary at DC. The hero is trapped in a missile as it's about to be launched, and Ditko brings us closer, closer, closer in on him, until all we see is his eye, opened wide with horror and ringed by sweat. In a field that liked its heroes cool and preferred the

Emotional intensity and oddity from an artist who was almost too good to work for the "respectable" companies, Steve Ditko. Script by Pat Masulli. (*Space Adventures* 33, Mar. 1960.)

objectivity of classical composition and the Hollywood medium-shot, this was a riveting focus on the individual and his most intimate reactions to a moment of crisis.

Pity, then, that the stories were only intermittently readable. Charlton's idea of keeping up with the times was to make everything "atomic"—it even had an Atomic Mouse and Atomic Bunny among its funny animal characters—so here we have an Air Force captain transformed by a nuclear blast into a being of pure energy with almost godlike powers. It was an interesting notion, promising a Green Lantern-like hero with an even more "cosmic" nature, but in practice it rarely transcended red-baiting jingoism. Charlton's editors and writers, like most of the denizens of the slapdash world of comics, were still stuck a few years in the past, reviving the aesthetic of the failed superhero comebacks of 1953, when everything stank of McCarthyism. *Captain Atom* lasted only nine issues, by which time Ditko was able to make a living almost entirely from the Goodman company.

Charlton steered clear of superheroes after that, sticking to its dependable printer-fodder, until DC's

continued success finally forced it to try a revival of *Blue Beetle* (June 1964), a '40s hero picked up cheaply years before when Victor Fox's clueless comics line went belly up. Now given a routine treatment by Joe Gill and artists Bill Faccio and Tony Tallarico, it lasted only a year and a half. The company also tried some superhero-influenced adventure comics: *The Fightin' 5*, a *Blackhawk*-style team; *Sarge Steel*, a superspy; and an unauthorized *Jungle Tales of Tarzan*, shortly crushed by the Edgar Rice Burroughs estate. Aside from the slick rendering of Dick Giordano on *Sarge Steel* and the distinctive art of Sam Glanzman on *Tarzan*, they were all just Charlton comics.

In the early '60s, with *Justice League* doing sensational business and *Flash* and *Green Lantern* selling well, every other publisher had to be considering superheroes, but also scratching their heads over how to avoid duds like Archie and Charlton's entries. Western Printing and Lithography, which for decades had been producing a line of comics distributed by the giant Dell magazine and paperback company, eschewed both DC and golden age models and found its own way.

Western was an anomaly in the business, a respectable children's press from Wisconsin—publishers of Golden Books, Big Little Books, Whitman Books, jigsaw puzzles, playing cards, and other family amusements—that had entered comics with high standards and solid capital. Through Dell it was hooked into the American News Company, making it the only comic book publisher with access to that erstwhile monopoly's high-profile newsstands. It had contracts with Disney (for *Donald Duck, Mickey Mouse,* and other comics), Warner Brothers (*Bugs Bunny, Daffy Duck* et al.), MGM (*Tom and Jerry*), Hanna-Barbera (*Yogi Bear, The Flintstones*), the most upright of kids' favorite movie stars (*Gene Autry, Roy Rogers*—but it let DC have the sleazier *Bob Hope* and *Martin and Lewis*) and almost everybody else who owned a property with wholesome comic book appeal. It employed some of the true masters of the comics medium: Carl Barks, the genius of the "Disney Ducks," Walt Kelly and his *Pogo*, and John

Stanley of the immortal *Little Lulu*. By the '50s it was the giant of all comics publishers, at times reportedly outselling all its competitors combined. It was said to cancel any title that sold under 600,000, which, by the mid-'50s, was more than just about anything but *Superman* sold for anyone else. It had offices in four cities, including New York and LA. When Dell got into paperback reprints of quality books, it turned to Western. The same editorial office that would handle *Tubby and His Clubhouse Pals* did the first mass edition of Mary McCarthy's *The Group* (how sad that no one was doing crossovers then). This was an old-line "class" company. Remarkably few Jewish and Italian names appear in Western's credits in the early days, quite a contrast to the competition.

Perhaps Western's emblematic figure was Gaylord DuBois, a living contrast to the hustling urbanites who filled other publishers' lurid pages: born in the nineteenth century and raised on a remote farm in the Adirondacks, he'd been a lay minister, epic poet, range rider, Wyoming deputy, necktie salesman, and social worker before the Depression and illness drove him into writing Big Little Books and then comics. Before he retired in 1977 he wrote over 3,000 comics stories, making him one of the most prolific writers ever in the field, if not in any American entertainment industry. Yet he was also among the most obscure, for Western obsessively denied credit to its creators to project the image of an editorial monolith and avoid possible ownership disputes. DuBois's work was dependable, sometimes elegant, informed by classic literature and early American virtues, but usually stodgy and without flair. Such was Dell/Western, and it's no surprise that even in the explosive '40s, it felt no need of costumed crimefighters. So established and parent-friendly were its comics, in fact, that it alone could ignore the Comics Code Authority and sail through the '50s with nothing more than the self-advertisement, "Dell Comics Are Good Comics."

The closest Dell came to superheroes was a steady set of adventure comics that plugged along through the '50s and into the '60s: *Turok: Son of Stone, The Phantom, Tarzan,* and *Korak: Son of Tarzan.* The last two were the best, and the most indicative of Western's distance from the rest of the field, with DuBois's well-researched and faintly didactic scripts, rendered by the stiff but idiosyncratic art of Jesse Marsh. Their highlight came with some contributions from Russ Manning, who had been drawing the *Tarzan* newspaper strip. His breathtaking scope and design made the lush foliage, sweeping veldts and mountain vistas of his fantasied Africa a world of beauty—but little mystery or surprise. Sales on such old-style adventure were softening as DC's snappy new superheroes rose, but still Dell wasn't worried. In fact, Dell's success finally went to its corporate head.

With America's new prosperity bringing inflation, nearly every comics publisher nervously raised its price from ten to twelve cents in 1961 or '62. But Dell had been selling a lot of twenty-five cent Giants, and the magnificent *Uncle Scrooge* went for fifteen cents in a format with more story and no ads; obviously kids were willing to pay more for "good comics." So, over the objections of Western Printing and Lithography, Dell confidently boosted its regular price straight to fifteen cents. Sales collapsed. As much as kids may have loved Donald Duck and Tarzan, they couldn't see passing up Casper and Flash for three cents less (after all, that dollar it took an hour to wheedle out of Mom would buy only six Dells, but eight of anything else). Western and Dell broke their alliance in a series of subsequent business disputes, and Western started publishing its own comics under the Gold Key imprint. Dell lost the most in the divorce: a nearly effortless stream of profit. It even tried to recover by cobbling together its own line, coming close to a superhero comic with *Brain Boy* in 1962, about a telepath who battles foreign spies, with a first issue drawn by DC darling Gil Kane. But the hero was costumeless, the story wasn't much, and it only lasted six issues. Western lost a well-known trademark and its place in the American News distribution machine. Gold Key started well, but it would never have the commercial clout Dell

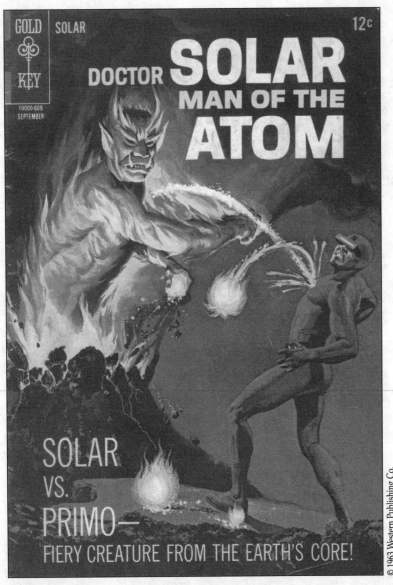

GOLD KEY

SOLAR

12¢

DOCTOR **SOLAR**
MAN OF THE
ATOM

SOLAR
VS.
PRIMO—
FIERY CREATURE FROM THE EARTH'S CORE!

The Gold Key editors always seemed determined to sell their products as more than 'mere comic books.' Their spooky, painted covers looked back to the prewar pulp magazines—all too fitting for a company with its glory days behind it. Painting by J.P. Sternberg and/or George Wilson. (*Dr. Solar* #17, Sept. 1966.)

a human reactor with a host of energy-related powers. The writers—principal among whom, as far as anyone can tell, was Paul S. Newman—played a number of clever variations on Solar's pseudoscientific nature in tightly plotted stories reminiscent of the Schwartz approach. Yet Western still seemed to resist the superhero aesthetic, keeping the Doctor in lab coat and slacks until his fifth issue (Sept. 1963), when he was finally given a standard spandex suit and cowl. Western also kept to its tradition of lush, painted covers, as if to lend an air of class to the pulpy proceedings within, and kicked the series off with handsome, dignified art by Bob Fujitani. Later artists—Frank Bolle, Alden McWilliams, and the promising young Ernie Colón—maintained the same air.

Two months after *Dr. Solar* premiered, Western made another step into the '60s with *Space Family Robinson*, created by Del Connell and written by Gaylord DuBois—the latter in his mid-'60s but still young enough to imagine Johann Wyss's Swiss family adrift in the cosmos—and drawn by Dan Spiegle in one of his less impassioned efforts. Aside from inspiring TV schlockmeister Irwin Allen to steal the idea for *Lost in Space* (which the show's owners acknowledged by allowing Western to add "Lost in Space" to the comic's title), it gave little to the burgeoning silver age. Two months after its debut, however, came another futuristic adventure story that would prove to be the finest Gold Key contribution to the genre: *Magnus, Robot Fighter* (Feb. 1963).

had taken for granted. Dell had made National the king of the industry again, and suddenly there was much more room in the marketplace for it—and perhaps other competitors—to grow.

Western's editors (particularly Marquis M. Morse, Del Connell and Chase Craig), were no fools. They realized they'd have to catch up to contemporary kid tastes in a hurry. The same month the Gold Key imprint debuted, it appeared on the company's closest approximation yet of a superhero, *Dr. Solar, Man of the Atom* (Oct. 1962). The first issue echoed *Captain Atom* as the hero, a nuclear physicist actually named Dr. Solar, survives exposure to what should have been a lethal dose of radiation and is turned into

Set in an idyllic fortieth century where robots do all the labor for mankind, *Magnus* relates the exploits of a man raised from infancy by a wise robot to guard against insurrections by our automated servants. Such uprisings, of course, happen routinely—sometimes led by renegades among the robots themselves, sometimes by evil humans—and Magnus is always there with his steel-tempered hands to stem the metal tide. The assorted writers, including artist Russ Manning, managed to vary the one-note concept in clever ways, and for the duration of its twenty-one-issue tenure they entertained readers with deftly crafted tales of futuristic mayhem. More than anything, though, *Magnus* brought readers back for Manning's smooth, sunny art. With an optimism that exceeded even the Schwartz stable's, he charmed readers with soaring skyscrapers, floating nightclubs and Byzantine catacombs in a wonderfully integrated futurescape. His action sequences of Magnus tangling with hulking robotic opponents had an almost classical quietude and grace.

Western avoided the failures of Archie and Charlton, but it also failed to kick off a heroic boom like DC's. Only two more fantastic adventure series would follow. *Mighty Samson* (July 1964) starred a superstrong survivor on a postapocalyptic earth, with decent stories and competent but constrained art from Frank Thorne and Jack Sparling. And *Total War* (July 1965), beautifully rendered by Wally Wood, featured a paramilitary group repelling an alien invasion of Earth (shortly retitled *M.A.R.S. Patrol* and solidly continued by Dan Spiegle). Western's adventure line was ever thus: finely wrought, never electrifying.

For all their efforts at modernity, what's astonishing in these comics is their profound conservatism. *Dr. Solar* was fairly basic good scientist-bad scientist stuff, but *Space Family Robinson* was a restaging of a nineteenth-century Swiss celebration of bourgeois ingenuity (which, in turn, was an homage to Defoe's assertion of the superiority of the eighteenth-century English colonialist, repopularized in 1960 by Walt Disney). DuBois used it to valorize the self-sufficiency of the enterprising American family and the preindustrial values in which he had been raised. *Magnus* was at once a man-versus-machine tale with nineteenth-century echoes, a work-ethic warning of the dangers of indolence, and a flashback to aristocratic terrors of losing control of the workforce—not excluding the white terror of a slave insurrection from the antebellum South. One can read Magnus himself as a sort of ultimate overseer, raised by a slaveowner's fantasy of the loyal slave to battle renegades and abolitionists. This was not, of course, the intention of the creators, but Western's traditional adventure aesthetic carried with it old cultural shadows. Western's heroes were paragons of antique

virtue, utterly lacking in individuality, without the wry charm of the Flash, the sentimentality of Superman, or the sweaty intensity of Captain Atom. These comics were well-intended and well-composed, but almost impossibly out of step with the youth culture of the 1960s. No surprise that none of them ever attained better than quarterly publication (whereas DC's popular series came out eight or twelve times a year) and that Gold Key's story through the '60s was one of slow decline.

No one else seemed in position to give DC any trouble. Surely not the American Comics Group, partly owned by National's Donenfelds, which hired mostly artists left unemployed by the death of Fawcett, like Kurt Schaffenberger and Pete Costanza. ACG's handful of titles were edited by one man, Richard E. Hughes, who also wrote all the

The relaxed, open art of Southern Californian Russ Manning contrasted with the tighter, more vertical looks of the New Yorkers who worked for DC and Marvel. It was perfect for the bright, clean world of Gold Key. Script credit obscure. (*Magnus, Robot Fighter 17*, Feb. 1967)

© 1967 Western Publishing Co.

45

Richard F. Hughes and Ogden Whitney deride, deconstruct, and destroy superhero story-telling. (*Herbie* #8, Mar. 1965.)

Worlds (35, Nov. 1964) and other titles. He then tried a couple of bona fide costumed heroes. Nemesis (*Adventures into the Unknown* 154, Feb. 1965) and Magicman (*Forbidden Worlds* 125, Feb. 1965) were both concerned with righting wrongs in the mystical realm and were both played largely for laughs—with villains like the Tittering Texan—as if the only way Hughes could write superheroes was by ridiculing them. Pete Costanza, who drew the early adventures of all three of them, seemed to share in Hughes's resentment—or maybe it was just failing eyesight—because he turned in some of the roughest work of his career.

Hughes's one truly brilliant contribution to the superheroic icon was born as an act of angry mockery. In a bizarre little story called "Herbie's Quiet Saturday Afternoon" (*Forbidden Worlds* 73, Aug. 1958), the discontent and throttled subversiveness that underlay Hughes's horror stories bubbled up in the fat, bespectacled, depressively languid person of young Herbie Popnecker. Herbie's parents attend a PTA meeting at which a messianic inspirational speaker of a particularly horrible '50s sort declaims, "What this country needs is boys of action! Get them out doing something!" This rallying cry, which could be called the impetus for DC's heroic revival, only inspires the ever-bilious Mr. Popnecker to denounce his own child: "Good gosh! That I should be the father of a LITTLE FAT NOTHING!" Pushed into "getting out and doing something," the doltish Herbie inexplicably—and inexpressively—defeats a tiger bare-handed, walks on air, saves a drowning senator, destroys a force of invading aliens, and is yelled at by his father: "It's about time you got home! Where were you?" "Just around," Herbie says. The effect, especially as drawn by the excruciatingly naturalistic Ogden Whitney, is hilarious and disturbing.

Herbie returned periodically, by readers' demand, always sucking lollipops, speaking very strangely (upon sighting countless duplicates of himself: "Odd. Other Herbies."), performing the impossible without explanation, winning the heart of Elizabeth Taylor, dropping worms in Mao Tse-tung's mouth and taking

stories under a bizarre panoply of multiethnic pseudonyms: Zev Zimmer, Pierre Alonzo, Kurato Osaki, Shane O'Shea, and about two dozen others. With *Adventures into the Unknown*, way back in 1948, he'd helped launch the horror craze. After the Code, his energies turned to "mystery" stories with a wistful and melancholy air, sometimes with absurd humor; many were about put-upon souls receiving justice in the afterlife. He reportedly hated series characters, but tried acceding to the times with *Magic Agent* (Feb. 1962), about a supernatural adventurer in a trench coat named John Force. It didn't take, but Hughes tried him again as a backup in *Unknown*

verbal abuse from his father. In early 1964 he got his own regular comic, where in his eighth issue (Mar. 1965) he first appeared as the Fat Fury, Hughes's ultimate derision of superheroes: barefoot, in red underwear, with a toilet plunger on his head. Hughes was a mysterious figure, but surely here was the lifelong rage of the persecuted loner turned not only against the get-up-and-go Organization Men of the '50s but against the superheroes who brought vicarious solace to other, less bitter loners. As if too attuned to misery even to believe in heroes, Hughes reveals an angry subcurrent of those "sunny" times. Herbie gives us a clue that not every comic book reader bought into the DC worldview—a teenage fan named Marv Wolfman went to a masquerade as the Fat Fury—but he was never more than a cult favorite. He was too estranged to threaten the mainstream.

And what of Leon Harvey, who pronounced aloud the death of superheroes in 1959? His company ventured no closer to the genre in the early '60s than a few casual reprints of *The Black Cat*, its most popular golden-age crime fighter. Heroes may have been alive at DC, but it seemed everyone else had to concede that only DC could make them work. Comics on the whole were rebounding from their near-death experience in the mid-'50s. But when a young publisher named Jim Warren decided it was time to create a new comics line in 1964, he avoided the full-color comics of the spin-racks and instead went after the market for oversized black-and-white comics racked among regular magazines, a niche until then owned solely by *Mad* and its imitators. Warren's *Creepy* was modeled after the EC horror comics of a decade before, and was launched with the help of EC veterans Wally Wood and Joe Orlando. Most of the scripts were by EC fan Archie Goodwin, with art by Wood, Orlando and fellow EC alumni Frank Frazetta, Johnny Craig, Jack Davis, Al Williamson, Reed Crandall, George Evans, John Severin, Russ Heath, and Alex Toth. *Creepy* sold well, and Warren soon followed with *Eerie* and *Blazing Combat*. But no one of consequence imitated him, and he never tried to go head-to-head with the superhero merchants. Clearly DC owned the field, and nothing was coming from any of its competitors that anyone could expect to change comics significantly.

It's funny what happens when you're least expecting it.

CHAPTER 7

WITH THE SUDDEN FURY OF A THUNDERBOLT

It's fitting, somehow, that the strangest and most influential superhero comic of the last fifty years should have origins as shrouded in mystery and conflict as the origins of its characters themselves. It's beyond our powers to unravel the whole truth, but we can begin by looking at what is known.

It starts with Martin Goodman's tattered and nameless line of comics. Comics historians call his organization's '40s incarnation "Timely," but that was only one of many corporate names that appeared on Goodman's publishing indicia. Goodman was a binge-and-purge publisher, always incorporating multiple companies simultaneously so one or two could go broke without dragging down the whole operation. Two comics produced by the same staff in the same month might be published respectively by "CanAm Publishers Sales Corporation" or "Vista Publications" or any of at least fifty other Goodman entities. He flirted with a company identity only twice, once for a moment in the '40s, slapping a "Marvel" logo on his covers, then in the '50s trying "Atlas." Logos didn't help when two distributors in a row went belly-up on him in 1956 and 1957, and every one of the "Atlas" comics was axed. Rumors flew that Goodman was getting out of comics, even selling off the office furniture. His money came

mainly from the publication of "slick" magazines, most featuring bad jokes and female skin, which in those debased days of comic book history were considered more prestigious and legit than comics. Comics had become a sideline that he left to Stanley Lieber, his wife's cousin, (or nephew—everything about Goodman is slightly obscure) to edit all by himself. It may have been true that he hooked up with Independent News for one last low-budget shot only because he didn't want to have to tell his wife he'd fired poor Stanley. For Lieber and his small pool of freelance artists, comics looked like a dying concern, a place to pay your bills while you hustled for a new career on the side.

Goodman had always been one of the most aggressive trend-chasers in the business, but his faith in the cheap and lurid made him hire raw young cartoonists—exploding with visceral imagination—who could bring an odd twist to those trends. The original *Marvel Comics* featured Carl Burgos's Human Torch, an android who, at least at first, was both a menace and a guardian to mankind. Backing him up—and sometimes engaging in elemental battle with him— was Bill Everett's Sub-Mariner. More antihero than hero, this pointy-eared, human-hating half-breed offspring of the queen of an undersea race and a human ship's captain was no friend of mankind, routinely assaulting the cities of surface-people to avenge the contamination of his beloved ocean. (Contrast him with DC's imitation, the handsome, curly-haired, pro-social Aquaman, complete with kid sidekick, and Goodman's line begins to seem like the Anti-DC.) Soon after, young Joe Simon and Jack Kirby brought Goodman their Captain America, a violent superpatriot who had no compunction about beating up Nazis nearly a year before the U.S. entered World War II.

By the late '50s Lieber, under the pen name Stan Lee, was writing virtually every comic published by Goodman, along with some cheesy humor for Goodman's "slicks." Whatever he couldn't handle be farmed out to his brother, Larry Lieber, who had nothing better going. In his teens Stan had won major essay contests and dreamed of "writing the great American novel." He'd married a beautiful English girl, who had aspirations to write and act. But he'd always been eager to be liked, too quick to lose his own way in his nervousness to fit in, and that office-boy job he'd taken from cousin Martin had ended up taking him over. He'd turned from an ocarina-playing imp to a tired drudge, already middle-aged at thirty-six.

Then the first thunderbolt: Jack Kirby came back.

Simon and Kirby had been Timely's editors in 1941 and 1942, but they'd left for National when they discovered that Goodman's people weren't paying them all their promised royalties. For years Kirby refused to go back, but now, with comics in collapse and strained relations with National, he didn't have much choice. It was a blessing for Lee. He had hardly any artists of distinction working for him, except the young Steve Ditko, who was just beginning to shift his workload over from Charlton. Kirby was not only good, with a proven commercial record, but incredibly prolific. Once he'd produced a staggering 142 pages in a single month, the equivalent of nearly seven complete comic books by 1959 standards. Even more importantly, Kirby was a man who could conceive and plot—and even write—his own stories. Lee discarded the full-script method that was standard in the business and developed a new method

with Kirby and Ditko: writer and artist would discuss a story (or Lee would type a plot outline), the artist would go off and draw it, and then Lee or his brother would supply the words. That not only saved Lee time and increased his income (for Kirby was never paid any part of the writer's fee, and Lee could now increase his already frightening output), but it also freed him from the banal plot formulas that repetition had pressed into his brain. Working with Jack Kirby would teach Lee just how much could be done with a comic book.

There wasn't much sign of that in the beginning. In 1959 and 1960, Kirby, Lee and Larry Lieber cranked out a ton of entertaining but routine Westerns and a weird cycle of dark, grandiose horror stories about monsters with names like Xom, Grottu, and the Creature from Krogarr. Most of the creatures were huge and blocky, sometimes made of stone or earth, and they cast huge shadows over the hordes of panicky, ant-like humans whom they threatened. It was a strain of gigantism that had been hinted at in *Challengers of the Unknown* but now came to full flower, as though Kirby were responding to the desolation of the once-fertile comic book field—and his own relative powerlessness in it—with apocalyptic nightmares of invincible destroyers. Yet for all that, the stories were short and formula-bound and added up to very little. Then in late 1960 or early 1961, from either Lee or Kirby, came the germ of a new superhero team.

Kirby told it like this: seeing the company slumping, he was determined to create something new and startling, "with a real human dimension." He thought superheroes were still viable, and envisioned a team of explorers of the outré, much like his Challengers, but with strange powers. He'd long been intrigued by the Frankenstein theme, a monster with the soul of a man, and created a character accordingly. He knew Goodman still owned the rights to the Human Torch, so he added him for visual impact, but made him a teenager because teen culture was so prominent at the time. He added a couple more characters: an "everyman" with the power to stretch and a woman who

49

A hero with a "human dimension," but with his roots in monster stories...

turned invisible. Then he started to draw, and when he had a whole issue, he took it to show Lee.

Lee told it like this: Martin Goodman came back from that apocryphal golf game with Jack Liebowitz and promptly ordered Lee to whip up an imitation of this *Justice League of America* Liebowitz was bragging about. (Others involved with the company have said that Goodman had a paid informant within Independent News.) Lee, however, had just had a conversation with his wife that changed everything. "Joan wanted me to bear down and make something of myself in the comic book field," Lee said. "She wondered why I didn't put as much effort and creativity into the comics as I seemed to be putting into my other freelance endeavors. The fact is, I had always thought of my comic book work as a temporary job—even after all those years—and her little dissertation made me suddenly realize that it was time to start concentrating on what I was doing—to carve a real career for myself in the nowhere world of comic books." Never a pulp writer or a science fiction editor, never a client of Julius Schwartz or an associate of Mort Weisinger, Lee was the only prominent writer or editor in the field who had been with comic books his entire working life. That drove him to do what no one else in the field would have considered: write for himself. He said he put his new determination to work in a two-page plot summary and handed it to Kirby.

The extent of Lee's and Kirby's respective contributions is the subject of an acrimonious debate that has recently cooled off but will never be resolved. Kirby claimed that he conceived and plotted every story he did with no assistance from Lee. As the debate grew more ferocious in his later years, he eventually claimed that he wrote them as well, that Lee never did anything but edit and steal credit. In early interviews, Lee admitted that Kirby sometimes produced entire stories after only the most minimal discussion, or even no discussion at all. Later, in response to Kirby's escalating claims, he declared that he had originated all the important characters and at least conceived most of the plots (and since Lee is still a Marvel officer, the official company position is that Lee is the "creator" and Kirby only the "artist"). What we can venture to say, after comparing their work together to their work with others, is that Kirby clearly appears to have done most of the plotting, and probably created most of the principal characters, but that Lee supplied all the dialogue and most of the character nuance. And that's probably enough to know, because it was their two talents together that made the Lee-Kirby, or Kirby-Lee, superheroes the most potent since superheroes were born.

The time was right for a revolution. Comic book sales were starting to pick up, buoyed by a burgeoning youth culture. In 1961 the baby boom was still going strong—its eldest members were only fifteen—and superheroes were seizing kids' imaginations. A desire for change was in the air, a desire exploited by young John Kennedy in capturing the presidency just that past November. There were storm clouds too, for Kennedy was a pugnacious president, spoiling for confrontations with the Soviets and the old guard. This new generation, these privileged "boomers" entering adolescence, was beginning to display a sense of identity, a self-involvement, and a fascination with existential crises that its elders just didn't comprehend. America's kids were being moved to new suburbs and force-fed the New Math, and now they were showing an appetite for the shocking and new in their own culture. With a comics line like Goodman's, there was little to lose, giving Lee and Kirby a freedom to experiment—to discover what could be shocking and new—that their rivals at prosperous National would never have. What they discovered, what they created, appears in huge smoky letters over a terrified city in the first panel of the comic book: "The Fantastic Four!"

"With the sudden fury of a thunderbolt, a flare is shot into the sky over Central City! Three awesome words take form as if by magic, and a legend is born!!" "Look! In the sky—what in blazes does it mean?" "I dunno, but the crowds are gettin' panicky!" "Rumors are flyin' about an alien invasion!" "Above all the hubbub and excitement, one strange figure holds a still-smoking flare gun! One strange man who is somehow *more* than just a man—for he is the leader of . . . the Fantastic Four!" "It is the first time I have found it necessary to give the signal! I pray it will be the *last*!"

Over the next few pages, society girl Sue Storm turns invisible and races through a crowd, knocking people over to reach the source of the flare. "So it has happened at last!" she cries. "I must be true to my vow! There can be no turning back!" Ben Grimm casts off his hat, dark glasses, and overcoat to reveal a monstrous orange, rocky body, smashing through walls and streets ("Bah! Everywhere it is the same! I live in a world too small for me!"), terrifying passersby, smashing cars, and being fired at by police—while he rushes to answer the same flare. Then fun-loving, car-crazy Johnny Storm bursts into flame, horrifying his friends and melting his car to a metal puddle, roaring off through the sky as bystanders scream, "Unless we're going mad—*it's something human!*" (*FF* 1, Nov. 1961). An ominous beginning, far from the thrill of "No, it's Superman!"

Yes, they were a team of superheroes, just like Goodman wanted, and the cover definitely echoed that of the first *JLA*. But this new group was like no set of superheroes anyone had ever seen. They had the powers of superheroes, but they didn't act like superheroes. They acted something like monsters—and something like real people.

The four were created, we learn, when maverick scientist Reed Richards took his fiancée, Sue Storm, her little brother, and an argumentative pilot on a flight in an untested rocket in an obsessive quest to beat the "commies" into space. Bombarded by cosmic rays, the four crash-land and discover that the mysterious rays have given them amazing powers.

Reed's body stretches like rubber (a power borrowed, like the Elongated Man's, from Plastic Man of the '40s, but here given an odd, almost sinister quality); Sue can turn invisible; Johnny becomes a new Human Torch (like Schwartz's Flash, a modern version of a '40s hero, but more radically modernized— a member of the youth culture, not a square police scientist); and Ben becomes a monstrous muscleman with rocky orange flesh, who in his rage lashes out savagely at his friends. Once tempers cool, they pledge to help mankind, following old superhero tradition. But there the tradition ends.

Heroes, in the gospel according to DC, wear costumes and use secret identities, but the Fantastic Four fight monsters and aliens in their street clothes. Although they take the dramatic titles Mr. Fantastic, the Invisible Girl, the Human Torch, and the Thing, they never consider concealing their true identities. Heroes never quarrel with one another, yet the Human Torch and the Thing are always at each other's throats. Most of all, heroes are handsome and well-loved by the world, more content with their lives than most of us can ever expect to be. Until 1961, no superhero writer would have suggested that acquiring strange powers might drive a wedge between a man and his society, bringing him more misery than contentment. But Ben Grimm has paid for his powers with an unalterably monstrous appearance; his enormous strength cannot console him for the loss of his humanity. Resenting the world as strongly as he feels

... there had never been a comic book star like the Thing: ugly, savage, terrifying, and tragic.

Jack Kirby's art was sparse in the early '60's, as he turned out enough pages for four mortal artists, but the energy was still compelling. Inks possibly by Christopher Rule, dialogue definitely by Stan Lee. (Fantastic Four #1, Nov. 1961)

bound to protect it, he has to struggle as fiercely against his own bitterness and self-pity as against any villain. Herbie Popnecker might have revealed a strain of bitterness in young people that prevented them from believing in the traditional "hero," but Ben Grimm gave that bitterness dramatic force within a superheroic context. This was a turning point in comic book characterization.

Goodman had reservations about the new comic, but Lee pushed for it and won his point. In the late summer of 1961, *Fantastic Four* 1 hit the stands. After thirty five years of change in comics, it's difficult to appreciate the impact that first issue must have had on the young fan spinning the rack in search of something new to read. Turning from *Justice League* to *Superman*, or even to *Captain Atom*, would have been an obvious shift to a different editorial style. But turning from any of them to *Fantastic Four* would have been like stepping through the gateway to another dimension. The emphasis of the stories was completely reversed: plot, pace, and mystery were shunted into the background while brawling, bickering heroes took center stage, soaking the pages in pathos, anger, and romantic melodrama. Jack Kirby was no rationalist like Schwartz or Weisinger, no taker of notes and writer of outlines like Fox or Broome. He would spin stories off the top of his head and draw them by the seat of his pants, planted at his drawing board from afternoon to dawn, making up the plot as he drew it, often cranking out pages at an astounding pace of six a day. He rejected DC's use of the "sym-

bolic splash" and mannerly "One day in Metropolis" openings, forcing himself to find a riveting visual moment to start every story. While DC's heroes still rarely threw a punch, Kirby's could brawl for pages. He was an emotional man, and it was powerful emotion that drove his stories. His heroes didn't save the day by deducing the chemical behavior of a sodium-based dust devil, but through a burst of rage or desperation, or the hubris or madness of the villain.

The plots in those early issues weren't much. The Fantastic Four spent a lot of time battling big monsters that looked like leftovers from Kirby's horror stories. Both creators were overworked and flying blind. Kirby's art was rough and sparse (and seemingly inked by whoever was hanging around the office that day). Lee's writing was often clichéd and overdone, and he had no editor to catch his blunders. The production was cheap, and the coloring was dreary. The paper was trimmed smaller than National's, to save a tiny fraction of a cent per page, and more of the pages were given over to ads (and from only the tawdriest advertisers, at that). But what those comics lacked in prettiness they made up for in innovation and raw enthusiasm. There was a sense of life, not corporate craftsmanship, in those pages. They were even signed "S. Lee & J. Kirby," in a field where anonymity was the rule. It was a sense not of something realized, but of something happening, something big coming. Even their crude, dingy look somehow added to the sense of mystery, of ominous and promising strangeness. As the story itself says, with four times the exclamation points DC would have used, "And so was born 'The Fantastic Four!!' And from that moment on, the world would never again be the same!!"

Even *Fantastic Four* owed a debt to the past, of course. The antihero at odds with society, the superpowered being who is frail at heart, heroes who fight one another—the seeds of those themes could be found all the way back in the *Marvel Comics* of two decades before. Young Stan Lee had helped write and edit some of those stories, and the themes no doubt echoed in his mind. Kirby, for his part, brought ideas over from *Challengers*, including the use of full-issue stories and an origin story centering on four heroes crash-landing after a daring flight. Yet until the Fantastic Four, those elements had never been so fully and dramatically exploited.

The peculiar Kirby-Lee collaboration made these the most purely visual creations in comics at the time, and yet they had a verbal texture and daring like no others. Kirby was free to tell stories of unprecedented sweep. Lee was free to forget about plots and to make his characterizations and human interactions as colorful and dramatic and funny as he could. It was rough going sometimes, as when a big block of Lee verbiage would descend upon a Kirby character's head, clearly intended to accomplish something in Stan's agenda to which Jack was indifferent. More often, it paid off: Kirby said he wanted to make an "everyman" of Reed Richards, but the words Lee put in his mouth cast him as a dark and obsessive genius, a far more interesting figure.

In discovering a new approach, Lee and Kirby also began to discover a new audience. The number of older comic book readers had been growing since the Flash first appeared. Many of them were teenagers, still fascinated by the sheer fantasy of costumed heroes but more aware of the real emotional stresses of living, less comforted by familiarity than children are and more hungry for novelty. To the adolescent eye, DC comics were beginning to look simplistic and clichéd. The Fantastic Four came like a revelation: heroes were human too, they could suffer and still be heroes, and comic books could experiment, could even aspire to be taken seriously (and what adolescent hasn't aspired to be taken seriously?). The *FF* gripped an audience smaller than DC's, but it was generally older, more vocal, and more conscious of what it read. Letters began arriving, unsolicited, at Lee's little office. He promptly instituted a Fantastic Four Fan Page, bearing such messages as "You are definitely starting a new trend in comics, characters who act like real people, not just lily-white do-gooders who would insult the average reader's intelligence." [1]

Lee and Kirby made a couple of compromises with superhero tradition or got Liebowitz to allow them (blue uniforms and a superscientific headquarters). But the fans encouraged them to keep pushing the boundaries. Issue 4 (May 1962) placed the *FF* specifically in New York City, not a generic city in the tradition of DC's "Metropolis." It even took us into the Bowery district, with its men's hotels full of derelicts, a place Green Lantern would never venture. More important, it featured the return of the Sub-Mariner—soon after Schwartz's revival of the original Flash, and under the prodding of fan Roy Thomas—but this was more than a revival. This was an antihero, something new to the silver age. The Sub-Mariner declared war on all mankind, and therefore had to be fought as a villain, but his motivation—vengeance for the devastation of his people by an underwater atomic test—could not be dismissed as simple evil. His tragic nobility also appealed to Sue Storm, the Invisible Girl, who grew infatuated with him, beginning three years of discord with her teammates and tension with her fiancé. Here was a whole new complex of ideas: heroes who might be in the wrong, who are ambivalent about their enemy, who disagree about their plan of action, who are even caught in a romantic triangle with a villain. The fans were ecstatic.

The Sub-Mariner returned for "The End of the Fantastic Four," a story that even now remains remarkably offbeat. In a few bad stock speculations, Reed Richards loses all the team's money and gets them evicted from their skyscraper headquarters. Their only recourse is to hire themselves out as actors in a science fiction movie being promoted by a mysterious movie mogul. The mogul proves to be the Sub-Mariner, maneuvering to attack them, not—as the traditional villain would—to destroy them, but only to assuage his wounded pride for his earlier defeat at their hands. He battles them all to a standstill and goes his lonely way back into the sea (*FF* 9, Dec. 1962).

[1] Marvel freelancer Dick Ayers has reported that many of those early fan letters were in fact written by Lee himself, but some, including one from DC fan Roy Thomas, were undoubtedly real.

The stories were getting better. With the introduction of the Sub-Mariner and Dr. Doom, a tormented mastermind obsessed with Reed Richards (*FF* 5, July 1962), the villains were getting better, too. The art was getting a little better, as the inking chores were handed to Dick Ayers who, although overworked and not the best in the business, was steady and dedicated. Most importantly to Martin Goodman, sales were getting better. His opening print run had been modest, but few copies were returned, and even as he increased print runs the returns stayed small. Ever in love with volume, he doubled the frequency of *FF* from bimonthly to monthly and was pressing Lee to produce more superheroes as soon as his contacts in the distributing game told him *FF* 1 was moving. By the end of 1962, Lee had already obliged with four of them.

Lee's products still lagged far behind National's in both sales and craftsmanship. Even a mediocre Julius Schwartz comic showed far more coherence and polish than the best Lee and Kirby work of 1961 or 1962. But the energy was infectious, and kids began talking about these weird new comics. Lee himself was not the type to sit shyly in the corner waiting for someone to notice him. The cover of the third issue of the Fantastic Four screamed, "The Greatest Comic Magazine in the World!!" Every issue from then on was mantled with a similar motto—and Stan Lee was just getting warmed up. The best promotion of all, though, was between the covers: vivid characters that kids could bond with, characters who became more solid, beloved, and believable, more independent of their creators, than any before them in their genre. When Stan and Jack themselves appeared in a story, menaced by Dr. Doom, they felt no more real—and no less mythic—than their creations (*FF* 10, Jan. 1963). When they took us on an eleven-page "Visit with the Fantastic Four," in which nothing but conversation took place, they made it as interesting as any battle with a monster or mad scientist (*FF* 11, Feb. 1963). Three months later, Lee finally gave his new line a name—the Marvel Comics Group, harking back to the vigorous beginnings of the golden age—and his fans were instant loyalists.

Lee and Kirby had sounded a bell for the end of one era and the beginning of another. Maybe it was best that Broome, Fox, and all their cohorts were too busy meeting deadlines to ask for whom it tolled.

CHAPTER 8

OF AMAZONS AND ALLOYS

Stan Lee and Richard Hughes weren't the only writer-editors in the business. Even in the well-staffed halls of National Periodicals, in yet another company-within-a-company, editor Robert Kanigher wrote nearly all his own scripts, while handling the broadest range of genres of any DC editor. He discovered the same freedoms and pitfalls as Lee and Hughes. Editing and writing war stories, superheroes, romances, and historical adventures—sometimes all at once—could lead to any of three results: crank-it-out mediocrity, wild innovation, or incoherent chaos. Lee was mired in the first until Jack Kirby prodded him to the second. Hughes had occasional bizarre flashes of the second but generally settled for the first. Only Bob Kanigher managed all three.

Kanigher started writing for several comics companies in 1940, quickly distinguishing himself for his speed and versatility. Only three years later he felt experienced enough to write a book called *How to Make Money Writing for Comic Magazines*. That same year, 1943, marked the beginning of his association with National, for whom he would later estimate he created, wrote and edited at least twenty three series. He claimed he wrote at least two scripts a week for forty years (most of them, reportedly, on the subway on his way to work). Garrulous, passionate, versed in history, often pretentious, he wrote the way he talked, in a torrent of images and concepts that was never guaranteed to coalesce into a single stream. He could be volatile, even infuriating (Gil Kane reported that Alex Toth once had to hold him out a window to get his paycheck), which may explain why he was never given a front-line DC title, why he worked with hardly any writers but himself,

and why he had his greatest successes with tough-guy war artists, most of them military vets. He shared an office for years with Julius Schwartz (and if we admire Schwartz for nothing else, let us admire him for that), often writing for him and even helping develop the new Flash, but Kanigher never did well with superheroes. He displayed, in fact, an almost Hughesian contempt for the genre, which was never more painfully apparent than with *Wonder Woman,* which he took over writing and editing in 1947.

The original conception of Wonder Woman could not have survived the '50s. She was created by William Marston, a psychologist with a keen interest in the female psyche, and her adventures were full of veiled sexual and fetishistic themes that had Fredric Wertham calling her a veritable lesbian recruiting poster. In purging the series of these subliminal contents, however, Kanigher also bled it of the mythological and political themes that had made it unique. Wonder Woman now became just another invincible hero, whose gender was functionally irrelevant. Instead of grappling with such questions as whether the way of women could bring peace to earth, the "Amazing Amazon" spent dreary years fighting Angle Man, Mouse Man, and other hastily conjured bad guys, along with enough extraterrestrial creatures to make Batman's adventures seem provincial by comparison. Gender may have been part of the problem: superheroes and superheroines had always been models of exaggerated male and female traits, and had appeared just as American culture entered a particularly confusing passage in sex-role transition (about the same time that people like Wertham were declaring loudly on the "pathology" of homosexu-

Just when DC artists were straining to make their work more textured and "artistic," along comes Roy Liechtenstein to remind them just how flat and technology-bound it really was. Some comic book people would take the lesson to heart. Here Liechtenstein turns assorted art by Irv Novick and Russ Heath, words by Robert Kanigher, and letters by Gaspar Saladino into one of the great American cultural icons: Okay, Hot Shot. (Oil and magna on canvas, 1963. Collection of Mr. and Mrs. S.I. Newhouse, Jr.)

ality). For all the bizarre transitions that superheroes have been put through, gender boundaries have not only rarely been blurred, they've been steadily reinforced. For Kanigher, the master of the war story, Wonder Woman may have inspired contempt at more levels than one.

Among the costs of Kanigher's shoddiness was a spectacular collapse of his craft. He called himself a "spontaneous, instinctual writer. I'm not a writer who sits down knowing what he is going to do in advance. That is not a writer but a *typist*." That would make James Joyce a typist, but never mind. Kanigher's plots hurtled from event to event with an illogic that even the most lax editor couldn't have approved (had he not also been the writer). One story opens in the past, with the teenaged amazon watching her future self in a "time and space screen." Wonder Woman rescues her female fan club from kidnappers, then saves the life of her boyfriend, who just happens to be crashing in an experimental jet at that very spot. Seeing this, Wonder Girl is filled with a sense of inferiority (to *herself*) which sends her off to perform a series of random feats, involving a "merboy," a "crack in time," and a dinosaur that gobbles up an island from beneath their feet. Just then, a messenger bursts into the chamber of our heroine's mother, Queen Hyppolyta, crying, "Satellite Lookout Station No. 3X22 reports hostile spacecraft heading directly toward our island!" So the queen flies up to fight a robot from Pluto, when, mercifully, page twenty-five arrives and the story is quickly wrapped up. Kanigher titled this concatenation "The Island Eater," presumably because, of all the disjointed episodes, that one allowed the biggest, ugliest monster for the cover (*WW* 121, Apr. 1961).

Although limping along with moderate sales from an audience who had no other super females to buy, the more astute fans screamed their discontent, and Kanigher was courageous enough to print their letters and rebut them frankly. His most regular critic, Paul Gambaccini, once appeared in print saying, "It's too bad Mr. Kanigher cannot accept our criticism, and it's too bad we cannot accept his philosophies." All the criticism in the world, however, couldn't make Kanigher give a damn.

When Kanigher did give a damn, he could write—and he proved it a thousand times by bringing craftsmanship and even flashes of passion to his war comics: *All American Men of War, G.I. Combat, Our Fighting Forces, Star Spangled War,* and *Our Army at War.* They were as far from *Wonder Woman* as anyone could get, at their worst too predictable, at their best naturalistic and emotional. The artistic standout was Joe Kubert, whose rich inks and subtle character nuance made him the ideal war man, but all the art— by Irv Novick, Ross Andru, Russ Heath, Jerry Grandenetti, Mort Drucker—was sober and masculine, always well crafted, with flourishes of individuality. (Although one observer, circa 1962, was less interested in their individuality than their iconic repetition. A young painter who had served under Irv Novick in an art unit in the army, Roy Lichtenstein, was drawing highbrow attention with his Pop Art reworkings of images from DC comics—most famously the girls from Tony Abruzzo's romances but also war scenes by Novick, Heath and others, all originally edited by Kanigher.)

Kanigher did manly adventure, too, in *The Brave and the Bold*. Its running series, like *Silent Knight* and *Robin Hood,* were rich in heroism and historical detail, but the best was *Viking Prince*. There were elements of superheroism in it, suggesting what Kanigher might have been able to do if he'd taken Wonder Woman seriously: the hero has to perform "Thor's twelve tasks" to reclaim the throne usurped by a villain. The stories were elegantly scripted, and atmospherically rendered by Kubert. Kanigher moved closer to creating his own superheroes with *Suicide Squad,* starring some altruistic daredevils, with Ross Andru art (*BB* 25–27, Sept. 1959–Jan. 1960), and with *Sea Devils* (*Showcase* 27–29, Apr.–Aug. 1960), about a squad of divers, with some fine art by Andru, Russ Heath, and Gene Colan. Kanigher's basic credo was an unusual one at National: "True plot is determined by characterization. A character who acts and reacts makes a story." If he could find a character he believed in, he could do something vibrant. If he couldn't, he'd just throw garbage at the page. He simply didn't seem able to find a superhero he could believe in—until he found six of them, almost by accident.

The story goes that Irwin Donenfeld stopped by Kanigher's office one Friday afternoon in late 1961 with a problem: some scheduling mix-up had left the next issue of *Showcase* without a feature, and less than two weeks remained before the deadline. They didn't need anything with a future, just a quickie filler with a superheroic slant. Kanigher's reputation as the company's speed demon won him the job of doing something about it, and he came through with a completely original feature, spun off the top of his head, by Monday morning. He handed the new script to his workhorse artist Ross Andru, who raced

through the twenty-four pages by the end of the week (despite the fact that, even under such pressure, Kanigher continued to scrutinize the art and demand revisions). By the time Mike Esposito finished the inking, only ten days had elapsed since Donenfeld's request. The biggest surprise of *The Metal Men,* however, was not that Kanigher and his men had gotten the job done on time, but that it was *good.* Donenfeld decided to keep it in *Showcase* for four issues (37-40, Apr.-Oct. 1962), which sold well enough to earn them their own title in early 1963.

It was a concept that could probably have found its way into print only that way, because it would

The pencil/ink team of Ross Andru and Mike Esposito was always fast, always energetic, and always a little scary—as if something big and strange were about to happen. They were perfect for the Metal Men. Script by Robert Kanigher. (*Metal Men* 8, Aug. 1964.)

never have passed an editorial conference at conservative National. Kanigher had always liked to find a physical object as a hook to hang his plots on—a typical war story might be about a pair of dog tags, or narrated by an M-1 rifle—and for some reason that weekend his mind had wandered to metals. So his heroes were a sextet of robots, each composed of a single metal that determined its powers, name, and, fortunately for Kanigher, personality: Iron was strong and silent, Lead sluggish but effective against radiation. Tin was the least useful, but Kanigher played off that by making him stuttering and self-effacing. Platinum, nicknamed Tina, proved to be a "very female" robot. Thanks to a "faulty responsometer," she fell immediately in love with her maker, Doc Magnus, making lighthearted soap opera a part of the stories. Andru drew them all as extravagant caricatures.

Kanigher was impudent with superhero tradition from the start: in the Metal Men's first appearance, which he expected to be their last, he even killed them all. He paralleled Stan Lee and his collaborators in playing with such novel structures as multi-issue stories and running subplots. He claimed not to read comic books, which, if true, would suggest that he could not have been influenced by *Fantastic Four*. Maybe it was just the increasingly irreverent, individualistic tenor of the times, or maybe it was the recklessness required by their respective circumstances, that encouraged both him and Lee and Kirby to throw themselves into character-driven creative free-for-alls that broke down the bounds of convention. Whatever the cause, *Metal Men* startled DC into a new perspective on heroes, speeding the transition of emphasis from SF to characterization and opening the gates to real innovation.

Yet Kanigher himself, flying without instruments as usual, was never able to follow up. Fans like Paul Gambaccini liked *Metal Men*, and Kanigher not only happily printed their letters but began shifting his stories more and more to meet their demands. At the fans' urging he eventually tried to deliver an old-style *Wonder Woman*, setting the adventures in the '40s and making the loose and wild Andru-Esposito team draw in the quaint style of the amazon's original artist, Harry G. Peter (*WW* 156 and 159–163, Aug. 1965 & Jan.–Aug. 1966). The effort only made the art as false and wooden as the stories. Even on *Metal Men*, his screwiness began to cross the line into self-parody and nonsense. As much as he may have liked his odd characters, he seemed unable to take them seriously as Lee and Kirby did theirs.

It took Roy Lichtenstein to turn Kanigher's products into gallery art, and it took other DC editors and writers to understand how to apply what Kanigher had stumbled across to superheroes. It wasn't Schwartz and Weisinger, with their well-oiled machines and the security of success, but others who'd struggled with superheroes, who may have questioned if they knew what they were doing, and who were under less scrutiny from management because they had no major heroes in their custody.

CHAPTER 9

THE HERO WHO COULD BE YOU

Fantastic Four had promised glories to come. Within a year, another Marvel comic delivered them. This one wasn't just innovative, but was executed with a craftsmanship Stan Lee had never hinted at possessing before—although that sudden improvement probably owes less to any increase in Lee's own ability than to his union with an artist/plotter better suited to his interests than Jack Kirby.

Steve Ditko had distinguished himself with science fiction at Charlton, and when he shifted to Lee's stable during 1959 and 1960, that genre became his stock-in-trade. His work for Lee was his best yet, combining a pervasive eeriness, a disconcerting sense of unreality in both figures and compositions, and a highly stylized brand of characterization that squeezed the perversities and weaknesses of his characters into every line. An undercurrent of madness seemed to flow through his stories. All that was known about Ditko was that nothing was known about him: he refused to let Marvel publish his photograph, or even a caricature, and told interviewers, "I never talk about myself. My work is me." The thought of a strange loner creating these odd visions in the solitude of his studio only added to the mystique. He still remains, though his reputation as an artist is universally high, one of the least-known people in the field.

Nonetheless, he and Lee became friends, and it's been suggested that Lee adopted much of Ditko's conservative individualism and pessimistic view of human institutions. Lee certainly considered Ditko his favorite collaborator, above Kirby, and almost never tossed the scripting of a Ditko story to his brother Larry. Stan used the artist's peculiar talents in a body of science fiction stories far more subtle and unsettling than those cranked-out Lee-Lieber-Kirby monster yarns—morality tales about the costs of vanity and greed, with *Twilight Zone* set-ups and O. Henry endings. The market preferred monsters, however, and the one title solely devoted to the Ditko stories, *Amazing Adult Fantasy* (subtitled by Lee "The Magazine That Respects Your Intelligence," a clear bid for the atypical comic reader), quickly dropped off in sales. But Lee would make the most of his failure. He'd been trying to sell Martin Goodman on an idea for a superhero even more daring than the Fantastic Four, and now he had the final issue of a dead series to test it with.

The origin of the new character is about as murky as that of the Fantastic Four. Jack Kirby claimed he pitched the "Spiderman" idea that he and Joe Simon had developed in 1953, and that Stan ran with it. Lee says he thought of it himself, inspired by the Spider of the pulps he'd read as a kid. Kirby said that by the time the idea was approved he'd become too busy—developing heroes called the Hulk, Thor and Ant-Man for Lee—so Ditko got the job. Lee claims Kirby drew some pages but Lee thought the character looked too noble and heroic for what he had in mind, so he turned it over to the quirkier Ditko. What counts is that Lee and Kirby probably both had a hand in creating the character (and Kirby definitely drew the first cover) but the job was quickly given to Ditko. And it was Ditko who enabled "the amazing Spider-Man" to be what he was.

The first page suggested that "we think you may find our Spider-Man just a bit . . . different!" We meet Peter Parker—skinny, bespectacled, a brilliant science student—who is doted on by the elderly aunt and uncle who raised him but is ridiculed by the cal-

low kids at his high school. "Someday I'll show them!" he sobs. "Someday they'll be sorry!" During a science demonstration, when Parker is bitten by a radioactive spider and granted "the proportionate speed and strength" of that creature, he gets his chance. In any other comic book story Parker would have immediately donned a costume and dedicated his life to fighting crime. But not this bitter little egghead. He does make a strange costume, and invents a device to shoot sticky webs from his hands, but only to make himself a show-business sensation. He conceals his identity, but only because he worries, "What if I fail? I don't want to be a laughingstock!"

Parker doesn't fail, and gets invited to show off his powers on *The Ed Sullivan Show*. While he gloats at the TV studio, a thief runs by him. A security guard hollers, "Stop him!" Parker blows him off: "I'm through being pushed around—by anyone! From now on I just look out for Number One—that means . . . me!" But pride does come before a fall. Peter's beloved Uncle Ben is murdered by a burglar. Insane with grief, Parker hunts down the killer, only to find that it's the same thief he allowed to escape. And so, Lee tells us, Parker is dev-

astated by guilt, "aware at last in this world, with great power there must also come—great responsibility!" (*Amazing Fantasy* 15, Aug. 1962).

Here was a solo hero, not a kid sidekick or a team member, who was really a teenager, and a teenager who wasn't happy-go-lucky or goofily cute but truly complex and tormented. Spider-Man's meek alter ego that was the character's reality, not a coyly fabricated disguise. His first thoughts were of money and glory. Here was a believably ambivalent hero, who grew into his superheroic role by way of his personal life. Thus a need for growth had been programmed into his personality. Unlike the set personalities to which even the Fantastic Four had been limited, Parker's character would have to change to cope with the problems life threw at him. It was a daring concept, but it was also tailor-made for Lee's adolescent readers. This was a scary new world. Here science didn't get you gorgeous girlfriends like Iris West or Jean Loring—it made you an outcast. It was also a dark and unpredictable thing, where hideous spiders and unleashed radiation threatened the young. The voice of authority—the security guard—was hollow, and the hero must find his own morality through the agony of subjective experience. Power and knowledge brought not freedom but pain. This was a full Romantic Rebellion against DC's '50s-style Enlightenment. Though Spider-Man was tossed out without fanfare or plans for a future—like the Metal Men earlier that year—letters and sales figures made it clear that the fans wanted more of him. Seven months later, Lee and Ditko launched him in his own title.

Parker's powers put him through a tumultuous series of changes in just his first year. He goes back to show biz to support his Aunt May, but a yellow journalist named J. Jonah Jameson, envious of Spider-Man's higher ethics, attacks him as a menace to society and a bad influence on children, and Parker finds his career hopes ruined. He tries to join the Fantastic Four, but backs out when he discovers that it isn't a paying job. He laments, "Nothing turns out right . . . (sob) . . . I wish I had never gotten my super-powers!" Then Parker hears that Jameson, his nemesis, is eager for pictures of a new villain. Spider-Man tracks the villain down, not to bring him to justice but only to take pictures of him. He ends up beating the bad guy, selling Jameson the photos and embarrassing him at the same time. Now his power goes to his head. "It's almost too easy!" he says, after rounding up a gang of thugs. "I almost wish for an opponent who'd give me a run for my money!" In his cockiness he even beats up people on the street just because they look suspicious. His world comes crashing down in self-doubt: "Am I really some sort of crack-pot, wasting my time seeking fame and glory?" He's genuinely tempted to team up with the FF's archvillain, Dr. Doom, but finds it in himself to refuse. In the following issue, when he risks his life to come to the aid of a scientist who has unwittingly turned himself into the evil Lizard, Parker finally becomes a true hero. The cost of his altruism is shown vividly when he sprains his arm in a return match with the Vulture, giving us the rare but moving sight of a hero struggling to overcome physical injury. At last, making money as a photographer and at peace with his motives, Parker develops a little confidence in his private life, discarding his oversized glasses—suddenly looking a lot like James Dean—and making a successful play for Jameson's pretty secretary, Betty Brant (*ASM* 1–8, Mar. 1963–Jan. 1964).

No comic book character had ever grown so organically. Ditko's art improved almost monthly, his action growing more dynamic, his melodrama more concentrated. Whereas Kirby filled virtually every panel with action, forcing Lee to stick his character development in edgewise, Ditko wove emotional scenes into the stories and infused the layout and rendering of every drawing with mood. He melded symbolic images with his realism: when the specter of Spider-Man haunted Parker's life, Parker might be shown with a web-draped shadow, or overshadowed by a phantom Spider-Man, or with his face half-covered by his spider mask. Lee felt comfortable enough to offset the drama with a breezy humor, while his fascination with irony and fate, themes he'd struggled with before now, became a genuine strength. The supporting cast brought the adventures to life

and gave them an unprecedented complexity. A musclebound oaf named Flash Thompson persecuted Peter but loved Spider-Man. Flash's dizzy girlfriend Liz Allan joined in teasing Parker but was secretly intrigued by him. Parker had a grown-up rival for Betty's affections, and Betty had a brother with criminal connections. Ditko and Lee kept all their subplots in constant flux. Ditko brought them all to life with the unheroic mien of his characters, which Lee complemented with a down-to-earth, confiding tone. We didn't read about Spider-Man; we gossiped about him with our good friends Stan and Steve. And it wasn't a bigger-than-life titan we gossiped about, but someone very much like us—perhaps, as Lee wrote, "the hero who could be you" (*ASM* 9, Feb. 1964). It was this intimacy, more than anything, that opened the field of superheroes to an adolescent readership.

Steve Ditko could run the emotional gamut even when his characters had no faces. This is part of the sequence that Gil Kane called "the greatest thing Marvel ever did," one of the most often-cited achievements of visual storytelling in the history of the medium. Subtle "camera movements" and unapologetic symbolism would convey all of Spider-Man's desperation and courage, even without Stan Lee's dialogue. (*Amazing Spider-Man 33*, Feb. 1966.)

Stan and Steve didn't let their hero sit complacently on his successes. In later issues Aunt May falls desperately ill, causing Spider-Man to run away from his archfoe, the Green Goblin. He's branded as a coward in the eyes of the world, finds his own confidence shattered, and is reduced to cowering in fear from his enemies, before Aunt May inspires him to affirm the course of his life: "Fate gave me some terrific super-powers, and I realize now that it's my duty to use them . . . without doubt . . . without hesitation! For I know at last that a man can't change his destiny . . . and I was born to be . . . Spider-Man!" (*ASM* 9–18, Feb.–Nov. 1964).

Ditko and Lee were connecting with every picked-on nerdy comic book reader over the age of ten, but never condescendingly, always respecting and valorizing those readers' lonely fantasies. They were also echoing the concerns of the youth culture with a conviction that suggested they were wrestling with the same moral and societal questions as some of the brighter high school and college students, even if Ditko's position, at least, was far to the right of theirs. These were years when the civil rights movement was exposing an American hypocrisy, when Kennedy's rhetoric inspired people to action and his murder left them angry. Even kids too young for sit-ins, free speech, and *Walden Pond* felt the rumblings. If nothing else, the pop music of the "British Invasion" was transmitting an edgy message of generational rebellion into their brains. How could images of Spider-Man pilloried in the press and fired at by the cops while running desperately, torn between his own life and his duty to his Aunt, trying to find his own "higher morality," not resonate?

Ditko and Lee brought to Spider-Man many other virtues that the other early Marvels lacked. Ditko's plots were neater and more complex than Kirby's, turning on several interlocking mysteries. There's no doubt that most of this came from Ditko: throughout his career he showed a fascination for secrets and intrigue, for hidden identities and characters caught in complex moral and ethical webs. Spider-Man's nemeses were colorful hoodlums, not monsters or Communists—and it was Ditko who always believed that our greatest enemies were among us, in our corrupt institutions and our own frailties, while Lee harped on his evil Reds. Beginning with issue 25 (June 1965), Ditko even started getting credit for "plot," something Kirby never got. No one has ever said why, but it may just be that Ditko, with his quiet but strong sense of justice, pushed for it, while Kirby (typically for him, and unfortunately) was content simply to do the work and leave the details to others.

Without fanfare, Ditko and Lee were bringing a structural innovation to superhero comics that would change the genre fundamentally and forever. Comic book stories had often been built upon earlier stories, as in Weisinger's construction of Superman's world, and Kirby and Lee were already playing with running emotional subplots in *Fantastic Four*. Editors occasionally continued stories over two issues, and in the '40s Captain Marvel had engaged in a two-year-long serial. But *Spider-Man* depended more and more on an ongoing "continuity" woven of multipart stories, cliff-hangers, foreshadowing, endless soap operas, and sustained character development. This made the stories slightly more inaccessible to casual readers but far more compelling to regular fans. It increased interest in back issues and helped turn used comic book sales into a cottage industry. For the moment it was simply an experiment, but eventually it would help save comics and would, for better or worse, change everything.

It seemed change would always swirl around Peter Parker, shaping not only his world, but his heart. His life as Spider-Man would drive Betty Brant from him, and he would graduate from high school to pick up a new cast of characters in college. But there were cracks showing. Lee had new projects to distract him, and Ditko was growing quietly, mysteriously discontented. Something was in the winds. In comic books, as in the greater world, the early '60s had seemed like a time of ferment and change, but the late '60s were going to make them look like nothing.

CHAPTER 10

THE BIRTH OF FANDOM

Although "fans," in the sense of a self-consciously active and vocal body of readers, weren't altogether new to comic books, neither were they at all common. In the early 1950s, EC Comics—gory, funny, smart, subversive, beautifully drawn—inspired a voluble body of "fan-addicts" to send in letters and create their own mimeographed "fanzines." But then came Wertham, the senators, the parents, the Comics Code. Bill Gaines and EC withdrew to the safety of the magazine racks with *Mad*. Harvey Kurtzman, *Mad*'s founder, withdrew to satirical books and magazines. Paul Krassner, a former EC fan and office boy who claimed to have lost his virginity on Gaines's office floor, withdrew "underground" with *The Realist*—featuring subversive articles and art by the likes of Wally Wood. The fan-addicts followed their example and withdrew to producing dittoed or cheaply printed "satire zines," like Robert and Charles Crumb's *Foo*. For a few years it seemed that the only comic book readers with opinions worth considering had been driven from the field, and dispirited editors had no interest in the remaining readers' thoughts.

Then came Mort Weisinger's letters pages and Julius Schwartz's collegiate JSA fans. And more: At a Pittsburgh science fiction convention in September, 1960, two young couples simultaneously conceived fanzines that devoted regular attention to comics: Dick and Pat Lupoff with *Xero* (a science fiction "zine" with a comic book column called "All in Color for a Dime") and Don Thompson and Maggie Curtis with *Comic Art*. It was a coincidence. The golden age had apparently been dead just long enough for Dick and Pat to start yearning wistfully for Captain Marvel and

The Crumb brothers fled from a horrific family life into comic books, and from a collapsing comic book industry into "zines" like this, which they sold door-to-door. (Foo #3, Nov. 1958.)

for Don and Maggie to start craving their ECs, just as Jerry Bails and Roy Thomas were aching for the Justice Society. They were far removed from Weisinger's young letter-writers: the new fanzine publishers were adults looking back, with little emotional investment in the present or future of the medium, while Weisinger's kids were the opposite, all waiting for the next issue of *Superman* with no sense of comics history. Before fandom could have any real effect on the field, the gap between them would have to be bridged. And who else could engineer that bridge but Mort's old partner in fandom, Julius Schwartz?

By the time Schwartz followed Weisinger's example with his own letters pages in 1960, he and Gardner Fox had already put Jerry Bails and Roy Thomas in touch. In 1961 Schwartz expanded his let-

Aquariuman, Green Trashcan, Lean Arrow, Wondrous Woman, The Cash, and S'amm S'mith, the Martian Manhandler, catch a Sekowskyan robot. Roy Thomas's cover for the first true superhero fanzine, published by Jerry Bails, pays tribute to Schwartz, Fox, and company. (*Alter-Ego* 1, Mar. 1961.)

ters sections to two pages, printing longer missives in full, even giving away original Infantino artwork as prizes for clever letters. Weisinger may have been content with "boo boo" letters from the kids who bought most of his comics, but Schwartz wanted to cultivate his older readers. So it always was: Mort with his sales and Julie seeking to recreate the thrill of his own early days as a fan, twenty-five years before. He encouraged the criticism of *Mystery in Space*, the controversy over whether Joe Kubert was the right artist for *Hawkman*, and the fight about whether superheroes were better suited for science fiction or human-interest stories in *Green Lantern*. He built up a regular stable of "letter hacks" who stayed with him through the 1960s. Guy H. Lillian III emerged complaining about the "idiotic epistles" sent in by the "clods" among his fellow readers (*Flash* 133, Dec. 1962), and would go on to set the standard for fan letters as Schwartz's "favorite Guy." Along with him came Donald MacGregor, Buddy Saunders, Kenneth Gallagher, Gary Friedrich, Bob Butts, and others. A slightly later generation would include

Mike Friedrich, Marvin Wolfman, Irene Vartanoff, Peter Sanderson, Marty Pasko, David Cockrum, Joe Staton, and many more who would make their influence felt—and not just as readers.

In the second appearance of Hawkman (*BB* 35, May 1961), Schwartz made a slight adjustment that could have easily been overlooked by a casual reader, but that had a catalytic effect on his readership. Until that time, all letters pages had published only the name, city, and state of the correspondent. Now Schwartz included street addresses. For years fans had nurtured their obsessions alone in silence. Now, suddenly, they'd found their lost race. Bails immediately wrote to the other letter-writers in that issue of *Brave and Bold* with his plans for a "comics fandom," for he had just returned from Mecca with the fire of the believer in his eyes. In February of that year, while the street-address-bearing issue of *Hawkman* sat at the printer, Bails had attended a science conference in New York and paid a visit to the National offices. Schwartz and Fox had taken him to lunch, where Schwartz explained the ins and outs of "fanzines" and fan networking. "I know now (for sure)," wrote Bails to Roy Thomas, "that I want to bring out a 'fanzine' devoted to the Great Revival of the costumed heroes." Roy was just the man he needed: an incessant talker and indefatigable writer, exploding with an intense desire to share all his minute research and speculations on the continuity of obscure superheroes. A few months later, they were publishing *Alter-Ego*, the first fanzine dedicated to studying "comic heroes of the past, present, and future."

Other fanzines popped up like mushrooms all across the country: *Komix Illustrated*, *The Rocket's Blast*, *The Comic Reader*, *Batmania*, and scores more. Most were done by adults, but some came from precocious kids just discovering comics, like the prolific Steve Gerber, writing for *Alter-Ego* and publishing his own slightly oddball *Headline* while still in junior high. Bails even added two more fanzines to his little home publishing business: *Capa-Alpha*, a sort of communal fanzine called an "amateur press alliance" or "apa" and *The Comicollector*, "the companion to

Alter-Ego," featuring ads for people selling, buying, and swapping old comics. Soon ads for overpriced back issues began appearing in the comic books themselves, and some bookstores began to sell old comics as premium items. Bails and Thomas formed an Academy of Comic Arts and Sciences—all fans—to give out "Alley" awards. Not surprisingly, Julie Schwartz and his freelancers won every category the first year, except for "Worst Comic Book," which went to Robert Kanigher's *Wonder Woman.* Bails's *Who's Who in Comics Fandom* counted more than a thousand Academy members by 1964. Prominent fans drove cross-country to visit each other, tally votes, and plan conventions. Snapshots from the time show groups of clean-cut young white men, occasionally with a rare woman or black man, sporting a few more eyeglasses per capita than the population at large, posed against the wood paneling of suburban rec rooms, grinning with the joy and fervor of camaraderie newly found.

But something was still missing. Despite the attention Schwartz and Kanigher paid to them, these "superfans" knew that they were a barely significant minority of comic buyers, that faceless little kids still ran the show. Teenage and young adult fans were craving comics to fulfill their more complex demands. Stan Lee looked at this new subculture and saw more than a rooting section: he saw a market. And more than that, although he'd probably never have said it out loud, he may a seen a chance at validation for all those years in the schlock heap.

Stan had always loved to win the affection of people around him, and now he could try to win the affection of thousands of strangers. When Schwartz starting publishing street addresses and promoting *Alter-Ego* in print, so did Lee, but he went further. In late 1962 he wrote, "Look—enough with that 'Dear Editor' jazz," and switched the salutations on published letters to "Dear Stan and Jack." To make the fans feel involved, he raised his pencilers and inkers from anonymity to give them—and himself—credit at the beginning of every story. This wasn't new: Schwartz had been giving Gardner Fox, Gil Kane,

and Murphy Anderson credit for *The Atom* for more than a year. But Schwartz's credits seemed intended to acknowledge only especially committed work, while Lee gave everyone—soon even the men who lettered the word balloons—not only credit but cute nicknames and ostensible attributes, obviously to create a sense of family. Kirby was "Jolly Jack" or "the King." Ditko was "Sturdy Steve." Even Lee's secretary got plugs as "Fabulous Flo" Steinberg. Lee himself was "Stan the Man" or "Smilin' Stan," and eventually Lee's own caricatured image, with his squinty eyes and impish grin, began to pop up in the comics. Credits like, "Written and edited with loving care by Stan Lee, plotted and drawn with talent rare by Steve Ditko, lettered and bordered with a vacant stare by Sam Rosen," made readers feel like they were part of a chummy gang.

Soon Lee was even giving nicknames to his heroes—"Stretcho" for Mr. Fantastic, "Ol' Greenskin" for the Hulk, "Web-Head" for Spider-Man—to be tossed around not only by editor and fans, but by characters in the stories. He knew just when to bring the readers into his confidence by revealing the men behind the curtain, just when to steal the spotlight from his characters. When Kirby rather gratuitously drew Johnny Storm and his friend Wyatt Wingfoot racing off in a sports car, Lee added the caption: "Jolly Jack informs us that he has drawn Wyatt driving a Ferrari Dino V-6 Berlinetta Special—given to him, no doubt, by an oil-rich grandfather who is definitely with it. This has nothing to do with our tale, but we thought you'd like to know. —Non-Sequitur Stan!" These were irreverent tactics for an irreverent time, and they made Marvel's bizarre stories palatable to skeptical older readers. Irreverence was all over teen culture then, from the Beatles' revolutionary *A Hard Day's Night* down to drive-in junk like *The Incredibly Strange Creatures Who Stopped Living and Became Mixed-Up Zombies.* But Lee may also have owed a debt to the Pop Art of Roy Lichtenstein, Mel Ramos, and Andy Warhol. Comics, that "respectable" art seemed to say, were machine-made and soulless, dead and laugh-

[1] That was the mainstream press' reading of it. Lichtenstein himself said, "All the works I appropriate are works I admire."

able.[1] With the nervous self-mockery of the ridiculed outsider who wants to fit in, Stan—who had once so longed to be a "real writer"—began simultaneously calling attention to the vapidity of his work and scrambling to bury it. No wonder he began getting more and more letters from college kids.

Lee's letters page persona was easy, hip, familiar, and he strove to impress his readers with his honesty and self-effacement. He admitted goofs openly and mixed unabashedly negative letters with the complimentary ones, even when DC fan Paul Gambaccini let him know that he was not impressed with the "new realism": "I have tried to hold back for months but can't do it. My hatred of your mags has caused me to write . . . Your heroes are lily-lily with obvious faking of emotions. . . . [your] so-called heroes who act like 'real people' (if so, I pity the human race)" (FF 9, Dec. 1962). This humble pose, however, stood in amusing contrast to the growing hyperbole of Lee's self-advertisements. Ever since he had plastered "The Greatest Comic Magazine in the World!!" on the cover of the Fantastic Four's third issue, he had been screaming for the attention of fandom. With the May 1963 issues, he finally gave his line the name Marvel, and only six months later his covers announced, "The Marvel Age of Comics Is Here!" Within another six months we saw issues that were "Bringing the Marvel Age of Comics to a Lofty New Pinnacle of Greatness!" (Apparently even this was too modest, for "The Brutal Betrayal of Ben Grimm" in FF 41, Aug. 1965, was proclaimed "Possibly the most daringly dramatic development in the field of contemporary literature!" Not even Thomas Pynchon or le roman nouveau could keep up with Smilin' Stan and Jolly Jack.)

To give the young stable an image of identity, Lee added a Special Announcements Section in 1963, then a checklist of Marvel titles, then the Bullpen Bulletins, full of hype and backstage gossip and references to pop culture figures from the Beatles to Mickey Spillane, bearing headlines like "Nutty Notes and Nonsensical Name-Dropping, Featuring Naturally Non-Essential News of the Nation's Top Non-Entities!" He created Stan's Soapbox to expound on

whatever caught his restless mind that month, mostly hype at first, but as he tried to swing with the youth culture, he started making glib pitches for brotherhood and tolerance that seemed almost to disavow the red-baiting of his scripts. In late 1964 he created a fan club called the Merry Marvel Marching Society, which offered, along with the usual pins and certificates, records called The Voices of Marvel and Scream Along with Marvel. He began filling his writings with esoteric slogans ("Face front, True Believers!" "Excelsior!" "'Nuff said!"), with references to an invented company mascot named Irving Forbush, and with florid promotions of the "Marvelous Marvel Manner." He made a joke of offering "no prizes" for boo-boo letters, and was soon mailing out empty envelopes proclaiming, "Congratulations! This envelope contains a genuine Marvel Comics No-Prize!" Most important, he addressed the fans directly with gratitude and praise, as in this blurb from the first page of a Spider-Man comic: "Dedicated to the new breed of comics magazine reader—to you, the modern Marvel fan, who will accept nothing less than the best in story and art!" (ASM 23, Apr. 1965).

The pride and pretensions of his readers were so well-fulfilled by these noble sentiments that a fierce loyalty to Marvel grew in their young breasts. Lee was always eager to publish letters attacking the unnamed competition, particularly when they came from converts like the former DC booster Gambaccini: "I don't know if their stuff has deteriorated or whether you have improved that much, but the competition now seems like ecch!" (ASM 7, Dec. 1963). At first Lee modestly disagreed with the detractors of his "Distinguished Competition," but by 1965 he found it impossible to keep himself off the bandwagon. "Chee!" he wrote. "Have you noticed the sorry mess of Marvel IMITATIONS making the scene lately? . . .We wanna make darn sure no dyed-in-the-wool Marvel madman gets stuck with one of those inferior 'Brand Ecch' versions of the real thing!" Pretty soon he was even attacking the competition's fans as "the bubble gum brigade," brainlessly gobbling "pablum" until they were ready for the *real* stuff from the "House of Ideas." The battle between "Brand Ecch" and "Mighty Marvel" became such a rallying point for loyal Marvelites that letters pages soon abounded with credos from kids echoing Lee's own hyperbole. "When you're reading a Brand Ecch comic," wrote Matt Emmens and Jimmy Luzzi, "you're just reading a comic book, but when you're reading a Marvel mag, you stand a little taller, walk a little straighter, and talk a little prouder" (*ASM* 33, Feb. 1966).

Whereas DC had quietly opened its doors to allow the fans in, Lee had gone out stumping for Marvel fans by whatever means he could find. He was winning, too: in 1961, DC had made a clean sweep of the Alley Awards, but only two years later Marvel won ten of fifteen categories, with Lee even beating Julie Schwartz as Best Editor. In winning the fans, he succeeded not only in selling his own upstart company, but in giving the fans themselves a greater sense of identity and a confidence that they had clout in the business.

As early as 1962 the fan guru Jerry Bails had declared, "Comic fandom will never be a fandom in its own right until it holds its own convention." Now regional "cons" were doing well, so in 1964 fans organized the first New York Comicon, with professionals invited. Unfortunately, no pros showed except Steve Ditko—the most reclusive of artists, but one whose private sense of honor must have made him see the debt he owed his fans. Within months, however, the mainstream press was discovering the new subculture. The Pop Art movement got it rolling, marking comics as cult artifacts, semiotic midden, novelties for highbrow curiosity.[2] Stan Lee, never missing a trick, actually labeled his comics "Marvel Pop Art Productions" in 1965, but dropped it when fans protested, suspicious of Pop Art and anything else that seemed to mock their beloved heroes. Then a middlebrow angle was found: in 1965 countless newspapers reported with incredulity that some people were actually paying as much as a hundred dollars for old comics, like *Action 1*, Superman's first appearance. *Newsday* and *Newsweek* profiled the "comic book cults," the latter

snickeringly suggesting that some of these "cultists" were homosexuals (well, of course, that explains *everything*). Jules Feiffer, who'd done work in superhero factories before becoming an intellectual darling as a cartoonist, wrote a series of fond reminiscences of golden age heroes for *Playboy*, which were republished in book form as *The Great Comic Book Heroes*. Thus, when CBS sent cameras to the second New York Con in 1965, the guests on hand included Mort Weisinger, Gardner Fox, Gil Kane, Otto Binder, Bill Finger, Murphy Anderson, and Jim Warren.

Weisinger (looking, said Roy Thomas, "like a malevolent toad") reminded the assembled fans that DC still outsold Marvel seven to one. But when someone asked him how to get work in comics, he said, "by way of the fanzines. . . . [Editors] are quick to note a good writer or good artist or even a darn good critic." Mort never forgot his own origin story. Already, in 1964, he'd hired his favorite *Superman* letter-writer, E. Nelson Bridwell, as an editorial assistant. Bridwell was like many an adult fan, an isolated man, wracked since childhood by medical problems, whose sustenance seemed to come solely from a mastery of literary minutiae and a love of precisely crafted stories. He could take abuse without eruption, subversion, or even humor, but as much as Weisinger no doubt appreciated that, he was looking for someone with a little more creative energy. In May of 1965, he turned to the elite fan writer himself, Roy Thomas. Thomas was at an interesting juncture: he'd just completed his first year of teaching high school, and he'd also won a writing contest put on by Charlton in its own effort to woo fans. But there was no question in his mind. Working for a DC editor was the fulfillment of a dream, not only his own, but that of thousands of other fans. Mort, unfortunately, was a nightmare of a boss, and within a week Thomas was desperate to get out. It didn't matter. The signal had been sent. Fans could become pros. They could actually *shape* the comics.

Thomas had a better offer, anyway. He'd gotten a phone call from Stan Lee, and Stan was ready to spring a surprise.

[2] Pop's roots stretched back to England in the mid-'50s, and what may have been the protean "quotation" of a comic book was a Jack Kirby romance cover in Richard Hamilton's *Just What Is It That Makes Today's Homes So Different, So Appealing?* It seems that Jack just couldn't help changing the world, even when he was totally unaware.

CHAPTER 11

THE MARVEL AGE OF COMICS

How do you follow up *Fantastic Four*? Lee and Kirby did it with an explosion of new heroes, the first of which ventured even further from tradition. They took the idea of the Thing and pushed it, mixing some Dr. Jekyll with their Frankenstein, and came up with a respectable scientist, Bruce Banner, who changed unwillingly into a savage green brute. They called him the Hulk, after one of their monsters, gave him a twisted mind that drove him to acts of magnificent destruction, and dropped him into the middle of a competition between the American and Soviet militaries to capture him— superhero as superweapon. The only one who cared was a teenager, Rick Jones, whose life Banner saved in the accident that made him the Hulk, and Rick's sympathy could barely penetrate the monster's hate-clouded brain (*Hulk* 1, May 1962). Potent stuff, but Stan and Jack may have launched it too quickly, for they seemed to have little idea what to do with it. The Hulk wobbled from eloquent-but-evil to inarticulate beast, then fell under Rick's mental domination, was hit by a ray that preserved the mind of Bruce Banner in the body of the Hulk, and finally reverted to bestiality, scorning Banner and his entire weakling species—all in five issues. Even the art was inconsistent, as Steve Ditko had to pinch-hit the sixth issue. Retailers returned *The Hulk* by the ton, and it was canceled after six issues.

Still, *Fantastic Four* was gathering steam, and Martin Goodman wanted Lee to kick a superhero line into full gear. Trouble was, he didn't have a lot of room to kick. Goodman had gotten Independent News to allow him more than his original eight titles a month, but not many more, and for every new series

added an old one had to go. *Teenage Romance* had made way for *The Hulk*, and *The Amazing Spider-Man* was going to end *Life with Millie*. Goodman had Lee add superhero series to the monster comics, still cautiously leaving some monster stories in the back. That caution seems to have spread to creative decisions as well, because for a while it looked as though Lee and his cohorts were turning their backs on the very daring that had won them their first success.

The same month that Spider-Man got his first trial story, Lee and Kirby plugged the Mighty Thor into the regular lead slot of *Journey into Mystery* (issue 83, Aug. 1962). He was a lame physician who finds a mysterious stone hammer that transforms him into the Norse god of thunder, complete with massive muscles, golden locks, and a winged helmet. He even discovers that he can fly by hurling the hammer with all his might and letting it pull him through the air by the wrist strap—the kind of thing an eight-year-old would try in his backyard. It was a rich idea, reflecting Kirby's growing interest in mythology, but he and Lee seemed to have even less of an idea what to do with it than they had the Hulk. Thor battled some standard Kirby monsters, then a Commie dictator in the improbably named republic of San Diablo, then Loki, the trickster-god, who gave Thor his first decent story (*JIM* 85, Oct. 1962). But only two issues later we find "Prisoner of the Reds." Lee threw most of the writing to his brother Larry, and Kirby drew it only occasionally, leaving the art to whoever was asking Stan for a favor that month. For his first year and a half, Thor was a disappointment to readers who wanted to see what Lee and Kirby could do with a hero who was also a god.

Lee was already deep into two more series for the monster comics: *Ant-Man* (*Tales to Astonish* 35, Sept. 1962) and *The Human Torch* in solo adventures (*Strange Tales* 101, Oct. 1962). The first was about a scientist who shrinks himself and uses insects to fight crime, apparently doubly inspired by an earlier Lee-Kirby horror story and by DC's Atom. Lee put no effort into the project, giving the writing almost immediately to his brother. Kirby stayed for only six issues before Don Heck—who called himself Stan's "utility man"—jumped hastily in. A flirtatious female sidekick called the Wasp didn't help much (*TA* 44, June 1963), nor did the conversion of the hero into Giant-Man (*TA* 49, Nov. 1963). At any size, this was the least of Marvel's successes. The Human Torch (joined by the Thing with *ST* 125, Oct. 1964) received even less attention from his creators. Lieber wrote it, and Dick Ayers, who was better used as an inker, drew it from the beginning. The stories consisted of colorless battles with such one-dimensional foes as Plant-Man, the Beetle, and Paste-Pot Pete. They were also oddly disconnected from Marvel continuity, with Johnny Storm and his sister Sue living a quiet suburban life apart from Reed and Ben, and maintaining secret identities even though they were known to the world in *FF*.

Despite it all, sell-through jumped on all those titles as soon as the superheroes took over. Goodman boosted print runs and told his editor to come up with still more heroes. It was then that a light seemed to go on for Stan. With Spider-Man succeeding and the Fantastic Four still rising, he took a look at the elements that made them so potent and knew that if he and his collaborators couldn't or wouldn't create anything else quite so fresh and risky, they could at least shape new ideas around a vital formula of their own. The key to it was the flawed hero, and formula or no, it came from the heart. Lee knew the social defenses of the glib but vulnerable soul, Kirby the silent anger of the outsider, Ditko the melancholy wisdom of the loner, the observer. The Thing, the Hulk, and Spider-Man had shown them the way. Now they developed heroes who were more subtly impaired, either by

physical handicaps or spiritual unease. In doing so, they not only set Marvel thoroughly apart from its competition and opened the doors to the soap opera that older fans were coming to love, but created icons of increasing immediacy to self-involved young people in the fragmented '60s.

Lee's first calculated uses of the formula were a pair of heroes developed largely apart from Kirby and Ditko, although Kirby appears to have been involved in the cocreation, or at least the design, of both. Iron Man, who took over the one monster title left vacant (*Tales of Suspense* 39, Mar. 1963), is really Tony Stark, millionaire munitions inventor, who is

Jack Kirby's rage, terror, power. Did DC's politeness stand any more chance than Rick Jones? Dialogue by Stan Lee, inks by Dick Ayers. (*Hulk* 3, Sept. 1962.)

injured while inspecting his weapons in Vietnam and captured by "Wong-Chu, the Red guerrilla tyrant." Even though shrapnel imbedded near his heart will soon kill Stark, the fiendish "warlord" demands that he devise weapons for him. "My last act," thinks the noble American, "will be to defeat this grinning, smirking, Red terrorist!" He builds a suit of electronic armor that keeps his heart beating and gives him tremendous powers. He escapes, reborn as a superhero, "but in order to remain alive, I must spend the rest of my life in this iron prison!" Here was another hero both blessed and cursed by his powers. Without his iron device, Iron Man was actually more vulnerable than a normal man, cut off from humanity—or at least from the women he was accustomed to romancing—by the massive chest plate under his clothing.

Lee strove for emotional realism with Iron Man, having Stark afflicted by dangerous heart attacks while lashing out defensively at his loyal chauffeur—sad-faced "Happy" Hogan—and his cute but unglamorous secretary, Pepper Potts, who's in love with her boss. Lee tried for political reality, too, opening in Vietnam and continuing with a parade of Commies: the Red Barbarian, the Crimson Dynamo, a red version of Fu Manchu named the Mandarin, and a Russian seductress called the Black Widow. Having an emotional and political focus made Iron Man more interesting than Ant-Man, the Torch, and the early Thor, and the fact that Lee quickly took the writing back from his brother shows what really mattered to him. Unfortunately, his emotional scenes broke down into predictable melodrama, and his Communists were swallowed up by the vicious jin-

goism that would have been obnoxious in any age, but was also grossly out of fashion by 1963. It was so incongruous for a man who tried to impress his readers with his hipness that we're left wondering: was Stan really, as some old coworkers have suggested, a political *naif* who was seduced by friends in the John Birch Society into propagandizing for them? Or did he sense the subversive nature of his comic book experiments and, fearing the wrath of parents or the Comics Code, seek the protective coloring of red-baiting? He wouldn't have been the first frightened progressive to do so.

The visual storytelling wasn't up to Kirby or Ditko standards, either. Don Heck was a naturalistic penciler with a subtle grace and a lovely line derived from Milton Caniff, and he'd done fine work for Lee on Western and romance stories. But when the small size of the Marvel "bullpen" pressed him into superhero work, it exposed a reticence in his action and nothing to compare with Kirby's relentless narrative push. He was unaccustomed to plotting like Kirby and Ditko did, which forced the stories to depend more on Lee's cranked-out synopses and on fight scenes that Heck didn't "feel." In Iron Man's first great battle, he's hit by nothing more terrifying than a file cabinet pushed down some stairs by Wong-Chu. Lee and Lieber made things worse in trying to save the situation by having Iron Man declare, "Ugh!! He weighted each drawer of this cabinet with rocks!" (Just like a red barbarian to keep rocks in his file cabinet!) This sort of thing would be a problem for Marvel whenever Lee had to stray from his two best collaborators.

Nonetheless, the theme of a hero having to overcome a physical handicap struck a chord with Lee, and he promptly repeated the idea with Daredevil (who, because of production delays, would not appear on the stands until the next year). Blind lawyer Matt Murdock, his remaining senses miraculously heightened by radioactivity, avenges the murder of his father by training himself Batman-style and donning a flamboyant costume to fight crime (*Daredevil* 1, May 1964). In fighting style and attitude, Daredevil resembled Spider-Man, and even his foes—the Owl, Stilt-Man, and the Fellowship of Fear—were much like the Lee-Ditko Vulture, Doctor Octopus, and the Enforcers. The series was graced by lively art, first by Bill Everett and Joe Orlando, a couple of veterans between jobs, and then for nine issues by Wally Wood, the elegant artist who had, among much else, given polish and restraint to Kirby's work as an inker on *Challengers*. Ordinarily Lee couldn't have attracted an artist of such high reputation, but Wood was a temperamental alcoholic who'd made himself hard to employ.

Unfortunately, Lee's imitative instincts tripped him up. Daredevil's private life—with sad-faced Foggy Nelson and Karen Page, the secretary who loves her boss —was Iron Man redux, and his "radar sense," reminiscent of Spider-Man's spider-sense, soon undermined the innovation of his blindness, turning his handicap into just a vehicle for bathos. "Farewell, Matt . . . my darling!" Karen thinks during one parting. "If only you could have *seen* me . . . seen the *lovelight* in my eyes!" And Matt thinks, "For a time I almost dared to hope . . . that Karen might feel about me as I felt about her! Yet the emotion I mistook for love was merely pity . . . pity for a man without sight!" (*Daredevil* 12, Jan. 1966). Lee had spent his career imitating other people's successes, and now that he had some of his own, he was imitating those. He did far better when he stuck with Kirby and Ditko, who tapped into the icon of the flawed and alienated hero more viscerally and symbolically, sparing their creations such calculated baggage.

With Kirby, Lee created three new series in 1963, starting with *Sgt. Fury and His Howling Commandoes* (May 1963). World War II was selling well then in movies, TV, and comics, maybe in response to Kennedy's efforts to get us involved in Vietnam, and now Stan and Jack wanted to put their own spin on the genre. "The War Mag for People Who Hate War Mags," they called it, a Kirbyesque romp through the battlefields in which tough, cigar-chomping Nick Fury led a squad of fanatics on impossible raids. It read sometimes like an offbeat

superhero series, sometimes like a gleeful riff on bad war movies, and sometimes like heartfelt memoirs—for Kirby based some of the material on his own war experiences. But whatever mood it was in, it was startling for its brazen acknowledgment of ethnicity: in the comic book world of Clark Kents and Peter Parkers, Izzy Cohen was explicitly fighting the Nazis because he was a Jew, Dino Manelli because the fascists were betraying his ancestral land.

More startling still was Gabe Jones. In those years comics publishers forbade portraying black people, unless bongo-beating "natives" were called for, fearing that Southern retailers would return the books unsold. The same year *Sgt. Fury* appeared—the year after the Civil Rights Movement's March on Washington—DC reprinted an adaptation of Ian Fleming's *Dr. No*, originally published in England, and had all the locals colored *pink*, even though they were obviously drawn as black people, and the story was explicitly set in Jamaica. Here, though, was Gabe—played a bit stereotypically with his jazz trumpet, but nonetheless a fully equal member of the Howlers—not just in the pages but right on the cover. Jack and Stan weren't just doing "realism," either: the US military had still been segregated in World War II. Even if this was Kirby's idea, Stan was with him. When the color separators made Gabe look white, Stan wrote memos until they got it right. He and Kirby were doing more than selling comics, they were making a statement. Gabe stayed when Kirby pulled out and Dick Ayers took his place, but unfortunately *Sgt. Fury* then became little more than a war mag for people who love war mags.

Two more Kirby series followed in the summer of 1963. *The Avengers,* a teaming up of Thor, Iron Man, Ant Man/Giant Man, and the Wasp, was a clear imitation of *JLA*, but with the Hulk thrown in as a kind of quasimember to add some Marvel-style conflict. *The X-Men* however, was the "alienated hero" concept par excellence. Its teenage stars were labeled "The Strangest Super-Heroes of All," and all shared a common affliction: they were mutants, young people born with weird powers because of abnormalities in their parents' genes. Cyclops fired beams of destructive energy uncontrollably from his eyes; the Angel had huge wings sprouting from his back; the intellectual Beast possessed massive legs and feet that gave him phenomenal agility. All were scorned by their peers and feared by society until brought together by a mutant telepath in a wheelchair—Charles Xavier, or "Professor X"—to learn to control their powers and use them constructively. Xavier considers mutants to be *"Homo superior,"* the next step in human evolution, but believes that they must for the present live in harmony with *Homo sapiens*, even keep watch over them, and resist the temptation to take advantage of their powers. Unfortunately, the Brotherhood of Evil Mutants—led by Magneto, and including the confused but basically decent Quicksilver and the Scarlet Witch—believe that the destiny of *Homo superior* is to rule. Mutants have enemies, too, like the fearful scientist who develops the murderous robots called Sentinels. So Professor X must send his young charges out to defend a world that fears them.

Lee and Kirby gave us some of their liveliest, sloppiest soap opera in the rivalry of the silent, brooding Cyclops and the rich, frivolous Angel for the love of Marvel Girl. The Beast, his intellect and baroque vocabulary ("Your powers of deduction," he tells Iceman, "are exceeded only by your affection for the obvious!") contrasting with his brutish appearance, was one of the most delightful surprises in comics. And the oddly dignified villains, with their zealous devotion to their people, afforded the clearest blurring of good and evil yet in superhero comics. Disappointingly, the stories rarely exploited the element that made the X-Men unique: their alienation. Except for the paranoid air of the Sentinels story, the so-called "uncanny X-Men" often behaved like just another band of costumed crime fighters. Part of the problem was that Kirby was clearly overstretched by Marvel's burgeoning growth. By early 1964, he was doing *Fantastic Four*, *Avengers*, *Thor*, *X-Men*, and covers for most other Marvel comics. The less accomplished Werner Roth began finishing the pen-

cil art over Kirby's layouts, and replaced Kirby completely with issue 18 (Mar. 1966). Perhaps, too, alienation was not yet quite acceptable enough in American children's entertainment for Lee and Kirby to feel bold enough to pursue their idea to its logical conclusion. The X-Men was a great idea that would have to wait for its moment.

With Ditko, Lee played a peculiarly '60s variation on the outcast hero, one cut off from society not physically but spiritually. Stephen Strange is the world's foremost surgeon, yet also the most arrogant and greedy of men—until an injury prevents him from ever operating again. His world falls apart, and he drifts as a derelict, until one day he overhears two sailors talking about an Indian sorcerer who can cure anything. He finds his way to the Ancient One's, but the mystic refuses to help him because he senses Strange's selfish motives. When Strange discovers that the Ancient One's pupil, Baron Mordo, is planning to overthrow his master, however, he risks himself to stop him. The old guru at last makes Strange his disciple in the mystic arts. Dr. Strange returns to America and takes up residence in a mysterious old house in Greenwich Village, but the eldritch forces he tampers with leave him alienated from his fellow man, more completely removed from society than any hero before him.

Lee launched *Dr. Strange* as a backup strip in *Strange Tales* (110, July 1963), where it drew an esoteric body of fans and won a regular berth, squeezing out the remaining monster stories. Its hero was odd even for Marvel, with his eye not on our world, but on weird dimensions hidden from normal men, even the realm of sleep, where he battled Nightmare, the personification of evil dreams. It was Ditko's fantastic landscapes that stole the show—if landscapes they can be called, for his otherworlds were vast, open spaces with no up or down, no horizon or vanishing point, only floating pathways linking one aerial island to another. These pathways were impeded by doorways set in space, where disembodied snake-jaws waited to snap down on the unwary traveler, guarded by legions of mindless, horrid creatures hearkening to the commands of dark lords. Battles were never fought with fists and feet, but with incantations ("In the name of the dread Dormammu . . . of the all-seeing Agamotto . . . "), with plasmic blasts of mystic force, with undulating webs of magic, with hypnotism and astral projection. The effect of these brief, tightly plotted stories was an eeriness that bordered on the hallucinatory, a genuinely disturbing air very rare in comic books.

If Strange was of a different ilk, then so were his most loyal fans, hard to confuse with the clean-cut Roy "the Boy" Thomas. Cartoonist Trina Robbins remembers the day she and some of her East Village freak friends—many of them cartoonists for the underground newspaper *The East Village Other*—made a pilgrimage to Marvel Comics to meet the acid-dropping, long-haired creators of Dr. Strange, who had obviously somehow infiltrated the establishment world of superhero publishing. They were stunned to find the crew-cut conservative Sturdy Steve and the lovable but politically vague Stan the Man. Lee dabbled at the hipster role, but where had he and Ditko come up with these powerful echoes of the beat, drug, and Eastern spiritualism scenes? No one knew, no one cared. Pretty soon the collective Family Dog was putting on a concert in Haight-Ashbury called "A Tribute to Dr. Strange," and Ken Kesey was saying the Marvel

superheroes were modern gods. Marvel had begun a journey into a kind of hipness that Lee himself could never have conceived.

Next Lee and Kirby found yet another new spin on the alienated hero. The successes of the revived Human Torch and Sub-Mariner made inevitable the return of the company's third golden age star, Captain America, particularly since Jack Kirby had helped create him—so the Avengers find him frozen in an

Arctic ice block, preserved at the peak of his career by a plunge into an icy sea at the end of World War II. Though still filled with fighting spirit, Cap is a man reborn into a strange era; and reborn alone, for he learns that his beloved sidekick, Bucky Barnes, died in the same act of sacrifice that left him frozen. "What happens next?" he ponders. "Can't return to my career as Captain America—it would be meaningless without Bucky! I don't belong in this age—in

This guy's an objectivist? Somewhere within the quiet recesses of Steve Ditko lay the wildest visionary in comics history. Dr. Strange explores those recesses, with dialogue from Stan Lee. (*Strange Tales* 126, Nov. 1964.)

this year—no place for me—if only Bucky were here—if only. . . ." Cap joins the Avengers and finds a surrogate Bucky in the Hulk's young friend, Rick Jones (*Avengers* 4, Mar. 1964), but this is no easy solution for Cap's almost morbid grieving. His transfer of emotion to the unwitting Rick soon take on a powerfully creepy tone.

The formula was working. Since the failure of the Hulk, Marvel's superheroes had enjoyed nothing but climbing sales. By early 1965 Captain America was backing up Iron Man in *Tales of Suspense*, Thor was filling all of *Journey into Mystery*, and the Hulk had returned to help Giant-Man sell *Tales to Astonish*. The monster stories were gone. Suddenly Lee found himself with a problem that would have been inconceivable to him four years before: he had too much work. Goodman's company always had been the House of Volume, and just about every Marvel series was monthly now (whereas DC's only monthlies were multiple-series titles like *Action*, and its single-

character comics came out only six or eight times a year). Stan knew he couldn't let Marvel's writing quality slip too far if he was to keep his demanding fans, and his brother Larry hadn't exactly been setting the world on fire. He needed a second writer, one who could handle the characters, the aesthetic of innovation, and maybe most important, the "Marvel method" of dialoguing finished pencils. He'd auditioned a few veteran writers, but they just couldn't adjust. Now this superfan, Roy Thomas, who'd just helped hand Lee his second Alley Award in a row as best editor and writer, was in town for a job with Mort Weisinger. Thomas had been hoping to meet Lee for lunch or drinks, but Lee had no time for socializing. He sent Thomas some Kirby art pages and asked him to try his hand at dialogue. Thomas finished them all that same night. Two days later, Lee was asking Thomas if he wanted to write for him. An hour later, Weisinger was raging: *nobody* quit DC for Marvel. E. Nelson Bridwell's job was safe. A new age had begun.

CHAPTER 12

THE WORLD'S STRANGEST HEROES

Schiff on Skates was slowing down. "On a small scale," he said of the editorial group he'd developed at National with Murray Boltinoff and George Kashdan, "the cooperative aspect was good in many ways, but on the large scale that emerged, it became unwieldy." He wanted to return to overseeing a few comics from start to finish so by 1963 he'd turned *Challengers of the Unknown*, *My Greatest Adventure*, *Tomahawk*, and *House of Secrets* over to Boltinoff and *Aquaman*, *Blackhawk*, and *Rip Hunter* over to Kashdan, leaving himself with a manageable load of five titles. The change showed quickly, as Schiff's anthology series shifted from monster mayhem back to moral tales, and his supernatural-hero series, *Mark Merlin* and *The Enchantress*, returned to preeminence. Marvel's success with characterization may have encouraged him in stories like "Missing: One Alien," a romp in which the monstrous but comical buddies L'on and Vaar became appealing, distinctive characters (*Tales of the Unexpected* 84, Sept. 1964).

Murray Boltinoff, although mainly an art director, was not without editorial experience. He'd been editing the popular *Adventures of Jerry Lewis*, in fact, and one must conclude that even the most indirect exposure to the tortured idiocy of Lewis will eventually twist a man's sensibilities, for Boltinoff's stable immediately produced "The World's Strangest Heroes." So they were advertised, at least, and they did their best to live up to the claim. A movie star inhales jungle vapors that cause her to grow uncon-

DC proves it can do weirdness, too, although always with more restraint. 'The World's Strangest Super-Heroes' drawn by Bruno Premiani. (*Doom Patrol #92*, Dec. 1964)

trollably to monstrous size. Weird waves in the atmosphere create a "strange duplicate," a "negative man," inside a pilot. An adventurer is mangled in a car crash, and can be kept alive only by installing his brain in a robot body. Outcasts from mankind, embittered by their fates—the first DC heroes to pick *upon*

75

[1] The astute reader will also note a strange, or shall we say uncanny, resemblance to Marvel's X-Men: "The World's Strangest Heroes" and "The Strangest Super-Heroes of All," each a group of freakish outcasts drawn together in a secret hideout by a genius in a wheelchair and taught to use their powers to defend a hostile world, specifically against a gang of enemies called "The Brotherhood of Evil (Mutants)." The Doom Patrol first appeared three months before the X-Men, which, given production schedules in comics, makes it only dimly possible that Lee and Kirby could have plagiarized it, and the first appearances of the "Brotherhoods" were simultaneous. In any case, we doubt that Lee, Kirby, Boltinoff, Drake, or Haney, even in the imitative world of comics, would ever stoop to such gross theft. Either this was all just a wild coincidence or some unknown someone who had the ear of parties on both sides was sprinkling ideas.

the Ben Grimm dynamic—they draw deep into self-exile until gathered together by a mysterious, wheelchair-bound genius whom they call the Chief. He trains them to use their freakish natures for the good of mankind as Elasti-Girl, Negative Man, and Robot Man. The press christens them "The Doom Patrol." "Life isn't over for us!" Elasti-Girl decides. "It's just beginning!" (*My Greatest Adventure* 80, June 1963).

Even though DC's world was far more charitable than Marvel's in embracing these outcasts as soon as they prove their heroism, the Doom Patrol brought an air of darkness and mystery into that usually sunny world. Boltinoff and the series' creators, Arnold Drake and Bob Haney, showed that they were the only men in the company who understood what Robert Kanigher had discovered with *Metal Men* and what Lee, Kirby, and Ditko were opening up at Marvel. Drake, whose *Space Ranger* had shown him to be Schiff's freshest and most imaginative writer, soon took over all of the writing. Uncommonly literate and versatile, a teacher and charity organizer as well as a writer, he blossomed on *Doom Patrol*, not only inventing strange plot twists and menaces, but evoking his outcasts' anguish with a rare intensity. "When they write about our 'daring exploits,'" says pilot Larry Trainor about the press, "what do they call us? . . . [They] never use our human names! We're still just freaks to them!" To which Robot Man replies, "That's all we'll ever be—misfits—so get used to it!" Robot Man was graphically melted and smashed; in one story he even tore himself apart to use his own arms and legs as weapons (*DP* 87, May 1964). Their principal villains were the Brotherhood of Evil, a freakish bunch consisting of a disembodied brain, an intelligent but murderous gorilla, and a woman with putty-like flesh who could mold her face into any visage (*DP* 86, Mar. 1964). Boltinoff, with an eye for unusual art, assigned the job to Bruno Premiani, an Italian newspaper cartoonist who taught at Argentina's National School of Fine Arts. Using a careful, classically based approach, Premiani prevented *Doom Patrol*'s oddity from turning into *Metal Men*'s comicality. His use of deep shadow and expressive faces deepened the mystery and dramatic power of the concept. At last the bizarre and outlandish elements that had run through the comics of Schiff and his associates were put to good effect. The new heroes, in fact, forced a whole new approach to superhero stories.[1]

Bob Haney followed quickly with another weirdo, this one daring to flirt with Marvel's brand of ambivalent morality: Eclipso, "Hero and Villain in One Man" (*House of Secrets* 61, Aug. 1963). Initially drawn with some vigor by Lee Elias, he was reworked by Alex Toth—making one of his rare visits to superheroes—into a truly spooky binary being of equal parts dark and light. Eclipso was a law-abiding scientist when solar eclipses weren't releasing his powerful evil side—and he had to use all his intellectual resources to keep that shadow-self in check. DC was still rationalistic, but it was acknowledging the power of the irrational now, and the results were exciting.

George Kashdan seemed to have less to offer as an editor—although the fact that he was a pro-freelancer gadfly at National ("his attitude was not to kiss ass," said Haney) may have limited his chances. He got not only Schiff's cast-offs but Kanigher's (*Sea Devils* in 1967) as well, and all of them declined under him. He served *Aquaman* better: the Sea King got married in comics' first big "wedding issue," and when Ramona Fradon quit to have a baby, Nick Cardy stepped in with his graceful art. Kashdan also turned *The Brave and the Bold*, into a showcase for superhero team-ups (from *BB* 50, Nov. 1963), bringing together the likes of Green Arrow and the Martian Manhunter, the Metal Men and the Atom, Batman and Aquaman. The idea was fun for kids, and the tales were entertainingly written by Haney, but the overall quality wasn't high.

Finally, after more than a year of success for *Metal Men* and *Doom Patrol*, Kashdan took a whirl on another weird Haney hero: a living periodic table called Metamorpho, the Element Man (*BB* 57, Jan. 1965). He was like a kid's chemistry set come to life, a multicolored, hideous-looking composite creature who shifted to the most bizarre extremes of shape and substance.

With such a screwy protagonist, Haney could only play upon that screwiness with a rollicking self-mockery. Wisecracking like Dean Martin in a bad crime flick, the "Fab Freak" breezed effortlessly through tangles with power-mad scientists, goofy-looking aliens, and subatomic universes, but he was unable to cope with Sapphire Stagg, armed with "curve power" and a great deal of money. Kashdan cajoled Ramona Fradon back to draw a few issues with a comical grotesquerie that was almost beautiful (after which she was unfortunately replaced by Sal Trapani). Metamorpho did well enough to win his own series (Aug. 1965), but there was an ominous note here for DC's new style of hero. In the hands of writers and editors who didn't have the deep empathy for outcasts that Lee, Kirby, and Ditko shared, this self-conscious "weirdness" could easily break down into self-parody.

The rising youth culture posed another challenge that DC didn't quite seem up to. *The Teen Titans*—sidekicks Robin, Kid Flash, Aqualad, and Wonder Girl—grew out of a team-up in *The Brave and the Bold* (54, July 1964) and started in its own comic in late 1965. It enjoyed solid art by Irv Novick and Nick Cardy, but quickly became a vehicle for pop-culture references and cute slang that could have seemed convincing only to kids too young to know better. The "Fab Foursome" met the "fabjous D.J. Deejay . . . the world's first disc jockey in space," whose "dreamy sounds" send "Wonder Chick, Gillhead, Flasheroo, and Robin-O" off on an implausible battle with an alien that is described by Deejay as "groovy! So gear and ungrotty! Marv and fab!" Stan Lee was winning teens over with a writing formula that he called "the Three H's: Honesty, Humor, and Hipness." But Haney forgot the first H, consciously "writing for the twelve-year-old in Ohio." The Titans won a regular following (many of whom debated in the letters pages whether the Titans were better than the Beatles—although without specifying at what), but they drove away more demanding fans.

Even the Doom Patrol was not immune, as their adventures began stepping over the fine line between the bizarre and the ludicrous: they encountered the

Animal-Vegetable-Mineral Menace, (*DP* 89, Aug. 1964), a millionaire named Mento who possessed a silly-looking purple hat that gave him undefined mental powers (*DP* 91, Nov. 1964), a giant jukebox (*DP* 96, June 1965), and a wacky teen hero called Beast-Boy (*DP* 99, Nov. 1965). Wooden humor replaced character-delineating dialogue. It began to seem that Boltinoff and Drake may have understood *Metal Men*, but they didn't quite grasp the Marvel mystique after all. It was as if DC's editors—even its liberal gadflies—couldn't view outsiders as anything but comical, couldn't simultaneously endorse the power structure and the "weirdos" who challenged it, but could only trivialize their weirdness.

Ramona Fradon's flamboyant cartooning and sensual decorativeness proved perfect for a swingin' '60s freak—but pointed DC toward a deadly goofiness. Script by Bob Haney. (*The Brave and the Bold* #58, Mar. 1965.)

Meanwhile, 1964 had seen another editorial earthquake. Despite the reversion to vintage supervillains and mystery stories, sales had continued dropping on the Batman line until Irwin Donenfeld and Jack Liebowitz decided Schiff was no longer the man for the job. *World's Finest*, which costarred Superman, was given to Mort Weisinger; Julius Schwartz was handed *Batman* and *Detective* and told to bring them up to date. In exchange, Schiff got *Mystery in Space* and *Strange Adventures*, as well as taking *House of Secrets* back from Boltinoff.

Schiff was shaken and started asking himself when he could afford to retire—but he did his best. When Alex Toth left *Eclipso*, Schiff brought in the best of his regular artists, Jack Sparling. His figures and layouts were built on a rounded line—fleshy, full-bodied people and lush, sloping backgrounds—along which the action rolled at breakneck speed. *Adam Strange* changed radically, with Lee Elias replacing Carmine Infantino on art and the plots departing from their ingenious scientific bent, but it now shared *Mystery in Space* with *Space Ranger*, drawn in a fanciful, style—reminiscent of Dick Sprang in its detail and charm—by veteran Howard Purcell. *Atomic Knights* and *Space Museum* were dropped, but *Star Hawkins* ran intermittently in *Strange Adventures*. Its art now included some of Gil Kane's finest work. Schwartz dropped the Martian Manhunter from *Detective,* so Schiff put his green-skinned sleuth in *House of Mystery* (143, June 1964), where he, Jack Miller, and Joe Certa bucked the sophisticating trends of the time with a series more fanciful and juvenile than anything they'd done in the "monster" days. The Manhunter and little Zook now spent their time among the creations of the magical Idol Head of Diabolu, including such dreamlike images as an orchestra of living musical instruments and a hole cut out of the sky, leading to a world above the stars. It was one of the most distinctive series of the silver age, but the kids didn't seem to notice it.

In 1965, in a burst of inspiration—or desperation—Schiff and his writers created six more strange new heroes. Immortal Man had the ability to die and return to life again and again, always remembering his last life—and always in love with the same mortal woman— but each time in a different body. He appeared in *Strange Adventures*, along with Animal Man, whose main attraction was superb art by Carmine Infantino and Gil Kane. Other titles showcased the less interesting Ultra, the Multi-Alien, the telepathic Prince Ra-Man, and Automan, an amiable robot. The only success of the six was Dial H for Hero, in *House of Mystery,* which Schiff and writer Dave Wood created as a wide-open forum to experiment with strange heroes. Advertised as "The Most Original Character in Comic History," Robby Reed is a teenager who stumbles across a telephone dial from another world. Whenever he dials the letters H-E-R-O, he is transformed into a different hero, and invariably an outlandish one— Radar-Sonar Man, Velocity Kid, Baron Buzz-Saw, Quakemaster. The scripts were energetic, and so was Jim Mooney's art. DC was proving it could deliver more than just elegant revivals of classic heroes.

But were weirdness and originality enough? None of these new creations were setting the field on fire and fans were starting to feel insulted by their increasingly goofball tone. It was the first hint that when DC's editors decided to loosen up and change with the times, they just might not *get it*.

CHAPTER 13

MAN AND SUPERMAN

While the weird heroes of Lee, Kanigher, Schiff, *et al.*, were fighting for the new breed of readers and tearing away at the foundations of what Julius Schwartz had built—while fans handed out their Alley Awards and argued over whether Spider-Man was more realistic than Green Lantern, or the Doom Patrol more piteous than the X-Men—one hero stood calmly above them all, fatherly smile on his face and cape floating in an endless summer breeze.

Mort Weisinger did it his way. Teenage and adult fans called his work childish, one-dimensional, repetitive, boring, ludicrous. But Superman consistently blew every other superhero away in sales, and as the '60s went on, he soared even over the heads of Donald Duck and his brood to become the best-selling comic book character of all. Mort had been here before. He'd started his career by running counter to science fiction fans and selling *Thrilling Wonder Stories* to teenagers; now he ignored the slings and arrows of comics fans to go straight for the increasingly neglected masses of little kids. While Marvel and the Schiff-group were experimenting with deeper emotionality, Weisinger was making the same qualities—in an utterly different manner—the very basis of the Superman mythos. The Man of Steel still fought crime and saved the world from natural cataclysms, but his stories rested firmly on his relationships with friends and foes alike. He developed a paternal concern for Jimmy Olsen, and entered unspoken but turbulent affairs of the heart with Lois Lane and Lana Lang. He toiled ceaselessly, through agonizing failure after failure, to restore his countrymen in the bottle-city of Kandor to their normal size.

His clashes with Lex Luthor took on an odd ambiguity as the archvillain displayed a broader humanity. From all this poured more grief, rage, love, and irony than even Marvel comics could boast of, yet—and this was Weisinger's genius—it was all crystal clear to a young children.

Weisinger and his writers had developed a narrative technique to dramatize heroic passion almost to the exclusion of violent action. The stories were told in fairy-tale fashion, with the significant events presented directly and in isolation, at the expense of mood-setting cinematic flow. In the Imaginary Story "The Three Wives of Superman" (*SGLL* 51, Aug. 1964), just five sequential panels take us through a critical turn in the hero's life. In the first, Superman mourns the death of Lois Lane on a "heartbreak asteroid." In the second, he returns to his Fortress of Solitude, and in the third he relives old times with Lois. In the fourth he discovers that she was killed by a serum of his own devising. The fifth finds him at her grave, where he makes peace with her memory by rededicating himself to his Superman role. As in a child's storybook, such sequences were essentially static, but through his endearing characters and his growing Superman lore, Weisinger gave them a vitality that gripped his young readers—and makes them delightful to adults who can get in synch with his odd aesthetic. Weisinger broke the one seemingly immutable rule of the genre—that the superhero has to fight somebody sometime in every story—and still sold more comics than Jack Kirby's brawls and Carmine Infantino's speed-tricks combined.

He and his scripters forged an appealingly goofy style of scripting engineered to make every aspect of

[1] Although he's been accused of taking ideas pitched from one writer and giving them to another writer as his own, while "rejecting" the first writer's pitch in favor of something stolen from still a third, leaving all questions of authorship muddy. Has there ever been a field in which so many wars were fought for so little glory?

[2] Joe Shuster wasn't even that lucky. His art failed to keep up with fashion and his eyesight gave way; he spent most of his life in errand-boy jobs and poverty. The disposable-culture factories of comic books were not kind to their creators.

a story clear. Lines like "We're leaving the past! (Choke!) There's the explosion that destroyed our native planet Krypton! (Gulp!)" drew jeers from older readers, but the little kids didn't care. (Amusingly, Weisinger was also given to interjecting lines to cover apparent "goofs," as if all those cute "boo boo" letters actually jabbed at his sense of invulnerability. Why else, when Bouncing Boy's power kicks in suddenly, would a bystander cry, "Look . . . he's expanding—like a balloon!! He's lucky he's wearing clothing made of stretchable fiber!" except to keep kids from asking why his clothes didn't tear? This appeared in *Adventure Comics* 301 (Oct. 1962), but we could have pulled a hundred—nay, a thousand—other examples.)

Weisinger did nothing halfway. At eating, at obscenity, and at work, he was obsessive. He was a major mover-and-shaker at the Magazine Writer's Association, and whipped out dozens of articles for *Esquire* and *Colliers* and others, along with books as divergent as a diet plan, a sleazy novel called *The Contest*, and the best-selling *1001 Valuable Things You Can Get Free*—although he reportedly farmed out much of his "writing," including that of his novel, to desperate freelancers and sold the finished work under his own name. *The Contest* was reportedly written by SF and comics veteran Dave Vern. He not only edited his comics, but personally fed his writers many of their plots.[1] Nor was he above browbeating and manipulating his freelancers to make sure the control—and the credit—remained with him. Artist Curt Swan described him as "very opinionated and difficult to deal with. And if anyone showed any weakness, he loved that, because then he would really lean on them." And Swan stayed with him longer than anybody. Some, like Otto Binder, couldn't stand it, but those who could were given steady work, and the result was a vast, consistent, and intricately interwoven body of comics that boys and girls supported for years.

Weisinger worked best with men he had known since his youth. Binder had been a fellow SF fan in the 1930s, Edmond Hamilton one of his most reli-

able writers for *Thrilling Wonder Stories*. But the man whom Weisinger called—in very rare praise—"the most competent of all the Superman writers" had known not only the editor, but the hero himself longer than any of them. Young Jerome Siegel had traded fanzine ads with Schwartz and Weisinger's *Time Traveler* in 1933, the same year he dreamed of his hero from another planet and got his friend Joseph Shuster to draw him, never imagining that five years later that hero would create an entire industry. In retrospect we can say that they should have fought to keep the rights, but then would they have even made the sale? There would always have been someone else willing to fill the pages for just cash, as Siegel and Shuster had been doing for three years. Being paid for creative work was even more miraculous in the Depression than now. They never questioned National's policies at the time, and happily made money off their long-term contract to supply Superman stories, until Siegel met a lawyer in the Army who told him he could get him his gold mine back. Jack Liebowitz took it personally when Siegel sued. He felt he'd been living up to an honest agreement, and now Siegel was getting greedy and reneging. He fired him. Siegel sold scripts to other publishers, but by the late '50s those other publishers were folding, and it took his wife's intercession to get him off the blacklist at National. Weisinger came to like him, though, not just as a writer but as a man. Siegel was about the only comics freelancer Mort would keep visiting, even after they no longer worked together.[2] "Siegel was the best emotional writer of them all," the editor said, "as in the unforgettable 'Death of Luthor'" (*Action* 318, Nov. 1964). Siegel knew about loss and longing. He was a shy, fragile man with a feverish inner life who watched his alter ego make millionaires of Liebowitz and Donenfeld—and a powerful editor of Weisinger—while he hustled work-for-hire gigs. Yet, the Man of Steel must still have spoken to him, for he threw himself into the burgeoning Superman mythos, with affection and humor, going unabashedly for the heartstrings.

One less venerable member of the stable was Leo Dorfman, a writer for Fawcett and Dell Comics in the 1950s whom Weisinger hired to fill Otto Binder's shoes in 1961. Dorfman was at his best in romantic, domestic stories like "The Amazing Story of Superman-Red and Superman-Blue" (*Superman* 162, July 1963), and he was given the regular *Supergirl* job. Other writers worked for Weisinger in the 1960s—including Otto Binder off and on—but Siegel, Hamilton, and Dorfman were his creative core.

Curt Swan was a penciler who never set out to draw comics. His dream was to be a magazine cover artist, his youthful heroes were such illustrators as Al Parker and John Whitcomb. But while drawing for *Stars and Stripes* in Paris during the war, he met France Herron, former editor of *Captain Marvel*. When Herron joined National after the war, he recommended that the jobless Swan show his portfolio to Weisinger, who promptly hired him. Swan drew *Jimmy Olsen* in the 1950s, bringing in his love of quiet scenes and human expression, never warming to DC's increasingly fantastic approach. "To me the . . . supporting characters really had a personality . . . . Somehow they became a part of me. Then, when they started this business of flying around and Jimmy Olsen becoming some creature, Elastic Lad, I'd want to take the script back and slam it down on Mort's desk." He never did take a script back, however, and certainly never slammed Mort's desk. When Wayne Boring moved full-time to the *Superman* newspaper strip in 1961, Swan became the Man of Steel's main artist.

Swan's penchant for realism gave him more in common with Norman Rockwell than with Infantino or Kirby, but Weisinger's new humanism made him and Superman a perfect match. Teamed with inker George Klein, whose neat, unassuming lines blended wonderfully with the pencils, Swan gave Superman

his quintessential look, and for all the killing and resurrecting of the character in recent years, that look is still Superman's basic visual template. Swan was unable to draw every Superman story, of which there were several each month, but Al Plastino, who had made a career out of more or less imitating Wayne Boring in the '50s, shifted to more or less imitating Swan in the '60s and kept the overall look consistent in style (if by no means in quality).

All these writers and artists built on the elements that Weisinger and Binder had created in the late 1950s. Not all their stories were good ones, by any means. The sheer number of stories was mind-boggling: eight issues a year, year after year, of *Superman*, *Superboy*, *Jimmy Olsen*, and *Lois Lane*, each usually with three stories, plus twelve a year of *Action* and *Adventure*, each with one or two Superman family stories, and starting in 1964, *World's Finest* as well. At least 1,600 silver age stories, and plenty of them soporific potboilers, most

No one ever did quaintness and intimacy like Curt Swan. He can still make us want to be bundled up, zipped to the Arctic, and shrunk into that bottle-city. Inks by George Klein, script possibly by Jerry Siegel. (*Superman* 158, Jan. 1963.)

built on a handful of too-often-repeated gimmicks (like the plot in which a character is hit on the head or drugged, wakes up to find him or herself in a historical epoch, and amazingly finds that a hero of legend—Samson, Robin Hood, George Washington, ad infinitum—is really just like Superman, and all his friends are just like Jimmy and Lois and Perry, after which said character wakes up, relates this experience, is told it was only a dream, and then—astonishingly—discovers a scrap of tunic or hair or plume that could only have come from the hero of legend). But when Weisinger's comics were good, they were unlike anything before or since. And when they rounded out Superman and his world by building on his unique mythology, they were very good indeed.

The central focus of Superman's development continued to be his Kryptonian origin, especially stories in which he discovers new details of both his native planet's and his own personal histories. He learns that an Earthly professor had traveled to Krypton to save his young life after a bite from a "fish-snake" (*Action* 281, Oct. 1961), and that a second Krypton was created and populated with androids to decoy against an alien armada, a world that Superman unwittingly destroys (*Superman* 189, Aug. 1966). In the archetypal Weisinger story (and title), "The Day Superman Became the Flash," he learns that his father used a "computer forecaster" to pick the planet to send him to, rejecting five on which he would have become other DC heroes—a speedster, a sea king, a tiny titan, a super archer, or dark-night detective—but on which he would have been unhappy, alienated, or killed too young. Finally, his father settled on Earth (*Action* 314, July 1964). The shadows of fate and tragedy fell everywhere.

As Kryptoniana abounded, the town of Kandor became more prominent, and kids were delighted to discover new details about the Bottle City nearly every time they visited. In just a handful of stories, we learn of telepathic police hounds that can locate fugitives at any distance by reading their minds, of duels fought with stun swords, of statues erected in honor of Kryptonian heroes, of bizarre native flora

and fauna, and of the scientist Van-Zee, who is Superman's exact double, and his wife, Sylvia, who is a double of Lois Lane. The most fun of all these tales were the ones in which Superman and Jimmy Olsen, borrowing from Batman and Robin, assume the secret identities of Nightwing and Flamebird, Kandor's greatest crime fighters.

One of the few bits of Superman lore introduced after Otto Binder's exit was the Phantom Zone, a "twilight dimension" where Krypton's worst criminals are banished as "disembodied wraiths" (*Adventure* 283, Apr. 1961). This was the dark flip side to Kandor, a nether realm preserving the most horrible aspects of the Kryptonian soul. Some prisoners gain wisdom through this purgatory and are freed by the Kandorian Phantom Zone Parole Board, but most, led by Jax-Ur—who gleefully boasts of his destruction of an inhabited moon—only allow their hatreds to stew. Although they can speak to our dimension only through the Zone-O-Phone in Superman's Fortress of Solitude, they can see and hear everything that transpires here, enabling Jax-Ur to devise horrible schemes of vengeance against Superman, whose father was responsible for his conviction. The occasional escape of these criminals provided Superman with foes of equal power to fight and brought new revelations of Krypton's past.

Weisinger particularly liked "red sun" stories. "To make him more of a likable character," he explained, "the type of story I became fondest of was the one where . . . Superman lost his powers and had to survive on his natural wits. . . . You could identify with him then, an outstanding character deserving of your admiration, a real hero because of the clever things that he did when deprived of his super-powers." When he's captured by the primitive populace of a red-sun planet, he fakes magic powers to win his freedom (*Superman* 184, Feb. 1966). When the Superman Revenge-Squad tricks him into traveling far into the future, when Earth's sun has turned red with age, he has to battle his way across a barren wasteland, warding off mutated beasts, to reach his Fortress of Solitude (*Action* 300, May 1963).

Lex Luthor found himself deep in the Superman mythos of the '60s, with a body of lore that paralleled Superman's own. He had his own fortress (Luthor's Lair, an abandoned museum in the heart of Metropolis, with statues honoring Attila the Hun, Genghis Khan, Captain Kidd, and Al Capone), a futuristic gang called the Legion of Super Villains, and even a planet, Lexor, on which he is respected as a hero and Superman detested as a villain (*Action* 277, June 1961). Although they scarcely ever threw a single punch, he and Superman became the mightiest rivals in comics, their clashes so monumental that the Earth proved an inadequate arena and they raged across time and the universe. In one true Weisinger classic, Luthor teams up with the evil android Brainiac, and their struggle with Superman ranges from Lexor to Kandor (*Superman* 167, Feb. 1964). In the very next issue, Luthor returns for another epic that originates on Lexor but climaxes in the San Francisco earthquake of 1906 (*Superman* 168, Apr. 1964). With the dense narrative that Weisinger favored, these issue-long stories packed an amazing complexity and texture into just two dozen pages.

The so-called "Imaginary Stories" showed off Weisinger's techniques best of all. These purported to be not actual Superman stories, but "what-if" stories showing what would happen to the Man of Steel if certain cataclysmic events should occur in his life. They covered years, often following characters from birth to death—and indeed, there was a lot of death in them, but almost always in acts of heroic self-sacrifice, fulfilling a fate foreshadowed from the start. Although told in a bald-faced style that made every detail clear to six-year-olds, they still managed to be genuinely bittersweet, usually by following the model of the heroic epics of antiquity, in which defeat made the brave even braver and neatly concluded their personal destinies. Tragedy, failure, and irony in its truest sense drove these stories, and in tales like "The Three Wives of Superman"—wherein Superman marries Lois Lane, Lana Lang, and the mermaid Lori Lemaris in turn, only to have each die tragically—the intense sorrow of the characters tran-

scends even the narrative voice. Only a teenager could laugh at "The Death of Superman," when Luthor finally succeeds in killing his foe and Supergirl must carry on the heroic mission, thinking, "Choke . . . all I feel is a great sorrow at the passing of the strongest, kindest, m-most powerful human being I've ever known! Sob—M-my cousin Superman . . ." (*Superman* 149, Nov. 1961). Luthor was a powerful figure in these stories, sometimes even getting to be a good guy, as when he's adopted by Clark Kent's foster parents and eventually sacrifices his life to save that of Superman, his brother (*Superman* 175, Feb. 1965). Weisinger was a believer in nurture over nature, it seems; maybe the Imaginary Stories gave him a place to consider what would have happened had he been adopted by a kindly farm couple.

Much of the joy of Weisinger's comics lies in the huge and bizarre supporting cast and their countless unexpected guest appearances. They included not just the usual gang in the newsroom but Kandorians and Atlanteans too, and even pets: Streaky the Super-Cat, Comet the Super-Horse, Beppo the Super-Monkey, and of course the original, Krypto the Super-Dog (who would even join his own team of superheroes, the Space Canine Patrol Agents).[3] Every one of them was caught in a web of interlocking relationships and ironic coincidences, sometimes ingenious and satisfying, other times outlandish—like Superman's occasional musings on the astounding number of people in his life whose initials are "L.L." Once a Cybernian Predicting Machine claims that Superman's life will be saved by one of those "L.L.s," but as he lies dying of kryptonite exposure, he uses his telescopic vision to see that each of them—Lois Lane, Lana Lang, Lex Luthor, Lori Lemaris, Linda Lee, Lightning Lad, Luma Lynai—is unaware of his plight. Who (choke) can save him now? Why, a young baseball player who conveniently happens by to toss the kryptonite away—with the capitalized words "Little League" conspicuously embroidered on his jacket (*Superman* 157, Nov. 1962).

Jimmy Olsen, Superman's pal and a cub reporter at the *Daily Planet*, had been given his

[3] At this point the perfect Weisingerite finds him or herself silently chanting the oath made by the SCPA on the constellation Canis Major: "Big Dog, Big Dog, bow wow wow, we'll stop evil now now now!"

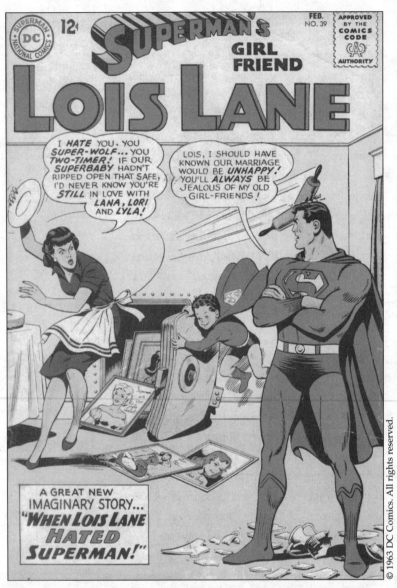

The other Kurt, Schaffenberger, was unparalleled at humor, vivid emotion and sheer sensuality of line. This is from when it was okay for girls to read comics, and okay for everybody to be amused by superheroes. (*Superman's Girlfriend Lois Lane* 39, Feb. 1963.)

to impress his girlfriend Lucy and end up fighting a kangaroo in an airplane. He worked better in cute riffs on human relationships, like the trio of stories in which he and Lucy fall in love while in disguise, never realizing with whom they're enamored and suffering great guilt for their infidelity.

Even Jimmy, however, made his contributions to the growing Superman legend, especially to Kandor, where the quaintness and gimmickry of his stories worked well. He introduced the gnat-sized superheroes from the Bottle City who call themselves the Superman Emergency Squad (*SPJO* 44, Oct. 1960), and four tiny desperadoes weirdly transformed by red kryptonite (*SPJO* 63, Sept. 1962), and in the one great epic of his series he enters the bottle with Superman to become Flamebird (*SPJO* 69, June 1963). Unfortunately, the good stuff wasn't to last. Curt Swan had done his first regular Superman work on *Olsen*, and for more than a decade he filled it with character and beauty. In 1965, however, Swan moved to *Adventure Comics* and was replaced by Pete Constanza, at the rough end of his career. The stories grew daffier, and by the mid-'60s the adventures of Superman's pal became Weisinger's least appealing and lowest selling.

Olsen's early success had prompted *Superman's Girlfriend Lois Lane* in 1958. Lois was put through the same weird transformations as Jimmy—Lois the Super Brain, the Phantom Lois Lane, Baby Lois—but the two main emphases of her stories were more domestic: her never-ending scheme to discover Superman's secret identity and her dream of marrying him. Complications usually swirled around either threats to her feminine vanity or wacky schemes to trap Superman, reminiscent of Lucy Ricardo. It could get awfully repetitive, but at times her adventures had a real sweetness and humor. The best were her Imaginary Stories, which originated with her series and from the beginning displayed a variety that lifted them above the grind. In the first installment she finds that being married to Superman is not the bed of roses she'd always imagined. Fearing that his enemies will strike at him through his wife, Superman

own title in 1954, an unprecedented move for a supporting player, but frequent Superman appearances and a set of special Olsen gimmicks made it successful. At first Olsen's specialty was disguise, playing such diverse roles as a TV actor, a spy, a rock-and-roll star, and—in drag—a mobster's moll, to get scoops and foil crooks. Then in the late '50s he fell prey to the same foolishness that afflicted Batman, with Olsen transforming in nearly every issue into a Giant Turtle Man, Human Porcupine, Flame Boy, Tom Thumb Jimmy, Living Pinocchio, or most often, the stretchable superhero Elastic Lad. The madness of a fever dream always threatened to engulf his stories: he'd try an Apache dance

insists that she publicly marry Clark Kent, not the Man of Steel. While gossips whisper, "Poor thing! She's marrying Clark because she couldn't land Superman!" and other women boast about their successful husbands, Lois must bite her lip and hide all signs of her husband's powers, even burning a beautiful extraterrestrial gown he bought her. By the end she is shrieking in frustration (*SGLL* 19, Aug. 1960).

Lois's greatest distinction was its art, some of the most charming and seductive ever in comics. Kurt Schaffenberger had developed his style while drawing Captain Marvel for Fawcett, and he brought to the Superman family the same humor, quaintness, and vivacity that his friend Otto Binder had brought with his writing. He also brought the greatest dynamism of his career. His emotionally lively, caricatured style suited the light touch of most Lois Lane scripts, while his pristine simplicity made a smooth match with Swan's more restrained work. While Weisinger hired Swan to draw nearly all the Superman family covers, thus reinforcing the Superman "look," he made an exception with Schaffenberger's sumptuous covers for *Lois Lane*.

The *Supergirl* series, running in *Action* from 1959 to 1969 before moving to *Adventure*, was pointedly aimed at young girls, a market Weisinger valued highly. Unfortunately, he and his all-male staff slipped too often into boyish condescension. The stories revolved largely around family problems, teen romance, and peer relations, and although much Superman lore found its way into those pages, it usually provided only a backdrop to Supergirl's latest heartthrob. Jim Mooney's art here was flat and constrained—as she was told to mimic Swan—although his faces were expressive enough to capture all the sorrow, irateness, and wide-eyed delight that Leo Dorfman regularly made his heroine undergo. Supergirl suffers agonies when her flying stallion, Comet, is sold to a Hollywood producer and subsequently seems to prefer the company of Liz Gaynor, his costar, over hers (*Action* 294, Nov. 1962), but that's nothing compared to what she suffers in "Supergirl's Rival Parents" (*Action* 310, Mar. 1964).

There she is overjoyed to find that her real parents have survived the destruction of Krypton—but then she must choose which set of parents she'd rather live with. Although her adventures were never the best crafted, Weisinger and his writers did manage to tap into the deep unconscious stuff of children's minds. Countless kids have fantasies about "real parents" who will come back to claim them one day, and such yearnings can lead to agonies of loyalty. And what could resonate more powerfully for a girl at the verge of puberty than a magnificent white stallion who can bear her on its back into the sky, then transform briefly into a beautiful but tragic young man?

The Superman mythos expanded in different directions with *Superboy*, "The Adventures of Superman When He Was a Boy," also featured in *Adventure Comics* until 1962. There Weisinger introduced the assorted new colors of kryptonite (red, blue, white, and gold), the origins of Lex Luthor and that fifth-dimensional imp, Mr. Mxyzptlk, and the Bizarros, who even had their own would-be humorous series in the back of *Adventure* (185–199, June 1961–Aug. 1962). This often created paradoxes in continuity, at least for older readers, who wondered how the Mxyzptlk whom Superman first met as an adult in 1944 suddenly proved to have been a pest to Superboy since high school. But to the vast bulk of Weisinger's young readers, every new issue was like the beginning of history, and these paradoxes went unnoticed. Complementing all that was a distinct Superboy lore, centering on his hometown of Smallville, with a cast of characters that included his kindly foster parents, his devoted dog Krypto, a juvenile Lois Lane named Lana Lang, and Clark Kent's loyal pal Pete Ross (so loyal, in fact, that although he once accidentally discovers Clark's true identity, he never reveals the fact, even to Clark himself). It all added a new dimension to the Man of Steel's personality, broadening the stage on which he acted and giving Weisinger a chance to fill in biographical gaps that no other editor enjoyed. The Smallville tales exuded an old-fashioned charm that, if not as enveloping as *Kid Flash*'s mystique, made them a cozy retreat. The run-of-the-mill Smallville story, in fact, was generally much more entertaining than the Superman stories that ignored the "mythos," and in the grim days of the '50s, *Superboy* was Weisinger's gem. The art, by George Papp, couldn't stand up to Swan's and Schaffenberger's, but still had its own funky charm.

Among the many innovations of 1958 was an intermittent series called "Untold Tales," in which we discovered episodes in Clark Kent's life between his careers as Superboy and Superman. Weisinger took his revelations further back in time with stories of Superbaby, cute tales of Clark's early experiments with his powers. Occasionally we took a step back even further, to see baby Kal-El on Krypton, giving us an infant's view of that advanced planet, with such amazing toys as a pipe that blows soap bubbles in complex geometric forms (*Superboy* 79, Mar. 1960).

Having given us the past, how could Mort not give us the future? In *Adventure* 300 (Sept. 1962) the Legion of Super Heroes, until then limited to occasional guest appearances, premiered in a series of its own. The original members of that thirtieth-century team—Lightning Lad, Cosmic Boy, and Saturn Girl—were now joined by more powerful teenagers, among them Brainiac Five, whose "twelfth-level brain" makes him a human computer, Sun Boy, who can generate heat and light, Triplicate Girl, who can split herself into three identical bodies, and Chameleon Boy, Shrinking Violet, and Bouncing Boy, whose names say it all. Around them Weisinger and his writers—first Jerry Siegel, then Edmond Hamilton—wove a vast lore. They had a clubhouse, a vast array of superscientific gadgets, regular elections for team leader (later voted on by the fans), the Legion of Super Pets, the Legion of Substitute Heroes (Legion applicants who had been turned away), and a cast of diabolical foes. About the only thing the Legionnaires weren't provided with were personalities, but each possessed a unique origin and a complex personal history around which some fun, if goofy, stories were spun. Superboy himself figured prominently as a member of the team—as well as its

historical inspiration—and of course there were guest appearances by Supergirl, Lana Lang, Jimmy Olsen, Krypto, Comet, and Streaky the Super-Cat. The time barrier was a revolving door in Weisingerland.

Regular Legion writer Edmond Hamilton had been, since 1928, one of science fiction's main inventors and popularizers of classic "space opera." His love of grandiose, cosmos-spanning adventures earned him the nickname "World-Wrecker" from his peers. With Weisinger he created the pulp series *Captain Future* (for which his agent was Julius Schwartz), and then followed his editor to comics in the early 1940s. His old predilections now surfaced in Legion stories that spanned space and threatened great cataclysms. The man who had to draw such things, and consistently failed to make them impressive, was John Forte, a stiff penciler with a flat style that made everything smaller than life. Still, he had a weird, archaic imagination for costumes and paraphernalia—like the clubhouse that looked like a Buck Rogers rocket jammed upside down into the ground—and the frozen caricature of his faces left no doubt of his characters' passions.

Passions there were, maybe more than in any other Weisinger series—for weren't these supposed to be teenagers, locked in battle over peer status and cliquish loyalty? Take the "Death of Lightning Lad" sequence, in which the eponymous lad dies in battle and is later resurrected through an act of self-sacrifice by another hero (*Adventure* 304–312, Jan.–Sept. 1963). Heavy enough for any comic book, but twists and turns along the way build the emotional stakes. Saturn Girl is warned by aliens that a Legionnaire will die using his powers against Zaryan the Space Conqueror, so she tries to rob her teammates of their powers so that she'll be the one to fulfill the prophecy. Lightning Lad discovers her plan and sacrifices himself in her stead, but soon after seems to revive and take up where he left off. "He" is revealed to be his sister, who shares his lightning powers and is then inducted into the Legion as Lightning Lass. Then a new member, Mon-El, discovers that Lightning Lad really *can* be resurrected if a living being uses his own body to conduct a lightning bolt —and thus his own life force—into the corpse. Mon-El wants to sacrifice himself, of course, but the other Legionnaires decide to let fate, in the form of a stray lightning bolt, determine the martyr. It's Saturn Girl—but no! It's actually Proty, Chameleon Boy's shape-shifting pet, impersonating her after he caught her tampering with the steel wand so that *she* would attract the lightning bolt and be the one to die so that Lightning Lad might live. Ultimately, it only cost readers one shape-shifting pet, but it gave them almost more nobility and tragedy than they could stand.

The Legion hinted at an even greater potential, and after three years that potential was realized, thanks to a veteran artist and a teenage boy. In 1965 John Forte succumbed to a long illness, and Weisinger, seeing the building popularity of the Legion, moved Swan over from *Olsen* (*Adventure* 340, Jan. 1966). Hamilton continued as writer for another half-year, but the stories immediately read better, as Swan made the Legionnaires look older, the thirtieth century more sleekly futuristic, and the menaces more threatening. Then, when Jim Shooter delivered his first story with issue 346 (July 1966), the writing itself took on a new sophistication. The series became one of Weisinger's best, and his most distinctive—distinctive in part because Jim Shooter was only thirteen years old.

Young Jim had been in the hospital, reading comics, and discovered that the ones he liked best— the Marvels—were also the most beaten up, the most read by other kids. Then "I was reading *Adventure Comics*, and it occurred to me that somebody got paid for writing this. . . . I thought, 'I can write better than this. . . .' My family needed money, and when you're thirteen years old, what can you do? Nobody will give you a job." He was from Pittsburgh, a big kid, craggy-featured and older looking than he was, with an angry streak and a confident manner. He was never easily daunted. Already wizened by an unsentimental world, ready in eighth grade to surrender his youth to the breadwinner's role, Jim realized that by learning how to craft what the popular comics did

well and selling it to the publisher of the less popular comics, he might get paid. He submitted a complete comic book, fully scripted and illustrated, with remarkably slick writing and visual storytelling. Weisinger knew that Hamilton was about to retire from comic book work, and he needed a replacement. He had already initiated the policy, new at National, "of combing the slush pile to discover new talent." He'd found fans E. Nelson Bridwell and Roy Thomas, and now he must have figured he'd found the best yet in Shooter.

Though never one of DC's best sellers, the Legion had inspired its own cultish fan movement since its earliest appearances. Fans didn't just vote for team leader, but flooded the mail room with requests for more background, sent in ideas for new Legionnaires (some of which Weisinger used), and suggested romantic match-ups between heroes and heroines. It would be hard for an adult, especially one of Hamilton's grandfatherly age, not to find such things simply "cute." But a junior-high kid could understand how vital they were to his peers, how seriously the fans took their heroes, and how achingly important were the social intrigues of adolescent cliques. Though mainly a loner, Shooter could intuit that the Legion was a perfect fantasy for the youth culture—a community composed of and run by teenagers, to whom adults were irrelevant except as villains. Not surprising, then, that he "got it" where Hamilton didn't. What is surprising is how well the kid could craft a story. He was a quick study, learning storytelling and editorial skills from Weisinger—and perhaps picking up a bit of the autocrat's nature from him as well—and getting the content from Marvel.

Shooter knew how to use Marvel tricks and then top them. Stan Lee had introduced a hero named Wonder Man into *Avengers* just to startle readers by having him die in the same issue. Steve Ditko, freelancing for a new publisher called Tower, then killed a hero who'd been around for a few issues. So Shooter allowed readers to bond with a new hero named Ferro Lad before having him die to save the galaxy from a huge cloud that devoured suns

(*Adventure* 353, Feb. 1967). It was the first time a DC good guy had died in a "real" episode—not a hoax, not a dream, not an Imaginary Story. Fans kept waiting for him to come back, like Lightning Lad, but he never did. As it dawned on them that Ferro Lad was really gone, he stuck in their minds like a lost friend.

The Legion was an exception in Weisinger's world, in that it was aimed at slightly older fans, but in a way it only proved the success of the rest of the Superman line. For all of Shooter's innovations, the Weisinger style and mythos still filled and surrounded the Legion. After all, these were Superboy's friends in the far future, and maybe the future would be a little more like Marvel. In any case, the Legion never rivaled Superman in sales. Maybe, ultimately, it was just something to lure older fans into Superman's world.

While storms buffeted comics in the 1960s, Weisinger held steady to the course he had plotted at the beginning of the silver age, keeping his big ship calm in the wild seas. He let the fanzine crowd mock him, preferring to spark the imaginations and touch the emotions of young boys and girls. His work still stands, unmistakable and nearly untapped in its richness of invention, passion, and lore. The critics never knew what to do with him. His successors have never quite seemed to know what to do with Superman. Uncle Mort knew it all.

CHAPTER 14

BUILDING A UNIVERSE

Marvel didn't stop with its offbeat new heroes. Stan Lee innovated as if he were racing against time, as if he weren't bringing enough frantic energy to beating his deadlines and hyping his comics, but had to rewrite the rules of superhero storytelling with each passing month. Now he was trying to unify the whole "Marvel Universe," trying to sell not just a set of comics, but an entire line to his fans as one inseparable unit. Mort Weisinger had given Superman a consistent universe that linked seven titles, but Lee was after something even bigger. He and Jack Kirby had already left no doubt that all their heroes coexisted in the same world, and that that world included all the real places and social realities of ours. By 1965 Steve Ditko was even giving that world a metaphysics. It still wasn't enough. Lee and his collaborators wanted to redefine the way heroes related to each other, their opponents, and their society.

Guest appearances by heroes in each other's stories were old hat, but no one had done them as often or as casually as Marvel started doing. Marvel heroes wouldn't just get together for periodic team-ups, as Flash and Green Lantern did twice a year; they'd bump into each other on rooftops, and call on each other for help—and sometimes get rebuffed. Most of all, though, they fought. DC's heroes were always as chummy as could be, but nearly every time Marvel heroes met, some plot twist had them pounding each other, often tearing up whole city blocks in the process. In the first two Marvel team-ups, a cocky Spider-Man fights the Fantastic Four to prove his worth (*ASM* 1, Mar. 1963), and then the military uses the FF to wrestle the Hulk into submission (*FF* 12,

Mar. 1963). That kicked off an almost ritualized series of Thing vs. Hulk battles, each longer and more apocalyptic than the last, until finally entire issues were given over to their wild, funny, verbose, concrete-shattering slugfests. Sometimes battles were brought about by a villain's schemes, other times by a simple misunderstanding. But such things were never quickly cleared up. When the villainous Chameleon fools Iron Man into believing Captain America is a phony, Cap obligingly waits until five pages of fight scenes have passed before setting the record straight (*TS* 58, Nov. 1964).

Whether the heroes were fighting, joining forces, or just catching up on gossip, these crossovers were among Marvel's most popular features. Lee and Kirby quickly created a regular forum for such team-ups with *The Avengers*, in which the heroes joined forces to battle cataclysmic threats that are too much for each alone. They were an effective mix: the two Lee-Ditko loners, Spider-Man and Dr. Strange were left out, and with Thor and Iron Man's might, Giant-Man's size, and Captain America's gymnastic agility, there was plenty of opportunity for Jack Kirby action. They did not, however, give Stan Lee much room for his emotional developments. When Kirby left to launch Captain America's own series, Don Heck took over the penciling chores, and although he had a good touch with human emotion, he lacked Kirby's punch. To keep the series entertaining, a change would have to be made.

Lee had the tools at hand: Quicksilver and the Scarlet Witch, those noble but confused siblings from *X-Men*, had won the affection of fans. Lee decided to make heroes of them, another Marvel first. He had all the Avengers but Captain America resign, to be replaced by the two formerly evil mutants and Hawkeye, a Green Arrow-like Iron Man foe who'd also proved to have his heart in the right place (*Avengers* 16, May 1965). The main thrust of the "New Avengers" was Lee's favorite thing: character conflict. Hawkeye was an abusive show-off with a chip on his shoulder, Quicksilver a proud, humorless outsider, overly distrustful of mankind and protective of his sister. The Scarlet Witch was a naïve, nervous soul, and Captain America the weary veteran trying to turn them into a team. Their discord was perfect for a team of insecure, overambitious misfits, but it continued with very little development until it became grating. Even the return of Giant-Man, now called Goliath, and trapped in a freakish ten-foot height (*Avengers* 28, May 1966), wasn't enough to overcome repetitive shtick and an uninspired run of villains. It was about time for Stan to hand *The Avengers* off to someone else.

That someone, Roy Thomas, was coming along nicely. After proving he could write on *Sgt. Fury*, Roy was able to give that series to a protégé of his own, Gary Friedrich, and relieve Stan on *X-Men*, a low-selling title and a complicated one to write. From his first appearance on *X-Men*, Thomas showed himself to be as detail-obsessed as a writer as he'd been as a fan, intent on covering everything imaginable in dialogue, adding touches of characterization even to the most insignificant background characters. The opening splash panel of his first issue sports eleven word balloons and captions—totaling nearly two hundred words—which allow us to understand the depicted bank robbery from the point of view of villains, victims, and bystanders alike. Over the next nineteen pages, the X-Men and their foes not only talk endlessly but give us the "origin" of Professor X's paraplegia. (*XM* 20, May 1966). An adolescence spent in the solitary hunt for back issues in the flea-market wilderness of Missouri, an adulthood forged in the flame of a mocked and outcast subculture, Roy had a mental and emotional immersion in his material that even Jerry Siegel couldn't approximate. For Thomas,

and many of the fans who followed him into the business, the stories were of less importance than the *stuff*: the texture, the background details, the "continuity" of old comics to new ones. To hard-core fans, this had the effect of making Marvel stories seem not just like entertainment, but like the historical documents of some other world, a world whose possible reality they dearly wanted, in their secret hearts, to see reinforced.

Thomas promptly resurrected "a stampede of yesteryear's most sensational super-villains," six old Iron Man and Human Torch foils whom Lee had wisely left forgotten (*XM* 22, July 1966). He set about linking up scattered pieces of the Marvel universe with knowledge and careful thought, where Lee had done so impulsively and only when his faulty memory was up to the task. Thomas launched a back-up feature detailing the origins of the various X-Men, which Lee had left unexplored (*XM* 38, Nov. 1967). And he worked to make his adolescent mutants more convincing than Lee had, drawing on his high-school teaching days. Fans were biased toward their own "Roy the Boy" from the beginning, but all this guaranteed that he would instantly be among their favorite writers—even though he was still struggling with the basics of storytelling.

Meanwhile, Marvel's past and present were being linked by *Captain America*. Lee tried to remind us occasionally of the poignancy of Cap's displacement as a World War II hero stuck in the '60s, but Kirby dominated the series with action that must have had his adrenaline pumping as fast as his hero's. In Cap's first solo adventure, he's attacked by a gang of thugs armed with automatic pistols and an electronic suit of armor, and Jack treats us to seven pages (of a ten-page story) of flying bullets, hurtling bodies, judo throws, crunching fists, bulging muscles, and collapsing furniture, all free of the encumbrance of plot or captions and executed with the exuberant abandon of a saloon brawl in a big-screen Western (*TS* 59, Nov. 1964). By this time Marvel was making enough money that Lee could begin giving Kirby some significant raises in his page rate, eventually the highest in the business. Kirby could cut his workload without cutting his income, concentrating on pumping up his art and moving into a monumental, high-velocity storytelling style that would set the comic book world just as violently on its ear as his early work had a quarter century before.

For three more issues Cap fought a gang of acrobatic Nazi assassins, a Communist sumo wrestler in Vietnam, and a whole cell block full of convicts. But with the retelling of his origin (*TS* 63, Mar. 1965), he began a ten-issue sequence set during World War II, in which he and Bucky gaily turned back the tide of fascism. This allowed no room for characterization, alienation, and mourning, but in return Lee got a little more unity for his Marvel Universe. Cap and some of his villains had already appeared in the World War II of *Sgt. Fury*. And Nick Fury himself—now a colonel and a CIA agent—had appeared in the present when Adolf Hitler resurfaced to annoy the Fantastic Four for an issue (*FF* 21, Dec. 1963). Lee wasn't just uniting the past and present of his own world, but stirring them both up with our world.

In the summer of 1965 he found an even more immediate way to keep Marvelites in touch with the past. He'd already given *Fantastic Four* and *Spider-Man* giant-size annuals, but decided to show up DC by filling his with original material instead of reprints. Seeing DC's continued success with its *80 Page Giants*, he now matched them with *Marvel Collectors Item Classics*. There was some *chutzpah* here, because National had more than twenty-five years of Superman, Batman, and all to pull from, whereas the earliest "Marvel" stories were fewer than four years old. But Lee knew there were fans out there discovering his comics every day, reading the references to past adventures that he now sprinkled liberally through his scripts, desperate for back issues that they couldn't find. The cynic may have called it just a stunt to sell old material at a ridiculous markup, but for new Marvel converts it was a chance to get hip in a hurry. Anyway, it said right on the cover that these were "Collectors Items," and didn't the *Times* say comics were collectible? Lee followed soon with *Fantasy Masterpieces*, featuring reprints from the

golden age and the monster comics, and forever after Marvel would have a profitable sideline in reprinting its own product *ad infinitum*.

The Marvel Universe was woven still more tightly by its two preeminent antiheroes, the Hulk and Sub-Mariner. After the cancellation of his series, the Hulk made almost monthly guest appearances in other comics, always battling the hero but protesting that he only wanted to be left alone. At the same time, in the first *Fantastic Four Annual* (1963), the Sub-Mariner found his lost race of Atlanteans, relieving him of his main source of rage and enabling him to don the noble robe of Prince Namor of Atlantis. When he encountered the Fantastic Four next after the reunion, it was

Captain America's first appearance in his own series in over a decade, and not one that any Marvel fan could forget. Jack Kirby begins to show the big, face-punching, Pop Art style that will change comic book art forever after. Inks by Chic Stone, words by Stan Lee. (*Tales of Suspense* #59, Nov. 1964.)

as an arrogant but admirable ally (*FF* 33, Dec. 1964). Of the two, the Hulk seemed to provoke a greater response from the fans, for each of his appearances was followed by a flood of "bring back the Hulk" letters. Perhaps the lumbering beast who only wanted society to leave him alone said more to the adolescent psyche than did the proud ruler of a wronged people. Thus, when Lee decided Giant-Man could no longer carry *Tales to Astonish* alone, he added the Hulk as a second feature (*TA* 60, Oct. 1964).

Here was the Marvel mystique personified in green. It started with a shock: the Hulk, the seeming epitome of big-muscle Kirby characters, was to be drawn by Steve Ditko. And it read like a Ditko series, with a vivid cast of characters interwoven into a complex soap opera and an ongoing plot overshadowed by the evil of the mysterious Leader, bringing to mind the Green Goblin and Dormammu. Building upon the continuity techniques of the other Ditko strips, *The Hulk* broke new ground as the first superhero series in which the stories never ended, but rather ran from cliff-hanger to cliff-hanger in a continuous narrative. It was an effective device for making a long saga out of half-length stories and a clear bid for the attention of "loyal Marvelites" over casual browsers, an indication of where Lee and Ditko thought their success would lie.

With Ditko's departure and Kirby's return to the character (*TA* 68, June 1965), the series took a dramatic turn. The Hulk's mammoth fists pounded the soap opera to nothing. Lee and Ditko had had the Hulk traveling around the world in his tangles with the Leader, but Lee and Kirby sent him to the moon, a distant solar system, the far future, and the Earth's core for an orb of cosmic knowledge (*TA* 73, Nov. 1965). Can there be any doubt as to whether the artists or the writer were really conceiving the stories? Stan, meanwhile, was going through his usual confusion about the Hulk's personality, starting him off with fairly eloquent anitsociality, then switching to dumb thuggishness. "I'll show 'em!" he cried in *TA* 65, Mar. 1965, then "Dead! Saved my life! Died for Hulk! Was friend! Died for Hulk!" an issue later. For a time he

regained the mind of alter ego Bruce Banner, but gradually it degenerated—and Lee at last began to find the note of angry, injured alienation toward which he had seemingly been groping all along.

The Hulk's failure to understand why mankind hounded him became more poignant. It was almost heartbreaking after Rick Jones, believe his monstrous friend dead, finally told the world that Banner and the Hulk were one and the same (*TA* 77, Mar. 1966). From then one Banner could have no peace either as human or as monster. The following issue, Bill Everett began drawing over Kirby's basic layouts, Everett's bold, cartoony pencils emphasized the power and brutality of the character, while the subtleties of his inks were able to bring out an undertone of sadness. When the Hulk huddles in misery under a desert sky, moaning, "No place to go! No one to turn to! The world hates the Hulk! Why? Why does it never end—?!!" (*TA* 80, June 1966), our hearts go out to this big brute. Even though Kirby and Everett left the series after six issues, this combination of puppy-dog misery with destructive force became, at long last, a consistent characterization. Thus, readers who had followed Marvel from the beginning—or were following it retroactively through back issues—had seen a character evolve through two series and many guest appearances, interpreted by both of Marvel's protean artists. It was only four years and about four bucks worth of comics, but to a Marvelite it felt like a lifetime.

The Sub-Mariner was a different icon. In his guest appearances, he usually served as an antagonist, though with noble motives. But when he squeezed Giant-Man into oblivion to begin his own series alongside the Hulk, he was purely the hero of Atlantis (*TA* 70, Aug. 1965). His specialty was highfalutin' gladiatorial adventure, hyped up with jet-speed swimming that approximated flight. Again what Lee lost in depth he gained in breadth, for now the oceans were added to the past, the netherworld, and our own world as integral parts of the Marvel Universe.

Sub-Mariner's most astonishing feature may have been the art of Gene Colan, newly arrived at Marvel from Robert Kanigher's war comics and Jim Warren's line of black-and-white horror comics. He was a master of mood who thought in terms of light rather than line, a painterly sophisticate with no use for the "just keep it clear" aesthetic of early '60s comics. His deep shadows, fluid figures, and almost photographic faces gave his undersea scenes a mystery and an odd believability that never let the reader forget he was in a strange, exotic land. More astonishing than the quality of his work, however, was the mere fact that Marvel had hired him. With modest page rates and the stink of death about it, the Goodman line hadn't attracted top-flight artists for a while. Lee had never been able to make himself hold out for the best, anyway; he was just a boy who couldn't say no, wanting to be seen as a great guy by everybody, and the sadder the case of the artist asking him to toss him some work the more likely he was to find something for him. He'd been astoundingly lucky to hook Kirby and Ditko at low tide, and Heck and Ayers' loyalty was valuable, even if the fans didn't like their styles. Beyond them, though, he tossed his plots to a pool of burnouts and misfits that no better publisher would have hired, the likes of Paul Reinman and Chic Stone, once-respected guys whom only Lee or ACG's Richard Hughes would hire now. And then there was Brother Larry, who could always be counted on to draw as blandly as he wrote.

Now, finally, he had some more money to spend, and a look of stability, even heat, around him, and artists who actually had other options were starting to make themselves available. One of the first was Frank Giacoia, a quick and efficient inker and one of those guys who knows everybody. He'd say, "Hey, Stan's looking for people and he's a cinch to work for," and suddenly DC hands like Mike Esposito and George Roussos were inking for Marvel. They didn't give Stan, the old softie, the same careful work they gave people like Bob Kanigher, and they didn't give him the use of their real names, either. Giacoia, Esposito and Roussos became "Frankie Ray," "Mickey Demeo" and "George Bell," fearing the wrath of the ever-explosive Kanigher, and when Colan first joined the crowd he called himself "Adam Austin"—as if

anybody in the business couldn't recognize Colan's art from across Grand Central Station. But as he discovered Lee was easy to work for and almost never asked for a redraw, he dropped his other work and let Stan brag openly about having Gene Colan in his stable. Soon two of Lee's favorite artists from the early '50s—John Buscema and John Romita—would return to him, the first from many years out of comics, the second from eight years of drawing romances for National. Stealing Romita wasn't like stealing Carmine Infantino; at the boys' club of National, romances were a bottom priority, usually edited by converted secretaries (after all, what did girls know about art and stories?). But still, Stan was stealing DC

Marvel begins to steal DC's thunder: Gene Colan's mood, subtlety, and elegance are worthy of the Distinguished Competition, but are here devoted to the antiheroic Sub-Mariner. Dick Ayers's inks are a bit out of their element here, but the Colan touch shines through. The self-proclaimed "superfluous wordage" is, of course, by Stan Lee. (*Tales to Astonish* #84, Oct. 1966.)

artists. Marvel was starting to look like a contender.

In the new milieu of consistency and connected-ness, one series stood out like a sore thumb: *The Human Torch and the Thing*. Weakly drawn, dully written, and irreconcilable with *Fantastic Four* con-tinuity, Lee gave it the ax the same month the Sub-Mariner replaced Giant-Man. Larry Lieber was sent to the Siberia of Marvel's fading Western line, and it was to give himself time to develop a replacement series for *Human Torch* that Lee handed *Sgt. Fury* to Roy Thomas. Lee didn't have to abandon his crusty, nail-tough commando, though, because the replace-ment he and Kirby came up with was *Nick Fury, Agent of S.H.I.E.L.D.* (*ST* 135, Aug. 1965). It was set in the present and featured a middle-aged, eyepatch-wearing Fury as head of a superscientific spy group reminiscent of TV's U.N.C.L.E., and it contained a wonderful surprise: not a Commie in sight. Maybe it was Jack who insisted on pitting S.H.I.E.L.D. against a mysterious fascist enclave called Hydra, but one suspects that a year or even a few months earlier Stan would have stuck in dialogue linking it to the inter-national Red conspiracy. Things were happening, though: Barry Goldwater's "extremism in the name of liberty" and Lyndon Johnson's vicious attacks on it had polarized the country, and the former's crush-ing defeat showed that Americans really weren't ter-rified of Pinkos anymore. Now Johnson was seizing people's imagination with his quasisocialistic War on Poverty, while that other war of his, in Vietnam, was beginning to stir up some vocal opposition. Dedicated conservatives dug in defensively, while "soft" conservatives suddenly felt like they'd missed the bus. The high school and college kids whom Stan loved to reach were swinging way left in a hurry, and the Commies were all but vanishing from Lee's scripts. When Ditko caricatured some scruffy-look-ing college protesters in *Spider-Man,* Lee dialogued the scene with light humor, as if not wanting to com-mit himself to a position. Those were days when Stan often drove Jack home from visits to the office in his big convertible, and Roy Thomas remembers that "everybody was walking on eggs around Steve Ditko

by the time I arrived, because he and Stan had not been speaking in months." Welcome to the mid-'60s.

Freed from jingoism, Lee could have fun devis-ing secret oaths and improbable tech-speak for S.H.I.E.L.D. and its foes. Kirby invented a whole arsenal of miracles like a flying sports car, ESP-amplifying machines and an airborne "Heli-Carrier" headquarters. The cantankerous Fury and a comical supporting cast—including a middle-aged Gabe Jones, now a high-ranking government agent—gave it all a blue collar New York feel that made it a charming counterpoint, not just to the increasing grimness of America's real government work, but to James Bond and Napoleon Solo's world of baccarat and martinis. Explicit connections to Tony Stark and Captain America tied Marvel's world still more closely together and gave that world a touch of absurdist technologism that made it seem a lot more fun than our own. Kirby was visibly losing interest in Marvel's vaunted "realism," and that was exciting to watch even when his plots were boring (and for *S.H.I.E.L.D.* they were).

So where was the Fantastic Four during all this universe building and character development? Where they'd always been, right at the front. The foursome proved to be Lee and Kirby's most flexible characters, growing together as distinct but insepara-ble members of a family. Sue Storm's ambivalent feelings for the Sub-Mariner finally settled down after his reunion with his people removed her princi-pal reason to pity him, and at last she told him that it was Reed Richards with whom she wanted to spend her life (*FF* 27, June 1964). It took Reed a while, but he managed to step out of his rigidly cerebral role long enough to ask her to marry him (*FF* 35, Feb. 1965). Ben Grimm, the tragic Things remained the team's emotional nexus, but now a gruff sense of humor was balancing his misery. Stan gave him a Brooklynesque speech pattern that included wise-cracks about his old haunts on Yancy Street, oaths sworn on a mysterious Aunt Petunia, and William Bendix's old catch-phrase, "Wotta revoltin' develop-ment this is!" Ben's running hostility to the Torch evolved into an affectionate needling, and their all-destroying battles inside FF headquarters put a wonky spin on Marvel's usual hero-against-hero brawls. To cope with it all, Reed had to grow into a harried father-figure, loving but losing patience with the goons under his command.

As Lee and Kirby found their footing, the stories and art took a wide turn for the better. Dr. Doom, the evil scientist in cape and armor, obsessed with humbling Reed Richards, gradually unfolded as a real character: we discovered his Gypsy origins, and the source of his evil in the wrongs suffered by his family in Europe, then saw him become the perversely benevolent tyrant of the Balkan land of Latveria (*FF Annual* 2, 1964). In the FF's finest hour yet, "A Blind Man Shall Lead Them," they were forced to defeat Doom without their powers in an impressive, two-issue, all-out battle that helped set a dark, monumental new tone for all Marvel comics (*FF* 39-40, June-July 1965). Doom also became a villain-at-large for the growing universe, tackling Spider-Man and then nearly everyone else. Later it even emerged that the Avenger's time-traveling foe, Kang the Conqueror, was some sort of temporally displaced manifestation of Doom, drawing everything still tighter together.

To Marvel's undersea, transtemporal and transdimensional realms *Fantastic Four* began to contribute a consistent vision of outer space. In *Flash* or *Green Lantern*, whenever an alien race was needed a new one was invented, and Infantino or Kane would whip out yet another set of creatures with long fingers and no hair or bug eyes and reptilian lips. DC's heroes took these countless visitations pretty much in stride. But Kirby and Lee returned repeatedly to the Fantastic Four's first alien foes, the Skrulls, and the moon-based cosmic sage called the Watcher. A visit from above was a rare thing, and even the Fantastic Four gazed at the stars with some awe. Jack and Stan hadn't yet begun to chart the outer realms—but they were ready.

The first phase of Marvel's growth was consummated and brought to a close by the Fantastic Four's third giant-sized annual (Summer 1965), featuring the wedding of Reed and Sue. This was the guest-star phenomenon taken to its extreme, "the world's most colossal collection of costumed characters, crazily cavorting and capering in continual combat," a riot of twenty-one villains and their hordes of acolytes, thugs, and deadly beasts. Not to mention another cameo by Stan and Jack. It wasn't much for plot, but twenty-five cents for forty-two colorful characters was the best buy of the year for hero-hungry kids. And the best part wasn't just that there were a *lot* of heroes. It was that readers in the know, "True Believers," understood how they all fit together.

Superheroes were getting hot. Fandom and now even the mainstream press were fueling the flames. In 1965 Tower Books announced that it was going to launch its own comics line and hired Wally Wood to put it together. Charlton was gearing up for another run, this time looking to hard-core fandom to support it. Archie had brought back the Fly—as Fly Man—and in late 1965 followed with more superheroes under a "Mighty Comics Group" logo blatantly imitating Marvel's. Four, or even two, years before, the suggestion that anyone would imitate Stan Lee would have been a cruel joke. But there it was. He'd hooked the new youth with agonized heroes and reeled them in with a self-contained fictional domain that reflected the clannishness of the new youth culture. If Julie Schwartz was Dixieland, and Mort Weisinger was the funk of klezmer and the wail of a cantor repackaged as bubblegum pop, then Marvel was self-pitying Beach Boy ballads and electrified folk and the smirk of the Beatles and even a precognition of psychedelia. Revivals of '40s heroes and mature craftsmanship weren't where it was at. "Mighty Marvel," in Lee's own later estimation, had become "a lusty, gutsy, irreverent mischief-maker in the wondrous world of comix," and it had survived all the second-rate art, hasty writing, and crappy production of its early days to leave the also-rans in the dust.

Lee had to be wondering: could he actually challenge DC?

CHAPTER 15

POW!

It was March 1965, and Bill Dozier had a plane to catch. A comic book caught his eye, and he grabbed it. Dozier was no kid, and he was no fanzine publishing friend of Jerry Bails. He was a Paramount Pictures veteran and a TV producer with a résumé of cheesy kids' shows going back to *Rod Brown of the Rocket Rangers* in 1953. Now kid stuff was big

money, and superheroes were happening. Any idiot in an alligator shirt and topsiders could tell you that. Somebody was setting up a *Superman* musical on Broadway. ABC, the kid-vid network, had already optioned *Batman*. A superhero TV show? It could happen, with the right hook. It couldn't hurt to kill a few minutes on a plane reading this *Batman* with this wild-looking character, this Riddler on the cover. There was a *look* here: a multiple-image drawing of a guy in a green and purple suit covered with question marks, spinning like a top against a neon fuchsia background, with Batman and Robin belting him and huge words floating over his head, "HA! HA! HA! HA!" It was Pop Art, it was Lichtenstein. There was a full-page ad on the back for an Aurora Batman model. That meant kids were *buying*. And the writing inside was . . . well, not like the old way of writing for kids, it was . . . *kooky*. Riddles, puns on every page. The bad guy said, "Maybe you don't quite recognize me because I'm out of uniform!" The caption read, "Yes—the RIDDLER! The question-marked costumed criminal whose delight it is to confound and confuse law officials with conundrums!" This stuff could be hilarious if it was read the right way. It could be . . . *high camp*. And high camp was happening. Susan Sontag said so.

Events that come from nowhere often seem inevitable in hindsight. It was strange, but it was fitting, that what catapulted superheroes into a national craze was the steady Julius Schwartz stable that had gotten the silver age started.

As experimentation swept the field, Schwartz went virtually untouched by it. His popularity continued, as did the quality of his output, and he maintained his titles on the same smooth road. He and his freelancers had brought American comics as close as they would ever come to a classical style, with their emphasis on grace and clarity. Their stories had steady rhythms and balanced proportions, with a sense of unchanging and unhurried calm. Schwartz's heroes were neoclassical rationalists—a police scientist, test pilot, museum curator, physicist—and even their girlfriends were reporters, technocrats, and lawyers, all seekers of knowledge or truth. His writers and artists hewed to the form, except for a slight accentuation of their archness: not self-parody by any means, but an amused delight in their own facility and predictability.

From 1961 to 1964 Schwartz's roster of comics went unchanged. Then came the fall of Jack Schiff and the mandate to salvage *Batman* and *Detective Comics.* All Schwartz had to do was remold Batman into his own style and call it the "New Look." He made one dramatic change, both to get the fans' attention and to add a feminine element to what had always been an austerely male series: he had Bruce Wayne's loyal butler, Alfred, die in an act of heroism, to be replaced in the household by the dithering Aunt Harriet (*Detective* 328, June 1964). Since Batman had no superpowers to play variations upon, Schwartz asked his writers to supply more fisticuffs—not wild Kirbyesque brawls, but choreographed gymnastics cleverly exploiting props and settings. Otherwise, he stayed with the screwball costumed villains and gangs of hoodlums to whom Schiff had returned at the end, asking only that John Broome and Gardner Fox (with Ed Herron and Bill Finger) heighten the complexity of the mysteries and the ingenuity of the gimmicks on which they turned.

The art chores were shared, too. Carmine Infantino drew every other issue of *Detective Comics,* bringing a sleek, modern style to Batman, unlike any the Caped Crusader had known in his twenty-five years. At the editor's suggestion, he even added a bright yellow oval to Batman's gray chest for a very Schwartzian splash of gaiety. Tellingly, Infantino was the first artist to demand that the "Bob Kane" signature be left off his work, and Schwartz came through for him. Kane's studio kept providing, but more and more of the work shifted to Joe Giella, Schwartz's old reliable inker, and with time Bob Kane—and his name—were shuffled off the scene. Whether by Giella or by Kane's ghost artists, this was the weakest art Schwartz had overseen in a long time, but at least Carmine did all the covers.

Backing up Batman in *Detective Comics* was now the Elongated Man in his own series, written by Fox and penciled and inked by Infantino. In nearly every episode Ralph Dibny and his wife, Sue, drove into a new town just in time to encounter a puzzling new mystery—for Ralph and Sue were inveterate travelers, and the locales they visited, rural or urban, desert or tropical, were evocatively rendered by Infantino.

It was a winning package. Sales climbed, and soon Batman merchandise, like the Aurora model, began to appear. Schwartz was also picking up a new kind of fan: college kids who read comics not because they missed the heroes of their childhoods, but because they found them absurd. A bunch of dorm girls from Bennington College wrote in with delight when the Elongated Man stretched his ear down a chimney to eavesdrop on some bad guys and the thugs exclaimed, "An ear—in the fireplace! He must be up on the roof!" Fox probably hadn't meant it to be funny, but he and his editor knew praise when they saw it, and the Bat-scripting got sillier. "Out of uniform," quoth the question-marked, costumed criminal.

All else was sweet in Schwartzville. Simultaneously with the new *Batman* and *Detective,* Hawkman finally "won his wings" and started in his own comic by Fox and Murphy Anderson. In his established series Schwartz began to allow readers more and more glimpses into the personal lives of his heroes. Although without a glimmer of Marvel-style melodrama. His character stories seemed to flow from the same suburban ease and middle-class optimism that had informed his late '50s work, as if his heroes, now well established and secure in their abilities, felt they could take a little time for their family and friends. In *Green Lantern,* Broome wrote stories featuring Hal Jordan's brothers and uncle, and his sister-in-law's conviction that her husband is Green Lantern. It was fun stuff, as assured and warm as Broome and Gil Kane ever got. For *The Flash*, Broome turned in beautiful stories about movie actress Daphne Dean, a former sweetheart of Barry Allen's (*Flash* 126 and 132, Feb. and Nov. 1962), and spun some yarns around Iris West's father, an absentminded scientist whose dizziness always landed him in a jam (beginning *Flash* 134, Feb. 1963). In *The Atom*, Fox introduced the "time pool" invented by Professor Hyatt, one of Ray Palmer's colleagues (*Atom* 3, Nov. 1962). The mighty mite would use it repeatedly to travel back in time in the interests of scientific curiosity, meeting the likes of Ben Franklin, Edgar Allan Poe, and Henry Fielding—and how wonderfully Foxian that is, for Weisinger would have used Samson and Lee would have used Hitler, and not even Gold Key's Gaylord DuBois would have considered an eighteenth-century satirist. Flash and Green Lantern guest-starred regularly in each other's titles. Atom and Hawkman shared a few adventures. The Elongated Man visited the Flash, Green Lantern, Batman, and the Atom. Not once did they quarrel. These were self-assured grown-ups, not Stan Lee's arrested adolescents. In a typical setup, Barry and Iris visit Hal and Carol in Coast City, taking time for some swimming and archery. When an alien invasion begins, Barry and Hal have to sneak away from the girls to don their costumes and repel it (*Flash* 131, Sept. 1962).

With each passing year, Schwartz's comics grew sleeker and more gorgeous. He finally listened to Gil Kane and assigned Sid Greene to ink *Green Lantern*. Not only did Greene improve the polish, but Kane seemed willing to draw a little better, too. DC had long been distinguished by high production values, under the conservative but exacting eye of production manager Sol Harrison, and Schwartz always seemed to get the best of the best: brilliant but tasteful coloring by Jerry Serpe and Jack Adler, lively lettering by Gaspar Saladino.

At last Schwartz pressed on with the golden age revival. To the joy of Jerry Bails and Roy Thomas, the return of the original Flash was followed by a team-up between the Justice League and the Justice Society: Dr. Fate, Black Canary, Hourman, the "Earth-2" Atom, Flash, Green Lantern, and Hawkman (*JLA* 21–22, Aug.–Sept. 1963). Sales were huge, and the JLA/JSA crossover became an annual summer event—two issues every time—to keep kids haunting the newsstands. Next the golden age Flash, Green Lantern, and Atom visited their "Earth-1" namesakes. In *Showcase* (55–56, Apr.–June 1965), Schwartz tried another relaunch, teaming Dr. Fate and Hourman for a 1940s-style adventure by Fox and Anderson. The same creative team followed with a Starman/Black Canary team-up (*BB* 61–62, Sept.–Nov. 1965), then a three-issue tryout for the Spectre, the nearly omnipotent crime-fighting ghost of the 1940s (*Showcase* 60–62, Feb.–June 1966). They were all pretty uninspired, but the Spectre stood apart, with an otherworldly flavor far different from Schwartz's usual scientific slant and he was the only one of the three to receive his own title, and even he had to wait another year and a half.

The fatigue showing in the new revivals wasn't confined to these titles, however. By the end of 1965, the whole Schwartz line seemed to be losing some magic. John Broome had always felt a little out of his element, and now he was burning out not just on comics, but on American culture. He followed the Beat trail, moving to Paris and traveling in Asia, cutting back on the number of scripts he sent to Schwartz. Gardner Fox would pick up the slack, but something was amiss with him. His oddball plots had always risked flying apart, but more and more often now they toppled over the edge of nonsense. Schwartz later said that sometimes he wouldn't let Fox leave the editorial office until he'd rewritten his scripts to make sense. Even Infantino was letting his inks get quicker and rougher on *Elongated Man*, the first time he'd shown less than total focus when inking his own work. Maybe the novelty of the silver age was just wearing off. Maybe it was the fact that even Jerry Bails was picking Stan Lee as his favorite editor; it's one thing to labor in anonymity, but quite another to taste a bit of glory and then have it withdrawn. Or maybe it was just the way of all art, for

[1] Is it an accident that when the original Rod Brown, Cliff Robertson, guest-starred on *Batman* it was as a villain named "Shame"?

every classical style ultimately becomes just an empty collection of gestures.

In another month it wasn't going to matter much. William Dozier had set his Batman idea up with ABC and 20th Century-Fox. He hired a comedy writer, Lorenzo Semple, Jr., to do a pilot script that took off from Gardner Fox's pixilated prose and pushed it into parody. Batman and Robin lost their above-it-all Schwartzy cool in favor of speech-making, palm-punching, and "holy conundrum"-ing that may have helped Dozier work off the embarrassment still lingering from *Rod Brown and the Rocket Rangers*.[1] A two-nights-a-week structure was devised to allow cliff-hanger endings in the spirit of old radio and movie serials. With Infantino's cover for *Batman* 171 as a visual template, art director Serge Krizman developed an artfully artificial look that exploited the lurid color biases of early color TV as no show had attempted before. Those big floating sound effects became its visual signature. Coolsters Neal Hefti and Nelson Riddle laid down some jazzy wax-tracks that would have met Schwartz and Broome's approval (if anyone had asked them). A parade of slightly ludicrous Hollywood almosts and used-to-bes (Cesar Romero, yet!) was trotted through to give it the tone of self-mockery. Dozier himself contributed a stentorian narrative voice.

Jack Schiff was engaged as official advisor—one last bone tossed him by National's management—and his earnest sense of Batman's wholesome value to children fed perversely into the creative loop. The questioning of authority on America's campuses was refracted through the mainstream as a nervous but amused queasiness about icons—icons of heroism, of national defense, and of justice—that had only recently been upheld with excessive seriousness. The James Bond movies skewered orthodoxy with a wry amorality, and *The Man from U.N.C.L.E.* and *Get Smart* had scored on the tube with progressively comedic spins. Cartoons like *Rocky and Bullwinkle* and *Underdog* showed that kids, and their parents, liked mock adventure. A spirit of burlesque—taking its name, "camp," from the gay community—was

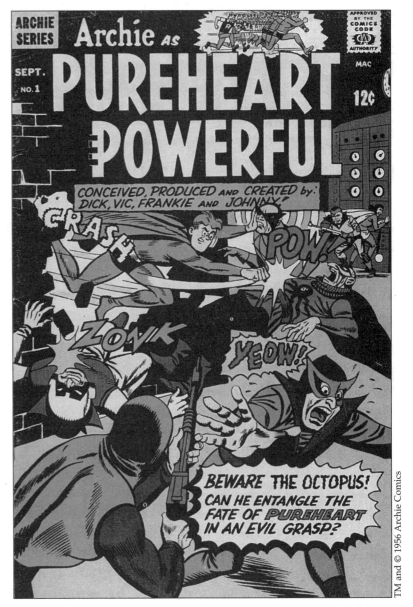

TM and © 1956 Archie Comics

spreading through the culture. This TV *Batman* was the most committed expression yet of mainstream camp, and indeed its heroes—Adam West's impossibly stiff Batman and Burt Ward's ludicrous twenty-something vamp on teenage innocence—gave their show of capes and tights the spirit of a drag ball.

It premiered on January 12, 1966, and it hit. It hit bigger than anybody expected, even Dozier, even ABC. Little kids, oblivious to the show's tone of mockery, were hypnotized by its color and flamboyance. Adults were titillated and relieved to find someone lampooning their own former naïveté. Only teenagers and precocious preteens, aware of the lam-

Campiness—and a blatant Marvel imitation—as "America's Typical Teenager" goes superheroic. All too typically for comics, the guys credited for conception and production include publishers and editors, but not the artist, Dan DeCarlo. (*Archie as Pureheart the Powerful* #1, Sept. 1966.)

Batmania brought C.C. Beck back to the medium after more than a decade of invisibility. He was still unsurpassed at the economy and vivacity of pure cartooning—an art disappearing as comic books became more sophisticated. Script by Otto Binder. (*Fatman, the Human Flying Saucer* #1, Apr. 1967.)

poon but too defensive and serious about their dreams to see them mocked, felt the dagger of betrayal.[2] More than just a popular kids' show, *Batman* became a national craze. Wednesday and Thursday nights became Batman nights, and Wednesday night's cliffhanger a subject for in-depth playground analysis everywhere. Adam West made the cover of *Life*. Batproduct gushed from every *tchotchke* house in America. A *Batman* comic strip hit the newspapers. *It's a Bird . . . It's a Plane . . . It's Superman* bombed on stage, but a *Batman* movie hit the big screen, the first time a feature film had ever been made about a comic book superhero (even if it was just a mechanical spin-off of the TV show). Superheroes old and new, straight and satiric, took over Saturday morning: *Superman*, *Space Ghost*, *Frankenstein Jr.*, *Batfink*, even a slate of *Marvel Super-Heroes* so cheesy they looked like Martin Goodman must have sold the rights for a cup of coffee and a back rub. Grown-ups, to the amazement and sometimes horror of their offspring, were saying "holy escalation" and "holy generation gap." "Biff! Bam! Pow! Comics Take Over the Campus!" became the ubiquitous puff-piece of American journalism, usually mentioning not just Batmania, but the collegiate set's love of those wild new Marvel superheroes.

Sales soared on *Batman* comics, hitting levels no comic book had touched in more than a decade. Superhero comics in general took off. Archie had already started its Marvel-imitating Mighty line with *Fly Man* and *Mighty Crusaders*, and now it added *Mighty Comics* and *Superheroes vs. Supervillains*, with a horde of heroes. Jerry Siegel wrote them all, but hardly one was worth reading. Even the regular Archie-and-Jughead line jumped onto the craze, as Archie sometimes found himself transformed into a mock-hero called Pureheart the Powerful. Harvey Comics, finally deciding that superheroes weren't dead after all, bought some characters from an advertising artist named Jim Steranko and pumped out *Jigsaw*, *Pirana*, *Spyman*, and *Bee-Man*—but its only worthwhile contributions were reprints of Joe Simon and Jack Kirby's *Fighting American* and Will Eisner's *Spirit*. Western/Gold Key added *The Owl* and *Tiger Girl* (Jerry Siegel again). Dell, Western's ex, set up its own shop to produce *Dracula*, *Frankenstein*, and *Werewolf* (attempts to fuse the superhero craze with the concurrent monster fad),[3] plus *Nukla*, *Neutro*, and the generic *Super Heroes*. The King Features newspaper syndicate quickly brought out an unremarkable *Mandrake* and *The Phantom*, but its *Flash Gordon* did boast some stunning art by Al Williamson, Reed Crandall, Wally Wood, and Gil Kane. Some old Fawcett alumni, including Otto Binder and C.C. Beck, produced *Fatman, the Human Flying Saucer*, and *Super Green Beret*. Somebody named Milton Fass published a new, wretched *Captain Marvel* and the well-named *Terrible 5*. Wham-O, America's hippest toy maker (the Frisbee, the Super Ball), slapped together a twenty-artist, fifty-page, two-foot-tall monument to schlock called *Wham-O Giant Comics*. Charlton was beginning a major new superhero push, with its eye on older fans. Tower Comics expanded its line. Cheap book-publishing houses were rushing paperback collections of comic book stories onto the stands. Tower got right to the point with *Dynamo, Man of High Camp*, while Belmont snuck knockoffs of DC and Marvel's logos onto the cover of *High Camp Super-Heroes* although it only reprinted Mighty Comics. This was a superhero orgy. Had it really been only ten years since *Showcase* number 4?

National's management hadn't had to deal with an opportunity like this since Superman's first burst of fame more than twenty-five years before, and the world had changed a lot since then. Surviving the '50s had taught Liebowitz and Donenfeld to be penny-wise and conservative. They'd never done much to promote their line as a whole, as Stan Lee had. Now, infuriatingly enough, it looked like Lee might be the biggest winner in the sweepstakes. He had momentum with the older crowd going into the Bat-craze and was hooking curious readers seeking something truer to the TV show's antiheroic irreverence than DC could provide. For the first time in a long time—maybe ever—National Periodicals had to make changes to head off a competitor. Right before the show premiered, black and white "go-go" checks were stripped across the top of every DC cover to make them stand out on the racks. To reinforce the new identity, editors jammed the phrase "go-go" into characters' mouths at least once an issue; when the fans screamed out what a pathetically unhip attempt it was, they dropped it. The Caped Crusader guest-starred everywhere. He virtually took over the covers of *JLA*, and *Brave and Bold* became entirely a vehicle for "Batman and . . ." team-ups. Covers now sported flamboyant, slogan-laden blurbs, imitating both Marvel's hype and Dozier's pompous TV narration. Soon art changes were being demanded: bigger panels, bigger figures, in-your-eye foreshortening, more Pop Art, more *Kirby*. To make matters worse, during a cost-cutting binge to stave off another price increase, DC made its artists use art boards one-fourth smaller than they'd always used. The effect on the art was awkward and unpleasant.

Editors Jack Schiff, Murray Boltinoff, George Kashdan, and Robert Kanigher made their comics even goofier than they had been. In *Challengers of the Unknown*, tough Rocky Davis tried to wow America's kids with hip jive only about ten years out of date—("Drop him, cat—I mean like make with the splitsville!"). Bob Brown was asked to draw not just with bigness, but with wacky humor, which killed whatever charm his work still had. Bruno Premiani, whose *Doom Patrol* work was already suffering from his failing eyesight, was just about destroyed by the same demands. When Batman guest-starred in *Blackhawk*, it was to announce, "The Blackhawks are washed-up has-beens, out-of-date antiques. . . . To put it bluntly, they just don't swing!" (*Blackhawk* 228, Jan. 1967). So Andre, Olaf, Stan, and Hendrickson became way-out superfreaks: Weapons Master, Golden Centurion, the Leaper, and M'sieu Machine (*BH* 230, Mar. 1967). They were way-out, all right, and by the following year they were way out of print. Boltinoff tried to revive the looney *Plastic Man*. Jack Miller was made an editor to produce the superhero humor of *The Inferior Five*. Yet Miller also seemed to anticipate a reaction against camp, when he and Schiff converted the goofy *Maritan Manhunter* into a crime series in early 1966.

Julie Schwartz played it cool. The *Batman* show had forced him into a couple of changes, but he made the best of it. Dozier and company thought Alfred would be an asset, so Schwartz's men contrived to reveal that Alfred's "death" had actually only injured his brain and driven him to attack his old friends as the mysterious "Outsider" before coming to his senses. Later the producers wanted a Batgirl to shore up both their female and pubescent male audiences. She was secretly the daughter of Police Commissioner Gordon, and in the comics (beginning with *Detective* 359, Jan. 1967) she was a source of lighthearted fun and classy Infantino cheesecake.

When the new "bigness" threatened the pristine lines of his artists, Schwartz shook up the inking chores in his stable to compensate. Sid Greene was reassigned to Infantino and Sekowsky, and succeeded admirably in tightening up their new work. Gil Kane had been pressing for a long time for a chance to ink his own pencils, and now it came, on *Green*

[2] Talk to comics fans born from about 1954 to 1960 and you'll find that they generally love the show, may even have become fans because of it. Talk to those born in the five or six years before and watch them blanch with rage at the memory. Most of them will tell how the show misrepresented comics, refusing to acknowledge that its greatest sin was taking the weird aesthetic of comics and transferring it all too faithfully to live action.

[3] Vampires, werewolves and "walking dead" were forbidden by the Comics Code, but the Dell folks evidently thought they were still big enough not to need Code approval.

Lantern. Kane was one DC artist who admired Jack Kirby, and as Kirby's action art made quantum leaps at Marvel, Kane's followed suit. Kane now filled every panel with the same fluidity and punch he had long shown in his covers. When Green Lantern let loose a roundhouse right at an opponent, the reader almost found himself rolling with the impact. But GL was no mindless brawler: Kane imbued him with heroic nobility and savage determination. His inking made it all look even bigger with its rough and masculine, nearly sculptural quality. Soon Kane would be inspiring nearly as many imitators as King Kirby himself.

Then Schwartz dropped his bombshells. His fictional world of eternal stability had to make room for change. First Barry Allen married Iris West (*Flash* 165, Nov. 1966) and soon after revealed his secret identity to her. The very next month, Schwartz's other eternal romance spun the other way. In *Green Lantern* 49 (Dec. 1966), Carol Ferris, Hal Jordan's sweetheart, suddenly takes up with another man. Devastated—and the sight of a distraught hero at the end of a Schwartz comic was an image to shake up the most jaded fan—Hal decides he must leave Coast City. In the very next issue, we find him on the road, away from his entire supporting cast, even from his job as a test pilot. In his desperation to prove his worth to himself as a man, not just a superhero, he vows to rely more on his fists than his power ring. It was a purely emotional reaction, the kind of thing Marvel's heroes would do. It was also a way to let Gil Kane strut his action art, the kind of thing Marvel's editor would do.

Although Fox was filling in often now, the best of the stories were by Broome. He neatly caught the challenge of the open road and the new life, suggesting Hal's grief, excitement, and confusion with masculine dignity. It was a perfect metaphor for Broome himself as he moved toward a life beyond comics and America. It was also a perfect metaphor for DC, although surely no one saw it that way then. DC was still the king, and it was fighting back against the upstart. Who could guess that its entire twenty-year status quo was about to blow apart?

CHAPTER 16

THE COSMIC SAGA

During the early days of Marvel, Jack Kirby's workload had been so great—so *staggering*, turning out more than a thousand pages a year—that his art was rough and hurried, his plots thin, his overtaxed imagination never able to equal the feats it had performed for *Challengers* and earlier series. Now he could winnow his work down to what really mattered to him. Finally, by 1966 he brought the full force of his talent and vision to bear on his three favorite creations: *Fantastic Four*, *Thor*, and *Captain America*.

In the process, he effectively took over the whole job of conception and plotting. Lee still felt he was co-plotting because he and Kirby shared story conferences, but John Romita remembered some of these "conferences" as happening while Lee drove him and Kirby home from work: "I would be in the back seat of Stan's convertible, and these two giants were up front plotting the future of the Fantastic Four, Thor, or whatever they were working on. And I would listen, absorbing all of that stuff and getting a big kick out of how they ignored each other. Sometimes I could hear that one of them was talking about one story and the other one was talking about something completely different. . . . It appeared that they would finish their conversation, each thinking that he had convinced the other, when it was obvious to anybody else that they hadn't." Kirby was now turning in stories straight from his own imagination. All Lee could do was try to give the dialogue his own voice, and even there he could only be a servant to Jack's ideas, for the ideas were now so strange, so powerful, and distilled to such intensity. All by himself, Kirby was blowing open the boundaries of the Marvel universe and creating comic books almost mythological in scope and strength.

Since Thor's conception in 1962, Kirby and Lee had flirted with mythological themes, but they nearly always kept to the safe ground of traditional superhero settings. They finally broke the bonds of Earth with the inception of a backup series called *Tales of Asgard* (*JIM* 97, Oct. 1963). Each of these five-page episodes featured either an actual Norse myth retold or an episode from the early days of the Asgardian gods, in which writer and artist could let their imaginations run wild. These stories were full of the trolls, dwarves, giants, and valiant heroes of European fairy tales. and were some of Marvel's most charming achievements.

The absence of Earthly concerns didn't appear to bother readers, for *Tales of Asgard* was a letters-page success. Soon Thor's regular adventures took a turn toward the mythological, beginning with the attack of a pair of Asgardian villains, the seductive Enchantress and her would-be lover, the brutal Executioner (*JIM* 103, Apr. 1964). With trickster-god Loki's transformation of a thug named Crusher Creel into the powerful Absorbing Man (*JIM* 113, Feb. 1965), the affairs of Asgard and Earth began overlapping into such a complex pattern that the story line could no longer be contained in a single issue. Before the completion of the three-issue Absorbing Man story, Thor was already engaged in a contest with Loki to procure some magic stones. That tale wended its way through Earth and Asgard for the next five issues. And before Thor settled *that*, events had been set in motion that would take him to Olympus for a battle with Hercules, and then to the farthest reaches of space to meet a godlike experimenter called the High Evolutionary. By the time the sprawling, interweaving plot lines finally converged to a kind of solution (*Thor* 135, Dec. 1966), twenty-three comics and nearly two years had passed.

Although not a single story by any definition, those twenty-three comics were connected by far more than Marvel's earlier emotional subplots. This was a completely new approach to comic book story-telling. The precedent had been set by Steve Ditko and Stan Lee's use of movie-serial continuity in *The Hulk*, but this free-flowing narrative, bluntly and dar-ingly rejecting the basic unit of comic book story-telling—the single issue—was forced into existence by Kirby's exploding imagination. With this open field, Kirby was able to create vast, strange worlds and hordes of creatures that readers had never seen. The only types of stories that could do justice to these worlds were long quests, epic battles, and grand schemes that set the whole cosmos in motion.

To tell these stories, Kirby increased the range and force of his art to match the scope of his vision. He wove his mythical realms of rugged, barbarian majesty and fantastic splendor. Savage landscapes of fire and ice, wild seas, towering palaces, and the boundlessness of space sprawled across huge panels, some covering full pages, some covering two. The forms were stripped down, pure comics, as if Kirby had picked something up from Pop Art himself. He pushed his figures into the foreground and tilted his perspectives to thrust monumental forms into the reader's eyes and send the vanishing point dropping back endlessly into space. His characters had a sense of gravity that mere comic books had never before conveyed. His gods and heroes were awesome in repose and explosive in action, giving his scenes a strange sense of importance, as if they truly were the stuff of legend. There were no more "everymen" like his original Reed Richards. These were icons of human traits, more than human, and the worlds they roamed were distant, endless, and beyond time and corporeality. Here was Kirby at forty-eight, an age when most artists would be content to find a niche and coast to retirement. Instead, he reinvented him-self, his art, and comic books themselves.

Like all powerful creators, he lifted up the people around him. His inker on *Thor* was Vince Colletta, who ignored most of the line work of the pencilers he worked over in order to increase his own rate (after all, he needed time for his other calling, taking nudie pictures for skin mags and "managing" a stable of "models"). But on Kirby, on *Thor*, his minimal inks took on a "once upon a time" quality and became somehow oddly appealing. At the same time, Lee responded effectively to the new Kirby scope with a serious, sometimes ponderous tone of writing that always reminded the reader that these were the adven-tures not just of a costumed crime fighter, but of a leg-endary deity. Gradually, he developed for Thor and his fellow gods a pseudo-Shakespearean speech pat-tern that set them amusingly apart from the rest of the superhero pantheon. "Evil one!" Thor cries. "'Tis no ordinary mortal thou hast attacked—but the mighty God of Thunder!" (*Thor* 135, Dec. 1966).

The most productive union of Kirby and Lee's tal-ents, however, came as Kirby began to feel comfort-able with his new approach to *Thor* and brought the same wave of creativity crashing over *Fantastic Four*. In an immensely complicated seventeen-issue sequence, Kirby told many stories and yet united them into one (*FF* 44-60, Nov. 1965-Mar. 1967), even more so than they had in *Thor*. Lee fleshed out Kirby's mind-boggling creations and plots with memorable personalities and a constant undercurrent of mystery and suspense. First there were the Inhumans, an ancient race of weird creatures from a hidden city in the Himalayas, no two of whom were remotely alike: Gorgon, whose thick legs and cloven hooves gave him a devastating kick; Lockjaw, resembling a giant, frog-mouthed bulldog, who could teleport throughout the universe; their brooding king, Black Bolt, whose voice could destroy a city; Medusa of the living hair; Crystal, mistress of elemental forces. Crystal soon captured the mad love of the Human Torch, and when she was taken from him, his quest to find her—accompanied by a stoic American Indian friend named Wyatt Wingfoot—became the most powerful unifying element of the series.

Then Kirby gave us the first black superhero in comics, the Black Panther (an animal after which, as Jack probably knew, a radical black self-sufficiency movement in Mississippi had named itself). The Panther was the king of the hidden, superscientific jungle land of Wakanda, a scientist, a warrior, and a gentleman, drawn as all muscle and blackness by Jack and finely scripted by Stan—a heartfelt conception from creators who clearly supported black peoples' struggle for power and dignity.

But the best example of the magic of their collaboration was born at a lunch conference, according to Lee, in which the two set themselves to the creation of the most awe-inspiring menace imaginable in the Marvel Universe: Galactus, a giant who roams the cosmos, taking sustenance by devouring the life forces of entire planets. Kirby made a veritable god of the grandiose being—and a god, logically, required an angel. "When he brought [the art] to me so that I could add the dialogue and captions," Lee recalled, "I was surprised to find . . . a silver-skinned, smooth-domed, sky-riding surfer atop a speedy flying surfboard." Always pulling from the cultural ether around him, Kirby was obviously riffing on the surfing craze—but nothing was ever just "what it was" by the time it had gone into Jack's head and surfaced on paper. This Silver Surfer, Kirby explained, was the herald of Galactus, an angel who warned each world of its impending doom. "I was wild about the new character," Lee said, sensing the mythic power of Kirby's creation. "I found a certain nobility in his demeanor, an almost spiritual quality in his aspect and his bearing . . . something totally selfless and magnificently innocent." As the story develops, the Surfer, moved by the innate nobility he senses beneath the fear and hatred in the hearts of mankind, joins with the Fantastic Four to help repel Galactus. For this mutiny, his master robs him of his freedom, confining him forever to Earth by an invisible barrier (*FF* 50, May 1966). Thus cut off from his beloved outer space by a sacrifice he never dreamed he could make, the Surfer became Marvel's most tragic and philosophical figure. "There is still so much I do not

know . . . about mankind!" he says. "But now, I shall have the rest of my life to learn—for in finding a conscience, I have lost the stars!" It was ironic, and yet somehow appropriate to the strange collaboration of Lee and Kirby, that the character who would prove to be Lee's personal favorite came to him as a complete surprise. Perhaps it was more ironic still that this character would eventually be the flash point that would destroy the Lee-Kirby collaboration.

Through all this, of course, the personal melodramas of the Fantastic Four continued, now complicated by the dilemmas of the Silver Surfer and Crystal. Structurally, Kirby's telling of these tales was unorthodox, improvisatory, and at times seemed even

Jack Kirby as mythmaker in "Tales of Asgard." In stretching and simplifying his visual sense to capture godhood, he brings to the comic book page a grandeur no one had ever dreamed of before. Inks by Vince Colletta, dialogue by Stan Lee. (*Journey into Mystery* #120, Sept. 1965.)

the solid inks and warm craftsmanship of Joe Sinnott. Through the alchemy of his pencil, Kirby transformed clunky cubistic forms into all-destroying devices and architecturally impossible cities. He experimented with collages of magazine clippings that became bizarre vehicles and incomprehensible otherworlds.

These were comics that rewarded reader loyalty. To the Marvel fan who had followed the plot developments from their inception, these two years of *Thor* and *Fantastic Four* were like a wondrous tapestry of lost worlds, distant galaxies, and magnificent beings. A trip to the newsstand or the drugstore each month became a new step in a voyage into uncharted realms that seemed to have no bounds.

Even Kirby's third title, *Captain America*, enjoyed its share of grandeur. Although restricted by the limited powers of its hero and its the ten-page-per-issue format, it gave us the return of the ultimate Nazi villain, the Red Skull (*TS* 72, Dec. 1965), and the reawakening of some monumental horrific Nazi death machines called the Sleepers—brilliantly conceived as huge, abstracted metal skulls—and a quest for the "Cosmic Cube." Even with all that, Jack found room for Cap's struggle with his past, his affair with a woman who was an eerily perfect double for his lover of the 1940s, and his involvement with S.H.I.E.L.D.

This one-man revolution of Kirby's could not have been better timed. Fandom was already buzzing about it when suddenly—right about the time the Silver Surfer was appearing, the Sleepers were waking, and Thor and Hercules were nearly leveling New York with the force of their fistfight—*Batman* appeared on TV and sent little kids and college students fanning out to the comic book racks. America was in love with new ideas and cosmic mind-blowers, and Jack was pumping them out like an artillery barrage. It was an apocalyptic time, with the government escalating its first unwinnable war, the country's first major wartime peace movement catching fire, teenagers dropping out to build a new culture based on the revelations of a high-tech drug—and every Kirby page was an apocalypse. With his reduced workload, Jack must have been finding time

An angel on a flying surfboard warns a suddenly insignificant human race of the coming of a space-god who eats planets for lunch—and "the King" makes it believable. Inks by Joe Sinnott. (*Fantastic Four #77*, Aug. 1968.)

haphazard. The conclusion of the first three-and-a-half-issue Inhumans story came seven pages into issue 48, whereupon the Galactus plot appeared literally out of a clear blue sky (Mar. 1966). Lee was troubled enough by the hopscotching narrative that one caption read, "Forgive us if our tale seems to ramble . . . but we have so many elements to introduce . . . so many loose ends to tie up!" (*FF* 50, May 1966). Yet, Kirby somehow held all the threads, and when he dropped a single-issue story into the middle of it all, bringing Ben Grimm's agony of identity to a head, it was one of his best comics ever (*FF* 51, June 1966). Kirby's art took on still more intensity, aided here by

for some long-deferred reading, too, because his work was suddenly exploding with ideas torn from religion, science, and history—the Living Planet, hyperspace, Prester John—all thrown together with the fervent abandon of the autodidact. All the cultural buzz of the moment was scrambled, melted, blended, and grafted in the mind of Jack Kirby and hurled with seeming unconsciousness onto his pages in the forms of technopop gods.

Marvel was hot, and Kirby was its hottest flame. Inside Jack, however, a colder flame was burning. He started seeing sweatshirts, T-shirts, and posters with his art on them, and toys and models based on his characters. Those cheap *Marvel Super-Heroes* cartoons from Grantray-Lawrence Productions just took panels straight from the comics and faked the most minimal animation. That was *his* art in syndication across America, and now network *Fantastic Four* and *Spider-Man* cartoons were in the works. He'd heard that Lee was telling other artists to "draw like Kirby." For all this, Jack was paid nothing. He remembered the days when he'd been a partner with Joe Simon, when they'd been able to own some of their own creations, selling only publishing rights. What was he getting from Marvel—glory? Kirby rarely looked at his published work, but he was becoming increasingly aware that every issue of every comic he created in the solitude of his home had "Written and edited by Stan Lee" plastered above the "Drawn by Jack Kirby" credit. Then came the big write-up on Marvel in the New York *Herald-Tribune*. This was no puff-piece on those kooky komics kultists. Kirby and Lee were both interviewed, but Stan was a glib salesman, always attuned to others' perceptions of him, while Jack's words often followed the widening gyre of his mind. "The resultant article," said Kirby's friend Mark Evanier, "made Stan look like a genius and Jack, a buffoon." *Esquire* did an article too, full of color Kirby drawings, but the emphasis again was on Stan Lee's hip new Marvel Comics. Serious fans knew what Jack was all about—a couple of teenagers named Len Wein and Marv Wolfman would hang around his studio, learning the art of comic book storytelling from the master—but

that was small consolation when Stan started getting invitations to speak at colleges, and nobody asked for Jack. Kirby began saving Lee's interviews, building a record of how he felt he was being slighted, and every new piece of paper fueled the hidden flame in his gut.

Then, out of the blue, came a signal from a colleague he respected: Steve Ditko quit Marvel. His exit has been blamed on an argument between Lee and Ditko about the Green Goblin's secret identity, and on Ditko's displeasure when Marvel, like DC, made its artists switch to smaller-sized art boards, but with the mystery that always surrounds Ditko, no one knows quite what happened. Despite the apparently seamless union of their talents, something was coming between him and Lee. It may have been a woman: Ditko had discovered Ayn Rand and her objectivist philosophy, as had many in the increasingly subjectivist '60s, and was becoming unhappy with Lee's humanized villains and fallible heroes. Both men, obviously, were concerned with the individual's quest for right and the unreliability of general opinion, but the mid-'60s had polarized liberal individualists like Lee and conservative individualists like Ditko. Whatever the cause, when Charlton invited Ditko to come back, promising him the freedom to tell his own stories and to use whatever art materials he wanted, he was gone.

Jack wasn't the type to up and leave. He was still creatively attached to his Marvel creations, and still feeling loyal to the company for giving him the chance to survive and prosper during the industry's greatest crisis. Nor was he the type to complain about credits or to go head-to-head with Stan over perceived injustices. He was, however, the type to worry about supporting his family. He was pushing fifty now, so he started to press for some sort of long-term contract from Marvel, or some way to see a piece of long-term profits from his creations, some protection against being booted into the unemployment line next month because they wanted some new hotshot on *Fantastic Four* or *Thor*. He got vague promises that he'd "be taken care of." He got page-rate increases. He didn't get security. Stan told him there was

The creator and his creatures: "Jack Kirby and Marvel Characters," a self-portrait from 1970. All characters © and ™ Marvel Entertainment Group except for the guy at the drawing board.

nothing he could do. Martin Goodman didn't want to waste his time with some damn artist. Jack burned.

Meanwhile, Ditko's *Spider-Man* went on under Lee and new artist "Jazzy Johnny" Romita (from *ASM* 39, Aug. 1966), who'd also replaced Wally Wood on *Daredevil*, but it was a whole different show. The old subplots were tied up all too neatly, characters were abruptly changed, and Peter Parker was robbed of much of his complexity as he became a hip, motorcycle-riding Joe College. The art was sleek and "jazzy" indeed, but nothing of Ditko's intensity was left. And sales went *up*. It had to make Lee think: could it be that once the Marvel formula was in place and the concept fleshed out, a comic might actually do *better* without the idiosyncrasies of a visionary artist? Would Marvel be smart to pursue a more uniform, quickly accessible style across the board? It was the sort of thing that could make an editor reconsider his own value, and that of his artists.

From the summer of 1966, a bifurcation appeared: Jack's three comics were more than ever

Jack's, but all the rest of the Marvel line belonged more than ever to Stan.

During 1967, as Kirby's feelings about Marvel grew more ambivalent, the boundaries of his universe began to show. The stories grew simpler, the new inventions fewer, and the straight-ahead fight scenes gradually more prevalent. New ideas continued to appear in *Fantastic Four*—a star-spanning race of experimenters named the Kree, a test-tube-born messiah called Him, a sub-atomic "microworld," a topsy-turvy world called the Negative Zone, and the hint of strange abilities in Reed and Sue's baby son, Franklin (*FF* 64-77 and *Annual* 6, July 1967-Oct. 1968). *Thor* continued at a grandiose level for a time, with a story about Ragnarok, the doom of the gods, and new revelations about Galactus and the Inhumans. (*Thor* 146-169, Nov. 1967-Oct. 1969). Kirby's storytelling was always irresistible, his fight scenes always earthshaking—he adjusted wonderfully to the smaller art boards by making his action even bigger and bolder— but the creative intensity was dropping.

Then, in early 1968, came the blow: as Kirby was working on the Silver Surfer origin story for an issue of *Fantastic Four*, he learned that Stan Lee was writing the first issue of a *Silver Surfer* comic book. The art would be by John Buscema. The story contained the Surfer's origin, and it contradicted everything Kirby thought about the character. His Surfer had been a being of pure energy who had to learn from Earthlings what emotion and individuation were all about. Stan's was a man from another planet who'd made the supreme sacrifice in becoming Galactus's herald. Stan's was well in keeping with what had now become the Marvel formula, a formula Jack had left far behind.

It was like a hammer to Kirby's skull. He abandoned his story in progress, feeling that he could never use the Surfer again. "I already knew," he said, "that a concept I contributed was instantly lost to me in a legal sense, but to lose it creatively as well. . . ." It was too much. He gave up on creating anything new for Marvel.

But what was Jack Kirby without new creations? And what was Marvel without Jack's heart and soul?

CHAPTER 17

ARTISTS AND HEROES

For all the Archies and Milton Fasses jumping on the superhero bandwagon, hardly any new creative blood was coming in. There were writers Roy Thomas and Jim Shooter and, over at Warren Publishing, Archie Goodwin, but nary a new artist to be found. So many old hands from the 1940s boom years were kicking around looking for work, that a few phone calls and a little bit of money were all an inexperienced publisher needed to slap together a squad of veterans who could crank out a passable-looking comic book with no supervision. But you have to be careful when you let artists, even comic book artists, go unsupervised. You might let something out of the bottle that can never be put back in.

Wally Wood was one of the most respected artists in the business, at least among his peers if not among the more deadline-minded editors. He'd become a favorite of fan-addicts for his science fiction work for EC, with its wonderfully controlled surfaces but seething masses of detail and horrifying undercurrents. His own surface was mild, his emotions turbulent. Once an unwitting editor tried to suggest improvements to a Wood page in front of other artists; without a word, Wood grabbed the page and walked out, never to return. He alternated days-long marathons of sleepless work with drinking binges, so that even by the '60s, when he was still shy of forty, his art was showing a loss of intensity and detail (although that line work was still pristine). There's no telling what demons haunted poor Woody, but he always showed an obsession with hordes of vile aliens attacking the Earth in waves of fire and bloodshed. He'd created and packaged a series of trading cards, a masterpiece of luridness called *Mars Attacks*,

with a writer named Len Brown. Then, with his old art assistant Joe Orlando, he helped Jim Warren set up his *Creepy* and *Eerie*, bringing in nearly all his old EC cronies. He may have been a problem as a staff artist, but as a free agent he could perform miracles.

In 1965 Harry Shorten of Tower Books, one of the most trend-conscious of low-end paperback publishers, decided he'd better get in on this comic book boom. His plan was to publish his own comics and then collect them in paperbacks like the extremely popular *Mad* books, which were helping make Bill Gaines rich. His gimmick was a regular comic book series in the double-size-for-a-quarter format that other publishers used for specials and reprints, figuring America's affluent and comics-hungry kids could find the extra thirteen cents for something they *had* to have. To make sure they had to have it, he called on an *Archie* cartoonist named Sam Schwartz to launch *Tippy Teen* (a title hilarious to all those eight-year-olds who remembered the big song hit of 1938) and hired Wally Wood to help Schwartz create a superhero line. Wood said he "functioned as a freelance editor and did as much of the art as I could." For the art he couldn't do, he and Schwartz brought in Wally's old cohort Reed Crandall and got Gil Kane and Mike Sekowsky to squeeze a few pages into their schedules, promising them a lack of editorial interference that they found quite refreshing. Soon enough, that other singular force, Steve Ditko, was on board, along with Wood's assistant, Dan Adkins, and a lot of experienced hands to help out: Mike Esposito, Joe Giella, Paul Reinman, George Tuska, Ogden Whitney, and more. Not surprisingly for an artist who resented all intrusions into his private

Wally Wood wasn't what he had been, but he could still sculpt a hero of grace and power like no other artist. (*Dynamo* #2, Oct. 1966.)

that created its own super-operatives (*T.H.U.N.D.E.R. Agents* 1, Nov. 1965). The creators couldn't take the superhero stuff seriously, playing their star, Dynamo, as a bit of a goof. The stories were at their best in their little humor bits. Jumping into the air, Dynamo cries, "Now to get back up to the penthouse . . . in a single leap!" The next panel shows him standing on a ledge halfway up the building, saying, "Hmmm—might take two leaps." The big selling point, though, was the art: Wood and Crandall creating sleek and gorgeous, Kane strutting his action-chops like Julie Schwartz had never let him. And it did sell. Tower followed with *Undersea Agent* (Jan. 1966), *Dynamo* (Aug. 1966), and *NoMan* (Nov. 1966), along with a war comic called *Fight the Enemy* (Aug. 1966). Harry Shorten got four paperbacks out of them.

Wood and his crew plotted and drew with an abandon that showed they were having a great time, even if they didn't expect this to last long. They were also willing to break the rules. Dynamo went up against one of Wood's patented alien invasions, but this time the aliens were unseen infiltrators, Wood substituting a truly eerie paranoia for a blood feast (*Dynamo* 1-4, Aug. 1966-June 1967). NoMan was an android hero who "died" at least once per issue as his bodies were destroyed. Once, when down to his last body, he thinks, "If they kill me now, I'm dead!" Later, in angry resentment of his own android nature, he hurls one body after another to its destruction in a globe-trotting orgy of suicide (*TA* 7, Aug. 1966). In that same issue, Steve Ditko shocked everybody in fandom by showing the hero, Menthor, shot six times at close range—and dying. No superhero who'd been around for more than one issue had ever been killed before—Jim Shooter's Ferro Lad story was still six months away—and it happened with brutal Ditko intensity. There was a message here: the artists had something to say, and they were restless to say it.

Charlton Comics got the same message. It had been limping along with its cheap war and Western comics, only cautiously adding to its small quasisu-perhero line—*Blue Beetle*, *Fightin' 5*, *Sarge Steel*—with *Son of Vulcan* in early 1965. Editor Pat Masulli

visions, Wood didn't pursue veteran writers. He brought over his partner from trading cards, Len Brown, and raided fandom for a few more hands—Larry Ivie, Roger Brand, Bill Pearson—who could string the action scenes together with a few functional words.

The funny part about hiring this crew for this job was that Wood and Crandall didn't like superheroes and usually strove not to do them, while Kane and Sekowsky had been doing nothing else lately and were getting sick of them. So Wood compromised, combining the cape-and-cowl icon with the more reality-based spy genre, and cooking up a sort of U.N.C.L.E.

tried tapping into the new fan market, luring Ditko back for a few issues of a revived *Captain Atom* in 1965, and creating the fan writing contest that Roy Thomas won before Stan Lee stole him away. Masulli also let old hand Frank McLaughlin write and draw a new series called *Judomaster,* the first comic book to grab the martial arts fad that was germinating in the spy movies. But nearly the whole line was still boringly written and drawn, dragged backward by Charlton inertia to the feel of the early '50s. In fact, the only other title likely to make a picky '60s reader pause was *Sarge Steel,* and that was only because of the art of Dick Giordano. Like Ditko, he was one of the last artists to break in when the business was collapsing in the early '50s, and every line of his work showed his debt to the Milton Caniff imitators and the B crime movies of that time. He'd developed a sophisticated action style, though, and a high gloss in his inking. Besides that, he was a guy with ideas, trying in spite of his own style to keep his gruff cop apace with James Bond and Peter Gunn. In short, he was too good for the company, but Charlton found a way to keep him. Masulli stepped down in early 1966, and Giordano was named editor.

He turned out to be a dynamo. He was tuned in to fandom, and he immediately committed Charlton to what he believed fans wanted—or, at least, the parts of what they wanted that he wanted, too—characterization, innovation, and a much bigger dose of reality. He banished all temptation to be a DC-style editor. "I prefer to work with people whose work I admire and let them do what they do best," he said. "I am not interested in having them do my book. . . . I'm interested in creating an atmosphere in which a freelancer—an artist, writer, letterer, colorist—will feel comfortable doing things the way he feels they should be done. . . . I tried to establish a situation where we were all working together, perhaps having some fun in the process." He started by promising Ditko the control of his work that Stan Lee wouldn't or couldn't, and Ditko promptly left Marvel to revamp Captain Atom and to relaunch the tired Blue Beetle. Masulli had wanted Roy Thomas to work for

him and lost out, but now Giordano hired three young Missourians whom Thomas recommended: Gary Friedrich, Dave Kaler, and Denny O'Neil. He brought in another young writer named Steve Skeates and managed to lure away one of DC's better war comics creators, Sam Glanzman.[1] He hired some oddball new artists and gave others a freer reign: Pete Morisi, Pat Boyette, Jim Aparo. He encouraged his friend Frank McLaughlin to run wild on *Judomaster,* giving it a rough pizzazz. It was a low-rent bunch, all either too unestablished or, in Ditko's case, too independent to work at the bigger companies. But it was a vital bunch, ready to try anything, and most of them turned out to be pretty good.

The Giordano group revamped Charlton's whole line: Western, war, and science fiction. The contrast between the titles of their new creations and the titles of the established comics in which they appeared shows how profound the revamp was. Denny O'Neil and Jim Aparo's humorous science-fiction Western, *Wander,* was in *Cheyenne Kid*; Sam Glanzman came as close to antiwar comics as anyone ever had with his heartfelt *The Lonely War of Pvt. Willy Schultz* in *Fightin' Army.* For most fans, though, it was the new Charlton superheroes that were attracting attention. There was Morisi's *Peter Cannon, Thunderbolt,* about a man able to draw upon huge reserves of strength through willpower alone, a visceral tapping of the new individualism (Jan. 1966). And *Peacemaker,* about a master of weapons who hates violence and dedicates himself to spreading peace; Joe Gill, the tired old Charlton workhorse, revealed a side he'd never shown before in some thematically driven and almost intellectual scripting (Mar. 1967). There were the backup strips, too, like Gary Friedrich and Sam Grainger's *Sentinels,* about a folk rock trio with superpowers, not to mention *Tiffany Sinn* and *Peace Corps Patsy.*

It was Ditko, though, who carried the line. Stan Lee had always brought his own vivid touch to *Spider-Man* and *Dr. Strange,* but at Charlton Ditko's scripters—Kaler, Friedrich, and Glanzman—stepped back and contented themselves with helping the artist

[1] Glanzman was a bit of a maverick. Freelancers used to caution each other that they'd better use pseudonyms when moonlighting for upstart publishers lest they offend their principal employers (when Mike Esposito and Gene Colan first started working for Marvel they were Mickey Demeo and Adam Austin), so Sam, to "conceal" his defection, had Charlton call him "D.C. Glanzman."

Away from DC's restraint, Gil Kane flexes his muscles—as penciler, inker, and writer. (*T.H.U.N.D.E.R. Agents* #14, July 1967.)

TM and © 1967 Tower Comics, Inc.

realize his singular vision. First Ditko and Kaler revamped Captain Atom, giving him an opponent who was also a love interest, Nightshade (*Captain Atom* 82, Sept. 1966), and then—at the instigation of Giordano, who openly disliked overpowered characters—they stripped away most of his nuclear might and made him fight with his wits and determination (*Captain Atom* 83, Nov. 1966). Nightshade was the first heroine of the silver age who fought with her fists and feet instead of ladylike thought projections or invisibility. (Golden age heroines had been a tough bunch, but the '50s had made comic book women less threatening.) Amusingly, Stan Lee promptly con-

verted his Black Widow into a similar Emma Peel type in the pages of *Spider-Man*.

Ditko developed a new Blue Beetle as a backup in *Captain Atom,* a Beetle as besieged and misunderstood as Spider-Man, in adventures nearly as complex. The fans loved him, and soon he had his own title (June 1967). Here the Ditko theme of themes was played to its fullest: Captain Atom, in his series, has already been painted as a menace by a hysterical press, and now the new Blue Beetle is suspected of murdering his predecessor. Then a gang of clownishly attired thugs called the Madmen—Ditko's visualization of his increasingly self-absorbed countrymen, one suspects—use fear to turn the public against him. "Get him, Madmen," they cry. "He's trying to stop us from making a living!" Such moral relativists, indignant that a representative of law and order would interfere with their God-given right to make a living by any means necessary, were becoming central figures for Ditko.

Most conservatives of the time contented themselves with worrying about acts of aggression from the urban poor, but Ditko's vision was bigger. Ever since J. Jonah Jameson, he'd been railing against those who distort our public information or cultural mores for their own corrupt or irrational reasons. Now, in a backup strip called *The Question*, he brought those issues to the very heart of his stories (*BB* 1, June 1967). Vic Sage is an incorruptible TV reporter devoted to exposing crime among the rich and powerful, surrounded by the venality of his own audience and employers. "You, the enraged public, wonder how a leech like Dicer and his ilk can thrive so readily among you!" he roars on the air. "How many of you willingly support his gaming tables . . . or play a number daily? . . . You are willing partners in Dicer's crimes!" When words prove insufficient, Sage spritzes himself with a chemical that turns his suit to the Question's trademark light blue. The Question then roots out corruption with his brain and fists, terrifying his targets by flipping a blank card at them—on which, as they touch it, emerges a question mark.

If Vic Sage always defeated venality in his adventures, it wasn't so in the real world. Jack Liebowitz and his friends at Independent News didn't like this threat from the self-distributed Charlton and the rival independent distributor PDC, which handled both Tower and Harvey Comics. They reportedly suggested to their major wholesaling clients that they overlook superhero product from these other distributors, and sales promptly began dropping. Harvey, feeling the squeeze, pressured PDC to underplay Tower to retailers, and by late 1968 *T.H.U.N.D.E.R. Agents* and its kin were gone (*Tippy Teen* actually outlived them by a year). Their deaths may have been fore-ordained, though, because the *Batman* craze was burning out, as all overheated crazes must. Charlton was even less lucky: it canceled its entire new super-hero line in late 1967. A year later though, it released two final issues that enabled Ditko to make his most unambivalent statement yet.

In a Question one-shot called *Mysterious Suspense* (Oct. 1968), we find a TV sponsor with mob ties trying to suck Vic Sage into his corruption. When Vic proves unattainable, the sponsor gets him fired. In a tremendous story of suspense and violence, the Question brings them all down. Then, in a final issue of *Blue Beetle* (5, Nov. 1968), the beleaguered hero comes up against Our Man, a purposely flawed role model who calls himself the "destroyer of heroes." As if engaged in some private dialogue with Stan Lee, Ditko (through Glanzman) has one simpering bystander whine, "The only good man is one who has faults, like Our Man. Any person without faults would be such a disgusting spectacle!" To which a clearer-headed citizen retorts, "That's why you're always complaining about stupid sales clerks, idiotic drivers, or dumb politicians? You're knocking your GOOD MAN'S virtues!" They were scary times for American conservatives, and Ditko obviously felt that subtlety could no longer be heard above the noise in the streets.

Ditko's absolute heroes show just how much freedom Charlton and Giordano were allowing their freelancers, because one gets a very strong feeling that everyone else in the bunch had little use for that kind of heroism. Giordano didn't like characters with powers. Peacemaker didn't like violence. Steve Skeates's one-shot *Tyro Team* tried to show what would *really* happen to college kids who got super-powers: no sleep, blown exams, disastrous dates (*Charlton Premiere* 1, Sept. 1967). Denny O'Neil and Jim Aparo's Prankster (*Thunderbolt* 60, Nov. 1967) was a wacky cut-up on the outside but a man of sorrow and anger on the inside. He was devoted to overthrowing Bane, the tyrant of Ultrapolis, who worships a female computer and has forbidden his subjects to partake in anything personal or creative. "Love, laughter, art," bemoans the Prankster, "everything that lends dignity to human beings outlawed! People made to work like animals . . . slaves to Bane and his dream of power!" The Prankster fights to free the human spirit from technocracy, not just with violence, but with humor and color and purposeful irrationality. We were a long way from the eager futurism of Adam Strange.

Here was a creator reaching for a new relationship between hero and culture, but in a direction quite opposite Ditko's, and quite a bit more in tune with the mood of young Americans. Denny O'Neil was young, but cut from old cloth. In college he'd had big dreams of writing journalism and fiction, but he was just a small-town Missouri reporter when he did a "local boy makes good" piece about Roy Thomas's job at Marvel Comics. Thomas was so pleased with the article that he got Stan Lee's approval to offer O'Neil a job, and O'Neil "thought it was too good a caper to pass up." He moved in with Thomas and Dave Kaler in New York, figuring to write comics for a year or two. He was no comics fan, and was an outsider among them: an Irishman among WASPs, a drinker, Jesuit educated and intellectually ambitious, left wing in a prehippie way, prone to guarding his words where Roy couldn't staunch the flow of his. Like Otto Binder and Gardner Fox and the other old-timers, he'd gotten into comics just because they were there, but being a college kid, he romanticized them as "blue-collar literature." *Newsday* caught it perfectly in a picture accompanying a 1965 piece on the comic book "cult": O'Neil sitting in the background puffing his pipe, looking arch and aloof, as a gleeful Roy hands Dave a copy of *Spider-Man*.

In a more perfect world, O'Neil would have been another Norman Mailer, or at least a Midwestern Jimmy Breslin, but in the real world he married young and had a kid young and had bills to pay. His stint at Marvel was short, and his most lasting contribution was a letter in *Fantastic Four* wittily excoriating Marvel's portrayal of '60s college kids as fun-loving louts (but what did Stan and Jack, those Depression boys who'd been fighting deadlines since their teens, know of college beyond Ruby Keeler in *Sweetheart of the Campus*?). When Giordano needed cheap writers with something to say, O'Neil was there, and Charlton was the place for him: a low-rent Italian *famiglia* business in a field run by Jews, running its own printing press with old-country cousins and their cousins' cousins who couldn't even speak English, the air thick with ink and Catholic proletarianism. Denny might never be another Mailer, but at least he could cloak himself in a pseudonym pulled from Mailer's *Deer Park*: "Sergius O'Shaughnessy."

The market just wasn't there for experimentation of Tower's and Charlton's kind, thanks at least in part to people like Jack Liebowitz (whom Arnold Drake called "the bottleneck of the '60s . . . [for] his failure to see comics in its fullest context"). But Wally Wood believed that the readers were there, and that maybe someday a market could be created that would reach them. He'd tasted the thrill of creating his own projects and keeping some control over them, but even Tower hadn't let him own his own creations. Even there he hadn't felt he could give his best and most personal artistic gifts. Now comic book fandom was showing him a way. Most fanzines included amateur art. Some were devoted entirely to it, and many of the boldest fans had persuaded their favorite pros to contribute. Steve Ditko had been one of the most generous. Some zines, like Bill Spicer's *Fantasy Illustrated*, had almost commercial-quality printing and production and sold for much more than the comics themselves. With mail order, the whole print-and-return, minimize-your-losses system of newsstand distribution could be avoided. A publisher could advertise, take orders, and then print just as many copies as were already pre-sold. Wood's former assistant, Dan Adkins, had come up from fanzines himself, and now he invited Wood to take over an idea he'd had for a "prozine."

Wood called it *witzend*—for surely with the troubles besieging Tower, that's where he was—and gathered Frank Frazetta, Roy Krenkel, Al Williamson, and Archie Goodwin to contribute material. In 1966 he brought out his first issue, selling for a whole dollar. In his opening editorial, he thanked "all you horny-handed, ink-stained editor-publishers, demon reviewers, and wild-eyed mimeograph machinists" in fandom and committed his publication to not-for-profit personal projects, creator ownership, and the development of independent artists who weren't considered "commercial" by the big publishers. The first contributions weren't much—pretty but vapid science fiction stories with some pointlessly bare breasts—but soon Wood found what he'd been looking for, "the closest I've come to the real stuff," his Tolkien-influenced fantasy *The Wizard King*.

At the same time, Ditko came in with his own real stuff, *Mr. A* (*witzend* 3 and 4, 1967 and 1968). This was the Question redux, except that Mr. A tosses a half-white and half-black card, symbolizing his worldview: "Fools will tell you that there can be no honest person! That there are no BLACKS or WHITES . . . that everyone is GRAY! . . . When one knows what is black, EVIL, and what is white, GOOD, there can be no justification for choosing any part of EVIL! Those who do so choose are not GRAY but BLACK and EVIL . . . and they will be treated accordingly!" Sure enough, Mr. A not only coolly watches a cop-killer fall off a skyscraper, but berates the liberal welfare worker who wants to save him—she's unable to make a rational choice, he says. "I'll kill anyone who gets in my way—AH!" yells the punk as Mr. A punches him off the building. "Your goals never were realistic," says Mr. A without a touch of humor. Says a gangster, again with no irony, on his way to bribe or kill Mr. A's reporter alter ego, "We won't touch him unless he insists on remaining poor and honest." Character and story disappear into dogma. The subjective focus on individual pain that had originally made Ditko so powerful vanishes into objectivism. Young lefty cartoonists of the time congratulated themselves on their subversion and daring, but what could have been braver or more honest than this blast of right-wing absolutism that assaulted both the establishment and the rebels? It was so damn brave, in fact, that Ditko alienated the college readers whom he'd been so vital in seducing into comics in the first place. The great loner was disappearing into himself, away from comicdom and the fractious greater world.

witzend struggled along despite Wood's deteriorating health. Wood took whatever job he had to—inking at DC, cheesecake for GIs,—to buy time for his *Wizard King*. Bill Pearson, a fan who organized a monthly salon for comics pros and elite fans to discuss their beloved art form, helped out with the publishing when Woody couldn't handle it. It was an amazing message for a commercial artist like Wood to be broadcasting: it's better to struggle and starve for the personal work that earns you nothing than to sell your skill for an easy living.

Gil Kane liked Wood and Ditko's spirit of independence, but his formidable energies were directed toward the outer world, not inward toward the studio, bottle, and philosophy. He was a self-formed man, an immigrant kid remaking himself into a figure of professorial dignity, a natty dresser with a sculpted nose, a Stan Kenton haircut, a regal bearing, and a golden tenor. After Tower, he took a long break from *Green Lantern* and *The Atom* to work for Marvel, Warren, and others who would give him more freedom. Developing a project for Warren that never saw print, he started working away from home for the first time, in a midtown studio, and, he said, " it changed my life." Kane saw new vistas opening in that exciting time, not only on his art board, but in his career. He'd already become known as a vocal critic of the DC

way, calling its stories "banal" (which was to become almost a Kane catch phrase over the years). "They don't sell people," he said, "they sell puzzles." Now he could do something about it. He found financial and distributing support for a black-and-white magazine of his own and set about creating an action hero for adults.

Kane's thematic models were the hard-ass action movies then selling to the Sinatra-and-booze set—*Point Blank, The Professionals*—and his visual model was Lee Marvin, the epitome of the scary, amoral he-man. He brought in Archie

Cartooning as a plastic expression of social philosophy. Free of commercial publishers, Steve Ditko's work becomes more personal, and yet less *about* the personal: Mr. A is pure icon. (*witzend* #4, 1968.)

115

Speech bubble: "Awright, Miss Mace! What's goin on? Where's Hu—"

Panel captions:

The door burst open, slamming into the wall on protesting hinges, and the one called Eddie lunged forward, squinting eyes darting suspiciously around the room...

Savage's backhanded swing ripped through the air, driving the gun's cold steel into Eddie's face with catapult force, flattening the soft flesh of his nose into a bubbling smear of shattered bone and torn cartilage.

But as the gunman slumped limply to the floor, a giant vise of flesh clamped around Savage's wrist with numbing strength...

A vicious whirling motion that seemed certain to tear his arm from its socket jerked Savage off his feet and sent him hurtling across the room to collide with a coffee table with bone-rattling impact...

Rolling with the momentum that had sent him tumbling, Savage came to his feet, shaking his head to clear his swirling vision, to face the lumbering charge of the mountainous Oriental. Once the huge, hamlike hands caught him, it would be over...

Dodging their crushing grasp, Savage gambled everything on the spike-like stab of his fingers through sweaty folds of flesh into the giant's solar plexus, digging high under the ribs toward the heart. He made a sharp jerking motion and deep within the hulking body there was a soft snap...

With a short, rattling intake of breath, the mammoth figure stiffened, unable to straighten up. Hands locked together, Savage pounded at the muscular folds on the back of the Oriental's neck with sledgehammer fury as the massive hands still clutched and grabbed at him...

The huge form sagged to the floor still fighting to rise, like some prehistoric beast caught in quicksand. Savage dropped on top of him, knee driving sharply into the small of the broad, expansive back, hand slicing at the neck like a falling guillotine blade...

...And the human mountain ceased to move.

Cover up those blocks of redundant words and this becomes as fluid a narrative sequence as comics had ever seen. Such prolonged "continuous action" was almost never possible with standard comic book scripts. Words by Archie Goodwin, but plot and art by Gil Kane.
(*His Name Is...Savage* #1, 1968).

Goodwin, the EC fan-addict who'd won a reputation as the best short story writer in comics, to write the text— not just dialogue, but heavy captioning with the flavor of a pulp novel. There were far too many words, but Kane's cinematic narrative had never been more focused. He reached back to old masters like EC's Bernard Krigstein for devices like holding a steady "camera angle" across successive small panels to slice a continuous action into visual "beats."

Kane's *His Name Is...Savage* was the first mass-market, self-published comic since the big publishers had seized control of the business at the beginning of the golden age, and it hit the newsstands in the spring of 1968. Unfortunately, it didn't hit very many news-

stands. According to Kane, unnamed people associated with the Comics Code Authority "decided to act in order to suppress publication . . . having people make phone calls and suggest that I was turning out a pornographic book." Distributors avoided it, and Kane gave up after a single issue.

Kane saw Wood's *Wizard King* and also noticed the big sales on paperbacks about a barbarian named Conan. He sold Bantam Books on a fantasy book in comics form called *Blackmark*, but that went nowhere, too. He returned to work-for-hire jobs, especially for Marvel, turning his frustrated energy toward working faster, making his drawings more simple and powerful, more stripped down to the essence of anatomy and violence. His studio attracted bright young assistants who thrived in Kane's air of superiority to the banal business around him, especially one brilliant young smart-ass named Howard Chaykin. Kane wouldn't return to self-publishing, but young artists like Chaykin remembered *Savage* and thought about the possibilities.

They were times that changed people and separated them, and comics artists were separating now into those who just wanted to pay the bills and those who wanted to advance their art form. Fandom was changing and dividing, too. Jerry Bails, after years of fervent leadership, suddenly announced in early 1966 that he would "all but retire from comics fandom." Roy Thomas was already gone into "prodom" and others of the old guard were drifting off. Now new breeds were coming up. There were the intellectuals, not content to bring back their old heroes, but determined to push comics toward literary and artistic worth. One such was Richard Kyle, who invented the terms "graphic story" and "graphic novel" for works that deserved better than "comics." Another was Bill Spicer, whose subsequent *Graphic Story Magazine* (1967) was devoted to all that was "artistically serious" in the medium. "Like the novel and the drama," wrote Kyle, "the graphic story's limitations and strengths are only those of its creators and their insights into the essential human substance: Art does not make truth, truth makes Art." Kyle and Spicer called young readers' attention to the riches of comics before the Marvel Age, like the work of writer/artist Will Eisner, whose *Spirit* Kyle saw as a "complete personal statement." It was the sort of thing to make fan cartoonists wonder if their greatest goal should be to draw a Stan Lee plot after all.

Comics were already more intellectually respectable in France (of course), and in 1968 a high-school drama teacher and used-comic-book dealer named Phil Seuling—a sort of loud-mouthed, Brooklyn-accented version of Bails and Thomas—hooked up with Maurice Horn, who had just organized the landmark *Bande Desinée et Figuration Narrative* show at the Louvre, to form the transatlantic Society for Comic Art Research and Preservation. SCARP didn't last long, but it organized the 1968 New York Con and gave it a tone of cosmopolitan culture. And then there was Gary Groth, a bright-eyed little squirt of a teenager with big ambitions, living the nomadic life of a military brat in which comics were the one great constant. By the age of fifteen, he was publishing one of the slickest of zines, *Fantastic Fanzine*. He gushed with semiliterate self-congratulation for his own discriminating taste, but he also cadged interviews with hotshot artists and showed a precocious interest in the business of comics and the limits publishers put on creators.

The subject matter of the zines was expanding, from Vietnam War stories to Carl Barks's *Donald Duck* to Conan the Barbarian. A few of the new fans were longhairs, uniting their love of comics with the drugs, visions, and values of the counterculture. Fanzine art had nearly always been restricted to clunky imitations of mainstream superhero drawings, and no fan artist had yet broken into the pro ranks. But suddenly there were these talented kids—Jeff Jones, Berni Wrightson, Jim Starlin, Mike Kaluta—drawing from Kirby and Ditko and old ECs and head-shop posters and Aubrey Beardsley and erotica and whatever else was being shoved into their eyes in those vision-hungry years, and forging a new look unique to the fanzines. Furthest out was George Metzger, with his compelling but barely comprehen-

© 1966 Jeff Jones

Jeff Jones turned out to be too good an illustrator to stay with comics, but he arose when fans—and American youths in general—were discovering that there had been life before the Ike Age. (*Fantasy Illustrated* #5, 1966.)

A fifth grader named Don Dohler scribbled a character in 1958 who caught on with his classmates. By eighth grade, Dohler and Mark Tarka were using this "Pro Junior" as the Alfred E. Newman of their dit-toed fanzine *Wild*—which showcased smart-alec kids like Jay Lynch, Skip Williamson, and Art Spiegelman. (*Wild* #1, 1961.)

© 1961 Don Dohler

Pro Junior became a symbol of the undergrounds' fanzine roots. Here Robert Crumb uses him to skewer the superhero icon. Two years later, Denis Kitchen would publish *Projunior Comix* with contributions from some of the undergrounds' best. (*Bijou Funnies* #4, Bijou Publishing Empire, 1969.)

ground newspapers. Hippified and radical cartoonists (like Trina Robbins, who had made the pilgrimage to meet Lee and Ditko) were turning those into vehicles for a new kind of comic strip. Then, in 1967, that geeky, Luddite, acid-dropping, priapic genius from the Midwest named Robert Crumb—who'd been doing *Foo* nearly a decade before and had been cranking out his own obsessive, subversive, masterfully drawn comics ever since—looked around his new San Francisco digs and figured that all these poster-loving, comics-reading freaks might pay real money for a whole comic book full of satire and sex. He found someone to print a bunch of copies (actually, he found two someones, but the first one took his art and disappeared), and he sold them on the streets, out of a baby carriage. He sold them, and sold them, and sold them. Within weeks they were all over the country, and cartoonists everywhere were getting their minds blown by *Zap Comix #1*. By 1968 everybody was getting into the act, and "underground comix" was a cottage industry.

These were no superhero comics. About as close as they got was Gilbert Shelton's brutally funny *Wonder Wart-Hog*—which he'd been doodling in private since 1959, when DC's revived heroes were just gearing up—and that was no less than a laying bare of the whole genre as a tool of the repressed, hypocritical power structure. The Hog of Steel dresses as a little girl to catch the vile pornographic cartoonist "R. Scum," and then he jumps up and down on him until he's pounded to jelly. When voluptuous reporter Lois Lamebrain laughs at his tiny male member, he explodes in rage and rapes her with his snout (*Zap 4*, 1969). Later he leads a patriotic sing-along of the most hawkish, segregationist Dixiecrats in the US government, in a story called "Believe It or Leave It: You Don't Know How Good You Got It Here in America, Bub" (*Zap 5*, 1969).

Poster shops and head shops quickly began carrying these things, opening up huge audiences for cartoonists, far beyond the reach of mailing lists and baby carriages. Smarter cartoonists and publishers, like Denis Kitchen and Ron Turner, started publish-

sible acid-head visions of EC science fiction stories, a true '60s son of Wally Wood. Soon, though, he and Vaughan Bodé and Grass Green and Mike Vosburg and others were crossing over into another comic book world: the one growing out of the "satire zines" inspired by Harvey Kurtzman. (After all, hadn't Adam West and Burt Ward blurred the line between superheroes and satire?)

The satire-zine and related college-humor scenes had been spawning iconoclastic, small-press comic books at least as far back as Frank Stack's *Adventures of Jesus*, published by his friend Gilbert Shelton in 1963. Meanwhile, Paul Krassner's *Realist*—including cartoons by Wally Wood and a new kid named Art Spiegelman—had kicked off a wave of left-wing, satirical, pop-oriented under-ing and wholesaling not just their own, but other people's comics, so that artists could forget about distribution and just draw. They didn't allow returns, as the big "independent distributors" did, meaning that retailers had to figure out in advance what they could sell, gamble on buying it and put some energy into selling it. But head shop owners found that these comics were worth the risk and trouble. The undergrounds sold for far higher prices than "overgrounds" and the readers who wanted them, wanted them badly.

Soon a new business started appearing: young guys looking for a way to make some bread—or tired of the nomadism of dealing old records at flea markets—saw the underground boom and decided they could combine publishing and retailing. A depressed little man named Gary Arlington, who'd been drifting through life without purpose or passion for fifteen years since his beloved ECs had been killed, had an idea. He persuaded a number of underground cartoonists who had started out as EC fans—and there were a lot of them—to create a "Nickel Library" of new comics paying tribute to EC in their own styles. The Nickel Library never happened, but Arlington found himself opening the San Francisco Comic Book Company, a hole in the wall selling old comics, new undergrounds, and soon, to keep the rent steadily paid, the hip Marvel comics that many of his young customers picked up along with their more radical stuff. Fifty miles to the south, in a dying downtown neighborhood near San Jose State College, a hippie-fringe sharpie named Bob Sidebottom set up a publishing venture called California Comix and a retail outlet for it called the Comic Collectors' Shop. He got Bob Crumb to draw him a business card (showing a

comics fan grabbing a comic book with a huge price tag and drooling, "I wan' it, I wan' it!") and blasted old jazz at the timid teenagers picking through his huge stacks of twenty-five-cent old Marvels. In the same town, seven teenagers, including a kid named Bud Plant, opened a short-lived store to sell old Marvels and DC's. Then Phil Seuling, still teaching high school, opened a shop in Brooklyn. Soon they were popping up in LA, and Chicago too, "comic shops" appearing like spots of mildew on the maps of America's low-rent neighborhoods.

To call the undergrounds a product of the Bat-craze would earn a derisive snort from the passionate partisans of the form, who prefer to see them as the heirs of EC or Kurtzman's *Trump* or the pornographic "Tijuana bibles" of the Depression. Those are all truer thematic progenitors, indeed, but they were long gone by 1967. Yet, barely a year elapsed between the first "Careful, Boy Wonder!" and *Zap #1*. *Batman* had made America's youth comic-conscious, and when comics appeared that were more consistently in tune with their sensibilities, the audience was ready for them. Now *Batman* was vanishing, the new superheroes were fading, and Wonder Wart-Hog was prospering. This was an antiauthoritarian generation, and the superheroes, no matter how many different ways they'd been handled, had a built-in authoritarian element.

This was not lost on the new "overground" comics creators. Denny O'Neil and his peers saw the undergrounds, and that hatred of authority struck chords with them. This was even funnier than Wally Wood launching a superhero line: the young people who didn't believe in heroes were poised to take over the whole genre.

CHAPTER 18

THE DC EXPERIMENT

It was a tumultuous and confrontational time in America, and even the halls of National Periodicals were not immune. But the last thing anyone at National wanted to fret about in 1967 was Vietnam or the Black Power movement or the Yippies or the War on Poverty. *Batman* ratings were plummeting. Comics sales were slumping. And Marvel was coming on strong. Martin Goodman made it all very simple for Jack Liebowitz: let him publish as many comics as he wanted, or lose his distributor's cut on Marvel's fifty-million-unit sales per annum. Liebowitz took the brakes off, and suddenly the comic book world was facing Goodman Unleashed again. DC would need new product, maybe a lot of it, to keep its dominance of the newsstands, and to make that product sell, it would need a new approach.

"What's Marvel doing right?" became the question of the year at editorial meetings. An apocryphal anecdote has it that production manager Sol Harrison once answered, "Bad art." True or not, it shows the smugness of National's old line, with their high page rates and elegant illustrators. To them Kirby was rough and out of control, and the newer Marvel artists like John Romita were just second-stringers they didn't need. One man at the meetings saw it differently, the only man with the eye of an artist: Carmine Infantino.

Infantino was in his forties now. He'd been fighting monthly deadlines for more than twenty years, he'd brought his art to a glittering peak, and he was losing the fire to keep improving. It was time to think longer-term. Dick Giordano and Wally Wood had recently landed editorial gigs—why not him? He was a smart guy, well-liked by management and loyal to the firm. He'd started attending editorial meetings at his own request, and now he felt he understood what DC needed: an infusion of Marvel's in-your-face vigor without a loss of what he called "the DC touch," with all its Lubitschean implications of nuance and sophistication. He noted that until recently all Marvel covers—except for Steve Ditko's series—had been drawn by Jack Kirby, with forward-thrusting action and powerful central figures. Now, with the arrival of the new wave of Marvel artists—Gene Colan, John Buscema, and John Romita—that forcefulness was being combined with baroque body language, heavy rendering, and a dose of realism. Infantino sketched his ideas for giving that look the "DC touch." As Julius Schwartz recalled, "He unveiled them at a meeting, and everybody applauded." When they hit the stands, sales rose. Irwin Donenfeld, spurred by news that Stan Lee was offering Infantino work, told him that if he wanted to give up his regular art assignments, he'd pay him to redesign DC's covers and to scout new talent to draw them. Infantino didn't have to think very long. He blew through his last assignment—the first issue of a weird new hero for Jack Miller—and bid the Flash and Elongated Man good-bye.

DC's editors were groping for new kinds of heroes. They came up with a couple of jungle gimmicks: *B'wana Beast*, a creation so awful that Mike Sekowsky reportedly refused to draw the last issue, so a three-issue tryout became a two-issue filler (*Showcase* 66-67, Apr. 1967), and *Bomba the Jungle Boy*, George Kashdan's trendy update of Roy Rockwood's teenage Tarzan (Oct. 1967). Bomba bombed. Schwartz finally got his *Spectre* going as a

The teenagers wanted angst? Neal Adams and Deadman delivered—as not even Ditko, Kirby, and Lee had ever dared. (*Strange Adventures* #212, June 1968.)

series (Dec. 1967), but Gardner Fox's lighthearted writing and Murphy Anderson's restrained art weren't adequate for such a mystical concept, and the "Discarnate Detective" felt like just an old Schwartz hero out of his element.

It was Arnold Drake, brainstorming with Carmine Infantino and Jack Miller, who nailed what the fans were looking for. Shrill letters decrying "camp" were coming in by the truckload; even fans who liked the TV *Batman* hated DC's lame attempts to capture the same irreverence. Drake had just taken his *Doom Patrol* through its campiest period, but he was smart enough to see that a lot of readers were starving for the opposite. Now he, Bruno Premiani, and Murray Boltinoff were pulling back to its darker, more disturbing orientation. Miller edited the goofiest of all DC titles: *Inferior Five* and the Archiesque *Swing with Scooter*. But as DC's first new editor in an eon, he was determined to do something startling, and his late work on *Martian Manhunter* showed an interest in crime stories. Infantino believed DC's brain trust could out-Marvel Marvel at sophistication and dramatic realism, so they pushed the new aesthetic all the way.

The cover of *Strange Adventures* 205 (Oct. 1967) pictured a costumed acrobat plummeting from a trapeze. From a corner, the barrel of a rifle protruded into the picture. The caption read: "This man who was just murdered is our hero! His story begins one minute later." Thus were launched the revolutionary adventures of Deadman.

Boston Brand is an acrobat for a "struggling, fleabag circus"—until a rifle shot sends him hurtling to his death. When his fellow circus performers crowd around his corpse, however, Brand discovers that only his body has died. His spirit has somehow survived, and Rama Kushna, "The Face of the Universe," has a special fate in store for him. Manifesting himself as a baby elephant, a trained mouse, and finally as a tree, Rama Kushna explains that "you shall have the power to walk among men until you have found the one who killed you." To aid this "Deadman" in achieving his quest, he endows him with the capacity to enter anyone's body and take control of it. Shortly afterward, Deadman learns that witnesses claimed the killer had a hook in place of a hand. The quest begins.

121

Deadman's origin, powers, and quest weren't all that made him startling. Miller, who took over the scripting after Drake's pilot issue, responded to a reader who suggested teaming Deadman up with the Spectre: "*Deadman* [is] done in a highly realistic manner, while *Spectre*, although just as effective, [is] done in the more traditionally super-charged and imaginative manner. . . . If you tried to mix [the styles], all you'd have left is hash" (*SA* 211, Apr. 1968). Deadman's mission brought him up against dope dealers, motorcycle gangs, evil circus performers, and smugglers of illegal immigrants. The scripting went for blunt, blue-collar emotionalism, avoiding both the formal, explanatory quality of most DC writing and the heavy-handed melodrama of Marvel. Captions were merely crisp stage directions that sped the action along. Deadman communicated his rage and self-pity more through action than chatter.

And then there was the art. After Infantino's one issue, the job was handed to his favorite new "find," a young man who'd been bopping around comics for a few years, developing his own style but attracting little notice. His name was Neal Adams, and he would prove to be the most influential artist of the next decade.

Adams, born in 1941, was the first artist of his generation to become prominent in comics. His was the first new pictorial vision in the field since Ditko had appeared more than a decade before. He'd refined his chops on a wide range of advertising art, humor comics, and newspaper strips—perfecting his line work under Stan Drake on *The Heart of Juliet Jones*—so within a few issues of his first regular superhero series, he was a full-blown phenomenon. He was handsome, confident, good enough to take comics or leave them, and unafraid to do anything. He combined a startling naturalism with flamboyantly experimental layouts. In one of his pages, the images in all five panels combine into a huge abstracted head of Deadman. He showed a flair for action, and didn't confine it to individual panels. His figures literally burst free of the borders, flying and throwing punches clear into the next page. To that he added his *Juliet Jones* emotional nuances, his ability to bring out the idiosyncrasies of every character through a full range of passions. His line work caught every detail. Clothes were made of real cloth, hair blew in a breeze or became matted with sweat. Adams himself once said that if superheroes really existed, they would look the way he drew them.

With the passage of time, Adams's work has become far less intoxicating. His blend of naturalism and superheroics is often uneasy, and the relentless detail of his work can be tiring and bottom-heavy. But in the late '60s, when camp-weary fans were hungering for a new "seriousness" in comics, when the simple pop graphics of the TV *Batman* had become a symbol of everything that was baleful in the world's perception of comics, he was the messiah.

As a letters page later revealed, "Deadman was *intended* to appeal to the sophisticated and alert reader." It did. In his first letters page Miller wrote, "Deadman has literally opened the floodgates to a torrent of fan letters that is smashing all records around the DC offices" (*SA* 209, Feb. 1968). Marv Wolfman, a superfan already angling to write comics, wrote, "After having read comics for over sixteen years, I can honestly say that Deadman is, without a doubt, the greatest character I have ever seen. . . . Never did I expect such an adult theme in a comic mag." Joyce Wakefield offered, "*Deadman* is an example of what *can* be done." No less than Jerry Bails's wife, Jean, wrote to say that she'd been an inconvertible Marvel fan until *Deadman*: "For one who has 'faced front,' I've been turned around." And Adams's art, they all agreed, was "tremendous," "startling," "realistic." The powers-that-be were happy to concur. Adams was allowed to write some issues himself, and got credit for it when Miller and others sometimes didn't. When one fan lamented that the first issue hadn't been worthy of what followed, the editorial response was, "The first *Deadman* was drawn by Carmine Infantino . . . one of the 'big guns' in our field. Be kind to him . . . everyone can't be Neal Adams!" As pianist John Lewis said of the first major concert by jazz revolutionary Charlie Parker, "He made everybody else look like old men."

In one stroke DC had leapfrogged over Marvel, abandoning adolescent fantasy to grasp at adult adventure—even if "adult" only meant a supernatural spin on TV's *The Fugitive*. It had stolen the hearts of hard-core fandom from Lee and Kirby. It was a triumph, marred by only one little disappointment. It didn't sell. Three issues after Deadman premiered, *Strange Adventures* was cut back from monthly to bimonthly. Seven issues later (*SA* 216, Feb. 1969), it was canceled. The older fans were noisy, but it looked like there just weren't enough of them. *Superman* was still the backbone of the company.

DC didn't retreat into juvenility, however. *Deadman* had shown writers, artists, and editors "what *can* be done," and they weren't ready to give up on it. Neal Adams was assigned to nearly all the covers in the Superman line, DC's cash cow. He would soon rework the Spectre into a more atmospheric style, recast Green Arrow as a goateed hipster, and then redesign Batman himself. One gets the impression that DC's editors would have liked nothing better than a whole army of Neal Adamses, even if their best-selling comic was still drawn by Curt Swan.

The old guys were getting nervous. Even before the Deadman/Adams bombshell, Marvel and fandom were sending the message that the DC style just wasn't cutting it anymore. Gardner Fox and Otto Binder were fifty-six years old in 1967, and their cohorts weren't far behind them. Their thoughts inevitably drifted to questions of retirement and security. As with Kirby, too, there was the money thing. National's owners had made a ton off the Batman craze, and the editors had probably seen some bonuses, but for freelancers it was just page rate, page rate, page rate. Those freelancers had always been isolated, working out of their homes and often going months without bumping into each other. But 1967 was a year in which trod-upon Americans were pulling together to air their grievances, and suddenly, in a remarkable show of solidarity, nearly the entire DC writing staff— Fox, Binder, Arnold Drake, John Broome, Bob Haney, Ed Herron, Bill Finger, and Dave Wood—started talking about a union. They wanted some ownership of their creations, or at least some kind of retirement or health plan, and some recourse from the abuse of Mort Weisinger. Drake and Haney went to Irwin Donenfeld—whom Haney called "a terribly stingy little man"—but Donenfeld tried a divide-and-conquer stunt, telling them that he'd give out dollar-a-page raises but to only one writer at a time, starting with Haney. They went over his head to Jack Liebowitz, but after some condescending paternalism—"I'm very sympathetic. . . . When I was a young man, I was a Socialist too!" (said Drake: "The problem was that Liebowitz had a youth of twenty minutes")—Liebowitz said he'd have to refer it to his lawyers. Knowing they were being stalled, the writers started talking about a strike. To have any clout, however, they knew they needed artists in their corner. After all, anyone can write a fight scene and stick some words in it—all those young guys doing the fanzines, to name a few hundred—and maybe the little kids wouldn't notice for a while. But bad art by scabs would jump out from the cover.

The trouble was, management knew how to play writers and artists against each other. Artists were paid a little better, and no one had been complaining about DC's art nearly as loudly as they had been about the writers and their fab, gear, go-go, kooky, camp attempts to keep up with the times. A lot of the artists were a little younger—having started in the postwar boom days, whereas most of the writers went back to the prewar pulps—and maybe they weren't yet as frightened of the future. Anyway, what artist could really feel loyal to the guy who made him draw crowd scenes and cities and giant living jukeboxes when what he really wanted to draw was a beautiful dame and a tough guy throwing a punch? Only one artist joined up: Binder's friend Kurt Schaffenberger. Drake tried to woo Infantino, knowing that where he went others would follow. But Infantino said, "I'm sorry, but I'm on the other side." The unofficial "cover editor" already saw himself as management.

123

Then, before the writers could pick another course, it all came apart. Binder's daughter was hurt in a car wreck, and he had to bail out. Drake went to London on personal business. Broome was already living in France, able to contribute less and less. Herron's fragile health broke. Finger's drinking was destroying him. Fox was losing his clout as Julius Schwartz became increasingly unhappy with his work and started looking for replacements. The writers had some editorial support, but not from the right places. Jack Schiff backed them at first, but after years of having his workload jerked around, his favorite projects taken from him, he was all out of enthusiasm. When Liebowitz refused to create an "educational office" even in the flush Bat-days, Schiff knew it was hopeless. In 1967 he retired to political activity and philosophical writings. Jack Miller, who'd been a writer longer than an editor, left after contracting cancer. George Kashdan proved to be the writers' biggest advocate—and suddenly he was fired, officially because his titles weren't doing well enough. Kanigher was shifting back to freelance writing. Schwartz and Boltinoff either didn't want to fight or didn't know what was happening. (Schwartz has denied that there ever was a writers' uprising.) That left Mort Weisinger, of whom Haney said, "He was buddies with Jack Liebowitz.... He despised writers, he despised artists." In 1968 the movement dissolved. After a while, some of the participants began to notice that they were getting fewer script assignments.

Irwin Donenfeld had the last laugh. *Doom Patrol*'s late shift from campiness back to darkness had not been enough to save it, and the series was ordered canceled. In the last issue, Drake redeemed it with a finale as unconventional and disturbing as the series' beginning. The Brotherhood of Evil lures the heroes to a desert island and tries to break their wills by offering them a deal: they'll live if they approve the murder of fourteen innocent, ordinary, "useless" people. But the Doom Patrol, defenders of the damaged and outcast, will not submit, and the Brotherhood torpedoes the island, killing them all. It

was a grand moment, and fitting that the three "freaks" who had survived their respective tragedies to lead second lives as superheroes should be the first titular heroes actually to die on the comic book page. Yet, there was a very DC gimmick to it: on the final page, Drake had Premiani draw the writer and artist themselves looking out at the readers, asking them to write in and beg for the Doom Patrol to be returned to life and publication. Donenfeld saw it, and in a last shot at the uppity writer, he demanded that Drake and Premiani's pictures be erased and Murray Boltinoff's substituted. And that's how Arnold Drake's last DC series ended (*DP* 121, Oct. 1968).

If National's bosses seemed unconcerned at the discontent of their writers, it may have been because they had other things on their minds. A phenomenon like "Batmania" attracts bigger players than the Wham-Os and Tower Books of the world. The discovery that DC comics meant big money brought the investors sniffing around. To Liebowitz and the Donenfeld family, it looked like a good time to sell. The TV *Batman* was canceled after only two and a half years on the air, and a lot of kids were finding comics boring in the way that only last year's fad can be. And inflation was pushing up paper and printing costs, threatening another price increase that might scare the readers. Only an idiot would pass up a good buyout offer to risk enduring anything like the '50s again. Thus, in early 1968, the deal was complete: National Periodical Publications and Independent News were absorbed into Kinney National Service, a company with an obscure financial background tied into the New York City building trades. It had grown rich on funeral homes and parking garages, and now its owners were looking to diversify into the rather more glamorous communications industry. Its charismatic leader was a forty-one-year-old whiz named Steve Ross, a name straight out of the comic books (although back in Brooklyn he'd been Steve Rechnitz, a name that would've been more at home in the credits). His mode of operation was to hire smart executives, offer them big incentives, and then back them up and let them run their own show until they forced him to do otherwise.

Ross didn't know comics, and he didn't seem to care much how the business ran. He had his eye on buying Warner Bros., and saw DC mainly as just a valuable source of properties. So when it came to picking a smart executive, he left it up to the man who'd kept National afloat for so long: Jack Liebowitz. Irwin Donenfeld was taking the money and running, but Liebowitz wanted to remain publisher for two years to groom his successor as editorial director. There were a couple of obvious choices: Schwartz and Weisinger. But Schwartz just liked to tend his own garden, do the comics he cared about, and then go home to play pinochle with his wife and the Besters. And Weisinger? Well, he'd just had an adventure on a red sun planet of his own: a nervous breakdown.

If Mort loved anything, it was control. He'd worked himself half to death making sure he maintained it over his seven comic books, and now maybe the changing times, the new forces in the market, the apparent lunacy of America's new youth, were just too much to handle. In psychotherapy, he said later, he discovered that he'd been identifying dangerously with his alter ego, Superman. His detractors would have howled at the thought of the "malevolent toad" as the clean-cut defender of Earth, but for Weisinger this Kryptonian Moses, this great Jewish hero disguised as an office shlub—struggling to fill the hopes of a lost father, watching for threats from his Fortress of Solitude, terrified of the weakness that lay buried wherever chunks of his shattered childhood world had struck, his loss and grief shrunken into a bottle from which he could never release them, straining to maintain the order of the whole world with his power—he'd become Weisinger's soul, and it was too much for a mere Earthling to carry. Could he have been wrestling, too, with some shame that he fell so far short of the Mensh of Steel, that he never allowed his people even the dignity that Clark allowed Jimmy—or do we just wish it were so? Whatever was happening inside Mort, the outside results were clear: he cut back his workload, handing *Superboy* to Boltinoff and surrendering more and more workaday details to E. Nelson Bridwell. Surrendering, however, was not Weisinger's way, and he still couldn't do anything halfway. Retirement had to come soon.

The reasoning is clear in hindsight, but at the time there were few people in the comic book business who weren't shocked to hear that Liebowitz had given the job of editorial director to Carmine Infantino. Here was the august giant of the business, with its tradition of hiring pulp editors and literary agents as editors, handing the reigns to a freelance artist. But this artist was a New York Italian of the old school, the school of debts and *padróni*—"not a bad guy," said Bob Haney, "[but] he was very beholden to Jack Liebowitz, he was loyal to Jack Liebowitz . . . loyal to those kinds of old principles that were not even principles, they were just rotten paternalism, and did not work very well for anybody, including the paternals." In the old school of National, loyalty was rewarded. In the spring of 1967, Infantino was drawing the Flash fighting the Mirror Master for Julie Schwartz. In the spring of 1968, he was Julie Schwartz's boss.

One of his first acts was ending the assorted payola and double-dipping schemes that had become part of the business of comics. The new owners loved him for that. A more pleasant job was filling the editorial void left by the losses of Schiff, Kashdan, Miller, and Kanigher. He may not have been a friend to writers, but he soon proved to be one to artists. Maybe it wasn't just that he was an artist himself. He must have known how much creative direction Kirby and Ditko had given Marvel, and of course there was Giordano, whom Donenfeld had already been wooing over from Charlton. In any case, his choices had résumés. His fellow Schwartz veteran Mike Sekowsky had shown some brains and creativity in his Tower work. Joe Orlando had helped Jim Warren and Wally Wood set up *Eerie*, and Joe Kubert knew the war comics as well as Bob Kanigher. All the new editors—taking their cues from Marvel, from *Deadman*, and from Giordano's work at Charlton—worked aggressively to bring to DC a tone of realism

125

So much promise: Steve Ditko had never been better than when he launched his first DC title. He would never again be this inspired. (*Beware The Creeper* #1, June 1968.)

fruitful at Charlton, and it looked like it might pay big dividends.

Ditko's first DC creation, the Creeper, carried echoes of both the Question and Spider-Man: a hard-boiled journalist who terrifies criminals and police alike with a demonic yellow costume (*Showcase* 73, Apr. 1968). With a complex supporting cast and a many-faced villain called Proteus, this was a seeming return to Ditko of the Marvel years. Denny O'Neil's scripting was solid and tough, and soon enough he was even willing to have his real name put in the credits. Ditko's next creation went straight for the social issues of the time. Two superheroic brothers are radical extremes: the Hawk believes that force is the only effective tool of justice, while the Dove says that "violence only begets more violence" (*Showcase* 75, June 1968). They argue constantly about the rightness of violence, calling each other "coward" or "witless barbarian." The stories seemed slanted somewhat toward the Dove—at least after Steve Skeates applied his dialogue, with a sly tone that mocked the Hawk. A close look at the plot and the drawings, however, suggests that Ditko saw at least equal virtue in the Hawk, willing to repel "irrational" violence with "rational" violence. Giordano, politically left of center himself, let Skeates's scripts go through. For Ditko, it was a betrayal. He quit as soon as he saw the dialogue. Gil Kane contributed some of his most energetic action art to the next four issues, but the now overtly liberal bias lacked texture. The subtext of Ditko's and Skeates's "collaboration" made a more interesting comment on the national dialogue of the time than anything either of them did intentionally.

Ditko's dissatisfaction with his collaborators soon spread to *Beware the Creeper*, as well, and he quit after the fifth issue. Infantino pulled the plug on it and *The Hawk and the Dove*. Ditko went back to *Mr. A* and paid his bills by drawing Joe Gill horror stories at Charlton. From then on, he left his politics in his self-published work, reducing his commercial work to simple adventure. He would always be a skilled and distinctive illustrator, but the late '60s had

and a keen attention to character. Most of all, they experimented as no one had done since the desperate early days of Lee, Kirby, and Ditko. Under them, new kinds of heroes, even new genres, were created, and old ones were recast in a completely new light. Infantino may have felt loyal to the old guard, but obviously not to the old DC.

Giordano looked like the greatest catch at first, because in addition to his own creative energy and motivational skills, he brought the best of his free-lancers: Denny O'Neil, Steve Skeates, Jim Aparo, Pat Boyette, and Steve Ditko himself. Giordano rejected National's philosophy of editorial control, sticking to the hands-off style that had been so

fragmented the Ditko that was. He would never again be a creative force in comics, would never again combine art, theme, and plot with the unparalleled power he once had.

While Ditko was launching his two series, Giordano kept scouting new talent. E. Nelson Bridwell, Frank Springer, and Jack Sparling turned in *The Secret Six,* a gutsy riff on TV's *Mission Impossible,* in which a mystery-man blackmails six mismatched people into taking on cases of international intrigue (May 1968). It was good but only lasted seven issues.

Giordano also played out the string on *Blackhawk, Bomba, Spectre,* and *Deadman,* all doomed to cancellation. He took over *The Teen Titans* but was unable to give it a direction or a steady creative team, due to Infantino's "constant interference," he said for the anxious new editorial director was having trouble keeping his hands off. He revitalized *Aquaman* — CBS had spun it into a Saturday morning cartoon, but it was a measure of Infantino and Giordano's beliefs in their aesthetics that the new version never even flirted with the fish and octopus stunts that made the hero work on TV. Steve Skeates and Jim Aparo launched the Sea King on a richly tapestried, suspenseful quest to save his abducted wife. With that adventure concluded, though, things became a little disjointed. The individual stories displayed the same verve, but the series seemed headed nowhere.

None of the ambitious new superheroes, in fact, seemed headed anywhere. The question began to be heard: were superheroes dying? It was a reasonable one. Every veteran had seen the cycles come and go—superheroes, crime, horror, superheroes again—and fully expected that the wheel would eventually turn again and readers would tire of capes and cowls. The post-*Batman* slump could have been the first sign, and the continued success of Jim Warren's horror magazines an indicator of where the future might lie.[1] Infantino hired Joe Orlando—with his *Mad* and horror résumé—specifically to develop nonsuperhero material. He took over *House of Mystery,* dropping *Dial H for Hero*

and *Martian Manhunter* to remake the magazine in the dark, eerie cast of EC and Warren (although the Comics Code still didn't permit any real blood or nastiness, making it all rather pallid). It being an anthology series, Orlando was able to turn it into a testing ground for new talent, especially talent that would have been considered wrong for DC's heroes, like those new EC-influenced fan artists, Mike Kaluta and Berni Wrightson.

Next Orlando moved on to new titles, trying to break new ground and to revive genres forgotten in the shadow of the heroes. *Anthro,* by newspaper strip veteran Howie Post, was the appealing story of "a lusty young man of prehistory," (Aug. 1968). It was canceled after issue 6. *Bat Lash,* DC's first Western since the 1950s, was plotted by *Mad* cartoonist Sergio Aragonés, scripted by Denny O'Neil, and gorgeously drawn by Nick Cardy. The protagonist, owing a debt to TV's *Maverick,* walked the line between hero and scoundrel, bringing some of the character-driven quality of the new superheroes into the Western genre. This was the pinnacle of the new DC aesthetic. And it lasted only seven issues.

DC tried two toy tie-ins: *Captain Action,* drawn and partly written by Gil Kane, showing how artist-friendly the new DC was (Nov. 1968); and *Hot Wheels,* with some of the most glorious art in years by Alex Toth (Apr. 1970). Both died quickly. Some creations were tested in *Showcase* in 1968 and 1969, but never graduated to their own comics: *Johnny Double,* a private detective story; *The Dolphin,* the tale of an odd, water-breathing woman; *The Nightmaster,* a sword-and-sorcery saga; and *Firehair,* about a half-breed Indian, featuring some of the finest art ever turned in by Joe Kubert.

Then there was Mike Sekowsky. Jack Miller had just begun to oversee dramatic revamps of *Wonder Woman* and *Metal Men* when he left DC and Sekowsky ended up drawing both. In the first, Denny O'Neil had the Amazons run out of magic and leave the Earth, and Wonder Woman renounce her powers and costume, quit the Justice League, and study with an Asian martial arts master named (alas) I Ching

[1] Although, confoundingly, Warren was finally starting to play with superhero-like material, launching a costumed vampire-heroine called Vampirella in 1969.

(*WW* 179, Dec. 1968; *JLA* 69, Feb. 1969). Then Sekowsky took over the editing and writing, and the amazing Amazon took over a boutique to sell mod clothes of Sekowsky's own bizarre design (*WW* 182, June 1969). In the late '40s Big Mike had been Stan Lee's main man for teenage girl humor comics, with a nice touch for fashion and femme fluff. Now he was just another DC guy who was going to find out how much the world had really changed in twenty years. This was like a superhero version of *That Girl* with a twist of Emma Peel and although it had a goofy charm, all its own, it sent male fans screaming for the hills and failed to captivate many girls.

The "New Hunted Metal Men," who had become persecuted outcasts under Miller, were now outfitted by Sekowsky with human appearances and faddish secret identities: folksinger, artist, tycoon, and engineer. Tina, of course, was a fashion model. *Metal Men* was canceled (41, Jan. 1970), so Sekowsky took a shot at *Supergirl*, where again his emphasis was on frequent changes of wardrobe—in this case, the Girl of Steel's costume—each change weirder than the last (with *Adventure* 397, Sept. 1970). He also created a pair of new concepts, a *Then Came Bronson* motorcycle riff called *Jason's Quest* (*Showcase* 88-90, Feb.-June 1970) and a science fiction adventure, *Manhunter 2070* (*Showcase* 91-93, Aug.-Dec. 1970). Nothing took.

Murray Boltinoff, the only old Schiff associate to survive the purge of '67-'68, tried hard to swim with the new tide. He pumped more action into *Superboy* and knocked about twenty years off Ma and Pa Kent's ages, evidently fearing that young readers wouldn't trust any foster parents over sixty. He turned *Challengers of the Unknown*'s direction back toward its original, slightly supernatural conception, it was canceled in 1970. Boltinoff brought Kanigher and artist Frank Thorne in to revamp *Tomahawk* as a mature, realistic Western, but it soon passed to the editorship of Joe Kubert. He revived an old hard-boiled strip called *Johnny Peril*, with Sparling art, in *Unexpected* (107, July 1968), but it soon vanished. Boltinoff then followed Orlando's example in revamping *Unexpected* as a 1950s-style "mystery" anthology.

The other DC launch of the period had an even shorter life. Orlando brought out *Brother Power, the Geek*, Joe Simon's return to comic books after nearly a decade. The story of a living bundle of rags that purported to tell the truth about the underworld of hippies and "flower power," it was a weird and embarrassing attempt to tune in to the youth culture of the times, and the most vivid sign yet that the veterans of the business were falling out of step with American kids—or at least a nervous editor could read it as such. For whatever reason, it was killed after two issues, before sales reports could even have been compiled. "Poor sales" is always the excuse for the comic book cancellations, but the new DCs were so short-lived, without one exception, that some observers wondered if Infantino intended them as nothing but finite market tests—unannounced "miniseries" before such existed.

No one ever knew quite what Infantino was up to, because although he came across as a regular guy in the office, he was no babbler. He hid his thoughts behind a mask of aloofness, of old-country *lontananza*, and his decision-making process was mysterious and seemingly arbitrary. The result was the beginning of a perception that still brands the Infantino administration: great starts but little follow-through. It began to seem that, for an editorial director, Infantino had little direction.

One thing was clear: setting the old guys free to experiment had produced an explosion of exciting comics, but no commercial successes. Editors started looking harder at the fans who wanted to write, giving assignments to Len Wein, Mary Wolfman, and Mike Friedrich. Bob Haney quoted Orlando as saying, "I won't work with anybody over the age of thirty-five." A generational shift was shaking the freelance community.

Blaming the old guys may not have been fair. There had been a price increase from twelve to fifteen cents, a full twenty-five percent, the boredom with *Batman* was extending to other superheroes, as well, and the economy was in a state of "stagflation" now that the artificial boost of the Vietnam War was getting old. Many store owners were abandoning comics in favor of higher yield-per-unit items that could occupy the same space. Even such stalwarts as the *Atom* and *Hawkman* had vanished in a general reduction of titles at DC, while all the new publishers of the mid-'60s boom had folded, ACG along with them. Gold Key, Charlton, Archie, and Harvey were cutting back on their titles, abandoning superheroes in favor of their familiar horror, funny animals, and humor. From 1964 to 1969 the number of comics titles published annually dropped by a full third, from about 300 to 200, and the next year would drop below 200 for the first time since 1941.

Infantino's first year in charge had been an exciting but confusing one. The field seemed suddenly flushed with a recognition of its expanding horizons. Creators were taking greater pride than ever in their artistry, encouraged by Infantino's new policy of giving credits in all DC comics. With old editors leaving and new ones rising from the ranks of the artists, the creative impetus was shifting from the offices to the freelancers. DC was going after the fans. "The Wonderful World of Comics" was now a regular feature in DC's pages, plugging fan events as well as DC's own projects. A giant-sized comic called *DC Special* reprinted high-quality work in fan-targeted groupings. The new boss made the first one, with a show of the true artist's bravado, an "All Infantino Issue." Yet nothing aimed specifically at older readers, nothing that broke the Batman-Superman mold, was finding enough buyers to survive. Marvel was still gaining.

The editors may have been getting panicky, but not Infantino. Behind that mask of his, he had a plan. He had his sights on Jack Kirby.

CHAPTER 19

THE MARVEL EXPANSION

It was a wild time for Stan Lee. Cousin Martin Goodman was unchained again, and he wanted more superhero product in a hurry. At the same time, Stan was eating up the adoration of college kids, making the lecture circuit almost a second job, and fielding overtures from the movie and publishing worlds.[1] Maybe he can be forgiven for failing to comprehend either the nature or the depth of Jack Kirby's discontent.

A new Marvel creative staff was already developing. Roy Thomas began to hit his stride when he took the helm of *The Avengers* with issue 35 (Dec. 1966). Here he showed that he could invest more of himself than just his passion for research, heightening the conflicts between the characters and deepening their emotional turmoil, pushing them even further than Lee had. Hawkeye remained the group's rebel but now revealed reasons for his ambivalence—especially the torch he carried for the beautiful Russian spy named the Black Widow, who was now turning against her old country. Shortly afterward, Thomas introduced the Red Guardian, a proud Soviet counterpart of Captain America, who proved to be the Widow's estranged husband. Although the Guardian's goal is to destroy Captain America, ultimately he gives his life to prevent an unconscious Cap from being blown up by a cowardly Russian officer. In the aftermath, the Widow must make peace with her memories and old loyalties, Cap must live with the knowledge that he owes his life to the enemy of his country, and Hawkeye must learn to submerge his pride in his love for the Widow (*Avengers* 43-44, Aug.-Sept. 1967). In such towering dilemmas, Thomas brought an air of profundity to

Marvel melodrama. He pushed Lee's scripting style another few notches, using a flowery self-importance that underlined his serious intentions ("Never, accursed one," cries the Guardian at his death, "not till the heavens crumble, shall Captain America be killed by one so craven as you!"). Philosophical conversations and literary references—a whole page quoting Shelley's *Ozymandias*—gave collegiate readers something to chew on, and an increasingly learned tone in the letter pages suggested that such readers were taking notice.

Thomas used Goliath and the Wasp to try his hand at some heavy marital drama, culminating in a nervous breakdown that caused Goliath to take a new identity, Yellowjacket, and to temporarily turn against his teammates (*Avengers* 59, Dec. 1968). He brought the Black Panther from his fanciful Kirby kingdom to the tense streets of New York. Stan and Jack had broken taboos by bringing Gabe Jones and the Panther into comics, and now Roy wasn't going to back down from the next challenge: he had the Panther clashing with racists, had characters arguing racial issues on the comic book page, and sparked a debate among black and white readers in the letter columns. The writing was a little clunky, the stories a little evasive, but Thomas was pulling comics into the scary heart of the angry American dialogue, where no comics had dared to go since the Comics Code destroyed EC.

The character the fans fell in love with was a new one, an android called the Vision who was somehow given human memories and, as a consequence, human feelings. He agonizes about his true nature, especially after he learns that his brain waves were taken—in a distinctly Thomas twist—from those of

[1] The most intriguing of which, at least to us, was a proposed collaboration with the filmmaker Alain Resnais, and what a tragedy that it never came through. Surely the product of those two minds—*Yancy Street Mon Amour?*—would have been among the most bizarre, not to mention the most God-awful, products of the cultural revolution of the 1960s.

that forgotten, dead one-shot character called Wonder Man. His brain, he notes, "is not truly a brain at all, but a maze of printed circuits . . . . I wonder . . . is it possible to be . . .'basically human'?" The Avengers reassure him of his humanity and welcome him to their ranks, drawing a tear from his synthetic eye and, thus, the title of the story: "Even an Android Can Cry!" (*Avengers* 58, Nov. 1968). What a metaphor for teenagers struggling with the "plastic world" and their own authenticity. What a metaphor for repressed young comics fans whom the world ignores but who know what loves and agonies churn in their own hearts.

With the origin of the Vision, Thomas showed himself in possession of imagination, emotional force, and plotting talent, well able to bring life to his bibliographic mastery of comics. Although the Vision's confusion was eventually to break down into self-pity (particularly in an interminably frustrated romance with the Scarlet Witch that would drag on for more than a decade), and his tragic alienation was to be badly overused, his early appearances brought a new weight to comic book characterization. Thomas, like Lee before him, overstated his themes to get them across, often to the point of mawkishness. But the popularity of *The Avengers* proved that the superhero genre and its audience were capable of concepts far more ambitious and intelligent than the previous generation had ever thought.

Thomas was aided on *The Avengers* by the arrival, soon after his own, of penciler John Buscema. Buscema had been one of Lee's favorite young pencilers in the early 1950s, but he had left comics during their shaky years for the more secure field of advertising. Now he unveiled a bold, masculine style, heavy on thickly muscled characters in dramatic poses. "Michelangelesque," Lee called it. Fans were thrilled by the huge, baroquely twisted hands and anguished facial features that he drew to give impact to Thomas's emotional scenes. He also helped Thomas—although Roy may not have seen it that way—by stripping his panels down to one or two figures, usually leaving out background characters alto-

"...EVEN AN ANDROID CAN ...CRY!"

gether, keeping his scripter from going overboard with the dialogue. In short order, reportedly at Lee's urging, he began incorporating Kirby's action techniques into his art, combining the best of Marvel's melodrama and fisticuffs.

Thomas and Buscema were institutionalizing the Marvel style, distilling Lee, Kirby, and Ditko's work into one vision, addictive to older fans but still compelling for little kids. Both sales and letters suggested that this was the path of the future. But in 1966 and '67 Lee could still be seduced by the new and untested. Jim Steranko had been a carnival pitchman, stage magician, escape artist, guitar player, and most

John Buscema combined the power of Kirby with the naturalism and fluidity of the elegant DC artists to give a new sense of weightiness and emotional depth. Here he makes the Vision a star. Inks by George Klein, script by Roy Thomas. (*The Avengers* #58, Nov. 1968.)

131

recently, advertising artist. Coolly arrogant, wickedly handsome, surmounted by a grand pompadour and soon noted for appearing at comic conventions with voluptuous and exotic women, he was a self-made '60s playboy, a master of flash and misdirection in his persona and his art, a kind of working class Orson Welles. The Pop Art glamour of Batmania had drawn him to comics, and almost immediately he'd sold Spyman and other ill-fated characters to Harvey. With an eye for pop culture and a genius for learning anything in an instant, he saw that Marvel was the place to be and mastered a glitzy imitation of Kirby's style. According to Steranko, Lee was bowled over by his first glimpse of his pages, saying, "We don't have anything for you, but you're too good to get away." He started Steranko penciling and inking details inside Kirby's layouts on *Nick Fury, Agent of S.H.I.E.L.D.*, and as Kirby cut back his workload, Lee gave him the whole series to write and draw himself (with *ST* 155, Apr. 1967).

"Everything," said the new hot-shot, "from films, from radio, pulps, business, everything I could possibly apply from my background, including the magic I've done, the gigs I've played—everything goes into every comic story. Nick Fury became Steranko." Indeed, Fury quickly became slimmer, younger, and far more suave, cavorting with women straight off the covers of *Vogue* in some of the most slyly explicit pre- and postcoital scenes anyone had ever managed to slip past the Comics Code. Steranko exaggerated the series' spy-movie elements into an uninhibited, slightly facetious, James Bond-style romp, arming his agents with devices like the vortex beam (lifting objects through space), the aphonic bomb (exploding without sound), a pocket-sized electronic absorber (conveniently on hand to save Fury from electrocution), and a molecular disintegrator called the Q-ray —and that was all in his first story. The stories were high-speed blasts of technological combat, often jumbled and hard to follow, but written with a downplayed campiness that always let us know the writer was above this stuff, doing comics for kicks.

What truly blew the minds of fandom, though, wasn't Steranko's writing but his art. His draftsmanship wasn't perfect, and his anatomy and perspective were sometimes just downright *off*. But drawing from the psychedelic fashions of the moment, with a training in '60s graphic design that no older comics artist had, he gave his pages a visual punch like comics had never seen. Nearly every page was a tilt-a-whirl of action-crowded panels and flashy effects. Bodies hurtled and twisted around swirling conglomerations of machinery with an abandon that would have given Kirby pause. Like Neal Adams, his one contemporary, Steranko brought the same inventiveness to the layout of an entire page. The two relative youngsters— Steranko turned twenty-nine and Adams twenty-six the year they both exploded onto the scene—fed off each other's energy and competition. (In his last *Deadman* issue, Adams even drew some psychedelic rays that, if squinted at just right, spelled, "Hey, a Jim Steranko effect") Steranko used Kirby-style collages and op-art backgrounds that, to comics fans who weren't terribly hip to the hot New York design trends, looked revolutionary. He even insisted on controlling the coloring of his work, an aspect of comic book production that even the best artists usually took for granted. And he also claims credit for getting Marvel to drop the heavy use of gray, which dragged its art down so badly in earlier years.

No comics artist had ever been so concerned with the *whole* of the package, from story to layout to production to those covers of his that looked more like posters. With his diverse talents, Steranko could approach comics on his own terms, and he did so with a vengeance. "If you're a publisher, and you want my work," he said, "you get it my way or you don't get it at all." Of Marvel, he said, "We had disagreements about the way I told stories . . . and if I had to sit there and put a lot of Steranko blood, sweat, and tears into it . . . I felt that at least I had the right to say, 'No, you're not going to do this to my work.'" Lee said that Steranko " . . . would take forever to do a page, and you know what our schedule is. And I used to say, 'For Christ's sake, work faster! So don't put as much work in it!' And he couldn't care less about deadlines. He did it his way." Interestingly, Neal Adams was also beginning to develop a reputation for stretching his deadlines in the name of quality. A new attitude was being born. But as long as Steranko and Adams stayed one step ahead of the publication schedule, and as long as fans kept calling them geniuses, editors would do their best to cope.

Stan, on the other hand, seemed to be coasting. He did launch a *Mad*-imitative humor comic full of Marvel in-jokes called *Brand Ecch*, a clever way to use the camp craze for self-promotion instead of self-embarrassment, as DC was doing (Aug. 1967). With art by Jack Kirby, Gene Colan, Bill Everett, and others, it was a must-buy even for Marvelites uneasy with its echoes of Bat-humor, and it survived until a full year after the TV *Batman* was gone. Lee also converted *Fantasy Masterpieces* into *Marvel Super-Heroes*, a *Showcase*-style venue for new heroes. Expecting it to appeal to older readers looking for new thrills, and knowing that the profit margin on a twenty-five-cent comic was higher than on a twelve-center, Lee and Goodman kept it as a giant-size with reprint backups. It started strongly enough that *Brand Ecch* (called *Not Brand Ecch* by then) was converted to the same format. Lee created the first hero himself: having learned from Milton Fass's abortive *Captain Marvel* that that trademark was up for grabs, he gave his comics group its own namesake. This Captain Marvel, however, was really Mar-Vell, a noble warrior-scientist of the alien Kree, stranded on Earth by a scheming officer who coveted the Captain's beloved (*MSH* 12, Dec. 1967). Drawn by Colan and leanly written by Lee, the story was an instant hit. But when it came time to give the Captain his own comic, Lee gave the job to Roy Thomas.

On *Spider-Man* Lee continued Peter Parker's collegiate soap opera, but without the complexity or relentless change Ditko had given it. Many early villains returned for a few stories, but new menaces, such as a huge, petulant crime czar called the Kingpin, were less satisfying. It's hard to blame Lee, though. Despite a repetitiveness in the stories (Aunt

May's periodic bouts with death were becoming almost laughable), John Romita's breezy art and Lee's ability to keep his hero charming were continuing to push up sales. *Spider-Man* slipped ahead of *Fantastic Four* to become Marvel's best-seller.

Daredevil, except for Gene Colan's breathtaking art, never quite outgrew the shadow of Spider-Man. *Dr. Strange* was still blessed with lovely art by Bill Everett, Marie Severin, and Dan Adkins, who used the polished style he'd learned from Wally Wood. The writing, unfortunately, was only sporadically imaginative, as Lee repeatedly called for hasty pinch-hit jobs from Denny O'Neil, Raymond Marais, Jim Lawrence, and Roy Thomas. Lee turned *Sub-Mariner*

Like wow. Jim Steranko brings the late '60s to comics and fans begin to dream of real-world legitimacy. Dialogue by himself, inks by Joe Sinnott. (*Strange Tales* #167, Apr. 1968.)

133

"Jazzy" Johnny Romita strips down the art and the subtext of Spider-Man, makes it Marvel's best-selling title, and points the way to a new mainstream look. (*Amazing Spider-Man* #68, Jan. 1969.)

over to Thomas, who—with some issues by Everett, the character's creator—continued Lee's brand of gladiator battle (*TA* 93, July 1967). In *The Hulk*, Lee continued to play with his themes of alienation and persecution, with art by John Buscema and Gil Kane, and then Marie Severin, once the ace colorist at EC where her brother John had been a star penciler and inker. Now Marie proved to have a sensitive, naturalistic style of her own, which made the Hulk less awe-inspiring but far more sympathetic (with *TA* 92, June 1967). Sometimes her brother inked for her—or she inked his pencils—but usually she worked with Herb

Trimpe, a rookie artist with an organic, cartoony line that he would soon transfer to his own pencils. Trimpe and fellow inker John Verpoorten had both apprenticed under Tom Gill, a veteran Western/Gold Key artist, but when they went out on their own, they both went to Marvel. The comics world was narrowing to two hot publishers and a few also-rans.

By 1968 Lee was able to attract veteran writers, and he lured two of the smartest and ablest of them all. Archie Goodwin started pinch-hitting frequently, making his first forays into superhero writing. It was apparent that the genre wasn't his favorite or his best, although he did contribute a good set of stories when he stuck somewhat to reality and had Iron Man battle Marvel's regular crime syndicate, the "Maggia" (*TS* 99-*IM* 1, Mar.-May 1968). Lee also found Arnold Drake's odd imagination of some value to the Marvel Universe, after the cancellation of his *Doom Patrol* for DC. Drake did a year-long fill-in for Roy Thomas on *X-Men,* creating complex new mutants named Havok and Polaris, as well as a futuristic group called the Guardians of the Galaxy for *Marvel Super-Heroes.* The Guardians included various humans who had evolved to adapt to different planetary conditions, including a massive Jovian named Charlie-27 and a crystalline Plutonian called Martinex (*MSH* 18, Jan. 1969). It was only a one-shot, but it was so deftly written, and so stunningly drawn by Gene Colan, that it stayed in the minds of brighter fans—including the twisted mind of a college kid named Steve Gerber.

It was still rookie Thomas's work on *Avengers* that was thrilling most fans, though, and a lot of them were asking for him to return to *X-Men.* Lee must have seen where the future lay, but if he had any doubt about the need to bring new talent into the field, and fast, it was all swept away by the heady expansion of 1968—and the fiasco of 1969.

First there was a new war comic, *Captain Savage and His Leatherneck Raider*s (Jan. 1968). Then *Tales to Astonish*, *Tales of Suspense*, and *Strange Tales* were split into six separate monthly titles: *The Incredible Hulk* (Apr. 1968), *Captain America* (Apr.

1968), *Iron Man* (May 1968), *Sub-Mariner* (May 1968), *Nick Fury, Agent of S.H.I.E.L.D.* (June 1968), and *Dr. Strange* (June 1968). Meanwhile, *Captain Marvel* got his own series (May 1968).

The fans were thrilled at first, but there were trouble signs right from the start. To have time for *Captain Marvel*, Colan had to leave *Iron Man*. To replace him, Lee found Johnny Craig and then George Tuska, both good artists no longer doing their best work. Goodwin's scripts were pretty good, but not enough. Dan Adkins drew *Dr. Strange* at first, but when he couldn't maintain the monthly pace, Colan was shifted over there, taking him off *Captain Marvel*. Thomas took a very literary and cosmic approach to the doctor's magic, which was very nicely offset by Colan's mysterious art—with the dense, moody inking of Tom Palmer—but it was all a bit esoteric for the average reader. An attempt to make Strange a sort of superhero, complete with leotard and mask (*DS* 177, Feb. 1969), didn't help. *Captain Marvel*, meanwhile, was suffering from changing artists and pinch-hit writing as even Thomas found that there was a limit to the number of hours per day he could write superheroes. All this also screwed up Colan's *Daredevil* schedule, requiring some truly hideous fill-ins by a terribly raw young Kirby imitator named Barry Smith.

The Hulk plodded steadily along, with Herb Trimpe taking over the penciling, and the Sub-Mariner looked good under John Buscema. But Jack Kirby, his enthusiasm for Marvel already destroyed, soon left *Captain America* behind (*CA* 107, Nov. 1968). *Nick Fury, Agent of S.H.I.E.L.D.* started with promise, as Steranko used the new twenty-page format to experiment with some complicated, offbeat single-issue stories, but the sudden doubling of page production turned his deadline troubles into deadline disasters. Lee started pulling in whatever pinch-hitters he could find—Gary Friedrich, Frank Springer, Herb Trimpe, Barry Smith—but Steranko blew his top. All that Steranko blood, sweat, and tears alternating with all that deadline-beating pap? Steranko walked out, pausing just long enough to pay homage

to Kirby with three stylized, disturbing stories for *Captain America* (110, 111, 113; Feb.-May 1969) before leaving Marvel—and comic books—behind.

Lee got to pursue one pet project with *The Spectacular Spider-Man*, a magazine-sized, black-and-white, thirty-five-cent attempt to crash Jim Warren's niche and reach the untapped adult market that Lee was convinced was out there. The first issue (July 1968) flopped, largely because of distribution troubles, and a full-color second issue (Nov. 1968) followed suit. Ultimately, it only served to tax Lee and Romita for a few months.

The last of the new releases of 1968 was also the best, and the one that seemed to have the brightest prospects. It was Stan Lee's favorite and Jack Kirby's heartbreak, *The Silver Surfer*. Here Lee specifically wanted to write for his older readers, with no obligation to hew to the Marvel pattern of fight-driven stories and cliff-hangers. So he had it launched in the twenty-five-cent format, every issue with forty pages of the Surfer drawn by John Buscema and a ten-page science fiction parable called *Tales of the Watcher*, drawn by Colan. All fifty pages would be written by Lee, and here he really seemed to be conceiving and plotting his stories, not just letting his artists carry him along. Working on his beloved "Sentinel of the Spaceways," he was inspired to craft his most eloquent writing. He was obviously striving for poesy, but these stories required no hype or pretense to bring out their thematic force. In the hero's origin story, all the oddity of a shiny alien surfing through the sky disappears in a moving tale of a man losing both love and home, and then renouncing his last possession, his freedom, for a higher principle. "That which is mine for the taking is not worth the taking," he says, in one of many Lee maxims on the purpose of life. "Paradise unearned is but a land of shadows" (*SS* 1, Aug. 1968). Lee brought so much obvious passion to the story that we can almost overlook what it did to Jack Kirby. Lee called it "the most wonderful series I know," and it seemed, indeed, like the culmination of his career as a writer. Buscema kept up with him, turning in some of his own most sweeping landscapes, evocative expressions, and beautiful figures, superbly complemented by the inking of Joe Sinnott and Buscema's own brother, Sal.

The new format, however, didn't work. Apparently not enough fans were willing to cough up a quarter, not even for the apotheosis of Stan Lee. *Marvel Super-Heroes* had already been turned into a reprint series, and *Not Brand Ecch* was canceled. After issue 7, *The Silver Surfer* was cut down to normal size, and the reader could feel Lee's passion ebbing, could feel a personal work turning into just another nicely executed Marvel comic.

Lee had other reasons to lose his focus: in the fall of 1968, cousin Martin sold the company. DC wasn't the only property that looked like a good investment in the wake of Bat-fever, although it was the only one that could attract a player like Steve Ross. Goodman's buyer was the Perfect Film and Chemical Corporation, a low-profile operator in the publishing business, which reorganized Marvel as Magazine Management Corporation. Goodman was staying indefinitely as publisher, but Lee knew the ball game had to be different. Would this give him someone to appeal to when Goodman was being cheap and stubborn, or would it just mean more penny-pinchers holding him back? It's no wonder Stan started boasting about his Hollywood opportunities, even right smack in Stan's Soapbox. He had to see what his value was to his boss's new bosses.

Magazine Management had deep enough pockets to break completely from Independent News and set up business with Curtis Circulation, which would have none of Jack Liebowitz's conflicts of interest. Switching distributors during a market slump and a price increase may have been a bad idea for the short term, though: the casualties started piling up. *Dr. Strange* was canceled after barely more than a year (*DS* 183, Nov. 1969). That freed Colan to try to give some consistency back to *Captain America*, and Thomas to try to save *Captain Marvel*. Roy contributed five issues of clever science fiction ideas, aided by masterful Gil

Kane art, but that proved to be the Captain's finale (*CM* 17-21, Oct. 1969-Aug. 1970).

Thomas returned to the slumping *X-Men*, too, and seemed to be helping it rally—especially since he brought Neal Adams with him (*XM* 56, May 1969). Adams had been tempted into dropping some of his DC work, at least partly by Roy's enthusiasm and his popularity with the fans. Both writer and artist were under thirty, and it must have been fifteen or twenty years since such a thing had happened in the middle-aged world of comics. In 1969, those things mattered. The two Young Turks kicked into a hard-hitting, suspenseful story about the mutant-hunting Sentinels, one of the very few X-Men stories to make full use of the series' implicit theme of persecution, followed by an exotic adventure in a lost jungle world, featuring a rare glimpse into the mind and personality of Magneto (*XM* 57-63, June-Dec. 1969). For fans who'd endured the aimless rambling and ever-shifting personnel of *X-Men* for years, this was *it*: complex character interactions, big adventure, and a harrowing tone of paranoia. And as soon as they'd tasted it, it was snatched from them. After issue 66, the series went all-reprint, and the fans would have to content themselves with years of "bring back the X-Men" letters.

The Steranko-less *Nick Fury* went to reprint and died. Steranko hadn't even stayed in comics long enough to leave any imitators, though his quick flash across the firmament had suggested new storytelling dimensions and inspired a new attitude of cockiness and independence in young artists. Those would prove to be far more lasting gifts to the field than any of the new series launched in those years.

Not even *The Silver Surfer* could survive. In desperation, Lee pressed Kirby into doing an issue to give it a new direction. Kirby's attitude toward the project can be surmised by the fact that he had his embodiment of peace and nobility snap under constant abuse and declare war on the human race (*SS* 18, Sept. 1970). The "new beginning" proved to be the ending, though, and Herb Trimpe's follow-up issue never saw print. It was the most painful cancellation of all for Lee. He never really wrote a comic book with his heart again. He would return to the Surfer only incidentally, and yet he decreed him the only character in the Marvel universe that no other writer was allowed to revive. Fans would beg for the Surfer for a long, long time. It was all too sad and too fitting that the most agonized of heroes, robbed of his star-spanning passion and denied all love and fulfillment, should have brought such pain to both his creators and robbed from them both their passion to create Marvel comics.

The Incredible Hulk, Iron Man, Sub-Mariner, and *Captain America* survived, but none set the world on fire. Marvel finally had a wide-open distribution deal, but now it had holes to fill in its schedule just to get back where it had been. Goodman had always stepped backward in the face of trouble, and so he did now, with a Joe Orlando-style "mystery" anthology, and then dull romance, Western, and kid-humor comics, mostly reprints. When Marvel finally released new superhero series—*Amazing Adventures*, featuring *The Inhumans* and *Black Widow*, and *Astonishing Tales*, with *Ka-Zar* and *Dr. Doom*—they were "split books," a direct return to the format of *Tales to Astonish* and *Tales of Suspense* (Aug. 1970). It was probably under Goodman's pressure that Lee even tried rolling back the clock on the basic Marvel approach to storytelling, ordering everybody—even Kirby—to stick to single-issue stories and to cut down on the continuity. That only knocked sales down further. Lee told Roy Thomas to keep pushing his pet projects, but Stan himself seemed to be hanging back and checking the new territory.

For all this, the worst news Stan got didn't come from his bosses. His old partner Jack had become almost a stranger by then. He'd even moved to California because one of his daughters was suffering from asthma (and, although he didn't tell Stan, he hoped proximity to Hollywood might bring him some of the movie and TV contacts that Stan was boasting about). In that pre-fax, pre-FedEx era, hardly any artists were given work if they lived beyond commuting distance from New York, but Jack was so isolated from Marvel that it didn't much matter. Jack's work wasn't much to think about, either. Not only was he no longer giving anything new to *Thor* or *Fantastic Four*, but by late 1969 his stories had even ceased to be fun in a purely simplistic, action-packed way. Still, Stan was apparently quite unprepared for the phone call he got from Kirby one early March day in 1970. Jack was quitting. Carmine Infantino had made him an offer he couldn't refuse. After eleven years, seven or eight thousand pages, a whole comics line, a whole universe, Kirby was leaving Marvel.

He left a rich legacy behind him, and the fans who were turning professional were eager to play with Kirby's creations themselves as writers and artists. He dug a well that Marvel is still dipping into month after month, issue after issue, a quarter century later, and despite all its best efforts, still hasn't been able to drain dry. He loosed comics from their bonds, setting the art free to explode across the page and the stories free to sprawl across the years. He forced a fundamental change in the relationship of writer and artist. Marvel was still Jack's turf, it always will be. He just wasn't there anymore.

CHAPTER 20

THE END OF THE SILVER AGE

Suddenly they were gone: Carmine, John, Mort, Otto, Gardner, Mike, Sid, Jack, Arnold, Bob, Bill, George, Ramona, Russ, Carl, Richard, Ogden, Al, Steve, Bruno, Edmond, Jerry, Jim, France, Dave, and Wally—the editors and writers and artists who'd given the silver age its shape, its look, its energy. The comic book heroes—vanished in a span of three years.

They weren't all gone from comics, of course. Carmine Infantino's name appeared in the indicia of every DC product, but those beautiful pictures were no more to be found. Arnold Drake, ever versatile, was writing *Little Lulu* for Western and doing a solid job, but he'd never bring his odd sensibility back to superheroes. Some of the big guns were still where they'd been, but things were different. Stan Lee had lost his fire. Julie Schwartz had none of the writers or artists who'd made his stable what it was. Gardner Fox, finally cut loose by Schwartz, was scrounging work here and there, but he wasn't the same. Curt Swan was trying the new, bolder style and cutting back his workload after twenty years of herculean service. Kurt Schaffenberger bounced downward to backups and fill-ins. Gil Kane was doing more work than ever, but now mostly for Marvel, and in that ferocious new style so different from his *Green Lantern*. Murphy Anderson was prominent, but only as an inker, never again as a penciler. Steve Ditko was back on Charlton's horror comics, the next best thing to invisibility. Jack Kirby was rumored to be heading for DC, but no fan could even imagine what that would look like.

Some were decidedly gone. John Broome was in Paris, or India, or Tokyo, teaching English and mas-

tering Zen painting, bowing out with a few odd scripts in 1969 and 1970 that contained hidden references to Wilhelm Reich's radical psychological theories, among other things. Jerry Siegel took on another doomed legal battle with National when Superman's copyright came up for renewal, then fled comics and New York to see if he could find a new life in California. Mort Weisinger had unceremoniously dumped George Papp because he thought he was old-fashioned. Sid Greene was dead, and Bill Finger, France Herron, and George Klein would follow soon.

Even some of the ones brought in to make things new were gone. Dick Giordano found he couldn't work with Infantino, and when *Aquaman* was canceled in 1971, he formed an art studio with Neal Adams and gave up editing. *Teen Titans* wouldn't outlive him for long. After *Wonder Woman* was taken from Mike Sekowsky that same year, Big Mike headed west to work in animation. Jim Shooter retired younger than anybody. He moved to New York to work for Stan Lee, found the city a horrible place for an eighteen-year-old who didn't know anyone, and headed back to Pittsburgh, a "real" job, and perhaps a chance at a normal young adulthood. *The Legion of Super-Heroes*, which had already lost Swan, surrendered *Adventure Comics* to Supergirl and slipped first into backup status in *Action*, then into oblivion. Its fans were left aching.

Mort Weisinger finally retired in 1970. Editor Murray Boltinoff already had *Superboy*, next he got *Action Comics*, and now it appeared the whole Superman family would be carved up among different editors. (Was that really the only practical division of labor, or were Infantino and company specifically trying to avoid a monolith like Mort again?) The writers who might have rejoiced at Weisinger's departure were already gone, or going. Leo Dorfman said good-bye to an era with an epic, maudlin, and heartbreaking Imaginary Story. It was officially overseen by Boltinoff but was all Weisinger in spirit. The Man of Steel grows old and useless, the supertechnological Earth of the future having no need of his powers (*Action* 396-397, Jan.-Feb. 1971). At the end he zooms into space, saying, "Somewhere out there, among the millions of galaxies, there must be a world like the Earth I once knew...a world that still needs a Superman!"

Apart from Lee, the only veteran writers still working on superheroes were Dorfman and Bob Haney, and they worked only for Boltinoff. Rumors persist that National blacklisted all the participants in the writers' rebellion of 1967, but Haney's continued presence suggests that if there was such a list—and Schwartz and Infantino have insisted there wasn't—it wasn't strictly enforced. The writers surely lost some good will with their demands, but it's likely that a slumping market, the veterans' higher page rates, the rise of Marvel, the teenocracy of the times, and the cry of fans that DC was "corny" were enough to make the editors feel they needed new blood.

The new blood was very new, and mostly very inexperienced at anything except writing fanzines. E. Nelson Bridwell was suddenly pinch-hitting all over the place. He and Weisinger had also found a quiet young writer named Cary Bates, who could imitate the silver-age style quite convincingly, but it did always feel like an imitation. Schwartz was the only DC editor looking for experience in his new guys, bringing in newspaper cartoonist Frank Robbins, a first-generation Milton Caniff disciple, to write some *Batman* and *Flash* issues. He was a terrific storyteller but couldn't produce a whole lot of scripts. Weisinger had always liked quiet guys who wouldn't fight back, especially guys like Siegel who lived in terror that no one else would hire them, but Schwartz liked his people articulate and opinionated. Even his favorite artists—Infantino, Kane, Anderson, Sekowsky—

were an ambitious bunch with ideas of their own. Denny O'Neil, with his journalist's speed and restlessness and to-the-point punch, now became his man. "The best writer at the moment," Schwartz called him, and fired Gardner Fox from *Justice League* after eight unbroken years to make way for him. Bates and O'Neil were prolific, but there were still pages unfilled. Mike Friedrich, Len Wein, and Marv Wolfman were all teenagers, just know-it-all middle-class kids, when they started writing professionally in 1968. There were a lot more like them waiting in the wings.

Get a few drinks into most of these fans-turned-pros, late at night in the drained hours after comic conventions, and you'll learn that a lot of them had absent or emotionally remote fathers, and that their superheroes were important guides for them through adolescence. Those were hard years to be a young man: the hippie culture and the new mainstream feminism were challenging everything Americans had understood to be masculine. The superheroes had always been there to articulate ideals of American maleness to boys who needed clearer models or extra support: self-sufficiency, protection of the weak, the rational use of violence, reserved camaraderie, sexlessness in public (you only wear tights when no one can see your face), the mask to hide individuality and emotionality, the secret hideout to store unsuspected reserves of power. How do you sustain those ideals, those characters, when your whole culture is wallowing in a loud, emotional orgy of father-hating self-criticism? Yet, how do you surrender them just when you're venturing into a terrifying new world, leaving high school in the suburbs for the life of a self-supporting writer in Manhattan, leaving the sunny DC cities of your youth for the world of *Midnight Cowboy*? That was the agony and the challenge of those new writers, a challenge against which their inchoate skills and anachronistic medium would prove to be not enough.

These fans weren't interested in creating or reviving other genres. For them, Westerns and romances were just jobs to knock off during an apprenticeship before moving on to the superheroes who had gotten them into the comics business in the first place. There were also other, less emotional pressures to keep the superheroes alive, or at least to find similar heroes who could take their places: every other genre was dying. Dick Giordano's replacement at Charlton, Sal Gentile, asserted in an editorial, "Next time you're in a store selling comics, watch what sells most consistently. Not the Long Underwear Laddies. It's Romance and Marriage that keep the cash register ringing...[and] Western...[and] War books. The Super heroes were big for a while, but they're simmering down, going, going, gone to Valhalla." It was conventional wisdom—indeed, even in 1970, romance, Western, and war combined to account for more comic book titles than superheroes, while humor and TV adaptations together still accounted for, more than half the titles published—but it was soon to be wrong. The other genres had been so neglected during the long reign of superheroes, the art and stories had become so awful and so little effort had been put into keeping them vital to new generations of kids, that even as the superheroes simmered down, the cowboys and soldiers and young lovers were going ice cold. Marvel's Westerns were all '50s reprints or Larry Lieber doing pale imitations of Kirby stories from 1959—this when Westerns in the movies were Peckinpah and Eastwood bloodfests, and Newman and Redford romances. DC did solid World War II comics, but who wanted to read them while body counts were being tallied on TV in a hated war that was being dragged on just so Richard Nixon would have something to promise at reelection time? DC's humor line was dying. *Bob Hope* and the charming *Fox and Crow* were canceled in 1968, and *Jerry Lewis* and Sheldon Mayer's *Sugar and Spike* would follow in 1971. An attempt to do hip humor in the late '60s with *Stanley and his Monster* and *Swing with Scooter* had failed. To revive its romances, DC brought in Joe Simon, half of the team that had created the genre and made it a gold mine in its early days. But that was in 1947, when saving your purity for Mr. Right was the great American struggle, before

the Comics Code made comic book romance totally sexless and the Pill made real romance more sexual than ever. Simon gave us stories like "I Found My Love at the Woodstock Festival" (*Falling in Love* 118, Oct. 1970), where the same old chaste, petty, infantile girls played their love games in Pucci pants, without a mud-smeared naked flower child in sight.

Horror had some potential, because young artists like Berni Wrightson liked drawing slimy monsters and women in jeopardy. And Gil Kane, in his keynote address at the 1969 New York Comic Art Convention, predicted that superheroes would soon be replaced by barbarians and science fiction. But his *Blackmark* hadn't gone anywhere, and old-style SF had died when the space program became a daily reality, technology just a servant of war, and our own changing country a more alien world than any. "New Wave" science fiction was all about narrative devices and head trips that no one could draw.

The focus on superheroes had been so intense that most kids had ceased to think of comics as anything but a way to read stuff like that old *Batman* show. As comics disappeared from grocery and drug stores, casual readers saw them less and less, and sales depended more and more on hobbyists willing to hunt them down—which meant mostly male superhero fans. Gold Key was still selling a lot of humor and TV comics, but it was slipping: Carl Barks and John Stanley were both retired, and reprints were replacing new stories. *Archie*'s imitators were nearly all gone, and Archie himself—trying to keep a teenhood of malt shops and jalopies alive for kids whose older brothers and sisters were smoking dope and hitching to Big Sur—had the smell of extinction about him. Charlton cranked out its tired programmers, while switching its energies to distributing a magazine more in tune with its times, Larry Flynt's *Hustler*.

The aging editors still ran the show, but the new writers inevitably made their values felt. O'Neil was interested in people, not plot structures. "If you met a Marvel hero at a party," said he, "you'd probably have a pretty lively conversation with him. If you met his DC opposite number, you'd probably remember a dentist appointment after five minutes." On *Justice League* he immediately started making the conversation more lively. Green Arrow, once as cardboard as a superhero could be, suddenly became a hothead and a bit of a rebel. Black Canary moved from Earth-2 to Earth-1 following the death of her husband, lost her powers, was transformed into a modern young chick, and started a heavy relationship with Green Arrow. Wonder Woman—already robbed of her powers by O'Neil—and the cornball Snapper Carr hit the road. Martian Manhunter, whom O'Neil found too alien to flesh out as a character, headed off to a distant planet called New Mars. Batman became introverted and mysterious, more like the grim avenger his origin had suggested. The Atom told jokes. Flash had a married life to worry about. In O'Neil's first Justice League of America story, Green Arrow and the others with minimal powers felt the big guns like Superman were treating them condescendingly and fought back in anger (*JLA* 66, Nov. 1968). Was this also the anger of the Young Turks against the aging sultans of DC? It wasn't Marvel yet, but it was heading that way.

Cracks were showing in the editorial monoliths. Infantino got his hands into everything, and the new editors he hired were consciously less controlling than the old guard. The greater mobility of artists was breaking up the old stables. Infantino hand-picked Ross Andru and Mike Esposito to replace him on *Flash*, and to fill Infantino's shoes on *Detective* Schwartz had to reach for one of Jack Schiff and George Kashdan's regulars, Bob Brown. As *Batman* sales kept flagging, Schwartz bumped Joe Giella and the Bob Kane studio and brought in Irv Novick, long a Robert Kanigher and Kashdan man, to join Brown. Brown also replaced Papp on *Superboy*, while Andru and Win Mortimer did fill-in work on *Superman* and *Action*. When Sekowsky turned editor, Dick Dillin moved from Kashdan's canceled *Blackhawk* to replace him on *JLA*.

For readers it was confusing and unpleasant. After years of dependability, we suddenly didn't know what *Superman* or *Flash* would look like.

Andru, dynamic as he was, didn't have the fluidity or the quaintness that we expected from the Flash and Superman. Dick Dillin did a solid job, but could never wrestle the clutter of the JLA into shape with Sekowsky's panache. New inking styles were coming in, too. Infantino had always been frustrated by Sol Harrison's production department and its demand for clean lines that were guaranteed to print well, but now that he was in charge, he made sure there was room for more sophisticated rendering. Unfortunately, few comic artists had ever had the incentive or opportunity to develop a nuanced ink line like his, or even an intensely detailed one like Neal Adams'. Joe Kubert was liberated for his finest work ever, but Frank McLaughlin brought a choppy Charlton look to Dillin and Novick's pencils, while Jack Abel laid heavy blacks over Curt Swan's delicate lines where George Klein had once been so precise. They strove to make Swan's heroes more muscular, but only made them rough and muddy. It turned out that the production department had a point: the increase in blacks often did make the pages print too darkly, a problem only exacerbated by the new DC coloring philosophy, which was heavy on purples to give the work a moody, "serious" look in keeping with the oppressive tenor of the times. DC's sun-glinting polish and optimistic vibrancy were clouding over, its silver surface looking tarnished.

The dominant look of the time was no longer Dan Barry or Carmine Infantino's, but Neal Adams', and everyone seemed to accept it. Adams hadn't kept *Deadman* alive, hadn't saved *Spectre* or *X-Men*, hadn't made much of a difference in sales with his covers. In fact, he had no commercial successes to his credit in comics and never would. Yet, he had so knocked out the vocal fans and his artistic peers that the whole look of DC shifted in his direction. Schwartz started using him for *Batman* covers, on which he redesigned the hero into a fluid, spooky echo of the "dark night detective" of 1939, with elongated cowl-ears and a vast, all-enswirling cape. The Bat-artists quickly adopted not only the new design, but even Adams's style. Novick, an ex-Army officer

141

Neal Adams's Batman, all mystery, darkness, and sensual swirl, marks a change in the whole tone of superheroes. Inks by Dick Giordano, script by Denny O'Neil. (*Batman* #245, Oct. 1972.)

convention audience that publishers listen to fans "just to be polite." He and others pointed out that the fans hated *Superman*, but that *Superman* still outsold everything else. Why, then, was *Superman* being made to look more like *Deadman* and Marvel comics, while no one was trying to make *anything* look more like *Superman*? Call him "editorial director," but Infantino was an artist after all. He'd always insisted on strutting his sophisticated ink line, even when Schwartz told him the kids wouldn't buy "impressionism," and now he created an atmosphere of artistic ambition and integrity that was far more in tune with the fans who had failed to keep *Deadman* afloat than with the kids who'd made Weisinger powerful. No one ever said, "Let's blow off the half-million eight-year-olds who buy *Superman* and settle for a good review in *Fantastic Fanzine*." But with sales dropping anyway and the market changing in unpredictable directions, it was easy to hope that a growing fandom and a "new youth" would support the material that the artists and editors felt was ennobling and expanding their medium. In 1956 a man could settle for keeping his job, but in 1969 who could settle for less than a revolution?

Fandom was confused. Now that the mass-media eye had moved on, it was again a safely invisible subculture, an escapist haven. Yet, the haven was becoming a business: in 1970 a mail-order dealer named Bob Overstreet published a *Comic Book Price Guide*, which crystallized the condition-rating system and asking prices that had been evolving by general consent during the previous few years. Suddenly, any junk shop or used-book store owner could add comics and know what to charge for them, kicking off a spectacular inflation in back-issue prices— *Action* 1, which had raised eyebrows by selling for a hundred dollars in 1965, was suddenly selling for a thousand—and bringing a whole new population of borderline-loser speculators into the field. Comic shops began to detach from their underground roots, and soon it wasn't unusual to hear a retailer booking Super Bowl bets over the phone while he jacked up the prices on his Neal Adams comics yet again. In Eastern

and art teacher who always seemed to treat comics like a day job, and Bob Brown, always adaptable— would forever after draw like Adams on a bad day, and the Adams Batman is still the norm. Jim Aparo, on *Brave and Bold*, followed suit, though with more distinction, and one can even see Dick Dillin on *JLA* straining for an Adamsian attenuation of anatomy.

The chant in comics has always been that sales are the one, true God. But that has never been the grinning assertion of the true salesman; it's always been the self-consciously cynical snort of the artist trying to wrangle a compromise with his ideals. Why else would they say it so often? Jim Warren told a

and Midwestern cities, mob money was reputedly setting up some shops, to replace the dying candy stores as an easy way to launder cash. Better people were starting to find their way into the business, too. Phil Seuling in Brooklyn and his friend Bud Plant in California were expanding from retail into the wholesaling of undergrounds and "prozines" like *witzend* to comic shops, and they were looking for new ways to combine the retailing of new and old comics.

The silver age had been the most consistently satisfying period in the history of comics, a decade and more when unwaveringly solid craftsmanship existed side by side with the wildest experiments. It was what had given fandom life: its extravagant characters, its ingeniously plotted short stories, its unified editorial visions, its colorful and unabashedly cartooned art. The kids who became fans, and the fans who became pros, had fallen in love with the pristine Flash, the wonders of Kandor, the brawling Fantastic Four, the anguished Spider-Man, and the utterly bizarre Doom Patrol. Most of all, they'd fallen in love with comics' exuberant sense of fun. Now all that was going away. Those few but steady editorial visions of the '60s were being replaced by something more changeable, more driven by writers and artists, more "adult," and the fans felt they should want that. Denny O'Neil has said, "Maybe the audience was a little uneasy about liking comic books, so they would reject anything that seemed childlike to them." Little kids like clarity and simplicity, and are essentially unaware of the artist as a practitioner, but older kids want "realism" and stylistic pyrotechnics, the sense that an artist is really "good" and "worked hard" and isn't looking down at his readers. Jerry Bails had been able to like the Fox-Sekowsky *JLA* back when comics were understood to be kid stuff and fans were accustomed to being "kooks." Now that fandom was a publicly known subculture, it had its dignity to consider. And a terribly fragile dignity it was.

That the fans felt vaguely that they were missing something is suggested by the sensation caused by Jim Steranko's new project. After leaving Marvel, he formed his own company, Supergraphics, to publish product aimed at the overlapping comics, genre fiction, and horror movie fandoms, selling it via the comics shops and mail-order networks. Since it was all advance-ordered and nonreturnable, it was a pretty safe endeavor and could make him decent money without the huge capital required by a Marvel or a National. He started with *The Steranko History of Comics*, a proposed six-volume series of which only two would ever be published. The first, ecstatically recreating the golden age of National and Timely— glorifying the vigor and violence of the early superheroes, the atmospheric creepiness of Batman, and the sunny heroism of Superman—appeared in 1970 and set fandom aflame. The same year saw book publication of the unabashedly gushing essays of Dick Lupoff and Don Thompson's *All in Color for a Dime*. Among the contributors was Harlan Ellison, hotshot SF writer, culture critic, and *Star Trek* scripter, now becoming a deity to comics fandom simply by deigning to pay attention to it. Clearly what fans really hungered for was fun and creative abandon and clear-cut heroes, without the need of apologizing or painting over their passions with a veneer of maturity. They couldn't quite allow that in the comics of the present, but they could live it vicariously through the heroes of a long-gone age, when boys were boys and imaginary dads were killing Nazis, legitimized by the approval of a hip stud artist and a science fiction sex symbol whom no one could ever call corny or juvenile.

As usual, it was Julie Schwartz who was best attuned to his readers. Before Steranko made fans hungry for an old-style Batman, Schwartz had already realized that his "New Look" was as old as a Dior evening gown and decided on "going back to where Batman was at the very beginning." Adams had already given him (and Novick and Brown) a visual cue, so Schwartz and Frank Robbins hammered out a story in which Dick Grayson, AKA Robin, goes away to college, casting Batman in his original role as a loner (*Batman* 217, Dec. 1969). Bruce and Alfred then leave Wayne Manor to take up residence in a penthouse atop the Wayne Foundation building in Gotham City so as to live in "the heart of that sprawling urban blight—to dig...the new breed of rat...out where they live and fatten on the innocent." Bruce modifies his costume à la Adams, elongating the ears and cape and restoring its original purpose of "striking fear into the hearts of criminals" (for no one but Jack Schiff could have been unnerved by the "New Look" Batman). As a middle-aged New Yorker, Schwartz obviously understood how scary the city was becoming, how the country had suddenly awakened from its infatuation with the suburbs to realize that the urban core had been neglected. With the murder of Kitty Genovese—whose screams many heard but no one responded to—and other horrifying stories, the news media discovered that playing on Americans' fears of crime and social disintegration meant big profits, and they were determined to give Americans a profitable worldview. The quaint romanticism of Gotham City had been replaced by televised race riots, white flight, Johnny Carson's mugger jokes, and Razzo Rizzo's cough. Comics fans—mostly products of suburbs or small cities, like the bulk of American middle-class kids, for whom the Eastern metropolis was only an image of our collective imagination—took notice.

Schwartz was less sure what to do with the rapidly flagging *Green Lantern*. The general decline in science fiction had damaged it, as had changing art and writing teams. He lured Gil Kane back for a run of great issues, pairing him with fine inkers like Wally Wood and Murphy Anderson. But sales kept dropping. The avuncular chipmunk, who for fourteen years had always seemed to know his next move, was stuck. He figured it was time to learn what younger eyes might see in the character. He called in Denny O'Neil and asked him to "see what could be done with it."

Thus, the man who launched the silver age had now pronounced its end.

PART TWO
THE AWKWARD AGE

CHAPTER 21

RELEVANCE

The cover of *Green Lantern* 76 looked different. First, the emerald gladiator was no longer the sole star of his own comic book: he'd been joined by fellow Justice Leaguer Green Arrow. Second, the art had changed. The monumental heroism of Gil Kane had been replaced by a Neal Adams emotional study. And third, there was an odd note of discord. Why was Green Arrow shooting a shaft through his partner's power battery, crying, "Never again!"?

A bigger shock came with page one. The first words of the story were, "For years he has been a proud man! He has worn the power ring of the Guardians, and used it well, and never doubted the righteousness of his cause. His name, of course, is Green Lantern, and often he has vowed that 'No evil shall escape my sight.' He has been fooling himself."

Flying over Star City, Green Arrow's hometown, Green Lantern sees a "punk" attacking a fat man in a suit. He intervenes, expecting approval from bystanders, but is greeted instead with a barrage of cans, rocks, and bottles. Not only that, but his assailants are all black—and few black people had ever appeared in DC comics. He's about to retaliate when Green Arrow appears and stops him angrily. "Green Arrow!" cries Green Lantern. "You're . . . defending these . . . these *anarchists?!*" Green Arrow explains that the "fat cat" Green Lantern was defending is, in fact, a slumlord, and leads him through a crumbling tenement. When an ancient ghetto-dweller says to Green Lantern, "I been readin' about you . . . how you work for the blue skins . . . and how on a planet someplace you helped out the orange skins . . . and you done considerable for the purple skins! Only there's *skins* you never bothered with...the *black* skins! I want to know . . . *how come?!* Answer me *that*, Mr. Green Lantern!" Green Lantern hangs his head, gazes down at his feet, and says only, "I . . . can't . . ." The self-confidence that had bolstered the

emerald gladiator since 1959 crumbled in an instant—and a new wave of comics was launched (*Green Lantern/Green Arrow* 76, May 1970).

Taking over *Green Lantern* "was unusually interesting and potentially exciting," Denny O'Neil has said. "I had an idea. For a while, I'd been wondering if it might be possible to combine my various professional and personal concerns." He said he still "considered myself as much journalist as fiction writer," and drew on the "new journalists" he admired: Tom Wolfe, Norman Mailer, Jimmy Breslin, Pete Hamill, Hunter S. Thompson. "Could a comic book equivalent of the new journalism be possible?" he asked. "What would happen if we put a superhero in a real-life setting dealing with a real-life problem?"

To anchor the space-faring Green Lantern to Earth and human concerns, he was teamed with the new Green Arrow, whom O'Neil was recasting as a defender of the downtrodden in *JLA* and to whom Adams had already given a Robin Hood beard in *Brave and Bold*. "The lusty, hot-tempered anarchist," as O'Neil saw him, not only awoke the "cerebral, sedate model citizen who was the Green Lantern" to pressing social ills, but even persuaded one of the remote Guardians of the Universe to join the two of them in a journey of discovery across America. "Come off your perch!" he says. "Touch . . . taste . . . laugh and cry! Learn where we're at . . . and why!" "I feel," replies the Guardian, "there is wisdom in your words." And so the three hit the road in a big American car..

Every story strove to tackle a pertinent social issue. The trio defended a struggling mine workers' union, unmasked a phony religious prophet, and protected a tribe of downtrodden American Indians. The Guardian soon returned to the planet Oa, and Green Lantern and Green Arrow were joined by the latter's lover, Black Canary—like Wonder Woman, a superheroine deprived of her powers by O'Neil—as they went on to deal with pollution, overpopulation, feminism, race riots, and destructive industrialism. Running throughout these stories was the tension between the moderate Lantern and the radical Arrow as they butted heads over nearly every issue, turning the stories into a superpowered *Point Counter Point*.

Such "relevance," as the fans were calling it, was old hat at Marvel, of course. Stan Lee and company had always kept their stories better plugged into the youth culture of the moment than DC's, and in most ways O'Neil was only following their lead. Stan and Jack had been introducing black characters since 1963, and Roy Thomas had been explicitly writing about racial issues since 1968, while DC's world remained lily-white. Green Lantern was seeing not just his first ghetto, but his first African-Americans in *GL/GA* 76. Although O'Neil probably didn't consciously intend it, his opening sequence was less about heroes reacting to the real world than about DC reacting to a changing cultural scene. It was an abrupt and excessive moment, but O'Neil had the survival of a whole series—maybe even a whole company—on his hands.

The influence flowed both ways. Soon after Green Lantern's confrontation with black poverty, Stan Lee gave Captain America a black crime-fighting partner called the Falcon (*CA* 133, Jan. 1971) and made Cap the symbol not of the confident America of World War II, but of the conflicted America of the early 1970s. Cap became a motorcycle cop in his secret identity, enforcing the law but at an intimate level with the citizenry, often crossing paths with the Falcon in his secret identity as a Harlem social worker. As with Lantern and Arrow, the interaction between the stolid Cap and the fiery Falcon was the focal point of the series, although Cap kept his dignity and was never put through the crushing doubts and humiliations that Green Lantern was. O'Neil and Adams then picked up the baton with the introduction of John Stewart, Hal Jordan's backup in the Green Lantern Corps. Stewart is a black architect who says of his GL uniform, "These aren't any

threads James Brown would wear," and, "I won't wear any *mask*! This black man lets it *all* hang out!" (*GL/GA* 87, Jan. 1972).

With typical impudence, Lee quickly went after a "relevant" subject that DC hadn't dared to because it was specifically forbidden by the Comics Code: drug abuse. In *Spider-Man* 96-98 (May-July 1971), Peter Parker attempts vainly to save a ghetto kid from a heroin overdose and then—to drive home that this isn't just a problem of poor nonwhites—discovers that his affluent white friend Harry Osborne has become addicted to tranquilizers. It was a slightly clunky story, but fierce, and drawn with fire by Gil Kane, who believed that supporters of the Code had killed his *Savage*. It was the first time since 1955 that a publisher had dared defy the Code, and since that publisher, EC, had paid for its defiance by losing its comics, it took some courage. But Lee, as usual, had guessed the mood of his times correctly. Few distributors or retailers balked, media attention made all three issues big sellers, and the keepers of the law realized they'd better revise their rules or go the way of the dinosaurs. The Comics Code Authority promptly released the first new Code since 1954, allowing not only mentions of drug use (so long as the intention was anti-drug), but the use of subjects like vampirism and lycanthropy, which seemed less disturbing now that monster movies were all over TV (and EC was no longer a competitor). As soon as Stan opened the door, O'Neil tried to top him by revealing that Green Arrow's wholesome boy sidekick, Speedy, was in fact a heroin addict (*GL/GA* 85-86, Oct.-Dec. 1971). The "Speedy Is a Junkie" story, like Green Lantern's collapse at the sight of low-income black people, feels far more forced and overstated than Lee's equivalent, but then Marvel was coming from cockiness and DC from desperation.

Where DC outdid Marvel was not in introducing social relevance or even an open political bias—although O'Neil did advertise his liberalism in bigger neon letters than anyone at Marvel—but in making them the conscious focus of an entire series. Although action and adventure were still the bulk of

Humanism and reductionism: the iconic heroism of Gil Kane gives way to the torment of Neal Adams's '70s man. Inks by Dick Giordano, script by Denny O'Neil. (*Green Lantern/Green Arrow* #89, May 1972.)

So it seemed to the fans, at least, who gave *GL/GA* every award and accolade they could think of, and to most of the mainstream reporters who wrote about it with more gravity and respect than they'd accorded any aspect of comics during the Bat-days. One paperback publisher, perhaps anticipating another comics craze like '66, even repackaged the stories in book form. O'Neil and Adams were suddenly the stars of the field, and everyone understood that they were the ones—not Julie Schwartz, not Carmine Infantino—who were responsible. The old guys backed the kids to the hilt, promoted them and praised the hell out of them, and never tried to fool anybody about who had the creative vision. By sheer number and youthful energy, the new generation was winning all the most public fights in America—eighteen-year-olds were getting the vote, the government was giving up in Vietnam, moms were declaring their right to have orgasms, and Robert Reed was wearing bell-bottoms—and now they'd done it in comics, too. The fans and the creators all knew that the days when the editor made the comics were gone.

Too bad *Green Lantern/Green Arrow* wasn't as satisfying as it was important. It was wonderfully executed in its details. O'Neil gave us some nice character bits, like Arrow's lusty humor and love of chili, and Adams was particularly dazzling with Green Arrow's archery stunts. But Adams's naturalistic detail clashed with the fantasy inherent in Green Lantern's power ring. When GL creates a green flying horse to carry Green Arrow along, it's just *too* damn horsey. Adams thrilled fans hungry for "realism," but in retrospect he makes us yearn for the integrity of an earlier aesthetic, the purity of Gil Kane. Together, Adams and O'Neil could pull off some of the most potent visual moments ever in superhero comics. One issue features a Christ-like environmentalist vandalizing Ferris Aircraft, Hal's old employer, until he dies, self-crucified, on the tail of the new fuel-efficient jet he's trying to keep from production. The emotional tension of the whole story compresses into a tight shot of Green Lantern trying to contain his rage. Then it explodes in a glorious

every story, the *point* of the story was the political message. *Captain America* might broaden the scope of superhero adventures, but *Green Lantern/Green Arrow* suggested a fundamental new approach to them. Even Steve Ditko hadn't tried such ripped-from-the-headlines topicality. Here was a comic that would have to press the medium into a radical self-appraisal, a reevaluation of its purposes, just as the old man's "How come?" had pressed Green Lantern. It seemed inescapable now that the comics community—and the world at large—would have to grapple with the full potential of the medium.

half-page drawing as he rakes a green ring-beam through the jet from nose to tail with a SSCHHAAAAKKKKKKK. "That was a nine million dollar aircraft!" says a Ferris fat cat. "Send me a bill," says GL (*GL/GA* 89, May 1972). Unfortunately, to appreciate the moment we have to buy into a line of simplistic anti-industrial cant and some pretty forced behavior by the veteran hero.

Probably no hero in the DC universe could have been less appropriate to political relevance and gritty realism than the fanciful Green Lantern. The contrast could be effective when O'Neil kept his hero on Earth, but then he started weaving the old fantastic nature of the series in with his new approach. The overpopulation story was set on the Guardians' home world of Maltus, one of those standing-room-only worlds just like the one on *Star Trek*, typical of pop-culture reactions to *The Population Bomb*. The feminism issue used man-hating harpies, amazons, and an ersatz Medusa from another dimension (all being manipulated by a man, it turns out, and all talked out of their rage by the powerless Black Canary). It just stressed further the clash between what Green Lantern had been created to be and what "relevance" had forced him into.

With his power ring driven by his own will, Green Lantern had also, of necessity, been the most levelheaded and self-possessed of heroes. The collapse of his confidence and values could never feel organic. O'Neil was obviously uncomfortable with the character. "Green Lantern was, in effect, a cop," he has said. "An incorruptible cop, to be sure, with noble intentions, but still a cop, a crypto-fascist." He had trouble with Green Lantern's enormous power, too: "A writer must find a way to make a character symbolically real for himself. You've got to *connect* somehow...through your own deepest dreams and fantasies. Now, my fantasies are quite modest, generally concerned with human perfectibility. I might imagine myself training and training until some glorious autumn morning I run the New York Marathon in 1:59:59 . . . . It won't happen, but it *could*, to somebody, someday . . . . I have never fantasized about

having inhuman power conferred on me by an outside agency." He gave far more emotional power and consistency to Green Arrow, his headstrong left-wing mouthpiece. Yet, in keeping him strong enough to dominate Green Lantern—who would argue back pigheadedly and be ritually humbled in most issues—O'Neil had to push even him into caricature. At moments the series reads like a battle between a shrill pontificator and a manic-depressive loser.

There was also a strain of meanness coming in with the new "realism." Carol Ferris came back into Hal's life, but a villain promptly, and agonizingly, crippled her, leaving her trapped in a wheelchair and in big financial trouble. Green Lantern revealed his secret identity to her, and they became friends at a far more "mature" level than in the John Broome days—but she paid a heavy price for dumping our hero. These were dark days in the American mood and dark days for O'Neil, darkened by the fact "that I was playing the dreary role of the whiskey-swilling Irishman, that my marriage was coming apart like wet tissue paper, that a brief fling as a proto-celebrity had created terrible self-doubt." That his work was bitter is not surprising. But it was an ominous note of what might come when "reality" was mixed with the fantasies of power and violence that are integral to superheroes.

Green Lantern/Green Arrow did have its didactic virtues, introducing young readers to political issues, perhaps opening a door for readers who'd generally ignored reality-based fiction. Ultimately, though, it could never have hoped to be artistically satisfying or effective for most readers or even honest with its own content. When juvenile material reaches for an adult aesthetic, it demands to be viewed with adult eyes. The charmed suspension of disbelief that makes a purely fanciful battle of superhero and supervillain plausible can no longer be sustained when the hero starts grappling with unions and polluters. "Concretizing the symbol," the mythologist Joseph Campbell called it, and it's the quickest way to deprive any symbol of its genuine mythic power. These stories could never really be reality-based. If a man had a power ring and wanted to right social wrongs, think what he'd really do, how quickly his world would become different from ours (and how little he'd need the clown with the arrows). Nor were the worlds they created internally consistent enough to be fantasy. "Adult superheroes" were an uncomfortable compromise, neither fish nor fowl.

As the praise rolled in on *GL/GA*, O'Neil became the "revamp" man at DC. He'd already helped change Wonder Woman, revised JLA, and was contributing some acclaimed stories to Julie Schwartz's new Batman, so it was inevitable that he would be called on to write the post-Weisinger Superman. Schwartz had been given the Man of Steel's flagship title, *Superman*, and as he recalls, "The first thing I said when Carmine asked me to take over Superman was, 'I gotta change him.'" The old DC regime might have said, "Don't mess with success," but Infantino was all in favor. After all, where would DC, or Infantino himself, be if Schwartz hadn't changed the Flash in 1956 and Batman in 1964? Murray Boltinoff was getting gorgeous results from Curt Swan and Murphy Anderson on *Action Comics*, so Schwartz stuck with them. The hero himself, however, was dull to both Schwartz and O'Neil, "a chummy, white-bready sort of fellow," as O'Neil saw him, with "a large extended family and godlike powers whose activities had become nearly as predictable as Dagwood Bumstead's." Their aim, once again, was relevance: not political topicality, although they indulged in a bit of that, but a greater similarity between Superman and his flawed human readers.

They cut to the chase. From their first issue (*Superman* 233, Jan. 1971), they changed almost everything that Schwartz's older fans had been griping about in Weisinger's comics for years. All the kryptonite on Earth turned to iron in a chain-reaction blast. Superman was robbed of most of his powers by a "sand creature" formed by the same explosion. Clark Kent abandoned his career as a mild-mannered reporter for the *Daily Planet* to become a news anchorman for the Galaxy Broadcasting System. Imaginary Stories were eliminated, and a consistent, more Marvel-style continuity was set up, with mys-

teries about Clark's new boss and a new romantic heat between Superman and Lois Lane. Superman's hometown-in-a-bottle, Kandor, was rarely mentioned, and the only new contribution to Kryptoniana was a well-crafted backup series, *The Fabulous World of Krypton*, in which Cary Bates and various other writers and artists told the history of that planet in a far less fanciful way than Mort and his gang ever would have. O'Neil was having trouble, though, "spending up to three weeks on Superman scripts and not enjoying the work. By contrast, Batman scripts took three days and were often fun. . . . I couldn't find a connection with even a vastly scaled-down version of this demigod." He wrote thirteen issues, solid but unexciting, and he quit.

By then O'Neil was back on *Wonder Woman* (*WW* 197, Oct. 1971). Gloria Steinem had complained publicly that the hero of her girlhood, the strongest of all pop culture females, had been robbed of her powers and handed into the mentorship of a man, so O'Neil strained to prove that his amazon martial artist was, in fact, a role model for women who wanted to be self-reliant and strong. He even got Samuel R. Delaney—SF novelist, analyst of sex and gender issues, and husband of poet Marilyn Hacker—to write a two-part women's lib story. Unfortunately, perhaps because he felt he was writing to kids, Delaney fell into all the easy anti-machismo clichés of the moment with nothing to say about the whole of sexual politics.

Other writers were playing with relevance, too. Mike Friedrich, going to college in the San Francisco Bay Area while spending summers in New York writing comics, was O'Neil's most determined disciple. Nearly every story he wrote for Schwartz—during stints and fill-ins on *JLA*, *Flash*, and *Superman*—was laden with political stances, hip references, and contemporary characterizations, all too obvious. He showed how different the new wave of writers was from the old, seeking to legitimize the passions of his fan days with a seriousness beyond his ability. Gardner Fox once wove a cute tale around eighteenth-century novelist Henry Fielding meeting the Atom. In contrast, Friedrich had a dark, tormented genius named Harlequin Ellis—an homage to fan-god Harlan Ellison—help the JLA, even though he is ever haunted by "the crash-pounding of his creative soul." Meanwhile, the unrelated Gary Friedrich, at Marvel, was using *Iron Man* for topical stories, which the hero's true identity—the munitions maker and public figure Tony Stark—made quite easy. When Stan Lee stepped down from *Captain America*, Friedrich replaced him and went straight into a race-riot story line.

Many fans thought "relevance" was the dawn of a new age, but almost before they could say it, the whole thing ended. *Green Lantern/Green Arrow* was canceled in early 1972. At almost the same time, sales figures were slowly revealing that the new "humanized" Superman was just sitting on the racks, and returns were going up, so Infantino had to ask Schwartz to give him back his powers and his kryptonite. Within a few months, Wonder Woman had her powers and costume back, and I Ching was dead (*WW* 204, Dec. 1972). Once again a DC revolution, acclaimed by the fans, had dropped like a lead balloon. DC's writers and editors turned their backs on politics, and Marvel's went back to handling it as they always had, as just part of the fabric of the Marvel universe. The last gasp of the trend was *Prez*, a strange little thing from Joe Simon in 1973, half satire and half liberal flag-waver, in which a cute teenager is elected to the presidency and fills his cabinet with minority stereotypes in order to cleanse the corrupt establishment. It ran for four issues in 1973, and then Infantino pulled the plug. At Marvel, Lee, Ditko, and Kirby had spoken to their times just by doing what

they *felt*, but as soon as other people consciously *tried*, they fell short. It's an eternal pop culture pattern.

By then the big creative talent at DC was beginning to look exhausted. Schwartz assigned Cary Bates and a couple of new kids, Elliott S. Maggin and Marty Pasko, to maintain *Superman* in a sort of Weisinger-Lite style, and coasted on *JLA* and *Flash* while he looked for something new to excite him. O'Neil was still in demand, maybe too much in demand, cranking out a huge number of scripts but showing less excitement and daring all the time. In those days of few experienced comic book writers, those who were good got as much work as they could handle, and ended up following the old Stan Lee model: writing as much as they could for ten or twelve dollars a page, maybe four or five scripts a month, battling to stay ahead of rising New York living expenses.

America looked exhausted, too. With Watergate, our retreat from Vietnam, and the dismal economic and social environment we were mired in, few of us wanted to engage with anything in any particularly challenging way. It seemed that in the nation in general, and in comics in particular, the one hope of fulfillment might be to escape into private fantasy. Not the simple fantasies of the old days, though. "Relevance" may have ended, but the aesthetic of "realism," of darkness, of pain, of moral queasiness, and of ethical uncertainty remained. That, the fans all knew, was what made "mature comics," and that's what seemed to hit Americans in the gut. The fantasies of the '70s would have to be darker, more ambiguous, more cynical, more frightening than ever before.

CHAPTER 22

BARBARISM

Who can be a hero in unheroic times? If not an old galactic cop suddenly hurled into self-doubt, then maybe a savage out only for himself.

Fans had been writing to Marvel for a few years suggesting a comic in the "sword-and-sorcery" genre. Gil Kane said it was the next big thing. Robert E. Howard's Conan stories of the '30s pulps were being republished in paperback editions by the mid-'60s, and sold so well that new stories were commissioned to keep the series rolling. Other writers had jumped into this sword-and-sorcery genre too, including Gardner Fox with his barbarian Llarn; at the very end of his fan days, Roy Thomas had adapted a Llarn story for a zine. Now Roy was in the Marvel office full-time, officially a staff writer but also an informal assistant editor. Stan Lee was even encouraging him to generate some new projects of his own, probably wondering if Roy might be more in tune with the readers now than he was. Roy went hunting for the rights to Conan the Barbarian.

At the dawn of the 1930s, Robert E. Howard was a quiet young man who lived with his mother in the dust and depression of Cross Plains, Texas. But in his imagination, he lived in another place: the Hyborian Age, a fantasied time of brutality and chaos before the dawn of history, where Robert's alter ego, Conan, was a wandering thief and mercenary from the barbarous northern land of Cimmeria. Conan slashed his way through turbulent kingdoms and decadent empires reminiscent of Frankland, Rome, and Egypt, until he rose at last to be king of powerful Aquilonia. He and other Howard barbarians found a market in *Weird Tales*, reaching into the fantasies of other lonely young men in that brutal and chaotic American time. Then Howard's mother died, and young Robert put a bullet through his brain. Conan remained a legend in pulp fandom, but he was forgotten by pop culture at

large until *The Lord of the Rings* set the '60s generation afire. Conan's savage American individualism—cash worshipping, routine destruction of ancient gods, using and disposing of wenches like Kleenex—was far from Professor Tolkien's grand Anglican fantasy, but paperback publishers wanted fantasy and Lancer Books found Conan. To young white males in a world where the old structures were collapsing and weird new forces both threatened and seduced them, the Cimmerian was a gratifying fantasy indeed.

This was a genre comics had neglected, partly because the Comics Code had limited the sorcery, sex, and bloodshed that made the stories so much fun, partly because the few tentative stabs at it—from John Giunta's *Crom* in 1950 to *Viking Prince* to *Blackmark*—hadn't done very well. Thomas was determined to do it right. He pursued the Conan rights with the Howard estate himself, then "managed to sell Martin Goodman on the idea of actually paying a little money for it, which was my major accomplishment." Book adaptations weren't new to comics, but they'd never been done with a Marvel aesthetic or with superhero fans as a targeted audience. Thomas, displaying both his English teacher's training and his comics fan's instincts, worked hard to preserve the style and content of Howard's original stories while building the visual excitement and sense of ongoing narrative that Marvel fans expected. He pushed the Code as far as he could, and when it was revised, he took advantage. Although he'd never be able to capture Howard's content completely, he succeeded well enough to bring a refreshing new boldness to comics. It looked like he might even make Gil Kane's prediction about sword and sorcery come true.

Thomas retold Howard's tales in careful order, filling in gaps with stories of his own. His barbarian went up against an evil seductress, a minotaur, a spi-

[1] Jakes was a low-end genre writer at the time, so the rights probably came cheap, but by Bicentennial time he would discover that there was far more money in making a fantasy of history than in historicizing fantasy, with his "Kent Family Chronicles."

der-god, even a woeful extra-terrestrial imprisoned on earth. It all inspired him to the best scripting of his career, a bit too rich in adjectives but still with elegance and distinction. He paid homage to Howard with minute attention to the places and customs of the Hyborian Age, including maps and text features that provided a wealth of background information. Never, though, did his passion for detail overwhelm his sense of story, as it could when he wrote superheroes.

The real magic of *Conan*, however, lay not in Thomas's writing, but in his inspired choice of artist. Barry Smith was a young Englishman—an anomaly in that very American business, but the Marvel fad had taken London by storm in the late '60s, and Smith had reached across the Atlantic—who'd started as a crude Kirby imitator. Thomas knew Smith was interested in fantasy art, though, and allowed him to discard the "Marvel style" and follow his own influences. As early as issue 4, he revealed flashes of something unique, and by the time he left the series after issue 24, he was the new darling of fandom. His storytelling retained its Kirby-derived force, but now Smith drew heavily from the Pre-Raphaelite painters, with a good dose of the early twentieth-century school of book illustration that descended from *L'Art Nouveau*. These were sources that no American comic book artist of the time would have thought to use, or thought about, period. But for teenage and young adult readers of the early '70s, who had discovered the Pre-Raphaelites and nineteenth-century English illustrator Aubrey Beardsley through the head-shop culture, they resonated powerfully. Smith's pages were a delicate embroidery of stylized figures parading against beautifully ornate backgrounds—glass towers, bone-filled dungeons, lantern-lit bazaars—composed of small, dense panels in defiance of the current passion for the big and bold.

Conan started slowly, nearly unnoticed. But then it began to build up heat within fandom, and sales started to struggle upward. Thomas was emboldened to help launch more barbarians in *Kull the Conqueror, Gulliver Jones: Warrior of Mars, Thongor of Lost Lemuria,* John Jakes's *Brak,*[1] and *Skull.* He brought in SF writer George Alec Effinger

to help with some, but—like Samuel Delaney on *Wonder Woman*—Effinger showed none of the wit that marks his fiction. None of the barbarians took.

Conan, meanwhile, was demonstrating a disturbing new trend. In his fourth issue, Smith's art was effectively inked by Sal Buscema, but in the fifth he was massacred by Frank Giacoia, one of the old fill-in speed demons of the business. Inkers played musical chairs during Smith's entire stay, some right (Buscema, Dan Adkins, Smith himself), some wrong. This tendency plagued Marvel—and, to a lesser extent, DC—more and more as the '70s wore on, and

By Conan the Barbarian #21, Barry Smith was pushing his art to new heights of elegance and design. Thanks to the comics industry, we'll never know what heights he might have hit. (Nov. 1972.)

[2] How perfect, too, that where Marvel adapted the work of the dark, Oedipal, suicidal Howard, DC and Chaykin should choose the elegant Lieber, who sailed into his eighties as a wit and habitué of San Francisco watering holes.

if it wasn't a fill-in inker, it might be a fill-in penciler who changed the whole tone of the series. Much of the problem was the disorder created by the willy-nilly launching and canceling of titles, and the breakdown of the old editorial stables. But there was also a new attitude among the young artists coming into the field, the Jim Steranko attitude, which had also become the Neal Adams attitude and was being passed on to the kids who followed them. Their generation had an antiauthoritarian streak, and they didn't have their elders' Depression-vintage financial anxieties. Most of them were unfettered by the dependents and mortgages of earlier generations, and the popular ones knew that the passions of fandom would always make them desirable to editors, no matter what their work habits. For them, editors and deadlines simply didn't hold the same terror that they had for the scarred veterans of the lean years. They had the luxury to be *artists*, not just page fillers.

Smith knew that if he fussed over his pages to make them perfect he'd make the same money he made for zipping through an issue like Bob Brown or Ross Andru. And if that painstaking care caused the pages to be a few days late, he'd get nagged by his editor and risk an overnight ink job. Once, because Thomas couldn't bear to see bad inks on some heartbreakingly pretty Smith pages, he even had the issue shot straight from the pencils (and because Smith's pencils were so complete, it actually looked awfully good). Smith pushed for a deal that would pay him more for better work, but comic book accounting just wasn't set up that way. He didn't want to be like the old-timers, like Gil Kane, who was stripping his art down to keep up with the hunger of his publishers. So he left. He set up "The Studio" with Jeff Jones and other artists, from which, as Barry Windsor-Smith, he would sell illustrations and posters and fantastical paintings. It was Steranko all over again: coming out of nowhere, electrifying fandom, and then almost instantly gone. This kind of thing had happened before, when most of the EC gang had bailed out of the business, and the fans of the early '50s had lost a lot of enthusiasm then. Some '70s fans were now wondering how long they could sustain their interest in a field that couldn't keep its best and its brightest.

Smith's successor, John Buscema, recast the wandering barbarian in a brawnier, simpler mold. It was a blow to devoted Smith fans, and angry letters and agonized phone calls flooded the Marvel offices. For a couple of years, not a single convention question-and-answer session could pass without some fan asking some Marvel guest, "Why did you guys let Barry Smith get away?" Apparently, however, it was a blow only to devoted Smith fans, because sales gradually increased during Buscema's tenure, mostly among more casual readers, including a lot of women. Later, a Marvel sales executive would say they liked the barbarian's overdeveloped pecs and sinewy thighs, carved out in near nudity by Buscema's sculptural pencil (the '70s were bringing the bodybuilder in, sweeping the Pre-Raphaelite out). Fans of Robert E. Howard were also heard to say that the Buscema version was closer to the burly original.

Roy Thomas and Stan Lee both tried to sell Conan to the more grown-up, outside-the-Code market with a black-and-white magazine called *Savage Tales* (May 1971). It died. Maybe the biggest obstacle for dedicated Marvelites was that *Conan* stories were contained in single issues. Once that had been the way of all comics, which suited casual readers fine. Loyalists, however, were becoming the industry's mainstay. And the loyalists were addicted to their subplots, cliff-hangers, endless heroic agonies, arch nemeses, and casts of friends and lovers. Thomas would remember that when he launched another new genre.

DC hadn't seen enough heat from *Conan* to leap into barbarism, but Gil Kane's protégé, Howard Chaykin, took a stab at it in his own impish way. He and Denny O'Neil introduced their adaptation of Fritz Leiber's witty Fafhrd and the Grey Mouser stories in *Wonder Woman*, and then set them up in their own series, *Sword of Sorcery* (Mar. 1973).[2] Chaykin's art had a sweep and drama reminiscent of Kane but a humor and ingenuity all his own, and with O'Neil's effective scripting—plus some art assists from a couple of young hotshots from fandom, Walt Simonson

DOWN CORRIDORS RANK WITH INCENSE, STARBUCK BOUNDS TOWARD THE CABIN OF BROTHER TOMÁS...

...THERE TO FIND THE PLUNDER!

CODY!!

BACK OFF, HEATHEN...

© 1974 Howard Chaykin

The "ground-level" press sets a young Howard Chaykin free to explode with fantasies out of Toth and Kane, fantasies the mainstream couldn't contain. ("Cody Starbuck," *Star*Reach* 1, Apr. 1974.)

and Jim Starlin—the series was a charming counterweight to *Conan*. Yet, it lasted only five issues. Chaykin followed with a creation of his own, *IronWolf*, which got off to an exciting start but ran in only the last three issues of a title called *Weird Worlds*. Chaykin, loudly radical and famously fond of the female and the forbidden, didn't want to do superheroes—"I have no interest in Boy Scouts," he said—but he was having trouble getting DC to support his sword-and-sorcery and science fiction ideas. Yet another promising youngster was being disenchanted by his chosen field.

Gil Kane had said superheroes were fading, and few disagreed with him. He said barbarians were rising, but there he was wrong. Who or what could save this business?

CHAPTER 23

KIRBY WAS THERE

For months the ads read, "Kirby is coming!" "The Great One is coming!" "People! Places! Things! So powerful in concept—it's almost terrifying!" The word spread like wildfire through fandom in 1970: the King had signed a five-year contract with National that promised him unprecedented creative freedom. He would create, edit, and write new heroes all his own, and for the first time the world would see what the mature Jack Kirby could do without the influence of Stan Lee or anyone else. At last the long-awaited blurb appeared: "Kirby is here!" And it was appearing on the cover of . . . *Superman's Pal, Jimmy Olsen*?

No one will ever know quite what went on in the negotiations between Carmine Infantino and Jack Kirby. Here were the two quintessential artists of the silver age, the one who'd brought the heroes back and the one who'd revolutionized them. They were the embodiment of the DC Touch and of Mighty Marvel, forging a union that had the promise to transform and dominate the comics of the 1970s. It was a moment worth remembering, but unfortunately for us poor historians, Infantino's recollections have always been cryptic and Kirby's have always shifted from one conversation to another. That Infantino was looking to Kirby to give DC commercial blockbusters seems certain; the expectations placed on him were utterly different from those on the elegant illustrators like Howie Post and Nick Cardy, whose work the editorial director preferred. Infantino apparently tried to coax Kirby into taking over the Superman line, but that wasn't Jack's way. Once, when a young Marvel cartoonist announced that he wanted to continue some series "in the Kirby tradition," Jack chuckled,

"The Kirby tradition is to create a new book." He and Infantino compromised: Jack would take over one established title and create three of his own. Kirby then asked either for a series that had no regular creative team, so he wouldn't have to throw anybody out of work, or for DC's lowest-selling title, so he could prove that he could sell anything. Both the magnanimity and the pride are in character, and either way the result came up *Jimmy Olsen*.

If any readers doubted that the King could spring back from his late, stale days at Marvel, his *Olsen* put those doubts to rest. A revived Newsboy Legion—Simon and Kirby's 1941 version of the Dead End Kids—roar up in a high-tech car called the Whiz Wagon, exploding across a two-page spread. They drive Jimmy to the forested Wild Area, where a gang called the Outsiders lives in a colossal tree house called Habitat and battles the superscientific vigilantes known as the Raiders—all under the shadow of the semimystical Mountain of Judgment. Meanwhile, Superman struts his first fresh action stunts in years, and Jimmy and Clark Kent get a new boss: Morgan Edge, owner of the conglomerate that just bought the *Daily Planet*, but also a gangster who sets Jimmy up to be killed. And that's just the *first* issue (*SPJO* 133, Oct. 1970). In just twenty-two pages Kirby had turned the trite world of Superman's pal into one of the oddest melanges in comics history, uniting cosmic scope, gritty violence, topicality, and nostalgia. He began grappling with themes even more overtly mythical and symbolic than he had at Marvel, forging a writing style that oddly combined beat jive with blunt, savage philosophizing. "Go! Go! Go!" cries an ecstatic biker. "Death is *fast!* Death is

Jack Kirby's imagination leaves earth far behind. He drew "Man—Machine—Merger" as the centerspread for Kirby Unleashed (1971), a self-published portfolio for the fan market that testified to both the magnitude of his fame and the growth of the comic shops. Inks by Mike Royer.

loud! Death is *final!*" He borrowed more overtly than ever from the classics, which he called "the most powerful literature there is," as when one Outsider describes the Mountain of Judgment as "like Moby Dick! You go there to meet it—and die!"

Kirby would never know how well he'd succeeded in selling DC's losingest superhero comic. Infantino stuck to the time-honored comic book tradition of keeping sales figures secret—it wouldn't do to have artists knowing how valuable they were to the company, after all. We've learned since that sell-through was tremendous for the first few issues, but just as Infantino ordered print runs increased to take advantage of it, the sales began to drop. *Olsen* was suddenly selling well below 50 percent of its run, a money-loser. The likelihood is that back-issue dealers and hard-core Marvelites were buying multiple copies of the early issues, expecting them to inflate in value like the early Marvels had, but as they realized *Olsen* was "weird" and not very Marvelish, they backed off. At the time, no one knew that fans and investors were doing such things; new series and new directions were always expected to start a little low and then build as kids spread the word. Infantino stopped pushing Kirby to take over extant DC titles.

The pressure was now on Kirby's new creations—and those were already being compromised from what Kirby thought was his original agreement. He had wanted to edit his own stable, creating and directing several series to be written and drawn by others, but now Infantino insisted that he draw at least sixty pages a month and use no other artists. Kirby had wanted to branch into new formats, new sizes, and new markets, with magazines for adults and a self-contained epic, *The New Gods*, to be published in three rotating series of twenty-four comic books each, then reprinted in book form for sale through bookstores. National perfunctorily dispensed with the adult comics with a pair of black-and-white one-shots, *In the Days of the Mob* and *Spirit World*, dumped on the market under the imprint "Hampshire Publications." The epic, Kirby was now told, couldn't build to an ending and wasn't guaranteed any life beyond comics. Still, Kirby gave it his all. At the beginning of 1971, he pulled the veil from his grandest and most unified creation, one that came to be called "The Fourth World."

The greatest expanse of that realm unfolded in *New Gods*, telling of no less than "the titanic struggle for the fate of mankind." "There came a time

157

[1] Although when he spun a new variation on the Silver Surfer—the Black Racer, a skier as cosmic herald of death—he made him an injured man transfigured by Darkseid rather than a creature of pure energy as his Surfer had been. Jack could do anything at any moment, but never, ever what one would expect.

when the old gods died," says the opening narrative, and from the ruins of their domain arose two worlds: New Genesis, "a golden island of gleaming spires that orbits a sunlit, unspoiled world," and Apokolips, "a dismal, unclean place . . . . an armed camp where those who live with weapons rule the wretches who build them . . . . [where] life is the evil . . . . and death the great goal!" (*NG* 1, Mar. 1971). The master of Apokolips is the great, stone-faced Darkseid, a monumental, self-possessed embodiment of destruction. Arrayed against him are the glorious young gods of New Genesis, spearheaded by the scarred, grim Orion, who draws on a vaguely mystical power called the Source. Orion wields the powerful Astro-Force against Darkseid—and proves eventually to be Darkseid's own son. The New Gods and their foes resembled Kirby's earlier Inhumans in distinctness and variety—including the impetuous Lightray, the knowledge-seeking Metron with his universe-spanning Moebius Chair, the cruel scientist Desaad, and a group of undersea demons called the Deep Six—but the scope of their adventures was far greater. Orion's mission, which he must accomplish through subterfuge on Earth as well as combat in the Fourth World, is to prevent Darkseid's conquest of mankind and his acquisition of the dreaded Anti-Life Equation.

The same month came *The Forever People*, about a colorful group of superpowered flower children from New Genesis who are trying to frustrate Darkseid's agents on Earth (*FP* 1, Mar. 1971). As their most interesting member, a naïve, mystical woman called Beautiful Dreamer, comments, "We have fun names!": Big Bear, Vykin the Black, Mark Moonrider, and Serifan, the last a macho hippie-god in a cowboy suit. They also have screwball hippie speech patterns, sometimes striving clumsily for hipness but more often veering into the dream-speech of Kirby's mind. A giant tricycle teleports them through space and different dimensions, where they encounter adventures set against such mind-boggling backdrops as Desaad's horrifically jolly amusement park, Happyland.

Next came *Mr. Miracle*, the adventures of a super escape artist, Scott Free and his gnomish assistant, Oberon, travel America performing Kirbyed-out, high-tech versions of Houdini stunts, but are secretly agents of New Genesis (*Mr. Miracle* 1, Apr. 1971). Soon their lives are complicated by a partnership with a muscle-bound, hotheaded amazon named Big Barda (*Mr. Miracle* 4, Oct. 1971). Their greatest foe is Granny Goodness, whose matronly veneer hides the soul of a sadistic dominatrix, and who tenderly coddles a computer called Overlord while devising exquisitely horrible death traps for our Scott. Behind the façade of an orphanage, she trains brutal but infantile warriors for the service of Darkseid. This was the least mythically dense of the three but the most full-throttle fun, as *Captain America* was to *Fantastic Four* and *Thor*, but with its grotesquely funny characters and ingenious escape sequences, Scott's adventures were even more devilishly charming than Cap's had ever been.

Within these three titles and *Jimmy Olsen*, the vision that had begun growing in Kirby's work at Marvel six years before came to full flower. Some of his Marvel ideas resurfaced, now distilled to pure Kirby terms, bereft of Lee's inclinations toward humanization and internal agony.[1] The Marvel formula for characterization played no part in these new creations. The Fourth World was a theater for elemental drama, for the clash of absolutes, for grand symbolizing about the nature of life and death, good and evil. Beside the powerfully symbolic and multifaceted Darkseid, even the awesome Galactus began to seem like just another comic book villain.

Kirby was determined to use his unprecedented creative freedom to make his message unmistakably clear. "I felt there was a time," he later explained, "that a man had to tell a story in which he felt . . . . there was no bullshit. There was absolute truth." Even Darkseid told the truth for Kirby, as when he observed a funeral for a fallen New God, saying, "Oh, how heroes love to flaunt their nobility in the face of death! Yet they know better than most that war is but the cold game of the butcher!" (*NG* 4, Sept. 1971). "And he's right," said Kirby, remembering the day he "was handed a helmet, an M-1 rifle, and two chocolate bars and told to polish off Adolf Hitler." It was Darkseid—and not any of the many heroes who opposed him—who was ultimately the focus and the most fascinating personality of the Fourth World stories. It was a departure for comics but a logical result of Kirby's thought. "People like villains because they know that in us the villain lives," he said. "The villain is as valid as the hero."

Who were the villains and heroes here? Certainly we can read Darkseid as Hitler, the physically flawed Orion as Roosevelt, and Scott Free as Kirby himself, the seemingly trivial entertainer who is in fact speading the truth about good and evil. We can read them archetypically as well, with Darkseid as Kronos and all those other destructive father-figures, Orion as the wounded warrior-king whose wound is his strength, and Mr. Miracle as the poet or fool who reveals the truth but only through trickery. Kirby said Darkseid was everybody who'd ever abused him or stabbed him in the back in his career, which might make the wounded but unstoppable Orion Kirby himself. We can find deeper biographical echoes, as well: of the hurt artist against the father who wanted him bound to pragmatism, of the creative spirit of Scott Free having to free itself again and again. Then we see the Forever People as artists, maybe comic book artists, who for all their goofiness are essential players in the war against the oppressive industry of Apokolips. We can also see a broader critique: the "dismal, unclean place" not as Nazi Germany but as the whole industrial world, where machines "rule the wretches who build them," where the "life" of freedom and creation "is the enemy" and the "death" of mindless production "is the great goal." Orion then becomes industrial man, a creation of the system that has scarred him. Mr. Miracle becomes the visionary whom technology cannot hold, and the Forever People, like the real-world hippies, become the harbingers of a new culture for whom names aren't the brands of destiny, but "fun."

And *fun* was what Kirby brought to his stories, for all his moral intensity. His art was stripped down and powerful, his storytelling fast and compelling,

Pure Kirby. Inks by Mike Royer. (*New Gods* #7, Mar. 1972.)

his plots—the best-crafted of his career—abounding in fight scenes, extravagant costumes, and fantastic machinery. A deluge of ideas poured from every issue, always with surprising and slightly tongue-in-cheek names: the Boom Tube, transporting characters between the Fourth World and ours; Mother Box, keeping the New Gods in touch with their homeland; and Doctor Vermin Vundabar's Murder Machine, which the cover said was "like a diabolical car wash!! It traps you on the way in—and kills you on the way out!" (*Mr. Miracle* 5, Dec. 1971).

This was how to do comics that grappled with the great issues of their day, and all days—not with "relevance." This was the superhero *as* superhero, the comic book *as* comic book. It was one of the rarest and most meaningful moments in the medium's history: a truly individual vision, free of trends and fads, free of editorial policy and the demands of main-

[2] Kirby needed Sherman for a more immediate sort of reality-contact than just double-checking hippie slang: he tended to disappear so completely into the otherworlds of his imagination that it was unsafe for him to drive a car, and when his wife was unable to drive him, young brains who knew the L.A. freeway system could be the difference between life and death for him. The greatest compliment Jack could give in his later years was, "You can drive my car anytime!"

stream fandom. In those pages full of archetypal power, explosive action, and bizarre invention, Jack Kirby—the man who had been both workhorse and maverick, street fighter and mythic poet, salesman and creative genius during all of comics' most critical junctures—brought his tumultuous career to a dazzling consummation. In the process, he created three of the finest series of their time.

Kirby did have help, it should be noted. Steve Sherman and Mark Evanier—the latter something of a gag-writing prodigy, selling jokes to comedians and comedy magazines in his teens, soon to work for James Komack's sitcom factory and other TV venues—were doing some work for an LA company called Marvelmania, which had a contract to produce posters and other Marvel merchandise, until the owner disappeared with all the money (ah, comics!). Kirby drew posters for Marvelmania, met the two whiz kids, and invited them to visit him at his studio. Soon he hired them as assistants, which meant mainly they were sounding boards for his ideas and conduits to the West Coast youth culture, which surely helped Kirby attain a freshness and vigor that even the best of his New York peers couldn't approximate.[2]

Ultimately they became advocates, as well. When they saw that Kirby's pencils were being weakened by inker Vince Colletta, they pushed Jack to protest until the rough but more faithful Mike Royer got the job. They also tried to get DC to stop its insulting practice of having its staffers redraw all of Kirby's Superman heads so they'd look more like the "real" Superman, but production manager Sol Harrison, in Evanier's recollection, "sat us down for a ten-minute monologue on how everything Kirby drew looked like those lousy Marvel comic books." (They didn't even try to fight DC's insistence on turning Morgan Edge into a good guy; somehow, the idea of a publishing firm being bought out by organized crime just made DC management *uncomfortable*.)

For Evanier, it would be far more than a job. Even after Kirby no longer needed an assistant and Evanier was scripting *That's Incredible* and other weird '70s TV, he would be among Kirby's closest

friends and fiercest protectors. He was prominent in fandom, but was never suckered by pretension and faddishness. He was the only major fan who focused his energies on breaking into Western/Gold key, content to let his friends fight for *Spider-Man* while he wrote reams of *Mickey Mouse* and *Scooby Doo* scripts. He and Sherman encouraged Kirby to some of his wildest flights, including the one that outweirded even Weisinger's *Jimmy Olsen:* a guest appearance by Don Rickles and his evil twin, "Goody Rickles" (*SPJO* 139-141, July-Sept. 1971).

Evanier knew genius when he saw it, but the rest of fandom wasn't so sure. Accustomed to viewing Roy Thomas poetics and Denny O'Neil toughness as the twin peaks of "adult" comics writing, Jack's blatant thematic signposts and sometimes graceless dialogue looked unsophisticated. It became a cutesy cliché among fans to say, "We always knew he could draw—now we know he can't write." There's no better proof of the limitations of fandom's adolescent, insecure tastes than the fact that just as the greatest superhero cartoonist of them all was doing the purest work of his career, fandom's approval of him began to drop. *New Gods* hit its stride as *Green Lantern/Green Arrow* was hitting its head against its built-in limits, but it was the latter that the fans thought was proving the potential greatness of comics.

Carmine Infantino wasn't reading fanzine reviews, he was reading sales figures. Years later, new bosses at DC dug into those secret figures and discovered that the numbers were solid, enough to keep the series in the black, although they weren't the instant blockbusters that DC wanted. DC had started them with print runs appropriate for top-selling superhero series, and after returns they were selling only about 40 percent. Rather than lowering the print runs, Infantino wanted Kirby to justify his fat contract by selling more. Infantino thought the Fourth World had a "tremendous college audience, but the youngsters didn't dig it. They couldn't understand it." But then there had never been comics like this before. So many creations were being hurled out that readers would have to give them faith and time. *Fantastic*

Four had had to climb slowly up from the muck on word of mouth and its own continuous improvement. The Fourth World comics were steadily expanding their scope and tightening their focus, and with time they might have caught fire—but we'll never know. In 1971 Infantino gave *Olsen* to Murray Boltinoff (*SPJO* 149, May 1972) and told Kirby to come up with something more commercial. Most of Kirby's proposals were rejected, and the rest led to disappointments of other kinds. Evanier reports that Kirby thought of bringing Fawcett's Captain Marvel back to life with the original artist, C.C. Beck. "Infantino accepted the idea," reported Evanier, "made the deal with the characters' owners—and then . . . told Kirby that no DC comics would ever be edited outside the DC offices in New York." Julie Schwartz would get the Captain Marvel job.

Much worse news was on the way. In 1971 Jack Liebowitz finally stepped down, and Infantino ascended to publisher. Sol Harrison, the strongest link to the old regime, gained a more powerful voice in business decisions, soon getting a promotion to vice president, director of operations. The first challenge facing them was the necessity of another price increase, barely two years after the last one. Not only was inflation roaring now that President Nixon had suddenly discovered he was a Keynesian deficit spender, not only were retailers continuing to drop comics in favor of higher-yield items, but as sales dropped, so did advertising revenue. Look at '60s DCs and you'll find, mixed in with the whoopee cushions and sea monkeys, ads for high-profile kid-consumables like Tootsie Rolls, Hot Wheels, Cheerios, and CBS cartoons. Just a few years later, DC could boast little better than the Columbia House discount record club. Cover price would have to pay more and more of production costs. DC decided to attack the problems full in the face, increasing page counts and bumping the price all the way from fifteen to twenty-five cents. They were nice packages, filled out with well-chosen golden age reprints (boisterous Simon and Kirby stories for the Kirby comics, moody Jerry Robinson work for the Batman line).

Marvel followed DC's example two months later, in what proved to be Martin Goodman's last brilliantly sleazy stunt. After much hullabaloo about the new format, he suddenly, after a single issue of each title, pulled his comics back to their normal size with the proclamation, "Now only twenty cents!" It was a price increase of a full third from two months before, creating a fat profit margin that allowed Goodman to give his wholesalers a bigger cut. Not only were kids able to buy five Marvels to the dollar instead of four DCs, but now everybody who sold comics across the country had a motive to push Marvel at the expense of the competition. In the past, DC's only fear was that retailers would return too many unsold copies. Now wholesalers were returning DC books without even getting them on the stands. DC won points with fandom for class, but class didn't pay the printer. With Liebowitz gone, Goodman was the only old pirate still left from the cutthroat distribution wars of the '30s, and these postwar punks didn't stand a chance.

By early 1972 Infantino was showing signs of panic. He reportedly asked Kirby to devise new series that were simpler and more commercial than the Fourth World, meaning with single lead characters, one-issue stories, and easy-to-follow action plots. He said one had to be about a monster, because everybody thought horror was coming back, and one had to be a riff on *Planet of the Apes*, because he'd just failed to get the rights to that movie series (and Marvel would end up succeeding). Kirby responded with *The Demon* and *Kamandi, the Last Boy on Earth*. The former was the story of occultist Jason Blood, transformed by the ancient spirit of Merlin into a nearly uncontrollable demon named Etrigan, whose mission it was to battle the magical forces of darkness. The latter was about a human boy in a post-nuclear-war future in which other animals have gained intelligence and reduced mankind to bestialism. Kirby imagined editing them while others wrote and drew them—Mark Evanier and Dan Spiegle on *Kamandi*—but Infantino had other ideas. They sounded commercial to him, and he figured Kirby art could only help sell them. So to give Jack a little time in his schedule, he canceled *New Gods* and *Forever People*.

Evanier saw Kirby the day he got the news. "He was devastated. He looked like a man who'd been punched in the face repeatedly. He was very, very hurt." Even Infantino said, "Jack was in tears over it." Fans assumed *New Gods* and *Forever People* were killed for low sales. They were unsatisfied with the way countless plot threads were left hanging after only eleven issues of each, and began to wonder if Kirby had lost his touch. *The Demon* (Sept. 1972) was moody and entertaining, a rare and potent blend of horror and heroics. But the strictures placed on it kept it from building like other Kirby creations had, and it would only tread water until cancellation after sixteen issues. *Kamandi* (Nov. 1972) was a clever idea, but Kirby settled for a long series of different talking animals (even talking snails) instead of more complex plot variations. Kids liked it, but older fans saw talking animals as kid stuff and generally dismissed it. Infantino, however, had finally despaired of a Kirby blockbuster and lowered print runs to keep it in the black. Kirby would ultimately do forty issues. *Mr. Miracle* failed to carry the Fourth World torch, getting simpler and faster all the time. "Jack was getting panicked," Evanier recalled, "and was maybe trying too hard to please a lot of folks who had suggestions on how to make the books more commercial." After eighteen issues, it was canceled (Mar. 1974).

Then came *OMAC*, about a "One Man Army Corps" in a future of robotics gone mad. It was rich with ideas— a female "Build-a-Friend" with which the hero falls in love, and a sentient orbital satellite shaped like a giant eye—but it ran only eight issues (Oct. 1974-Dec. 1975). Then there was an oddly nostalgic run of World War II stories for *The Losers* in *Our Fighting Forces,* then a tryout called *Dingbats of Danger Street,* then *Kobra*, a cocreation with Steve Sherman about twin brothers, one good and one evil. Neither turned into much. Suddenly Kirby was reduced to doing art on other people's concepts just to meet his quotas. It was like MGM using Buster Keaton as a gagman.

Kirby had been undone by a company wanting to use him without honoring him, by the excessive expectations his own success had created. His arrival at DC had promised to champion the cause of the artist-creator, to further the shift of comics into a graphics-dominated medium, "to keep the medium," in his own words, "ever flexible and sustaining." Now he was beaten down, sick of this business. Even his craftsmanship suffered. The big images that had once been so powerful began to lose their focus and detail, and his compositions started losing some grace. His stories sped by too quickly to be satisfying, and his always-odd scripting began to swing toward the oblique and confusing. He had carried to a wondrous conclusion the explosive innovation of Marvel in the 1960s, but in the slick, serious days of Denny O'Neil and Neal Adams, Roy Thomas and Barry Smith, his rambunctious creations, so uniquely combining awe and delight, were being dismissed as "comic booky." In 1971 a portfolio of his work called *Kirby Unleashed* was a best-seller among fans and created a new market for comics art. Just a few years later, Marvel staffers were sneering in fanzines that they didn't miss Kirby a bit, that Stan Lee had been the genius all along. A fan named Joe Ferrara recalls going to a convention in those years to see his hero, Neal Adams, but when he found the lines for Adams wearyingly long, he wandered over to the other celebrity guest, the one with few fans around him. He still remembers Jack Kirby's friendliness and generosity, even after he confessed to him that "I just wasn't into the kind of work he did."

By 1974 Kirby was cranking out monthly *Kamandi* issues, doing *OMAC* with little support from DC, and looking back on his dead Fourth World. His five-year contract would be up soon, and he probably already knew he wasn't going to sign another one. He'd been here before: his reputation suddenly faded, slick young guys making him look like old news, relations poisoned at DC, nowhere to go but back to the company where they'd screwed him before. But the last time, he'd been sixteen years younger, sixteen years more hopeful. Sixteen years and two fictional universes.

What the hell had it all been for?

Chapter 24

MARVEL: PHASE TWO

Stan Lee was on top of the world. He was standing onstage at Carnegie Hall, the same Carnegie Hall where W.C. Handy had once legitimized the blues for bourgeois society, where Benny Goodman had done the same for jazz, and now he was doing it for his own bastard medium. It was called "A Marvel-ous Evening with Stan Lee," and a packed house of True Believers was eating up every smart-aleck, self-deprecating word he tossed across the footlights. Stan was graying now, a regular silver fox in aviator glasses, and that fit his new status. He'd been butting heads with Martin Goodman over the direction of the company. After *Conan* proved it would survive, Lee wanted to forge on, with Roy Thomas pointing the way, into new genres, new formats, and new audiences. Goodman was all for high volume, but only with time-tested content: horror, war, Westerns, and established superheroes. Once that would have ended the argument, but now Lee could force the new owners to make a choice. They chose the smile that every Marvelite knew and loved, the risk-taking energy that had made Marvel worth buying. It wasn't official yet, that January night in 1972, but the war was won. Goodman was about to get his golden parachute, and little cousin Stanley would become president and publisher of Marvel Comics.

It was the end of Stan Lee, editor, and Stan Lee, writer. Roy Thomas got the editor's chair and *Fantastic Four*, passing Stan's last two gigs, *Spider-Man* and *Thor*, to Gerry Conway. Stan had always put his own credit above everyone's, even when he was only the editor (while DC editors buried their names down in the fine print), but now every Marvel comic had the words "Stan Lee Presents" embla-zoned over the top of the splash page. He was a selling point, and he knew it. "Hang loose, heroes," he wrote in Stan's Soapbox, "and watch our smoke! Marvel's set to bust loose now, and that means the wondrous world of fantasy won't ever be the same!" 1972, he said, was the start of "Phase Two" of the Marvel Age of Comics.

Whatever the fate of the world of fantasy, Roy Thomas would never be the same. He'd brought his career as "just a writer" to a peak just before it ended. Lee had said goodbye to writing with some epics that exploded with death imagery, from the Norse death-goddess to Ragnarok, the doom of the gods, from Dr. Doom taking over the FF to the return of Galactus (*Thor* 184-200, Jan. 1971-1972; *FF* 113-123, Aug. 1971-June 1972). Thomas, though, wasn't going to be topped. He used his *Avengers* to weave what he intended to be the largest-scale, most profound cosmic saga ever to appear in comics, centering on a war between two alien races, the Kree and the Skrull, in which Earth, like some Pacific island in World War II, might be devastated just because it happened to be in the way. Some issues were drawn by Neal Adams, who, with the aid of Tom Palmer's inks, brought force and beauty to Thomas's far-ranging story line.

Unfortunately, the saga suffered from Thomas's determination to make the prose as grandiose as the story line. He crammed deep meditations into the mouths of whatever characters Adams had penciled into the panels, many of which managed to be simultaneously pretentious and silly. During one action sequence, for example, Ant-Man sees one of his ants killed and reflects, "Human beings are funny—they think no living things but themselves capable of feel-

163

ing pain. That's because—they've never heard an ant scream. Well, *I* have—and it's a sound to haunt a lifetime worth of dreams! A sound like lost souls in torment or the wailing of a forsaken child—and I don't ever want to hear that sound again—not EVER!" When not emoting, Thomas's characters were tossing out pop-culture references: the ant who was killed was named Crosby, to go with its partners Stills and Nash. The climax of the war represents the unification of all Roy Thomas's personal themes. Seeing that the war must end, the Supreme Intelligence of the Kree grants temporary mental powers to the only human at hand who's outside the whole mess, the annoying Rick Jones. From Rick's mind springs an army of forgotten heroes from the Goodman stable's golden age. It looked as though Roy hadn't had an organic ending in mind, and in attempting to top himself had thrown all of his recurrent motifs together into one big arbitrary plot twist. Still, the Kree-Skrull War, combining the greatest mythopoeic aspirations of fandom's favorite writer with some of the most atypical and ambitious work of its favorite artist, was immediately hailed as a masterpiece. Even now, older fans call it "the classic Kree-Skrull War," in the same meter that they employ for "the classic *Green Lantern/Green Arrow*."

Then began Roy Thomas, Phase Two. Before he could even climb on top of the regular slate of Marvel monthlies, he found himself supervising an explosion of new titles that had begun in Goodman's last days. These weren't just new *series*, but *Showcase*-style comics, such as *Marvel Spotlight*, *Marvel Feature*, and *Marvel Premiere*, which introduced new series every issue or two. Plus, there was *Marvel Team-Up* (Mar. 1972) and *Marvel Two-in-One* (Jan. 1974), based on DC's *Brave and Bold*, pairing Spider-Man and the Thing with a different hero—and often a different creative team—every month. Thomas was even supervising new genres, trying to launch a horror line. He needed a horde of new writers and artists. Gary Friedrich was there already, and now Mike Friedrich came over from DC, soon followed by his compatriots Marv

Wolfman and Len Wein—the freedom and fan-orientation promised by a Marvel playground under the supervision of Roy the Boy was irresistible. Closely following Thomas's style and example, and often collaborating with him, was the prolific Gerry Conway, only nineteen and already a rising star. Tony Isabella, Doug Moench, and Chris Claremont were also kicking around, selling an occasional story or trying to. Good young artists were still hard to find, but there were a lot of old hands—George Tuska, Syd Shores, Sal Buscema, Herb Trimpe, Gil Kane—to fill the pages until the fan-artists could come of age. It helped that Stan was making John Romita the art director, and Kane was now becoming so fast that he could not only launch several new titles, but crank out hundreds of punchy cover layouts. (The covers were repetitive, roughly executed, and plastered with blurbs, giving Marvel some of the ugliest packaging in comic book history, but at least there was a "look," as there'd been in the early Kirby days, and it promised a definite Marvel blend of action and angst.) Still, with a novice editor and the whole industry in flux, there was no way to avoid chaos. Thomas could never hope to be an editor in the traditional sense. He could only kick-start series, make assignments, and let the creators run free, hoping there'd be some gold in the rushing waters.

He found one decent nugget in a writer named Steve Englehart, who combined Thomas's love of comics arcana with a post-'60s impudence toward tradition. He was an Indiana boy but a '70s boy too, with a charged bundle of passions: sorcery, left-wing politics, desert backpacking, tantric sexuality, and conspiracy theories. His first chance to shine came on *The Beast*, starring the former X-Man (*Amazing Adventures* 12, May 1972), around whom he wove subplots involving the X-Men, Iron Man—two stars of Marvel's defunct romance comics line, Patsy Walker and Buzz Baxter. He didn't point out who Patsy and Buzz were, making an Englehart game of it by letting the fans discover it for themselves. The Beast's series ended after seven issues, but by then Englehart had proven he could make the fans notice him, and had already replaced Gary Friedrich on *Captain America*.

Then there was editorial assistant Don McGregor, a romantic anachronist whom at least one fan remembers giving tours of the Marvel offices in white ruffled shirt, black suit, and purple prose. When handed the job of writing a new *Black Panther* series (*Jungle Action* 6, Sept. 1973), he tackled it with remarkable energy and serious intent. He designed a complex geography and socioeconomic history for the kingdom of Wakanda, with an intriguing political situation: while King Tchalla lived out his infatuation with the West by joining the Avengers, his people began to feel he had abandoned them, and a brutal chieftain—Erik Killmonger—laid claim to the throne. The story took thirteen issues to resolve, most of them drawn by Billy Graham, whose startling angles, lush backdrops, and sinewy figures conveyed in a few panels more of the jungle's menace and the Panther's rage than could dozens of ponderous words.

McGregor, however, being a fan-turned-writer of the 1970s, felt that dozens of ponderous words were an essential addition. His Panther took an inward journey, trying to choose between the world— represented by an urbane American lover (a black woman; comics hadn't changed *that* much)—and his duty. For this, McGregor dropped all pretense of writing for children and put before the fans the most difficult and ambitious style yet employed in comics. He mixed verbiage more florid than Roy Thomas's, with huge lumps of pop psychology and philosophy, filling pages with discussions of values and self-perceptions, examining every nook of his characters, stalling his story and torturing grammar: "I'm afraid much of Killmonger's revolution has caused me to lose a great deal of my empathy," says Tchalla at the end of a very long exposition, "but Taku, he still listens, senses, evaluates. Inside he is simultaneously outraged by the savagery of men, yet, most often, I think he is merely bemused by their purposes and intrigues" (*JA* 16, July 1975). The acclaim that McGregor's writing won from many fans showed that storytelling was becoming less important to the

readers than exploration of the heroes' lives. Indeed, quite strangely for a genre that was once all about externalities, the inner lives of the super heroes were becoming the sole concern of some series.

Most other new series were battered by frequent changes of personnel and direction. The chaos had started before phase two, but now only got worse. *The Inhumans*, kicking off *Amazing Adventures* (Aug. 1970), had led with four issues of rapid-fire Kirby action. Now it made an about-face to a troubled, humanistic approach under Thomas and Neal Adams, and then ended after two issues by Gerry Conway and Mike Sekowsky. The *Black Widow* backup had lasted only eight issues under four writers and three pencilers. In *Astonishing Tales* (Aug. 1970), *Ka-Zar* began under Lee and Kirby, shifted to a fantastical tone under Conway and Barry Smith and then moved to New York City and into a semirelevant phase under Mike Friedrich and diverse artists. Its backup, *Dr. Doom*, which had looked interesting as the first series to star an outright villain, lasted only seven issues but featured three writers and two pencilers.

With Marvel's new market advantage, more old characters were given their own series. The only success, presumably on the strength of its characters, was *The Defenders* (*Marvel Feature* 1, Dec. 1971), a team of loners and oddballs: the Hulk, Dr. Strange. Sub-Mariner, an ex-villain named Nighthawk and a human woman possessed by an Asgardian soul, the Valkyrie. That such a group could become a team seemed unlikely even for Marvel, and indeed, writers Thomas, Englehart, and Wein often had to stretch the plots to make them work. Next came *Warlock,* about the mysterious golden messiah formerly known as Him, now a Christ-figure on an alternate Earth created by the godlike scientist the High Evolutionary (*Marvel Premiere* 1, Apr. 1972). Thomas wrote a thoughtful origin story, full of biblical parallels, Gil Kane added his dynamic art and Dan Adkins his fine inking, and the series showed tremendous promise. But when Mike Friedrich took over the writing and Bob Brown the art soon afterward, the Christ-figure was recast in a more standard hero role and rambled to early discontinuation. Friedrich and Herb Trimpe brought back Ant-Man (*Marvel Feature* 4, July 1972), an unsuccessful revival of an unimportant hero, which testified more than anything to Marvel's unwillingness to let any piece of its past fade away. Next came the return of Dr. Strange (*Marvel Premiere* 3, July 1972), with some gorgeous Barry Smith art. But Smith left almost immediately, and writers and artists started playing musical chairs.

The last feeble stab of the Goodman days was at reviving war and Western comics. *Combat Kelly and the Deadly Dozen* and *The Gunhawks* both attempted a cynical, modern look at historical violence—lots of Sam Peckinpah style in a Marvel narrative—but they weren't given to major creators, and both failed promptly. One other Western tells a great deal about the changing times: *Red Wolf*, about a semi-mystical American Indian hero in the Old West (*Marvel Spotlight* 1, Nov. 1971). It was written by Gardner Fox, now cut loose by DC, revisiting his *Super-Chief* and *Pow Wow Smith* work of a decade before, and what a long decade it had been. Fox's experience in pulps, paperbacks, and the varied comics of the past still served him well, gave his stories a texture that none of the fan writers had. With a colorful milieu, an entertaining story, and lush, quiet art by veteran Syd Shores, Red Wolf's tryout sold well enough to win him his own title. But the times being what they were, Fox struggled to jam his light style into the new seriousness—especially when, after seven issues, Red Wolf was moved to New York in the present. Two issues later, it was canceled (Sept. 1973). It would prove to be Fox's last series, the quiet departure of a seminal comic book writer who still seemed to have something to offer, but nothing that fandom was looking for.

Along the way, *Captain Marvel* returned from cancellation (*CM* 22, Sept. 1972) with a lot of fun ideas in its favor. Roy Thomas had even paid sly tribute to the golden age Captain Marvel by having his Kree warrior share the same space/time with Marvel's ubiquitous teenager, Rick Jones, just as the other captain had with Billy Batson. But now weak writing by Conway, Wolfman, and Mike Friedrich, along with sloppy art by the aging Wayne Boring, obscured all the cleverness. The presence, even preeminence, of Rick Jones also soaked the stories in excess emotion and with-it lingo: "A warm, loving chick shafted me last night—and that burns me—*bad,* man—*BAAD!*" (*CM* 25, Mar. 1973). Yet, the very same issue with that warm, loving chick brought in something new: a fanzine artist named Jim Starlin, then very slowly developing from a promising fill-in guy to a comic book visionary. He took over the plot line, turning in a nine-issue run that pushed the boundaries of the Marvel Universe for the first time since Kirby was still going strong. The structure owed a lot to Thomas's Kree-Skrull war, but the characters were all his: a bald, mystical, extraterrestrial woman named Moondragon and Thanos, a tyrant out to enslave the universe by obtaining an old Kirby creation, the Cosmic Cube. Along the way, Captain Marvel encounters a personified metaphysical force called Eon and is granted an extrasensory "cosmic awareness" (*CM* 29, Nov. 1973). The stories were hurt by a plethora of inkers, scripters, and guest-stars, but from underneath it all emerged a rich complexity and an evocation of an ultimate, implacable evil. Starlin seemed to be mixing Kirby, Ditko, and a vat of acid into a vision that was wholly, syncretically Marvel.

Once Stan Lee was firmly in charge, he pushed for new characters, some aimed straight at neglected demographic groups. *Hero for Hire* played off "blaxploitation" movies like *Sweet Sweetback's Baadasssss Song,* with a tough black protagonist who uses his strength and steel-like skin to clear himself of criminal charges. Having no job skills, he becomes a strong-arm for hire, working in Harlem on assignments involving pimps, racketeers, and ghetto parasites (*HH* 1, June 1972). The inker, Billy Graham, was a black man—one of very few in what was then an almost entirely white business—though penciler George Tuska and writer Archie Goodwin, were both white. Despite some forced "blackness" (Cage tended to holler "Sweet Christmas!"), Goodwin turned in some superb stories, gutsily preserving the opportunism and moral ambivalence of the character. He left after four issues anyway, leaving Luke to uncommitted stints by Englehart, Isabella, and others (with Billy Graham sometimes assisting). To forestall cancellation, Cage was renamed Power Man and made into a more standard hero.

Still less successful were Marvel's bids for a female audience. *The Claws of the Cat, Night Nurse,* and *Shanna the She-Devil* boasted some female creators, but not much else to bring readers back (except maybe Marie Severin's art on *Cat*). All died quickly. Girls had once bought comics by the millions, even superhero comics. Now the Marvel formula and post-camp grittiness were making comics more and more a "boy biz," and none of the passionate new talents seemed interested in a serious effort to reach female readers.

Young artists like Jim Starlin and his friend Howard Chaykin were pushing for more science fiction. Lee was reluctant: SF had never done terribly well in comics, and it wasn't catching fire in other media, despite a number of lugubrious Hollywood attempts, such as *Soylent Green* and *Silent Running* (whereas *The Exorcist* was very encouraging to Lee's support for a horror line). But Chaykin, along with Gerry Conway, and with an art assist from Neal Adams, got to launch a *War of the Worlds* series in *Amazing Adventures* (18, May 1973), positing what would happen if H.G. Wells's Martians attacked Earth again, and this time won. The stories were set in a hideously altered future in which a band of human guerrillas fights for emancipation, led by the brash and violent Killraven (after whom the series was shortly renamed). Conflicts pulled Chaykin away, unfortunately, and the series soon became another playground for Don McGregor. Again McGregor had good ideas, especially about how the cruel Martians might torture humans (McGregor showed a fascination for willfully inflicted pain that would influence later writers of "mature" comics). Again, too, he wrote as if adjectives were about to be banned, and tried to make each story a significant work of a different type: "social satire," "fantasy

© 1970 Jim Starlin

head trip," "realistic and relentless drama," "a bizarre love story," "a moralistic comic book of rather epic proportions." The series was almost saved by another new artist coming up from the intersection of fandom and freakdom, P. Craig Russell, a lover of opera and nineteenth-century illustration, with a delicate line and a haunting tone (from *AA* 27, Nov. 1974).

Starlin and Chaykin were discouraged that Stan wasn't throwing open the doors of comics as wide as they wanted. Although he'd experiment with demographics and tone, even he felt the need to stick to superpowers and "safe" genres. They missed the freedom of the fanzine days, and began talking about doing a "prozine" together. Among the people they

From his earliest fanzine days, Jim Starlin showed the Ditko-derived line and Kirbyesque cosmic sense that made him a hot recruit for the expanding Marvel. (*Fantastic Exploits* #16, 1970.)

told was Mike Friedrich, who wasn't crazy about the writing he was doing and was looking for something else to get him excited. He headed home to the Bay Area and looking into the possibility of publishing his own comic book.

During all this, Roy Thomas wasn't just juggling editorial chores, but still writing. He tried to give *Fantastic Four* a startling new direction, but all he managed to do was stomp on Stan and Jack's garden. He forced Reed and Sue to become bitter enemies and had Sue file for divorce. He made the Torch lose his beloved Crystal to Quicksilver of the Avengers, and threatened the Thing's manhood with the obnoxious Thundra in a truly dreadful reaction to the terrors of the feminist movement. There were some stresses and resentments showing here, but they didn't make for exciting stories.

Thomas had also been doing some fun, personal work on *The Incredible Hulk*, adapting *Moby Dick*, spoofing Tom Wolf's *Radical Chic* with a story about an Upper East Side cocktail party to benefit the Hulk, and cajoling Harlan Ellison into contributing a story called "The Beast That Cried Love at the Heart of the Atom." All very English teacherly, all colorfully drawn by Herb Trimpe. But then came editorship, and Thomas's imagination stalled out. He gave the Hulk to Len Wein, who wrote mainly routine adventures. From the time he became Marvel's editor, in fact, Roy Thomas lost touch with the enthusiasm that had once made even his most awkward work exciting. Only his *Conan* stories would remain well-crafted, and those had lost the magic of the Barry Smith years.

Gerry Conway was starting to show the strain of shouldering Roy's burdens. He'd reawakened Daredevil, whom he moved to San Francisco—thus making him the first Marvel hero to live in any city other than New York (*Daredevil* 87, May 1972)—and put him through a jet-set love affair with the dashing Black Widow. Aided by the sensitive, sophisticated art of Gene Colan, he was able to create a fairly convincing adult relationship between the two heroes. On *Thor*, however—and *Fantastic Four*, which Thomas eventually surrendered to him—he managed no more than potboilers, turning Kirby and Lee's work into a mere formula. He tried to keep the subplots lively on *Spider-Man*, though his villains and plots were uninspired, and went for Marvel's biggest shocker of the year: Gwen Stacy, Peter Parker's constant girlfriend since the late Ditko days, was killed by the Green Goblin (*ASM* 121, June 1973). It was a powerful moment, one still remembered by anyone who was reading Marvels then, but Conway had nowhere to go after it. What he gained in shock value he lost in the complexity of the series. Many Spider-fans began to lose interest, and that issue has gained a status among Marvelites as the milestone marking the end of Marvel's silver age.

Phase Two was full of ominous signs: the dangers of sudden expansion, of the generational revolution, of dependence on fandom, of "serious comics." Superhero stories were still juvenile adventures at heart, and always would be at some level, but they were being dressed up in stylistic tricks that were distracting, ill-fitting, sometimes ponderous, often poorly crafted. Most of the new writers were like rookies hurled from the sandlot to the big leagues, ill-prepared for the demands of professional storytelling, intoxicated by the new ambition of the medium, falling prey to pretension and self-indulgence. Even the best work from the new generation rarely amounted to anything, because the lunacy of assignments and scheduling seemed to guarantee that every series would quickly fall into less capable hands and, with no old-style editor to watch over it, veer off in a radically new direction.

The signs were there, but nobody at Marvel had time to read them. The more obvious signs were much happier: Marvel circulation had gone *up* in the wake of the price increase, the last gift of Martin Goodman, an unheard of achievement. Despite a few bombs, phase two had brought *The Defenders*, *Marvel Team-Up*, *Marvel Premiere*, *Marvel Spotlight*, and a few other solid successes. For months DC hung onto its twenty-five-cent format, waving that sad little imperative—"52 big pages, don't take less!"—in the face of the cruel facts of circulation, until the sales figures finally made clear what a disaster it had been. After a decade, Marvel had actually done it, had become the industry sales leader. DC was where Dell had been ten years before, in second place and dropping fast.

Stan Lee was on top of the world. Free of the nights at the typewriter, the headaches over deadlines, he could focus on creating a line of oversize magazines like he'd wanted to for years, on building smarter connections with the worlds of cartoons and TV than Goodman had ever attempted. As he stepped back into the wings at Carnegie Hall, it probably never even flickered across his mind that within just a few years of the W.C. Handy and Benny Goodman concerts on that same stage, their brands of urban blues and big-band swing were dead for the American public, preserved only as nostalgia items by those who didn't want to let go.

CHAPTER 25

HORROR FROM THE SWAMPS

If there was anything that could save comics from a downward spiral into the intensifying esoterica of superhero fandom, anything that could save the creative lifeblood of the field from an endless dittoing of Spider-Man team-ups and new Marvel teams, anything that could save DC from utter defeat, it was horror. By the early '70s every other genre was going nowhere fast. Julie Schwartz couldn't sell his two new science fiction comics, *From Beyond the Unknown* and a renewed *Strange Adventures*. The world of ghosts and skeletons, however, was actually showing some life. It was especially lively in the hands of Joe Orlando, the most durable of Infantino's editorial hires, never a first-rank artist, but an editor with an artist's eye.

He pushed even harder than Infantino at getting Sol Harrison and his production department to accept subtler artistic visions, so it didn't take long for the volatile Orlando and the stubborn Harrison to become office enemies. Orlando later said "I was an outsider," a role he and the rest of the EC gang always relished, "and that meant I wasn't getting the best DC artists and DC writers." He hired old comrades like Al Williamson, Wally Wood, and Gray Morrow, a paperback cover illustrator who never mastered comics, but who appealed to fans of tasteful lines. He also used some of the low-priced but elegant talent from Spain and the Philippines whom Jim Warren had been importing for his black-and-whites, artists like Alfredo Alcala, Nestor Redondo, Tony DeZuniga, and Alex Niño. Mostly, though, he scouted for new talent—this was the editor who said he wouldn't hire anyone over thirty-five—and he found Berni Wrightson, Don Newton, and Mike Kaluta, stars of the fanzines who harked back to EC and pulp illustrations in their dark, stylized, premodern moodiness. For writers he used the likes of Otto Binder and EC vet Jack Oleck while he developed Len Wein, a superhero fan with a particular fondness for monsters.

Anthro and *Bat Lash* had died quickly, but *House of Mystery* and *House of Secrets*, along with Murray Boltinoff's *Unexpected*, went on. Orlando tried to build the franchise, with gothic romances like *Secret House of Forbidden Love*, and genre blends like *Weird War* and *Weird Western*, but the markets weren't there. He had more luck with *Phantom Stranger*, introduced in *Showcase* (80, May 1969) and immediately continued in its own series (June 1969). This was a revival of a mystical DC character from 1952, an odd blend of anthology horror and a regular costumed star. The Stranger would flit in and out of tales of human greed, warning each protagonist of the danger of his evil ways, always to be ignored and see the character consigned to a horrible fate. The stories were predictable, but the presence of a "superheroic" star seemed to help sell them.

As good as Orlando was at reviving the flavor of the early '50s, however, he wasn't the man to understand what fans wanted in the early '70s. He was barely getting his horror line up to a level he could be proud of when Stan Lee and his boy writers stole his thunder. Their first efforts weren't much: uneven EC imitations called *Tower of Shadows* and *Chamber of Darkness* that folded quickly, then a bunch of reprint comics—*Creatures on the Loose, Monsters on the Prowl, Where Creatures Roam, Where Monsters Dwell, Fear*—mostly full of old Kirby and Ditko stories. Then came the black-and-white *Savage Tales*.

The lead feature was *Conan* but backup stories provided a chance to do horror outside the Comics Code. Stan didn't want just a throwaway "Good Lord! Choke!" story, though—he knew the value of ongoing characters. He also knew that his former production chief, Sol Brodsky, had jumped to a company called Skywald, which was planning to bring out some new horror comics, including a revival of a shambling creature of swamp moss from the early '50s called the Heap. Stan and others had profited from knockoffs of the Heap in the horror days, and now he wanted to make sure Skywald didn't establish any claim to the idea. Skywald was doomed to instant failure, but by then Gerry Conway and Gray Morrow had given Stan the Man-Thing, a scientist transformed into a moss-heap by his own disastrous experiment, incapable of speech or clear thought, but enough in touch with his dim human memories to try to do the right thing (*Savage Tales* 1, May 1971). The potential of a mute, expressionless heap to connect with readers looked pretty limited, but the story was taut and Lee said the fan mail was good.

Just a few months later, Orlando and Wein came out with an awfully similar "swamp thing" story of their own, eerily drawn by Berni Wrightson (*House of Secrets* 92, Sept. 1971). Orlando would say later that, since he was working with Otto Binder, he wanted to pay homage to Binder's Adam Link stories from the pulps about a melancholy robot with a human-like mind. We have to consider the fact, however, that Wein and Conway were friends, and Conway knew Marvel had series hopes for Man-Thing. The fans who were taking over the business in those days had no patience for the old competitiveness between the publishers. They were playmates from the fanzines, and Marvel and DC were nothing but neighboring playgrounds, the only difference being that the new monitor at Marvel was big brother Roy while DC was run by crusty old gym coaches like Orlando and Schwartz—but even they would grunt and give in if you changed the rules a little. The comics of the new generation were almost communally written, with ideas kicked around and series

passed back and forth among friends, with so much of the same excitement and chaos and ambitious verbosity that they (with the exception of Denny O'Neil's) usually read as if they were all written by the same precocious teenager.

Savage Tales had died, but within months two almost simultaneous events changed Marvel's whole game plan: Goodman's coup with the price increase and the loosening of the Comics Code in response to Lee's drug stories. The Code Authority withdrew its injunctions against "walking dead...vampires and vampirism, ghouls...and werewolfism." Marvel was in an aggressive mood, determined to beat everybody else to the punch, and before most readers even knew about the new Code, Roy Thomas was developing a whole horror line. With his pure superhero background, Roy understood what Orlando may not have: that selling a series to the Marvel audience required continuing, sympathetic, superpowered characters. Just because superheroes were losing their heat didn't mean the core audience, born after the start of the silver age and weaned on Marvel comics, would suddenly revert to the tastes of 1950. The sluggish start of Thomas's sword-and-sorcery comics, with their self-contained stories and self-contained heroes, only underlined the point. He made sure his horror series would have not only complex, angst-ridden protagonists, but supporting casts, running subplots, and recurring foes.

First came *Werewolf by Night,* tested in the second issue of *Marvel Spotlight* (Feb. 1972) and given its own title when the sales reports came in (Sept. 1972). Thomas developed the basic story line, as he would for all the new monsters. His protagonist was hip and alienated, cursed to turn into a werewolf. His link to the world and companion in Marvel agony is his sister Lissa, who loves him and wants to understand him but is always sundered from him by his curse. Thomas handed the writing to Conway, his designated mood-and-poesy man, who soon passed it to Len Wein, who handed it off to his buddy Marv Wolfman ("At last!" read the credits. "A werewolf written by a Wolfman!"). They all sustained the tone,

"Too cartoony" is an epithet defensive comics fans have applied to most of the great artists in the field. Art like this, by Mike Ploog, shows how much more horror, sadness, and sheer story can be contained in cartooning than in "realism." Dialogue by Steve Gerber. (*Man-Thing* #5, May 1974.)

but none of them could find a way to give the stories any direction. What made the series click was the art of a new discovery who probably never would have found work on superheroes, an artist with the wonderful name of Mike Ploog.

Ploog had a rich ink line and a sense of the grotesque that echoed the usual EC-revival style, but he brought in an odd humor and cartoony liveliness that prevented any writer from making the material too self-important or ponderous. He owed less to the elegant Al Williamson than to the funky Jack Davis, and he owed more than anything to Will Eisner's vivid characterizations and bouncy action art. His

stories moved like Marvel stories, with surprising poignancy in the "character moments," capturing the fun of monster stories without the static, shadowy gothic feel that DC favored.

Thomas felt a little more certain about his second launch, *Tomb of Dracula*, starting it off in its own title (Apr. 1972) and with art by Gene Colan, one of Marvel's most valuable resources and a horror fan who pushed for the job. Dracula, after all, not only had a certain literary respectability that Roy liked, but had been a proven draw in the movies for forty years. Colan, old pro that he was, would never miss an issue for the life of the series, turning in some of his eeriest and most dramatic art. Inker Tom Palmer, whose work with Neal Adams and John Buscema had made him a hot commodity, was a heavy user of Zipatone, an artistic aid few comic book fans had ever seen. In fans' eyes, Palmer gave clarity, solidity, and a veneer of even greater sophistication to Colan's often oblique images. Unfortunately, *Dracula* went through writers in rapid succession: Thomas, then Conway, then Goodwin, then Wolfman.

Then came *Ghost Rider*, by Gary Friedrich and Mike Ploog (*Marvel Spotlight* 5, Aug. 1972).[1] Friedrich had always liked to play riffs on the subcultures of young America, and now he did a decent job of nailing the outlaw biker world. Ploog turned in a gloriously lurid character design, a lean biker all in black leather with a flaming skull for a head, whipping around corners on his hog. His drunk, shabby, violent bikers were a hilarious bunch, some of them looking straight out of the underground comics of Rand Holmes or S. Clay Wilson. Friedrich and Ploog's boldest stroke of all was having Satan himself appear in the pages, and a pretty charismatic fellow he was. Such a thing would have been inconceivable in mainstream comics just a couple of years before, but this was the early '70s, conservative America was prostrate, hard rock was in, the Comics Code Authority was reeling, Roy the Boy had grown his hair long, and nobody seemed to notice. *Ghost Rider* didn't catch on much with the fans, most of whom would have been scared enough of a biker even without the addition of a flaming skull, but it found enough of a niche among bad boys and cyclists to cruise through the '70s.

Next, the Man-Thing started his own series (*Fear* 10, Oct. 1972). But with a protagonist who couldn't talk or think, drawn stiffly by Gray Morrow, followed by the scarcely more dynamic Val Mayerik, there wasn't much Gerry Conway could do but be dully poetic. The very next month, Conway's DC-employed pal Len Wein showed him how a moss-monster could be done, giving DC a shot at recapturing the low ground of horror.

Wein was already revamping *Phantom Stranger*, turning the ghostly nudnick into a hero as he battled a criminal cult called the Dark Circle. Now he, Orlando, and Wrightson were seeking a way to get a series out of their Swamp Thing, spurred on by the ecstatic fan response to their one-shot. Their hero, like Man-Thing, was a scientist made hideous (*Swamp Thing* 1, Nov. 1972), but Wein wisely gave himself a latitude that Conway hadn't, giving his Thing the power of speech and tortured thought.

It was a moving and well-realized idea, but it probably wouldn't have drawn much notice if not for the chillingly evocative art of Berni Wrightson. Wrightson was another of those late '60s kids who looked backward to find a sensuality and vitality that the pop culture of the late '50s and '60s had suppressed. There was some Al Williamson in his work, some nineteenth-century fantasy illustration, and a lot of EC artist Graham "Ghastly" Ingels, although he was twice the draftsman Ingels had ever been. He'd been a star in the fanzines and was already doing great horror work for Warren, where one of his collaborators, writer/artist Bruce Jones, said, "Berni Wrightson knows a lot about maggoty grave dirt. And he didn't learn about it by collecting Spider-Boy and Captain Jock-Strap . . . . He learned it in darkened rooms, sitting mesmerized by Karloff's performance in *Bride* . . . and by taking long, solitary walks through the neighborhood cemetery and wondering what your dead Uncle Chester looks like now . . . ." With lines twisted like jungle creepers and faces contorted in desperation, greed, and terror,

Wrightson was able to tear the fears from the hearts of his readers and send them flowing over the page. In *Swamp Thing* he made the bayous a single, malevolent organism, rich with the smells of rot and fecundity, from which the protagonist oozed like a wayward, sentient clump of moss.

Wrightson, Wein, and Orlando worked closely together, plotting the first nine issues page by page in the editor's office, thus bringing the artist into the process of creation at a more intimate level than DC had ever allowed. Wrightson even plotted the tenth issue mainly on his own when Wein fell ill. Orlando was an artist—a hands-on, intuition-driven guy, a talker and a listener much more than a script-reader or note-jotter—and the energy he could generate in late-night bull sessions with a couple of trusted associates would prove to be the greatest gift he could bring DC. He and his *Swamp Thing* kids proved to be clever and compelling plotters, able to keep a rather limited character fresh and unpredictable.

The monster even left his marshy roots, donning a trench coat and hat in a poignant attempt to move among men again. His adventures were wonderfully

Berni Wrightson was another of those '60s kids who reached back to the '50s and earlier to seize the morbid and erotic imagination of the '70s. Here he tips his hat to EC's "Ghastly" Ingels, but gives a very modern expressiveness and humanity to his "Thing." Script by Len Wein. (*Swamp Thing #2*, Jan. 1973.)

[1] It was a title Marvel had had kicking around from its old western comics, pulled from *Ghost Riders in the Sky*, and a desire to keep the trademark alive may have been the sand around which this pearl grew.

unsettling: in a strange village he meets the wife he believed dead, and then his own earlier, still-human self (they prove to be the creations of a mad clock-maker). Wein delivered florid descriptions in the pulp-horror tradition, as when a cry of fright "echoes through the ancient battlements like the death-knell of a dream," and gave his lonely monster moving interior monologues.

Swamp Thing became the sensation of the moment, Wein a hot writer, and Wrightson the "new Barry Smith." The good times, unfortunately, lasted only ten issues. Wrightson was caught in the same dilemma as Smith—pressured to work faster for the same money and not wanting to sacrifice quality—and so he followed Smith out of comics, joining him and Jeff Jones at The Studio. He would find he could make a living in book illustration and lithography, with rare dabblings in comics, while pursuing his love of antique draftsmanship and excruciating line work to a satisfying extreme. Orlando replaced him with one of his Filipino artists, Nestor Redondo, who did nice dark atmosphere but lacked all the drama and perversity of Wrightson. Wein left three issues later for a full-time spot at Marvel. The series lasted to issue 24 (Sept. 1976), but with none of its original impact.

Orlando tried to score again, turning *Adventure Comics* into a showcase for weird new characters, dumping Supergirl for Black Orchid, a super-heroine whose true identity was hidden even from the readers. The art was by Tony DeZuniga and the scripts by Sheldon Mayer, the man who'd given Julius Schwartz his first comics job, so Orlando obviously had some flexibility in his "nobody over thirty-five" rule. Orlando tried the Vigilante, Dr. 13, and Captain Fear, and even got some art out of Alex Toth, but nothing quite clicked.

Then he got a new idea, one very much a product of its sour, angry times: "I had just been mugged in broad daylight on upper Broadway.... The feeling of helplessness and anger and loss of manhood (my wife was with me at the time) as I watched the two muggers strutting away with my wallet gave me the

Walter Mitty idea of fantasy revenge." A young writer named Michael Fleisher was holed up in the DC library at the time, researching a projected seven-volume *Encyclopedia of Comic Book Heroes* (of which three—on Batman, Superman, and Wonder Woman—would be published). Along the way he sold some scripts to Orlando, and now he got the nod for a revived *Spectre* (*Adventure* 431, Jan. 1974). Fleisher threw himself into it with disturbing relish, writing of "the leeches of the underworld [who] crawl forth from their slimy crevasses to rob the helpless and slaughter the innocent." His ghostly hero dispensed a sadistic brand of magical justice, as when he turned one gangster into a wooden statue and then sliced him into little pieces with a buzz saw (*Adventure* 435, Oct. 1974). Jim Aparo's eerie art made the series fairly effective, but Fleisher's writing creeped out most of fandom.

There was trouble in the Marvel monster factory, too. Mike Ploog and Gary Friedrich had launched *Monster of Frankenstein*, a lovely and heartfelt adaptation of Mary Shelley's original story (Jan. 1973), but Ploog left after eight issues. Val Mayerik followed, and then cancellation. Ploog also left *Ghost Rider* and *Werewolf by Night*. Friedrich spun a series off *Ghost Rider* called *Son of Satan*, in which an exorcist discovers that he is, literally, the devil's son and uses his own diabolical powers to battle his father (*Marvel Spotlight* 12, Oct. 1973). But it had to be drawn by Herb Trimpe, who had some of Ploog's humor and charm but none of his mood or character nuance, and it didn't last. Ploog went on to do his own illustrating and movie storyboarding (eventually wrestling Milan Kundera into pictures for *The Unbearable Lightness of Being*). He was another one who was just too good for comics.

Marvel found a way to keep its monsters interesting, however: it allowed its writers to run unfettered, with no genre formula to constrict them. It wasn't a planned policy—Thomas just didn't have time to pay attention—but it sparked a moment of creative excitement, the likes of which Marvelites hadn't seen in seven or eight years.

With Marv Wolfman, *Tomb of Dracula* finally found a writer who'd stick around. Marv said he'd never read many horror comics, which "kept me from doing anything standard, because I didn't know what standard was." He decided to do "people-oriented stories" and quickly made *Tomb of Dracula* the best work he would ever do (from *TD* 7, Apr. 1973). He avoided centering his plots on Dracula himself, instead focusing on people whose lives had somehow fallen under the villain's shadow, either by losing a loved one to the vampire's bite or by fighting to destroy vampirism. He developed a large cast of characters whose paths would cross and recross in unexpected patterns over the years, including a jive-talking black vampire-slayer named Blade, a cowardly writer who wants to milk a best-seller out of Dracula, and a hard-boiled private eye who also happens to be a vampire, and who uses his investigative talents to destroy minions of Dracula. This was an ingenious application of the Marvel superhero style to horror: King as the flawed superhero, the man cursed by his powers but devoting them to the good of a world that has no place for him.

Dracula himself became multifaceted and capable of growth. Wolfman showed us the Count's ambivalent feelings about his bloody past, his proud adherence to the peculiar ethical code by which vampires live, his love for a human woman, his beloved son Janus and hated daughter Lilith, and the odd mixture of distaste and respect that he accords the people who are determined to slay him. He was Dr. Doom, Sub-Mariner, and a little bit of Galactus. His ability to die and be reborn was used to good effect, particularly when Harker and his other foes felt compelled to bring him back to life in order to combat a greater evil (*TD* 40-41, Jan.-Feb. 1976). This was a devilish echo of Stan Lee stories like the one in which the Fantastic Four have to ask Dr. Doom to lead them against the possessed Reed Richards. Unfortunately, the very number and variety of elements seemed to overwhelm Wolfman at times. Some subplots would be abandoned for a year or more, and then pop up unexpectedly with too much having been resolved "off

camera." Many issues ran mainly on subplot continuity, without much really happening. It became virtually impossible for a new reader to pick up a single issue and understand it, but that fact helped make it a cult favorite. Quite a few comics fans and professionals born around 1960 have said that *Dracula* was just about the only series that kept them interested in comics through the inconsistencies and disappointments of the '70s. The horror genre, it seemed, wasn't going to pull comics away from dependence on its hard-core fan base, but it was proving that fandom would be loyal to material written expressly for it.

The poor Man-Thing, meanwhile, had no idea what he was in for when Gerry Conway turned him over to a new kid named Steve Gerber. Gerber was another Missourian, but while Roy Thomas was teaching high school and Denny O'Neil was writing newspaper articles, Gerber was just an impish teenager, doing his funny and slightly twisted *Little Giant* for the fanzines. Anxiously funny, anxiously volatile, a chain smoker, a brainy Jewish kid from the dead center of the heartland, always the outsider in any group, he was more in tune with satire zines and undergrounds than superheroes. Gerber was uninterested in revising Marvel history or making political statements, but he was attracted to the bizarre creations of Lee and his cohorts precisely for their bizarreness. Desperate for a way to make *Man-Thing* interesting, Gerber took flight into the realms of magic, alternate reality, and hallucination.

The Man-Thing's swamp proves to be the "nexus point" for dozens of alternate realities, and efforts to build an airport there have disturbed the "cosmic balance." "The very structure of reality will collapse," warns a wizard. "A plague of insanity will sweep across the cosmos . . . . Your world will be inundated by a tide of blade-wielding barbarians...or beasts who walk and talk like men . . . ." It all leads to a dream-reality where barbarians, World War II dogfaces, old biplanes, and rocket ships all wage war on a "blood-red plain—'neath this verdant sky—among these stones surely sculpted by a somnambulant lunatic" (*Fear* 18-19, Oct.-Dec. 1973). The blade-wielding

175

barbarian appears when a butter knife left on a table becomes a sword—and then the peanut butter in the jar beside it swells up and becomes a savage swordsman. The beast turns out to be a smart-mouthed, cigar-chomping duck named Howard. "Finding yourself in a world of talking hairless apes," he says to Korrek, "now *that's* absurdity!" Val Mayerik, whose pencils weren't much more than perfunctory until then, suddenly came alive with a character design worthy of the undergrounds: an establishment version of Donald Duck, with fedora, suit jacket, and tie, but no pants. "Howard was created totally as a joke," Gerber has said, and when he saw the art his first thought was, "I'm in real trouble." Howard died before the story line was through, but fans flooded the offices with letters demanding that he come back.

Gerber's voice united the flowery Marvel style with a tongue-in-cheek wit and a truly audacious pretension. No one else would have begun a story with the declaration, "Reality: Plato found it in the shadowy confines of a cave—Descartes, in a syllogism . . . . 'Cogito ergo sum' . . . . 'I think, therefore I am.' They blew it—both of them." It was that audacity that made Gerber charming, and he ran with it until he overreached himself. For his big shock ending, he came up with the anticlimactic revelation that the gods who control the cosmos are a couple of dogs—in the last panel he even dares suggest that the reader spell G-O-D backwards (*Man-Thing* 1, Jan. 1974). Gerber's best stories were smaller, as in the haunting tale of a pathetic little carnival clown who commits suicide and then, as a ghost, compels four people and the Man-Thing to act out the story of his wretched life while three cloaked figures sit as "critics," judges of the clown's soul (*MT* 6, June 1974). As a moral fable, a supernatural story, and a very sad portrait of a man, it was a work of true feeling and originality. It helped, too, that it was drawn by Mike Ploog, pausing on his way out of comics to do his most evocative work yet.

Man-Thing was canceled after issue 22 (Oct. 1975), but by then Gerber was bringing his imagination to a team of major Marvel superheroes, and preparing a *Howard the Duck* series. For fans

despairing the losses of Smith, Wrightson, Ploog, and all, Gerber offered some hope.

Otherwise, the horror cycle was winding down. In 1972 and 1973, Marvel tried anthologies again with *Worlds Unknown*, *Journey into Mystery*, *Chamber of Chills*, and *Supernatural Thrillers*, ambitiously adapting works of horror by H. G. Wells, Theodore Sturgeon, Fredric Brown, and Robert E. Howard. Despite nice writing and art, they all failed. Gerber and Gil Kane produced *Morbius, the Living Vampire*, an intriguing series combining horror and science fiction (*Fear* 20, Feb. 1974), but it never gained its own title. A Haitian magician named Brother Voodoo had a series in a revived *Strange Tales*. In a weird twist on Marvel continuity, the son of newspaper publisher J. Jonah Jameson, Spider-Man's nemesis, found himself transformed into Man-Wolf (*Creatures on the Loose* 30, July 1974). One amusing idea that was doomed to fail was the resurrection of an old Kirby-Lee monster as the central character in *It, the Living Colossus* in *Astonishing Tales*. A few other horrors were given tryouts, including *The Living Mummy*, *Satana, the Devil's Daughter*, a Jewish monster-hero in *The Golem*, and even a team called *The Legion of Monsters*, with Dracula, Werewolf, and others. Not too surprisingly, none of them caught on.

Horror did finally give Stan Lee what he'd been wanting for so long: with Marvel's distributing edge, he was finally able to get a set of oversize black-and-whites onto the magazine racks to challenge *Creepy* and *Vampirella*. *Vampire Tales*, *Dracula Lives*, *Monsters Unleashed*, and *Tales of the Zombie* hit the stands in 1973 and actually sold pretty well. Soon would come the return of *Savage Tales*, then *Savage Sword of Conan*, *Planet of the Apes*, *Deadly Hands of Kung Fu*, *Unknown Worlds of Science Fiction*, *Marvel Preview*, and a *Mad* imitation called *Crazy*. Marv Wolfman was hired to edit them all, having shown facility writing both horror and humor, even though he had no editorial experience. He recalls being given six weeks to create *Crazy* and assemble an entire staff for it, while still editing the other series and writing his usual comics. A few highlights came from the chaos, though, including Barry Smith's finest Conan story, "Red Nails," in *Savage Tales*. Lee also flirted with pulp magazines and even published *The Comix Book* with Denis Kitchen, the savviest and least offensive of underground publishers (although Marvel's name was left off, and Stan was credited only as "instigator"). It failed in its attempt to sell undergrounds to the mainstream, but it set a precedent for Marvel in allowing cartoonists to own their own material, just like underground publishers. None of these magazines, in fact, would succeed especially well, but they were leading Stan toward the horizon, proving what he'd always tried to tell cousin Martin: that there was life beyond the spin rack.

By then horror was moribund at DC. Orlando tried to keep *Phantom Stranger* alive with a couple of good backup series—*The Spawn of Frankenstein*, with some beautifully ornate Mike Kaluta art, and *Black Orchid*, now written by Michael Fleisher—but it didn't survive 1976. One of Orlando's writers, John Albano, had come up with a popular character in *Weird Western*, a hideously scarred and brutal gunfighter named Jonah Hex. Michael Fleisher took it over after *Spectre*'s cancellation, winning it a loyal following with hard-hitting, nihilistic stories. It was a Western, the only one in comics to survive the '70s, using some horror and superhero conventions to hold its audience. In a "peek at the future" story, the sort of thing Mort Weisinger teased readers with, Fleisher smiled grimly and gave us a most un-Weisinger fin-

ish for his hero: stuffed and mounted in a Wild West show (*Jonah Hex Spectacular*, 1978).

They were dark days at DC, and darkness was what their people did best, what their fans responded to best. Things were brighter and hotter at Marvel, but they were wild, too, flying out of control. The '70s were on, and DC was the older generation, its whole world knocked out from under it. Marvel was the baby boom, burning itself out with a long, long party in the pad the '60s had given it. Roy Thomas was burned out already. He quit as Marvel's editor in 1974, after only two years. Gerry Conway was on vacation, so the job went to his friend, Len Wein. Stan's success had made everyone, even Stan, think that hot writers make the best editors—and *Swamp Thing* had made Wein the hottest of them. But Marvel was bigger now, and there was more to the job with Martin Goodman gone. "I'm not a person who's very interested in business," Thomas has said. "I felt that I was wasting too much time on things I really hated." He made a deal to become a writer-editor, essentially writing whatever he wanted without supervision, but the excitement that had left his writing when he took the editor's job would never come back. *Conan* was steady, rarely more. His superhero work would become overwhelmed by his passion for comics history. His first new creation was to be *The Invaders*, a team-up of golden age heroes set in World War II. Maybe it hurt that he didn't have to submit his work to Stan anymore. Or maybe he was just doing like the rest of young America: taking his toys into his room and closing the door.

CHAPTER 26

THE BATMAN

DC found one way to make darkness and bitterness work. The grim, post-camp Batman caught the imaginations of fans and pros alike. It looked, for a moment, as though Julius Schwartz might once again have found the key to a DC resurgence.

This was a new tone for Julie, not the brightly lit futurism of the 1960s but a return to the darkness and mystery of Batman's birth, and to the pulp novels and Victorian adventure stories that underlay the whole superhero genre. That—for young people discovering the roots of comics through the esoterica of fandom—gave this new/old Batman a sense of profundity and power. Denny O'Neil began to call him "the Batman" in his scripts, as Bill Finger had in the beginning, and the new appellation became a code phrase for fans to tell the lightweights from the fanatics. O'Neil's Batman was still an upstanding citizen, still a rationalist, but he was explicitly motivated by his rage over the murder of his parents. His milieu was the dark and gothic: the nocturnal city, lonely cliffs, the riggings of old sailing ships. His appearance, as he swooped from the darkness, all cape and shadow, inspired more fear than reassurance, even in the law-abiding. The playful Elongated Man was long gone from *Detective Comics*. He had no place in this new world.

Batman's enemies were the same costumed weirdos as ever, but now they were played as truly murderous psychotics. The Joker became a twisted genius, a Moriarty to Batman's Holmes. Two-Face, physically hideous and a diagnosed psychotic with a horrific backstory, returned after decades of absence, as shadows fell over sunny DC. O'Neil and Neal Adams gave Batman a new archnemesis in Rā's al Ghūl, a crime lord who can be restored to life endlessly with his Lazarus Pit. Batman and Ghul's daughter fell in love, adding another pulpy twist to the torment of DC's most complex hero ("*Leave*, Talia! Because if I turn around and you're still here, I'll have to make a decision that could *ruin* me! For both our sakes, *go!*"). O'Neil put "the Batman" through a gauntlet of illusions designed by a villain to drive him mad (*Detective* 408, Feb. 1971) and had him save a deformed, flipper-limbed child from a murderous crowd (*Detective* 410, Apr. 1971). Frank Robbins, the other Bat-writer, had the hero forced into a game of Russian roulette (*Detective* 426, Aug. 1972) and created the Man-Bat, a decent scientist who inadvertently transformed himself into a winged monster. Man-Bat was much like Ditko and Lee's Lizard, but he was something new to DC: a morally ambivalent foe. (And he provided a very different view of the effects of science from the Schwartz scientists of the past.)

The new Bat-tone, however, was more an ideal than a reality. Neal Adams had designed this Batman, and he still drew quite a few issues, always strikingly and to the excitement of the fans. But the regular artists were Irv Novick and Bob Brown. They did all they could to give Batman an eerie countenance and to fill his world with shadows and mystery, aided by the inks of Dick Giordano, now Adams's partner in Continuity Studios. The effect, though, was never as atmospheric as what the fans saw in their heads. The art was literalistic, with conservative storytelling, and never captured the design sense or creepiness of the golden age stories that DC reprinted. Robbins occasionally drew his own stories, with an angular, nightmarish effect. Those gems, however, were few and far between, because the fans, in love with Adams, found them "weird" and "cartoony."

Denny O'Neil was at his best here. He dropped most of the earlier mystery and complexity of Batman plots, but his scripts were fast and lean, his settings intriguing, and his action imaginative. Robbins wrote better plots, and high-impact scripts, even if they were nearly all drawn by Brown and Novick (the Adams issues were nearly all written by O'Neil, because Julie knew how hot that team was with fans). Yet the stories were still Schwartz stories, self-contained and gimmick-based, and the fans who wanted spookiness and psychological depth had to read a lot into the material. The occasional cover by Mike Kaluta, or Berni Wrightson's spooky rendition of a guest-starring Batman in *Swamp Thing*, showed what wonders of design and sensuality could be wrought with this swirling-caped, heavy-shadowed character. But the comics couldn't deliver on their own promises.

It was another editor, in a brief but startling stint on *Detective Comics*, who gave the fans their first glimpse of the promised land, a more exalted world of superheroes. Archie Goodwin had edited as well as written for Warren's war and horror magazines, so it was natural for Carmine Infantino to hire him to take over editing a couple of war comics that Joe Kubert had to drop. Then, in late 1973, Schwartz had a chance to revive his old *Strange Sports Stories* and needed room on his schedule, and *Detective* was shuttled to Goodwin. Goodwin had never really shone on superheroes, but here he used his skill at horror and suspense to bring out the creepiness that had been implicit in Schwartz's Batman without ever quite breaking through. His plots were as tight as Robbins's, his mood even more convincing than O'Neil's. At Warren he'd always worked on anthologies, trying to match the best artist available to each story, and now he flew in the face of every tradition of series comics by doing the same with *Detective*: Howard Chaykin, Alex Toth, Jim Aparo, and Sal Amendola gave him the best they had to offer. The fans were thrilled, and didn't much mind that each was just a one-shot. They were more interested, it seemed, in the best of the best, even if only as an "event," than in steady work by mediocrities. It became a pastime among fans to speculate on "who would you like to see draw a Batman story?" This wasn't what the old guard liked to see, since it gave more clout than ever to the sensational young artists who flitted in and out of the business—"bravura artists," as Chaykin called them.

Goodwin's greatest gifts, despite all this, were not to Batman himself. *Detective Comics* had showcased many backup features through the years, recently including solo adventures of Robin and Batgirl, but not until Goodwin's *Manhunter* (*Detective* 437-443, Nov. 1973-Nov. 1974) did any outshine the lead stories. This was a globe-trotting suspense story, full of clones and ninjas and Interpol agents, and was one of the most complex and intriguing mysteries ever in comics. It blended, like no series before it, the pristine craft of silver age DC with the artistic ambition of the Infantino years and Marvel's sense of the epic. Best of all, it showcased the talents of its artist and cocreator, Walter Simonson. He was a pleasant and unassuming ex-fan, introduced to comic book society by Chaykin and Jim Starlin, but he could strut as much "bravura" as either of them at the drawing table. From Gil Kane, especially the Kane of *Savage*, he learned to master brutally effective fight sequences. His violence seemed to transcend the merely visual and actually evoke sound—the crunch of bunched fingers driven into a throat, the clank of chains striking armor. From Alex Toth he learned economy of line and an almost impressionistic touch for setting and mood. From Chaykin and Starlin and Barry Smith, and from the old master Bernard Krigstein, he took complex page designs and the use of small panels to control the pace of his stories down to the millisecond. Simonson had been a Kirby fan as a kid, and somewhere under all that technique beat the action-pulse of a Kirby story. But he could slice that action into half-beats and quarter-beats, then hit with a sustained climactic note. The effect was cinematic, but the tools were pure comics.

The end of the series was sad to see, but it was also wholly satisfying. This was no ongoing series, recycling its own stories or running out of steam when its creators left or got bored. It was a self-contained serial, with a big finish guest-starring Batman, and it pointed the way to a new structure for comic book storytelling. It was the genre version of the "graphic novel" Richard Kyle had defined in the zines, that devoutly-to-be-wished consummation of the comic book form.

Walter Simonson's cartooning and hypnotic storytelling gave mystery, suspense, and a sense of coming greatness—not just to his stories, but to "the Batman" himself. Comics like this left fans hungry for years. Script by Elliot S. Maggin. (*Detective Comics* #450, June 1976.)

Goodwin wouldn't follow up on his breakthroughs. He and Infantino disagreed, politely but thoroughly, over the direction of his comics, and after a year he headed to Marvel. Schwartz came back to *Detective*, but was unable to sustain it even at the level he had before. Simonson left, except for the occasional isolated story. The other bravura boys—Chaykin, Kaluta, Wrightson—would do even less. Comics had no place for the talented and eccentric stylist who wouldn't grind out monthly series.

For Batman, though, the biggest blow was the resignation of Neal Adams. He did his last stories for Schwartz in late 1973, and then moved on to higher-paying advertising work. Unlike men of an earlier generation who'd made similar moves, however—Krigstein, Jack Cole, Harvey Kurtzman—he didn't just walk away from comics. Like Steranko, who continued to publish for the fan market, Adams responded to the sense of community and the admiration that fandom had given him. Adams's way, however, was less mercantile and more confrontational than Steranko's. He tried forming a guild for comic book artists, to push for the benefits that artists

in other fields took for granted: medical coverage, royalties, copyright ownership, the return of their original art. The last was becoming a flash-point in comics as art sales became common through mail order and at conventions. Fans who'd received art for writing clever letters, or staffers who pirated art from the editorial offices, were making money while the artists who created it got nothing. Adams found support. Older artists, dependent on comic book income, had refused to join the writers' movement of 1967, but the new ones, whom editors needed more than the artists needed editors, looked willing to fight.

For the fans, who knew little of the war behind the scenes, it was all quite painful. Soon the Batman line was falling into disarray, as Frank Robbins, Bob Brown and Irv Novick decided it was a good time to retire from a slumping business, and Denny O'Neil was lured away by new projects. Schwartz had to grab any writers he could find, some rookies and some tired Marvel hands, and had to settle for artists who could turn in steady work even if it was far less atmospheric than Adams's and not as solid as Brown's or Novick's. He tried shifting the emphasis back to Batman's detective abilities, but none of his new hands had the charm of Gardner Fox or the toughness of Robbins. The only reliably decent Batman comic became *The Brave and the Bold*, which coasted along for nearly the whole 1970s with teamup stories in a silver age mold under Murray Boltinoff, Bob Haney, and Jim Aparo. Even that was nothing to write a fanzine about. "The Batman," who had briefly offered the hope of revitalizing DC, had become a tired cliché.

Yet, fans would continue glancing at *Batman* and *Detective*, hoping that this would be the month for a new Simonson story, or the debut of some startling new artist. Batman's mystique transcended his treatment, and the first murmurs began of what would become a fan refrain: that "the Batman" was the one superhero who had the potential to be not just entertainment but *Art*. Fans in their teens and twenties were hungry for dark, stylized urban crime stories with the twisted psychology of *film noir*. If no one would give it to them, they might have to make it themselves.

CHAPTER 27

SAVE THE TALKING TIGER

There was one place where DC reigned supreme: the past. It virtually owned World War II. Marvel's *Sgt. Fury* had gone to reprint, and so had most of Charlton's fading war line, but DC continued to publish four regular war comics with new material: *Our Army at War*, featuring Sgt. Rock; *GI Combat*, with the Haunted Tank; *Star Spangled War Stories*, starring first Enemy Ace, then the Unknown Soldier; and *Our Fighting Forces,* home of the Losers. They'd been solid comics under Bob Kanigher, but when Joe Kubert took over the editing in 1968, he raised them higher. Aside from Kubert's own art, which was never better, there was abundant work by John Severin and Russ Heath and one-shot appearances by Alex Toth, Walt Simonson, Mort Drucker, Neal Adams, Ric Estrada, Frank Thorne, and George Evans. Kanigher reached his peak as a writer now that he was freed from editorial duties. His and Kubert's *Enemy Ace* was the most acclaimed war series ever, with the most human warrior in the genre, a World War I German flying ace who detests war so profoundly that he shuts down emotionally and is branded a death machine by the men who don't know the anguish that devours him. There were almost no Vietnam stories among Kubert's comics, but the spirit of the era informed them. Kubert stamped them with the motto, "Make War No More." Kubert overflowed with a robust love for comics that inspired his freelancers. His letters pages were the most intimate in comics, full of lonely GIs and military history nuts bonding with the sweetheart of an editor they addressed as "Dear Joe." Kubert's war comics still stand second in power only to Harvey Kurtzman's of the early '50s, but they were second to none in elegance and richness.

Kubert was a favorite of the fan elite, but since his abortive launch of Hawkman ended in 1963, his work had rarely been showcased in a genre that the fans had much interest in. He finally got his chance to break out of the military ghetto in 1972, when the slumping Western/Gold Key lost the rights to the creations of Edgar Rice Burroughs—and DC won them. For any artist who grew up on the work of Hal Foster and Burne Hogarth, *Tarzan* was a dream job, and Kubert promptly set about editing, writing, and drawing it all by himself. Here was a character, like Conan, who promised to give the fans the kind of solitary male heroics they loved, but without the trappings of a superhero, and it outstripped every superhero of the time in perfection of execution.

Kubert was faithful to both the plots and the spirit of the Burroughs originals, making the Lord of the Apes a quietly noble scholar and warrior, at home both in the jungle and in civilization (*Tarzan* 207, Apr. 1972). Kubert's writing was extraordinarily simple, dropping the baroque ferocity that made Burroughs so hard to read past the age of fifteen, but still lyrical and moving. After the new fan-writers, trying so hard to make literature, Kubert came as a shock: here was an adult, one who actually knew how to write, who knew that words increase in power as they are more sparingly used. He loosened and broadened his art, trading some monumentality for a panoramic sweep and tropical lushness. Stripped of clothing and hardware, his lean, attenuated figures danced gracefully in battle, flight, and tribal ritual. When Tarzan visited civilization, Kubert's early twentieth-century backdrops became a new kind of jungle, one of brick and wood and human malevolence.

Joe Kubert's classical composition and unambivalent storytelling marks him as one of the older generation, but his linework, atmosphere, and artistic ambition were the match of any young hotshot. His *Tarzan* embodied everything DC's most conscientious artists and editors had been striving for. (*Tarzan* #208, May 1972.)

Before the sales reports were in on *Tarzan*, Kubert was already building a Burroughs franchise, handing *G.I. Combat* and *Star-Spangled* to Archie Goodwin. *Korak* (June 1972) was a letdown, executed only competently by Kanigher and Frank Thorne. Then came a flurry of versions of some of Burroughs's more rarely adapted novels, faithfully written by Len Wein, Marv Wolfman, and Denny O'Neil. *Weird Worlds* (Sept. 1972) featured *John Carter of Mars*, gorgeously drawn by Murphy Anderson, and *Pellucidar*, adventures in a savage world at Earth's core, with attractive art by Alan Weiss. Backups in *Tarzan* and *Korak* were *Beyond the Farthest Star*, pristinely rendered by Dan Green,

and *Carson of Venus*, with the decorative and unmistakable art of Mike Kaluta.

Weird Worlds and *Korak* were canceled within a dozen issues, but *Tarzan* held its own. Carmine Infantino and his peers had to see it as a vindication, and a sign that DC might be able to gain strength for the future by reaching into the past. Fandom's interest in comics history was at a peak in 1972, evidenced by the excitement surrounding the second volume of *The Steranko History of Comics*, despite—or perhaps because of—its astoundingly wordy paean to the defunct Captain Marvel and other Fawcett and Quality heroes. Another collection of essays from Don Thompson and Richard Lupoff, *The Comic Book Book*, was in preparation. "Adzines," mainly a forum for selling old comics, were becoming large, regular periodicals, complete with news and editorials, led by Alan Light's *The Buyer's Guide for Comics Fandom*. Denis Kitchen, already emerging as a leading publisher of undergrounds, started reprinting Will Eisner's *Spirit* from the '40s, which shortly became *de rigeur* reading for anyone who would claim to be an educated fan or a superhero artist serious about his craft. Warren Publishing then picked it up, bringing what many considered to be the most artful masked-crime-fighter series of all time to a general audience. The greater world was interested, too: Gloria Steinem and the *Ms.* staff brought out a collection of the golden age *Wonder Woman*, and a British movie adapted *Tales from the Crypt* (followed by *Vault of Horror*), which inspired some reprints of great ECs.

DC tried to slake the fans' thirst with a whole series devoted to venerable reprints, *Wanted: The World's Most Dangerous Villains* (Aug. 1972), followed by *Secret Origins* (Mar. 1973) and then two titles reprinting old Simon and Kirby material, *Boy Commandos* (Oct. 1973) and *Black Magic* (Nov. 1973). Then Infantino and production manager Sol Harrison took a gamble on *Limited Collector's Editions* and *Famous First Editions*, huge reprint packages on tabloid-sized paper. Despite a hard-to-display size and a dollar price tag, they sold fairly well. When Jack Kirby proposed getting the rights to the original Captain Marvel, Infantino had to think the time was right to bring golden-age heroes back as new series. He acquired not only the rights to the Captain, but to all the Fawcett characters, and announced that the Quality heroes—which National had owned for a while—would be dusted off, too. Unfortunately, the trademark to Captain Marvel had been lost because of Marvel's hero of the same name, but thanks to Jim Nabors every kid in America would recognize Billy Batson's magic word, "Shazam!" And so the new series would be called.

This looked like a can't-miss. Julius Schwartz, who had brought superheroes back from extinction, saved Batman and helped make him a national craze, and now seemed to be saving Batman *again* from the consequences of that same craze, finally had his chance to revamp another major superhero. *Green Lantern/Green Arrow* had failed, and he'd had to reverse direction on Superman, but he was still doing pretty well with the latter: Superman's second title, *Action,* was taken from Murray Boltinoff and given to Schwartz in 1972. Now Julie had C.C. Beck, the original Captain Marvel artist, who'd emerged from nearly twenty years of obscurity to throw himself into the convention circuit, where older fans welcomed him like Richard the Lion-Heart back from the Crusades. Schwartz gave the writing to Denny O'Neil, of course, who was his John Broome and Gardner Fox combined in those days. Captain Marvel was unlike anything Denny had ever written, but who could doubt that DC's premier writer could handle anything he tried? Fandom was abuzz from the moment the news hit. Back-issue dealers were already imagining what *Shazam* number 1 would be worth in a year.

In January of 1973, Billy Batson said "Shazam" again for the first time in a generation. It was a thrilling moment for readers who remembered him or who had read about him—if they could find the comic book. So many dealers had rushed out through snow and sleet to distributors' warehouses and newsstands to stockpile copies for priced-up

© 1972 Will Eisner

After twenty years away from comics, Will Eisner created some new material for Denis Kitchen's *Spirit* reprints. This was a new use for superheroes: commenting on the changing times, and on the irrelevance of the superheroes themselves. (*The Spirit* #1, 1972.)

resale that astonishingly few made it to the intended readers. No one had realized that there were so many speculators, with so much capital and so much faith in new releases. The speculators, for their part, didn't realize that there were such things as rules of economics: they were pulling in good prices for recent comics like *Conan* 1 and the first appearance of Swamp Thing because those hadn't sold well when they first appeared, and new fans discovering them created more demand than there was supply. A couple of hundred thousand *Shazams* in the back rooms of comic shops would make for a whole lot of *Shazams* selling for nothing for years to come. And that's what they got: you can still find them in the five-for-a-dollar boxes at conventions. It meant wonderfully low return numbers on that one issue for DC, but judging the actual audience response became impossible. At conventions that summer, Marvel and DC staffers berated dealers for "not letting the comics get to the kids who they're meant for." But some people around the industry's fringes read it all a little differently. For people like New York teacher and retailer Phil Seuling, Bay Area retailer Bud Plant, writer Mike Friedrich, and artist Jack Katz, this was just more evidence that the comic shop demimonde was growing into a market unto itself, with its own information network and its own values.

Readers who did manage to find *Shazam* 1 found a fun little comic book, but nothing to match the hype. Beck's work looked wonderful, nearly as confident and economical as in his heyday, a forceful reminder in that over-rendered era of the power of sheer *line*. The DC production department, now run by Jack Adler, came through with a bright, buoyant look that no one thought DC could do anymore. The problem lay in a clash of aesthetics. Infantino, after four years of seeing nearly all his radical innovations and concessions to creative freedom fail, was now not inclined to mess with success—even if the success of Captain Marvel lay decades in the past. Schwartz had expected to be able to reinvent the Fawcett material in his own way, but "I was told to do it the same way it was done years ago, and I just couldn't recapture it." He and O'Neil tried hard, immediately and unapologetically bringing in Captain Marvel Jr., Mary Marvel, the talking tiger named Mr. Tawny, and the whole Sivana family of bickering evil scientists, but O'Neil just couldn't manage that "symbolic connection" with the material. The Fawcett style, he said, "was too sweet-tempered...too naive. It was a fairy-tale world, and I still find it charming, but I think the audience had leapfrogged past that in terms of sophistication."

If so, it was the sophistication of the Visigoth smirking at a piece of Byzantine glass because it breaks too easily. The old Otto Binder and Bill Parker scripts had a delicacy and knowingness that no one in

the hysterical '70s could approximate. O'Neil's scripts meandered, had little heart, and sometimes slipped into cloying self-satire. Great ideas—like the story in which a disaster will happen if anyone speaks Captain Marvel's name—somehow just never took flight as they would have in the Fawcett (or the silver-age Schwartz) days. C.C. Beck hated the stories and started making changes that Schwartz hadn't authorized. Schwartz called on Kurt Schaffenberger, an old Fawcett hand, to draw them as written, and Beck demanded an opportunity to write his own stories. His first script came back with massive rewrites, and he walked—though not without a few choice words for the benefit of fandom. The new Captain Marvel Family, he said, were "made to act like big fat slobs," in adventures that were boring and, most pointed of all, "childish." Schaffenberger wouldn't stay long, so most of the issues went either to Bob Oksner, once DC's master of humor comics but now losing his touch, or to Don Newton, with a style too '70s and too "serious." O'Neil drifted on, and Nelson Bridwell, the assistant Schwartz had inherited from Weisinger and DC's resident authority on comic book arcana, stepped in with some scripts that were truer to the old tone but not much for excitement. Schwartz ran more and more golden-age reprints. He called *Shazam* "a failure."

For many older fans, Beck's departure, although he'd missed the entire silver age, felt like the last symbolic sundering of the past. He'd been a master when comic book art was based on cartooning instead of fantasy posters or advertising illustration. "When you're reading a comic, you see the drawings only out of the corners of your eyes," he said. "If the story is good, nobody stops to admire the art.... I didn't try to make them gasp with admiration at elaborately detailed backgrounds or elaborately muscled figures in outlandish poses." The old son of a Lutheran minister from rural Minnesota had no place in this new subculture, and he didn't give a damn if he didn't. His fans were hurt and outraged on his behalf, and left comics more and more to the teenagers.

Old heroes were popping up in other quarters, as well. In 1972 Schwartz's *Justice League of America*, which had been hosting annual guest appearances by the Justice Society of Earth-2, revived the Seven Soldiers of Victory, a team of minor DC heroes from the 1940s (*JLA* 100-102). The next year came the return of the Freedom Fighters, a group of Quality heroes like Doll Man and Uncle Sam (*JLA* 107-108). A little later would come a team-up with Captain Marvel, Bulletman, Spy Smasher, and other old Fawcett heroes. The Freedom Fighters and the Justice Society would even have their own comics for a brief while. The ancestors of the comic book heroes, the crime fighters of the pulp magazines, rode this wave of nostalgia, too. Paperback reprints of Doc Savage and the Shadow had been selling pretty well since the '60s, and Jim Steranko had whetted comics fans' appetites further with a colorful chapter in his history book called "The Bloody Pulps." It was Marvel that actually struck first, with *Doc Savage* (Oct. 1972) during its "Phase Two" explosion. Steve Englehart and Ross Andru launched it entertainingly, and Steranko dropped in to draw a couple of covers, but they all left and it quickly died. A black-and-white *Doc Savage* magazine a few years later didn't do any better. DC seemed to understand that the type of fans who wanted to see pulp heroes come back would also want to see a sophisticated execution—so Infantino gave *The Shadow* to Denny O'Neil to edit and write, with Mike Kaluta doing the bravura art (Oct. 1973). The fans and dealers were primed for this one, and its first issue was horded nearly as badly as *Shazam*'s.

The stories were macabre mysteries and crime riffs in O'Neil's *Batman* style, but with a nice twist of '30s movie atmosphere. They worked because of Kaluta: sometimes his draftsmanship was a little soft—he was made for illustration, not pumping out sequential panels on deadline—but his surface work was ornate, seductive, and almost painterly, evoking the eerie covers of the pulps. He had a nice touch for historical detail, but he transcended mere accuracy with ornamental renderings that captured the

romance through which pop culture viewed the '30s. Unfortunately—and it was already an old song by then—he left soon to join The Studio with Barry Smith, Jeff Jones, and Berni Wrightson. Kaluta set new records for becoming a fan superstar and disappearing, drawing only five issues of *The Shadow*. Frank Robbins followed him for four issues, with better storytelling and a riveting tone, but the fans who'd fallen for Kaluta hated Robbins for his angularity and savage line. He was followed by E.R. Cruz, one of the Filipino artists to whom Infantino was giving more and more work, but with its twelfth issue *The Shadow* was dead (Sept. 1975).

Teenage fans loved this: lots of lines, lots of mood, and an air of seriousness. Michael W. Kaluta lovingly recreates the 1930s. Script by Denny O'Neil. (*The Shadow* #4, May 1974.)

O'Neil also tried an adaptation of the pulps' Avenger as *Justice Inc.*, with art by Al McWilliams and Jack Kirby, who was then just intent on finishing off his contractual obligations, but it ran only four issues (June-Dec. 1975). At about the same time, Kirby also drew Joe Simon's attempt to reawaken their old *Sandman*, but with similar luck. The "golden age revival" had run out of steam.

Even the Kubert stable was running out of steam. Kubert, Kanigher, and Nester Redondo tried for a female answer to Tarzan with *Rima the Jungle Girl*, based on W.H. Hudson's *Green Mansions* (May 1974). The backup strip, *The Space Voyagers*, showcased the florid art of Alex Niño. But *Rima* lasted only seven issues. *Korak* had been reduced to a backup in *Tarzan*, where Niño turned the jungle prince's adventures into little gems of tropical mood and atmosphere. That lasted only four issues (*Tarzan* 231-234, July 1974-Jan. 1975).

By then Infantino and Harrison were into another experiment in format: turning their highest-profile series—*Detective*, *JLA*, *Shazam*, *Tarzan*, and others—into one-hundred-page giants, mixing new material and reprints, selling first for fifty cents and then for sixty. DC was caught in a strange place. The price jump of 1972 had devastated it, but precisely because of that it could hardly hope to recover its position by offering the same package as Marvel, and there was no way DC's bosses could bring themselves to out-cheap Marvel. The OPEC oil embargo of 1973—aided by the short-sighted, quarterly-report-minded greed of the American corporations that tried to profit from it—along with a national paper shortage, had made a new price increase inevitable. Marvel was trying to forestall it by chopping down the number of story pages and substituting more ads; for most of the silver age DC had offered twenty-four pages and Marvel only twenty, but soon Marvel would be down to seventeen. The DC annuals and reprint giants were cheap to produce and were selling well enough, suggesting that recycling its past glories in jumbo economy packages might be DC's best bet to survive. The format didn't work on the

major series, but new giant series were created in 1975: *Batman Family*, *Superman Family* (replacing *Jimmy* and *Lois*), and *Tarzan Family* (beginning life briefly as *Korak*). Kubert filled his pages with beautiful reprints: Tarzan newspaper strips by Hal Foster, Burne Hogarth, and Russ Manning; and old DC stories with jungle or animal themes—including Infantino's *Detective Chimp*, where the artistic sensibility now dominating DC had first showed itself. The other "family" comics ran new material by second-stringers—increasingly poorly done—backed up by golden and silver age superhero reprints. The sad effect was to emphasize how far DC had slipped.

Even *Tarzan* suffered. Kubert stopped drawing it after issue 235 (Mar. 1975), turning the work over to Franc Reyes. Kubert and Joe Orlando were proving to be the principal employers of the Filipino artists whom Infantino liked so much for their smooth lines and moody styles—but most of all for their low page rates, because most of them worked from the depressed Philippines. Only Niño was a forceful stylist. Cruz, Redondo, Reyes, Pablo Marcos, Alfredo Alcala, and the others were steady but rarely exciting, and ultimately only contributed to the increasing perception of young readers that DC was "the boring company." Kubert would leave *Tarzan* as editor and writer after issue 250 (May 1976), leaving it to Joe Orlando to play out the string until the Burroughs estate sold its licenses to Marvel. Orlando found a truly great draftsman in the young José García-López, but he too was of the conservatively elegant school, echoing newspaper strips of the '50s, and the fans barely noticed.

Kubert himself, the man who had once bubbled over with such an evident love of comics, had been dragged down by the mood of the mid-'70s. He gave up writing and drawing for his war comics, retaining only the editorship of *Our Army at War* to keep his foot in the corporate door, while he focused on his new project, the School for Cartoon and Graphic Art. His relations with fandom had shown him that, whether the comics industry was dying or not, a lot of young people were eager to become artists, and except for the increasingly highbrow School for Visual Arts in lower Manhattan, there was no place specifically aimed at teaching them. He bought an old high school in New Jersey and started advertising.

By 1973, when the furor of the '60s had died down, middle-aged Americans were pausing to look around and to discover that the world they had made was gone. The past several years hadn't just been a scary and exciting time, but had shattered all the assumptions about America and citizenship and morality and their own kids that had kept them fighting in the '40s and working in the '50s. The economy was flat, but the market for "collectibles," including old comics, was growing. Nostalgia was in—big bands, Sha Na Na, old movie revivals—and so was the kind of maudlin lament that Jack Lemmon poured out about his lost boyhood heroes in *Save the Tiger.* The square culture that had looked so foolish in the swingin' '60s, that had been camped to death in *Batman*, was suddenly looking so sweet, and so long ago. DC's middle-aged editors never did any Jack Lemmon twitching and agonizing in print, but much of what they produced from 1973 to 1975 can be read as a backward glance, a good-bye to a comic book business and an America that they'd lost forever.

Even the project Infantino backed most energetically as a trend-catcher ended up looking like a scrapbook of the past. With crass comedy big on TV, *Mad* still selling hugely, *National Lampoon* taking off, and underground comics exploding, it seemed like a good time to try a sophisticated humor comic with a slightly offensive tone. *Plop* was a high-quality package, pricier than other comics and—like *Mad*—without ads (Oct. 1973). Edited by Joe Orlando, it included work by some new people, and by *Mad*'s Sergio Aragonés, but also by Alex Toth, Wally Wood, Steve Ditko, and other grand old-timers. For the covers Orlando and Infantino pulled Basil Wolverton out of semiretirement—Wolverton, whose revolting and hilarious caricatures had inspired much of the style of *Mad* and '60s hot-rod art and underground cartoonists like Robert Crumb. Sales were solid enough to keep it running for three years with some strong support from

Infantino. But was this the support of a publisher who thought he had a potential moneymaker, or of an artist who knew his era was drawing to a close and wanted to do one last thing he could believe in?

Hollywood was discovering a market in backward glances, too, not just pathetically as in the movies *Save the Tiger* and *Carnal Knowledge*, but amusingly, as in the film *American Graffiti* and the TV shows *Happy Days* and *M*A*S*H*. Even kids seemed to pick up on it somehow. Hanna-Barbera's *Super Friends*, a very unhip cartoon version of the Justice League, started quietly on Saturday mornings in 1973 but grew increasingly popular for years afterward; the comic book version, though fandom jeered at it, became one of DC's few steady sellers (written by Nelson Bridwell, who could always be counted on for workmanlike archaism). A live-action Saturday morning version of *Shazam* followed the next year, and did well enough to keep the comic book dragging on, and even to spawn a spin-off show and comic in *Isis*, neither of which is worth any comment. When the show died, Captain Marvel was consigned to the back of *World's Finest*, and then back to oblivion.

In 1971 Steve Ross reorganized Kinney National Services into Warner Communications, putting an aggressive former agent named Ted Ashley in charge of the Warner Bros. movie studio. National Periodicals had been placed under the aegis of Warner Publishing's William Sarnoff, but the parent company was more interested in licensing out DC's characters than in actual publishing income. With *Super Friends* and *Shazam* selling, Warner was fumbling to find a way to make *Wonder Woman* work as a TV movie, and its second effort, in 1975, did well with a self-consciously wholesome '40s milieu. Now there was buzz of Warner planning a major-league *Superman* movie. Nothing like that had ever been done before. Except for the 1966 spin-off of *Batman*, the only big-screen appearances of superheroes had been the no-budget serials of the '40s, where pudgy actors always seemed to be resisting the temptation to pull up their tights. But now Warner's huge success with *The Exorcist* and *The Towering Inferno* suggested that big action and big effects might do the job. It looked like pop escapism was getting hotter as America got more recessed and depressed: *The Six Million Dollar Man* was keeping kids glued to the tube, *Jaws* was setting box office records, the James Bond movies were enjoying a renaissance, and this hot new director named George Lucas had already spent two years developing some monstrous special-effects space adventure for 20th Century Fox. Now Ilya and Alexander Salkind wanted to produce *Superman*, coming off their slyly campy reworking of another heroic myth, *The Three Musketeers*. They were talking about attaching big names, starting with the hottest writer in Hollywood, Mario Puzo.

While the Warner lot was buzzing with Superman talk, just a few miles away a bitter little clerk/typist for the California Utilities Commission in Los Angeles had his own thoughts about the Man of Steel. Jerry Siegel had lost his second court challenge to National's ownership of his brainchild, and for a while he was in deep despair, even, by his own admission, "close to suicide." The comic book industry that he, perhaps more than anyone, had helped create may have had no work for a sixty-year-old former writer, but fortunately the California bureaucracy was a little kinder, and Siegel kept himself going with the routine of going to work and typing forms. But his creation would never let him rest. He'd moved three thousand miles away, and now Superman had followed him, taking up residence in the very air of LA—or at least the gossip that LA breathed as air. Hour after hour at his typewriter, Siegel brooded about what he felt DC had taken, what he thought should be his. And when the forms were done, he went on typing.

Newspapers, wire services, and TV networks started getting the letters: single-spaced, carbon-copied, six pages or longer, detailing forty years of the grievances and agonies of Jerome Siegel and Joseph Shuster in nonstop prose that would break an artist's heart and inflame a reporter's eyes. "The greatest emotional writer of all," Mort Weisinger had called him. The stories began to appear: here on the

verge of the nation's bicentennial, in this country that had just waged an ugly internal battle against hypocrisy and corruption, the creator of the greatest American hero of all had been cheated out of his livelihood by a massive corporation. Nearly everyone in comics saw the stories and was angered, and one of them was willing to act on his anger: Neal Adams, who saw in Siegel the first rallying point for the artists' guild he was trying to forge.

Few freelancers were willing to rock the already leaky boat of comics, but Adams did find a well-connected ally in Jerry Robinson—who had cocreated Robin and the Joker for the greater income of National Periodicals and Bob Kane before he moved into the newspaper strip field and became a prominent advocate of cartoonists there. Adams and Robinson were aided when Shel Dorf, organizer of the San Diego Con, then becoming the nexus of all West Coasters interested in comics, talked the shy Siegel into appearing there and giving comicdom a living symbol of the victims of corporate evil. History was revised in retelling that day of capitalist infamy: Siegel and Shuster, the twenty-four-year old comic book professionals who'd been happy to sell the universally rejected *Superman* after having sold several other concepts outright to National, who never questioned the system until a lawyer told them how much money they could make from a court case, were now transformed into a couple of naive nineteen-year-olds (in some stories, only seventeen-year-olds) railroaded by a slimy Jack Liebowitz, who knew exactly what a billion-dollar scam he was pulling on them. But so it is in all uprisings, and the revision was told often enough to become an emotional truth for a frustrated freelance community. It was the last thing DC needed.

While DC retreated to the comics of the past and dumped or ignored the men who'd created those comics, Marvel hurtled blindly ahead with only an occasional half-amused glance at its old "Timely" days. It continued to sell silver-age reprints by the ton, but with little evidence of reason or taste. It launched an ongoing relationship with Simon &

Schuster with *Origins of Marvel Comics* and then a series of sequels, but they were pure silver age. *The Human Torch* started out looking like a golden-age reprint title, but was soon showing a preference for the dreary Lieber-Ayers Torch stories of the early '60s. Roy Thomas showed some sentimentality when he gave Bill Everett his *Sub-Mariner* back, to write and draw (with issue 50, June 1972). Thomas had loved the character as a kid and had roomed with Everett for a while. Everett was ill from years of alcoholism, but his art was still gorgeous, less vigorous but lusher than ever. Unfortunately for his prospects, the semihumorous approach that he'd always used, and which now clashed so forcefully with the highfalutin tone Stan Lee had given the Prince of Atlantis—"Imperius Rex" now gave way to Everett's singular "Great Gar!" and "Sufferin' Shad!"—drove the fans nuts. Roy brought Steve Gerber in to update the dialogue, which only created an uneasy mix. Everett died soon after, and his creation shortly rambled into cancellation (*Sub-Mariner* 72, Sept. 1974).

Thomas's new role as a writer/editor enabled him to do *The Invaders*, where he and Frank Robbins pitted Captain America, the Sub-Mariner, and the original Human Torch against the hordes of fascism in World War II. The stories quickly lost whatever spark Thomas had first felt upon diving into his beloved golden-age comics, and when Robbins retired to paint landscapes in Mexico, his choppy, golden-age vigor was replaced by the more mechanical work of Frank Springer. Thomas's attempt to create a second golden-age team, *Liberty Legion* (*Marvel Premiere* 29-30, Apr.-June 1976) went nowhere.

Marvel's version of a blast from the past came at the end of 1975, when Jack Kirby returned to the company he had kept alive and turned into a winner. There was no welcome-home party, no "The Great One Is Coming" campaign. It was announced that he'd be taking over *Captain America* and create at least three new series, but that set off only a quiet ripple in fandom. Some young Marvel staffers were openly skeptical of Kirby's ability to do the company any good. Comics were saying good-bye to

everything before the bravura artists of the past five years, while all those bravura artists had already said good-bye to comics. Old-timers were vanishing too, and not just C.C. Beck and Bill Everett. Leo Dorfman was gone as Murray Boltinoff was stripped of his Superman family titles, and Gaylord DuBois was about to retire from Western/Gold Key, which would leave the increasingly marginalized Bob Haney and Robert Kanigher as the only writers of non-humor comics who'd been around for more than a decade or so. John Severin moved to humor work on *Cracked*, and the other Kubert war guys drifted off to various pursuits. Alex Toth ended his long flir-

Teenage fans didn't love this: lots of lines, lots of mood, and better visual storytelling—but all devoted to a charming, expressive and "cartoony" clarity. Bill Everett nears the end of his life with a last, sweet run on his favorite creation. Everett did the inks and dialogue—after being asked to try to write his character the way Stan Lee had. (*Sub-Mariner* #57, Jan. 1973.)

189

tation with comics, vanishing into his mind-numbing but less depressing animation work, saying that "the medium of storytelling I dearly love" was "without joy, love, incentive, high standards, ethics, quality of conception, and performance," filled with "vulgar, banal, negative concepts, writing, and characterization." Wally Wood was burning out: "Working in comics is like a life of hard labor in solitary confine-

ment," he said. "If I had it to do all over again, I wouldn't do it." When a stroke left him partially blind, there was nothing much left for him but porno comics, the bottle, and suicide.

Tarzan, *Shazam*, *The Shadow*, and *Plop* had set off a glow, had promised a dawn of new excitement and elegance at DC. It had turned out to be only a lovely sunset.

CHAPTER 28

DOWNHILL FLOWS THE MAINSTREAM

So where were all the heroes while all this genre-testing and reviving was going on? Where were Superman, Spider-Man, the Flash, and Captain America? Coasting, mostly. And coasting can only go in one direction.

Mainstream art got steadily worse as untrained new hands were pressed into service, old hands felt unappreciated, and pencilers and inkers played musical chairs. The only artists who stayed put were the likes of Sal Buscema on *Captain America* and *Defenders*, Herb Trimpe on *Hulk*, Ross Andru on *Spider-Man*, and Dick Dillin on *JLA*, inked by speedsters like Frank Giacoia, Mike Esposito, John Tartaglione, and Frank McLaughlin. All good artists, but the endless repetition of their sheer, dull competence was enough to put the most devoted fan to sleep. John Buscema—feeling disgusted, the story goes, when Stan Lee told him to "draw like Kirby" on *Thor* and *Fantastic Four*—lost his Michelangelesque adventurousness and just started cranking pages. (Marvel staffers soon learned that the really great Buscema drawings were now the doodles he did for his own amusement on the backs of his art boards—he still loved to draw, just not for the *company*.) Don Heck, attacked for years by Marvel fans who couldn't appreciate his busy, Milton Caniff-like line work, settled for life as a crank-it-out fill-in man. Overwork and hundreds of nearly identical cover layouts had even reduced Gil Kane to just a set of xeroxed Kane clichés: the cruciform figure to show agony,

the forward-thrusting brawler, the "nostril shot"— close up, head thrown back, huge mouth screaming—signaling emotional moments with the regularity of an applause sign.

Whatever charm the fan-writers had possessed when they were new and excited faded quickly as they ground out their four or five or six scripts a month. New writers kept coming in, but it rarely took long to become the same story. The new way of writing comics had become so established, and so worn out, that some of the newcomers couldn't manage any freshness even to start with. Although their plots were all locked into the formula that had sold Marvel comics to kids in the late '60s—open with action, fight a lot, end with the apparent death of the hero whenever possible—their hearts weren't with the little kids. They wanted to make their comics sell, as much as any comics were selling anymore, but deeper in their hearts they wanted to impress their peers. They'd spent their adolescences in the society of other "comics nerds" and in most cases had gone straight from their high-school comic-book clubs to the long isolation of the typewriter. When they did socialize, it was usually with their fellow fans-turned-pros. Their style and subject matter seemed to come entirely from other comics, especially Stan Lee's, and little from the broader world that even the worst of the old writers had moved through. There were exceptions, like Denny O'Neil, but he seemed to have used up the cache of themes that he'd brought into comics with him, and neither the community nor the discipline of comics gave him much room to expand his horizons.

The fan-writers remembered, more fondly than anything, the Kirby epics and Ditko melodramas of the mid-'60s, and so they went for continued stories, sometimes *extremely* continued stories, whenever they could. That might not have been such a bad thing if any of those writers had Kirby's vast imagination or Ditko's control of storytelling, but none of them came close. Continuing story lines became just a way of deferring having to think of an ending for another month or two. Most DC editors still insisted on self-contained issues, but the young writers just didn't think along those lines and their plots rarely managed to be more than efficient. The two-story issues that had produced so many eight- and fourteen-page gems disappeared, along with the symbolic splashes and so much else that had set DC apart from Marvel. As the '70s went on, and more editors left or gave in to the times, even the traditional self-contained story began to give way to Marvel-style cliff-hangers, ongoing plot threads, and "epics."

The cocksure Infantino boldness that had made DC so creative in 1968 had been pretty well broken down by market failures, and trying to be more like Marvel was an easy fix to any problem. Even when DC editors tried to keep the old ways, it was hard now that the freelancer pool was flowing so freely back and forth. In the '60s only a few artists, and even fewer writers, had moved from one company to the other, but now Len Wein and Marv Wolfman had jumped from DC to editorial positions at Marvel, and soon Gerry Conway and Steve Englehart would go the other way. Artists not only shuttled freely back and forth, but sometimes worked for both companies at once. They were like a single army of freelancers anyway, sharing ideas and tastes in a way the isolated older generation of writers never had. The old editors didn't stand a chance.

Just about everybody was doing big fight scenes to fill full-length or multipart stories with less plot than John Broome would have used on an eight-

pager. Brawls were a good way to stay on top of deadlines, especially for a writer working under the "Marvel Method" ("Pages 8-16: they fight. Go nuts!") The big fights had worked for Kirby, not just because he drew good punches, but because he understood the narrative and rhythms of violence the way Fred Astaire understood the dance number. But most comic book fights were drawn by old guys who'd come up through Westerns and romances and traditional DC superheroes, or by new guys who could ape Kane's or Kirby's fight compositions but never tapped into that "balance between power and lyricism" that might have made them worth reading.

Stan Lee's once-radical approach to characterization had become a set of stock gestures, dull enough in Marvel comics but downright clumsy when grafted onto the DC heroes. Giving individuality to those heroes who were often no more than plot functions in costumes wasn't a bad way of trying to keep up with an increasingly adolescent audience. But the results could only be embarrassing when the paste-on Marvel personalities—the hothead, the jokester, the bitter ex-friend, the hard-as-nails "liberated" woman—were tacked almost randomly onto the good-guy archetypes of Green Arrow, the Atom, and the Flash. Writers found themselves jamming overstated character bits in wherever a thought balloon could be squeezed and hammering them home with ponderous captions. Conflicts were contrived between chummy old heroes for no reason but to have internecine fights à la Stan. The innovations that had thrilled us in the 1960s could only make us wince a decade later.

There were some good stories mixed in, of course, but they were adrift in an ocean of creative confusion and endless superficial change. Roy Thomas had once said that the trick of writing Marvel-style superheroes wasn't change but "the illusion of change." Still, the same old illusions got awfully old after a decade or so.

The physical entity of the comic book was taking a beating, too. The publishers had always cheapened their product to avoid price increases, but into the mid-'60s they'd kept trying to improve the look of their comics. The reduction of original art size in 1966 had taken a lot of detail and finesse from the comics, but that was nothing compared to the price-saving tricks of the '70s: cheaper paper, low-budget color-separating, and finally, a switch from metal printing plates to plastic ones, which blurred lines and sometimes even made the lettering indecipherable. Staffs got smaller and cheaper, with the old production craftsmen gradually replaced by college interns, fans, and the spouses of other staffers. In an effort to outshout each other, Marvel and DC adopted increasingly ugly logos and cover formats. Then there were those huge, multiplying blurbs promising "Cover to Cover Action," "Magnificent Marvel Mayhem Like You've Never Seen It Before," and, of course, "Another Collector's Item Classic!" Marvel usually won the crassness competition hands down, but DC was unlearning its old standards in a hurry. Even Infantino's bold cover style of the late '60s had paled into formula. When Gil Kane finally burned out on Marvel comics, and joined a partnership to produce graphic novels, Ernie Chua, Ross Andru, and other artists stepped in to do the same kind of covers even more hideously. By the mid-'70s John Romita was shaping the Marvel look as art director, but though he was a good visual storyteller and character designer, his gentler touch—still showing those eight years of solid romance work in his youth—could never make anything graceful of the bilious rage of the new Marvel.

The result was a mud slide of violent, boneheaded comics, sloppily written, boringly drawn, hastily inked, artlessly colored, squeezed by tawdry ads, muddily separated, and blurrily printed on paper that seemed to turn yellow and stink while it was still on the racks, all wrapped in vulgar, busy covers that all looked alike and screamed like a barker at a strip show. And such small portions! The paper and image area were actually cut smaller, and both companies did everything they could to conceal the fact that they were slashing story pages and increasing ads (like numbering the pages to include ads so that the seven-

© 1974 Charleton Comics and 1985 First Comics, Inc.

teenth and last page of the story would actually be marked page "32"). One would be hard-pressed to find a single artifact of American mass culture—not power lawn mowers, not the Houston Astros, not Lucite platform wedgies—as ugly as a '70s comic book.

The chaos and despair swallowing the comics was only a reflection of the state of the industry. Magazines and paperbacks were caught in the same inflationary spiral as comics, and the independent distributors, trying to save their more lucrative markets, did nothing to save comics. As retail outlets kept abandoning comics, publishers had to shift from making their profits on volume to making them on

A rare bright spot: Joe Staton's faultless storytelling and vibrant cartooning. Joe, unfortunately, arrived a little too late to become a favorite of the new breed of fan. Script by Nicola Cuti. (*E-Man* #7, Mar. 1975.)

193

margin, which forced price increases well above the consumer price index—and therefore even further above kids' allowances, since parents ("a dollar a month was fine for *me* when I was a kid!") are always slow to pass cost of living increases on to their kids. By 1978 a twenty-five-page DC that would have sold for twelve cents only nine years before was selling for fifty, a seventeen-page Marvel for forty. As more kids chose to spend their entertainment dollars on the new generation of arcade games, even more outlets dropped comics.

The people running the business were unequipped for such a crisis. Gilberton Publishing, the *Classics Illustrated* people, had thrown in the towel in 1971. The classics concept was then picked up by a company called Pendulum, which gave it up within a few years, too. The once-invincible Western Printing and Lithography had canceled *Little Lulu* and surrendered its lucrative slate of Hanna-Barbera licenses to Charlton. Charlton was then emboldened to one last growth spurt, which produced one fun comic book in 1973: the humorous superhero *E-Man*, with delightfully cartoony and vigorous art by a new-comer named Joe Staton. Then Larry Flynt jumped his *Hustler* from Charlton to a new distributor, and in 1977 Charlton went broke. (A little later, in a bit of *karma Siciliana,* Flynt took a "hit" that deprived him of the use of that half of the body on which his prosperity was founded.) Archie Comics was trimming its product and experimenting with a "digest" format, pocket-size comics that could be racked in tiny spaces like supermarket checkout stands. Harvey Comics was soon following its example. In 1975 Chip Goodman, the son of Marvel's ousted master, got some financial backing for a quixotic mission to avenge his father and try to restore the family glory. Under the '50s Goodman name, "Atlas," and the editorship of Stan Lee's hapless brother Larry, his Seaboard Publishing stormed the spin racks with more than twenty new titles at once, in nearly as many genres, with art by Neal Adams, Steve Ditko, Wally Wood, Howard Chaykin, Mike Ploog, and others. The venture collapsed almost instantly.

The competition was folding, but that was small consolation to the publishers that the industry was now calling the Big Two. When Stan Lee stepped down as president of Marvel, content to be just the publisher, he was replaced by Arthur Landau, whose background was in licensing American publications for the international market. Cadence Industries (into which Perfect Film and Magazine Management had reorganized, in some tangled deal with Curtis Circulation) apparently saw comics much as Warner Communications did, as a farm for licensable properties. In a policy that sounds insane in retrospect, Landau encouraged Lee and his editors to, in Archie Goodwin's words, "add more comics when they needed more money." The fact that comics *cost* money to produce, that they're all returnable, and that retail space was rapidly shrinking, didn't seem to factor into anyone's calculations. By 1975 Marvel was pumping out new titles as if it were 1952 and Martin Goodman was in his prime. Most of them were recombinations of tried-and-true superheroes—*Marvel Two-in-One, The Champions, The Invaders, Super-Villain Team-Up, The Inhumans, Peter Parker the Spectacular Spider-Man*, and *Spidey Super Stories* (a tie-in with the Children's Television Workshop's *Electric Company*, using Spider-Man to teach reading lessons)—or new "showcase" titles like *Marvel Presents, Marvel Feature*, and *Marvel Chillers*. Then there were the new formats: *Marvel Treasury Editions*, reprinting recent fan-faves in twice-up size, and *Giant-Size Avengers, Giant-Size Captain America, Giant-Size Captain Marvel, Giant-Size Chillers, Giant-Size Conan, Giant-Size Creatures, Giant-Size Daredevil, Giant-Size Defenders, Giant-Size Dracula, Giant-Size Fantastic Four*...need we go on? They were double-size quarterly packages, filled up by overworked writers, raw new artists, and reprints.

Since horror had topped out, nonsuperhero genres had nearly been abandoned. The last stab was martial arts: *Kung Fu* was surviving on TV, and *Enter the Dragon* turned into a big crossover hit. Steve Englehart and Jim Starlin gave *Master of Kung Fu* an interesting texture by making their protagonist, Shang-Chi, the son of Sax Rohmer's Fu Manchu (*Special Marvel Edition* 15, Dec. 1973). The oedipal conflict was meaty, the cast of characters reminiscent of the anti-Dracula gang that Wolfman used so well. But the creators jumped ship almost immediately, and the series, typically, floundered. Next came the black-and-white *Deadly Hands of Kung Fu*, then Roy Thomas and Gil Kane's *Iron Fist* (*Marvel Premiere* 15, Nov. 1975). The latter quickly fell into the usual diverse hands, and was shortly folded into another series, *Power Man* (48, Dec. 1977). DC answered with *Richard Dragon, Kung Fu Fighter* (May 1975) and *Karate Kid* (Apr. 1976), a weird mix of the Legion of Super-Heroes and a bad David Carradine imitation. They were quickly gone, and it was back to superheroes for nearly all concerned.

Roy Thomas, Len Wein, Marv Wolfman, and Steve Gerber did their best work away from mainstream superheroes—as would new creators like Jim Starlin and Doug Moench—suggesting that immersion in the stuff of fandom was curtailing their growth and diverting them from the essentials of storytelling. Their venues for other writing were few, however, and getting fewer as fads blew through but still the superheroes abided. The superhero icon may have been creatively tapped out and incompatible with the '70s, but kids were still addicted to the Marvel Universe, and some to the DC pantheon. Casual readers were being lost so rapidly that the only comics to survive the '70s would be the favorites of those young costume-junkies, padding through the drugstores after school, looking for an angry fix. Wolfman has said he felt as though he were "dragged into the superheroes because everything else I was writing—horror, humor, kids comics—got canceled." The fans' favorite artists were already gone, and now their favorite writers were burning out en masse.

The editorial nightmare only made it worse: when Wein replaced Thomas as editor-in-chief, he discovered that he was "the sole editor of fifty-four titles a month. It was just outrageous. I had one assis-

tant." Not only were the contents of the comics a mess, but they were falling behind schedule, shipping late, skipping months, infuriating distributors and retailers, and alienating fans. Wein bailed out in the summer of '75, creating a writer/editor arrangement for himself, and soon he had sole charge of *Spider-Man*, *Fantastic Four*, *Thor*, and *Hulk*. Within two years that workload had burned him out and he'd gone back to DC, but nothing he did there showed any excitement. Back at Marvel, Wolfman replaced him as editor-in-chief, lured Archie Goodwin away from DC to take over the black-and-whites, and tried to do some creative things: three new Steve Gerber projects and a new African-American hero in *Black Goliath* (although the black experience was being interpreted by Tony Isabella). But he lasted even less time than Wein. Gerry Conway was hired away from DC to replace him, lasted three weeks, and went right back to working for Infantino, a job that suddenly seemed much saner. Next up was Archie Goodwin, who'd be good for about a year and a half. Stan joked about it—"Just tack his name to the door, don't paint it on"—but apparently neither he nor anyone else ever said, "Maybe we need a multiple-editor system like DC's had for nearly forty years."

The result of it all? Marvel was completely dominating the newsstands, selling huge quantities—and losing two million dollars a year.

DC was run with more order, but the results were no more successful. Infantino felt backed into a corner. Afraid of DC being so overwhelmed on the newsstands that wholesalers, retailers, and kids would forget about it, he felt he had to increase product. He gradually shifted popular titles like *Superman* and *JLA* to monthly publication in the marvelous Marvel manner, after decades of a DC policy dictating that any series without backups by separate creative teams couldn't come out more than eight times a year. Quality suffered, but quantity didn't.

Then he ordered new titles. There were revivals like *Blackhawk*, *Plastic Man*, *Metal Men*, *Freedom Fighters*, and *All-Star Comics* with the Justice Society of America. There were also villain-based series like *The Joker*, *Man-Bat*, and *Secret Society of Super-Villains*. There were spin-offs and repackagings like *Isis*, *Karate Kid*, *Super Friends*, *Tarzan Family*, *Batman Family*, *Superman Family*, *Super-Team Family*, and *DC Super-Stars*. There were a ton of barbarians (now that *Conan* was selling well for Marvel), like *Beowulf*, *Stalker*, *Warlord*, *Claw*, *Kong the Untamed*, *Hercules Unbound*, and *Starfire*. And there were *Richard Dragon*, *Justice Inc.*, *Ragman*, *Kobra*, *First Issue Special* . . . . dear reader, let us avert our eyes. No one with a love of art or humanity can gaze long at such a debacle of mediocrity and chaos befalling what had once been the cleverest and most elegant of all comic book publishers. Yes, there were things worth looking at here and there: Walter Simonson and Joe Staton art on *Metal Men*, a bit of Wally Wood on *All-Star*, Simonson and Wood (and José García Lopéz) on *Hercules*, Steve Ditko's return to DC (though not a very illustrious one) with *Stalker* and *Man-Bat*, the Jewish undertones of Robert Kanigher and Joe Kubert's *Ragman*, David Michelinie's Moorcock riff on *Claw*. But they were all brief, all interrupted, all going nowhere.

And what of our heroes, the old hands who had resurrected the superheroes and guided them through the turmoil of the '60s?

Julius Schwartz's career after 1973 is a blur. Irv Novick and Cary Bates carried on Flash's career year after year after year in complacent imitation of the silver age, rarely more or less than efficiently. *Green Lantern/Green Arrow* eventually returned as a backup in *Flash* under Denny O'Neil and various artists, now unburdened of relevance but with little in its place. It got its own title again in 1976, wherein Hal Jordan worked as a trucker (CBs and *Convoy* were in) and had various swashbuckling science fiction adventures that new artist Mike Grell, starting as a Neal Adams imitator, could never quite pull off. Through the pages of *The Justice League of America* marched Denny O'Neil, Mike Friedrich, Len Wein, Cary Bates, Elliot "S!" Maggin, Marty Pasko, Steve Englehart, and Gerry Conway in such quick succession that none of them could give it any direction or break from the

affectations and repetitions of the times. Goofy Snapper Carr became an embittered youth and turned against his old JLA pals. Ray "Atom" Palmer married Jean Loring and Adam Strange married Alanna of Ranagar, but it was hard to care.

Schwartz's *Superman* started off looking awfully good. With Murphy Anderson's precise finishing, Curt Swan was able to display his growing facility for bolder "modern" layouts. Then, in 1974, Murphy Anderson quit comics to pursue some entrepreneurial artistic adventures of his own. His successors, Bob Oksner and Frank Chiaramonte, had none of his elegance and polish. Bates, Maggin, Pasko, and other writers were rarely able to milk anything exciting out of an invincible hero now deprived of the emotionality and complexity of the Weisinger years. Schwartz and his writers had always been great at weaving power tricks organically into their stories, but now they started taking the cheap way out: Superman would spot a sinking ocean liner or an overheating nuclear plant on the way up to his Fortress of Solitude and spend a few pages strutting his powers on a dilemma with no suspense and no relation to the story. Soon Superman's adventures were duller and muddier than they'd been in the '50s.

Schwartz's workload got bigger as his creative fire burned lower. Aside from *Superman* itself, the Kryptonian universe had coasted along under Murray Boltinoff and other editors (where the backups were more interesting than the lead features: the dual-personality *Rose and Thorn* in *Lois Lane*, by Kanigher, Andru, and Esposito, and the amusingly magical *Zatanna* in a short-lived *Supergirl* title). Then Schwartz picked up *Action Comics* and *Superman Family*—where he also had to juggle stories about Krypto, Superboy, Nightwing, and Flamebird—leaving only *Superboy* and *World's Finest*, now Superman's equivalent of *Brave and Bold*, in other hands. In 1975, after another nowhere stint under Kanigher, *Wonder Woman* was bounced to Schwartz, too, and under him Marty Pasko and Kurt Schaffenberger would struggle to bring the amazon back to life with light charm and regular guest-shots by other heroes. Add to that Schwartz's old regulars, plus the two Batman titles, plus *Shazam*, plus a briefly revived *Strange Sports Stories* in 1973 (which lacked the fine polish of the '60s version and was completely out of step with unathletic '70s comics readers), plus the fact that one by one his titles were going monthly. Suddenly Schwartz wasn't tending a garden but running an agribusiness, relying more and more on E. Nelson Bridwell as his detail-minded but uninspired overseer.

Can we blame Schwartz and all his cohorts for coasting? Julie turned sixty in 1975, and not only was his industry collapsing, but his entire generation, spat upon by its children, was withdrawing to cruises and seniors' communities and political lobbies to suck out of the government every reward it could get for having won a world war and built the richest nation in history. As for the children, the great revolution of the late '60s hadn't won them much except a world of diminishing returns. It had been a lot to ask of a bunch of teenage comics fans who just wanted to keep playing with the toys of their childhoods: find a way to sell those toys to new kids in the '70s or watch the whole medium die. Most of them had been too young and excited even to realize that that was their job. It was impressive that some of them did well at all, at least in the first half of the decade, when their anger and disgust with the world could still energize them to rearticulate the authoritarian icons of their preteen fantasies in an antiestablishment form.

Steve Englehart, with a gutsiness no doubt honed by growing up radical and pagan in Indiana, was the best at it. He and the hippified Bay Area artist Frank Brunner recast Dr. Strange as a brooding, eloquent explorer of dank Lovecraftian nether realms (with *Marvel Premiere* 9, July 1973). His adventures peaked with an unsettling journey into a topsy-turvy world within a crystal ball, where Strange encounters Death himself (*DS* 1-5, June-Dec. 1974). Englehart's writing was vivid and surprising, Brunner's art bold and atmospheric, reminiscent of Neal Adams but less weighed down by naturalism.

Englehart managed to top himself on *Captain America*, where the villain turned out to be not Death, but Richard Nixon. The stage had been set by Englehart's predecessor, Gary Friedrich, in a long race-riot story that pulled off a fan-thrilling unification of Marvel's secret armies and criminal organizations of the 1960s: the Supreme Hydra proved to be the son of the crime czar called the Kingpin, while Hydra and affiliated cabals turned out to be controlled by that Nazi schemer, the Red Skull (*CA* 147, Mar. 1972). In the age of the Pentagon Papers and the building conspiracy theories about the Kennedy assassinations, any revelation of secret ties struck chords, and Englehart promptly put Cap and the Falcon through the same treatment. He started by solving a continuity problem that had been bugging minutia-minded fans since Stan and Jack's cavalier reintroduction of Captain America eight years before: how could Cap have gone into deep freeze for twenty years in 1944 when there had been a run of Captain America stories in the early '50s? Englehart introduced a McCarthyite nut who'd gone on a red-pounding rampage in the guise of Captain America—until the government had to put him in suspended animation, only for him to escape after twenty years and mistake the real Cap for a Communist-sympathizing '70s imitation (*CA* 155, Nov. 1972). In the course of fighting the phony, the real Cap comes to some distinctly Vietnam-flavored realizations about the dangers of patriotism and his own heroic role.

Then Watergate blew up, turning conspiracy theories into a national pastime, and Englehart's revelation that the head of the evil Secret Empire is really the jowly president of the United States leads to the collapse of Cap's belief in the nation he symbolizes—and thence to his resignation as a hero (*CA* 176, Aug. 1974). Cap actually withdraws from his own series to let the Falcon fight alone for a few issues—the kind of bold stroke that could only have seen print in the editorial nonsupervision of '70s Marvel—then he takes the new identity of Nomad, "a man without a country." He finally reaffirms his destiny when an overzealous youth gets killed trying to be the "new Captain America" (*CA* 183, Mar. 1975). Englehart's stories were nicely crafted, and Sal Buscema's art had a good narrative drive if not much sparkle, so sales climbed impressively (except when Frank Robbins filled in on the Nomad sequence, doing far more potent work than Sal, which the fans hated).

The fans also took to Englehart's infernally complicated, subplot-filled stay on *The Avengers* (105-152, Nov. 1972-Oct. 1976). He shook up the membership roster repeatedly, cutting Hawkeye and adding an arrogant ex-villain called the Swordsman and a mysterious Vietnamese heroine named Mantis (whose slowly unraveling origin would be a dominant subplot for a year and a half). Then he cut Captain America, the Black Panther, and others in order to add the Beast and another mystery-woman, Moondragon. Later he added the quasifeminist Cat and the formerly dead Wonder Man. He gave the Vision a shocking new origin and got him married to the Scarlet Witch (which did not, unfortunately, end the long agony of their melodramatic relationship). He wrote a four-issue crossover with *Defenders,* which he was also writing at the time, that ran from one title to the other. The fans loved it and the multi-series crossover would eventually become a Marvel staple. There was a lot going on, but unfortunately the sheer number of balls in the air and endless short art stints by Rich Buckler, George Tuska, Jim Starlin, Don Heck, Dave Cockrum, Sal Buscema, George Pérez, Keith Pollard, and Bob Brown—almost all badly inked—kept *Avengers* from jelling.

Englehart started showing from same problem befalling Roy Thomas and other continuity-minded writers: as he focused on subplots, the plots themselves suffered. Addicted Marvelites have confessed to skimming a lot of the issues just to read Englehart's clever revelations about their beloved characters, but as the revelations slowed down, so did the stories. Englehart found, too, that Death and Nixon are hard acts to follow. After Frank Brunner left comics, like every other young fan fave, to be replaced by Gene Colan, *Dr.*

Strange had to settle for being gorgeous but repetitive for the rest of the decade.

Captain America had a stranger fate. When Jack Kirby returned to Marvel in late 1975, he was given back the hero he'd cocreated in 1941 and revived in 1964—but a lot had changed for Jack since then. He tried to go back to his mid-'60s glory days, combining wide-open action with interdimensional adventure of the *Fantastic Four* kind, but his focus clearly wasn't there. The work was vigorous but not always coherent, and his Cap was as emotionally simple as if he were still bopping Nazis with his trusty sidekick Bucky. Kirby hated Nixon with the same passion Englehart did, but with the bicentennial at hand, there was no way GI Jack was going to let his red-white-and-blue hero be anything but a proudly waving banner. After three years of Englehart's tight interweaving of detail and heartfelt political probing, the fans reacted with outrage. Marvel staffers were apparently no more sympathetic, and at one point Kirby partisans even accused them of slanting the letters pages toward the negative in order to justify shoving Jack off the series. Kirby's efforts to give the Falcon the feel of a tough young black man of the '70s drew particular derision. When he blundered once and had the Falcon say, "Don't *jibe* me, man!" the fans howled. One has to wonder if such an error would have been sent to the printer uncorrected if it had been made by someone younger and hipper. After little more than a year, Jack was induced to turn his attention to new series, and Cap was pulled back to a more Englehartian track. The creative chaos of the time undid the hero, however, as Roy Thomas, Steve Gerber, Don Glut, Roger MacKenzie, Chris Claremont, and still other writers turned his adventures to hash.

Englehart, meanwhile, had visibly burned out on Marvel and moved to DC, where he found less freedom and less rich text to play with. His days of revitalization were over. *The Avengers* now fell into the hands not just of a parade of artists, but of nine different writers before the '70s finally stumbled to a close. And all of them seemed to want to continue the

Englehart pattern of rapid roster turnover and an almost obsessive revealing of hidden connections and secret origins. Like the new attention to characters' personal lives, it was a way of keeping long-time fans coming back for more ("the stories may be boring, but I've *got* to know how Wonder Man's connection to the Swordsman can be reconciled with what the Vision learned from Ultron-6 back in 1968"). But it only made it harder for casual readers to pick up an issue and want to read more.

Englehart did one last fan-favorite stint, this one on *Detective Comics*, playing with political corruption in Gotham City, exploring Batman's loneliness through an ill-fated romance, and delivering the most psychopathic Joker of all (*Detective* 241-246, Aug. 1977-Apr. 1978). The artist, Marshall Rogers, did "bravura" without the '60s passion, with a hyperconscious, cold-lined design sense that impressed hungry Bat-fans. Then he and Englehart were gone. Englehart moved to California, writing a fantasy novel and kids books, and picking up work writing those new things called video games for a company called Atari.

Gerry Conway found a simpler and more visceral way to plug superheroes into his times. Most of his work was just an attempt to do '60s Marvel in the same way that Cary Bates was doing '60s DC: all the right moves but somehow none of the heart. Replacing Thomas on *Fantastic Four*, he'd quickly wrapped up the marital agonies and rolled it back to a wide-open Kirby style with the aid of penciler Rich Buckler—a sort of Al Plastino of the '70s, who could swipe Neal Adams on *Avengers* or Kirby on *Fantastic Four* and still beat the toughest deadlines. But after an issue or two, it could only inspire readers to go pick up Kirby back issues. On *Spider-Man*, however, following the Ditko and Lee tradition of real-world engagement, he brought something more than pastiche.

Eight months after writing the death of Spidey's girlfriend Gwen, and right about the time the Orlando/Fleisher Spectre was starting to saw up bad guys, Conway introduced a new character, ostensibly a villain but signalling a new approach to heroes. He was an ex-Marine named Frank Castle whose family had been slaughtered by thugs, and so he called himself the Punisher, donned black commando garb with a huge death's head on the chest—the teeth of the skull being the shells in his ammo belt—and committed himself to gunning down criminals with a high-powered rifle. The old pulp heroes like the Shadow hadn't hesitated to shoot criminals, and even Batman—the source of all those superheroes who fought crime to avenge a murdered relative—had resorted to machine-gun fire against a monster in 1940. That Batman story, though, had gotten Bill Finger and Bob Kane called on the carpet by their editor, Whitney Ellsworth, who thought, in Kane's words, "that mothers would object to letting their kids see and read about shootings. The new editorial policy was to get away from Batman's vigilantism.... We made him an honorary member of the police force." That became the model of the DC superhero, and of all post-Comics Code superheroes, so that Spider-Man himself was lifted above selfishness by the murder of his uncle, vowing not to kill and remaining on the side of the law even when the forces of the law turned against him. The Punisher was an inversion of Spider-Man, and thus an ideal foe for him.

Spider-Man concealed his identity in doing good and allowed himself to be misunderstood (taking a very Ditkoesque "My work is me" attitude). The Punisher, pointedly unmasked, didn't much care if his identity was discovered, and was unnervingly frank about cold-bloodedly hunting down criminals, even taking their ill-gotten cash once they were dead in order to support his own crusade. Both Conway and Spider-Man took a standard early-'70s liberal-therapeutic view of him, Conway by dropping hints from the beginning that he was mentally ill and couldn't be happy unless he was killing (through which his former status as a Marine in Vietnam took on a sinister air), Spider-Man by commenting, "That man's got problems that make mine look like a birthday party" (*ASM* 129, Feb. 1974). Yet the impression the Punisher gave—especially when tested as a protagonist in the black-and-white, non-Code *Marvel Preview* (1975)—was of cool, supreme confidence. The Shadow of the '30s and Michael Fleisher's Spectre were mysterious creatures, stand-ins for divine justice, and generally killed their opponents as climactic acts, a thug's reward for a long trail of villainy. The Punisher's calculated hits—sometimes on Mafiosi and drug dealers who weren't even explicitly shown to be killers—was something new. The moral relativism that had spread so widely during the '60s with its left-wing message, "He only kills because he's poor or disturbed, and is therefore to be pitied," had stuck in the American mind. But now in a time of depression and decay, it was taking a strangely competitive, right-wing twist: "He's responsible for his own evil deeds, but since he has suspended the social code, so can I in killing him."

The Punisher was a singularly ugly and negative character, but well-developed as such by Conway and designed with brilliant directness by John Romita. The idea was pulled almost intact from the "men's adventure" paperback series called *The Executioner*, and it echoed the *Dirty Harry* movies and *Death Wish*, doing big business at the time. Castle's whole speech pattern, in fact, read like an extrapolation of Harry Callahan's "Are you feeling lucky today, punk?" Conway's great stroke lay in nailing the rage and sense of helplessness among young American men that made those icons sell, but wrapping them in a superhero costume that made it easy for preteen and teenage boys to connect with. "I wanted to do a dark, street-tough opponent for Spider-Man," said Conway. "From the moment that I wrote him, I thought he would become a star character." His guest appearances boosted sales from the start, but Marvel decided not to give him a regular series yet, since he had no superpowers and his violence couldn't be made adequately brutal and explicit under the Code. Conway was lured over to DC, where he'd find the same limitations as Englehart did, and his days as a creative force were done. He and his Punisher, however, pointed the way to the tastes of the new comic book audience.

Street crime would become a bigger and bigger part of the superhero milieu as the '70s went on. In the old days a hero rarely encountered a villain beneath his own level of power or fantasy. Ditko had occasionally pitted his heroes against safe crackers or burglars in masks and fedoras, to anchor them in social reality. Then came Batman's vow to fight the "new breed of rat" in the cities, and occasional scenes—especially in O'Neil stories—in which the hero would swoop down on a holdup in progress and send the startled thugs sprawling. Now the "dark alley" that seemed so germane to the retro-pulpy Batman started popping up all over the place. Any Marvel hero was likely to chance upon an innocent being menaced by "punks" and charge in to bust some nonsuperpowered heads. Pretty soon another variation was appearing: the hero being surprised by punks in his secret identity, revealing his power just as they were relishing their superiority ("You don't have a chance, WIMP!"), and giving them a pleasing moment of terror before pounding them insensible. To some extent this served the same function as Superman's flotation of ocean liners with superbreath—showing off powers without having to think too hard about plot—but it satisfied some obvious emotional cravings, too.

It was a hard time for America's urban and ethnically mixed areas, especially New York, which was facing bankruptcy and being told to get lost by the Ford administration. When "Fabulous Flo" Steinberg, Stan Lee's former secretary, pulled some of her comic book friends together for a just-for-fun underground called *Big Apple Comix*, she tapped a vein of bile and sickness, with outpourings of black humor from Denny O'Neil and others about New York's filth, poverty, and crime. Young writers from Midwestern suburbs riding the subway or picking their way through the East Twenties of Manhattan to the Marvel offices may have needed the fantasy of superheroes even more than their readers. Comics creators, ever nonconfrontational and desperate to be seen as pro-social, always avoided pointing out the racial undercurrents of urban fear, much more than

Dirty Harry and its ilk, drawing the gangs of "punks" as white, or as carefully racially mixed. Readers knew the subtext, though—Joe Orlando expressed it in '70s code when he talked about the "upper Broadway" muggers "strutting" away with his wallet. The new, angry superhero could fill in for the beleaguered, isolated young white male feeling his world being squeezed by a rising tide of assertive, no longer invisible "others." Denny O'Neil's Green Lantern had responded to the rocks and bottles of angry black people by turning his fear and rage on his own race and class, but the Punisher, and other heroes starting to take on the "real world," lashed out more viscerally, and more symbolically.

The Punisher suggested an effective strategy, bringing in a prospective star character as a villain so the kids could see him angry and fighting another hero right off the bat. And so when Roy Thomas decided Marvel should aim a character at its growing Canadian readership, he asked Len Wein to pit him against the Hulk. Foreign heroes were always based on symbols or animals associated with the country, and in this case Roy wanted a wolverine: ferocity, anger, characters with bared teeth and snarly mouths—that's what was selling comics. Gone were the manly grimaces of Kirby's heroes, here to stay were the twisted lips of John Buscema and Gil Kane. Wein's social demeanor was sweet and harmless even by the nonconfrontational standards of the new comic book crowd, but he was the Swamp Thing man, after all, and he said his favorite character was the Hulk—it was the only series he'd kept writing when he replaced Thomas as editor—so he knew something about the mute rage of the freak, the unwanted. He turned in an inversion of the Hulk much like the Punisher's inversion of Spidey. Where the Hulk was bestial but essentially gentle, exploding in rage only when provoked, the Wolverine was instinctively driven to kill ("claws bared, teeth clenched, his face awash with almost feral FURY!") and needed to hold himself back with all the humanity he could muster (*Hulk* 180, Oct. 1974). Romita turned in another tight character design, with emphasis on vicious metal claws that could have no purpose but to kill—a nastier visual concept than any on the market. He wasn't the instant hit the Punisher was, but Wein thought he had something. He and his friend Conway both seemed to know that anger was in.

CHAPTER 29

DON'T, HE SAID

For fans of an earlier aesthetic, it was a dispiriting time. The best of the fanzines had become places for would-be comics artists and writers to develop portfolios for "breaking in to the pros."[1] Fandom at large seemed far more bored and contemptuous than it had just a few years before, except when complaining about the loss of Barry Smith and Berni Wrightson and their peers, or carrying on internecine wars.

Gary Groth, having left his *Fantastic Fanzine* behind, tried college, dropped out, then tried to work for Jim Steranko and discovered he wasn't suited to working for anybody. He finally took over a failing adzine called *The Nostalgia Journal* in 1976. In his first issue he launched an assault on the business ethics of *The Buyer's Guide*'s Alan Light and threw down a challenge with his best Stan Lee imitation: "Beginning a New Era in Adzines! Watch out, *TBG*!" Soon he converted it to *The Comics Journal*, the first professional magazine devoted to the serious study of comics (although in the beginning that meant only the pretentious seriousness of the over-age Marvelite). Groth's first big coup was an interview with science fiction maven Harlan Ellison, the idol of all fans, who no doubt saw in Gary's precocious brains and ferocity a reflection of his own younger self, when he'd been *l'enfant terrible* of SF fandom. They played off each other, Harlan doing his opinionated shtick and Gary trying to prove he could keep up with him. While griping about how hack art was taking over comics, Ellison fumbled, perhaps rhetorically, for an example of the worst artist in comics. Groth gleefully supplied a name: "Don Heck." It was a typically smug Marvel-boy response, attacking an unfashionable veteran who, worn down by fan abuse and devastated by the death of his wife, was cranking out art-by-numbers.

Ellison, mistaking the name for someone else's, laughingly agreed. Groth published the whole exchange. Harlan would spend years apologizing to Heck whenever he saw him. Gary wouldn't.

In the same interview, Ellison tried to compliment the perverse daring of Michael Fleisher's *Spectre* by chortling that Fleisher was "bugfuck." Fleisher didn't take it as a compliment and leveled a huge suit for character defamation and career damage at Ellison and the *Journal*. No amount of logic or continued success in comics could dissuade Fleisher—as if he were determined to prove the very charge he was trying to refute—and nothing could make Groth or Ellison retract. It would take years to settle, but the whole mess sold a lot of *Journals* and enabled Groth to sell himself as the very embodiment of truth, taste, and journalistic integrity in comics. Marvel and DC insiders attacked him, but with every attack he grew more confident, more pugnacious, and more verbose. It was the start of a new mood in the comics subculture.

There was only one little pocket of fandom that preserved some of the spontaneity and sheer superhero worship of the old Roy Thomas and Jerry Bails days, and it revolved around the one '70s comic book that still had the flavor of the silver age. Six months after the cancellation of *Legion of Super-Heroes* in *Action Comics*, Murray Boltinoff, needing backup stories for *Superboy*, ran a short, one-time, and undistinguished story by Nelson Bridwell and George Tuska featuring a few Legionnaires (*Superboy* 172, Mar. 1971). It was just enough to remind Legion fans of what they'd been missing. A thirteen-year-old named Mike Flynn sent in a letter looking for other kids to join him in a Legion fan club, Boltinoff printed it, and within a few months Mike had more than two hundred letters. The Legion had never had an organized fandom in the '60s, maybe because Mort Weisinger's letters pages had been satisfying enough, but suddenly Flynn and his new comrade Harry Broertjes were creating a fanzine, *The Legion Outpost*, to be followed by Rich Morrisey's amateur press alliance, or apa, *Interlac*.

Flynn and his cohorts began deluging Boltinoff with demands for more Legion stories, and the more he published the more they demanded. Soon Boltinoff settled on a regular team, writer Cary Bates and artist Dave Cockrum. Bates could do the Weisinger style better than anyone left in the business, and Cockrum had been a big fan of Boltinoff's *Doom Patrol*, drawing with a bouncy sense of fun and an ability to juggle tons of characters reminiscent of Mike Sekowsky. Boltinoff, once one of DC's bolder editors, had been nothing but conservative and low-profile since the purges of 1967—reportedly even setting a policy against hiring anyone who hadn't proven himself by working for another editor—but in this case it served him well. Bates and Cockrum turned in stories that thrilled the fans who'd been carrying a torch for the Jim Shooter and Curt Swan days, and with *Superboy* 197 (Sept. 1973), Boltinoff gave the Legion the lead story in every issue. Cockrum was an unending fount of character designs, lugging around notebooks which he'd been filling with superhero ideas since high school. His new costumes and looks for the Legion were garish and weird, sometimes hideous—perfect for the '70s. He soon left to develop a pet project at Marvel, replaced by Mike Grell (*Superboy* 203, Aug. 1974), who made it all look Neal Adamsy. Most Legion fans complained about Grell, but they still found the thirtieth century to be a pleasant retreat from "realism" and dark alleys. The silver-age optimism and affectionate soap opera of the biggest teenage clique in comics provided a spirit on which they could build a dependable and nurturing fan community.

Legion fandom attracted a different crew from other comics: smart but modest kids who felt no affinity for the upheavals of the late '60s and whose fantasies still vibrated in tune with the simple superheroes of a more conservative culture. *The Legion*

© 1974 Dave Cockrum

Dave Cockrum kept the fan-pro connection strong with tons of art for *The Legion Outpost*, most of it remarkably joyful for such a grim decade. Characters © and ™ DC Comics. (*The Legion Outpost* #8, Summer 1974.)

Outpost was a more communal zine than almost any other with less of a centralized editorial viewpoint, reflecting the communality of the Legionnaires. And *Interlac* was a venue for arguments about characters and stories, and for typewritten socializing among isolated fans, much more than a place to strut a budding talent. There was little talk of "graphic novels" in either. One fan attributed the Legion's popularity to its "built-in 'nifty' appeal." A physicist in the works named Joe Filice, whose favorite artist was Carmine Infantino, submitted a mock article to *Outpost* on "The Physiological Nature of Super-Powers." Then a precocious kid from Tupelo, Mississippi—whose most contemporary hero was Elvis Presley (living proof that a kid *could* get out of Tupelo)—discovered the Legion and, through them, other fans of that silver age which had ended when he was only eight. The angry Marvel heroes meant nothing to him, but Superman and the Flash, settling problems through logic just as he struggled to use his formidable brain to bring some order into a chaotic relationship with his father, became his guides and inspirations. He even built a Phantom Zone projector out of Tupperware, just like the one that freed Mon-El into thirtieth-century bliss after a thousand years of being trapped outside time. If there was one thing this young Mark Waid could do, it was find the symbol to give form to his deepest needs.

A love of comics and a head for business have rarely coincided. Roy Thomas had quit his Marvel editorship because he hated the number-crunching, and Stan Lee had given up the president half of his job for the same reason. At DC, Infantino was losing power to the more business-minded Sol Harrison. Somehow, though, it's not surprising that Legion fandom would attract a kid like Paul Levitz, already planning a business career in high school and proving his organizational abilities as editor of *The Comics Reader*, fandom's source of inside news from the pros. The technocracy of the thirtieth century and the complex but consistent processes by which the Legion had run since its inception in 1958 would appeal to a young man who liked the tidal dependability of assets and debits, the manipulatable arcana of corporate systems. Before he'd even graduated from high school in 1973, Paul had landed a job as Joe Orlando's assistant, and already had his eye on somehow writing or editing the Legion.

Another young man who knew how to organize and function in the working world was suddenly made aware of the revived Legion in 1974. Jim Shooter had thought little about comics since he'd quit Marvel in despair five years before, at the age of eighteen, and his tough pragmatism and lowered expectations had done well enough for him since. Then *Outpost* contributors Harry Broertjes and Jay Zilber tracked him down in Pittsburgh for an interview. In the course of the questions and answers, they asked him why he'd never gone back to comics writing, why he didn't contribute to the new Legion. The old ambition woke up in Shooter, and within months he and Bates were sharing the series.

A new element came to the stories along with Shooter, an echo of fierce emotionalism that no one at DC had attempted since Weisinger. But now it had a disturbing '70s twist, maybe a taste of the anger and pain of a young man who'd never had a real adolescence. The Legionnaire Braniac 5 builds a robot of Supergirl in his sleep and later convinces himself that the machine is his real, flesh-and-blood lover (*Superboy* 204, Oct. 1974). Princess Projectra contracts a "pain plague," and to save her, four Legionnaires take turns diverting the unbearable pain into their own bodies (*Superboy* 209, June 1975). The Legion is attacked by Grimbor, the "greatest master of bondage, restraint, and security in the universe," and his woman, Charma, a mutant whose powers evoke abject devotion from men but violent hatred from women (*Superboy* 221, Nov. 1976). The form was pure silver age, but the content was the fantasy-life of the angry and isolated, linking love and sex with pain and delusion. They were slick and devilish comics, powerful for Legion fans for more reasons than they probably realized, and an intimation that Shooter could bring the fierce control of a Weisinger to stories that could hit a teenage post-'60s audience harder than any of the sloppy emoting of the Marvel mainstream.

But it was only an intimation, never a consummation. In 1976, with his footing now secure as both a writer and an adult, Shooter again took that job from Stan Lee. Grell added his own new series, *Warlord*, to *Green Lantern/Green Arrow* and dropped the Legion. Soon after, with *Superboy*'s sales and Boltinoff's stock at DC both slipping, Denny O'Neil was brought in as editor. He replaced Bates with Paul Levitz, who was writing a new *Aquaman* and other stories in Orlando's *Adventure*, and looked, at twenty years old, like promising new blood; he brought in a new find named James Sherman to give the art a sleek, science-fictiony look. But O'Neil may have pushed too hard for change and a weird sort of refracted twentieth-century relevance, and Levitz, by his own admission, wasn't ready yet. The Legion turned into another '70s mess: wobbly direction, plots with loud action but no complexity, overstated "personalities," an angry black member who could only irritate black kids and make white kids resent nonwhites more. Then O'Neil left, and over the next two years the Legion suffered through two editors, four writers, and seven artists. Sherman had turned into a terrific artist and so, of course, left the field. Such a decade.

It was the same with all the super heroes: even if something exciting was happening in the early or mid-'70s, it would all be over within a year or two. After Conway, none of *Spider-Man's* writers seemed able to distinguish between the classically pathetic and the just plain pathetic. The troubled but always determined Peter Parker of the early days became a whiner unable to tackle or even accept any of the challenges of life; it was a typical collapse for '70s heroes. His dead girlfriend Gwen Stacy returned, turned out to be a clone, and then—the *clone*, that is—went off to "find herself" (and no, she didn't mean to find the original Gwen). On *Daredevil*, Steve Gerber nuanced the hero's affair with the Black Widow by putting into quiet conflict their attitudes on crime fighting, partnership, and love. But then Gene Colan left, and Gerber left right after him, and the series fell into so many unconcerned hands that it became one of Marvel's worst. It was cut to bimonthly and seemed unquestionably doomed. Suddenly the dull competence of *The Incredible Hulk* or *Thor* was beginning to look like a triumph.

Who could care about quality when the market itself was disappearing? No matter what genres or gimmicks were tried, sales kept contracting and contracting, and when challenged to explain, editors could only grump, "Market conditions." There was one voice crying in the wilderness that "market conditions are just a cop-out for editors who don't know what they're doing": Mort Weisinger. He was retired and rich and sounding off to the fanzines, saying that if editors created comics that kids wanted, the kids would find them, and that if the kids bought them, then somebody would sell them. It had worked in the '50s, when the business looked doomed, and it could work in the '70s if anybody with *his* brains would

© 1972 Dave Sim

step forward. But nobody listened to Mort. He died soon after, hypertense, obese, and sour to the end. His only eulogies among his coworkers were bad jokes.

Comics needed a miracle, and it didn't look like anyone in charge was capable of producing one. Marvel president Arthur Landau's idea of a money-making idea was like this: create a team of international superheroes, representing all the major foreign markets in which he could sell Marvel product. He suggested it to Thomas, and Roy thought it would work with the X-Men, since there were already a Japanese and an Irish mutant hanging around the outskirts of Professor X's family. Thomas suggested that Len Wein develop it, and Wein lured Dave Cockrum over from *Legion*, complete with his notebooks full of weird character ideas. Somehow, though, either Thomas didn't mention or Wein didn't hear the part about "major foreign markets," and by the time Wein and Cockrum worked up a mutant group they liked, they had a Kenyan, a Soviet, and an American Indian in it. As usual with Marvel, it was too late to straight-

Legion fandom stirred discouraged fans of the '70s to action—among them, a teenage artist named Dave Sim. Characters © and ™ DC Comics. (*The Legion Outpost* #5, Fall 1973.)

205

en things out—Wein had replaced Thomas as editor by then anyway—and there was, at least, a German in the bunch, and Wein's pet Canadian, Wolverine, so that's how it saw print (*Giant-Size X-Men* 1, Summer 1975). Then Wein hit a workload crunch, had to dump the writing in a hurry, and tossed it to the guy closest at hand, his editorial assistant (*XM* 94, Oct. 1975). The assistant wasn't even a writer. He was a struggling actor named Chris Claremont, trying to save up some money so he could do summer stock. He'd read comics as a kid and had done a college internship at Marvel as a lark five years before, after which he sold scripts off and on, as "a convenient way to pay the bills while I was trying to get acting gigs." He projected an image of self-confidence, as actors often manage to do, occasionally finding ways to remind people that he was of recent English descent and to refer to Shakespeare with cousinly familiarity. The bravado came out on the page: he might have overwritten and underplotted, but his characters were vivid and his dialogue compelling, probably because he knew how lines sounded when said out loud. Come summer stock season, he decided to stick around, and between him and Cockrum, with his rough but lively visuals, the new *X-Men* looked like the makings of a modest success. But anyone could see it wasn't going to turn the company around.

Marvel's owners at Cadence Industries finally had to act. In 1975 they decided to replace Landau with someone who actually knew publishing and the returnable distribution system: James Galton, former publisher of Popular Library. His first job was to stop the hemorrhage by just canceling and canceling. Marv Wolfman fulfilled Galton's mandate to make the books run on time by creating an imaginary comic book—drawn by Sal Buscema and written by Bill Mantlo, one of the new writers who could do the institutional Marvel style by rote—every issue of which would be saved for emergency fill-ins on other titles. Stan Lee got into the act by hiring Jim Shooter as a floating associate editor. Even when Shooter had been just a teenager, Lee had admired his toughness,

his charisma, his cold practicality—he was the hard-ass editor Stan had never had the strength to be. He wrote a few series—*Avengers*, *Daredevil*, *Ghost Rider*—all well enough, but more importantly he lived up to the nickname Lee gave him, "Trouble" Shooter, by supervising writers, helping keep things on schedule, and studying why editors in chief kept burning out. You only had to look at Shooter to know that he was just training for something bigger.

Even while trimming the line, the new administration allowed some commercial-looking new series. Three were new superheroes with salable titles, because new trademarks could mean new licenses. *Nova*, Marv Wolfman's light story of a teenage superhero, was a natural for kid-vid, and *Spider-Woman* and *Ms. Marvel* wouldn't even need an explanation in a pitch meeting. Then there was *What If . . . ?*, aiming explicitly at heavy-duty Marvelites by tackling "imaginary stories" ranging from "What if the Avengers Had Never Been?" to "What if Sgt. Fury Had Fought World War II in Outer Space?" There were the new Jack Kirby creations: *The Eternals*, *2001*, and *Black Panther*. And there was *Red Sonja* a female *Conan* spin-off with almost pornographically voluptuous art by Frank Thorne. Roy Thomas, the writer, called Thorne's work "too sexy," and Thorne moved to Warren's new magazine, *1994*, and the sensual barbarism of his *Ghita*. Marvel comics were still seen as the province of presexual kids—but *Red Sonja* lost a lot of older readers.

Galton and Lee mainly, however, pushed Marvel explosively in new directions. They bought up Pendulum's Classics material for *Marvel Classics Comics*, pursued Hollywood licensing deals—*The Wizard of Oz*, *Godzilla*, *Logan's Run*—and took the Edgar Rice Burroughs rights from DC to do *Tarzan* and *John Carter* with art by Gil Kane and John Buscema. They also snagged Charlton's Hanna-Barbera package—*The Flintstones*, *Scooby-Doo*, *Yogi Bear*, and others, to be done by Mark Evanier, Scott Shaw, and other Gold Key aces—and contracted out for paperback novels based on Marvel characters and written by Marvel scripters. They arranged with Simon & Schuster for a bookstore-marketed *How to Draw Comics the Marvel Way* by Lee himself and John Buscema, and a *Silver Surfer* graphic novel by Lee and Jack Kirby. The latter wasn't especially successful either commercially or artistically, for Stan and Jack had grown too far apart aesthetically, but it was a small, pleasant vindication for two men who'd been saying for years that comics needn't be enslaved by the newsstands (and an extra little vindication for Jack, who shared a simple, equal "by" credit with Stan at last). Galton and Lee made deals with the rock group Kiss for a comic based on their likenesses, and with a real-life building-climber to do his life as *The Human Fly.* They even collaborated with DC on a couple of gimmicks, *The Wizard of Oz* and *Superman vs. The Amazing Spider-Man.*

But none of them worked miracles. The Classics and Hanna-Barbera comics bombed, and nothing else did spectacularly well. Galton had gotten Marvel back in the black, but it seemed to be a holding pattern.

Warner Communications was losing faith in DC's management almost as quickly as Cadence had in Marvel's. Warner Bros. had scored some major hits on the big screen, and Warner Books—which had been the obscure Paperback Library until Steve Ross bought it—was becoming a major player thanks largely to *All the President's Men*, a well-orchestrated tie-in between Warner's book and movie arms. Yet, National Periodicals was fading away just as its biggest opportunity in a decade was beckoning. By 1976 Mario Puzo was officially writing the movie *Superman*, and the producers had announced they were going after Gene Hackman and Marlon Brando in a hyped-up version of the old *Batman* celebrity-guest trick. With the success of *Super Friends,* animation companies were sniffing around: Filmation and DePatie-Freleng were planning to challenge Hanna-Barbera's hegemony with slates of adventure and superhero pilots. For all that, the plight of Jerry Siegel and Joe Shuster was getting more press than any of it, and Carmine Infantino was refusing to toss them any bones or express any sympathy. It was that old-country code again: a son never raises his hand to

his father, a worker never turns against the company that helped him. To him, Siegel and Shuster were only disloyal and embarrassing.

For William Sarnoff, scion of broadcasting moguls and head of Warner Publishing, all those ideals cultivated in the hard soil of Italy were just a PR disaster. He fired Carmine Infantino, fired the man with the DC Touch in his good right hand, the man who had given form to the new Flash, who had given the silver age its shine, who had launched "adult superheroes" and championed Neal Adams and made DC the artist's company, who had given his life to National Periodicals—now out, gone, passé, feeling bitter and betrayed, never to set foot in DC's offices again. Sarnoff made Sol Harrison president of the company, but for DC's new publisher he specifically sought someone from outside comics, someone with experience selling periodicals to children, for it was obvious that DC insiders didn't know their market, and they knew how to sell to kids least of all. Had it really been only ten years since Batmania?

In July 1976, as most of America was focused on the dreary anticlimax of the bicentennial, a sixteen-year-old named Dave Olbrich was making the long, flat trip from the farm country of Minnesota to the towers of Chicago. He'd hardly ever been farther than Rochester, but he was bound for the big city now because he was a comics fan—"I grew up on a farm five miles from the middle of nowhere," he'd say, "and the Marvel superheroes were my friends"—and because Chicago was the site of the biggest convention in comicdom. Olbrich would say later that only two or three comics kept him attached to the medium in the grim years of the mid- to late-'70s, and his favorite of those was Marv Wolfman's *Tomb of Dracula*. Wolfman was going to be at the con.

Marv had quit as Marvel's editor in chief just a few months before, and then he'd seen Conway come and go. He'd seen Jim Galton struggling with the company's mess, seen DC's reigns handed to a young publisher named Jenette Kahn who seemed to know nothing of comics, seen his own *Dracula* become a fan-favorite but begin to slip gradually downward in sales, and now he and his exhausted writer friends were seeing more than a potential short-term sales boost in Hollywood's interest in comics—they were seeing a way out. Bob Haney and George Kashdan were using DC connections to get script work for *Super Friends*, and now Marv and his buddy Len Wein, as writers and editors of *Fantastic Four*, would probably be huddling with DePatie-Freleng as they tried to develop it as a car-

toon. Their friend Evanier was already in the animation loop. All the hot comics artists had found other ways to make a living, and now the hot writers might have a chance to follow them.

Dave waited in the autograph line and finally got his chance to speak to Wolfman, one on one. "What can I do to get into comics?" he asked. "Don't," said Marv. "In five years there aren't going to be any comics."

CHAPTER 30

THEIR OWN DEVICES

When Denis Kitchen took Stan Lee up on his offer to fund the quasiunderground *Comix Book,* he neglected to mention that he was doing it out of fear: the undergrounds were collapsing in the "Crash of '73."

There were a lot of reasons: the Supreme Court's obscenity ruling, the fading of the counterculture after Vietnam, the fall of the head shops. But one of the biggest was a catch in the nonreturnable wholesaling system that people like Kitchen, Phil Seuling, Bud Plant, and Ron Turner had developed. So many cartoonists and publishers, most of them terrible, had jumped on the underground bandwagon that retailers were swamped with comics that they couldn't sell and couldn't send back. Head shop and record shop owners had over-ordered so badly, afraid of missing out on easy money, that their budgets were tied up in inventory, and they couldn't afford to keep buying even the good stuff. Success produced a glut, the glut produced a crash, and the industry was ruined almost as quickly as it had reached its heights. The best publishers—Kitchen Sink, Last Gasp, and Rip Off Press—would find ways to survive, as would the best of the cartoonists, but it would be a constant hustle for the rest of the '70s. Their only hope for the future was the growth of more comics-minded retailers, who would surely be smart enough not to buy into gluts of garbage.

Phil Seuling looked smart enough. He was making money wholesaling undergrounds and fan-market publications, but he knew that the big money at nearly every store he serviced came from the returnable Marvels and DCs that were bought from the "independent distributors." He also knew the hassles deal-ers had gone through to stockpile *Shazam* 1 from these "IDs", and he decided there had to be an easier way. All those *Shazam*s had been returnable, but comics dealers almost never returned their extras: they knew their customer needs far better than any 7-Eleven manager ever could, and they could always stick the extras in a bag and sell them later as over-priced back issues. He realized that if he could get Marvel and DC to sell direct to his Seagate Distributing at a discounted price, with no possibility of returns, he could resell to comic shops all across the country. More fans would go to those shops because they'd get their comics sooner and in better condition. The publishers would make more money because they wouldn't have to credit returns, would-n't have to print two comics for every one sold. He could be rich. He could even get out of his day job in public education, a dream worth dreaming for any big-city teacher in the 1970s.

The trick was getting Marvel and DC to agree. They knew the value of the fan market, and each even published a magazine for mail order and comic shops only: *F.O.O.M.* ("Friends of Ol' Marvel"), the zine of a fan club Marvel formed in 1973, and *The Amazing World of DC*, National's slicker and more history-minded answer to it. But to sell *comics* that way would require a fundamental change in the way the industry ran, and the industry leaders weren't good with change. It could also anger established wholesalers and retailers by essentially underwriting their competition. Marvel said no, but Sol Harrison, in charge of DC's business dealings, was desperate enough to take the chance. In late 1973 he approved the quiet sale of limited quantities of DC comics

© 1974 Jim Starlin

Bigness through smallness: Jim Starlin used tight control and cartooning to weave a cosmic vision. The worldview is Kirby's, but the technique is intimate and detail-conscious, perfect for super-attentive fans. ("The Birth of Death," *Star*Reach* 1, Apr. 1974.)

direct to Seagate, making everyone involved promise not to tell the IDs.

Three thousand miles away, writer Mike Friedrich was forging his own relationship with the "direct market" of comic shops. He'd come back from New York to the Bay Area determined to publish his own comic book, knowing that Jim Starlin and Howard Chaykin would contribute SF stories of a kind they couldn't sell to Marvel. *witzend* was still going, and Steve Ditko had begun publishing his own comics, including a whole book of *Mr. A*, but Friedrich didn't think he could meet anybody's expenses with a minimally distributed vanity project like those. He turned to Bob Sidebottom, the first comics-only retailer he'd met, an underground publisher who also knew how to sell

Spider-Man. Sidebottom drove him to the ID warehouses where he bought his Marvels and DCs, and showed him workers taking in returned comics by the thousands, stripping off the tops of their covers as proof of return, bundling the strips for shipping, and bundling comics by the ton for grinding into pulp. Then he drove Friedrich to Last Gasp, where Ron Turner, the great teddy bear of the undergrounds, just boxed up orders and sent them out. "I could see right away," said Friedrich, "that what Last Gasp was doing made a hell of a lot more sense than what the IDs were doing."

With that knowledge, he created a comic book in 1974 called *Star*Reach*—and it did reach for the stars, not just for star artists like Starlin and Chaykin, but for the glittering firmament of a comics field that Friedrich believed *could be*. He planned a big print run, and his contributors—Starlin, Chaykin, and Walt Simonson—put in sixteen pages each of their best-crafted work. Sidebottom bought about a third of his initial print run, and then Bud Plant bought a bunch, not only for his new Comics & Comix store but for mail order and resale to other California dealers, and then Seuling picked up some for distribution to the New York area. Friedrich and his artists actually made a little money, so he pressed on with a second issue, and orders went up. Eventually, he'd even bring out more titles, *Imagine* and *Quack*, and among his venues he'd publish not only more work by Starlin, Chaykin, and Simonson, but some by Neal Adams, Frank Brunner, and other hotshots. He gave up writing, dismissing his scripts for DC and Marvel as nothing but "adolescent fantasies." Star*Reach Productions, with its creator-owned, Comics Code-free, personal artistic efforts, was for him what Wally Wood had once called "the real stuff." "I think that if people are actually involved from the top to the bottom in a common endeavor, really involved," Friedrich said, "everyone is going to be more productive.... If the writers and artists have a piece of it, they're going to be more involved and are going to do a little bit more than if they don't."

Friedrich called his babies "ground-level

comics," for lack of a better word, and opened them up to less mainstream artists, as well. In New York he'd met Lee Marrs, a cartoonist who worked both under- and overground and who, along with Trina Robbins and others, had helped found the Women's Comics Collective. Now he gave a home to her *Pudge, Girl Blimp* after the undergrounds crashed. It was from Marrs and P. Craig Russell, an opera lover who worked in the mainstream but didn't aspire to stay there, that the best stories came. "It turned out," Marrs said, "that what a lot of the mainstream talent did when they were 'unleashed' was to do the same stories they had done before—only the girls didn't have clothes on. Wow—what a breakthrough!"

More mainstreamers would follow into the "ground level." Jim Steranko brought out a "graphic novel" (actually a pulp detective story with pictures over the text) called *Chandler*. Gil Kane and some partners founded Morning Star Press in 1976, planning an adaptation of Robert E. Howard's *Bloodstar*. (Gil never did give up believing in his barbarians.) Byron Preiss, a small-time paperback publisher who seemed perennially convinced that there was money in comics, contracted Chaykin to do fully painted "visual novels" of *Empire* by Samuel Delaney and *The Stars My Destination* by that old *Green Lantern* scripter, Alfred Bester. Joe Kubert even pulled some old-timers together—John Severin, Dick Giordano, Lee Elias, Doug Wildey—to publish *Sojourn: New Vistas in Narrative Art*. But none of them paid all their creators' bills or inspired any imitators, and none broke much artistic ground. Steranko moved on to publishing movie magazines, Preiss to new schemes, Kubert to teaching full-time, Kane to drawing *Star Hawks* for the newspapers and *John Carter* for Marvel. Fresher and more artistically satisfying than all those projects was *The First Kingdom*, a graphic fantasy novel brought out in 1974 by the Comics and Comix Stores by an obscure artist named Jack Katz. It did well enough to encourage him to publish sequels. It looked like it would have to be the newcomers, the fans, and the outsiders—with styles and ideas that hadn't already been published to death—who would

carve out a new place in the medium.

Berkeley Con drove it all home. By the early '70s comics conventions were regular events in every major city in the country. San Diego Con, with gorgeous weather and affluent suburban fans, was attracting pros and dealers from all over and growing by leaps and bounds. Companies like Creation were even packaging cons and sending them on tour. At nearly all such cons, comics-related merchandise and events blended with science fiction and *Star Trek* stuff. But until 1973, when one of Bud Plant's partners, named Bob Beerbohm pulled together some surviving underground dealers and publishers for a convention on the University of California campus, no one had tried to draw together the entirety of the comic book subculture. At Berkeley Con there were dealers hawking old *Fantastic Fours,* and the teenage boys with plastic-rimmed glasses and short-sleeved shirts buttoned to the neck who were hunting for them. But there was also Vaughan Bodé, a lightweight cartoonist but a heavyweight self-promoter, in gender-bending clothes and turquoise nail polish. There was an improv comedy troupe doing a bordello skit, a slide show on the Donald Duck art of Carl Barks (of whom few super-

Funkiness for the undergrounders, fantasy for the mainstreamers, and big breasts for both—Richard Corben beckons to both constituencies in his art for the Berkeley Con program (1973).

© 1973 Richard Corben

211

hero fans had yet even heard), and a showing of old Fleischer Studio cartoons with their jazzy, boozy surrealism. There were lots of undergrounds, spread out for every Marvelite to see. For fans it was a revelation, for publishers and dealers a chance to build distribution connections. From that point on, "comicdom" would begin to redefine itself as a subculture, the lines between "fan" and "pro" and between "overground" and "underground" blurring, and the doings of the superhero mainstream receding in importance.

It was happening within the mainstream, too. Jim Starlin shuttled back and forth between Star*Reach and Marvel, and in the editorial chaos of the latter he was virtually unsupervised. He and his assistants would send in pages completely lettered and inked, and as long as he didn't violate the Code (which wasn't very diligent anymore anyway), whoever was the editor in chief that month would shoot them straight to coloring. When he got his hands on *Warlock* (*Strange Tales* 178, Feb. 1975), he made it completely his own, as artist, writer, and de facto editor.

His eight-issue story was pure Kirby epic and pure '70s head trip: Adam Warlock versus the Magus, godhead of the Universal Church, bent on enslaving the cosmos. Warlock learns that the Magus isn't just an enemy, but the dark side of his own soul. Trying to stop his evil half but not daring to let him die, Warlock has to survive a kangaroo court—composed of a giant eye, a giant mouth, and a tentacled head—and the Land of the Way It Was, a realm of clowns and scarecrows, ruled by the Madness Monster. All of which turns out to have been created inside Warlock's head by a psychedelic helmet. Warlock himself became far more than the messiah Lee and Kirby had created, became, in his own words, "savior, god-slayer, demon, and the avenging hand of light!" Possessed of a vampiric soul-gem that could suck the soul of any being into his own, he had to keep his fury under control while fighting the ultimate evil.

Starlin's art finally came into its own. Every period of stylistic ferment in every field produces one synthesizer of everything, and Starlin was it for

comics at the end of the '60s revolution. Like Chaykin, he'd learned his elegant figure work from Gil Kane, to which he added a sense of page design and a use of small panels taken from Barry Smiths and Walt Simonsons. Yet, from his early days as a star of the Marvel fanzines, he brought the fluid-lined fantasy of Ditko's *Dr. Strange* and the blocky forcefulness of mid-'60s Kirby. There wasn't a trick he wouldn't use: poster art psychedelia, Ditko splitfaces, Sterankoesque shifts in visual and narrative viewpoints. Whether he inked himself or turned to Steve Leialoha, a mellow San Franciscan with underground connections, he rejected fussy Adamsderived rendering in favor of a clean "comic booky" line. He expanded the Marvel Universe from merely huge to seemingly infinite, and reasserted its roots in Kirby's vision just when Lee/Thomas melodrama seemed to reign unchallenged. At the very moment that Kirby fell completely out of fashion, Starlin took the Kirby cosmos, prettied it up, gave it a self-conscious wink and a big dose of hipness, and sold it to the very fans who found Jack embarrassing. He sold a revolution in a superheroic package, and by the time Warlock and Magus finally had it out (*Warlock* 11, Feb. 1976), all the fans could do was stare with their mouths hanging open. "The cosmic zap," Don McGregor called it, and to his mind it was the reason Marvel was blowing DC off the stands.

Again, though, the mass comic book market proved incapable of supporting what the hard-core fans loved. *Warlock* was canceled, and Starlin had to carry on his cosmic imaginings wherever he could: in *Avengers Annual* 7 and *Marvel Two-in-One Annual* 2 (1977). After four issues of *Dr. Strange*, Starlin looked for new opportunities in the "ground-level" press.

He'd had an influence, though. Clean, decorative, faintly humorous art—synthesizing Gil Kane and Barry Smith with a light touch—became *the* look of the teenage artists in *Capa-Alpha*, *Apa 5*, and the other fan venues that were becoming proving grounds for new Marvel talent. The market was responding to them, too. A Canadian artist named John Byrne particularly echoed Starlin's massive figures and fluid designs, and seemed to be following his cue in bringing a Ditkoesque charm to his faces but a Kirbyesque force to his action. He got jobs drawing *Marvel Team-Up* and *Iron Fist*, where he and British writer Chris Claremont hit it off. Both were stocky, bearded guys, a bit full of themselves, loud and assertive by comicdom's standards, cocky about their ability to impress the fans without straining too hard, and pretentious but defensive in the way that only Canadians and Anglophiles in the US can be. Soon enough they were doing *Star Lord* in the black-and-white *Marvel Preview*, created by Steve Englehart but now written by Claremont as "classic Bob Heinlein/Ed Hamilton space opera." Byrne showed a flair for charming characters in *Iron Fist* and for cosmic swashbuckling in *Star Lord*—if he could put them together, he might really do something.

A young New Yorker, George Pérez, took off from Starlin's small panels and fine detail to make his pages increasingly denser and more design conscious. He was picking up assignments on *Man Wolf* and a Doug Moench creation called *Deathlok*. A tense, wiry, caustically funny fan from New Jersey, Keith Giffen, mixed frank Kirby swipes with a small-figured control that showed debts to Starlin and Smith. He attracted Gerry Conway's attention and started working on DC's *All-Star* and *Kobra*. Other Starlinites were following the master's footsteps: Al Milgrom and then Pat Broderick taking over *Captain Marvel*. A new wave of inkers was coming in, too, picking up from Starlin and Leialoha's tight fluidity: Terry Austin working with Byrne, Bob McLeod and Bruce Patterson working with Broderick.

One of their peers, a teenage cartoonist in New Hampshire who seemed to be taking his cues mainly from Starlin's friend Simonson, was having worse luck. His attenuated figures, broad panels, and sweeping action had little of the finesse of Byrne and the others, and his layout gimmicks and time-slicing seemed to be reaching for the cinematic immediacy and funky physicality of *Manhunter*, a look that had already fled the field. It was no surprise that this Frank Miller couldn't find any work except for some *Twilight Zone* stories for the moribund Gold Key line.

This was a strange thing: talented young artists getting into the business just as the best of the old-timers and the early '70s sensations were getting out of it. This was a new generation, and Starlin was the perfect model for them. Adams and Steranko had almost overreached their medium, had inspired Smith, Wrightson, Kaluta, Chaykin, and the rest to be *artists* first, willing to leave comics behind if comics couldn't expand to contain their talent. When they were coming of age in the '60s, the whole of pop culture had been too exciting, and comics still too dominated by old hacks and sales-minded editors, for them to imagine that they could attain a fulfilling adulthood by drawing superheroes. These new kids had come of age in the dreariness of the '70s, tail-end baby boomers who felt no thrill in being part of a new "youth culture," who took the absence of heroic ideals for granted and sought a sense of order and community in the world-unto-itself of institutionalized fandom. Hitting employment age in America's worst economic times since the '30s, seeing people fight for gas with softball bats, and hearing parents agonizing that inflation was going to wipe out their retirement plans, can also make a young fellow more interested in finding steady work than in exploring his full artistic potential.

Starlin had been the last of his peer group to come into his own, slowly finding a way to unite the "bravura" spirit with the big, splashy fun of Kirby's Marvels, and he was the most commanding inspiration left in the field as the new fan-artists were coming up. They were too conservative and comics-bound to aspire to his acid-head visions, but they could follow his lead in wanting to do just *comics*, superhero comics, with whatever art they had for as long as there were still comics left to do.

CHAPTER 31

TRAPPED IN A WORLD THEY NEVER MADE

By now serious fans found themselves abandoning *Spider-Man*, *Batman*, and nearly everything generated by the big editors and the big writers, looking instead for things like *Warlock*, the little series at the neglected margins of the mainstream that the editors didn't care enough about to meddle with.

Doug Moench was a smart young man who could take advantage of such benign neglect, a writerly equivalent of the new artists who learned from both the successes and the mistakes of the first generation of fan-writers. The Thomases and O'Neils had had to learn from and at the same time rebel against the Lees and Foxes before them. But Moench could learn tautness from O'Neil, lyricism from Thomas, character writing from Wolfman, and mystery from Englehart. His generation hadn't internalized the traditional limitations of the medium like his predecessors had, and so could be bolder in drawing on movies and fiction for narrative devices. Growing up in rural Pennsylvania, where comics and fandom might be the only social lifelines for a bookish kid, Moench quietly made himself a holistic and expert comic book writer like there'd never been before.

With Rich Buckler he created *Deathlok the Demolisher*, about a man with a computer implanted in his head (*Astonishing Tales* 25, Aug. 1974). It was short-lived, but it wove a terrific internal dialogue between man and machine. Moench came into his own, though, on what must have seemed at first like

a ticket to oblivion: *Master of Kung Fu*. The cover of issue 29 (June 1975) didn't promise much: a typically cramped, vile Marvel factory-piece with its huge balloons reading, "Action as you've never seen it before!" and "Fists of fury versus slashing swords of death!" The caption on the splash page sounded like more Marvel hype: "Exploding—a blisteringly volatile new direction for mighty Marvel's dynamic master of kung fu!" But by the end of the issue, the few fans who'd bothered to read it realized that for once the hype spoke true.

The eponymous master, Shang-Chi, has joined the British spy agency MI-6—the contribution of artist Paul Gulacy, a huge fan of James Bond and the Steranko S.H.I.E.L.D. Through veiled allusions we can assume Shang's fellow agent Clive Reston to be the great-nephew of Sherlock Holmes and the illegitimate son of James Bond. His first mission is to infiltrate the island of drug dealer Carlton Velcro (a very Moenchian play on tax evader and emigré Robert Vesco), who now dreams of conquering the world. Gulacy strutted his stuff in Shang's battle with Velcro's thug, Razorfist: he took Steranko's style and grounded it in a cold, hard-eyed cinematic approach that showed a studious attention to Bruce Lee movies. He was learning from Jim Starlin and Walt Simonson, too, how to hold one "camera angle" through successive panels to freeze time or slow it down, and how to slice panels to make the readers feel a moment or a change in rhythm. But where others made comics, Gulacy made movies.

Moench picked up on the art, crafting a melodic but keen voice that fleshed out Shang-Chi through first-person narrative captions. As he fights Razorfist we feel Shang's conflict, his abhorrence of both violence and the drug dealer who's ruined thousands of lives—*feel* it, don't just read it in the expository thought balloons typical of '70s comics.

Moench and Gulacy were becoming close friends, bouncing wilder and wilder ideas off each other. There was Brynocki, a robot who looked like the Big Boy of the restaurant chain and controlled an arsenal of deadly choo-choo trains and other toys (*MKF* 33-35, Oct.-Dec. 1975). And there was Fu Manchu, Shang's father, who in the course of an eleven-part story tries to resurrect his warlord ancestor Shaka Khan (Moench did love his name play), blow up the moon, hurl the Earth into an ecological holocaust, and take over the planet to restore "the glory which was Old China." As loony as that sounds, Moench and Gulacy kept it intimate and atmospheric by telling each piece of the story from the first-person viewpoints of five characters. They even managed some grown-up presence with the death of Larner, an embittered alcoholic agent straight out of a Graham Greene novel (*MKF* 40-50, May 1976-Mar. 1977).

Gulacy left after that. It was a struggle to do his best comics on a monthly basis, and his run included some fill-ins by lesser artists. His successors, Jim Craig and Mike Zeck, more of those talented kids with the clean, dynamic styles and the smart narrative tricks, were good enough. Moench was able to give his series a rare integrity and a precious insularity from the upheavals shaking the business around it. Older and more sensitive fans, who would never have expected to find themselves reading a kung fu comic, embraced *Master of Kung Fu* as the consummation of what *Deadman*, *Manhunter*, and every other would-be adult comic had been striving for. Its letters pages were filled with long, thoughtful critiques from older readers who found little else in comics to cling to during those years. Cat Yronwode, living on a commune in Missouri, reading Kitchen Sink comics and Will Eisner reprints, was a regular letter writer to

Master of Kung Fu. Women were still rare in fandom, but as the more ambitious comics delved deeper into introspection and themes of community and personal change, more and more of them were popping up. It was Stan Lee's *Silver Surfer* that had inspired Wendy Fletcher, a talented young artist from Gilroy, California, to write a fan letter. That had led to her marriage to another fan, Richard Pini, and together they were trying to peddle a thoughtful fantasy series about elves to comics publishers. Yronwode would become involved with a man she met through fandom as well, a New York comics dealer named Dean Mullaney, who shared her desire to be involved

James Bond fan and Frank Sinatra imitator Paul Gulacy wrestles his Steranko roots into a style that's at once highly cinematic and purely illustrative. Inks by Dan Adkins, words by Doug Moench. (*Master of Kung Fu* #38, Mar. 1976.)

somehow in creating good comics, *heartfelt* comics. She and Wendy Pini were finding, though, that the comic book boys' club had little room for their dreams. Pini's *Elfquest* was rejected by everybody.

As Marvel and DC pumped out new product, it seemed like there should be more series like *Master of Kung Fu, Tomb of Dracula* and *Warlock*, personal works by creators ignored by overworked editors. Yet, most writers and artists seemed content just to crank out formula until the business collapsed. At DC there was only one really personal work, a barbarian series written and drawn by Mike Grell: *Warlord* (Feb. 1976). The idea was straight from Edgar Rice Burroughs: a modern soldier stranded in an inverted world inside the earth. Travis Morgan, the "Warlord" who dedicates himself to freeing people from slavery all over savage Skartaris, was a great Burroughs-like hero, roaring, "You have never lived until you've almost died! For those who fight for it, life has a flavor the protected will never know!" And Grell was the man who could pull it off, a hunter and woodsman, a conservative individualist, an impatient writer/artist, who kept a brisk pace and told his stories with pictures to keep words to a minimum (and how refreshing that was in the '\70s!). His ideas were clever, and if his art was never expert, it was always sweeping and expressive. With no editor riding herd on him, however, he often lost his way: just as a war is about to erupt, Morgan is snatched away by a giant bird and plunged into a rambling, eleven-issue interlude before finally getting back to the combat at hand. But Grell kept his creation purely his own, fending off guest appearances with DC heroes even when they might have boosted his sales. *Warlord*'s fans might have wished for a little more control, but surely none of them would have wished for the dead, depressing stuff of the mainstream. Every other DC barbarian bombed quickly, but Grell's distinctive vision actually hooked some readers, and his *Warlord* would hang in through the rest of the decade.

There was one other visionary in the back rooms of the mainstream, one whom Cat Yronwode and fans bonded with more fiercely than any other: Steve Gerber. His first forays into superherodom, especially on *Daredevil*, had been good but constrained by the norms of the genre. It was *Man-Thing* that revealed his true abilities, and fortunately he had the courage, or the self-obsession, to let his abilities lead him. When he took over the going-nowhere *Defenders* in 1974, he took a look at his implausible cast—Hulk, Dr. Strange, Nighthawk, and Valkyrie—and immediately started bending and twisting the established Marvel reality, blurring the lines between "serious" superheroes and satire. His Hulk was the most endearing ever, blending childlike innocence and dim-witted tenderness with savage strength—he even adopted a motherless fawn, named it Bambi, and thrust responsibility for its care on "Hulk's smart friend, Magician" (i.e. Dr. Strange; his custom of giving his own descriptive names to everyone he met was one of the great charms of Gerber's Hulk).

But just when he had his readers bonding with his characters, Gerber would turn around and do something like his eleven-issue "Headmen" plot, about a villainous crew of old monster-comics characters all united by their deformed heads (*Defenders* 31-40 and *Annual* 1, Jan.-Oct. 1976). Their plot involved switching Nighthawk's brain with one of their own, but Dr. Strange retaliates by sticking one of their brains in Bambi, kicking off a game of "musical minds." Somehow into this comes an EST-like, self-loathing, clown-mask-wearing cult called the Bozos, plus a bunch of interplanetary meddlers trying to obliterate mankind's passion and folly, plus an army of Marvel guest-stars. It concludes, in "World Gone Sane," with Gerald Ford sitting on an asteroid with Dr. Strange.

Gerber also took a stab at Arnold Drake's old *Guardians of the Galaxy*. It wasn't one of his most inspired jobs, but he did introduce such threats as the Planet of the Absurd and the anti-life Topographical Man, who ended up engaging in "the supreme affirmation of life," a "cosmic consummation" with the astral projection of a female character, which was so graphic it's amazing the Comics Code Authority let it slide (*Marvel Presents* 3-7, Feb.-Nov. 1976). With Sal Buscema and Al Milgrom doing steady, "sure it's just a regular superhero team" pencils on *Defenders* and *Guardians* respectively, both were weird and liberating spins on the genre. Less successful, and quite short-lived, was *Omega the Unknown*, a superhero of Gerber's own invention. His masterpiece, though—and the comic book so personal that he nearly disappeared into it and never came out— was *Howard the Duck*.

"There was a lot of negative feeling about *Howard* among the staff," said Marv Wolfman, "because nobody had done anything that ludicrous before." Wolfman and Gerber knew they had to make a talking duck interact effectively with the "real world," so they couldn't use cartoony or self-mocking art. The series started with Frank Brunner and then went to John Buscema before finally passing into the hands of Gene Colan, Wolfman's most valued collaborator (*Tomb of Dracula*) and the man without whom Gerber couldn't bear to continue *Daredevil*. With the aid of Steve Leialoha's clarifying and lightening inks, Colan made Howard astonishingly believable and expressive, even poignant, as he strove to find his "true self" in the mad society of humans. The result was a superhero comic that was an inversion and a critique of everything superhero comics had been, an incorporation of the spirit of Wonder Wart-Hog into a Code-approved Marvel milieu through which Spider-Man could swing without losing any of his unreal reality.

The story opens in Cleveland where Howard contemplates suicide, until he discovers a tower of credit cards in the middle of the stinking Cuyahoga River, ruled by Pro-Rata, a sorcerer bent on becoming "Chief Accountant of the universe" with his "prize of prizes—the Cosmic Calculator!" (*HD* 1, Jan. 1976). He forces Howard and Bev, the duck's human girlfriend, to dress like characters from *Conan* and then burns to death in a pollution fire on the Cuyahoga. Soon Howard finds himself nominated for president by the All-Night Party because they like his unrestrained honesty—until the campaign starts ("My God, he's telling the truth! He'll be dead in a week!").[1] He's sabotaged by a fake sex scandal, dri-

ven to insanity, and finally submits to drug therapy because he knows there's no place for sanity outside the structures of society: "If I skip out, I flip out." During this time Gerber also got the improbable job of writing the comic based on the prepackaged pseudo-satanist musicians Kiss, then a sensation among preteen boys, and so he wove them into Howard's world, too. Their advice—"When you meet reality head on, kiss it, smack in the face"—frees Howard from his quest for his "true self" and leaves him in a sort of existential hedonism. "Life's too far in the future to think about...right now, I could use a good cigar." (*Marvel Super Special* 1 and *HD* 12, 1977.)

Marvel had trouble getting the first two issues distributed, and the copies that did get to the warehouses were largely hoarded by dealers. (That had the same impact on Marvel that *Shazam* had on DC, Ed Shukin, Marvel's new sales manager, decided he wasn't going to let DC dominate the direct market anymore and started selling aggressively to Phil Seuling's Seagate Distributing.) Once readers started to get their hands on *Howard*, though—including collegiate readers who would otherwise have never bothered with an "overground" comic—it started to sell. Pretty soon there was a tabloid-sized *Marvel Treasury Edition*, then a Howard newspaper strip by Gerber and Colan. No mainstream comic book had ever tapped into its moment, into the adult culture beyond kids and fandom, like this one.

This was a long, long way from Jerry Siegel's Depression-era wish fulfillment. And yet, in another way, it wasn't very long at all. By writing for Marvel, Gerber had given up all ownership of his character. Marvel could reprint it (which it did), sell the movie rights to it (which it was working on), even fire Gerber from it, and all he'd ever see was his page rate, just like Siegel and Shuster forty years before. The more popular Howard became—popular as an assault on conformity, hypocrisy, capitalism, accountants— the more unhappy Gerber became serving the ends of a conformist, hypocritical, capitalistic, accountant-run business. He even wrote an artist into the series (whom Colan drew to look much like Gerber), a

[1] In the "real world," Howard picked up several thousand write-in votes that November, although not quite enough to tip the race to Ford.

smothered creative spirit named Paul Same, who can endure life only by sleeping constantly. In his sleep, however, he becomes Winky-Man, a supervillain who not only strikes back violently, but paints boldly enough to get a one-man show (*HD* 4, July 1976).

Then, in late 1977, came the bombshell: DC's new publisher, Jenette Kahn, expressed public regret for the way National Periodicals had treated Jerry Siegel and Joe Shuster and arranged for them to be paid a twenty-thousand-dollar-a-year stipend, with hints that more might be forthcoming. It was just the kind of PR stroke that Warner Publishing had hired her for, but it was also a crack in the monolith that DC's Jack Liebowitz and Marvel's Martin Goodman and all their peers had built: was a publisher admitting that retaining all rights to a lucrative product was *wrong*? It stirred Gerber into Winky-Manhood. He pressed Marvel to give him back the rights to Howard, Marvel refused, and he sued. Marvel fired him instantly, another blow to long-suffering fans, but Gerber didn't back down. Friends like Mark Evanier, Len Wein, and Marv Wolfman helped him get work in animation, and he soon found that among other admirers willing to go to bat for him were Cat Yronwode, Dean Mullaney—and Jack Kirby.

A few new fans-turned-writers tried to pick up on what Gerber had been doing. David Anthony Kraft and Peter B. Gillis brought some odd and charming slants to various superheroes, but they lacked Gerber's charisma. More typical of the new writers coming up was Roger Stern, who replaced Gerber on *Guardians of the Galaxy* and was soon moving up to higher-profile characters. He was a solid storyteller and a smooth scripter who liked his superheroes serious and noble, with the steady melodrama and heavy villains codified by the Lee/Romita *Spider-Man* and the Thomas/Buscema *Avengers*. It was becoming clearer and clearer to serious fans that nothing really worthwhile could come from an editor or a company anymore, that the only way to get good comics was for the publishers to hire creators with integrity and eccentricity and then get out of their way. The trick would be

creating a market that could encourage those writer/artists to stay and the publishers to respect them.

Now that Marvel and DC were both selling to the "direct market," new comic shops were popping up, even in communities where they couldn't sell undergrounds and even if they didn't have great back-issue stock, because they finally had something to offer that the local Walgreen's didn't. The market was still tiny, but the fact that one retail venue was growing while all others were shrinking was a miracle—and miracles, like we said, were what this business needed. Unfortunately for Phil Seuling, he didn't get the monopoly he wanted. DC and Marvel started selling to his friendly rival in California, Bud Plant, and then to others. As more and more back issue dealers and comics fans with a bit of business sense discovered that there was actually money to be made in just buying and reselling new comics, Seuling even found himself fighting for the East Coast market. He was furious, but now his brainchild was growing on its own and no one could control it.

Then, in 1976 and 1977, a new market began shooting up from the rotting stump of the undergrounds. An old friend of Robert Crumb's, Harvey Pekar, was self-publishing *American Splendor*, a coldly detailed chronicle of his life as a low-level civil servant in Cleveland. Art Spiegelman was using comics as a medium to examine the comics medium itself in a rigorously conceived and expensively produced book called *Breakdowns*. Jack Jackson was painstakingly unveiling some ugly truths about American history in *Comanche Moon*. A heretofore unknown artist named Larry Gonick started an ambitious but accessible bit of pedagogy, *The Cartoon History of the Universe*. Denis Kitchen had taken over *The Spirit* from Jim Warren and persuaded Will Eisner, one of the longest-missing but best remembered old masters, to begin producing new material. The result was *Life on Another Planet*, a science fiction political satire that wasn't a screed, but came from an older man's wisdom about human foibles, a viewpoint comics had hardly ever seen before. At the same time, Eisner was undertaking an extraordinarily personal project, a set of four novellas

Like a mighty engine of deconstruction, Art Spiegelman shatters the boundaries between past and present, action and narrative, Code and content, high art and low. As the comic book dies as a living form, it's reborn as self-commentary. (*Breakdowns*, Belier Press, 1977.)

about Jewish life in the prewar Bronx, the first time he'd done a job without a client in hand for nearly forty years. With the fall of the sex-drugs-and-laffs undergrounds of the early '70s, an introversion had begun, a serious exploration of the potential uses of comics.

Another child of the undergrounds washed up on America's shores in 1977 from France. The combination of the student revolt of 1968, the new dignity of comics fostered by critics like Maurice Horn, and the importation of American undergrounds had shaken the elegant but conservative world of French comics to its foundations. Some of France's most talented young artists broke from the establishment to form their own magazines, *L'Écho des Savanes* and *Métal Hurlant*. The latter—slickly produced and featuring the art of Jean Giraud, aka "Moebius," already internationally renowned among his fellow artists—drew particular attention in the US, inducing the comics-minded hipsters at *National Lampoon* to create an imitation called *Heavy Metal*. The American version was slick, full-color, rarely aesthetically challenging—*Lampoon* editors called it *The Naked Girls with Wings Monthly*—and a big success with the high school and college crowd. It got newsstand penetration like no comics publisher could dream of, and critically wounded all the Warren and Marvel black-and-whites.

Among the *Métal Hurlant* features that *Heavy Metal* reprinted were the lewd, muscular science fiction adventures of Richard Corben, a Kansas City cartoonist who'd won a French following. He'd emerged in SF fanzines in the '60s and discovered comics fanzines through a friend named Jan Strnad. He was pulled into the undergrounds by Gary Arlington of the San Francisco Comic Book Company, who could smell a fellow EC fan from half a continent away. Jim Warren soon went after him, and Gil Kane's Morning Star Press hired him for *Bloodstar*. Now here he was in *Heavy Metal*, like molasses shipped to Europe and returned as rum, his huge bald men chasing football-breasted women through apocalyptic landscapes and making him an adolescent idol of the late '70s.

The lines were all crossing now, the pieces falling into place for a new kind of comic book. Yet, still it all felt like isolated events, flashes of individual effort that could never save or replace the dying mainstream comic book. Then it all changed—and not by the efforts of any established giant or any sensational newcomer. It was because in 1978 a whole bunch of seeds planted in *Iron Fist*, *The Black Panther*, *The Legion of Super-Heroes*, the distributing racket, and the outskirts of fandom all sprouted at once.

219

CHAPTER 32

TROUBLE SHOOTER

Things weren't looking good in early 1977. Jenette Kahn had hit a rough road at DC almost immediately. She was unlike anything comics had ever seen: bright, attractive, and cultured, with the uncommitted smile and room-tracking gaze of a socialite but the instincts of an entrepreneur. She was unmarried, with no children, but enough in touch with her own girl-self, behind the bottle of Perrier and the brooch-heavy blazer of the '70s female executive, to put together a successful magazine by kids and for kids, called—deftly—*Kids*. She'd followed that with a couple of professionally produced magazines for the juvenile market, *Dynamite* and *Smash*. Her mandate now, obviously, was to sell DC comics to kids, but she'd hardly settled into her office than she realized that kids didn't buy these things anymore—not regular little kids, picking up comics on impulse in the supermarket like most Americans remembered buying comics. Her experience with the young contributors to *Kids* was of little help in understanding the fourteen-year-olds who liked to see the Punisher blowing away thugs and Captain America delving into his tangled past and Walt Simonson drawing Batman.

Kahn was good with the symbolic stuff: the settlement with Jerry Siegel and Joe Shuster, officially changing National Periodicals' name to DC Comics, commissioning a slick new DC logo, supervising the company's move out of its old haunts on Lexington Avenue into Warner's Tishman Building in the heart of Fifth. She was good with personnel, too: when Gerry Conway's brief stewardship of Marvel left her suddenly shy an editor, she didn't trust herself to hire someone new but instead made the versatile Joe Orlando into a sort of super-editor, with Paul Levitz and other assistants as editors reporting to him. Liking Orlando's "love of creativity" and ability to "rise to any challenge," she'd gradually expand his job into a managing editorship; Levitz, still studying business in college, would expand with him to become "editorial coordinator." That created some tension with DC's president, Sol Harrison, who'd often been a conservative counterweight to Orlando's ideas. Harrison was ostensibly Kahn's equal, but his experience and control of the purse strings gave him an edge. Orlando and Levitz would be valuable allies in educating Kahn to the subtleties of comics and backing her up when she decided to buck business-as-usual. The office lights that had once burned deep into the night for the loud plotting sessions of Orlando, Len Wein, and Berni Wrightson now burned for the new plots of Orlando, Kahn, and Levitz, plots for new ways of running the comic book business.

Kahn was good with writers and artists, too. Jack Liebowitz and Harry and Irwin Donenfeld were used to treating creative contributors like children, but Kahn was used to treating children like creative contributors. She was said to be doing the town with Neal Adams for a while, the last man in the business the old bosses would have considered socializing with, and no doubt her understanding of the needs of freelancers deepened over many a glass of chardonnay. She wanted to pay freelancers royalties on high-selling comics, but Sol Harrison dug in on that. She succeeded in pushing through medical plans for freelancers, tied to continuity contracts that would help keep creative teams in place.

Understanding what the market could sustain, however, was a bigger mystery, one that more experienced hands than Kahn were just as baffled by. Following Carmine Infantino's focus on market share and profit margin, she approved a slew of new series and converted established titles to "Dollar Comics," which were superior to Infantino's disastrous experiments in bigness only in that they contained no reprints. The "DC Explosion," she called it. The idea was to have a big presence on the stands when the *Superman* movie opened in 1978. It sounded good, but to experienced DC watchers it looked like a man who's convinced himself that lead weights will make him float: every time he sinks to the bottom, he drags himself out and says, "Damn, I guess I need still *more* weights!" Their new series included more revivals—*Challengers of the Unknown*, *Aquaman*, *Teen Titans*, *New Gods*, *Mr. Miracle*, and the New Doom Patrol in a revived *Showcase*—new team-ups—*DC Comics Presents*, *DC Special Series*—new superheroes—*Steel the Indestructible Man*, *Firestorm*, and Tony Isabella's *Black Lightning*—and a few oddball things, like *Jonah Hex*, Steve Ditko's persecuted interdimensional hero in *Shade the Changing Man*, and *Star-Hunters*, partly about corrupt corporations in the future. At least there were no barbarians. This time there was even less to look at than in the last explosion. Three fan-fave artists appeared: Marshall Rogers, Michael Golden, with his dynamism and organic decorativeness on *Mr. Miracle*, and Michael Nasser, taking over *Kobra* with charisma and energy. Golden, in particular, was taking Mike Kaluta's aesthetic and translating it into lucid and forceful comic book terms, and they seemed to point to a new visual synthesis that might be both "bravura" and commercial. But before the readers could blink their eyes, they were all gone. Golden stayed in comics for a while, but at Marvel. DC could find great young talents, but it could no longer keep them. It was even losing most of its solid workhorses, if not to Marvel then to retirement, and its editors had to rely on very rough youngsters like Alex Saviuk and Jose Delbo, hoping that some talent would emerge from them someday.

Most of the new series had barely gotten rolling when DC's profit-and-loss statements came in—and a massive slashing of product was ordered. From 1975 to 1978 DC had launched more than fifty new titles, and by the end of 1978 only a half dozen were left alive. (Marvel had equaled DC's profligacy in the same period, and of their combined new titles more than half perished within ten issues, more than two-thirds within fifteen, and all but seven by the early '80s.) Dollar Comics were abandoned, and older series like *Kamandi* and *Shazam* were cut along with the new stuff. The "DC Implosion," staffers called it. A lot of pros missed the work (one poor shlub named Mike Barr had uprooted from Ohio just to help with the Explosion as a writer, and suddenly he was wondering if there was even going to be a DC Comics to work for anymore). But hardly anyone missed the comics.

Hollywood seemed like DC's one hope, and DC was blowing it. *Wonder Woman* was doing pretty well as primetime TV show for kids, but when Denny O'Neil, Marty Pasko, and Jose Delbo tried to tie the comic book into it with a retro-'40s charm, they only managed to make *Shazam* look like a golden age gem. The *New Adventures of Batman* cartoon was on Saturday mornings, with Adam West and Burt Ward doing the voices, but DC's version, without Robin or humor, offered nothing to kids who liked the show. Now *Superman* was looking like a hit in the making. The producers had pulled a *Godfather*, investing a few million bucks in Marlon Brando and using his name to attract enough investors to pay for Christopher Reeve, Gene Hackman, Margot Kidder, Ned Beatty, Valerie Perrine, and the best special effects in the business. When Mario Puzo's script came in too sincere, they got Robert Benton and David Newman—who'd written Superman's Broadway turkey of 1966 and who'd been coasting on *Bonnie and Clyde* for a decade—to camp it up, with extra help from Newman's wife, Leslie. Then to pull it all together, Producers turned to Tom Mankiewicz, a James Bond veteran with a father who could advise him on cracking ambitious screenplays

221

(papa Joe had been called in to save *Cleopatra* and 20th-Century Fox a decade before). They attached James Bond director Guy Hamilton, and when he had to drop out, they brought in Dick Donner, a rising star thanks to *The Omen*. John Williams—of *Earthquake*, *Towering Inferno*, *Jaws*, and both of George Lucas and Steven Spielberg's new space movies—was doing the score. They were *serious* about this thing. DC should have had a ton of product ready to exploit "Supermania." And what did it have in the pipeline? Just Neal Adams's *Superman vs. Muhammad Ali*. DC was floating like a bee, stinging like a butterfly.

New Marvel publisher James Galton was pushing the Hollywood connection too, at first with comparably mixed results. Marvel's heavily promoted tie-in with *Logan's Run* had bombed, and the movie hadn't done much better. It was becoming accepted wisdom that people just wouldn't buy science fiction on the big screen or in comic books, so when Roy Thomas met with the 20th Century-Fox people about turning their new space movie into a comic book, Stan Lee and Galton couldn't get very excited. To them, *The Man from Atlantis*, based on a TV show in development, looked like a much better bet. But Roy was excited by what he'd seen and heard. This George Lucas liked Marvel comics—liked them a *whole* lot, as the movie would soon make obvious to every comics fan in the audience—and he'd loaded his movie with broad characters, weird creatures, and fussy visuals that would translate onto paper better than any science fiction movie had before. Thomas pushed, Lee and Galton resisted, Lucas made Fox concede and concede because he really wanted a Marvel comic to come out right before the movie opened to help prime America's kids—and finally Lee and Galton got a deal sweet enough to overcome their doubts.

Roy tackled the adaptation himself, talked Howard Chaykin into drawing it, and using his considerable craft to be commercial rather than bravura, and got Steve Leialoha to ink a few issues. It was a fun, solid comic book. Then the movie opened, and it seemed like every kid and young adult in America told his friends that it was the biggest thrill ever put onscreen. The comic's print run sold out, more printings were ordered—almost unheard of in comics—and before it was over, *Star Wars* number 1 had become the first confirmed million-selling comic book since *Batman* in 1966, maybe the biggest-selling comic book since the glory days of Dell in the 1950s.

It's hard to remember the impact *Star Wars* made on mass entertainment, now that the world it helped create has been in place for nearly twenty years. There'd been blockbusters before, but never a movie that set off such an instant explosion of toys and merchandise, that had young people buying a soundtrack album full of nineteenth-century symphonic pastiche and rushing home to listen to it again and again, that brought kids back to the theater five or ten or thirty times, that reoriented Hollywood's entire view of its audience and its own greatest gifts so quickly and completely. After a decade of youth movies about agony and grit—with "family entertainment" given to tired old veterans who could only think of putting Julie Andrews in another period costume, or to shlocksters who delivered crashing airplanes and burning buildings to audiences old enough to say, "Hey, that's Helen Hayes!"—after a decade in which the trappings of science fiction were used for nothing but apocalyptic screeds, Lucas had done the simplest but least expected thing of all: made a slick, high-tech movie that followed all the patterns of old-style, feel-good action movies, but that looked novel enough for the young American audience to embrace as its own. And he gave them fun gadgets right when the pocket calculator, the VCR, and the video game were making technology look friendly again. The hip, high-speed, FXed blockbuster for ten- to twenty-five-year-olds is Hollywood's meat now, but in 1977 it left the whole industry saying, "Oh...." It transformed commercial scriptwriting, development strategies, market targeting, character licensing—and comic books.

One man watching *Star Wars* with close attention was Jack Kirby. Everyone who knew Jack's work could see where Lucas got his central ideas. Darth Vader had Dr. Doom's scarred face, metal mask, armor, and cape, plus a trace of Darkseid's name and presence. The Death Star looked like a scaled-down Apokolips. Luke Skywalker, echoed Orion: the mutilated lost son of the villain, raised in ignorance of his destiny to fight his father to the death. Luke wielded "the Force." Orion wielded "the Astro-Force," derived from "the Source." Lucas said he took his inspirations from movie serials that were out of date before he was born, and the books of Joseph Campbell, which he'd read after his formative years, but then he surely knew how litigious Warner Communications and Cadence Industries might be if he said his billion-dollar baby came from the pages of *Fantastic Four* and *New Gods*. People asked Kirby if he was angry, but according to his old assistant, Steve Sherman, "Stuff like that didn't bother Jack . . . . It just gave him more ideas for other things." As with superhero art, romance comics, and all the rest Jack seemed content to let other people run with his creations for no credit or payment at all, getting angry only if someone dared to credit him as "just the artist."

Kirby was already doing a series about space gods for Marvel, spinning off from the ultimate conspiracy theory of the '70s: Erich von Däniken's asinine but best-selling hypothesis that aliens brought civilization to Earth. *Chariots of the Gods?* was fun reading if you didn't think too much, and so was *The Eternals* (July 1976), even if it wasn't Jack at full focus. He was also doing a project that should have had the potential to profit from *Star Wars*, an adaptation of *2001: A Space Odyssey* (Oct. 1976). After a fairly faithful retelling of the movie, he took off in a series of new stories in which the big black rectangle worked quasireligious transformations on the denizens of various worlds. It was all very metaphorical, and a little repetitive, but it had the Kirby passion and seriousness that hadn't been seen since the early days of the Fourth World. It wasn't superheroes, though, and it wasn't the Marvel style, so it didn't do much for people in the office or at the newsstands. Before he could process whatever ideas *Star Wars*

had given him, it was canceled, leaving him to spin off one of the characters into the lighter-hearted *Machine Man*, which had little room for cosmic adventure. Kirby's only other series was *Black Panther* (Jan. 1977), which seemed to fly out of control, with stories like "King Solomon's Frog," in which he tried to blend the superheroic and the fanciful. Just as *Star Wars* was hitting big, Jack Kirby had no place to do science fiction.

The first creators to bring *Star Wars* content into superheroes were Chris Claremont and Dave Cockrum. At first they'd pitted their "new X-Men" mostly against each other and the mutant-hunting Sentinels, until they needed a big event for issue 100 (Aug. 1976). They decided it would be the death of Jean Grey, the former Marvel Girl. Two months later, in the next issue—for *X-Men* was still a low-selling title, published only bimonthly—she turned out not to have been *permanently* killed by the "solar storm" that she flew her spacecraft through, but to have been filled with a power that enabled her to resurrect herself. "Hear me, X-Men!" she declaims. "No longer am I the woman you knew! I am *fire*! And *life incarnate*! Now and forever . . . . I am PHOENIX!" This awesome, but as yet purposely undefined power suggested a cosmic dimension to mutant powers that hadn't been explored. When the *Star Wars* advance material came into the Marvel offices, Claremont and Cockrum jumped on it. Now they gave Marvel a whole new galactic empire, the Shi'ar, complete with an Imperial Guard (a tongue-in-cheek spin on Cockrum's previous team, the Legion of Super-Heroes), and hired guns called the Starjammers, whose commander turned out—in shades of Luke Skywalker—to be the father of the X-Man Cyclops. The number of readers started to grow, but when *X-Men* finally went monthly, Cockrum was replaced by the quicker and slicker John Byrne, Claremont's friend and partner from *Star-Lord* and other comics (*XM* 108, Nov. 1977).

Byrne had no "bravura." He was pure comic books, but within that he covered all the bases. He had a Starlinesque bigness that made the cosmic stuff

Most artists would have objected to designing hordes of characters and stuffing panels full of them, but Dave Cockrum's willingness to do so made *X-Men* the perfect treat for fans hungry for new worlds in the wake of *Star Wars*. Inks by Bob Layton, dialogue by Chris Claremont. (*X-Men* #105, Jun. 1977.)

almost awesome instead of just fun. With the aid of his favorite inker, the smooth and stylish Terry Austin, he also gave a charm and nuance to the characters that brought Claremont's dialogue to life. He and Claremont had finally found a place to combine all their skills, and their *X-Men* blew the Marvel Universe wider open than ever before. Anyone reading it could feel the electricity, and didn't even have to hear sales figures to jump on the bandwagon. Paul Levitz on *Legion*, immediately gave DC its first ambitious "cosmic saga," the apocalyptic, eight-issue "Earthwar" (*Superboy* 241-248, July-Nov. 1978). The scope and structure that Jack Kirby had given to

comics had passed through George Lucas and was given back to comics in a way that excited a new generation of kids.

After *Star Wars*, Lee and Galton didn't have to be pushed into licensing science fiction properties, nor did the movie and toy industries have to be pushed into creating them. Marvel picked up *Battlestar Galactica* and three lines of action figures: *Rom*, *Shogun Warriors*, and *Micronauts*. The latter even go a majorpush, with gorgeous art from Michael Golden and Howard Chaykin, and a complex "microverse" courtesy of writer Bill Mantlo. Then Marvel took the *Star Trek* rights away from Western Printing, just as *Star Trek the Motion Picture* was going into production. That was just about the death blow for the Gold Key line.

Once it had been Stan Lee pushing Martin Goodman into starting new crazes against his more experienced judgment. Now it was Roy Thomas, the same age Stan had been back then, pushing Lee and Galton to do the same. Lee was shifting his emphases, and maybe it was the right time. By late 1977, after *Wonder Woman*'s success on the tube, *The Incredible Hulk* and *Spider-Man* were being made as TV movies, with *Dr. Strange*, *Captain America*, and *The Human Torch* in various stages of development. They were all cheap and lousy, but *Hulk* had a maudlin melodrama that translated well to '70s TV, a quality well-captured by the self-pitying "new man" vibes of Bill Bixby and the sadness of the deaf muscleman, Lou Ferrigno. It became a series in early 1978, making Marvel a sellable presence in Hollywood. And Stan Lee was proving to be the perfect salesman, grinning and glad-handing and reflecting back to Hollywood its own desperate need to be loved. He embodied the nonthreatening fun that everyone wanted to find in comics, and soon he was spending more time in California than New York.

He'd also found the man to pass the torch to. After Roy Thomas finished the six-issue adaptation of *Star Wars*, he gave the ongoing series—further adventures of Luke Skywalker and company—to Archie Goodwin, who also got the job when a newspaper strip was spun off. Goodwin had hung onto the editor in chief's job longer than anyone since Thomas, but with a couple of steady writing gigs, he decided it was time to quit. At the very beginning of 1978, Jim Shooter took command, and Marvel Phase Two was decisively done. Lee was still publisher, with Shooter nominally doing the same job that Goodwin had just vacated. But anyone paying attention could feel the company tilt toward Shooter's towering form.

Shooter had known '60s DC, and he'd known '70s Marvel. He was sensible enough to see that, although Marvel's content and creators had pounded DC's, DC's institutional structure worked a hell of a lot better. With Galton and Lee's support, he vowed to phase out the writer/editorships as soon as the contracts ran out and quickly started hiring editors and assistant editors to take over handfuls of titles. He set up stables in the manner of Julius Schwartz and Mort Weisinger, all under his central control. The guys who'd been running Marvel for five years were offended. Steve Gerber was already gone, and Gerry Conway and Steve Englehart were at DC. Roy Thomas, Marv Wolfman, and Len Wein started speeding up their efforts to get out of the business as their writer/editor contracts ticked down. The loss of Gerber made it clear that creators did matter: *Howard the Duck* immediately slumped under other hands, and an attempt to continue it as a black-and-white magazine failed quickly. So Shooter moved quickly to match DC's new freelancer benefits and tried to top them with incentives for remaining on series. He doubled page rates, with promises of more raises to come. He wanted a royalty system to reward success—but Galton said no. Publishers knew, if freelancers didn't, how much money could be made on a successful series, and they weren't willing to give that up yet.

Shooter still had to make do with a lot of raw young writers and artists, but he also saw a way to use that to Marvel's advantage. He took on the mentor's role, boiling down what he'd learned about storytelling from Weisinger, Lee, and John Romita into easily transmissible rules: open with the hero displaying his powers, end every page with a hook, catch new readers up on the status quo in every issue, and so on. The "Marvel style" had already been largely institutionalized by a sort of conspiracy of fandom, but never like this. "We want to make sure that everything is at least good," Shooter would say. "Our people have been encouraged to be the cutting edge of the medium, but I think they can do more with the fundamentals of their craft than in a scattershot way." His regime might never allow the wildness of a Gerber, but it also wouldn't allow the oceans of incoherent junk that had been tossed at the readers during five years. Marvel comics were products now, with minimum manufacturing standards.

Marvel's big superhero series were soon locked into a rhythm of action and subplot as secure and soothing and soporific as the ocean waves. It wasn't all formula with Shooter, though, especially where modestly selling titles with more intelligent followings were concerned. He reportedly suggested to Doug Moench the story called "Nightimes," the most offbeat *Master of Kung Fu* issue to that time and one that would change the tone of "sophisticated" comics in general. The entire issue spotlighted a quiet evening in the lives of Shang-Chi and his lover, scenes of training, dining, moviegoing, and lovemaking with a subtext of serene introspection (*MKF* 71, Dec. 1978). The reflective quality that Moench had always used as counterpoint to the action now became almost the point of the series.

Shooter had an eye for talent and new perspectives. He took a great interest in the young artist named Frank Miller, whose ambitions were still outstripping his control, but who was voraciously inquisitive about visual storytelling and really seemed to want to do more with comics than draw guys in spandex punching each other. He hired Marvel's first ever female editors, Jo Duffy and Louise Jones. Jones had distinguished herself at Warren for her human touch and her understanding of character-driven storytelling. Shooter broke the pattern of hiring from the fanzine network, helping

225

comics become more heterogeneous. Billy Graham finally ceased to be "the black guy" in the business: Jim Owsley was a clever and charismatic writer who could bring crackling humor and emotionality to formula superhero scripts; Keith Pollard was a solid penciler with some Gil Kane in him; Trevor Von Eeden was an aggressive, erratic artist with a startling sense of design; and Denys Cowan was a very stylish, very fly young penciler with a self-confidence that made his work charismatic even when the fundamentals weren't great. The increasing integration of American society probably deserves more credit for the change than Shooter, but Shooter helped.

In most of his editorial hires, Shooter didn't go for big-name fan-writers with their own agendas and bristling talents. His first two editors were Roger Stern and Bob Hall, a writer and an artist who liked the Marvel way. He did, however, approach Denny O'Neil, whom he considered one of the two best writers, apart from himself, in the field; Shooter, like his first mentor, Mort Weisinger, always liked tightly controlled craft more than freeroaming vision. Denny fended him off for a while, but then, as he neared forty, he woke up to what a mess his life had become. "I finally decided to go sober," he said, "and I needed structure in my life, which an editorial job seemed able to provide." In 1979 he took over a few series that Shooter felt needed stabilizing, including the disastrous *Daredevil.* As for Shooter's other favorite writer, Archie Goodwin, he was his and Lee's first choice to put together Stan's new pet project, *Epic Illustrated,* a full-color magazine to compete with *Heavy Metal.* Shooter also gave an assistant editorship to Mark Gruenwald, a fan who'd made his name with his "Omniversal Theory," a mock-scholarly attempt to all the fictional universes of comics, from DC's and Marvel's to Gold Key's and Harvey's. His attention to Marvel continuity and love of order made him a natural for the new regime. Tom DeFalco, who'd learned to write for kids at Archie Comics, became a full-time writer at Marvel and impressed Shooter with his grasp of the

Marvel formula and the business of comics. He became an editor, and eventually Shooter's most trusted aide.

Most of the new assistant editors, though, were names only dimly familiar to comicdom. They were young New York-area guys who'd written analytic letters or seemed eager to learn in interviews, guys eager to play with their beloved Marvel superheroes but willing to do it someone else's way. They flowed in over the next few years, one being promoted and two new ones taking his place, until it was impossible to distinguish their comics or even remember who'd arrived when: Ralph Macchio, Jim Salicrup, Bob Budiansky, Danny Fingeroth, Howard Mackie, Bob Harras, Mike Carlin. They were models of a generation, having internalized the anxiety of the '70s and the collapse of the counterculture at a crucial age, believing that if you worked hard and sublimated yourself to the corporate world, the corporate world would take care of you. Studying under Shooter was the comic book version of an MBA.

Shooter's editors were empowered to give directives to their writers and artists and even to rewrite dialogue as they saw fit, just like Weisinger and Schwartz always had but previous Marvel editors had rarely dared. At first they were an excited bunch of kids, taking over the clubhouse of the guys they'd idolized in high school, the Thomases and the Weins, and redecorating it their own way. Pretty soon, though, they became better known for their obsessive protection of Marvel continuity and their compulsive enforcement of Shooter's rules of clarity. Shooter was demanding, and had a temper—a real phone-throwing, desk-tipping temper—and the editors learned that to survive, it was better to err on the side of caution.

Editors and assistant editors were encouraged to write, too. Shooter himself was a perfect example of a craftsman who might not be lost in his own creative visions, but who had learned the rules by studying comics. He was now showing how it could be done with a stint on *Avengers* that most fans agreed was the best since Steve Englehart's, even better in terms of pace and control. He felt staffers would have more to teach writers if they did more writing themselves. And if the day came when *everything* was written by house-trained editors who spent forty or fifty hours a week together, the product could only be that much more consistent (and the continuity of the Marvel universe would be that much tighter). Denny O'Neil, who had always edited freelance at DC, usually writing his own scripts, admitted that he was now learning a great deal about the technical aspects of his own craft from the questions Frank Miller would ask him at the Marvel volleyball games. "Frank was a good volleyball player," he said, "and an even better student." It was a new role for Denny—as if he'd opened a bottle as a young hotshot, knocked back a few drinks, and awakened as an old master—but one he came to enjoy.

Most Marvels were still written by the remaining older guys or by Roger Stern, Bill Mantlo, Doug Moench, Chris Claremont, David Michelinie, Roger MacKenzie, and others whom Shooter had come to trust when he was still an associate editor. But names like Gruenwald and Carlin and Mackie would pop up in the "written by" space with increasing frequency. Their work was just what one would expect: well-studied, pieced together from old bits of Kirby and Lee and Ditko and Thomas, every piece laid so carefully in place that there wasn't a micron of space for an individual vision or a new idea to slip through.

Shooter valued the storytelling craft of veteran artists, but he didn't have many. He relied on John Romita to help him train new artists, keeping him far too busy as art director to draw comics anymore. He tried to lure Steve Ditko back, but for the moment Ditko only did a few issues of *Machine Man*. The Shooter years also saw the Marvel debut of another old hand with a touch for visual storytelling: Carmine Infantino. On *Nova* and *John Carter*, Infantino showed off a new style, mostly kinetic, without the evident thought he'd put into his work before he took that office job a long decade before, but more fun and compelling than 90 percent of what was filling Marvel's pages. On *Spider-Woman*, with Steve Leialoha softening and polishing him, he was a last

reminder that elegance and superheroes could still coexist. Shooter, however, was no less inclined to lecture his older hands than his younger ones on the "right way" to tell a story visually, and he'd soon learn that sixty-year-old vets who hadn't had a page bounced for redrawing in twenty years might not take kindly to the suggestions of a boss still shy of thirty.

Shooter knew he'd have to rely on new artists, and although he liked dynamic stuff when he could find it, he'd always pick boring but clear over flashy but challenging. Bob Hall, Ron Wilson, Alan Kupperberg, Ron Frenz—they were always clear. John Buscema and Stan Lee's *How to Draw Comics the Marvel Way* was helpful in bringing in a generation of kids who, talented or no, had some concept of why they were supposed to do what Shooter wanted them to. Simply by stating that there was a learnable "Marvel way," it significantly increased the number of youngsters showing up at conventions with portfolios, willing to draw however they were told and to meet all their monthly deadlines. For the first time since the '60s, editors wouldn't have to worry about finding hands to fill their pages. Once a kid had "broken in," Shooter walked him through some well-chosen old Marvels to teach him how comics should be done. Nearly all of them were by Jack Kirby.

But what of Jack himself? He was doing *Machine Man*, *Black Panther*, and *Devil Dinosaur*, about a tyrannosaur and his ape-boy companion. Everything was turning to dust in his hands. The day he'd called Stan Lee with his resignation in 1970, he'd vowed never to work "Marvel method" again, never to do all the storytelling for some "writer" who was only going to slap on dialogue that subverted his plot. Yet, there was no place in the new Marvel for a guy in his sixties spinning his own weird visions. His *Hulk* had become hot primetime kid-vid. It had spun off into *The Rampaging Hulk*, Marvel's first successful full-color oversize magazine, and now there was talk of a *She-Hulk*, with Stan Lee writing the first issue just to thrill the fans (because, after all, Stan *had* created the Hulk, hadn't he?). Kirby's *Fantastic Four* was becoming a cartoon with Stan Lee's development

227

help, leading Lee and Galton to explore getting Marvel directly into animation production. His *Captain America* was becoming a TV movie, and the ads actually read "created by Stan Lee" until he and Joe Simon had their lawyers fire off letters (Stan was just playing his ocarina on cousin Marty's file cabinet when Cap was already a best-seller). His Dr. Doom and Darkseid had helped make George Lucas a mogul. His *X-Men* was the fastest-rising series in comics. His *Avengers* was Jim Shooter's monthly demonstration of the "Marvel style." And here he was drawing *Devil Dinosaur*, being hooted at by the fans, taking crap from assistant editors who would

never create anything in their lives, seeing his original art being sold at conventions, collecting his page rates. It was time to go.

Mark Evanier helped him hook up with DePatie-Freleng Animation, where he did designs for the *Fantastic Four* cartoon. He liked it, too. He was respected, well-paid, and given time to think and to do redraws. He found more work with Hanna-Barbera and Ruby-Spears and switched to animation full-time, retiring without fanfare from the business he'd made what it was. In 1979, for the first time in forty years, there was no Jack Kirby in comics. No one even seemed to notice.

CHAPTER 33

LIKE A PHOENIX FROM THE ASHES

Marvel rolled on. It was becoming clear already that any Marvel title of the Shooter age could go one of two ways: overcrafted tedium or tightly focused energy of a kind that hadn't been common in comics since the silver age. It was also becoming clear that either one was going to appeal to readers more than the mess of the '70s.

In Shooter's first year and a half, Marvel canceled nearly twenty titles, but then the cancellations slowed almost to a stop. Sales on superhero series were slowing their decline, and in some cases were even coming back up. *Star Wars* had a lot to do with it: kids who loved the movie and collectors who wanted the merchandise went looking for comic book racks for the first time, or at least the first time in years. When the racks were sold out, or were too few to find, they started to track down the comics shops that were popping up in the yellow pages under "Book Dlrs, Used & Rare." Some of them then picked up other comics, especially the ones like *X-Men*, which had armored galactic warriors in them. But the Shooter approach had something to do with it, too: when kids could pick up a comic book for the first time and understand what was going on, they were more likely to come back, and when they could rely on the same steady stuff month after month, they'd keep coming back, at least until they outgrew it. For the first time in a long time, things were breaking the right way for comics. Comics shops were taking off, breaking out of college towns and cheap urban neighborhoods into suburban malls and small cities. Comics people were catching on that the market for things like *The First Kingdom* and *Star*Reach* was growing.

Up in the suburbs of Toronto in 1977, a young fan named Dave Sim—who'd been growing increasingly angry with the comics mainstream ever since his beloved Barry Smith had been driven from *Conan*—decided to do something with his passions. His friend Gene Day worked obsessively on ambitious, ornamental art samples, sending them out to every venue he could think of. Sim, shamed by Day's energy, tried to work just as hard, but discovered that the only thing that could keep him at the drawing board was his homage to Smith about a barbarian battling through a fantasied age. He could draw and he could write, and his pastiches of Smith and Roy Thomas were sometimes uncannily accurate, sometimes sharply parodic. He lacked a name for his barbarian, so his girlfriend, Deni Loubert, suggested naming him after the three-headed dog of Greek mythology. Unfortunately, she got the name wrong and came up with "Cerebus." So do revolutions begin. Sim couldn't come up with a publisher and decided to publish it himself. He sent solicitations to comics distributors and got initial orders of five hundred copies; it was nothing to get rich on, or even pay the printer with, but it hadn't been very long since the days when a fanzine that gradually built up to a circulation of five hundred would have been considered a hit. In late

Self-publishing set Dave Sim free to unite a Barry Smith surface, funny cartooning, and clever visual/verbal story-telling. Here Elrod the Albino rescues a midget priest in a Cerebus suit. (*Cerebus the Aardvark* #7, 1978.)

habitués of the comic shops responded instantly to this new-but-familiar work, which was both derisive and affectionate, which reaffirmed their status as knowing fans yet helped them laugh at the adolescent kitsch that they still tried to like but couldn't quite swallow anymore. ("It was, the thieves would later say, the first time they had heard an Earth-pig *laugh* . . . .") It was full of jokes, yet never became *Not Brand Ecch*, and never failed to deliver the visuals and fights and plot points of a well-crafted sword-and-sorcery comic. Sim also rarely failed to deliver it monthly—this was no vanity project, this was his whole career. Orders jumped quickly into the thousands and kept on climbing.

Sim got bolder and started displaying a manic sense of humor weaned on Warner Bros. cartoons. Michael Moorcock's Elric became Elrod the Albino, who for no particular reason talks like Foghorn Leghorn. He modified Smith into a style that could make Cerebus hilariously cartoony but his world shadowed and frightening. Ten issues in, he had Red Sophia—the lustful warrior woman in the obligatory metal lingerie—try to seduce Cerebus by whipping off her top with a cry of, "What do you think of THESE?!" When he had Cerebus reply, "They'll probably heal if you stop wearing that chain-mail bikini," the fans were *his*.

From there Sim could go anywhere: superhero parodies (the Cockroach), Groucho Marx (Lord Julius), even abandoning the Smith pastiche for a style of his own, which had far more of Neal Adams and Will Eisner and Gene Day in it. In 1979, when he announced that *Cerebus* wasn't just a comic book, but a self-contained, three-hundred-issue story that he wouldn't finish until the next century, no one took him seriously, of course. But it showed how connected an artist could feel to his material when it was all his. *Cerebus* wasn't selling nearly enough copies to keep it alive through normal comic book publishing, but thanks to the direct market, it was making Dave Sim a comfortable living and leaving him free of anyone's meddling.

Wendy and Richard Pini were soon thrust into the

1977, comic shop customers all over North America picked up this odd-looking thing and scanned the splash page: "He came into our city in the early dawn . . . . Though later he would be called the finest warrior to enter our gates, at the time, he was but a curiosity. . . . You see, he stood only five hands high, had a lengthy snout, a long tail, and was covered with short grey fur. . . . He was, in short. . . .Cerebus the Aardvark."

Sim was too smart, too disgusted, too much of his generation to do a straight homage like past fans might have done. *Howard the Duck* helped, too. The

same strategy. They thought they'd finally found a publisher for their *Elfquest* in a small publication called *Fantasy Quarterly*, but it went broke after a single issue, leaving them more frustrated than before. Thus, in 1978, the first black-and-white *Elfquest* from WaRP ("Wendy and Richard Pini") Graphics hit the direct market. It started a little bigger than *Cerebus* and built an audience a little more slowly but still steadily with its prettily drawn tales of love and adventure in a Tolkienesque fantasy world. It hooked female fans in particular, and gradually sent out tendrils, by word of mouth, into the subculture of junior-high and high-school girls, giving them a regular supplement to the Anne McCaffrey and other fantasy books that seemed to be taking the place of romances for a generation whose view of the real world had been allowed so little romance. A small but growing number of girls—those who could stand to enter musty shops full of obese clerks, awkward boys, and ugly superheroes—were being drawn into a field they'd never thought about before.

At the same time, Dean Mullaney, a passionate comic book dealer from Staten Island, was putting together a dream venture inspired by *Star*Reach*. He'd hooked up with Don McGregor and Billy Graham, now both gone from *Black Panther* and sick of the corporate grind. With the business assistance of his brother Jan, Mullaney created Eclipse Publishing to bring out *Sabre*, the first "graphic novel" aimed specifically at the direct market. It was tall, thin, and square-bound, with glossy paper and offset printing, which allowed for subtle, rich colors in continuous fields, none of the little dots that Roy Lichtenstein had made famous. The format was modeled after the "graphic albums" that had been selling well in Europe for decades. Others were playing with the format, or considering it: Richard Corben, with his old friend Jan Strnad as scripter, with his *Mutant World*; a company called Catalan, translating French and Spanish graphic albums for the American market; *National Lampoon* and Warren reprinting work by hot comics artists. But only the Mullaneys knew how to get it straight to superhero fans. *Sabre* was the

story of a black adventurer and his lover fighting for right and dignity in a chaotic future world. The lover was white, and their sexual relationship frank, which put in big bold letters the freedom possible outside the mainstream, even if McGregor's convoluted prose and Graham's strong but self-consciously daring art looked awfully familiar from *Black Panther*. It sold, and Eclipse pressed ahead with an even higher-profile project, *The Price* by Jim Starlin.

This was a variation on Starlin's *Warlord* work, with his cosmos of haunted messiahs, big bald villains, philosophical chatter, space adventure, grotesque little sidekicks, and wounded beauties, but this, he said, was all the really good stuff that he wouldn't surrender his rights to. It was obviously influenced by *Star Wars*, however, with the old head trips replaced by high-tech swordplay and zooming spaceships, his time-and-space defying compositional sense replaced by narrative linearity. Starlin had gained something in control but lost something in heart. Doing page-rate work for a fading field may have freed him up just to play with ideas. The success of *Star Wars* was the sort of thing that could make anyone, especially at the brink of the '80s, see creator-owned comics as a gold mine as well as a playground.

Will Eisner, a man who'd spent four decades mining superheroes, newspaper supplements, and instructional comics for the military—and piling up his share of gold—was looking for something different. He'd found a publisher for his Bronx reminiscences, *A Contract with God and Other Tenement Stories*, and in late 1978 it appeared quietly in bookstores. Baronet Books wasn't a publisher that knew how to hit the comic book market, but those comics fans who tracked the book down discovered a work of astonishing intimacy, maturity, and emotional power, a power that seemed to come without trying. It stole up on the reader from the simplest and most relaxed of visual and verbal strokes. In Gary Groth's *Comics Journal*, Denny O'Neil called it "a near masterpiece. . . . using the resources of. . . . language exactly as a novelist uses them." He politely refuted the complaints of pretentiously serious adolescent fans that the art was "cartoony," calling Eisner's style the "conscious decision of a thinking artist intent on introducing us to his private, interior experience...." Some old mavericks were thinking commercial, some old deadline-beaters were thinking artistic. Anything could happen.

It was all good timing. *Superman*, the movie, finally opened in late 1978, and just like its makers had predicted, it nailed the national mood. "You'll Believe a Man Can Fly," said the ads, and so we could, but that liberating moment of Superman's first flight was only part of what packed the theaters. Superman also made us believe that the story of a young man being raised in the vast American prairie by old-style farm folks could be an origin worthy of myth, that a square-jawed cornball who said "swell" could be a hero for our times, that all an overstressed career woman needed was a man who was infinitely stronger than her, and that a courtship without sex could be sweetly fulfilling. Somehow, with the passage of time—and the work of Mort Weisinger, and Curt Swan, and Hollywood— Siegel and Shuster's hero of the outcast had become a symbol of America's most conservative yearnings for a maleness, a naïveté, and a WASP confidence that seemed long gone. But then, wasn't the conservative WASP male beginning to see himself as the outcast in America now? It was all so seductive, and done so well, that it even survived Margot Kidder, Valerie Perrine, and Gene Hackman doing the *Batman* villain he never got to play. It became Warner's biggest box-office hit ever, and gave Ronald Reagan the visual template and tone for the most artful presidential campaign in history.

DC had nothing to offer people whom the movie had made curious about comics. There was a brief blip in the sales of those pleasant but forgettable Schwartz-Bates-Swan *Superman* comics, but nothing like 1966, nothing like *Star Wars*. Jenette Kahn and Julie Schwartz, realizing that the movie's opening scenes on Krypton had excited fans' interest, tried a three-issue *World of Krypton*, the first time a series had been explicitly limited in longevity,

reflecting both the hot new "miniseries" format on TV and the growing collector's market in comics that made low-numbered issues sell well. It didn't do much. Nor did Warner Books' tie-ins, like Elliott Maggin's novel, *Superman: Last Son of Krypton*. About the only other special projects DC had going were a set of books from Simon & Schuster, reprinting war, romance, and science fiction stories from the '50s. The editor, Michael Uslan, had taught America's first real college class on comic books (for Indiana University, no less), but now, in the dawn of the "yuppie" era, he had a law degree too, and his eye on turning his comics expertise into some sort of entrepreneurship. He discovered that DC still had some desirable properties unoptioned for feature development, and along with a producing partner, Benjamin Melniker, he picked up the rights to Swamp Thing and—yes—Batman for less than Warner had probably paid the caterer for the *Superman* opening party.

DC may have had no follow-through, but at least there were exciting things coming from other publishers, so the comic shops could take advantage. The shops were benefiting from a new back-issue boom, too. A couple of canny collector/dealers, Bruce Hamilton and John Snyder, had worked to push the price of *Action Comics* 1 to $10,000, to drive home what a lucrative field comics collecting was. When they succeeded, the news media made it an event, and investors started jumping into comics. That brought more money and more venues for new comics. There were distributors popping up all over the country as retailers branched out and affluent comics fans got their parents to bankroll them. From a clandestine arrangement between Sol Harrison and Phil Seuling, the direct market had become 10 percent of Marvel and DC's sales, and a 10 percent proportionately far more lucrative and dependable than the other 90. Seuling may not have liked what the industry was doing to him, but the industry loved what he'd done for it. After a liver ailment ended his life a few years later, he'd be eulogized like no businessman in the medium's history. To DC's Paul Levitz, he was "a pivotal figure in the evolution of comics," to Marvel's Ed Shukin, "a pioneer in our field."

By 1979 Shukin and Jim Shooter had decided it was time to see just how much potential the new market had. They hosted a "summit meeting" for retailers and distributors at the San Diego Comic Con, where they called the direct market the potential salvation of the industry and announced the formation of a new position in the company: direct sales manager. At the end of the meeting, Mike Friedrich walked up and asked for the job. Friedrich was burning out on the publishing grind, willing to let *Star*Reach* and *Imagine* go. The job didn't work out—after five years of self-employment, Friedrich wasn't meant for a corporate office—but it got things started, and direct sales climbed quickly. Somebody in the brain trust thought of launching a new series and selling the first issue only through comics shops. Newsstand distributors had always been hard to sell on first issues, but the direct market gobbled them up as potential collectibles. The character idea was awful—the Disco Dazzler, not only embarrassingly out of date, but aimed at trendy kids who would never have been caught dead shaking their booties near a comic shop—but the market manipulation was clever. Chris Claremont and John Byrne were asked to introduce her in their *X-Men*, which was gaining heat in the direct market. Other comics would then tease with her until the time was right to solicit advance orders.

By then Marvel was getting ready to launch *Epic Illustrated*, its answer to *Heavy Metal*. To get good work, Marvel had to break from its normal practice and do what the European and ground-level publishers did: let creators retain all rights. That, plus higher advances than the likes of Eclipse could hope to pay, enabled Archie Goodwin to snag some big-name material for *Epic* right off the bat, including *Metamorphosis Odyssey*, Starlin's continuation of the story of *The Price*. Although aimed at newsstand distribution, *Epic* was especially strong in the comic shops.

Comicdom still didn't know where the business was going. The comic shops were encouraging, but there weren't nearly enough to compensate for the continuing loss of newsstand outlets. It was still a subculture of outsiders—"geeks," as they were starting to call themselves, or at least one another—overwhelmingly male, overwhelmingly white (although more and more Asian faces were starting to appear at the cons), overwhelmingly underachieving. They weren't stupid guys, because it took some kind of mental superiority, or at least savanthood, to memorize the life story of the Vision, but they were guys who didn't think much of themselves or their chances in the real world. The mainstreaming of the counterculture had a hideous affect on those self-consciously nonconformist fans: while other young adults were trading T-shirts and jeans for power ties and penny loafers, comics geeks were liberated from any pretense of self-regard by the "I'm above caring about appearances" pose. Any halfway attractive fan could riff endlessly on the quintessential geek: unwashed and scraggly bearded, thick glasses taped together, baggy slacks slipping low, and faded T-shirt stretched not quite all the way over a bloated belly, mumbling pompously about the superiority of superhero stories to "the fiction of the mundane." The riffing, of course, was a way of covering for the shame that even the least geekish fans felt about sharing the hobby that dare not speak its name.

Even the stars of the field didn't look much better than their fans: ill-considered facial hair and over-stretched superhero T-shirts were the badges of the true comics visionary from early in the '70s until well into the '80s. The young executive types like Jim Shooter and Paul Levitz, who wore suits and ties and made noise about maintaining a professional appearance in the office, were considered rather suspect. Any attempt to dress up usually took the form of funny hats, a bit of '60s flamboyance that had finally trickled into comics just when it had died everywhere else. In a time when money and early success were becoming America's primary drugs (with cocaine just a supplementary rush), these guys all leveled off within a couple of years after breaking in, thereafter just trying to maintain their volume against a shrinking field and their own diminishing energies.

The entire disco culture and superheated mating game of youth-at-large completely passed comics by. The nasty joke ran that women got into comics only because it was the one place in *Charlie's Angels* America where fat and nerdy were considered attractive. If a female with any sexual charisma at all did pass through a comics conclave—a cute sixteen-year-old looking for *Elfquest* or a tired ex-stripper hanging out with the underground crowd—the geeks were said to freeze in place, turn red, and fumble for a copy of *Red Sonja*. Quite apart from the fact that very few comics had anything to say to young women, the subculture itself was a self-perpetuating fraternity—and if it had had letters, they'd have been Omega Omega Omega.

Yet, the world was starting to glance in. "Normal" people and popular kids and young arty types were starting to peek through the doors of comic shops, thanks to *Star Wars*, *Superman*, *Howard the Duck*, and all the rest of it. As horrible as the bulk of comics were, a vague excitement was starting to pass from fan to fan, from geek to geek, as if everyone felt that something could happen any minute, something great. All it needed was a spark.

Chris Claremont was good with women. In his personal life, who knows? It took him a long time to get married, and apart from that—well, comics people just didn't *talk* about such things. On the comic book page, though, he was very good with women. He worked on both *Ms. Marvel* and *Spider-Woman*, where many of his stories were fresh and pleasantly free of the need to hurl his characters into constant combat, and where much of his dialogue seemed uncommonly attuned to the fears and passions of young women. He was said to be very close to his mother, even in adulthood—an unusual thing in a field in which "mom" was hardly ever mentioned and surrogate-father myths dominated—and he liked empathetic characters who spoke openly of love, not in the "if only" drippiness of Stan Lee and most of his followers, but in terms of protection and loyalty. He

was also about the only writer in comics who came from theater, where dress-up and role-changing can bring a chap into contact with sides of himself that the tight surfaces of most mainstream comics people never could.

The '70s had wiped out a lot of traditionally feminine entertainment and given girls the message that they should have similar fantasies to boys—and boys were getting used to more emotional and female content in their mass culture. Claremont struck a national chord when he said, "It always seemed to me there was never any reason why a character should be any less heroic, courageous, intelligent, aggressive, simply because that character was a woman. It always seemed to me that...the characterization should evolve from the character itself and should not be bound by the fact that it is a male or a female." But Claremont's men were rarely as heroic or intelligent as Storm, the African mutant "goddess" with the element-controlling powers in *X-Men*. She had her flaws: she was torn between a motherly devotion to all living things and a lust for the power she commands, and was given to claustrophobic panics because of a horrendous incident from her childhood as an orphan thief in the slums of Cairo. It was always the goddess in her, though, that won out, as she soared into the air and threw lightning and declaimed regally in defense of her fellow mutants. Storm's teammate, Jean Grey, dominated her relationship with the doubt-wracked Cyclops even before she became Phoenix, and afterward she was almost too strong a personality for him, or for any mere mortal. Yet for all their incipient deification, Claremont saw no reason that his women shouldn't remain "compassionate, warm, humorous, witty, intelligent, attractive." It was a hard fantasy to make real: they were impossibly perfect, impossibly tragic objects of love, pity, worship, fear.

Luckily, John Byrne was good with women, too. The heroines and love interests he drew were beautiful, of course, but with a cuteness and expressive humanity that made them infinitely more appealing, to male and female readers, than the all-the-same-face-but-different-hair-color girls of most comics artists. They weren't slimmed-down versions of Kirby amazons, they weren't simplifications of Romita romance weepers, they were *cartoons*—and thus closer to being *people* than any cipher of idealized "realism." Byrne made Storm and Phoenix horrific in goddess-form, lovably vulnerable when they "came down" and needed their friends to hold them. He went to the other end of the spectrum with Kitty Pryde, a precocious thirteen-year-old mutant, based on a girl who lived in his apartment building. Alternately cocky and timid, cuddly and venturesome, she was the first truly convincing teenager in superhero comics, and brought an instant spark of lightness and humanity to the mutants' harrowing adventures.

The Claremont/Byrne goddess could take a form other than wife, mother, destroyer, and daughter, too: in Emma Frost, the White Queen of the Hellfire Club, she could be a whore, a deceiver, and a dominatrix, as well. The question of who contributed what is nearly as tangled with Byrne and Claremont as it was with Kirby and Lee, and there's no point in pitting their conflicting claims against each other (although, as a general rule in such disputes between writers and artists, it's smarter to believe the artist; since they're not expected to create stories and characters, they have no need to get defensive about not having pulled their conceptual weight). It's safe to say that Emma—who runs her own "private academy," with her nasty little costume echoing both bondage gear and a wedding dress—is a synthesis of the strongest meat that Byrne and Claremont had to offer. It could have been either one who watched the infamous "Hellfire Club" episode of TV's *Avengers*, with Emma Peel as an undercover leather queen, and thought of the character. Making her as creepy and funny as she was, though, required blending Byrne's character design, sly humor, and Ditkoesque touch for suspense with Claremont's oppressive seriousness and ability to make believable his male heroes' crippling attraction to an object of both lust and terror. In the direct market, dominated by male teenagers and young adults, she was a sensation. Only two years before, Roy Thomas had thought

Frank Thorne's Red Sonja "too sexy." The comic book market had made a subtle, but all-important, shift.

Fascinating females, however, wouldn't have been enough to make *X-Men* a blockbuster, and that may be where Byrne's more boyish sensibility really made the difference. When Claremont wanted to take Wolverine out of the group, weary of trying to do anything dramatic with such naked male aggression, Byrne said they couldn't dump his countryman, the Canadian. Instead, they started humanizing the little carnivore by giving him a girlfriend, a mysterious Japanese noblewoman—and having him bond with his German teammate, Nightcrawler. Tormented his

John Byrne showed some Barry Smith influence too— along with Starlin, Kirby, Ditko, and nearly every other great Marvel influence—in bringing the mutants to appealing life. Inks by Terry Austin, dialogue by Chris Claremont. (*X-Men* 139, Nov. 1980.)

235

whole life because his body looks like the devil's, Nightcrawler had been mainly a figure of pity, but now, with Wolverine, he discovered his "inner child" and a rude sense of humor, as they'd challenge each other to impromptu physical contests, the loser springing for beer (someone, probably Byrne, obviously understood what Canadians and Germans have in common). Wolverine always won, but Nightcrawler's cute chagrin and childlike love of the means and not the end made him endearing and Wolverine's smugness amusing.

Wolverine's transcendent moment came when Colossus, the naive Russian farm boy who can turn his body to steel, finds his confidence collapsing in the face of his star-spanning adventures. Wolverine parks himself in a death trap, smirking and smoking, refusing to move as Colossus begs him to get out, until Colossus's anger and terror finally give him the strength to destroy the trap that he didn't believe he *could* destroy. It was a glorious macho moment, maybe the kind of thing only a Canadian could have come up with in the days of the American "new man," and it made Wolverine admirable and sympathetic without the usual pop-cult stunt of showing his "tender" side. Suddenly Wolverine was a he-man girls could like, and the testosterone counterbalance that made Claremont's holy women and weak men acceptable to boys.

Relationships and surprises were what made *X-Men* tick. Byrne was a compulsive idea man, jotting down notes as they popped to mind until he'd find himself with two or three years' worth of plot material, plus ideas for revamping everybody else's comics besides. No artist since Jack Kirby or Steve Ditko had been so consistently and rapidly productive of new heroes, villains, and plot twists, and like them, Byrne was a storyteller first and an artist only in service to his stories. He even seemed to synthesize Kirby's sense of the grandiose and Ditko's love of the tiny human moment, and if he lacked Kirby's power and Ditko's intensity, that seemed OK in 1978 and 1979, when Americans wanted entertainment to be more about reassurance than challenge. If anyone was born

for Marvel Comics in that moment, it was Byrne. He was becoming a star, too, with a style far more "comic booky" than the bravura boys who'd all left the field. He had nowhere to go but comics, and he was staying on *X-Men*.

Claremont, for his part, understood what no *X-Men* writer, including Lee and Kirby, had ever understood: that if mutants are a persecuted minority, they should react to persecution in everything they do, and their "team" should be more than a team, even more than a family; it should be their definition and their culture. He, almost alone among comics writers, was brave enough to go beyond the compensatory fantasies of outcast adolescents and to dramatize their fear and self-pity. From his first big plot line, the attack of the Sentinels, he had his X-Men constantly react rather than act. Every story for years was kicked off by an attack upon the mutants, often in the peace and quiet of their own mansion, not a one by them going off on a heroic mission. He understood, too, that in a context of shared oppression, the relationship between Professor X and Magneto had to change. His Magneto wasn't interested in enslaving mankind, but simply in ensuring the survival of mutantkind— although he thought that might require conquering the world, because he believed that mankind was intractably bigoted. Claremont's Professor X believed that man could be taught not to hate if mutants could prove their differences could be beneficial. To achieve their desired ends, however, both he and Magneto could be ruthless, arrogant, and coldly Machiavellian—and both could display unexpected moments of warmth and nobility. This wasn't law against outlaw, but assimilationist against separatist. Claremont was affirming comics, not as universal entertainment, but as the esoterica of a subculture.

There was a lot to put up with in reading Claremont: those inevitable "Hear me, X-Men!" speeches, the heaped-on introspection and sensitivity, the paeans to his women in dialogue and caption, the fact that his people didn't just suffer endlessly but always had to think, "The *pain*! The *pain* is too *great*!" He either lacked Byrne's organic sense of storytelling, or he thought Byrne wasn't doing enough with the characters, or both, because he could outdo Stan Lee at jamming pop-psych reflections on romance, insecurity, and troubled friends into the heads of characters fleeing giant Sentinels or saving the universe. Despite it all, or because of it all, he could nail the subtext of a story and make it as hot and lurid as a fight scene.

"[W]hat we have here, intended or not," he said, "is a book that is about racism, bigotry, and prejudice.... It's a book about outsiders, which is something that any teenager can identify with." Especially comics geeks. Especially girls who didn't fit into a world that seemed to have slots only for Phyllis Schlafly or Farrah Fawcett (or a shrinking, rather hostile slot for Gloria Steinem). Especially members of other outcast groups whose plight was never explicitly portrayed in mass culture—like young men and women attracted to people of their own sex.

Marvel officers have never liked to talk about it, but anyone tuned into fandom knows that the X-Men has always had a strong gay following, as has the Legion of Super-Heroes. Both provided models of the families of peers that young gay people often have to create in early adulthood when they drop out or are driven out of "normal" society and their "real" families. Both are made up of high-school or college-age kids insulated from our world—one in Professor X's "School for Gifted Youngsters" in upstate New York, one in the thirtieth century—and both of them are free of the limited rosters of "normal" teams. The Legion is huge, and appended by Reserve members and Substitutes. The "X-Men" are less a team than a classification, mutants allied with Xavier and opposed to Magneto. In addition to Cyclops, Phoenix, Storm, Colossus, Nightcrawler, Wolverine, and Kitty, they were likely to be visited at any moment by past members—Iceman, Beast, Angel—or by scattered friends like Banshee, Havok, and Polaris. Byrne added a team of Canadian mutants called Alpha Flight, and there he hinted that he could read a queer subtext too, with a pair of fraternal twin heroes, one male and one female but both

rather androgynous. He has said that he saw the male half, Northstar, as homosexual from the start, and gay fans were picking up cues even though they were well coded.

The X-Men were a family, and like a family they kept growing and had to keep renegotiating their relationships. With fights and triumphant endings, they satisfied the superhero addicts who needed their familiar formulas, but with shifting alliances and enmities they hooked readers who were about to give up on superheroes, or who glanced at them only curiously, or who never much liked them but gave this *X-Men* a try when their friends insisted. Sales were rising quickly, but more than that, a new coalition of readers was starting to grow—*Elfquest* girls, *Star Wars* geeks, marginal fans, young women turned on to it by guys they knew—who had to see if the urbane Nightcrawler and the bumpkin Colossus could actually have fun doing the town together, if Kitty would accept Storm as her mentor, if Jean could get rid of her Phoenix power.

That, the Phoenix power, became the crux of the series, the biggest event in a Marvel story line in quite a few years. The "Dark Phoenix Saga," they called it, and anyone in fandom who hadn't noticed *X-Men* yet noticed it then (*XM* 134-137, June-Sept. 1980). Jean's powers, after months of growing increasingly awesome and unpredictable, finally explode and transform her into a Kali in tights, the all-destroying Dark Phoenix. Intoxicated and blinded by godhood, she devours a sun, obliterating billions of innocent aliens. The Empress of the Shi'ar clamors for her blood—and of course it falls to the X-Men, led by Jean's beloved, to bring her to trial. At last she's subdued, her power blasted out of her body, and she's forgiven. Or at least she was when Byrne and Claremont finished the issue. Then it hit Jim Shooter's desk for approval.

No forgiveness, the big man said. If a hero killed, "there had to be moral consequences." He called an emergency meeting with Claremont, Byrne, and the editor, Louise Jones. "Shooter wanted Jean punished," Claremont said. "He wanted her to suffer . . . . [He]

237

feels that it is his responsibility . . . to see that nothing goes out of the office that reflects a moral position that he does not think Marvel should take." What consequences would fit the murder of billions? Killing superheroes had always been seen as bad business: how can you license somebody who's not there anymore? Shooter had once milked a great stunt out of the death of Ferro Lad, but this was different, this was a key character in a very hot team, a seventeen-year veteran of the Marvel universe. It was against all the rules—so they did it. After being exonerated by the Shi'ar, Jean realizes that she can never be sure her destructive power won't return, and kills herself. Cyclops is left slumped on the ground, delivering a colossal monologue that ends with, "Oh, Jean . . . Jean . . . ."

It's what the fans said, too. The climax hit the comic shops right before the convention season of 1980, and it was all anyone could ask of any Marvel rep: "Why did you kill Jean?" "Is Jean really dead?" "*Why* did you kill *Jean*?!" Sales went through the roof—and kept going, because who could read the death of Phoenix without having to know what happened next? It sent buyers pouring into comic shops, because *nobody* could wait long enough for the next installment of *X-Men* to hit the drugstores. Back-issue sales boomed, because there were at least twice as many readers as there'd been when Byrne started, maybe four times as many as when the series had started. *Giant-Size X-Men* number 1, that meagerly suc-

cessful quickie that Len Wein and Dave Cockrum had whipped out five years before, became a legendary collectible, and that only added to the flame. Suddenly kids thought if they bought two or three or five copies of every issue starting *now*, in five years they'd be rich. *X-Men* became the best-selling series in the business, and then very quickly the best-seller in the business in a decade. It broke the 300,000 sales mark when even *Spider-Man* didn't always break 200,000 and when nearly every DC was under 100,000.

It was the spark. New and resuscitated readers couldn't be content with just twenty pages of mutants a month. They wanted *more*. Luckily for them, something similar, something that looked like it might be just as exciting, premiered the month after Jean's death. It was a team of teenagers, conflicted and volatile, with a cosmic dimension. It was edited by Len Wein, who'd cocreated the new X-Men, written by Marv Wolfman, fresh from his acclaimed *Tomb of Dracula,* and drawn by George Pérez, a rising Marvel star whom some were calling the next John Byrne; in fact, he'd just taken over *Avengers* after a stint by Byrne. There was just one funny thing: it was published by DC.

No one quite knew it yet, but a revolution had happened. The forty-five-year business of comics-as-usual was dead—it just didn't know enough to fall down yet. A new world had been opened up, and there was nothing to do now but see how much it could hold.

PART THREE
THE GILDED AGE

NEW ROYALTY

By 1980, Sol Harrison was ready to surrender the DC reins. He was the last of the old guard in a position of power, and although he'd made the decision that had created the direct market, it must have been as clear to him as to anyone that he wasn't the man to lead DC into the new world. Paul Levitz, at an age when other business majors had barely gotten their MBAs, took over most of Harrison's duties as manager of business affairs. It would still be a year before Harrison would officially retire, making Jenette Kahn president and publisher and Levitz executive vice president, but it was already their show. It was time to put all those ideas that had been tossed around in Kahn's office late at night into effect. Joe Orlando would soon be unhindered in running the production department. He and his staff, headed by fan/artist/writer, Bob Rozakis, could start to undo the cheapest measures of the last few years. Everything Kahn, Levitz, and Orlando wanted to do would cost more money and raise cover prices, but it would create the kinds of comics that the direct-market audience was clamoring for, and they knew that if DC was to have any chance at all after the pounding Marvel had been giving it on the newsstands, it was going to need the direct market.

They started by hiring Dick Giordano as an editor, hoping he could bring in the creativity he'd brought to Charlton and DC in the '60s. To lure him away from Continuity Studios they had to double their pay scale, but they expected him to be worth it More new editors had joined or soon would: Ross Andru, leaving Marvel's art burden to younger hands; and Len Wein, dropping the writing on which he'd burned out. To fans, the biggest news was that Roy Thomas, after fifteen years as Stan Junior, was moving to DC to become a writer/editor of the kind Jim Shooter wouldn't allow anymore. He immediately took control of all the characters who'd been his companions in small-town Missouri in another time DC's golden-age heroes.

Marv Wolfman joined his friend Wein in a writer-editor team that would bring out the best in each. Then came George Pérez. Then Gene Colan, whom the terrors of the '50s had left perennially panicky about losing his job, and who'd been getting nervous as Jim Shooter started demanding changes in his art.

The fruits of the migration showed up immediately in *DC Comics Presents* 26 (Oct. 1980). The story was by Jim Starlin, part of a saga pitting Superman against another of his big, bald bad guys, this one called Mongul. It was exciting to see Starlin tackling the DC universe, but it was overshadowed by the "Free Insert" giving a preview of DC's next release: *The New Teen Titans*.

The team of teen sidekicks had failed twice in the '70s, but now Wolfman and Wein added a cosmic twist in the persons of Starfire, a naive but powerful woman from another world (Light Phoenix, one might say), and Raven, a mystic "empath" with a dark side and a filial connection to an otherworldly demon named Trigon. Raven's power to take on her teammates' pain gave Marv a chance to challenge Chris Claremont at in-your-face torment. Cyborg, half man and half machine, had a bit of Colossus in his powers and look, (although he had the familiar personality of the angry comic-book black man). Changeling, the former Beast Boy of the Doom Patrol, was a cute prankster; to deepen him, Wolfman dropped in thought balloons to explicate the agonizing depression that drove him to joke compulsively (no one could be happy in post-Claremont comics). Robin, the team leader, was given a new intensity and some unresolved father-conflicts with Batman. Later he changed his name to Nightwing and his costume to a dark and spooky one. Aqualad and Donna "Wonder Girl" Troy were given questions of origin and purpose to deal with. Popping in and out was Speedy, putting his life back together a decade after Denny O'Neil's "junkie" story line. Wolfman has said that he never consciously imitated Claremont, and he probably didn't, but *X-Men* had redefined the superhero team and had generated so much energy among fans and pros alike that no one would ever be able to do a supergroup again without having it in mind.

Two things made *The New Teen Titans* more than an ersatz *X-Men*: Wolfman's skill at superhero plots, nurtured as a fan of silver age DCs, and George Pérez's visual storytelling. Pérez had been a good Marvel artist, but now he was developing an intricate, many-paneled style focused on the unfolding of a dramatic moment, the expressive face, the event within an event. He Harked back to Starlin and Barry Smith and Marshall Rogers, but to Curt Swan, as well. He blended Swan's quaintness with a new style of characterization, a hipper, post-sexual-revolution style, in a nonthreatening package that could stir up any pubescent reader without chasing away nervous prepubes (or nervous postpubes). Starfire was lush, nearly naked, her cups running over with fleshy sensuality; but her orange skin, Orphan Annie eyes, and vacant grin made her likable to girls and boys alike. The male Titans had square jaws but impish grins, soft features and *Teen Beat* hair, nothing too hip or slick or manly. Pérez's inker, Romeo Tanghal, was to him something like what George Klein had been to Swan: not a master draftsman, but preserving his outlines crisply. DC's improved production department helped enormously and got better month by month, with sharply printed detail, clearer and lighter colors, and purer color separation. The overall effect was a bit soulless, but more polished than nearly anything DC readers had seen since the silver age.

Pérez had come up from fandom in the '70s, inspired not by the explosive energies of the '60s, but by the insularity of a shrinking field supported by a subculture devoted to minutiae. He had a solid sense of movement, showing a debt to Gil Kane, but what thrilled the fans to the tips of their toes was his

astounding detail. Pérez could do twelve-panel pages that read as clearly as anyone else's standard six-panel grid, and contained more visual information per panel. His line work might have been constrained, sacrificing personality to control, but for pulling readers into the details of a story, leaving them with a sense of having gotten their sixty cents' worth, there was no one like him. He was also an energetic cocreator and co-plotter with Wolfman, bringing the same love of detail and structure to the plots that he brought to his page layouts.

A narrative device he and Wolfman introduced

Ferocious action contained in nine tight panels. Good art, novel storytelling, but especially impressive design, the George Pérez trademark. Inks by Romeo Tanghal, dialogue by Marv Wolfman. (*New Teen Titans* #9, July 1981.)

showed what may have been a bigger source of inspiration than Starlin or Smith or anyone else. A TV newswoman named Bethany Snow faces the reader through the intermediary of TV-shaded panels and fills us in on impending menaces through on-the-spot narratives. It was a way to reflect the video-addicted reality of young readers and to avoid the captions that Wolfman and a lot of fans were associating with the stodgy, sloppy days of the '70s. For Pérez it was another design element, another way to bring hyper-conscious structure to an essentially visceral form. The visual model for it was TV itself, not just the rounded rectangle of the screen—contained but uncommitted to angles, the visual metaphor of our new culture—but what TV does to its own content. TV is passion in a box, made smaller and moved across the room. But with VCRs and cable, a new generation was seeing that box as a mechanism not of passive receptivity, but of ultimate control. MTV and the first boom in video-rental outlets arrived at the same time as the explosion of comic shops and *The New Teen Titans*, and the audiences for all of them turned out to be the same.

This was Pérez's mastery: the taming of the beast, the structuring of violence, imagination and young emotion. In the heyday of Julie Schwartz, it had been the writing that provided the greater structure, the art allowed to open it up. Here it was Wolfman who ran a little wild with big, explosive, fight-filled plots, Pérez who broke it down and reassembled it with crystalline logic. The '50s and '80s were united in a venal, indifferent conservatism and pursuit of cash, but their tenors were as different as Eisenhower's military and Reagan's Hollywood. Americans in the '50s had been asked to sublimate their greed and viciousness to an appearance of restful conviviality, making the savagery of capitalism into an unspoken communal exercise. It had been the literal content of entertainment—the "left brain" content, to use an '80s buzz word—that had to hew to a structure, while the less conscious, the more physical, the visual, was allowed to carry the vitality of fantasy. Formula MGM scripts with the Technicolor Cinemascope

opulence of Vincente Minnelli. Formula John Broome scripts with the surging art of Carmine Infantino. In the '60s the gaps had widened, and styles had polarized—Lee and Kirby all passion, Weisinger and Swan all control, Lee and Ditko a spreading rift—but now it was snapping back, in a reversal of the '50s. Reagan-era Americans were encouraged to let their libidos, their cutthroat individualism, their hubris rise to the top, but to channel them toward puffing up the economy. In movies, people and events were outlandish—E.T., Indiana Jones, Jake LaMotta—but film styles were tight and glossy, calculated and edited almost to death. In comics, what the superheroes *did* got bigger and bigger, but how they *looked* got tighter and tighter.

New Teen Titans 1 (Nov. 1980) sold out in the comics shops, and fans and speculators spread out to raid the convenience stores and drugstores for any copies of *DC Comics Presents* 26 that might still be sitting around. Silver age fans who'd largely lost interest in comics immediately recognized Titans' clarity and tight stories—sometimes contained in a single issue, never sprawling even when continued—as a hipped-up version of what they'd loved in childhood. Kids who found *X-Men*'s continuity a little too heavy or complicated latched onto *NTT* as a more tightly packaged, more simply *fun* way to get into the same kinds of fantasies and vicarious relationships. Thousands who had found Claremont's tragic goddesses and ferocious adult males a little much bonded instantly with the cute guys and troubled-but-nice girls of *Titans*. The trickle of girls into superhero fandom sped up.

DC ventured back into the miniseries format of *World of Krypton* with *Tales of the New Teen Titans*, each of four issues focusing on a different member. It did better than any miniseries had yet. DC finally had not only a hit, but a franchise, and it had what it had lacked since the early '70s: a large and noisy body of partisan fans all its own. Pérez was an overnight star. Wolfman was *the* DC writer. And they stayed. In 1981, at long last Kahn was able to offer royalties for writers and artists. She knew the value of happy creators. American business in general was focusing on new motivational tools, on ways to beat stagnation and match the "Japanese Miracle" and the new generation didn't believe in job security. Personally vested, for the first time, in the continuing success of their comic, Marv and George kept signing continuity contracts, kept delivering issue after issue, giving the fans a safe place to go year after year. Wolfman had already showed a great loyalty to *Tomb of Dracula*, but he put even more of himself into *Titans*. He did so too literally, unfortunately, when he brought in a rather revolting character named Terry Long—a sort of prettified Marv-self by way of the Sensitive New Man—as an implausible lover for Wonder Girl. Terry and Donna's wedding brought together all the emotional shticks of '80s superteams, both cute and maudlin, as wholly as the wedding of Reed and Sue had brought together all the Kirby action schticks of the '60s. But maybe Terry was the necessary price to pay for the writer's intense involvement with the material.

Wolfman and Pérez proved to be masters of overlapping subplots and foreshadowing. They built slowly to the revelation of Wonder Girl's true origin, and paid off with "Who Is Donna Troy?", maybe the most potent story Marv ever wrote (*NTT* 38, Dec. 1983). Wolfman always saw himself as a distance runner: once he surveyed a convention crowd and mused, "Probably every one of these people can write one story better than anything I've ever written, but can they keep doing it book after book, year after year?" When he liked his artist and his material, he proved to be the only really steady writer of his generation, and he would stay on top of the pile at DC longer than anybody.

The rewards were considerable. Whenever royalties had been discussed, and deferred, in the past, freelancers had generally figured they were missing out on just a nice little bonus on top of their page rates. None of them ever dreamed just how little of corporate income those clever old accountants like Jack Liebowitz were paying out. Freelancers on popular series were suddenly getting royalty checks

equal to two or three or four times their total from page rates—and the page rates themselves were far higher than they'd been before Kahn and Levitz. Soon Marvel, to keep from losing every decent freelancer it had, came through with royalties, too, although it called them "incentives," a term that implied less legal claim to the material by the creators, the sort of thing Marvel management was becoming compulsive about, especially with Steve Gerber's suit pending. Its deal was stingier than DC's, but Shooter pointed to its across-the-board better sales to argue that working for Marvel would pay more. Artists and writers who for years had been hustling as hard as they could to afford modest middle-class lifestyles were suddenly making two or three hundred grand a year—in the year Wolfman had once predicted there wouldn't be any more comics. For all those childless, mainly unmarried guys who'd rarely aspired to anything more than a complete *Fantastic Four* collection and an unlimited supply of pizza, it was disorienting.

Most of them kept their mouths shut. They kept showing up at conventions in their faded T-shirts, kept eating at Wendy's unless they could find an editor with an expense account to take them to Marie Callender's. It was partly because they had no desire for Armanis and Rolexes, partly because they didn't want to distance themselves from fandom, partly because they didn't quite know how to integrate these new worldly rewards into their self-images as outcast geeks. As a result, there was no rush into comics by money-minded young punks. Not yet. Comics were still seen as something one created for love, in a spirit of sacrifice and solidarity. It was only once one was already in the fraternity of pros that the clues began to trickle out, that the new secret strategy of the business—get on a "hot book," or make a cold book hot—began to develop. Just a year or so before, old vets might have lamented the loss of humor and horror and other venues, but it was hard to resent the ubiquity of superheroes when your CPA was finding clever ways to whittle your tax payments down to merely double what your entire income had been back when you were writing humor and horror. Neal Adams's dream of an artists' guild vanished into smoke. It was the '80s, after all, and not just on TV or the comic book page.

Much of the cash came from the direct market, and there were signs that its financial potential had barely been plumbed. By the beginning of 1981, Marvel had finished its buildup of the Disco Dazzler, and although everybody in the field mocked her name and her powers and her white polyester jumpsuit, retailers and collectors couldn't shake the fear that she might turn out to be the next hot thing. She was a mutant, after all, introduced in *X-Men*, and she looked like a strong candidate for Saturday morning TV development. The news was out that Marvel had just bought the dissolving DePatie-Freleng and was setting up Marvel Productions to make its own cartoon shows. When Marvel announced the gimmick that the first issue of the Dazzler—someone had the sense to cut "Disco"—own series would be sold only through comic shops, creating a supply crunch and a possible historical mystique, they couldn't resist buying.

Dazzler number 1 sold more than 400,000 copies, soundly beating everything else on the stands—direct and newsstand combined—every one of those copies nonreturnable and at an inflated profit margin. There was gold in them there hills, and nobody was guarding it but a bunch of easily manipulated compulsives.

CHAPTER 35

ELEKTRA COMPLEX

Comic book retailers nearly all had their roots in fandom, and they would continue to, because no one else could master the arcana of what made for collectibility, but in the early '80s, a new wave of dealers was appearing. They'd grown up with institutionalized collecting, took new comics seriously as potential gold mines, and were starting to turn comic shops into streamlined, aggressive businesses. Comics & Comix, cofounded by Bud Plant but turned over to others when Plant decided he preferred mail order, was growing into a chain of seven stores all over Northern California. Gary Colabuono opened Moondog's in Chicago, then soon opened another one, and was on his way to being a legend in retailing.

Mile High Comics in Denver would become not just a chain of stores, but a giant in mail order and convention dealing, soon publishing its own commercially produced and vended newsletter. Cliff Biggers, Ward Batty, and others published *Comic Shop News*, monthly news and reviews written expressly for retailers. *The Comics Buyers Guide* was sold to a company specializing in collectibles magazines, and turned by Don and Maggie Thompson into a full-scale weekly newspaper on the industry. A former postal worker named Steve Geppi bought a bankrupt distributing company in Baltimore, called it Diamond Distributing, and had the revolutionary idea of running it like a serious business, selling good service instead of discounts. Eventually he'd be wholesaling comics from eight warehouses nationwide.

And the business was spreading overseas. British comics readers had always made do with home-grown comics, most of them lagging behind American fashions, and black-and-white reprints of outdated Marvels, DCs, and others. Now comic shops could get American comics to British readers almost as quickly as they got them to Americans, and the British industry started to reflect the ambition of the hipper Marvels and DCs. In 1977 *Warrior* appeared, a black-and-white magazine with some superheroish stories, and five years later *2000 A.D.* With a large body of older readers—Britain has always had more adult comic fans than in the US the failure to put aside childish things has always been more ridiculed in the U.S., in the pressure to grow up, move forward, make money—British comics nurtured a school of artists whose draftsmanship, detail, and control outdid even their American peers. Brian Bolland, John Bolton, and Dave Gibbons almost immediately attracted the attention of American editors. The editors were less sure of the British writers, who brought out of London's punk sensibility a darkness and a perverse fascination with the pathological and fascist implications of superheroes.

Forbidden Planet, an English science-fiction shop, moved to New York and ended up with a two-story emporium for comics and fantasy merchandise near Greenwich Village and the School of Visual Arts. It became a major information center for young creators and editors both in the mainstream and out. It was partly through the support of such urbane stores that Art Spiegelman and his wife, Françoise Mouly, were able to launch a magazine called *Raw* in 1980. It featured the best of the new European cartooning, some challenging young artists from the SVA, where Spiegelman taught, and Spiegelman's own self-referential brainchildren like *Two-Fisted Painters* ("In This Issue: The Matisse Falcon"). It

245

also featured a little insert called *Maus*, a project Spiegelman had been poking at since his deep underground days in 1973, about his father's experiences in Hitler's concentration camps. Superhero fans weren't ready for the jump yet, though; *Raw* would do better in bookstores than comic shops.

Meanwhile, in another world, Golden Apple on Melrose Avenue in LA was becoming a comics outlet and gift boutique for a graphics-minded new generation. It brought commercial hipness not just to fans and to comics-minded youngsters in the movie and TV businesses, but to the increasing number of comics professionals drifting west, either temporarily or permanently, to exploit their Hollywood connections: Jack Kirby, Steve Gerber, Len Wein, Marv Wolfman, Marty Pasko, and now Roy Thomas and Gerry Conway, working on treatments for a *Conan* movie. Gil Kane would follow, for animation work, and then Howard Chaykin and more. The "Golden Apple Party" after every San Diego Con became a bonding rite that began to give California, where computers and video games and Hollywood were making New York and its print-based media look positively archaic, the glow of the comic book future.

If the direct market could support *Raw*, it could support darker and more ambitious takes on superheroes. Doug Moench was guiding his *Master of Kung Fu* through its most introspective phase, supported by the gorgeously moody art of Gene Day. Now he launched another atmospheric exercise with *Moon Knight* (Nov. 1980), a twist on the icon of Batman and the Shadow, about a mysterious crime fighter who juggles three secret identities simultaneously. It was a complex, occasionally unsettling character study, with art by a vigorous Neal Adams follower named Bill Sienkewicz that knocked out a lot of older fans. Neither the character nor the art knocked out younger newsstand buyers, however, an old story that had led to the death of dozens of ambitious comics from *Deadman* on. It wasn't alone. *Ka-Zar*, in which the Lord of the Savage Land is joined by his chic but feminist significant other, Shanna the She-Devil, showcased urbane banter by Warren

writer Bruce Jones and elegant art by Brent Anderson. It was building good word of mouth in fandom, but not selling much. And *Micronauts* had lost its toy tie-in but still had a fan base. Instead of canceling them, Marvel tried an experiment: soon after the success of *Dazzler*, it increased the page counts and prices of all three and sold them exclusively through the direct market. They survived. On *Moon Knight*, Sienkewicz now felt free to drop the Neal Adams imitation and push his art outward in the direction of punky graphics and cartoonists like Ralph Steadman, who were thrilling the art school crowd. He showed that perhaps nothing, not even a superhero comic, could be "too daring" or "too sophisticated" for the new market.

The comic book where it came together—the sophisticated and the visceral, the daring and the familiar—was *Daredevil*. Since he'd taken over the art in 1979, Frank Miller had been developing a complex storytelling sense under Denny O'Neil's tutelage. He'd been honing his visuals, looking past Walt Simonson and the other inspirations of his youth to masters of economy and restrained impact like Alex Toth and Bernard Krigstein. He was hoping to develop crime stories as the vehicle for his vision, "about tough guys beating each other up in mean cities," but he couldn't find a place to do it in a comics field that was becoming nothing but superheroes. He'd loved *Batman* and crime movies when he was growing up in New Hampshire, and when he moved to New York, he discovered the *film noir* that cineasts were then reviving: the old Samuel Fuller and Anthony Mann exercises in minimalist mood and all-pervasive nastiness. The muse even paid him a visit in the form of a mugger soon after he moved into his Alphabet City apartment, giving him an unresolvable rage that made his crime stories hotter and more focused than any comic book pastiche.

More than anything, Miller had focus. Maybe it was from growing up viewing the world over a hawk-like nose and from under fierce dark eyebrows, or maybe it was just the tautness and self-containment that made him look taller and leaner than he was, that gave him a charisma like no one else in his generation of artists. He was opinionated, cynical before his years, hostile to the growing Christian Right but scarcely amicable to liberal views of crime and euphemistic pussyfooting—in that he was pure New Hampshire. Miller may have come up with the generation of Pérez and Byrne, and he may have shared their '70s cynicism about sweetness and idealism. But as he came into his own, he swung in the opposite direction. Where they synthesized, he eliminated. Where they played with toys, he reached for a gun.

His images got simpler, almost abstract. "I wanted to do a style where the reader had to do a great deal of the work," he said, "where a pair of squiggles and a black shadow became an expressive face in the reader's mind." In the process, his work became more about pure motion, pure violence, and pure narrative. Roger MacKenzie, *Daredevil*'s writer, was doing good superhero stories, but it was Miller who made them feel cinematic, immediate, brutal even to readers who'd been through comic book fight scenes a thousand times. MacKenzie was helping Daredevil develop as a driven but thoughtful loner, a slightly obsessive vigilante, and giving him an intriguing milieu.[1] But it was Miller who gave him soul, who squeezed that obsessiveness and smoldering violence into every one of those few, harsh lines in his face. It was Miller who made the once moribund *Daredevil* sell well enough to go back to monthly publication and start to get plugs from comics dealers. When MacKenzie and Miller's differences required O'Neil to make a choice, O'Neil made the only one he could. Miller took over the writing with issue 168 (Jan. 1981), and comics fans got a bigger punch in the face than any Daredevil villain ever had.

He brought in Elektra, the most fascinating woman in comics for many a year. Like *X-Men's* Emma Frost, she was proof that comics were now aimed at males from about fifteen to thirty. Miller said simply, "The idea of the old girlfriend gone bad was a lot different from what was coming out at the time." But that didn't do justice to this daughter of a Greek ambassador, filled with childhood rage after her father was assassinated before her eyes, who became a merciless bounty hunter after her ill-fated college love affair with Matt Murdock. Miller's beloved *film noir* had come out of the cultural dislocation, the exhaustion and disillusionment of postwar America, the frustration of hard economic times aggravated by the first tease of a new greed-driven boom. It was exactly the mood of cynical Americans coming out of the '70s, and Miller felt the parallel.

The ultimate sources of *noir* tragedy were the *femmes fatales*, all the fleshy pinup girls who seduced our boys into killing and suffering at the front, now transformed into messengers of death, punch lines to a decade-long joke. In the resentful, self-flagellating mood of crushed hopes, the male imagination nearly always turns to the metaphor of the treacherous seductress. In 1980 TV news stations hit us with a hysterical flurry of items on "The Epidemic of the '80s: Herpes." It seems rather silly in the wake of the epidemic that came soon after, but one suspects that even without AIDS or herpes the news industry would have come up with *some* sexual epidemic. AIDS wasn't known yet when Miller introduced Elektra, but *Body Heat* was, the angry conservative reaction to the sexual revolution was, and the whole culture was primed for a sex-equals-death message.

Elektra's life story tracks the cultural break: the innocence of childhood in the early '60s, then the assassination of a Greek politician, stirring up memories of American support for fascist coups that were so shattering to patriotism, then the love of a bitter woman and an idealistic young lawyer in college in the '70s, when hope could still live but was bound to be dashed—and now their first meeting as competitors in the world of individualized violence, in the first autumn of the Reagan age. The fight was gloriously brutal, gloriously romantic, gloriously and tersely cinematic, and it hit readers at more levels than they knew.

There were other vibrations in mass culture that Miller was picking up and transferring into Elektra. Pop psychology was beginning to talk about childhood trauma and the behavioral echoes it sends

[1] Including a faithful paraplegic assistant named Heather, the second time in an O'Neil comic that a rather indifferent hero had won the impotent devotion of a sadly yearning, wheelchair-bound woman.

Frank Miller captures the whole Elektra-Daredevil relationship in a few words, a few lines. Inks by Klaus Janson. (*Daredevil #179, Feb. 1982.*)

when he retroactively gave the hero a *sensei* named Stick, and the pieces fit perfectly. By connecting his lonely, tragic but invincible opponents to an unbroken line of tradition, Miller spared them the psychologizing that always surrounded the Punisher, and that made him both too unpleasantly real and too trivial. Miller took one of the dreariest passages in modern American history and turned it into true romance.

He hid the romance, though, in a criminal underworld of frightening believability, a shadow-realm of stoolies, enforcers, junkies, and pushers. He made an arch-villain of the Kingpin, a great John Romita character design who had never had a personality to match, until now. Miller's Kingpin was a grand paranoid fantasy, his power deriving not from superhuman strength but from his grasp of the system, his control of a corrupt society from which the blind, innocent Daredevil is excluded. Miller did it all with simple strokes, both verbal and visual. The latter were immeasurably strengthened by the inks of Klaus Janson, who was sensitive enough to bring grace to Miller's hardest lines, yet smart enough not to add textures where none were needed. The former showed O'Neil's influence captions clipped down to quick transitions, dialogue genuinely hard-boiled. In one issue, told mainly from his point of view, Urich keeps smoking and coughing and thinking, "These things are gonna kill me"—until the light from reporter Ben Urich's match enables Elektra to find him and slice him open. It was as funny and tough a piece of hard-boiled storytelling as any medium had produced (*Daredevil* 179, Feb. 1982).[2]

Miller had created what he and every fan of the '70s *Batman* had been dreaming of. He'd had to use a different hero, but he'd put Simonson and O'Neil together into the ultimate "dark knight detective." Far more than his predecessors, however, he united tone, plot, theme, and character, seemed to go all the way down to the root of his material and build it up in a singularity of vision. He managed surprise and tragic inevitability at the same time, which can only come from ideas growing from within, not growing inward from the boundaries of genre. He had thematic focus

through adulthood. Pop sociology, meanwhile, was fascinated by Japan—*Shogun* was an unprecedented across-the-demographics success on TV in 1980—and particularly its old code of *Bushido*. In the chaotic and relativistic new America, an ethic of manly conduct and loyalty that existed outside community and rationality was a compelling idea. Ninjas, the ultimate self-contained warriors, had found their way into comics as early as 1974, in Miller's most obvious inspiration, *Manhunter*. When Japan's economic ninja attack suddenly had the US flailing at empty air, stuff like Eric Lustbader's series of "Ninja" novels was everywhere. Miller built ninja training into Elektra's background—and then into Daredevil's, like nobody since Ditko, but unlike Ditko he had a worldview that was eminently salable to his audience. Anyone unimpressed by Miller's themes or technique had to be impressed by his brutality. Daredevil's battles with opponents were bone-breaking street brawls, and beautifully choreographed ones. When Elektra and a hit-man named Bullseye went head to head, Miller delivered a breathtaking ballet of violence, culminating in the most throat-clutching scene since the Comics Code. Bullseye breaks Elektra's jaw, slits her throat and—relishing every moment—shoves a knife through her body, killing her (*Daredevil* 181, Apr. 1982). Tender readers were horrified, tough ones were breathless, Elektra's fans were crushed and outraged, but *nobody* could put it down, and nobody could blow off the emotions with "It's just a comic book."

It seemed an impossible act to follow, but Miller kept fandom's attention with a Punisher story that drove home how sick and pathetic the character was, but somehow gave him more charisma at the same time. Then he brought a disturbing new note into the hero himself. Daredevil, like Batman, was driven by the death of a parent, obsessed with the dead. Miller showed a touch of genius in literalizing the symbol without robbing it of its power in having Daredevil become obsessed with Elektra's corpse, even digging it up in the cemetery and talking to it. Then came Miller's last issue, in which Daredevil sits at the bedside of Bullseye, whom he's beaten to within an inch of his life, and subjects him to a game of Russian roulette (*Daredevil* 191, Feb. 1983). Jim Shooter claimed to have suggested the story, as he suggested "Nightimes" to Doug Moench, and it's possible. For all Shooter's stress on straight-ahead Marvel storytelling, he knew that stars should be encouraged to do what they do best. He took Miller under his wing for a while, reputedly taking him on bacchanalian jaunts to Atlantic City, in itself a monument to a greedy, dispirited, and neo-*noir* America. Shooter once made a magazine's list of the "fifty most eligible men" in New York, and, in his own words, was "doing my best to prove it." Quite an education for a young cartoon-

ist from New Hampshire, but Miller didn't become a "Marvel guy." He was too focused on that vision of his to take much notice of success, or of stardom.

And he was a star, of a magnitude that even Byrne and Pérez hadn't approached. Part of it was the manner, the laser gaze, the fact that he dressed casually bohemian and accessorized like an artist. Even more, though, it was the sheer purity of the work, the fact that he fit no established category or house style and seemed to come not as a development but as a revolution—or even a revelation. Fans didn't seem to want to allow him any antecedents: one boneheaded but revealing review of a reprint of *Manhunter* praised Walt Simonson and Archie Goodwin for "brilliantly anticipating Frank Miller's use of ninjas," as if Miller's *Daredevil* was a verity even when Frank was still in high school. *X-Men* changed the dynamic of comic book teams and relationships, but *Daredevil* changed the basic narrative. The dialogue got crisper, the captions got smaller—some writers started eliminating them completely, striving to tell their stories more "cinematically"—and violence and evil were looked more squarely in the face.

A new machismo started showing up even on the Marvel staff, in the persons of conservative young assistant editors with a love of the manly toys that older comics fans—the ones who hadn't come of age with the Punisher and Wolverine—rarely shared. Larry Hama was a rock musician, a gun collector, and a fan of war stories who wanted to get a venue for Vietnam stories going at Marvel. Carl Potts had been a rocker, "the world's straightest hippie," as he put it, until he put music aside for writing, drawing, jet-skiing, creating a science fiction riff on the French Foreign Legion, and pushing for a regular Punisher series and an anthology of historical adventure stories. They were '80s guys, part of the generation that helped put Reagan in the White House and then made fun of everything he said, and in that they were much closer to the mainstream than comics fans usually are. It was a strange thing that as the direct market encouraged comics aimed only at hard-core collectors, it thereby encouraged more adult content (or late

[2] With typical American reductionism, that issue was entered in the Congressional Record and listed in the Overstreet Price Guide as "anti-smoking issue." The last thing Miller seemed inclined to do in those years was preach against private vices.

249

adolescent content, at least), which enabled comic-dom and the rest of the young adult world to find more common ground.

All this was good timing for Marvel. At the same time Miller was taking over the writing of *Daredevil*, John Byrne was leaving *X-Men* to write and draw the favorite toy of his childhood, *Fantastic Four*. *X-Men*, with Dave Cockrum now rejoining Claremont, kept going strong, but there had to be some worry that it would begin to lose its momentum, as it was already losing some of its focus in plot and theme. Miller came to the rescue. Marvel had plunged into the miniseries format, teaming up all its big heroes for a cranked-out stunt called *Marvel Super Heroes Contest of Champions*. Now it teamed up its real heroes, Miller and Claremont, for four issues of *Wolverine*. They—mostly Miller, we hazard to guess—turned the Canadian "berserker" into a *Bushido*-driven mystic of violence, pitting him against evil ninjas in defense of his girlfriend, Mariko (Sept.-Dec. 1982). The plot was thin, and Miller's intensity just wasn't there. But the fights were fun, the character was made more intriguing, and Claremont, with Miller's example staring him in the face, turned in the tightest writing of his career. It was another monstrous success, bridging the gap between *X-Men* and *Daredevil* fandoms, synthesizing "grim and gritty" (as fans were calling the Miller tone) with "angst" (as they were calling Claremont's content) into a new Marvel style. It also turned Wolverine from a popular character on a hot team into the favorite of seemingly every male fan from eight to twenty, and pushed *X-Men* to even higher sales.

By then Miller was gone. Jenette Kahn had taken him to dinner to tell him what DC could give him: in short, anything he wanted. To get him, DC would blow its budget, invent new formats, develop new production techniques to make it possible for him to tell any story in any way he wanted. It was exactly what an artist like Miller dreamed of hearing, what Jack Kirby had wanted out of Carmine Infantino and never gotten. Miller went to DC.

So, about the same time, did Doug Moench, after "creative differences" with Shooter about the future of *Master of Kung Fu*. DC gave him Batman, among other jobs. Bruce Jones quit *Ka-Zar* when Shooter wanted it more standardized. It was becoming a pattern. Don Heck and Carmine Infantino soon followed Gene Colan and Ross Andru to DC. After a series of conflicts with one of his editors—a big, impatient, opinionated Irishman named Mike Carlin, who may have been almost too much like Shooter, not only in taste but in certainty about his own judgment—Shooter fired him. There were a few rising Marvel creators with styles of their own: writers Alan Zelenetz and J.M. DeMatteis, artists Bob Layton, Bill Sienkiewicz, and Butch Guice. But none showed the commitment to remaking comics that Miller, or even Claremont and Byrne, had. One had to wonder if any distinct new Marvel talents would be around long once they hit their strides, or if they'd start to crimp their strides to stick around.

Here was a conflict. The direct market had reached critical mass. The more product put out for it, the more readers would find their way to it, the more shops would leap into it, the more product it would demand. By 1982 Marvel's Ed Shukin estimated that the direct market accounted for 50 percent of the company's sales, an exponential increase from year to year. Marvel created a new direct-only series, *Marvel Fanfare*, anthologizing stories of Spider-Man, the X-Men, and other hot properties by fan-fave artists and writers, printed on up-scale "Baxter" paper with offset printing and sold for a stunning $1.50. It sold well enough, even without continuing stories or subplots. The new market was making possible an upheaval in comics. Even Miller's intense violence probably wouldn't have been dared had not both Marvel and the Comics Code Authority known that a series could now survive even if jittery news-stand distributors wouldn't handle it. Yet, at the same time, the improved health of Marvel's mainstream was pressing everything less than sensational into safe little packages. There was a war brewing.

CHAPTER 36

INDEPENDENCE

Kirby was coming.

In the summer of 1981, Dean and Jan Mullaney, having had some success with their Eclipse graphic novels, took on the challenge of *Eclipse Magazine*, a black-and-white serializing the pet projects of some disaffected professionals: Steve Englehart and Marshall Roger's *Coyote*, about a young man in contemporary Las Vegas with the personality and the magic powers of the mythical Indian trickster; Don McGregor and Gene Colan's *Ragamuffins*, about real kids in 1950s America; and *Ms. Tree*, a hard-boiled detective series about a woman out to bring down the mobsters who murdered her husband. The latter was by Max Allan Collins, mystery novelist and author of the *Dick Tracy* newspaper strip, and Terry Beatty, a young cartoonist with a style based on humorous cartooning and Johnny Craig's EC work, which wasn't likely to get him any work at Marvel or DC.

Around the same time, John Davis's Capital City Distributing in Madison, Wisconsin, ventured into publishing with a black-and-white magazine of its own: *Nexus*, a futuristic superhero series by a couple of local boys, Mike Baron and Steve Rude. Baron was a high-strung, angry guy, into martial arts, older than most comics newcomers, working as a reporter at an alternative newspaper in Boston and looking for a way, he claimed, to make a living without being hassled or having to work hard. Not the sort of person who'd have gotten into comics writing before, but Dave Sim had opened up a whole new world to pissed-off smart-asses who were intrigued by modern comics. Steve "the Dude" Rude was a mellower soul who shared Baron's interest in martial arts and bizarre imaginings, but was more the typical comic book fan. He grew up with a love of *Space Ghost* (designed by Alex Toth) and of Russ Manning's elegant *Magnus, Robot Fighter,* then he moved on to

Jack Kirby's Fourth World and to Neal Adams and his assorted followers. He was enormously tall, attenuated, naturally graceful and confident, and it flowed into his art. He didn't put it all together at the beginning, but anyone glancing at *Nexus* knew he was a major find. And anyone reading the tight, cutting, funny but melancholy dialogue—or even just discovering the aliens named Dave and Tyrone—knew that Baron was, too.

Baron and Rude blended their bitter ruminations and goofy imaginings into the adventures of the twenty-fifth century's Horatio Hellpop, who was driven by strange dreams to hunt down and kill heinous criminals. Because he never chose to be a "superhero," his character could transcend the acting-out of power fantasies, he could be a superhero for grown-ups.

Publishing in black and white made *Nexus, Eclipse Magazine, Cerebus,* and *Elfquest* cheap to produce and somewhat low-risk, but it also kept them away from the masses of superhero readers. Another set of brothers, distributors from San Diego named Steve and Bill Schanes, decided it was time to try regular color superhero comics for the direct market, with all the creator-ownership benefits of the "independent press."

All the time he was designing characters for *Fantastic Four* and other cartoons, Jack Kirby continued playing with ideas for graphic novels, keeping alive the dream of modern myths for the mass market that he'd nurtured with *New Gods*. Once he thought he'd found a publisher, who pushed for "something like *Star Wars*," and Jack came back with *Captain Victory and His Galactic Rangers*, a superheroic twist on space adventures. The project fell through, but then the Schanes brothers asked him to kick off their new Pacific Comics line. Jack reached for *Captain Victory*. So much for retirement from comics.

It wasn't great Kirby material. His eyes and his energy were beginning to fail him, and animation was still his principal job. Fans who'd been saying, "He can draw but he can't write" were now smirking, "He can't draw anymore either." Premiering in late 1981, *Captain Victory* was out of step with its moment, looking like some strange reprint from another era next to *Daredevil*, *X-Men*, and *Teen Titans*. But the fans *noticed* it, and a fair number of them bought it, so refreshing was it to have something other than Marvel and DC to satisfy their superhero cravings. *Captain Victory* hung in, and after about a year Pacific was bringing out a second cosmic Kirby superhero series, *Silver Star*. Neither, however, amounted to much. The impact of Kirby's return wasn't going to come through his comics.

Kirby had gotten Pacific noticed, and almost immediately it was moving to take advantage of that notice. In early 1982 it brought out Mike Grell's *Starslayer*, about a Celtic barbarian whisked to the far future, full of the swashbuckling that *Warlord* fans expected. Its second issue featured a backup called *The Rocketeer* from a young animation artist named Dave Stevens, unknown in comics but well-known in his own circles for his stunning draftsmanship and evocation of prewar elegance. Older fans took to his witty story of a stunt aviator in the '30s who comes into possession of an experimental rocket pack and zooms around old Hollywood like Buck Rogers— and they took to the cheesecake shots of the hero's love interest, a "glamour model" identical to '50s nudie queen Bettie Page. Coming on the high heels of Emma Frost, Starfire, and Elektra, she proved that the days of comic book heroines as fantasy-models for girls was over, and the days of comic book "babes" as fantasy-objects for boys had begun.

The announcement that *The Rocketeer* would lead off a new anthology comic, *Pacific Presents*, set off a buzz. Unfortunately, Stevens turned out to be an excruciating perfectionist, and very busy with animation, so after an exciting first issue, *Pacific Presents* disappeared for months. With his Hollywood connections, Stevens picked up a movie deal for *Rocketeer*, which might have given him a little more incentive to keep the comic visible, but then Marvel's legal depart-

ment discovered that it had once published a story or two about some forgotten character with the same name, and a legal disentangling began that threatened to hold the movie up forever. Meanwhile, in October 1982, Pacific released a new Neal Adams creation: *Ms. Mystic*, a lightweight "babe" spin on Dr. Strange. Comics were just a sideline to Adams too, though, and it would be more than a year before the second issue appeared. It seemed that artists were willing to work with independent publishers to get their pet projects into print, but delivering comics on a regular basis, as the fans had come to expect, was another matter.

Pacific, luckily, had caught Bruce Jones on the rebound from *Ka-Zar*. Jones had made his name with horror stories for the Warren and Marvel black-and-whites, and now, along with a partner, April Campbell, he wrote, edited, and packaged a pair of anthology titles in the EC tradition. With great Jones stories and stunning art from Al Williamson, Richard Corben, Mike Ploog, Tom Yeates, Rand Holmes, Tim Conrad, Scott and Bo Hampton, John Bolton, Ken Steacy, and Bill Wray, *Twisted Tales* and *Alien Worlds* kept Pacific going. Jones and Campbell, now writing together, followed with *Somerset Holmes*, a limited series about an amnesiac hunted by unknown assailants. Both the writing and the art, by Jones's *Ka-Zar* partner, Brent Anderson, were as cinematic as movie storyboards, and the series picked up a Hollywood option. *Somerset Holmes* showed the comics world that the storytelling tricks and literalism of movies could not only make a comic book feel slick and sophisticated, but could make it an easier sell to other media. And if a creator owned his own property, that could mean more income and more career opportunities. Comics were going West.

Eclipse Comics went West, not to the glitz of Southern California but to the laissez-faire rusticity of the Russian River country north of San Francisco, where Dean Mullaney set up business and housekeeping with Cat Yronwode. Yronwode had left her commune in Missouri, written a biography of Will Eisner for Kitchen Sink (which clinched Eisner's status as an example to mainstream and independent creators alike), and now stepped to the fore of the comics revolution as editor of Eclipse. Independent publishers and creators could work from anywhere—the *Ms. Tree* team lived in Iowa, pleasantly isolated from the comics mainstream—and Yronwode and Mullaney carved out a niche in a uniquely '80s "alternative" culture (nothing so confrontational as a counterculture): leftist but not angrily engaged, structured around pop culture and materiality, though in the form of ancient jazz and revival cinemas and Depression-era pottery. Eclipse Comics would be individualistic, funky, commercial in a fun way but without pretensions to slickness, by big names if they wanted to drop by but more likely by pleasant youngsters with fun stories to tell.

With one dramatic exception. Yronwode and Mullaney were serious about creators' rights, and when they sank their teeth into a cause, they could get as angry as any old hippies. When Steve Gerber needed money to help pay his legal bills for the fight for *Howard the Duck*, Eclipse and most of the California comics community came to his aid. His *Destroyer Duck*, about an enraged waterfowl on the rampage against corporate America, was drawn by Jack Kirby and Alfredo Alcala, and if it was never subtle, it was certainly biting. Sergio Aragonés and Mark Evanier contributed a more veiled metaphor of the plight of the artist in modern society with their backup series, *Groo the Wanderer*, about a stupid barbarian wandering through a fantasy world of pettiness and corruption that he can't comprehend but that he always brings to its knees with his sword and dumb luck. Other allies—Neal Adams, Frank Miller, Dan Spiegle, Joe Staton, Steve Leialoha—contributed covers, backups, statements of support, and anecdotes about the horrors perpetrated by publishers on creators. The Duck rampaged for seven issues, all heavily bought by retailers and fans who wanted to support the cause, and all the income went straight to Gerber's legal fight.

Like every superhero story, it had a happy ending: Gerber got his rights back and soon optioned *Howard the Duck* to George Lucas. Marvel and DC set their lawyers to drawing up more thorough work-for-hire contracts, as well as contracts with creator-friendly clauses built in. The "independents," as everyone was calling the small publishers now, weren't much of a threat to Marvel and DC's market share, but they were competitors for properties—and now creators knew that their ideas were indeed their properties. "In the next few years," said Mark Evanier, "conditions for writers and artists...went through more improvement than in all the years since *Detective Comics* 1, combined."

The independents had made an impression—and so had Jack Kirby. Now he wasn't just the old guy who "can't even draw." He was a member of the older generation who'd publicly gone to bat for a maverick fighting the giant of the industry. Not only that, but there was *fire* in those pages, the most committed work he'd done in years. As fans and pros talked about *Destroyer Duck*, they began to consider why Kirby might have done it, and what grievances he might have against Marvel himself. It all fed into a resentment of Marvel's bigness, an uneasiness about its new factory-like production, and rumors about Jim Shooter alienating writers and artists.

One Marvel fan had already formulated some very clear beliefs about commerce and art and knew which side of the divide he stood on. Gary Groth was pushing his *Comics Journal* away from mainstream fandom, giving more and more coverage to independents and undergrounds, peppering his editorials with references gleaned from his dabblings in ever-more-highbrow culture, and gradually attacking bigger and bigger sacred cows. His politics were sharpened by the Reagan years to an angry leftism with a libertarian streak, a hatred of all things "middlebrow," and a romantic fervor for the starving artist. He began to attract an odd crowd of contributors and passionate letter-writers, bright misfits with one foot in fandom and one in autodidactic intelligentsia. Robert Fiore, who developed a charismatic critical voice in shocking contrast to his imploding social self, laced his comics reviews with witty references to William Faulkner, Cole Porter, Marxist anthropology, and

253

Jaime Hernandez and his *locas* get the superhero fantasies out of their systems before moving on to pro wrestling and punk music and other things more or less real. His fluid anatomy, bold blacks, and deft expressions influenced a lot of '80s superhero artists, and could have made Hernandez a successful mainstreamer—if he'd valued money more than art. (*Love and Rockets* #3, 1984.)

whatever else he happened to be reading. Heidi MacDonald—archetype of a new breed of "geek-girl," a cute young thing who hung out with guys, collected baseball cards, and read superhero comics—couldn't rail against "The Bane of Comics: Endless Fight Scenes" without showing off her knowledge of obscure Celtic folklore.

Groth and his business partner, Kim Thompson, launched a second magazine, *Amazing Heroes*, to exploit the fan market that the *Journal* was abandoning (initially hiding the connection between the two magazines to uphold the image of spotless integrity that was becoming one of their key selling points). Dave Olbrich, the Minnesotan who'd ignored Marv Wolfman's warning to stay out of comics, soon became its editor. Groth published books like *The Art of John Byrne* to keep the coffers filled, but Byrne wasn't where he saw the future of comics. Groth was even falling out with fan-fave writer Harlan Ellison in the stressful buildup to the Michael Fleisher lawsuit. Ellison was just too much a "lover of trash" for Groth, and maybe too successful in the mass media. Groth was looking at Art Spiegelman as a better

model, a cartoonist and publisher who'd found a place in academia and the world of legitimized intellectualism as Gary never had, but who'd kept his anxiety and angry politics intact. In 1982, when three brothers named Hernandez sent in their self-published comic book, *Love and Rockets*, for the *Journal* to review, Groth knew it was what he needed to kick off the Fantagraphics line of comics.

The oldest Hernandez, Mario, put the magazine together but was rarely more than a part-timer in comics. The second one, Gilbert, was the visionary, with his "BEM," a compelling but nearly incomprehensible fever-dream of old monster movies. The youngest, Jaime, was the instant selling point. "Los Bros Hernandez" had all grown up on comics—especially Kirby, Ditko, Dan DeCarlo's *Archie*, and *Dennis the Menace*—and they all showed their influences in powerful styles. But it was Jaime who combined it all into a dense, slick, dynamic, perfectly composed, and intricately textured package that any superhero fan would identify as "good art." Jaime's people in "Mechan-X" were more fluid, natural, and expressive—and his women more real and luscious—than anything else on the comic racks. He showed the influences of superhero comics more vividly than his brothers, jumbling up the shabby suburban reality of a young Latina mechanic and her friends with dinosaurs, flying machines, a corrupt billionaire with horns, and mysterious islands. He even introduced a fantasy figure named Atoma, the ultimate comic book amazon. Within a few issues, though, he left most of the fantasy behind to follow his *vatos* and *locas* through their chaotic modern romances and lousy jobs and gigs in punk clubs and brushes with *barrio* gangs. Gilbert, who quickly proved himself to be the most powerful storyteller in comics, abandoned his monsters to create "Heartbreak Soup," a drama of life in a Latin American town.

This was a new America: quiet, bookish Mexican-American brothers from Oxnard, an LA backwater, watching professional wrestling and reading comic books, get into the LA punk scene and get their heads blown open. A scene that the mainstream says is all about nihilism and stupidity throws these kids into a world where gender and race and class lines are blurred, where the scattered pieces of rich, idealistic America's junk and glory become the stuff of a new kind of found art. For people like "Los Bros," he comic book wasn't something to be elevated, but just *affirmed*. When they later listed their influences, they included Federico Fellini, *Little Archie*, Luis Buñuel, Harvey Kurtzman, Sophia Loren, Robert Crumb, the Sex Pistols, Jesse Marsh's *Tarzan*, Elvis Presley, and Kirby and Ditko.

For readers, and for Gary Groth, we suspect, *Love and Rockets* was the ideal bridge from the higher levels of superhero fandom to the more challenging work of engaging with individual visions of the real world. *Raw* was too hard: "The Graphix Magazine That Overestimates the Taste of the American Public . . . That Lost Its Faith in Nihilism . . . " (and so on) was a bridge from art and academe to comics. But Jaime's art could get a reader to look more closely at Gilbert—whose work, to an eye trained on John Byrne, was harsh and choppy—revealing its humor and vitality only in the reading. A lot of those readers got hooked. To a small but growing subculture within the subculture of fandom, *Love and Rockets* was becoming a litmus test of hipness. Formerly apolitical Marvelites, collectors, and geeks were turning on to the new alternative scenes, the resistance to the wholesome America advertised by Reagan. It was still OK for them to like *Daredevil*, but when the subject of *Love and Rockets* came up, there was no question that it lived in a plane far above—and here one needs a certain condescending snort—"superhero comics." A new word crept into the lexicon: "fanboy," meaning anyone who was too passionate about mainstream comics, who lacked the ironic remove that allowed the hip to read *X-Men* without seeming to buy into its fantasies. Issues were rising that could inflame all their passions: Gerber's *Howard the Duck* battle, Shooter's standardization of Marvel, Kirby's diminishment as Marvel grew. Once the word got out that Frank Miller was leaving, too, he or she could only see "Shooter's Marvel" as everything that was diseased in '80s America.

Then a funny thing happened: Marvel started sending original art back to the artists, with a little release form giving the artist permission to dispose of it however he saw fit but retaining the ownership of the image for Marvel. It happened because freelancers had been agitating for it, and because Shooter was willing to fight for creators' rights, because he understood the freelancer viewpoint and didn't want to alienate people over something so small. It was a quiet gesture of good faith and respect, and no one was more pleased to hear about it than Kirby, who'd given Marvel thousands more pages of art than anyone else.

When the Marvel legal people got to Kirby's release form, however, they found it inadequate. Kirby had had his attorney send notices to Marvel on occasion when he felt his rights were being infringed (like the time Marvel cobbled a story out of Jack's cartoon storyboards and advertised is as new work he'd done for Marvel Comics). Wanting to cover all contingencies, Marvel prepared a special document, an enormous document, just for Jack, essentially asking him to sign away his rights with regard to Marvel forever—including his right to sue over future wrongs. He pushed for a normal release form, but Marvel wouldn't budge. A stand-off had begun.

Destroyer Duck rampaged on, and Captain Victory ranged the galaxy, both gloriously indifferent to lawyers. Eclipse was ready to attempt ongoing color comics now. The first was *Sabre* in late '82, a carryover of the pompous '70s aesthetic, but then *Eclipse Magazine* switched to the color *Eclipse Monthly*. A more playful taste showed itself there immediately, in Marshall Rogers's cartoony fantasy *Cap'n Quick and a Foozle*; in B.C. Boyer's tribute to Eisner with *The Masked Man*; in Doug Wildey's elegant '50s-style Western, *Rio*; in Trina Robbins's dreamlike adaptation of Sax Rohmer's *Dope*; and in *Static*, a remarkably apolitical creation from Steve Ditko (who, ever supportive of independence, was also doing *Missing Man* for *Pacific Presents*). *Ms. Tree* got its own series, somehow uniting the texture

255

The new independents had room for old-timers, too. Working with Mark Evanier, Dan Spiegle got to stretch his muscles on material Gold Key never would have dared. (*Crossfire* #1, May 1984.)

of Mickey Spillane, charmingly timeless cartooning, and the character-driven continuity of modern comics.

When Eclipse did superheroes, they were the brainchildren of Mark Evanier. He'd generally avoided working for Marvel or DC—he didn't like the way they'd treated his friends Kirby and Gerber, or what he was hearing about Shooter from all his old friends. DC was looking better now, with Siegel and Shuster's *Superman* deal settled, and some rumblings that Paul Levitz and Jenette Kahn might want to accommodate Kirby similarly for his creations, so when Evanier wanted to create a project with Dan Spiegle—a Gold Key veteran who wasn't finding much work lately— he sold DC on a revamp of *Blackhawk*. It was fun, but it didn't last long, and Evanier came away feeling that DC hadn't supported it.

How natural, then, that his superhero creation for Eclipse would be *DNAgents* (Mar. 1983), about a team of genetically engineered operatives with super- human bodies but the naïveté of five-year-olds, strug- gling for freedom from the huge, merciless corporation that created them. The all-powerful cor- poration would become one of the most common and most ponderous clichés of '80s pop entertainment, as self-pitying Americans strained to externalize our anxiety about the Faustian bargain we'd made for prosperity, but Evanier was enough of a wiseass to keep it fun. Will Meugniot and Al Gordon's uninhib- itedly sensual art brought it to life, and *DNAgents* sold well enough for Evanier and Spiegle to spin off a supporting character in another new comic, *Crossfire* (June 1984). Spiegle wasn't the slick new stuff the fans were looking for, but he was one of the

best storytellers in the business, fluid and racy and naturalistic, perfect for Evanier's tales of the under- side of Hollywood. Evanier's scripts had a relaxed voice full of sarcasm, satire, and an insider's love of Tinseltown, unlike that of any other comic book writer in the hyped-up '80s.

The boom kept booming. Eclipse brought out Doug Moench's time-travel adventure, *Aztec Ace*, and P. Craig Russell's *Night Music*, devoted to pret- ty neo-Victorian adaptations of operas. Pacific turned Aragonés and Evanier's *Groo* into a regular series and launched an *Elric* series and more anthologies, with work by Roy Thomas, P. Craig Russell, Jack Kirby, Berni Wrightson, and a flashy young find named Paul Smith. Capital switched *Nexus* to color, just as the hero picked up a magnifi- cent sidekick, an apelike alien in a Mohawk named Judah Maccabee.

Hero, professional wrestler, gourmet cook, and self-proclaimed adjudicator, Judah was an explosive bundle of humor, rage, appetite, and braggadocio, hamming his way across the cosmos: "Not now, my little potato-bug," he tells his amorous girlfriend. "Papa's wrestling with an existential dilemma.... Yes! Yes! I shall inculcate Great Nexus in the art of tavern- hopping! The lad hath ne'er tasted aught but table wine!" (*Nexus* 5, Jan. 1984).With the astonishingly tasteful editing and art direction of Richard Bruning, not just a fan but an honest-to-God trained graphic artist, *Nexus* won the undying love of its followers. Capital followed quickly with a pair of new titles: *Badger*, by Mike Baron and diverse artists, about a psychotic superhero, and *Whisper*, by Steven Grant, one of the first new writers to show a strong Frank Miller influence.

Soon enough Fantagraphics was expanding its line. Two series were grown-up twists on funny animals: *Don Rosa's Comics and Stories* and *Dalgoda*, about an appealing, dog-like alien who comes to Earth for military aid. Jan Strnad wrote it with a quiet wit and a Midwestern gentility quite new to space adventures, and Hawaiian artist Dennis Fujitake drew it with organic funkiness. Everyone was getting into the act— everyone who'd ever run an apa or a fanzine and could borrow a thousand bucks from dad. And wherever a publisher appeared, promising kids showed up to fill the pages with their private dreams, for comicdom was becoming broad enough for fans of any taste and talent to break in. Phil LaSorda, off in the Philadelphia suburbs, formed Comico to publish the didactically named *Primer*, and immediately there they were: Matt Wagner with his dark *Grendel*, as cocky in his visual storytelling as if he'd been doing it in diapers, and Sam Kieth, as driven as he was insecure, with his funny yet somehow haunting monster, the Maxx.

Elfquest and *Cerebus*, meanwhile, were cruising along. From his five-hundred-copy beginnings, Dave Sim was now selling more than 20,000 copies a month of his aardvark's adventures, even with a drastic change in tone. With long, intricate, rambling story lines like "Church and State," he'd abandoned his *Conan* pastiche for cynical political satire, weaving in his own "fanboy" self-indulgences with characters like Keefe and Mick, his homage to the Rolling Stones, and Wolveroach, satirizing Miller and Claremont. With his opinionated letters pages, championing self-publishing and ridiculing corporations, he was becoming a spiritual leader of the independents, and in 1983 he decided to put his newfound money where his mouth was.

With Deni Loubert as editor, Sim created the Aardvark-Vanaheim line to publish the deserving misfits of the field: *Journey*, in which a Will Eisner follower named Bill Loebs spun stories out of his love of Michigan's pioneer days; Arn Saba's *Neil the Horse*, "Making the World Safe for Musical Comedy"; and *Ms. Tree*, which wasn't selling well enough for Eclipse to sustain it in color but did fine in black and white (and its ability to jump from one publisher to another was the clearest proof yet that creator ownership was good for the fans as well as the artists). Then there were two series that picked up on Sim's own roots in fanboy parody but took it in very different directions. *Flaming Carrot* was a hallucinatory and hilarious reconstruction of pulp stories, golden age superheroes, and '50s science fiction movies (with stories like "The Dead Dog Got Up and

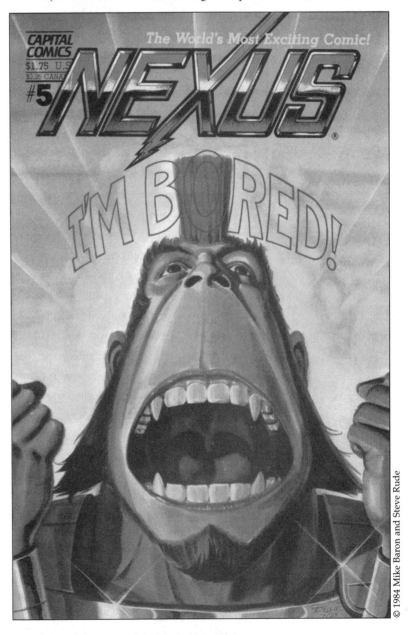

Steve Rude was a *Dr. Solar* and *Magnus* fan, and here he revives the painted-cover style of Gold Key in his own broad, loony way. The fellow with the ennui is Judah Maccabee. (*Nexus* #5, Feb. 1984.)

© 1984 Mike Baron and Steve Rude

257

Flew around the Room!"), written by an eccentric Georgia comics dealer named Bob Burden. *normal-man* was an ongoing parody of Marvel and DC heroes by an off-and-on Disney cartoonist named Jim Valentino, who showed more yearning to be in the heart of the mainstream than to reconfigure it.

The independents were revealing whole new outlooks, new regional tones in comicdom. The sweetest vision of the time, the most cheerfully comics-loving aesthetic anyone had seen in a long time, came from the Massachusetts suburbs. It was a high-tech area, growing around Harvard and M.I.T. the way California's Silicon Valley had grown around Stanford, and through the '70s and '80s it slowly rose from industrial bust to electronic boom. It was the sort of environment that could make a kid feel optimistic about the future, even in the '70s, especially if that kid was the son of an engineer and inventor, as was Scott MacLeod.

Scott was prone to analysis, to the invention that comes from the sudden perception of hidden relationships, to the belief that happiness and wisdom lay in understanding the hidden patterns in architecture, technology, storytelling, and personal development. Scott, though, was drawn more to art than to the cold externality of physical systems, with a sweetness passed down from the mellow liberal academic culture he grew up in. He faced the world with the kind of huge grin that grandmothers and babies love, but behind his glasses there was always something restless, edgy, desperate for answers. He thought comics were beneath him until the day in junior high that his friend Kurt Busiek—another brainy kid, but with sharper edges, more evident anger, a passion for "big guys hitting each other over the head," as he would later describe his beloved superheroes—finally got him to read some of the classier comics that were coming out circa 1973. Within a year they were collaborating on a "superhero epic" called *The Battle of Lexington*, and even as they headed off to college they both had an eye cocked toward comics. By 1981, Kurt was selling backup stories to Julie Schwartz, beginning a long process of knocking around the edges of mainstream comics, and Scott was in the DC production department. He imagined himself rising through the ranks—assistant to letterer to inker to penciler to *auteur*—along the sort of plannable track that had worked for his father and the other successful professionals of his hometown. Then life sent one of its harsh messages: his father died, too young, with too many dreams unfulfilled. Scott dropped out of the career track, out of DC, out of '80s America, and started work on the project of his dreams, even if he wasn't sure his skill was great enough to pull it off yet.

His *Zot!* appeared from Eclipse in 1984, under the pen name Scott McCloud. Cat Yronwode said she knew instantly that the creator was "a genius" (and Scott must have sensed it too, for how many unpublished twenty-two-year-old cartoonists would give themselves a trademarkable name that reached so explicitly for the skies?). *Zot!* was untouchable for sheer delight, its hero an exuberant teenager in a costume evoking the original Captain Marvel's, its setting the "far-flung future of...1965!" Zot's world was a playfully postmodern puree of art deco and naive futurism, a distillation of all the clean, gorgeous, adventurous futures Americans were promised by '30s Worlds Fairs, Schwartz science fiction comics and Disney's Tomorrowland. Into this world was thrust a sad thirteen-year-old girl named Jenny and her belligerent older brother, Butch (who is promptly turned into an articulate ape). They join Zot in his mad pursuit of the key to the Doorway at the Edge of the Universe—which, in McCloudian whimsy, turns out to be an old wooden door with a skeleton-key lock, sitting amidst the vastness of outer space. Standing in their way is the mad artist Arthur Dekker, who developed a hatred of life after a bout with cancer and a tragic love affair, and became obsessed with the inorganic decorativeness of art deco, transforming himself into an image of the Chrysler Building. McCloud drew not only on America's past but on Japanese comics, especially the work of the seminal Osamu Tezuka, which a few adventurous comics fans were beginning to discover amid America's fascination with all things Japanese. He brought as much

As Scott McCloud built to *Zot's* climax, his love of formal analysis blossomed. Sequence and time are suspended here in a single infinite moment, which can only be done in comics—and young Scott already knew it. (*Zot!* #8, Mar. 1985.)

new content into comics all at once as any of his peers, yet it all read like a return to the fundamentals of comics and cartoons.

Apart from *Zot!*, McCloud invented a game called *Five Card Nancy*, using panels from the bizarre *Nancy* comic strip. He promoted self-published "minicomics," like the stick-figure stories of Matt Feazel which rebelled against the steroid-pumped bigness and slickness of the '80s mainstream. He became a social nexus for the new cartoonists and critics who corresponded through the *Journal* and various letters pages, who came together and scattered and came back together through the never-ending party of the convention circuit, all the Hernandezes and Yronwodes and MacDonalds who conspired to transform comics from the bottom up. They were seeking their own Doorway at the Edge of the Universe, the key to the infinite future of comics. How could anyone reading their comics and their screeds, meeting them at cons and seeing the excitement in their eyes, not believe that they were about to find it?

259

CHAPTER 37

FLASH OF SILVER, FLASH OF GOLD

In the 1970s it was easy to imagine that a band of bellyaching impostors had supplanted the great heroes of the silver age. Easy, at least, for old-time fans, and apparently for writers and artists and editors as well, as they awoke from the near-death experience of that horrible decade and found themselves stronger, more confident, better skilled, and richer than ever. Suddenly the comics they thought they had outgrown became the symbols of a lost vibrancy. The adolescent may find childhood embarrassing—and for most baby boomers, adolescence lasted well past thirty—but the adult can reach back for childhood's clarity and sheer joy in being what it is.

It helped that one of the most exciting editors of the '60s was back in place at DC. In 1981 Dick Giordano became executive editor, in charge of new talent, new material, and creative coordination for the whole company. He was an energizing force, a stocky New York neighborhood guy with a big voice and a big grin who could talk football, wife-and-kids, or art. He'd lost much of his hearing in an illness, so everyone had to speak up around him, and he was always in the company of his assistant, Pat Bastienne, a neighborhood gal who matched him perfectly. It was impossible to be meek around Dick and Pat, and they emboldened people not just to talk, but to perform.

"I have a vision," he wrote in a message to the fans. "A vision of comics being all that they can be . . . . I want to publish a line of DC Comics . . . that will have people working together who care about their material, each other, their reader, and comics in general. Creators who work toward a common goal for love of the work and a desire to entertain and please an audience . . . as well as themselves."

Between Giordano's essays, Jenette Kahn's "Publishorials," and occasional messages from Paul Levitz, DC readers began to feel like they were part of a crusade. Giordano's echoing of both Dr. Martin Luther King's "I Have a Dream" speech and an Army commercial may not have been intentional, but they reveal the fervor for both uplift and recruitment that was gripping DC in the post-newsstand euphoria.

The enthusiasm was catching, even for old-timers. Now that the company had more editors, Julius Schwartz could go back to a small stable—just the Superman family—and focus his energies like the old days. His approach was like the old days, too. He launched *The New Adventures of Superboy* (Jan. 1980), written by Cary Bates in a light spin on the Weisinger *Superboy* style and drawn by Kurt Schaffenberger. When Julie talked Jim Starlin into doing an issue (for Julie could still charm the youngest and brightest), it wasn't for a cosmic head trip, but for "The Computers That Saved Metropolis" (*NAS* 7, July 1980). On *Superman*, he found better inkers for Curt Swan and coaxed Gil Kane into coming back for a few savage, high-powered takes on the Man of Steel. Schwartz dedicated an issue of *Action* to Superman's creators, to which Siegel and Shuster themselves contributed an essay and a pinup. Then he corralled every big name in the business into working on *Superman* 400, including the elusive Jim Steranko. Schwartz converted *Action Comics* into a two-story-per-issue format, featuring self-contained tales in his old tightly plotted, kid-oriented style. It became his place to try out new fan-writers. Julie still loved nothing so much as arguing plot with bright young weisenheimers: Kurt Busiek, Robert Loren

Fleming, a writing team with a touch for humor in Dan Mishkin and Gary Cohn, and the witty young star of Legion fandom, Mark Waid.

Cary Bates, after years of chugging through fairly uninspired recyclings of old villains and themes, now started picking up the pace, sharpening the humor, and seemingly having a pretty good time. In 1982 he turned in a terrific Superman Revenge Squad saga (*Superman* 365-368, Nov. 1981-Feb. 1982) and a truly Weisinger-style riddle about a pair of evil Kryptonians who claimed to be Superboy's true parents (*NAS* 27-28, Mar.-Apr. 1982). It could have been the hope of royalties, or the excitement of having *Superman II* doing big box office or just the cocky mood around DC—maybe the old DC way wasn't wrong after all.

Bates brought the same spirit to *Flash*, even after Julie left as the series' editor, and especially after the dream of the silver-age fans came true: Carmine Infantino returned to the art. He still never set foot in the DC offices, and whether he felt any sentimental pleasure at returning to the signature character of his greatest years as an artist, or took it as a sour reminder of his fall, Infantino wasn't the type to say. He just did his job and did it well, loose and wild and without the intricate speed effects of the old days, but still high velocity, still alive with the presence of an artist's hand, the sensual abandon of the act of drawing that the modern control freaks would never know. Dennis Jensen inked him sometimes, smoothing him over and fleshing him out like a ghost of the silver age.

Bates took advantage instantly with a delightful Elongated Man story (*Flash* 296, Apr. 1981), then with Captain Cold, and then with his masterpiece, the giant-size *Flash* 300 (Aug. 1981). There he united craftsmanship reminiscent of John Broome's with an '80s consciousness of what the medium could do and what the fans would expect. He and Infantino led the Flash on a harrowing internal journey that both recapped the hero's career and raised the chilling suspicion that that career might have been no more than a delusion of a demented Barry Allen (Aug. 1981). It may not have gripped young readers, but for many of

us, for many of DC's most hopeful supporters, it felt like going home again.

Infantino did other work for DC, but usually where the target audience was younger kids, like Marv Wolfman's entertaining revival of *Dial H for Hero* in *Adventure*. It was a flaw in DC thinking that would haunt it every time it tried to draw a new generation of kids into the medium—an assumption that because '60s DCs had been the favorites of editors and writers when *they* were kids, the kids of the '80s must want to read comics reminiscent of those '60s DCs. Marvel would make a similar blunder when it based its juvenile Star Comics line on the style of the antiquated Harvey Comics. The fans-turned-pros had little interest in the realities of modern childhood, preferring to imagine sentimentally that kids never change. As a result, any hope of comics being anything other than a field for adolescent and adult hobbyists vanished.

Infantino was better used when the target audience was the inner children of the writers themselves, as with the *Justice League* issue in which Gerry Conway brought back the Space Museum, or Mike Barr's homage to Gardner Fox in *Brave and Bold*. Such stories collared wistful fans in their twenties and thirties and had them watching every DC title for signs of another "silver age revival." Some series let them down: when Conway later tried to vamp up the sagging *JLA*, he turned in a painfully "relevant" mess in which the heroes relocate to a Detroit ghetto and hook up with a super breakdancer named Vibe. But then there were Gene Colan and Don Newton's stints on Batman, and Colan's redesign of Wonder Woman, and Roy Thomas's *All Star Squadron*, in which the old JSA battled Nazis against the backdrop of real history and Gardner Fox continuity. Roy muddied the story with excruciating detail that only someone with a few thousand dollars' worth of old *All-Star Comics* could appreciate, but Jerry Ordway's art made it a comfortable read.

Ordway was the champion of a new middle-of-the-road style. He was a Midwesterner, confident, unpretentious, genially conservative. He'd admired

Rich Buckler, that synthetic artist of the '70s, even inked over him early in his career, and was now weaving together all the popular threads of a decade's worth of superhero art: the bigness of Buscema and Kane, the balance of Swan, and that intricate but controlled surface, as smooth as a plastic action figure, of Byrne and Pérez and the new inkers like Bob Layton and Bob McLeod. His style did what the fans wanted: made the heroes look "real" without depriving them of their superhuman perfection, made the stories feel "serious" without dragging in the messy humanity that had made Neal Adams so exciting to a less insular fan culture. Kids and old-timers alike could settle warmly into him, be impressed with his draftsmanship, and then forget about it to slip into a nostalgic superhero story.

From all those discoveries, the "DC Dinosaurs," as we came to call ourselves, could shuffle on to find *Titans*, or the gutsier new version of *Green Lantern* that Marv Wolfman and Joe Staton were doing, or Thomas's *Infinity Inc.*, the slightly livelier adventures of the children of the JSA, or Wolfman and Colan's *Night Force* (although it never quite recaptured the magic of *Tomb of Dracula*), or Thomas's *Arak* (although it never quite recaptured the magic of *Conan*). There was even a flashback to DC's early '70s glories: Michael Uslan and Benjamin Melniker hadn't gotten anywhere with a Batman movie, but they had gotten *Swamp Thing* set up as a cheap horror flick with Avco-Embassy Pictures, which attached Wes (*The Hills Have Eyes*) Craven as director and Adrienne ("The Hills Have a Career") Barbeau as star. DC quickly brought out *Saga of the Swamp Thing* (May 1982), edited by the eponymous Thing's cocreator, Len Wein, written by Marty Pasko, and drawn by some of the first alumni of the Joe Kubert School: Tom Yeates, Stephen Bissette, and John Totleben. The comic was better than the movie, and the pencil-ink team of Bissette and Totleben showed some promise—if a horror genre should ever come back—with a postpunk morbidity given mystery and elegance by Kubert's lofty hopes for comics art.

We dinosaurs weren't huge in number, but we talked to retailers, wrote for fanzines, and had a dis-proportionate amount of money to throw around. We were good ambassadors spreading the impression in fandom that DC was the classier publisher. It was just the impression DC needed to win over the direct-market audience.

Marvel was still bolder in attacking that market. With Stan Lee spending most of his time with Marvel Productions in LA, a new vice president of publishing was hired, Mike Hobson, and he was proving to have the same aggression and business sense as Jim Shooter and James Galton. Mike Friedrich had left Marvel's sales force by then to convert his Star*Reach into a talent agency and packager to help creators deal with the suddenly diverse market and its multiplicity of legal and financial arrangements. The heir apparent in direct sales was Carol Kalish, a serious, handsome, prematurely graying woman, whose demeanor said "business sense" from across a convention floor but hid a genuine love of comics. She was part of the new breed of comic book women, plugging into the community but not hung up on childhood fantasies like her male counterparts, and she knew how the direct market worked. "Going into a comic book store is like going into a private club," she said. "Friendships start among the customers, and marriages have even occurred." Kalish herself lived with Richard Howell, an artist, writer, and a collector of Jack Kirby's work. She was the one who figured out that Conan kept prospering (with the aid of the 1982 Conan movie, and the sudden popularity of its star, Arnold Schwarzenegger, with American women) at least partly because women liked his exposed torso. "People tend to like their fantasy objects nearly naked, because that makes them vulnerable," she said, slicing through a lot of feminist objections to partly-clad women in comics with a blunt '80s pragmatism. She would build an aggressive sales staff of brainy, pushy, verbally deft superhero fans who could communicate with dealers in their own language: among them Peter David, a fanboy supreme with a booming voice and a gift for funny pop-culture references, and later Kurt Busiek, the cockiest struggling writer in the business.

When DC tried to top *Dazzler* with a direct-market-only one-shot by Englehart and Marshall Rogers, *Madame Xanadu*, Marvel topped that quickly with its first graphic novel: Jim Starlin's *The Death of Captain Marvel*. Phoenix, in *X-Men*, had proven the value of the "Death of" gimmick. Starlin's approach was typically weird—the hero died not of the ultimate cosmic zap, but of cancer—but if it didn't make for much of a story, it generated some talk. Marvel immediately protected its trademark by introducing a new Captain Marvel, less entangled in religious symbolism ("first of all, she's black") and installed in the Avengers.

Next came an *Elric* story, and then Starlin was back for *Marvel Graphic Novel* 3, this one a continuation of his *Metamorphosis Odyssey* from *Epic*. This *Dreadstar* was even less about metaphysics and psychic sacrifice, even more about a band of space-guerrillas fighting a big, bald bad guy with laser-swords. It was fast and fun and more tightly, conventionally crafted than anything Starlin had done before, and no one was surprised to hear that Starlin, Shooter, and *Epic* editor Archie Goodwin were developing it into an ongoing series to launch a new Marvel line of comics.

The key to Epic Comics was the crowning glory of Shooter's battle to keep Marvel creator-friendly, and to counteract the bad publicity he was getting: full creator ownership and control. Epic's focus was more market-driven than the independents, and it attracted mainly Marvel insiders interested in doing science fiction adventures. *Dreadstar*, the series, hit in late 1982 on slick paper, with a high price tag and for the direct market only, and did well out of the gate. Next *Coyote* moved over from Eclipse, without Marshall Rogers but with Englehart, Steve Leialoha, and Chas Truog. Then came *Alien Legion*, editor Carl Potts's concept and property, though executed by Alan Zelenetz and a cartoonist named Frank Cirocco (Potts was trying to get his friend Cirocco into comics, and the style Potts called "heroic realism," but Cirocco preferred doing more flamboyant cartooning and saw no place for himself in modern comics). Then Doug Moench and Paul Gulacy got together again for *Six from Sirius*,

impressively slick but much colder and more overworked than their old *Kung Fu*. With each successive title, the fans seemed less excited. Maybe it was too much space adventure, or too much polish. Sales were never better than decent.

The Marvel Graphic Novels, meanwhile, chugged on with a mix of upscale Marvel Universe stunts and creator-owned properties with Epic potential: yet more teams of science fiction adventurers from Walt Simonson and Dave Cockrum, which didn't become series, suggesting that after two *Star Wars* sequels and a host of imitations, George Lucas wasn't the only one exhausted by the theme. Then Marvel announced, wonder of wonders, a forthcoming new creation by Steve Gerber, fresh from his *Howard the Duck* courtroom victory. It wasn't the days of Jack Liebowitz and Jerry Siegel anymore.

Jenette Kahn and Paul Levitz had a problem. Warner Communications, well aware of how much more money it was making off the Superman movies and other licensing than off the publishing of comics, wouldn't allow them to grant creator ownership. They knew they couldn't take Marvel's breakthrough lying down, though, so they found other ways to attract freelancers to DC for direct-market projects: better royalty and first-refusal deals, higher page rates, and high-profile venues for British and other little-seen artists.

Mike Barr had been a DC editor and writer for a few years, and all the while had been trying to sell his idea for a science fiction spin on the Arthurian legends (an alien invasion prompts the heroes of the Round Table to return to life in new bodies). Now that one of the hot new British artists, Brian Bolland, was interested, it looked like a sure bet for the fan market. Bolland was synthesizing "mature" art as expertly as Jerry Ordway was synthesizing the mainstream, starting from the politely finished art of British series like *Dan Dare*, picking up Marvel bigness, then some bravura and some punky darkness from the '70s, and responding to the improved reproduction processes that the direct market made worthwhile with a violent but pretty ink line. Bolland and

Ordway and several of their peers were forging an ultimate mainstream look—Carl Potts's "heroic realism"—that perfectly met the needs of the totally immersed superhero fan. They were setting a standard for new guys coming up, like Dan Jurgens and Todd McFarlane, a standard for serious-but-not-challenging draftsmanship that would codify an unofficial "house style" for DC in the '80s.

When *Camelot 3000* appeared in late 1982, a twelve-issue "maxiseries" on Baxter paper, all those precisely reproduced and vividly colored pages of Bolland virtuosity knocked the fans on their seats. For a silver age fan, Barr held up his end well, with plenty of scenes of combat and mass destruction and some startling twists on his reincarnated heroes. His Tristan was somehow reborn into the body of a woman, and so was his Isolde, and so their ageless love became a lesbian infatuation that left both parties agonized and the fans buzzing. Not bad for an Ohio boy who'd once nearly joined the priesthood. *Camelot* was a bigger hit than any of Marvel's direct-only series. DC, as one ad campaign would put it, was "on the move again!"

It followed quickly with a whole "Adult Line" of miniseries, maxiseries, and open-ended series. Marv Wolfman and Joe Staton created the Omega Men, another band of freedom fighters in another galactic war, for *Green Lantern*, and they were soon spun off into a Baxter-paper, direct-only series of their own (Apr. 1983). Gerry Conway and Dan Jurgens pitted more renegades against another Hitlerian galactic warlord in the *Sun Devils* maxiseries. (Conway and José García-López did the same in *Atari Force*, a video game tie-in outside the Adult Line, which became the most fun of all the *Star Wars* imitations.)

When DC continued milking the superteam boom with *Batman and the Outsiders*, published on upscale paper to appeal to the direct market, Mike Barr got the writing job—and won over the younger fans with an ability to counterpoint the solitary intensity of the Dark Knight against his team of misfits. Wolfman and Pérez cobbled together the Vigilante as an answer to Marvel's Punisher in *Teen Titans* and

spun him off into his own slick-paper series (Oct. 1983). (For a while Titans and *Legion of Super-Heroes* were even tried in separate editions, upscale for the comic shops and cheap for the newsstands.) DC staffer Robert Loren Fleming hit with a proposal for a maxiseries called *Thriller*, a suspenseful and challengingly oblique story set in an apocalyptic New York, full of pulpy crime and Elvis Presley doubles. It seemed like a good idea when the forcefully innovative Trevor von Eeden signed on for the art, but the fact that both he and Fleming were trying to be artfully cryptic made it nearly incomprehensible.

The inevitable DC Graphic Novel line started at the end of '83 with more science fiction adventure—and some great visual storytelling, by García-López on *Star Raiders* and Ernie Colón on *The Medusa Chain*—but it trickled out only slowly. Meanwhile, DC tried "limited series" for other chunks of the readership. Dan Mishkin and Gary Cohn created *Amethyst, Princess of Gemworld* (May 1983), along with Colón, one of the most graceful and ornamental cartoonists left in a business that seemed to have little room for anything but the ponderous and over-controlled. It told the charming story of a thirteen-year-old suburban girl who discovers that she is secretly the rightful ruler of a fairy-tale land of magical jewels, and won DC more goodwill from fans who wanted to see comics less dominated by testosterone. A sequel followed, and Mishkin and Cohn launched *Blue Devil*, "Bringing Fun Back to Comics," about a Hollywood stuntman who becomes a "weirdness magnet," vigorously cartooned by Paris Cullins. It wasn't quite as much fun as it strove to be, and it didn't become a hit, but it made DC look even more like the place where the new and exciting could happen any minute.

Jan Strnad pulled off a clever piece of networking: he was getting to know Gil Kane, whose cantankerous elitism was making him a favorite of Gary Groth and the Fantagraphics gang. Strnad said he thought he could give Kane a chance to draw some of the barbarian sword-slinging he loved. Then he told DC he could get Gil Kane to return to the Atom, with which silver age fans identified him. The result, the *Sword of the Atom* miniseries (Sept. 1983), had the Mighty Mite dumped by his wife Jean, running off to the Amazon, getting stuck at his six-inch height, and becoming the sword-wielding champion of a race of nearly naked Lilliputians. It sold well, even though most of the buyers griped about Ray and Jean breaking up. The powers at DC didn't see series potential, not if Kane couldn't commit to it, but it taught them that a drastic, high-concept reworking of even a rather obscure silver age hero had a good-sized, built-in audience of older fanboys. They wouldn't forget the lesson.

Of all the direct-only projects at all the companies, though, nothing generated the talk and anticipation of Frank Miller's first DC project. When the news of his defection from Marvel first hit the grapevine, every fan had the same dream: Miller on Batman. Then it came out that he was going to do a miniseries of his own devising, called *Ronin*, but it had something to do with ninjas, so that was OK. It was going to be fifty-two pages, slick in every way, a shocking $2.50 per issue, and nonreturnable. It was a big risk for retailers, but when *Ronin* 1 (July 1983) was finally solicited, the orders were tremendous. This was already a gold mine for Miller and DC, even if the fans didn't buy it. The dealers couldn't wait to see it, but when they did—they started getting nervous. With good reason, it turned out: some fans, mostly older ones, hailed *Ronin* as a revolution in the medium, but most of them, the ones who wanted more of the urban sex-and-death of *Daredevil*, flipped through it and put it right back on the shelf.

Ronin was set in a post-holocaust New York City, where a samurai from feudal Japan was hurled by an ancient demon. It was all just a further distillation of the themes that had dominated *Daredevil*: the lone man in a decaying city whose evil he can't fully grasp, who has only his *Bushido* guiding him through its unseen but all-pervasive machinations. The telling of the tale was perhaps too much distilled, too style-conscious and intellectualized, not visceral enough or grounded enough in the trash of the real streets that

had sent Miller off on his wonderfully paranoiac day-dreams in the first place. And the art was like nothing Miller's fans had ever seen: he'd been studying "Moebius," the science fiction persona of Jean Giraud, whose restful, organic art had been inching its way into the consciousness of the more ambitious American comics artists since *Heavy Metal* first made it accessible. Miller had gone deeper into his study of Japan and Japanese comics, especially the samurai and gangster comics with their minimal lines and detached, almost ritualized violence. He also had a new collaborator: his colorist and soon-to-be wife, a painter named Lynn Varley, who broke all the

A global visual style: Frank Miller kept his feet in American superhero comics while he reached for Japanese art and the French fantasies of Moebius. Plus street dialogue of an '80s kind like no one had ever seen in an "overground" comic. (*Ronin* #3, Nov. 1983.)

265

ancient rules of comic-book coloring and turned Miller's ink-etched world into a mist of dreams and half-remembered emotions. The result was fascinating, liberating, and ambitious, but it was also transitional, not wholly integrated, and not nearly as riveting to the gut as to the eye.

So there were failings. But the excitement that *Camelot 3000* stirred up, the arguments that *Thriller* started, the critical prestige that *Ronin* brought, and the huge sales of *Titans*, were enough to turn DC's two decades of downward momentum around. It was indeed what the cover blurbs said: "The New DC!"

It was looking like Jenette Kahn and her colleges might actually know what they were doing. She'd been mocked a bit in freelance circles for her Upper East Side manner, her Jackie Kennedy voice, her costume jewelry with its Kirbyesque monumentality. But it turned out that she wasn't just smart and well-attuned to the times, but actually had integrity, and a desire to see her company well-perceived among freelancers, fans, and the world outside comics. It was officially a secret—but really no secret—that she and Levitz were giving far more to Jerry Siegel and Joe Shuster, including full medical benefits, than was called for in the original settlement. It was also no secret that Sheldon Mayer, one of DC's founding editors, was being given work drawing *Sugar and Spike* stories that might never see print. Kahn had a broader cultural perspective than any of her predecessors. An artist would probably never have found himself talking to Sol Harrison or Jack Liebowitz unless it was to fight vainly for employee benefits, but he could well find himself talking to Kahn about the Louise Bourgeois installation at the Guggenheim or the collectability of old Bakelite radios. Jenette dropping an observation that the history of DC superhero art paralleled that of Western painting—Joe Shuster as Giotto, Neal Adams as Michelangelo, Marshall Rogers as Caravaggio—was enough to set a young art-school graduate's blood boiling to become DC's Delacroix, Ingres, or even Cézanne.

Paul Levitz, meanwhile, was growing up in full view of comicdom. He was not only young, but short

and very slight, and in the early days he seemed determined to make up for his lack of natural presence by screaming and throwing people out of his office. Now he was developing his executive persona: cool, watchful (sometimes eerily aware of the little goings-on in the office), honest even with freelancers, apologetic but immovable on unpleasant business decisions. Whereas Jenette was the ambassador of the company, wooing talent and pointing directions and cultivating Hollywood opportunities, Paul was the tough guy, canceling and limiting budgets, and so he inspired most of the griping among freelancers and staffers. But when you bumped into him among the aisles of back-issue dealers at a convention, and he explained very simply why your baby was canceled, it was hard to walk away hating him. He and Kahn were both smart enough to see that if DC couldn't offer the sales figures and royalties that Marvel did, it could at least be the "freelancer friendly" company. Luckily for them, Jim Shooter was helping out.

If nothing else, Levitz was more believable as a fellow freelancer than Shooter was. As fine a craftsman as Shooter was, there was always something cold about his work; it was almost didactic in the way that it demonstrated its technique. When Levitz returned to *The Legion of Super-Heroes* in 1981, he was obviously doing so as a fan-writer. His passion was matched by that of the new artist, Keith Giffen (*LSH* 287, May 1982).

Giffen was growing up, too, pulling together his awkward synthesis of '60s Kirby and the post-Starlin school into a style that—although still a little too synthetic to be quite "all his own"—was at least unlike anything else in the business. Sleek futurescapes, sight gags, ingenious visual transitions, minimal but appealing faces, sometimes little Pérezian conversation beats, sometimes explosions of Kirby grandiosity—it was perfect for a bunch of thirtieth-century teenagers. He was also a plotter, or at least a co-plotter, whipping out stories on sheets of 8 1/2-by 11-inch paper, indicating figures and calling for dialogue bits with broad strokes that kept it all moving with a more purely visual flow than was likely to come from any writer's word processor. He and Levitz perfected the vignette, the short, self-contained scene ending with a punch at the bottom of a page, segueing with a cinematic cut to the next page, which reflected the modular editing of TV shows like *Hill Street Blues*.

When they decided to get grandiose, they topped even Marvel. In "The Great Darkness Saga," the Legion battled Darkseid and the minions of Apokolips (*LSH* 290-294, Aug.-Dec. 1982). It was Giffen's chance to "do Kirby," and he did him about as well as anybody has, well enough to spark a new buzz of conversation among older fans about how great Jack used to be. Demands for more Darkseid starting pouring in, until DC responded: the entire run of *New Gods* would be reprinted in gorgeous, slick new editions. Not only that, but Kirby himself would be hired to write and draw a new ending to it. It had taken a decade, but a little piece of Jack's dream was coming true.

The Great Darkness Saga also had both young and old fans buzzing about the ending, a mystery about the child of Saturn Girl and Lightning Lad, the first time DC had ever delivered a real continuity shock that stopped the fans in their tracks. For many fans, it was the first time they realized DC even *had* a continuity, certainly the first time they'd realized that worlds as disparate as Mort Weisinger's wonky thirtieth century and Jack Kirby's metaphoric otherworlds could be united into a single cosmology. The Lee-Kirby torch had been passed from Marvel to Giffen and Levitz. *Legion* did big business in the comic shops. Here was another lesson that Levitz, in particular, wouldn't forget: a continuity "event" would make this new breed of fan check out even the most neglected old series.

Giffen was hot now, and knew how to take advantage of his opportunities. He started calling for color-holds, ersatz computer graphics, and other tricks from DC's improved production facilities that made *Legion* look as futuristic as it was supposed to be. He even knew how to take advantage of Julius Schwartz's sense of humor, doing a story in *Action* in which

Superman is tormented by an insane creature called the Ambush Bug, popping in from some realm to point out the fiction of the comic book and to poke holes in Superman's sanctimonious purity. Schwartz loved it—he still thought Superman was a dullard—and so did fans who both hated and loved the Man of Steel. Giffen drew it in a flat, jagged style that the fans called "weird" and "cartoony," but the thing was so funny that they forgave him and bellowed for more.

The lines were being drawn: DC was going for the older, pickier, and less superhero-obsessed fans, and Marvel for the kids who wanted spandex, fights, and angst. Marvel's hottest new title of the period

Action, design, humor beats: Keith Giffen synthesizes Pérez storytelling, Kirby bigness, and silver age DC clarity, then throws in some amusing twists of his own. Paul Levitz contributes his tightest dialogue, Larry Mahlstedt his cleanest inks. (*Legion of Super-Heroes* #294, Dec. 1982.)

was *G.I. Joe, A Real American Hero* (June 1982), tying into Hasbro's revived toy line and a syndicated cartoon (the writing staff of which included Marv Wolfman and some of his cohorts). Larry Hama wrote and drew straight-ahead macho adventure for boys; Joe's enemies now weren't the Krauts, but Cobra Command, providing knee-jerk nationalism without messy political entanglements (rather like the U.S. government with its unconsummated battles with the Evil Empire, the Ayatollah, and the Sandinstas). The direct-market crowd mostly sneered at it and then went back to their far more "adult" reading, like *X-Men*, but *Joe* went on to be the top seller on the newsstands. Another big-action toy tie-in, *Rom*, kept doing well and was cleverly made "synergistic" with the Marvel Universe through guest appearances by X-Men and the like. Galton, Hobson, Shooter, and Shukin were mastering their market.

Marvel's direct-only products were mostly reprints, tons of things like *Phoenix: the Untold Story*, a glossy reissue of the Death of Phoenix from *X-Men* with the original ending intact, selling for two bucks when regular comics were sixty cents. Independent publishers were screaming that crap like that was squeezing them out of the market and doing comics no good at all, but Marvel kept it coming. When Marvel did create new products for the comic shops, they were usually fan-clubby things like *The Fantastic Four Roast* or *The Marvel No-Prize Book* or *The Marvel Fumetti Book*, with Marvel staffers mugging in photographs. Then there was Carol Kalish's *Marvel Age*, a whole magazine promoting the Marvel line as Bullpen Bulletins had once done, and Mark Gruenwald's baby, *The Official Handbook of the Marvel Universe*. Gruenwald by then was editing *Thor*, *Iron Man*, *The Avengers*, and *Captain America*, and was about to dig in as Cap's seemingly permanent writer, but the project that really got all his love and devotion was his encyclopedia of heroes, villains, planets, weapons, and everything else. Not even heights, weights, or the total poundage a hero could bench-press were left up to the readers' imaginations any longer. And the readers loved it.

The difference between companies was clear when Marvel started paying sales incentives to editors. DC editors got better base pay, and could be rewarded with bonuses and promotions, but royalties, and the burden to sell, were the province of freelancers. After all, was Len Wein the reason kids bought *Teen Titans*? At Marvel, the example was the Death of Phoenix issue, which the freelancers hadn't wanted to do, and the improved sales of the whole line. Shooter saw his comics as editorially generated; Kahn and Levitz saw theirs as creator generated. Maybe it was natural, after the hard times of the '70s, that both companies would reverse their old approaches, but seeing them trading roles still took some getting used to.

The Marvel mainstream mostly just ground on. If a series flew briefly over the mountains of pulp to catch the eye of fandom, it was usually because of a sensational twist, like Tony "Iron Man" Stark's battle with alcoholism by scripter David Michelinie. New attention to the series, though, also meant attention to Bob Layton, an inker with a lush but lively style who'd been making *Iron Man* look pretty for a little while and was gradually getting involved in the plotting. After a while he was the sole plotter, and the series kept selling. Shooter liked him: he was proof that the Shooter style of storytelling and training could really turn into something in the hands of a gutsy and imaginative creator. Pretty soon Layton had a miniseries to write and draw himself: *Hercules, Prince of Power* (Sept. 1982). It was robust, funny, and wonderfully told, taking the spirit of Kirby and Lee's Hercules into the '80s: he defeats Galactus by getting him drunk. Layton started work on a sequel.

Tony Stark wasn't so lucky. He fell back into alcoholism, for a very long time, as the new writer, Denny O'Neil, worked through some personal demons. In general, Marvel's editor-driven mainstream seemed as grim and full of self-pity as in the '70s, despite the better-turned plots. But some Marvel mainstreamers were doing a silver age revival of their own—although to them that meant Stan and Jack, not Gardner and Carmine.

John Byrne took his *Fantastic Four* "Back to Basics," as his first issue was titled (*FF* 232, July 1981), with a playful pastiche of the mid-'60s Kirby work that had gotten him into comics in the first place. He threw out the mawkish emotional developments of the '70s, and all the dreary repetitions of subplot and continuity with them, and dove into the Marvel Universe as if it were a toy box. He found amusing new spins on Galactus, Dr. Doom, and the Skrulls, opened up his full talent for mystery and suspense, and stripped his art down to a buoyant simplicity that evoked vintage Kirby without losing its Byrne cuteness. He was just in time for the FF's twentieth anniversary, and turned in a mystery that recapped their history but raised spooky questions about it, much like Bates's *Flash* 300 (*FF* 236, Nov. 1981). The fans ate it up. Byrne's credentials and the mystique of history made it OK for comics to be just plain fun again.

Unfortunately, Byrne added a second series as writer/artist, *Alpha Flight*, and started writing the new *Thing* series. He was trying to be Kirby in a way no mortal should ever attempt, and he lost his verve on all three series.

Meanwhile, Chris Claremont was going back to basics, too. He and Bob McLeod—laying down big, Buscema-like pencils to round out and polish up with his inks, for an effect much like the Ordway look—created *New Mutants*, an X-Men spin-off about naive mutants newly arrived at Professor X's school (Mar. 1983). Its stories were only mildly interesting, but it crossed over with *X-Men*, gave Claremont a chance for some of his tenderest character writing, and was a lead-pipe cinch with the Marvel audience.

Another hotshot artist had emerged, Paul Smith, and he replaced Cockrum on *X-Men*. His stuff was flashy, brave, and aggressively designed. Older fans who'd been losing interest in *X-Men* were suddenly curious again. Smith, it turned out, just wanted to pile up enough royalties to hop on his motorcycle and disappear into the great American nowhere for a year or two. His replacement, John Romita Jr., was as professional as a kid working for his father had to be, and

showed some promise for a potent design sense, but the plotting immediately meandered and the characters grew cold (evidently Claremont was hardly Claremont without the right collaborator). Sales, however, stayed high. It was a good discovery. *X-Men* would sell a quarter of a million copies no matter who drew it, thanks to mutant addicts and naive speculators who bought multiple copies; but the occasional hot new artist or major continuity event—like Cyclops falling in love with a woman who looked uncannily like Jean Grey (was she *back*?!)—could add tens of thousands more to that almost instantly. Fandom never forgot the passion of 1980, and always had one eye furtively on the X-Men. A really clever editor would know just how to exploit that.

Walter Simonson surprised everyone when he went back to his Kirby roots. His art had always shown humor and a pleasure in cartooning, but his early love of Kirby's Marvels had always been sublimated to an Adams- and Chaykin-like devotion to mood and cynical sophistication. Now he was married—to Marvel's most charming editor, Louise Jones—doing creator-owned work for the Marvel Graphic Novels, getting sales incentives, and just generally feeling good. We have to assume he was, at least, because there's never been a more joyous or exuberant run of a comic book than Simonson's first year on Thor (with *Thor* 337, Nov. 1983).

Thor had become Marvel's Hamlet in recent years, always agonizing about his dual life or the fate of the gods or something or other, so Simonson immediately bumped him out of his own title, gave his costume to an alien adventurer named Beta-Ray Bill, and cranked up the action. When Thor came back, he was a tough guy worthy of a Viking's worship. Simonson had Norwegian blood and wanted things right. His Asgardian buildings were based on medieval stave churches, his sound-effect calligraphy had a hint of ancient woodwork, and Thor even grew himself a real Viking beard. Loki had always been putting spells on his virtuous half-brother, but nothing like the one Simonson came up with: "What do you call," asked the cover, "a 6'6" fighting mad

Walt Simonson announced his presence in a hurry, as Beta Ray Bill smashed his way into Thor's life. It's raw Kirby, with a twist from Simonson's odd humor. (*Thor* #337, Nov. 1983.)

FROG?" It was no gag. Simonson's once-intricate art was now big, loud, and funny.

While Walter Simonson proved he could write as well as draw, Louise Jones Simonson proved she

could write as well as edit. She created *Power Pack* in 1983, an endearing series about four ordinary siblings who gain superpowers and have to figure out what to do with them. She found an artist named June Brigman who did wonderful characters—kids who actually looked like kids. It looked like a bid to reach a new audience of children, but *Power Pack* only did well enough to hang in; children definitely weren't finding their way to the comic shops. Those shops were still the turf of the big burly superheroes, and Marvel knew it. By late 1983 the word was already getting out that Marvel was preparing something huge, a maxiseries that would involve all its heroes and probably change the Marvel Universe forever. Even the name sounded ominous: *Secret Wars.*

Whether the mainstream changed for good or ill, it didn't matter with artists like Byrne, Simonson, and Layton being set loose, artists writing their own stories and having a blast at it. Critics had always said the best comics were the work of a single vision, and now there were venues enough and incentives enough for a lot of them to try proving it. Interesting that they, and Giffen at DC, were all drawing their inspiration from the same writer/artist: Jack Kirby. As the oppressive self-questioning and pseudo-enlightened pretension of the '70s lifted, Jack was looking awfully good.

"The prevalent mood of the business, for the first time in many years," said one book about comics from the period, "is one of soaring optimism." Between the Kirby kids, the new DC, and the independents, there was real reason to hope that, as that book's last line put it, "the true Golden Age of Comics might lie just over the horizon."

CHAPTER 38

THE REVOLUTION EATS ITS CHILDREN

Idealism may discover money, but it rarely hangs onto it. Cartoonists and distributors who really loved comics and the people who created them had discovered the gold mine of the direct market, but inevitably others came along who knew how to mine it faster and keep more of the proceeds. Quite a few others, as it turned out.

As the direct market grew, the newsstand market fell even further. Charlton had reorganized, tried to rally, and died again. The rights to its characters were sold to DC, where Dick Giordano figured he knew what to do with them. Warren dropped its comics in 1982. Harvey folded the same year; no more *Casper*, *Richie Rich*, *Sad Sack*. Marvel hired one of its veterans, Sid Jacobson, to build a line of kids' comics under the Star imprint, some original and some cartoon tie-ins like *Strawberry Shortcake* and *Fraggle Rock*. Even with Marvel distribution, it didn't last long; comic shops couldn't sell "kid stuff" and newsstand comics just weren't in the minds of kids much anymore. Western had abandoned the Gold Key imprint at the end of the '70s, along with all its non-humor comics, and switched to the Whitman name it used for its coloring books and other kids' products. It tried to get around the whole comic book distribution problem by selling its remaining comics only in plastic-bagged "samplers" of a few comics each, often on sale in toy stores. Marvel soon invaded the same market, squeezing Western even further. In 1984 Western abandoned comic books. For the first time since the dawn of the industry there was no *Donald Duck*, no *Bugs Bunny*, no funny animal comics at all. Collector/dealer Bruce Hamilton picked up the Disney and *Little Lulu* licenses, but only to publish beautiful hardbound reprints at a hundred dollars a pop. Archie was still around, barely, the last refuge for kids who wanted kids' comics, girls who wanted girls' comics. It even tried to crash the resurgent superhero market with a Red Circle imprint, but it was just the usual "Time to bring back the Fly!" stuff, and it bombed. All the money was in the comics shops now.

A group of comics dealers and investors in Chicago, seeing the instant success of Pacific and Eclipse, decided the time was ripe for a more professionally managed "independent" with strict monthly schedules, market-targeted product and heavy promotion. They'd offer more money than the others, publish on cheaper paper to keep cover prices lower, and give creators only *co*-ownership of their creations (and creators were still naive enough about the opportunities of the new market to agree to that).

271

SOMEONE'S GOTTA PUT IT ALL BACK TOGETHER...

...REUBEN FLAGG JUST MIGHT BE THE MAN.

BACK IN THE USA!!

© 1983 Howard Chaykin

A graphic sophistication unprecedented for comics announced that Howard Chaykin was hip, satirical, and not for children.

(American Flagg! #1, Oct. 1983.)

Their editor would be Mike Gold, a veteran '60s radical who'd become a nexus of the Chicago comics scene, but the owners themselves were a different breed. One had a habit of swaggering up to young artists at conventions with a huge cigar between his teeth and grinning, "I'm here to make you rich"; another created a stir at a convention by hitting on a competing editor's thirteen-year-old daughter; they lured Mike Grell away from Pacific and let him farm his *Starslayer* out to other hands while he created something more superheroic for them; and pretty soon they'd be famous for withholding royalties until

creators threatened legal action. But when their First Comics hit the stores, they seemed to signal that the independents had come of age.

Warp, an adaptation by diverse hands of a cycle of fantasy plays, was only a tease (Mar. 1983). *E-Man* was better: brash, tongue-in-cheek, boldly cartooned by Joe Staton and wittily scripted by Nic Cuti and Marty Pasko, it was the only comic anyone remembered from post-Giordano Charlton, and it was good to have it back (Apr. 1983). Then came the new Grell: *Jon Sable, Freelance* (June 1983).

Sable was the perfect bromide for the nausea of Miller's *Daredevil*, a blithe evocation of a conservative America newly contented with its resurgent economy and saber-rattling stance, enjoying its greed and violence while playing at innocence. Ronald Reagan even appeared in its pages, munching jelly beans and giving instructions like everyone's favorite boss. The hero, like the country, led a double life: Sable is an ex-mercenary who works as a bodyguard, detective, and adventurer on jobs too dangerous or specialized for other men, yet he also has a knack for writing children's stories, and so masquerades as a bland kiddie novelist named B.B. Flemm. Grell brought everything he'd learned from *Warlord* here, handling action, suspense, and emotional nuance with an easy, minimalist grace. Sable's background is tragic, and much like America's. While working as a ranger in East Africa his wife and children are murdered by poachers; not unlike a country that went to the tropics to play ranger and lost its confidence and innocence. But his present is happy: success in two jobs, an easy going girlfriend who's also his agent (sex and money in one package, with no emotional drain), a likable neighbor who turns out to be gay and helps Jon overcome some of his silly inhibitions.

Grell handled it all—rage and grief in the flashbacks, amused embarrassment with the neighbor—as if he hadn't a care in the world. Living in northern Idaho, making money off his fantasied alter ego, taking pages from his stories to tell his readers about his African safari, how could he not? He'd created a mid-'80s TV world for himself and his hero, a comic book *Cosby Show* or *Miami Vice*, and *Sable*, sure enough, got picked up for TV development, the first independent comic to crash the Big Time.

First kept pumping, and *Sable* was only four months old when its counterpoint arrived. Howard Chaykin had been knocking around comics for over a decade now, showing off some great art, great storytelling, punchy ideas with a hint of the perverse, a willingness to change and improve his own work, but somehow it had never all come together. He needed his own world, and finally found it in the collapsing, corrupt Chicago of the early 21st Century. *American Flagg!* began its history with 1996 "the year of the domino—when *everything* went to hell," a year that left the world's political structure in a shambles, the Soviet Union gone, most of the United States decimated and the remainder under the control of an octopuslike corporate entertainment complex called Plex-USA. What's left of our culture is a gross, wicked caricature of consumer society, a world haunted by the random violence of "gogangs" like the Genetic Warlords and Ethical Mutants, by insane political groups like the Arab Nazis, Animal Mutilators, and Gotterdammercrats, by everyone's favorite video show, "Bob Violence," packed with subliminal messages like "Kill, rape, death, sex, mutilate." It's a world that runs on sex and drugs, two of Chaykin's great passions in those years, a world where the brutal police force, the Plexus Rangers, rely on the wonder drug Somnambutol ("The Tender Riot Ender: It's like a wet dream . . . without the hot parts!"). Promiscuity, backstabbing, and official corruption are simply understood in a society that runs on a ceaseless barrage of hormonal stimulation.

Into this mess comes Reuben Flagg, a nice Jewish actor who once starred as a Plexus Ranger on video and is now, through a universal confusion of image and substance (and where would a satirist get an idea like that in Reagan's America?) pressed into actual service with the force. Flagg is Chaykin as much as Sable is Grell: smart, caustic, "basically well intentioned but easily seduced," as Chaykin once described either himself or his hero. He can expound

like an old Leftie on the betrayal of the American dream ("The American spirit—the honest, openhanded driving force of solidarity—has been castrated . . . by slimy fat cats who use patriotism like a tart uses cheap perfume") and then tumble into the sack with a fascistic German dominatrix. The sense of liberation was explosive as Chaykin, after decades of Jewish comic book creators doing *goyishe* heroes, allowed his Russian Jewish left wing New York world view to run loose. The bad guys' names were nasty German puns ("Scheisskopf"), the mayor of Chicago and Flagg's boss was an unctious machine politician, a perpetually grinning black man with a German surname and an out-of-control, violence-loving daughter named Medea Blitz.

The art was wonderful. Still some of that Kane dynamism but no more of the fussy Adams rendering. Chaykin had always admired Alex Toth, was even able to get along with him personally, and he'd finally really integrated the Toth lessons and made them his own, knowing just where to strip down, to leave out, to hit straight at the point. His layouts were very high design, very '80s, very commercial, just right for the Plexmall world. His sound effects lettering was ingenious, even beyond his friend Simonson's (and the effects themselves were worth reading, like the guns that go "pop-a-oo-mow-mow"). What reached into his fans' chests and ripped out their hearts, though, was his sexual iconography. No cute Byrne babes or spandex supersuits for him—his women were grown up, a little rotten, a little vicious, a little ugly, and all decked out in teddies, garter belts, and spike heels. Everything in Flagg's world was fetishistic—sex, violence, even politics—but with none of the clunkiness or naiveté of the true fetishist. Chaykin was too damn clever, too on to himself for that. "I put something behind my ears that drives men wild." "What's that?" "My legs."

He was a satirist, a smut monger, almost an intellectual, but he was also just having fun. In the first issue, with no explanation at all, a cat named Raul begins to talk. He talks well, too, becomes a voice of sardonic reason and a crucial character. Soon comes

Design as satire. The verbal and visual wit of Howard Chaykin were one. (*American Flagg!* #1.)

shape through crowded panels, compulsive word-play, sly background detail, and impossible plots. "The Superjew from the future," Chaykin was heard to call himself—or was it Flagg he called that?—and here he played the whole role: outsider, assimilator, entertainer, radical, rag-seller, scholar, money-changer, and seducer of innocent gentiles.

Once thing for sure, he could sell a comic book. Within days after hitting the stores, *Flagg* was being talked up by every fan with half a brain. It was the first huge hit of the independent movement, and was quickly outselling several Marvel and DC series, despite having no newsstand distribution, no big company label, and no market with kids. With Sable, Flagg, and more on the way, First looked like it was making a bid to turn the Big Two into the Big Three.

First took a chance on its next launch: *Mars*, by a couple of unknowns named Marc Hempel and Mark Wheatley (Jan. 1984), a journey through a hallucinatory world, the storytelling eerily ambiguous, the art stylishly cartooned. It didn't sell well. Nor did *The P.I.s*, in which Ms. Tree teamed up with Joe Staton's parodic detective, Michael Mauser (and Staton teamed up with Collins and Beatty). First would never be so daring again.

Grimjack was spun off from *Starslayer* after proving it could bring the young male fans in. It was a great high concept: a hardboiled troubleshooter in a place called Cynosure that crosses dimensional barriers, a hyped up metaphor for a ghettoized American city. The writer, John Ostrander, was a friend of Mike Gold's, a Chicagoan, who knew the archetypal ghettoized city all too well. He had a lean, macho, tough-guy style that owed about equal parts to *Jonah Hex*, *Mad Max*, Sam Peckinpah, and Mike Baron. The quintessential Ostrander scene—whether he ever actually wrote it or not—was the tired hero, elbows on the bar, drink nearly to his lips, the stranger saying something nasty, the hero flattening him with a wisecrack, and all hell breaking loose. Ostrander even wrote a backup strip, *Munden's Bar*, set in the rowdy saloon that Grimjack owns in the sleaziest quarter of Cynosure. He did fast plots with predictable beats,

the ultimate Ranger, Luther Ironheart, the embodiment of purity and innocence; except, of course, he's a robot with a cartoon face, a naïf and an incompetent. Flagg and his mechanical and animal friends fought a never ending battle for . . . well, that was hard to say, because Chaykin's plots didn't make much sense, so complex, cropped-close and full of digressions as they were. Which was fine. Coherent narrative would only have diminished the chaos and agitation of his America, and would have told a lie about the postliterate world. It was hard even to say who Flagg was, because the central character of *American Flagg!* was the society itself, and it took

tightly turned tough guy lines and colorful violence. It was all drawn, and well, by Tim Truman, another tough guy stylist but with less of the urban barfly than the backwoods survivalist. He was good with big guns, battered vehicles and shabby neighborhoods, but even better with Grimjack, the meanest, shaggiest, most self-contained antihero on the stands.

It was comfortable stuff for American guys, the cowboy icon transferred to a multiethnic modern city without the reality of modern cities to make it all spooky and ambivalent, the way '70s culture had done. It was *G.I. Joe* for eighteen-year-olds. The style was catching on: a little after *Grimjack* debuted, a movie called *48 Hours* made a producer named Joel Silver into a major Hollywood player by pitting a bitter white cowboy-cop and an amusing embodiment of the new urban America against characterless bad guys in two hours of destructive action through a fantasy San Francisco. It was a comic book movie, Silver was a comic book reader, *Grimjack* was a comic book comic. That same summer, James Cameron, another comic book reader, clinched his spot as The Action Director with *Terminator*: cartoony muscleman, terse catch phrase ("I'll be back"). "See ya at Munden's" became a catch phrase and a letters page sign-off for the fraternity of fans who were tired of art and ambition and just wanted their junk culture junky.

The direct market just seemed to keep paying and paying and paying. More comics and more publishers were popping up, but few were like Eclipse or Aardvark-Vanaheim. Comico, a company that had come out of nowhere with *Primer*, suddenly unleashed three regular color comics, and all three were all slick and commercial: *Evangeline*, by Judith Hunt and another tough-guy writer named Chuck Dixon, about a killer nun in a hostile future; a superhero team, *The Elementals*, by an artist who looked like he should already be working for Marvel, Bill Willingham; and the best of them, *Mage*, by Matt Wagner, who didn't have a lot of content to share yet but taught everyone some new tricks about pacing and sucking the reader into the suspense.

There was a new Canadian company, Vortex. It dropped a huge chunk of money on the slickest comic book ever seen, *Mister X*. Dean Motter and Paul Rivoche, a couple of graphic designers intrigued by the death of modernism and the apocalyptic social visions of hip young urbanites, conceived of a model city gone wrong, haunted by its amphetamine-buzzing, guilt-ridden designer. They went for the postmodern contingent by hiring the Hernandez brothers to execute it, and it did make a wonderful piece of cerebral paranoia—but it was also commercial Hip, more package than substance. Los Bros got screwed on the deal, too. They took it as a betrayal of the whole spirit of the independent press and never again left Fantagraphics.

More publishers: there was Bill Black, an old time superhero fan, with his Americomics line. There was Megaton Publications, bringing out heroes from a Marvel name, Butch Guice, and a new kid who obviously wanted to be a Marvel name, Erik Larsen. There was Mirage, with a fanboyish Frank Miller parody. There was Spectrum, Just Imagine, The Guild, Southstar, Chance Enterprises and more, most of them doing superheroes or things very much like them, most of them vapid and visibly yearning for Marvel or DC to notice them. Then came the word that Continuity Comics, Neal Adams' studio, was about to release a line of its own slickly-produced commercial series. All that on top of Capital, Aardvark-Vanaheim, Fantagraphics, and the booming Eclipse and Pacific. Underground publishers were starting to pick up. Denis Kitchen had dropped *The Spirit* magazine in favor of an upscale *Will Eisner Quarterly* and a Baxter-paper, offset-color *Spirit* comic book; he'd collected *Life on Another Planet* into a full color hardbound book called *Signal From Space* and was planning more Eisner books. Now he was talking about new Kitchen Sink comics with a more mainstream orientation. Even foreigners were getting into it: Catalan was translating its European albums, Japanese comics were starting to be imported (especially after Frederik L. Schodt's new book, *Manga! Manga!*, made them sound so exciting), *Judge Dredd*, *Warrior*, and *2000 A.D.* were invading from England, and now Eclipse was arranging to reprint British superhero series like *Axel Pressbutton*. And piled on top of all of it, the vast and expensive new products of Marvel and DC. How could a direct market that had been almost invisible only five years before possibly support all this?

It couldn't.

Retailers bought and bought until their stores were choked with unsellable small press junk. They had money sunk in that junk, and money sunk in copies of *Ronin* that were just sitting in the back room, in issues of *Camelot 3000* that hadn't even been drawn by Brian Bolland yet, in Epic comics and Marvel Graphic Novels that weren't flying off the shelves like they expected. Now Marvel was pouring out its overpriced reprints, on Baxter paper and with slick new covers, the kind of thing a Marvelite might think he just had to have. And now the killing blow: *Secret Wars*.

Mattel Toys had cut a deal with Marvel for action figures and wanted a comic book to help push them. The title, *Marvel Super Heroes Secret Wars*, and the concept, all the heroes in one big story, came from Mattel. Shooter and crew decided on a twelve-issue maxiseries with art by Mike Zeck, the best of the slick superhero artists who wasn't already on a valuable property, and inks by John Beatty, one of the very sleek, clean new guys. The scripting, allegedly, was assigned to one of Marvel's regular writers until Shooter discovered something: one copy of *Secret Wars* was going to be bundled in every plastic-bagged "sampler" for sale in toy stores, guaranteeing sales of at least a few hundred thousand copies. In any case, Shooter was the writer, and the twelve issues all together sold about eight million copies. That was a lot of incentive for an editor-in-chief.

Marvel hyped *Secret Wars* to the direct market for months, and much of the hype suggested that it would be a major continuity event. One great gimmick made every Marvelite feel he or she *had* to pick it up. In every major superhero series—*X-Men*, *FF*, *Thor*, *Avengers*, all of them—the issue on sale right before *Secret Wars* number 1 would show the hero or

heroes suddenly vanishing into thin air, the story to be carried on by supporting characters. As annoying as the interruption was, how could you not want to know what happened to them? As it turned out, they were only whisked into outer space and put through some pointless battles by the poorly-named Beyonder, then returned to the place and time from which they were whisked (*MSSW* 1-12, May 1984-Apr. 1985). One died (the nearly forgotten Wasp) and a new one joined (a new Spider-Woman, of no consequence). The biggest change was that Spider-Man's costume changed to an all-black ninja look, which helped launch a third title about the character, *Web of Spider-Man* (Apr. 1984). And readers had known about that from the start. It was all very efficiently done, with Shooter's well-tooled character bits and Zeck doing that Byrne-plus-Buscema look that he used when he knew he was selling to hardcore Marvelites. No one could really love it or hate it.

Except independent publishers. The crunch might have happened without *Secret Wars*, but it was the final money-sucker that left profligate retailers dry. They cut their orders for everything else, starting with the independents, and still hundreds of them failed to pay their distributors. Distributors then failed to pay publishers. Capital immediately stopped publishing its comics. The Schanes brothers had grossly overextended themselves with Pacific, renting a huge office space and hiring extra staff and pumping out new comics when things were going well. Now they folded, and left a lot of creators waiting for their checks. Other publishers survived, but they'd have to start thinking more commercially. The comic shops and the independents, it seemed, had to learn for themselves the same lessons about booms, gluts and busts that the undergrounders had learned a decade before.

Some in the independent press, including Cat Yronwode and Dean Mullaney, accused Marvel of trying to flood the market intentionally by pumping out all its overpriced reprints. Shooter responded that "I'm doing my job, which is making money for my company," and that the little guys had better wake up to the fact that this was a competitive business, not a commune.

The guys at First understood it, and prospered while others were panicking. Within the next year First picked up *Nexus*, *Badger*, and *Whisper*, and got a solid, long-running success out of the first. Chaykin, suddenly the hottest thing in the direct market, signed a deal with DC to revive his favorite old pulp character, the Shadow, and left the running of *American Flagg!* to other writers and artists. Steven Grant of *Whisper* was one of his designated heirs, and was quickly becoming a tough-guy-in-demand at Marvel and DC. Mike Baron took over writing DC's *Atari Force*, making it faster and funnier, and started getting offers for superhero work.

It seemed like all the artistic adventurers were suddenly thinking more commercially. Frank Miller took some time to review where he stood, what it might mean to follow a superhero success with an artistic adventure that the kids didn't buy, and then announced his three new projects: writing and drawing a Batman miniseries for DC, and writing an Elektra maxiseries and an "arc" of *Daredevil* issues for Marvel. He obviously wasn't going to risk becoming a low-income cult favorite.

Eclipse picked up some of Pacific's titles, tried to carry on the commercially successful horror and science fiction anthologies, even after Bruce Jones eased himself out of comics. Yronwode and Mullaney picked up *The Rocketeer*, collected it into a beautiful graphic album with a Harlan Ellison foreword, then got the rights to *Airboy*, a '40s aviation adventure that they hoped would appeal to the same crowd. They began shifting more toward book publishing, a steadier field that could take them outside the insecure comic shop market: *Will Eisner's Comics and Sequential Art,* immediately hailed as the Bible for all serious comics artists and writers, and *Women and the Comics* by Trina Robbins and Cat Yronwode herself, an exciting job of exhuming a buried history. They seemed, in fact, to be responding to the stresses of the present by going deeper into the past, bringing out slick reprints of obscure old comics in a sort of old-

hippie rejoinder to Marvel's crassness. Eclipse's most adventurous new series was Michael T. Gilbert's *Mr. Monster*, a tribute to pre-Code comics.

Eclipse did continue going out on a limb for female writers and artists, mostly in its anthology comics, including Trina, Lee Marrs, Shary Flenniken, Sue Cavey, and April Campbell. Wendi Lee, Sandy Saidak, Elaine Lee, and Christy Marx wrote historical adventures for them, the last two slickly enough that they were soon being lured away by Marvel. Most of Eclipse's first wave was canceled, however, including even *Zot!*. The world of Zot would return, it was promised, in a cheaper and more adventurous black-and-white line, spearheaded by McCloud. That line's first acquisition was *Tales of the Beanworld*, into which a successful Chicago advertising maven, Larry Marder, chopped and stirred tribal art, ecological philosophy, Marcel Duchamp, and plain goofiness. He became an instant standard-bearer of the alternative set, but he wasn't quitting his day job. In fact, he was very clear that he viewed his day job as a way of supporting his art, "the work that future generations will judge me by."

For their color comics, Cat and Dean hired editors more in tune with the mainstream: Sean Deming, who created a house-owned superhero team for them, *The New Wave*, and James D. Hudnall, a computer programmer and comics fan who started negotiating with Shoghukan, the giant of Japanese comics, to publish translations of action-adventure *manga*. Tim Truman left *Grimjack* to do *Scout* for them, the kind of lone tough-guy stuff they'd shown no interest in before. Through Scott McCloud they came to know Kurt Busiek, and published his superhero team, *The Liberty Project*. It had some unusual characters—a speedster who can't stop moving or he'll die and a heroine who loves him but will never be able to hold him—but the style, like the art by James Fry, was solid mainstream stuff.

Comico had been commercially minded from the start, but now it shored itself up by acquiring the rights to *Robotech*, a Japanese cartoon, and to *Gumby* and *Jonny Quest*, two favorite cartoon shows of the baby boom, eternally returning to life through reruns. The writer of the latter was Bill Loebs, who was having trouble keeping his humorous historical adventure *Journey* afloat. He proved to have a touch for whimsical action stories, generally pleasing the *Journey* fans who were worried that the mainstream would steal their Bill. Loebs had piled up some debts in the course of telling his tall tales about Wolverine MacAlistaire, however, and that sleek color mainstream was starting to look awfully seductive.

Dave Sim and his wife Deni were trimming the Aardvark-Vanaheim line, letting *Journey* go to Fantagraphics. Dave was doing well with *Cerebus*, finding a steady market in reprints of the early issues, but found he wasn't comfortable with the publisher's role, believing "it is the creator's obligation to make his own book work, to stay in touch with everybody, to do his own promotion." Deni liked the role, however, and this was one of many disputes developing between them, and not just about business. Others were following them into black-and-white publishing, like fellow Canadian Derek McCullough with his Strawberry Jam, but seemed to be perpetually hanging by a thread.

Denis Kitchen, meanwhile, was expanding Kitchen Sink's line, but not just with Will Eisner books and undergrounds. *Megaton Man*, by a raw but powerful cartoonist named Don Simpson, was a loud and bizarre parody of superheroes. It owed a bit of its look and tone to Gilbert Shelton's *Wonder Wart-Hog*, but it wasn't so underground in either style or sensibility. Simpson clearly had a background in fandom, although he was too disgusted by the superhero mainstream to want to get into it except on its own terms. Megaton Man wasn't a one-joke destruction of superheroes like the Wart-Hog of Steel but an ongoing character whom older superhero fans could find rather lovable.

The key to success in the failing independent market was discovered by Kevin Eastman and Peter Laird, a couple of reasonably capable, if not terribly original, fan artists who wanted to honor Frank Miller in the same way Dave Sim had Barry Smith. They didn't ape Miller's style as well as Sim had Smith's, they didn't build anything as clever on top of the parody as Sim had, but when their fellow Miller fans saw their homemade comic, they got the point. A first printing of 3,000 copies sold out. Fans and retailers were spreading the word: this thing was pretty fun, and with no Frank Miller on the stands it soothed the itch. A few months later, a second printing of 15,000 copies sold out. Now the word getting out was that this could be the next *Cerebus*, and since *Cerebus* 1 was selling for up to three hundred dollars, how could you not buy it? In early 1985 they came out with a third printing, 36,000 copies, probably more by itself than any independent to date. It sold out. They prepared a fourth printing of 50,000 copies. Over 100,000 copies of a black-and-white thing called *Teenage Mutant Ninja Turtles*. At a dollar-fifty a pop, the publisher's forty per cent going to the creators, you didn't even have to do the math to know that these kids were getting rich.

The direct market hadn't proven that it was good for supporting revolutionary art, not even ambitious ninja comics by Frank Miller, but it was great for creating collectibles.

One independent publisher stuck to his guns. Gary Groth, image conscious and contrary as ever, paid some bills with *The X-Men Companion*, but he also tackled some truly ambitious projects: Rick Marschall's *Nemo* magazine, devoted to newspaper comics of the past; a series of books reprinting two of the greatest newspaper strips in full, E.C. Segar's *Popeye* and Hal Foster's *Prince Valiant*; *The Ditko Collection*, devoted to all those *Mr. A* stories with politics so opposite to Groth's own. Groth kept *Journey* going as long as he could, despite Loebs' insertion of a truly wicked caricature of Groth himself, a pompous poet railing about Art and Truth in a wilderness fort. He reminded fandom that Gil Kane was a pioneer of the whole independent scene by reprinting *Savage*, and let Gil sound off in a *Comics Journal* column. He published *Honk!*, edited by his art director, Tom

Mason, devoted to humor cartoons and the study of same. He bridged the last remaining gap between different factions of comicdom, the new fandom and the old undergrounders, by publishing Jack Jackson's *Los Tejanos* and by giving a young genius of a cartoonist named Peter Bagge, editor of Robert Crumb's *Weirdo* magazine, a chance to do his own comic book. *Love and Rockets* survived the crash, broke the twenty-thousand copies barrier, spawned a set of reprint graphic albums. Groth was reeducating the whole comics field about its roots, its hinterlands, and its future.

He was also starting a war. He lived in one big house in Connecticut with his staff and assorted hangers on, a kind of boy's club, kibbutz, and bunker where self-styled rebels could keep each other's timid hearts from failing as they lobbed grenades at the mainstream. A few of them—Mason, who wanted to be a mainstream magazine cartoonist, and Dave Olbrich, the pragmatic farmboy who was now the sales manager—were more in love with comics in general than with Groth's mission, but most of them acted like they'd have given their lives to level *X-Men* and raise *American Splendor* in its place. When Gary decided it was time to move to L.A.—where more and more smart mavericks, like Chaykin and Kane, were heading—the entire household moved as one. Others in Gary's orbit, like Jan Strnad and Heidi MacDonald, moved out around the same time, adding to Evanier and Ellison and Kirby and Los Bros and still others to make L.A. the land of comic book dreams. Some of them played themselves as hip Angelenos—Groth looking quite the '80s man in polo shirt and flashy car, MacDonald discarding her Mets cap and geek look for a studied Melrose trendiness, declaring herself "the ambassador of comics" to the hipper world outside—although spouses who survived brief residences at the Fantagraphics Mansion describe a bachelor pad full of flatulence, snorting laughter, bitchy arguments, and borderline psychotics who talked to garden snails. Whatever they were, they took their sense of purpose from conflict, and Gary picked the tar-

Kevin Eastman and Peter Laird were just a couple of nice fanboys trying to get a little closer to the Great God Miller by spoofing Ronin. Little did they dream.... (*Teenage Mutant Ninja Turtles* #1, 1984.)

© 1984 Kevin Eastman and Peter Laird

gets. He'd been railing at crass comics for a long time, but attacking old guys like Don Heck hadn't really made the point he wanted. He liked fights, liked getting personal, liked specific objects to crystallize his righteous fury. He found that object, his personal symbol of everything fascistic and capitalistic in '80s America, in Jim Shooter.

They were made for each other: Shooter huge, dark, scarred by ancient acne, Groth slight, light and boyish; Shooter cold, deliberate, expecting the crowds to part for him, Groth watchful, as if always ready to throw—or dodge—a sudden punch; Shooter the walking corporation and Groth the guerrilla. To Groth, Shooter represented Marvel fighting Gerber, flooding the market, wasting its creator-owned line on *Star Wars* rip-offs and, maybe worst of all, outselling everybody so hugely with "adolescent trash." Groth had come to

279

hate superheroes now, not just bad superheroes but all of them. He'd outgrown them, and there's nothing the perpetual sophomore feels more contempt for than the passions of his freshman days. The ugly truth, however, was that without superheroes, without Marvel superheroes in particular, the independent market would vanish in an instant and Groth and all his colleagues would be working on doing paste-up at ad agencies. Nothing eats at your guts like depending on someone you hate. So Gary struck out, in editorials and articles in nearly every issue of the *Journal*. And Shooter rose to the bait. He made snide remarks about "fanzines." He came out in support of Michael Fleisher's lawsuit, made himself available to testify against Ellison and

Groth. He was said to be getting harder to deal with around the office.

Most of Fantagraphics' allies just shook their heads and smiled at Gary's humorless, adjective-clotted attacks on those "odious" superheroes (after all, most of them were dying to see what Frank Miller did with Batman). When it came to villifying Shooter, though, they found it easy to go along. Anyone who'd loved the chaos of the '70s that had allowed *Howard the Duck* or *Warlock* to happen could see Shooter as the Man Who Ruined Marvel, and it was easy to separate the Shooter who'd encouraged Frank Miller from the one who'd later lost him. They needed more than Gary's shrill editorials to stir up their anger, though. They needed Jack Kirby.

CHAPTER 39

COMICS GET HIP

Looking at Jerry Bails and Roy Thomas and the other officers of the Academy of Comic Book Arts and Sciences in 1965, one would probably never have called them a crazy bunch of swingers. Looking at Marv Wolfman and Len Wein on a convention panel in 1975, one might have thought they were mellow enough, but not the first dudes one would want to get down with. Looking at the comic book groups in an East Village bar or a Covent Garden pub or a West Hollywood beanery in 1985, on the other hand, one might almost—*almost*—have thought they were downright cool.

It had all happened so quickly, in such profusion—how could they not think they were the vanguard of an artform about to sweep the world? In 1979 comics had little to offer anyone but the most desperate superhero junkie, and the few good things had been hell to find. Then came Phoenix and *Titans*, then Frank Miller and the "new DC" and *Captain Victory*, and suddenly in 1982 it was exploding. Every month seemed to bring a new company or a new line, a new talent or another giant returning to the fold, a new format or a whole new kind of comic book. A fan could drop a fortune on *Love and Rockets*, *Flagg!*, *Thor*, *Zot!*, *Legion*, *Will Eisner Quarterly*, and dozens more—and a lot of them, Gary Groth and Jim Shooter aside, were doing it. Fans of every stripe were finding their ways from superheroes to the independents to the new undergrounds, from undergrounds to the independents to the new superheroes. Being a serious comics person meant being eclectic, and the kids who thought Marvel was the only cool game in town were branded with a nasty nickname: Marvel Zombies.

The great cosmopolitan comics conventions—like the San Diego Con, now the annual must-do of the business, drawing as many as 15,000 fans and nearly every creator in North America for four days and nights of nonstop shop talk—were like one huge community, like a mobile Brigadoon than vanished in one place and appeared in another with all the same people, all the same conversations picking up as if they'd never been interrupted. The business was growing, but it was still possible to know every editor, creator and critic who worked in it, and some people did. There were squabbles and heartbreaks and nasty gossip, but they felt like the stuff of high school. You always knew that the next day you'd see all the same people again, and probably be friends with most of them. *The Comics Journal* had become a forum for endless overwritten editorials and letters quibbling viciously over comics as if the world was at stake.[1] Crusty undergrounders, cadaverous punklings, stud superartists, square Superman fans, mutant-lovers, cheesecake artists, angry feminists, sneering *Comics Journal* reviewers—if they were in comics, they were part of the same world, and the relationships they forged in that world were the most real of their lives.

The "real world" didn't notice. Despite series of Superman and Conan movies, and Stan Lee's Marvel Productions getting *Spider-Man, Hulk, G.I. Joe* and other cartoons on the air, mass-media interest in comics had stalled. Roy Thomas and Gerry Conway had scripted a cartoon movie, *Fire and Ice*, but that didn't open many doors. Conway would gradually go on to be a TV writer, but Roy stayed with comics. Even after *Swamp Thing* did pretty

[1] And many of those letter writers, upon discovering their own overwrought epistles in the yellowing pages of the *Journal* a decade later, feel the same fond embarrassment that they would upon reading their inscriptions in a friend's high school yearbook.

well, Michael Uslan and Benjamin Melniker were unable to get a Batman movie going. Jenette Kahn hired Steve Englehart to write some treatments just to try to get it moving, but no one bit. Uslan and Melniker unloaded the rights on producer Peter Guber, who took it to Warner Bros. in an effort to do *Superman* redux. Tom Mankiewicz wrote a script and Ivan Reitman agreed to direct, but no one could find a workable angle. A then-young screenwriter and comics fan named Sam Hamm said that the old *Batman* TV show "really poisoned Hollywood's perception of the property; the studio zeitgeist watchers never even noticed all those alienated college kids with nose-rings parading up and down Melrose Ave in their black Bat-signal T-shirts."

Funny to think that there was a time in Hollywood when an association with an old TV show that baby boomers loved as kids but mocked as adults was a reason *not* to make a movie. The people controlling the money in Hollywood persisted in seeing alienated young people as angry and earnest, and didn't understand the intersection of late-punk and new-wave irony with the visceral kicks of junk culture. The next generation, though—the overeducated but mass-market minded Hamm, the ex-Disney cartoonist Tim Burton, who was translating Pee Wee Herman to the big screen, the rising Warner executive Bonni Lee, who was mentoring them both—did understand it, and knew they had an audience for it.

When other media did notice comics, it wasn't cause for celebration. Culture critic Benjamin DeMott took a pretty good look at *American Flagg!* and other hot comics for an article in *Psychology Today* and concluded that they were literature for losers, the community college crowd, bright under-achievers who took solace in cynicism. It provoked the outrage of fandom, became a subject of fierce discussion among elite fans as they counted out their cash register drawers and hurried for the bus to get to class. The article drew an indignant letter from a couple of writers named Will Jacobs and Gerard Jones, who were hoping to get their new book noticed. They were of that '80s breed, widely educated in a dilet-

tantish way, equally fascinated by art and junk but having trouble taking either seriously, desperate to be novelists but killing time with a satire of TV sitcoms. When *The Beaver Papers* sold, they cast around for another book to pitch and came up with a history of the silver age comics they'd been such huge fans of in their childhoods. Now they were getting excited about the new comics, and saw it as their mission in *The Comic Book Heroes* to make the world aware of the glories hidden in the comic shops. The current scene was overwhelming even to them: "It must remain for future historians to pick out all the patterns, all the causes and effects, that are even now molding comics into unforeseen new forms."

Well, here we are. And even from a decade's distance, it still seems like one of the most baffling, most exciting, most unpredictable, most productive three or four years in the history of any medium.

The ambassadors of comics to the hipper world would turn out not to be Heidi MacDonald in her lime-green bicycle shorts and purple Converses, but those eternal coolifiers of American youth culture, the British. Alan Moore was a towering, shaggy, charismatic cartoonist and rock singer who'd grown up on American superheroes and on Marvelman, England's vapid imitation of the original Captain Marvel. He'd come of age in the gender-bending, anarcho-nihilist youth culture of the British '70s. He was effusively warm, but even when he was just chatting about the weather, his eyes seemed to be boring into you, peeling aside skin and muscle, following the pulsing loop of your arteries or riffling the mucusy crevices of your brain. He loved to play with the implications of narrative structures and the after-effects of words, and his head seemed to fill up with electrically detailed vistas that demanded transliteration. There was no better receptacle for his imaginings than comic books, although he continued to move in the more creative circles of London music. He was a living conduit, in fact, from one world to the other: he recommended *Love and Rockets* to some members of the rock group Bauhaus, and when they broke off to form their own band, they stole the name.

Moore quickly became the star of *Warrior* and *2000 A.D.*, nailing the nightmares of young English readers with the paranoid urban suspense of *V for Vendetta* and his horrific revelations of the implications of superhuman power in his reworked *Marvelman*. American comics writers had never attempted such a prolonged and profound plunge into the darkness at the bottom of childhood fantasies, the understanding that the dream of power exists only against a reality of powerlessness, that the gift of fictional order is most precious in lives of chaos. The American comics market was big and built on formula, that was part of it. But Americans were still craving a strong, simple man to lead them out of confusion and doubt, and had even found an actor to cast as Mr. President. In England, the image of male heroism was more past its prime: a motherly sovereign had been joined by a motherly prime minister, who promised a return to the glories of the mother of all sovereigns a century before. There the Imperial Self was a source of mingled shame and nostalgia.

Len Wein read Moore's stories and recognized "a brilliant writer." Wein knew that power fantasies were about alienation and anger, although he'd never ventured all the way down into that knowledge, even with Swamp Thing or Wolverine. He needed a writer for *Saga of the Swamp Thing* now, as Marty Pasko headed off for TV work, and figured that with the wonders of FedEx, he could work with a writer in London. Would Moore be interested in writing for DC and perhaps playing with the potent foreign icons of his childhood? Indeed, there were no limits to the amount of playing he wanted to do.

For the first issue of *The Atom* in 1963, Gardner Fox had created Jason Woodrue, a villain obsessed with plants, one of Fox's countless characters based on index-carded facts. The story was typically light, but Gil Kane's cover showed a desperate Atom being devoured by a Venus flytrap as Woodrue grins in evil, eye-popping glee. To a little kid it could be a horrific image—and, indeed, twenty years later, Moore made Woodrue a morbidly flesh-hating, self-hating misan-

thrope, burning for communion with the ever-renewing, all-devouring world of vegetation. Moore's Woodrue helps dissect the Swamp Thing, and exposes the truth that the hero has long denied to himself: he is not scientist Alec Holland, transformed into a plant, but a *plant,* given sentience by the chemicals that killed Holland and erroneously believing himself—no, *itself*—to be the scientist. The Swamp Thing rages against the truth, murders one of his captors in his rage, as Woodrue coolly narrates from a safe remove, imagining the bloodshed that he knows must come. The narration and the visuals interlace

The demented gentlemen with leaves and wine glass is Jason Woodrue, an old Gardner Fox villain, significantly reconsidered by Stephen Bissette and John Totleben. The visual imagery of the script and the rhythmic interplay of words and pictures is the mark of Alan Moore. (*Saga Of The Swamp Thing* #21, Feb. 1984.)

283

like creepers as a relentless summer rain pounds the windows and the hero kills the villain whose crime was revealing the reality beneath the lie of comic book fantasy (*SST* 21, Feb. 1984).

The story was called "The Anatomy Lesson," and it had all the genuine creepiness of the Rembrandt painting after which it was named. After decades of comic book horror about the explicit and external, about the human body threatened by the *other*, this was a subtler and more modern horror: the threat here was from the implicit made explicit, the body exposed in all its primordial nastiness and inconstancy to a "rational" mind that bases its shaky stability on illusions of self, separation, and permanence. In seventeenth century Holland, at the birth of "modern reason" and the bourgeois redefinition of self and body, the paradigmatic image was Rembrandt's doctor holding aloft a slimy heart with pedagogical detachment. In the 1980s—amid postindustrial reconsiderations of the body, ecologically-based philosophies of humanity and nature, feminist critiques of gender constructs, and the dawn of AIDS consciousness—the new image was of the same doctor holding aloft his own heart, discovering a plant-tuber, and howling in horror.

That one story was a startling achievement, but Moore's Swamp Thing was only beginning a monthly journey of philosophy and psychological horror, shambling through the dark undersides of the modern world, of the DC universe, and of his own soul. Ultimately it was a heroic story, as the Swamp Thing came to recognize and affirm his place within the world of "the green." He would attend a Council of Trees, unleash a plague of plants upon mankind to send a warning about out despoilation of the earth, and become the world's great hope for bridging the artificial gap between "man" and "nature." *Swamp Thing* used the trappings of the horror genre and the form of a nineteenth Century "philosophical romance," but it gradually unfolded as a superhero story of surprising optimism. Moore did it all with pungent dialogue, lyrical captions, a sense of the swamp not just as setting but as American metaphor,

and a great imagination for original stories. No one could remember a time that a writer, just a writer, had had such an instant impact in comics. Stan Lee, Denny O'Neil, even Roy Thomas, had taken a while to build up heat, but while "The Anatomy Lesson" was still on the shelves, fans were shoving it into each other's hands and saying, "Read this."

Moore wasn't the only reason—artists Steve Bissette and John Totleben were both superb at realizing his visions and were active collaborators in the creation—but he was the difference. He was no Marvel Method plotter like Chris Claremont who needed an artist to give him structure and visual sense. DC staffers would pass his massive scripts around the office and mail them to favorite freelancers so they could all read Moore's two-page descriptions of single panels, with the visuals pouring out in a torrent of unedited, compulsive verbiage, down to the color of the lizard on the rock in the background. Most writers gave their artists a narrative box to fill up with the necessary detail. Moore gave his a block of granite, more visual information than could possibly fit into a panel, for them to hack at like Michelangelo until the story within was set free.

The effect was hypnotic, like some narcotic poem of Coleridge or Baudelaire, but it wasn't in the words. Critics always quote Moore to try to prove his eloquence, and certainly he wrote some artful lines. When the Justice League guest-starred, they and their orbiting headquarters were described with images full of the terror of an ancient contemplating his gods, images that made longtime fans' heads explode: "There is a house above the world where the over-people gather. There is a man with wings like a bird...there is a man who can see across the planet and wring diamonds from its anthracite. There is a man who moves so fast that his life is an endless gallery of statues.... In the house above the world the over-people gather...and sit...and listen...." (*SST* 24, May 1984). But Moore's writing was like the alternative-rock songs with which it shared a worldview, with those lyrics that sounded profound until you read them on the liner notes. His vision was as organic as the Swamp Thing, as symbiotic as the Louisiana bayou from which his hero grows and into which he decays. Moore has said that when he writes, he'll adopt the body language of his characters, shambling and striding around the room, to bring their minds into his own. Reproducing a page can show the compelling counterbalance of words and pictures that was Moore's art, but even that doesn't capture it. It was the rhythms of his whole stories that made them live. When the Swamp Thing revealed his true nature to his human lover, Abigail, she ate fruit that sprouted from his body. The moment was spooky, revolting, sexy, and poignant at once.

Swamp Thing wouldn't come close to rivaling X-Men or even Teen Titans in sales, would never have optimistic collectors buying five copies of every issue. Nor was it much use in pulling new readers into comics, because the subtext of Moore's stories and his narrative vocabulary were so much *about* the medium and directed at readers already overly fluent in its esoteric language. But it did seem to have every adult and precocious teen in comicdom picking it up, even most of the nonsuperhero crowd, and that was enough to make Moore a hot commodity. He and Brian Bolland were offered a Batman graphic novel, and he and Dave Gibbons were given DC's newest acquisition, the old Charlton characters. Fans could dream, but barely imagine, what Alan Moore would do with Captain Atom, the Question, and Blue Beetle. They knew it would have to be astounding after Eclipse started reprinting his *Marvelman* (under the less legally thorny title *Miracleman*). It was such a shocking exposure of the superhero as a god without wisdom that Mark Waid, reviewing it for the fan press, said that 1985 would be remembered as "the summer of *Miracleman*."

Wein's hiring of Moore was perfect timing for DC, allowing heat to build toward 1985. That was the company's birthday, fifty years since Major Malcolm Wheeler-Nicholson had written his first bad check, and Dick Giordano was calling it "a critical year." "The key word to DC's direction," he said, "is diversity. Diversity of format, of genre, and of style." He

announced plans for a humor line, beginning with the return of Sheldon Mayer's *Sugar and Spike*. He said he wanted to pursue mystery readers and women with detective stories, sophisticated romances, and humor with a female slant, all to be marketed through bookstores. Giordano thought that comic books were poised to break through into the wide-open spaces of adult mainstream entertainment, and that DC had the resources to make it happen. He assigned Sal Amendola, one of his old Charlton artists, to launch a highly touted talent search, with *New Talent Showcase* to publish its discoveries. And he announced a maxiseries called *Crisis on Infinite Earths*, which was going to revitalize the entire DC mainstream.

A new editorial crew had been coming into place. Mike Gold was hired away from First Comics to develop new material. Mike Carlin had been hired after Shooter fired him, and immediately showed a pragmatic eye and inexhaustible energy for straight-ahead superhero adventures. A bigger coup was luring Denny O'Neil back from the increasingly tense atmosphere of Marvel to take over the Batman line. Bob Greenberger, creator of *Comics Scene*, an effort at a slick, newstand magazine about comics, was hired to police schedules and continuity. Joe Orlando was turning production over to Bob Rozakis and his crew, becoming a vice president for special projects to help Giordano achieve his diversity. A graphic designer named Neal Pozner was hired to jazz up the design department. He was joined, after Capital Comics' collapse, by Richard Bruning. With additional help from Dean Motter, of *Mr. X*, DC was suddenly the most graphically sleek and daring publisher in the field. Although it still used the old printing presses at World Color Press in Sparta, Illinois, for its standard product, its fancy new direct-only comics were done by Ronald's Printing, a quality-minded Canadian company. Much of DC's color separating, traditionally grunt work, was now sent to Murphy Anderson, who ran his own art firm. The packaging of high-end comics was starting to rival that of the slickest magazines and trade paperbacks, looking

2 Giffen even swiped panels at random from the great Argentine cartoonist Carlos Muñoz, who was known only to the most cosmopolitan fans. The *Comics Journal* crowd, always missing the joke, screamed as if Giffen had stolen the bread from Muñoz's mouth, but Giffen just laughed it off and Muñoz discovered he suddenly he had a large and very curious American audience.

better than anyone had ever dreamed comics would.

The embodiment of the new DC, and the new comics subculture, came in a Rasputin beard and a bundle of cultivated eccentricity named Andy Helfer. He'd plant himself at his desk and survey his office—usually overcrowded with loitering freelancers—listening to rap or world-beat or punk rock, tossing out plot ideas, joking, digressing, and rewriting dialogue on already-lettered pages. Sometimes all at once. He was the axis of a group of highstrung creators, too smart for the work they were doing, needing to blow off their frustration in cutting humor. A new generation of bravura artists was trying to break into comics, kids who'd been inspired by Frank Miller and Howard Chaykin to push their work beyond superheroes, but in the age of John Byrne and George Pérez they were having trouble getting noticed. Mark Badger—a Cleveland boy who'd fallen in love with Barry Smith's *Conan*, gone to art school to learn to draw comic books and had the misfortune to discover the glories of Klee and Rothko and DeKooning, permanently ruining him for superhero work—found a rejuvenating intellectuality in Helfer. Mike Mignola, a Bay Area kid with a passion for the sensual mood and anatomy of Al Williamson and Burne Hogarth but a frenzied need for plastic toys and junk culture, took reassurance from Helfer's own schizoid tastes.

Most of the Helfer gang, though, were Jewish and urban, sardonically conscious of their roots, and of the roots of their medium in the crass mercantilism of the world from which their parents came. Helfer had a Freudian view of the material—"I think most of the people who are into this stuff have problems with their fathers"—and used it cleverly in his plots, although he rarely revealed anything about his own upbringing. A few conversations with the others in his circle would support the analysis, though. Josef Rubenstein was one of the sleekest inkers in the field, but he was an intense and cerebral exception in a specialty that usually attracts easy going sensualists. Mindy Newell was a single mom, a bundle of conflicting energies, and one of the writers Chaykin picked to succeed him on *Flagg!* (as Badger was one

of the artists). Chaykin would head for Helfer's office when in New York. He was doing *The Shadow* with him, and praised him publicly for, essentially, being too intelligent for comics. Julie Schwartz functioned as a sort of avuncular mascot, sticking his head through Helfer's door to make sure he could still fence with the young wiseasses.

Helfer's friend and favorite writer, J.M. DeMatteis, was becoming a fan favorite for his intelligent takes on Marvel superheroes. He was an adherent of the Indian spirituality of Meher Baba, but for all his meditation he had one of the most active monkey-minds in the field. His most heartfelt stories worked through agonies of human identity and purpose, and he once said that his ideal dramatic image for Batman would be the hero breaking down, curling into a fetal position, and wailing, "Why?!" This was a depth of personal exploration through superhero comics that ventured far beyond what even Roy Thomas or Steve Gerber would have contemplated, one that would have seemed impossible—or ridiculous—to Gardner Fox or John Broome.

DC had the spirit, but it didn't have the venues. With no creator-ownership contract or equivalent to Marvel's Epic imprint, there was no place to put into action the ideas that were kicked around in offices like Giordano's and Helfer's. DC's "critical year" wasn't turning out to be much. The romances never happened. The detective stories were limited to *Nathaniel Dusk*, a '30s pastiche by Don McGregor and Gene Colan in standard comic book format (Feb. 1994 and Oct. 1995). *New Talent Showcase* had nothing to show but fan-writers and fan-artists doing superheroes in the established way (Jan. 1984). *Sugar and Spike* never came back. One humor miniseries made a splash, Keith Giffen's *Ambush Bug*, but it was self-satire for comic book fans (June 1985).[2] One ongoing humor series was put out with little fanfare, *'Mazing Man* by Bob Rozakis and a wonderful cartoonist named Stephen DeStefano (Jan. 1985). Like *Ambush Bug*, and Roy Thomas's slightly earlier *Captain Carrot and His Amazing Zoo Crew*, it was a spin on superheroes, afraid to stray too far from what the comic shops were supporting. Neither series did very well, and no other humor was forthcoming. Great young talents like DeStefano had no place in comics, and he headed for animation.

Paul Levitz was looking at the bottom line, and he just didn't see any evidence that enough people who went to comic book shops were looking for anything other than superheroes. It was the superhero audience that made the direct market work, and anyone looking for humor or romance or anything else simply didn't think about comic books, or wouldn't have known where to find them if they had. DC wanted to crack the bookstore market, but bookstores didn't know what to do with comics. The only safe bet, the project DC was promoting as its big event of 1985, was *Crisis on Infinite Earths*.

The one "off" genre DC would gamble on was science fiction, figuring comic shops would buy it even if the bookstores didn't, and it had at hand the one man who'd been able to sell the stuff in comics. Julius Schwartz turned seventy in 1985. He'd lost his wife not long before, and now the comic book and science fiction communities were his life. For his birthday his coworkers surprised him with *Superman* 411, "A Tribute to Julius Schwartz." Julie himself got Alan Moore to write *Superman Annual* 11, an eerie and wistful story in which Superman dreams of his life had Krypton not exploded. Despite Moore's devilish narrative tricks, the story was a look backwards, the first one in fifteen years to tap fully into the symbolic power of the Weisinger Superman. And now Schwartz got to fulfill an old daydream: creating the *DC Science Fiction Graphic Novel* line. He picked up stories from his friends and favorites, Ray Bradbury, Harlan Ellison, Robert Bloch, Robert Silverberg, and art from the likes of Keith Giffen and Marshall Rogers. (He was no sentimental softie, though; he wasn't going to adapt anything by his friend Alfred Bester because "It's not visual enough!")

Comics fans had never much liked literary adaptations, and it seemed that hadn't changed. The SF line died after seven issues and never got deep into the bookstores. It had, however, allowed Julius Schwartz

to pull together his avocation and his vocation, to unite the two fields to which he'd given over fifty years of his life. He'd lived his three score and ten, and had to wonder if there was anything left to do.

DC gave Jack Kirby a bittersweet goodbye, as well. Kenner Toys had launched a set of action figures called the DC Super Powers Collection, and for its second wave it would use Darkseid and some of the other characters from Kirby's Fourth World. Kahn and Levitz gave Kirby a retroactive character interest contract, giving him a chunk of the income off all his DC creations, even though he'd sold all those characters to DC long before such contracts existed. He was

Jack wraps it up. Kirby's final visit to his mythological realms, synthesizing his vision of techno-violence and making an explicit—if typically enigmatic—statement about the symbols themselves. Inks by Mike Royer. (*The Hunger Dogs*, 1985.)

287

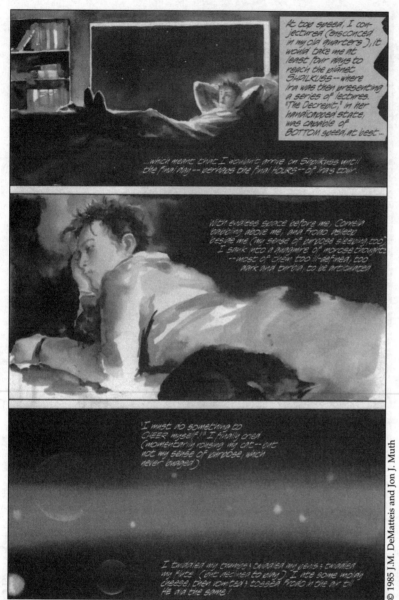

At top speed, I conjectured (ensconced in my old quarters), it would take me at least four days to reach the planet SHALKUSS—where Ira was then presenting a series of lectures. "The Decrent," in her handicapped state, was capable of BOTTOM speed, at best...

...which meant that I wouldn't arrive on Shalkuss until the final day—perhaps the final HOURS—of Ira's tour.

With endless space before me, Cornelia orbiting above me, and Frodo asleep beside me (no sense of purpose sleeping, too) I sank into a quagmire of morose thoughts—most of them too ill-defined, too dark and turbid, to be articulated.

"I must do something to CHEER myself!" I finally cried (momentarily rousing my cat—but not my sense of purpose, which never budged.)

I twiddled my thumbs, twiddled my dials, twiddled my hair (she declined to play.) I ate some moldy cheese, then counted, tossed Frodo in the air 51 He and the same!

© 1985 J.M. DeMatteis and Jon J. Muth

New technologies, a new fan base, and a new seriousness of artistic intent made possible a comic book that looked more like an album of antique children's book illustrations. Art by Jon J. Muth, script by J.M. DeMatteis. (*Moonshadow* 9, 1985.)

also hired to plot and draw the *DC Super Powers* limited series that would tie in with the toy-launch, and his wrap-up of the Fourth World storyline was expanded to include, not just the last issue of the *New Gods* reprints, but a separate graphic novel as well. Marvel wouldn't even return Jack's original art, but DC was freely handing him money and creative opportunities. It added fuel to fandom's sentimentality about Jack, and resentment against Marvel.

Kirby reportedly ended his graphic novel, *The Hunger Dogs*, with Darkseid and Orion killing each other in the ultimate father-son conflict, leaving the destinies of New Genesis and Apokolips in the hands

of a new generation of gods. Jack was nearly seventy, was seeing a new generation of artists incorporating his work, and may have been sending his last message: let *Kirby* die—let go of Thor and the Fantastic Four and Darkseid—and continue his legacy by making your own worlds. Unfortunately, the message was horribly mangled by DC. The deaths of two characters about to be sold in toy form was apparently considered bad business, so Kirby's pages were shuffled and rescripted, and new pages were hastily commissioned to create a story that ended up making very little sense. All the pages were then "improved" with a painterly coloring effect that only subverted the graphic simplicity that had always been among Kirby's greatest gifts. Still, there are a few images within the mess from which Kirby's power shines. He still had the gods inside him, and he was strengthened by DC's efforts to do right by him—strengthened for the big fight yet to come.

Those gestures toward Schwartz and Kirby were pleasing to old-time fans, but they didn't stretch the medium or the market. The Shooter-haters in comicdom didn't like to admit it, but Marvel was the company doing that. Wendy and Richard Pini, after seven years of battling in the direct market and having told all the *Elfquest* stories they wanted to for the moment, signed with the Epic line to reprint the whole series in color. Epic explored fantasy further with other creator-owned series, including Christy Marx's wonderfully entertaining *Sisterhood of Steel*, and projects by Mike Kaluta and Elaine Lee. When Keith Giffen and Cary Bates wanted to own their *Video Jack*, they took it to Epic.

It was also to Epic that J.M. DeMatteis took his most ambitious ideas. He turned to Mark Badger to draw his *Greenberg the Vampire*, a sweet little riff on Jewishness, nerdiness, and the supernatural. His big project, though, was a collaboration with a fantasy painter named Jon J. Muth. For many comics artists, painting had always been "real" art, the subtle and unattainable medium that could never be properly reproduced in comics and would always be too time-consuming to be economically practical. With better paper, better reproduction, creator ownership, and royalties, Muth was willing to tackle a twelve-issue Epic series called *Moonshadow* (May 1985). A reworking of an autobiographical novel DeMatteis had always meant to write called *Brooklyn Dreams*, *Moonshadow* told of a naive boy losing his family and being raised by strange aliens. He falls under the protection of a crass, stinking, hairy monster, and discovers his true nature through fantasy literature, William Blake, and the Romantics. The captions overflowed with rhapsodies to literature, the pages flowed with misty colors and *echt*-Victorian studies on the big-eyed wonder of the boy. It was all rather precious and rambling, but it was pretty and passionate and sometimes rescued by DeMatteis's blunt humor. Most of all, it was unlike anything comics fans had ever seen, easy to embrace as the next breakthrough toward the full potential of the medium.

Steve Gerber pushed in a different direction. His *Void Indigo* came out as a graphic novel in late 1984 and quickly became an ongoing Epic series, but fans hoping for the Gerber of the pre-lawsuit days were disappointed. It was a dark, bitter story, and the second issue contained violence and sex so graphic that retailers in conservative areas screamed until Marvel gave credit for returned issues. That helped kill the series and woke the business up to some new realities. Creators had been blaming the publishers and the Code so long for tying them down that they hadn't quite realized that once the publishers started allowing anything, commerce and culture would set limits of their own. Even when comic books were intended for adults, Americans at large still perceived them as being for kids. Comics wouldn't be allowed the same freedom as books or movies, unless they were slapped with "adults only" labels and shelved with the undergrounds, which many comic shops didn't carry and which never sold well. Marvel and DC began to consider other ways of labeling their products, and creators began to wonder where their real audience lay.

Meanwhile, the readers of comics like *Swamp Thing* and *Moonshadow* were beginning to wonder where their real interests lay. For years editors, writers, and artists had been trying to bring genres like horror and fantasy back to life. Now Moore and DeMatteis were succeeding, not by bringing in non-superhero readers but by leading older superhero readers to more complex and subtle material. Once those readers tasted that material, they found it increasingly difficult to return to the world of superheroes. Especially since superheroes were about to make a sharp turn in the other direction.

CHAPTER 40

DEATH AND PAIN

Chris Claremont never rested. He'd shed all his non-mutant work to focus on *New Mutants* and *X-Men*, and he was keeping those at the top of the comic book sales heap. The stories might not have been what they were in the John Byrne or Dave Cockrum days, but Claremont never failed to play surprising twists on the characters, and he never failed to keep everything at a screaming intensity, with the world ever hanging in the balance and our heroes ever at the brink of death. It got awfully goofy, at least to the eyes of older readers: Kitty Pryde, Byrne's cute and convincing little thirteen-year-old, now ended up single-handedly saving the universe (the *universe!*) and fretting sagaciously about what that implied, at least when she wasn't worried about why her best girlfriend, Magick, who was raised by a demon in another dimension and was terrified that he would use her limitless power for apocalyptic purposes, was mad at her. Got all that? It was simple compared with the explanation of how Madeleine Pryor, the double of Jean Grey, ended up being Phoenix and how the *real* Jean Grey, who turned out to have been lying on the bottom of the ocean for years and *was never Phoenix at all*, came back from the dead. That, in turn, was a snap compared with Cable, Storm's lover and trainer of new mutants, who came from the future and was apparently Cyclops and Phoenix's son from the future, where mutants are put in concentration camps, which may or may not happen—or maybe he isn't!

The sheer complexity of the plots, which conventional wisdom held was "too hard for kids," proved to be exactly what the kids loved: a fictional world that could strain their supple memories and organization-al faculties to the limit, but all laid out in big black outlines that they could grasp. And if longtime readers often got frustrated by plot lines that dribbled away and disappeared for years while new ones were started up in their places, it didn't matter much because those same plot lines were constantly hooking new sixth-graders.

Claremont kept hurling out new characters, until mutants became the fastest-growing ethnic group in Marvel America. He twisted their relationships and identities endlessly. Storm became Rogue Storm, and Ms. Marvel became Binary, both delivering the usual speech—"Hear me, X-Men! No longer am I the woman you once knew!"—in screaming full-page splashes. Rogue, a drawling Southern belle (for Claremont never wearied of using accents as a way to distinguish characters) with the power to suck the life forces from others with her touch, started as a villain, became a tormented antihero, and finally became the most pathetic of all the X-Men, for she couldn't *stop* her power from sucking energy. When she later fell in love with a Cajun mutant named Gambit (with an accent), she knew she could never, ever touch him, and the agony that that brought them both overflowed onto the pages and pooled on the floor. Agony was what Chris did best, or at least did most, and he could keep teenagers begging for relief and then hungering for more, because he simply had no shame. Despite some comic relief and some tough guy talk, the overpowering seriousness of every character and every scene made *X-Men* the purest drug on the comics market, uncut by Stan Lee self-parody or Denny O'Neil tautness or Frank Miller sophistication. Even the other soap opera masters, like Marv

Wolfman, stopped at the brink of total excess, but total excess was what hundreds of thousands of young people in the 1980s wanted.

Claremont shouldered the whole burden of the mutants, too, scouring for hot artists, recruiting them with whispers of how big *X-Men* sales incentives were getting. It was sometimes said at Marvel that the *X-Men* editor's job was "to take Chris to lunch." To keep Tom Orzechowski, the best letterer in the business and the only one who could make something readable of Claremont's piles of prose, he cut him a piece of his own incentives, something nobody did for a letterer. The verbiage was what mattered to Chris: his wife once led off a biographic sketch of him for a convention program with a lengthy boast about the sheer number of words he'd had published, something that no one else in a visual medium would have worn as a badge of pride. But he knew that hot artists were what brought new readers in and kept former ones wandering back. The artists rarely stayed long, usually just long enough to pick up some heat and some money and then move on to where the plots were more visually conceived and less crowded with characters. As a result, Claremont got to practice adjusting his style to a lot of utterly different artists—though none was as different as the rising star of the direct market world, Bill Sienkiewicz.

On *Moon Knight*, Sienkiewicz had been breaking out of his Neal Adams imitation, experimenting with huge fields of black and reductionist imagery, and playing with tricks from current graphic design. Sienkiewicz was a natural artist, one of those who could look at a piece of art and reproduce it as if it were his own, from whose hand graceful images flowed like water. He was a small man, he liked attention, and he got it by tanning himself deep orange-brown and dying his hair tangerine to match—this when hardly anyone in the nerdy comics mainstream was getting into either new-wave flamboyance or the California tanning cult. His art was challenging, but for a moment still superheroish enough to please *Moon Knight* fans.

The minute he took over *New Mutants,* Sienkiewicz went nuts (*NM* 18, Sept. 1984). There were broken and indistinct panels, figures reduced to jagged ciphers, and sweeps of aggressive black borrowed from those of Ralph Steadman. He overwhelmed both writer and characters, left Claremont and all his words helpless, brought storytelling to a standstill, but burned images into readers' brains. One issue left nothing in mind but the full-page drawing of a demon bear emerging from a night of shattered ink, another nothing but Warlock, not Jim Starlin's Warlock but an alien made up of countless little hunks of circuitry that no other artist has ever been able to make sense of. "Artists," he said, "have an obligation in society to help people see things in new ways," and he wasn't going to spare superhero fans. Older fans, whether out of genuine enjoyment of his work or just a determination to prove that they weren't scared or unhip anymore, called him a genius. Younger readers started to drift away as they discovered that the stories were getting harder and harder to follow and the characters were getting uglier and uglier. Luckily for the mutants, Sienkiewicz didn't stay long. Luckily for the superfans, he announced that he was joining Miller on his *Daredevil* projects.

Pretty soon Claremont turned the writing of *New Mutants* over to his editor, Louise Simonson, to concentrate solely on *X-Men*. When Marvel wanted a new X-title, Louise and her husband, Walter, shared its scripts. Walt gave up *Thor* and Louise gave up her editorial position. Marvel was growing again, not insanely as in the '70s but under Jim Shooter's tight guidance, and he'd hired another wave of young editors. Some were from fandom, but some were from the "real world," truly blank slates to be trained in the Marvel way. Simonson's heir on the X-franchise was Ann Nocenti, who had a sharp mind and some experience in publishing and media criticism, but no experience dealing with the likes of Chris Claremont or the X-universe. Claremont was one of the reigning stars of the business, and the only one who knew how to act like it. In bush jacket and safari hat, brooding

[1] Even poor, nonwhite neighborhoods that weren't geographically "inner" at all but sprawling away from the center, as in Los Angeles, Boston, and San Francisco, were lumped into this iconic "inner city."

and booming on convention panels, upstaging everyone around him like a master ham with his slow burns and vast sighs of impatience, flashing with defensiveness at the first hint of a slight, intoning, "Shakespeare was never anything but a working writer," he was a force not to tangle with. Nocenti left him alone and focused on writing her own mutant miniseries, *Longshot*, with another offbeat young artist, Art Adams (Sept. 1985).

Claremont's work only got more extreme, more intense. Pain and rage were becoming his stocks-in-trade, and although he still kept them within a context of familial devotion and community, it was surely as clear to him as to anyone at Marvel that the moments of sheer violence were selling well. Wolverine releasing his claws with a "snikt" and a nasty grin, the slimeball muggers about to jump Storm without knowing her power or rage—they were becoming every Marvel Zombie's favorite moments, because they promised releases of pure mayhem. Marvel's official position was that no hero ever kills, but it was a position kept in the drawer until parents complained. Wolverine's claws slashed deeper and more often, the black-ink blood splashed more freely, and readers were free to conjecture whether he was wounding or killing his foes. Most readers preferred the latter.

Those readers were young teens and preteens. They were born from about 1970 to 1975, maybe the most neglected generation in American history, certainly the most divorce-battered, with the fewest siblings and the most confused and self-obsessed parents. They grew up in front of TV sets, trained their synapses with *Space Invaders*, went through puberty with MTV ("sex is everything") and AIDS ("sex is death"), and heard the great national father figure (almost the *only* national father figure) simplify it all into Us and the Evil Empire. Another devil in their Manichaean media cosmos was the "underclass," as it was being called, the dark, tormented souls beneath our feet, their lives lived in violence and hedonism in a place called "the inner city," with all its Dantean implications.[1] It was an American ter-

ror stretching back to slavery and the Indian wars, one that had come back forcefully in the late '60s but was now achieving truly mythic power with the spread of crack cocaine and automatic weapons, the televised hysteria about "gang wars" and their drive-by shootings. "Inner city violence" became somehow the same thing as AIDS: to radicals both were CIA conspiracies, to the Christian Right both were the just desserts of sinners, to the news-addicted middle class both were "epidemics," ready to explode through the mainstream if we didn't maintain vigilance. It was the tautness of Puritan New England or medieval Europe, the digging in of people on the edge of a physical or social wilderness, and it called up the same angry fantasies and sudden explosions of violence that such tautness always did.

Bill Mantlo was a comics fan with a law degree and a law-and-order bent who liked to pit his heroes against "urban scum," that "new breed of rat" that Julie Schwartz and Frank Robbins had set their Batman against in 1969. He and many others in comics were particularly affected by one of Miller's *Daredevil* issues, a throwaway story for him but one that codified one of the nightmares of Manhattanites in the '80s: Daredevil descends beneath the streets to rescue a woman from the worm-like hordes who burrow into old sewers and subway tunnels. The creatures are shambling, cadaverous horrors with pustulant sores and hollow eyes snaring the innocent and dragging them down. The idea came from news stories; with the slashing of America's public health and welfare systems, many homeless people were sleeping in tunnels to avoid the violence of public shelters and the streets. It gave a locus for all the vague fears of New Yorkers, especially white male urbanites, who felt their world squeezing in on them. Mantlo worked the theme in a *Dr. Strange* story in which the Sorcerer Supreme of the universe is revolted at the sight of the tunnel people and screams, "They *find* what they *eat*—they *eat* what they *find*!" Then he and Ed Hanigan, an artist with vocally right-wing politics, an enthusiasm for guns, and a touch for drawing naturalistic violence, created a whole series around their urban nightmares, called *Cloak and Dagger* (Oct. 1983, July 1985).

The heroes were a pair of teenage runaways who had the powers to devastate people with pain and terror, and used them to save other young people from urban evil. The first cover shows them surrounded by a gang of snarling street thugs—all white, because Marvel wanted no trouble with ethnics. One of the thugs wears a colossal mohawk, an icon that would become standard for muggers in Marvel comics, along with weird tattoos and other vaguely punk-rockish accessories. It's unlikely that any mohawked white kid in America would ever pull a switchblade unless he was posing for his friend's indie record jacket, but it was an easy code for "the other," for a subculture that young mainstream readers could instantly label as too different and too visible, and therefore threatening. In the real world, the fantasies of rage might be more directed at guys who wore Jeri curls and listened to funk, or who cut their hair very short and listened to disco or Streisand, but the punks were a safe surrogate. *Cloak and Dagger* had the sort of reality-based milieu and odd, high-concept characters that usually added up to a bomb, like *The Hawk and the Dove*, but Mantlo and Hanigan let their heroes let loose with rage against real people, and it was a hit.

Carl Potts had been pushing for a long time for a *Punisher* series. His bosses were still afraid of public reaction and the Comics Code, but Potts thought he knew how to do it. He was a warm but reserved man, who left his flirtation with the counterculture far behind in favor of a gentlemanly and intelligent conventionality. He was encouraging to freelancers but angrily protective of his corporation. Later, he would say, "I always believed that if you were just loyal to your company and worked hard, everything would work out." He was moving slowly but steadily toward marriage, fatherhood, and an executive position, and he liked a world of clear rules. Potts had beaten the odds to get Marvel to publish *Amazing High Adventure* (Aug. 1984), a high-quality anthology of historical adventure stories by the best in the business, a celebration of Napoleon and George Rogers Clark

and others who had set the pattern for bourgeois masculinity. His friend Larry Hama, the *G.I. Joe* man, soon launched a new *Savage Tales*, Marvel's first war comic in more than a decade (Nov. 1985). It included *The 'Nam*, a sympathetic, heartfelt, and gorgeous look at GIs in Vietnam, by Doug Murray, a Vietnam vet himself, and Michael Golden. Potts and others like him were restoring the pre-'60s man, the American soldier, to dignity as a bulwark against conservative fears. The Punisher, a Vietnam vet in stark black and white, the image of death on his chest, blowing away people who crossed the line ("only wounding," said Marvel editors with a wink), could be the ultimate image of that man. He didn't prey on desperate street punks, but on mob fat cats who didn't have to break the rules but chose to. If he were made less insane, relieved of the ambivalence that Gerry Conway and Frank Miller had felt for him, he could be a salable version of Steve Ditko's Mr. A. No one at Marvel admired Ditko more than Potts, but Potts was never one for political confrontations, and he knew his readers weren't either.

The times were right, as Hollywood was proving that same year. A couple of ambitious producers, Jeph Loeb and Matt Weissman—the former a longtime comics fan—had written a script called *Commando*, in the which the hero is a CIA agent who casually and premeditatedly kills the pathetic henchmen who've kidnapped his daughter. The movie starred the former barbarian and robot assassin, Arnold Schwarzenegger, who made the brutality somehow charming. When he holds a terrified, unarmed bad guy over a huge ravine and wisecracks that he's going to kill him ("You know when I told you I'd kill you last, Solly? I lied."), the Hollywood-trained audience expects the bad guy to humiliate himself comically and then be spared. When Schwarzenegger drops him, and then wins us over with that "it's all just a game" grin, it's horrifying and yet intoxicating, even liberating as the ethical and genre constraints of generations are blown away. *Commando* came out in early 1985 and created a whole new cycle of "comic book movies." Pretty soon Hollywood would be

293

coming out with *Robocop*, which somehow combined a lefty satire of mass media—clearly influenced by Chaykin's *American Flagg!*—with a hyped-up *Dirty Harry* fantasy, partly by having the hero's opponent be a greedy corporate yuppie. On TV, *Miami Vice* was the same: bad guys you could hate either because they fed the "drug epidemic" or because they were rich and protected by a corrupt establishment, brought down by an angry white cracker and a slick urban black.

Potts found the perfect man to write his Punisher: Steven Grant. Grant was avowedly left-leaning but with an imagination that ran to shoot-'em-ups, and whose *American Flagg!* was much like *Robocop*, a distillation of Chaykin's satire into a simpler us-and-them conflict. To draw it, Potts hired Mike Zeck and John Beatty, fresh from *Secret Wars*, who could make it as glamorous and easy as *Miami Vice*. The Punisher finally got his own miniseries in late 1985. It sold, and it didn't set off an uproar.

Yes, 1985. And what had become of DC's critical year? The key word wasn't to be "diversity" after all, because all the money and promotion came down on one critical project. While Dick Giordano had been thinking about romance and humor, others had been thinking about *Secret Wars*. As soon as it became clear that it wasn't going to deliver on any of its hype, old superhero veterans like Marv Wolfman and Len Wein started thinking what a huge commercial event it could have been if it had. Marvel may not have wanted to monkey with its highly successful universe, but DC's was tattered with forty-seven years of continuity, managed by editorial stables that often didn't even talk to each other. There wasn't much evidence that anyone was bothered by the confusion, except Roy Thomas, who was simultaneously trying to write *All Star Squadron*, set during World War II on Earth-2, and *Infinity Inc.*, about the children of that same Squadron, but apparently set on Earth-1. Readers always seemed to have fun learning to keep the two Earths straight, along with Earth-3, Earth-S (for "Shazam"), and a few others, but DC people were in the habit of asking themselves what Marvel

was doing better. Some feared that the complexity of the DC "multiverse" was an obstacle to young readers climbing aboard. Wolfman and Wein began to speculate that if they could streamline DC continuity retroactively with a huge time-twisting event, it could not only be a hit but could make DC as reader-friendly as Marvel for new kids.

The fatal flaw, of course, was that it would also invalidate all of DC's past comics, leaving Marvel as the only company with a history available in reprint and back issues, which any Marvel Zombie could tell you was one of its biggest appeals. At the time, though, everyone at DC was eager for Something Big. DC had narrowed the gap with Marvel. The passion of American business in the '80s, the yardstick for measuring success in a culture based more on competition than overall prosperity, had become market share. DC's had been less than half of Marvel's when the decade began, but thanks to its aggressive push in the direct market, it had gone to more than 30 percent of the whole, while Marvel's hovered around 50 percent or below. Retaking the top spot began to seem not only possible, but urgently desirable. Even fandom starting talking about market share, rooting for DC to prove that creativity and integrity and respect for older fans could triumph over venality and juvenility. To do it, though, everyone felt that DC couldn't just go after its usual older readers, but had to steal the kids away from Marvel.

DC took no chances: *Crisis on Infinite Earths*, as the new series was called, would be by Len Wein, Marv Wolfman, and George Pérez. Marv would essentially be in charge of DC continuity for the duration, usurping one of Giordano's functions. The twelve issues of *Crisis* would involve just about every character in the DC universe, just to prove there really *was* a DC universe, from Superman and Darkseid down to the Trigger Twins and Animal Man. Every single DC title, even *Swamp Thing*, would tie into it, and not just at the start as with *Secret Wars*, but off and on for the entire year it ran. *Who's Who in the DC Universe,* an answer to Marvel's *Handbook* series, would run simultaneously. *Crisis* would be set up for months before its preview in every hot title, as cosmic beings called the Monitor, Anti-Monitor, Pariah, and Harbinger warned various worlds of a coming cataclysm, and then the sky turned red and signs of the apocalypse appeared. And to make sure no one dismissed it as just another fake, DC very clearly promised two big events: the Flash and Supergirl would die.

The news was greeted variously with excitement and dread by superhero fans, but none of them could ignore it. When it emerged that the whole crisis turned on an obscure event from a mid-'60s issue of *Green Lantern*, that *GL* issue's price-guide value jumped from four dollars to sixty, and sold for more than a hundred through some dealers. Creators couldn't ignore it, either. Steve Englehart had taken over *Green Lantern*, and he and Joe Staton had generated some interest with a bad-attitude version of Hal Jordan's backup GL, Guy Gardner (largely because of Staton's wonderful work with Guy's pugnacious expressions). Now Englehart would be a major custodian of the cosmic complexity of the crisis, his issues doomed to be swamped by continuity detail. When Cary Bates learned far in advance that *The Flash* would be canceled with issue 350, he lost all passion for it. His storyline rambled, and soon Carmine Infantino was just hacking out his pages, too. The cancellation ended Infantino's last regular assignment.

The first issue of *Crisis* hit the stores at the beginning of 1985. It opened huge. Sales jumped on every "*Crisis* Crossover" issue of every series. It won a fan award as "Best Limited Series" before it was halfway done. And it stayed huge, even when the sheer, preposterous complexity—the charting of the pasts and futures of dozens of characters, the folding together of parallel Earths, the mountains of exposition, the endless fight scenes—made it impossible to understand. Flash died, taking the brightness of the silver age with him. Supergirl died, killing the last remnant of an era of kids' and girls' comics. Others died, characters no one cared about, just to make it all feel more dramatic, but none of the nasty ones did, not the Vigilante or Deathstroke the Terminator or Guy Gardner or the feral Lobo from the Omega Men. As the series wound down in late 1985, it became clear that every hero had lost his past, that any or all could change fundamentally. Rumors began that Superman, Batman, and all the other big heroes might be starting over with new directions and new creative teams. The company had made progress as the "new DC," and although its first flush of joy had inspired a fond looking back, a recovery of some of what had made it great before, it was the "new" that was expected to sell to the kids. *Crisis* was to be the death, not just of Earth-2, Earth-3, and all the rest of them, but of the DC that was.

Goodbye to the fun old days, hello to the pyrotechnic new ones: the Flash crumbles away like yellowing newsprint. By making panels objects within the composition instead of mere containers of objects, George Pérez leapt into "postmodern" narrative, conspiring with readers as mainstream artists never had before. Marv Wolfman's straight-ahead dialogue and Jerry Ordway's rounded, conservative inks kept it all quite salable to superhero fans. (*Crisis on Infinite Earths* #8, Nov. 1985.)

295

CHAPTER 41

OUR FAVORITE YEAR

*D*ark Knight. Watchmen. The Kirby wars. The Fleisher case. The labeling fight. *The 'Nam.* The New Universe, the new Superman, and New World Pictures. Miller back on *Daredevil. The Shadow* and *The Dreamer.* The Hamsters and *Maus,* a Cat Dancer and a Dark Horse. *Playboy* and *Spin* and *Rolling Stone* and *The Village Voice.* Was it really just one year? To a lot of us who were in comics in 1986, it still feels longer and fuller than all the years since.

There had been exciting new releases for years, there'd been a star system building for years, but there'd never been releases or stars like this before. Despite the mixed reaction to *Ronin,* every superhero fan and borderline superhero fan was dying to see what Frank Miller would do with Batman. Even the title promised a return to glory: *Batman: The Dark Knight Returns* (Mar. 1986). When it hit the stores, fans were on the phone to each other instantly—"Did you get it yet?" Anyone hoping for the old Miller, the Daredevil Miller, didn't get what he wanted—but no one was disappointed. Miller had added a monumentality, power, and rough-hewn blockiness that he'd only hinted at in *Ronin.* In a sense, he was following Walt Simonson's footsteps again, as Simonson returned to his Kirby roots on *Thor.* Kirby was the new element in the Miller style, and it pushed him to a level of sheer graphic power to equal the force of his story. When Superman appeared in the story, he was the Superman that Kirby might have done if Carmine Infantino and Sol Harrison had let him. Kirby was obviously at the center of Frank's thoughts—but how could he not be? For Kirby was at the center of the comic book universe that year,

that most explosive, most monumental, most Kirbyesque of all years.

Dark Knight was about obsession. Obsession with urban violence, obsession with Batman—do we have to say that Miller brought the greatest energy of his career to it? A middle-aged Bruce Wayne has given up his Batman identity but finds it clawing its way back ("the beast," he calls it). Gotham City is at the mercy of corrupt officials and homicidal teen gangs—called "Mutants," amusingly. The Joker appears on a talk show with a caricature of Dr. Ruth Westheimer, a hideous little woman who chants endlessly about "zex, zex, zex, und more zex." He murders her with a drug that leaves her grinning horribly. Next he murders a platoon of Boy Scouts in a scene fairly leering with perverse glee. "Sex equals death," even "sex equals evil," continued to be Miller's leitmotiv. A few years before, Warner Communications, which continued to sell Batman and Robin merchandise licenses, had pressured DC into giving Batman a new Robin; that Jason Todd was a bad mixture of old and new, an angry smart-mouth in little green shorts, and no one liked him. Now Miller revealed that in the future of *Dark Knight,* Jason was dead—kidnapped, raped, and murdered by the Joker. DC made Miller remove the implications of rape, but allowed the death to remain. When a fan at a convention panel asked Miller what he thought would eventually happen to Jason in regular Batman continuity, Miller grinned, "He's history." The room exploded into laughs and applause.

Miller's Joker is a pederast, a slayer of the innocent, and a corrupt, implicit homosexual. Quite a villain for the '80s. Miller's Bruce Wayne finally allows "the beast" to take him back and finds that with the surrender to brutality comes a sense of power: "the night is mine again." Quite a hero for the '80s. *Dark Knight* sprawled so widely that the story disappeared in the middle, but, thematically, all the anger and chaos resolved into a single point: at the end, Batman fakes his death and goes underground to lead an army of Mutants in a violent campaign to clean up the city. The celebration of violent male youth and massive male leadership in opposition to female and homoerotic "degeneracy," the celebration of conflict over pleasure—these are fantasies that rise when societies are conflicted, when traditional male hegemonies are threatened, and when gender roles are being questioned. They emerged in European politics in the '20s and '30s, in the shape of fascism, and here they were emerging in the '80s in mass entertainment.

The impact of *Dark Knight* was beyond what anyone would have guessed. It not only took the comics community by storm but it seized the imagination of the hip popular press, and then of the mainstream media. Miller was featured in *Spin* and *Rolling Stone*, and then the *Dark Knight* phenomenon, if not Miller himself, was everywhere. It was the first time a Batman comic book had been noticed since the Batmania of '66, and it came as a huge shock to the world that comic books had "grown up," that they were sold in three-dollar packages with square binding like books—a "Prestige Format" that DC had invented just for *Dark Knight*—and that they were full of hideous but kinky violence, parodies of Dr. Ruth, and overpowering graphics. All those same headlines from '65 and '66 ("Holy Revisionism, Boy Wonder!" "Biff, Bam, Pow, Comics Aren't for Kids Anymore!") were everywhere, but what they were reporting was very different. The "zeitgeist watchers" of Hollywood, as Sam Hamm called them, noticed. Warner Bros' Bonni Lee got a *Batman* movie into development, attaching Tim Burton as director. Miller himself was fielding screenwriting offers, and moved to LA. Even non-superhero comics were benefiting from the attention. Joyce Brabner had a gift for publicity, and got her husband, Harvey Pekar,

noticed by media trend-watchers—although his autobiographical *American Splendor* was *Dark Knight*'s diametric opposite. Pretty soon Pekar was on David Letterman's show, as an aggressively funny countervoice to '80s hype and greed.

Orders from within the comics community for *Dark Knight* 1 had been big, but not big enough. It sold out, more customers showed up demanding it, and a second printing was run. Then the world at large discovered it—people who'd never been in a comic book shop were coming in and asking for this

Frank Miller's Batman makes his entrance. Kirby size and Kirby power. (*Batman: The Dark Knight* #1, Mar. 1986.)

297

new Batman thing—and it went to third, fourth, and fifth printings.

It was Frank's year. *Dark Knight* alone would have made him the star of the field, but before it had finished running, there was *Elektra: Assassin*, and then the graphic novel *Daredevil in Love and War*, and then his seven-issue run as scripter of *Daredevil*, and before '86 was over there'd be the beginning of his *Batman: Year One*, a reworked, post-*Crisis* origin story, stunningly drawn by David Mazzucchelli. *Elektra* was rambling, chaotic, and often vapid in its cynical libertarian satire of modern politics, but it was

Runnin' wild: the adult audience of the "direct market" allowed ambitious artists to develop visions that would be incomprehensible to children. And no one was more ambitious or incomprehensible than Bill Sienkiewicz. (Elektra: Assassin #1, Aug. 1986.)

forceful and challenging, with Bill Sienkiewicz opening up all his '80s graphic design gimmicks. Paint splashed and flowed and splattered, photos were scanned and collaged in, Elektra's childhood memories were drawn like a first-grader's crayon pictures, slammed alongside airbrushed and hyper-rendered paintings of the present (Aug. 1986). Miller apparently started with a plot, but Sienkiewicz ignored it and let the pictures—more than that, the media and the materials—lead him. Miller adjusted as best as he could with the dialogue, suddenly playing Stan Lee to Sienkiewicz's Jack Kirby, but facing narrative challenges out of Stan's nightmares. The result was a mess, but it was an invigorating mess. Fans who wanted to see comics, especially superhero comics, grow into something hip and artistically valid and respected by the world, and who wanted to congratulate themselves on their own ability to appreciate the daring and the difficult, hailed it as another masterpiece.

Love and War was a throwaway, a smaller version of the same chaos as *Elektra*. The seven issues of *Daredevil* (227-233, Feb.-Aug. 1986) were the ultimate working out of Miller's paranoiac nightmares about modern society, the control of our lives by bureaucracies and master criminals, and it was the best-crafted storytelling he ever did. *Year One* was an exploration of the themes of obsession and anger in Batman's origin, and a daring play on the *femme fatale* in Catwoman, whom Miller cast not only as Batman's enemy and would-be lover, but as a murderous prostitute and dominatrix (*Batman* 404-407, Feb.-May 1987). The whole '80s construct of sex, death, violence, competition, urban decay, and class war came together in one nicely-crafted hard-boiled package. Denny O'Neil justified his salary by calling in some favors and getting Miller and Mazzucchelli to let him run it as four issues of *Batman* instead of as a miniseries, and then he followed immediately with *Year Two* and *Year Three* story arcs by other creators. *Batman* and *Detective* shot from moribundity to being two of DC's best-selling comics.

Frank had won the triple crown: critical raves, big sales, and real-world attention. Panderers and "serious" comics creators alike fell at his feet. Suddenly darkness and violence seemed like the only ways to go.

On top of all that, Miller had nearly as much impact as a corporate adversary. Once again, the critical element was Jack Kirby. In February 1986, Gary Groth's *Comics Journal* detailed the story of Jack's battle with Marvel over his original art. Or, rather, it beat the drum, it called for action, it focused the whole industry's resentments of Marvel and Shooter down to a single issue—a single battle between artistic David and corporate Goliath. The response astonished even the *Journal* staff. Letters of support poured in. Dave Olbrich, Groth's sales manager and head of *Amazing Heroes*, cruised the conventions with a petition demanding that Marvel return Kirby's art. Both the number and the magnitude of the names on it amazed him. For the love of Jack, even enemies worked together: Groth found himself on the same side as Mark Evanier—Kirby's friend and advisor, and a consultant on the comic book industry to Kirby's lawyer—despite the fact that each disliked the other, and everything the other represented. The crusade seized the imaginations, not only of discontented pros and the fan elite, but of rank-and-file fans who'd never before shown much interest in comic-book politics.

Frank Miller stepped to the fore. He wrote an impassioned article for the *Journal*, reminding fans of Kirby's fifty years of creative generosity and unparalleled importance to comics, vilifying Marvel and all corporations that suck the blood of artists—this despite the fact that Gary Groth was never anything but derisive of Miller's superhero obsessions and obliquely right-wing fantasies. Freelancers who'd been afraid to criticize Marvel for fear of economic reprisals were emboldened by Miller's courage and anger. Anti-Marvel sentiment was whipped into a flame. Most astonishingly, Miller used his clout as DC's prize freelancer to push the company into publishing an excoriation of its own and every other publisher's practice of keeping original art. The art, said DC unequivocally, was and always had been the right-ful property of the artists. It was a shockingly bold move by Jenette Kahn. Any other publisher would have let Miller quit rather than print such a statement, for it threw DC wide open to lawsuits by all the artists whose originals had been lost or destroyed over the previous fifty years. But no one sued. It wasn't a year for pettiness. Marvel had been trying to use its return of original art to prove that it was an artist-friendly company, but the releases it made its artists sign still asserted the company's rightful ownership. DC and Frank Miller had turned Marvel's PR move into a PR disaster. Fans started organizing a boycott of Marvel. DC was closing the sales gap.

The conflict was getting ugly, and Kirby himself was making it uglier. Decades of resentment geysered up from his belly. His memory had always been lousy, and now his rage was twisting it into self-aggrandizing improbabilities. He started claiming to have created things he couldn't have created. He wanted a piece of the income and a "created by" credit for all of Marvel's major characters. He was Orion fighting Darkseid now, and comicdom, in an unprecedented show of solidarity, was eager to be his army of New Gods. Deeply trenched Marvel freelancers who were getting rich on Kirby's creations, like Chris Claremont, were uneasily silent on the battle, and their mere silence made them the object of attacks from Kirby partisans. Walt and Louise Simonson came out in favor of the return of Kirby's art and the greater recognition of Jack within Marvel, but even they took heat for profiting from Kirby characters with *X-Factor* and *Thor*. John Byrne, on Kirby's *Fantastic Four*, was silent at first—until he announced that he was leaving Marvel for a major DC project. Then he spoke out for Kirby, and against Jim Shooter.

Invariably, Jack claimed to have "written" every issue of every Marvel comic he'd ever worked on. "I've never worked with a writer," he said. "Written" had always meant "plotted" to Jack, for words to him were just an addition to a visual story. Comicdom seemed to know what he meant, and accepted his shift in priorities. An installment of the *Hour 25* radio show was devoted to Kirby, joined by Frank Miller, Steve Gerber, and Mark Evanier. It was Jack, three writers, and a writer/artist who understood the writer's side of the relationship from his work with Sienkiewicz—and none of them disputed Kirby's claim to authorship. Comics fans had always seen artists as illustrators and felt that the appeal of the story and characters was solely the writer's contribution, but now they began to reconsider what comics really were. So did artists: although the examples of Miller, John Byrne, and Walt Simonson certainly helped mainstream artists consider writing their own comics, it was the Kirby furor that made them ask whether any comic book should be primarily a literary creation. Young pros like Todd McFarlane and would-be pros like the kid in San Diego named Jim Lee began to see "true comics" as sequences of powerful images with a few words attached. Just like Jack did.

Comics people like heroes and villains, and now whoever failed to defend Jack became an enemy of everyone. Stan Lee was hurt and bewildered to find himself vilified by a community that had loved him for over twenty years. He, Mike Hobson, and Marvel's other staffers could only spread the word off the record that they were privately on Kirby's side but had to back Marvel's lawyers. This was all happening at the worst possible time for them. Marvel had reached such heights of profitability that Cadence Industries had decided to put it up for sale. The pressure to do everything right was intense, and there's nothing more likely to make people do everything wrong.

The pressure was worst on Jim Shooter. He'd always presented himself to fandom as the driving force at Marvel, and he'd have loved to make that the reality—to take Hobson's, or even James Galton's, place. The last change in ownership had led to Martin Goodman's ouster and Stan Lee's ascendance. Could he play Stan's role this time around? Or might he end up playing Goodman's? Shooter's contract would expire in early 1987, and he was under scrutiny. He has said that he was making his bosses uncomfortable by fighting to have Kirby's art returned, and to

have other creators' rights recognized. But there were also rumors swirling of ex-employees suing him, and there were questions about the sweetheart deal he'd given Vince Colletta, an inker with a questionable reputation whom no other editor would hire any longer. This was the time, if there'd ever been a time, to be loyal to Marvel.

Unfortunately, being loyal without being defensive—and angry—was a hard thing for Big Jim. Everything he did went against him. He wrote an editorial defending Stan Lee and it read to his opponents like a slap at Kirby. He saw himself as a tireless creators' advocate, as the spearhead behind Marvel's freelancer health coverage and financial incentives, even as an advocate of creative freedom and experimentation—hadn't he been one of Frank Miller's first proponents, after all? But here was his Frank, using the clout he'd gained at Marvel to deliver a huge hit for DC and turn the whole industry against his old company. Shooter himself was being demonized—not just by Gary Groth, not just by stupid fans, but by some of the smartest professionals in the field—as the dictator of the one evil corporation in the business.

Stories began to circulate of Shooter exploding into rages over minor insubordinations, of him rewriting dialogue on already-lettered comics—an incredibly costly procedure for the company—to make them Right, to make them Marvel, to make them Shooter. When he and Kirby met at the San Diego Con that August, they exploded into a shouting match so angry that Mark Evanier had to push himself physically between them. And that was just the first day of the convention. A little later, at a panel devoted to the Kirby issue, a member of the audience asked Gary Groth, "How should we approach Marvel representatives about this?" Groth replied, "With two by fours." It was obviously just a nasty crack, but the word spread among Marvel staffers that Groth was inciting fans to riot, and at a later panel a group of Marvel editors denounced Kirby. Marvel couldn't have looked worse.

DC was pressing its advantage. Denny O'Neil

used *Batman* 400 as a "Dark Knight Special" to keep fans flowing between the new hip stuff and the mainstream; he got Stephen King to write the introduction. He keyed *Batman* and *Detective* to Miller's dark tone. An even nastier reworking of a '30s vigilante came from Howard Chaykin's miniseries *The Shadow: Blood and Judgment*. Chaykin was hot, he liked pushing boundaries, and he was supported by the impudent Andy Helfer. DC's logic was that since this was a high-priced item available only in comics shops, little kids wouldn't be buying it anyway, so Chaykin pushed the violent and sexual implications of superheroes as far as anyone had in the mainstream: the hero sexually exploiting his female sidekick, the villain sadistically shoving the Shadow's old agents into water coolers and other visually intriguing but sickening spots. It was clever, with flashes of prewar romanticism, yet ultimately so cynical and willfully shocking that it even put off many of *Flagg*'s fans. It attracted attention, though, and it sold. Chaykin started a revamp of *Blackhawk* and Helfer developed a new *Shadow* series with Bill Sienkiewicz.

DC was determined to deliver on the promises of *Crisis on Infinite Earths* with major continuity events. *Batman: Year One* wasn't enough. A new *Hawkman* wasn't enough. Trina Robbins and Kurt Busiek's *Legend of Wonder Woman*, a paean to the golden age that gave the amazon a chance at a new start, wasn't enough. Even a miniseries called *Legends* that would try to clarify the new continuity and launch a new *Justice League* and *Flash* wasn't enough. DC wanted a mass-media hook, some hugely collectible first issues, and an event that would shock even *Crisis*-weary fans. Luckily, it had a way to get all them all with almost no risk of loss.

The staid Superman line had lost the interest of fandom. Julius Schwartz had agreed that it was time to move on. "I believe in the Biblical idea of seven fat years and seven lean years," he would say. "After seven years on one property, you just don't have anything else to bring to it." He'd been on Superman for over twice that long. His new role, as part-time "senior editor," would mainly involve going to conventions,

giving interviews, and generally serving as proof of DC's geniality and continuity. His reputation as a teller of tales about the prehistoric days had grown to the point that a fan had stumped him, at a convention panel a few years before, by asking him to "tell an anecdote." Julie was never stumped twice: he'd since refined so many anecdotes that he could do one-man panels with names like "Strange Schwartz Stories" at every convention on the circuit and never tell the same story more than, well, four times. It was a good time to give the Man of Steel to Andy Helfer, the only DC editor with the chutzpah of a young Julie Schwartz. Helfer, in turn, gave it to the man who'd been lured away from Marvel for just this job: John Byrne.

Few fans would really miss the tired Superman of the '70s and '80s, but the mere fact of his inevitable and unchanging presence, half-lost among more exciting comics, had always been reassuring. In a quiet way, a half-conscious way, the announcement of a new *Superman* number 1 was for superhero fans the most potent symbol of the revolution transforming comics. It was hard to feel excitement for the new without some grief for the old, and Schwartz knew exactly how to help the fans through the passage. To draw the final issues of *Superman* and *Action*, the final issues in a continuous run of nearly fifty years, Schwartz turned, of course, to Curt Swan. To write them, he turned to Alan Moore.

Moore was the perfect grief counselor. "What I enjoyed about comics as a youngster wasn't just that adolescent male power fantasy element," Moore said, "the biggest element for me was the world of *imagination* that comics opened up! It was not the fact that Superman could push planets around that impressed me, but that he had a Fortress of Solitude . . . and a bottled city, and that he could travel back and forth in time . . . and that the planet he came from had a gold volcano and a jeweled mountain. And this was incredible, fantastic stuff that took my mind into all sorts of interesting places!" Moore had Superman and his world destroyed by a deranged Mr. Mxyzptlk, revealed now as an immortal demon driven to madness by a boredom that cannot be relieved.

Indeed, it was Superman's, and Schwartz's, boredom with a fictional reality that seemed as though it could never change that had destroyed them both in the end. It was a haunting story, as full of heartbreak and terror as the greatest Mort Weisinger Imaginary Stories, touching on every bit of the Weisinger mythos, but in the self-reflective terms in which every adult fan had to view the heroes of his youth. It was the end of Kandor, Krypto, Superboy, and "ye editor," Julius Schwartz. It was a communal farewell for everyone in comics.

Byrne's *Man of Steel* miniseries took Superman back to his pre-Weisinger basics: no super-identity until adulthood, no other survivors of Krypton, limited powers (Sept. 1986). His art was charming and his plots were solid, but he left himself no room for that "world of imagination" of Moore's. He doomed Superman to play out a dully conservative version of "that adolescent male power fantasy element." He even undermined the psychological heart of the myth, the Clark-Lois-Superman triangle. Although Lois Lane was part of the mix, Clark Kent had his own love interest in the aggressive Cat Grant. Clark, in fact, was generally sexier, more confident, more yuppified than he'd ever been before. In the short term, that proved to be Byrne's canniest move, because that's what the news media seized on— "Super-Yuppie," "Superman Eats Brie"—and it heated up the speculator frenzy in the comic shops.

Man of Steel was a giant hit, and the frenzy happened all over again when the new *Superman* 1 came out, along with a new *Action Comics* and *Adventures of Superman* by Marv Wolfman and Jerry Ordway (Jan. 1987). Byrne added the *Legends* miniseries to his workload, to make sure every fan knew that DC had a new universe. Jenette Kahn, Paul Levitz, and Dick Giordano had deployed their biggest guns and fired them all at once. In 1986, after an eternity in second place and seemingly no way out of it, DC overtook Marvel in market share.

Had it really been only ten years since Carmine Infantino was fired?

Jim Shooter felt the heat. The Marvel mainstream was sailing along, thanks largely to the new "grittiness." Peter David, one of Carol Kalish's sales department fanboys, had pitched his way into a few script assignments and showed a gift for blending traditional Marvel superheroics with Steven Bochco-style realism. He had just knocked Marvelites out with a storyline in *Spectacular Spider-Man* called "The Death of Jean DeWolf" (*SSM* 107-110, Oct. 1985-Jan. 1986). It was pure *Hill Street Blues* with Spider-Man swinging through, and Marvel had a new writing star. When Doug Murray's *The 'Nam* spun out of *Savage Tales* and into its own title, it made a hit not just with GIs and war buffs who'd been reduced to *Sgt. Rock* and no other war comics, but with fans who loved Michael Golden's art, critics who wanted to see comics grapple with reality, and the mass media (Dec. 1986).

It wasn't enough for Shooter. This was his time to show the world, to blow DC back to the corner and prove to fandom that Marvel was the company to follow. The Marvel Universe was twenty-five years old in 1986, if one counted from *Fantastic Four* number 1, and to celebrate Shooter was going to give it a second universe. This New Universe would be his creation, with support from Tom DeFalco and some other trusted aides, so there would be no question of riding on Kirby's or Ditko's or anyone else's unappreciated genius. More than that, it would be a message to DC: *this* is how to do comics. He was going to do versions of Green Lantern, the Spectre, the Doom Patrol, and other venerable DC concepts, but do them the right way, the Marvel way, and show they could wipe DC off the stands. He'd write the flagship title, *Star Brand*, himself, and make it the best and most heartfelt writing he'd ever done. The artist would be the rising *X-Men* star John Romita Jr., following every one of Shooter's storytelling dictates. It would be *Green Lantern* done right, and the ultimate Marvel comic. Shooter predicted it would sell a million copies.

More money was pouring into comics shops than anyone had thought possible. Even with all of DC and Marvel's expensive new products, another boom was hitting the independents. Not the slick color independents, however. Only Comico was ascending, with its licensed properties and its new hit, Matt Wagner's *Grendel* (Oct. 1986). Part horror, part superheroics, and part realism, *Grendel* was the dark and literarily intense story of a demonic force that possesses ordinary people and allows them to straighten out their messy lives—or make them worse—with superpowers. It may not have been the best or the most successful of the ambitious comics of 1986, but it seemed to synthesize everything they aspired to, and bright teenagers seized on it.

First Comics was still cruising, and even lured Jim Starlin's *Dreadstar* away from Marvel, but it failed to come up with any more huge hits like *Flagg!*—and *Flagg!* was losing ground without Chaykin's scripting and art. Its attempt to jump on the data revolution with the first computer-art comic, *Shatter*, had scored some attention in 1985, but now it offered only clunky visuals and dropping sales. Eclipse, by going deeper and deeper into adventure and superhero comics, was losing its old loyalist audience without gaining much of a new one. Even finds like James Hudnall's intelligent *Espers* weren't enough to reverse the trend.

The boom was in small-press black-and-whites. The astonishing *Teenage Mutant Ninja Turtles* phenomenon was only getting bigger, now that Kevin Eastman and Peter Laird had signed with a licensing maven and were fielding interest in Saturday morning cartoons and toys. Collector fever was making the early *Turtles* issues into major investments, inspiring a hunger among dealers and speculators to find the "next *Turtles*," maybe even a chance to make back the money lost in '84. Publishers responded with mountains of imitations—or, as they presented themselves, "parodies." Eclipse had launched a black-and-white line with high artistic aspirations, including the new *Zot!*, *Beanworld*, the surreal *Reid Fleming, World's Toughest Milkman*, and the clever *Stig's Inferno* by actor/cartoonist Ty Templeton. But suddenly it was publishing *Adolescent Radioactive Black Belt Hamsters*, *Naive Interdimensional*

Commando Koalas. and *Guerrilla Groundhog.* Sales were huge, driven less by readers than by investors, and snatched Eclipse from the jaws of disaster.

There were dozens of others, from small publishers and from self-publishing creators. The genre and the phenomenon both got names: "anthropomorphics" and "the black-and-white boom." Some were by cartoonists who actually cared about their funny animals and their medium, and those sold extremely well. Steve Moncuse, a talented but unknown cartoonist, sold 60,000 copies of his first issue of *Fish Police* and soon had a Saturday morning cartoon in development. He thought he'd found himself a career, and was soon publishing Steve Purcell's *Sam 'n' Max*, about a dog and bunny police team. Fantagraphics, where Kim Thompson was determined to elevate the funny animal genre just as fan faves were elevating superheroes, did an ambitious anthology called *Critters,* Stan Sakai's lovely *Usagi Yojimbo*, and Jan Strnad's *Dinosaur Rex*—in what other medium would an homage to P.G. Wodehouse be combined with a *Lost World* spoof?). Dan Vado, a retailer in San Jose, California, used *Samurai Penguin* to make enough money to fund Slave Labor Graphics, which he'd devote to more artful black-and-whites like Scott Saavedra's screwy *It's Science with Dr. Radium.*

Dave Sim's *Cerebus* enjoyed another sales jump, introducing many *Turtles* fans to a kind of complex, subtle storytelling they'd never imagined before. Sim also proselytized for self-publishing in his letters pages and encouraged idealistic publishers like Vado to stick by their principles. His ex-wife, Deni Loubert, was expanding her Renegade Comics, throwing her doors open to every oddball, unsalable new comic seeking a home. (Some were good, like the graphically innovative and paranoiac *Silent Invasion.* Some weren't.) All you needed to get your own comics, it seemed, was a good heart and a willingness to live cheaply.

There were even cartoonists who used anthropomorphics for erotic fantasies. "Furverts," they called themselves, and since many of them are very sweet and talented people, we will refrain from speculating as to what this implies about their personal lives. Kitchen Sink's *Omaha the Cat Dancer*, beautifully written and drawn by Reed Waller and Kate Worley, was a gracefully pro-sex, pro-tolerance soap opera about the life of a feline stripper and her animal friends and lovers. It won over fans of the independents, the undergrounds, and even some of the mainstream, and helped fund Kitchen Sink in an ambitious expansion into projects as diverse as the Depression-era realism of *Kings in Disguise*, Don Simpson's science fictional *Borderworlds*, several "neo-undergrounds," and *Xenozoic Tales*, the exquisitely drawn eco-fantasy of an Al Williamson protégé named Mark Schultz. *Omaha* also inspired new ventures into sexually explicit comics, some even with human protagonists, that lacked both the satiric abandon of the undergrounds and the crassness of traditional pornography. So primed was the comics community for the new and ambitious that it was as though every new comic set off a revolution.

One retailer saw a chance in the anthropomorphic fad for something more lucrative than underwriting oddball black-and-whites, and something more lasting than a quick in-out. Mike Richardson of Dark Horse Comics in Portland, Oregon, formed a publishing company to bring out James Dean Smith's *Boris the Bear*, rigorously parodying every current schtick of the hot superheroes in a bid for mainstream readers. It was a successful bid, and Richardson suddenly had the money to lure young artists like Mark Badger and Chris Warner away from Marvel and DC for his black-and-white anthology, *Dark Horse Presents*. The "better" black-and-whites, thanks to the crusading of Dave Sim, Scott McCloud, and the Fantagraphics set, were gaining a cachet of superiority in the minds of the fan elite, and Richardson figured that if he published well-promoted, well-executed black-and-whites aimed at that mid-range between the *Turtles* and the *Zot!* and *Beanworld* crowds, at the Frank Miller and Alan Moore fans, he could carve a niche in the market. It worked. *The Mask*, with Badger's art, was a modest hit. A bigger one was *Concrete*, by a

movie storyboard artist named Paul Chadwick, who took a chance in comics to tell some personal stories. His low-key but very intelligent tales about a man placed in the body of a rock monster by aliens played with themes of isolation and "otherness." It won the hearts of intelligent fans, unifying the *Zot!* crowd and the *Dark Knight* crowd, and made Dark Horse an instant success.

With media interest in *Turtles* and Frank Miller, and with Chadwick's Hollywood connections, Richardson saw potential for his Dark Horse creations and instantly started exploring other media opportunities. It helped that his friend and would-be comics writer Mark Verheiden had moved to LA, to try to be a screenwriter. Verheiden had tried to crash comics with various proposals, including one for *Captain America* that had created some buzz at Marvel, but that had been rejected because Mark Gruenwald was solidly in place with his more conservative take. When Richardson agreed to publish Verheiden's reworked concept as *The American*, he and Verheiden both knew they were angling for Hollywood interest.

The best of the black-and-whites sold the best, but even the worst sold well. The speculator market was a gold mine for slickers like Steve Geppi of Diamond Distributing, who found ways to create false impressions of rarity and thus manipulate the market and make himself a small fortune. Diamond thus confirmed itself as the great opportunist of the market place. John Davis and Milton Griepp offered their Capital City Distributing as an alternative, a friend to more artistically committed comics. As the "Big Two," Diamond and Capital would battle for dominance in the market—but it was Diamond that inspired the most imitators.

The guys behind the late Pacific Comics reappeared with the hasty, black-and-white Blackthorne line. A clever cartoonist named Ben Edlund conceived a *Dark Knight*-cum-Dave Sim parody called *The Tick*, which he would eventually publish as a limited, numbered edition to make it an automatic collector's item. Scott Rosenberg, a twenty-three-

How comics had changed: a powerful rock-man highly reminiscent of Jack Kirby's Thing—used for conversation and gentle humor. (*Concrete* #1, Apr. 1987.)

year-old born into money and hungry for more, created Sunrise Distributing in LA. Sunrise quickly boomed, then ran into trouble from overexpansion, and Scott decided distributing was too precarious; he shut down Sunrise to go into publishing, owing tens of thousands of dollars to assorted publishers. He wounded Gary Groth's Fantagraphics and virtually destroyed some of the idealistic smaller presses like Strawberry Jam. To run his publishing company he hired away Fantagraphics' Dave Olbrich, one of the best people in the business at dealing with distributors and retailers.

Groth felt betrayed—not just for thirty pieces of silver, but for thirty pieces of silver from a distributor who owed him money. Then Jan Strnad left Fantagraphics to jump on the black-and-white boom with his Mad Dog Graphics, bringing along his *Dalgoda* collaborator, Dennis Fujitake, and Groth's art director, Tom Mason. Groth attacked Rosenberg, Olbrich, Strnad, and Mason in print, creating a schism that made the *Journal* still more bizarrely entertaining, the line between fanboys and elitists still

sharper, and comicdom still more energized. When Olbrich helped organize the Eisner Awards, the first comic book awards voted on by industry professionals, Groth sneered that they were worthless, since commercial souls like retailers and publishers' employees were allowed to vote. He answered with the Harvey Awards, voted on only by writers and artists.[1] Soon partisans of each set of awards called for boycotts of the other.

For a tense, crackling moment, everyone was united, even by hostility. One embodiment of that brittle energy was Mark Waid, a fanboy who'd been electrified by Alan Moore and dreamed of bigger things for comics. Groth hired him to take Olbrich's place at the head of *Amazing Heroes*. That had always been Fantagraphics' straight-up-the-middle fan magazine, best known for the reviews of R.A. Jones, who'd been voted fandom's favorite critic for an approach that he said "never tried to be intellectual." Now Waid brought in the spirit of '86, and turned it into an impudent, intelligent, controversial forum for the improvement of the mainstream, a superhero-

[1] The names say it all. Olbrich's awards were named, of course, for Will Eisner, master of sentimentality and maven of rationalized storytelling, who always owned his properties and never got the bum end of a business deal. Groth's were named for Harvey Kurtzman, master of withering satire and creator of *Mad*, who missed out on the uncountable riches of his invention and ended up doing *Little Annie Fanny* for *Playboy*.

© 1986 Scott McCloud

Scott McCloud not only mocks superhero convention and tries to out-Kirby Kirby...

because of the medium as because of the intensity of the people." He tried to shove so much knowledge about the medium into his head all at once that his critiques exploded out in twisting, emotionally volatile, self-contradictory, self-aggrandizing, but never predictable torrents.

It was the fanboys' year. Paul Levitz said as much in one of DC's Publishorials. He reminded the younger generations that it hadn't always been like this, that comics fans had once been isolated and scorned, that they had no influence on the business, that only shoddy kid stuff could sell. In those days, fans could only dream hopelessly of shops devoted to comics, giant conventions full of accessible pros, gorgeously produced comics worthy of adult fans, and fans themselves becoming writers, artists, editors, even publishers. Now those dreams had come true, more grandly than even the most naive optimist could have imagined. His closing words were, "We won."

The victors were having fun, celebrating their medium. In Southern California, Ray Zone was reviving the 3-D craze of the early '50s, doing specials for various publishers which evolved into a whole series, *The 3-D Zone*, from Renegade. He did several reworkings of old Kirby comics, and paper 3-D glasses reading "Jack Kirby, King of the Comics" circulated everywhere, even turning up on Johnny Carson's head during a *Tonight Show* routine. Bruce Hamilton's Gladstone line brought back affordable Disney Comics; Carl Barks finally got his due, as fans who'd been trained to see humor comics as inferior to superheroes began to realize that talking ducks might have at least as much artistic potential as what Jan Strnad called "people who dress up in costumes and beat each other up." Will Eisner stole the hearts of comicdom with *The Dreamer*, a "graphic novella" sentimentalizing the birth of the comics industry and the early superhero factories. Kitchen Sink gambled on a hardback edition, $17.50 for forty-six pages of comics, and grown-up fans ate it up.

Then Scott McCloud hit with his new project, *Destroy!*, a tabloid-sized one-shot labeled "The

oriented equivalent of the *Journal*. For his chief critic, Waid turned to another (and unrelated) Jones, Gerard, who was unqualified but was eager to get into the comic book world. "I'd been living the isolated life of the writer, dealing with the publishing world at a purely business level," Jones said, "when doing *The Comic Book Heroes* started drawing me into this bizarre other world. At the '86 San Diego Con, I fell in love with it, felt like I'd found a creative community for the first time in my life, like I was part of a *movement*. I made friends in every subset, talked until three in the morning every night, got a crush on the first fangirl who paid attention to me. I knew I wanted to be part of that world—not nearly as much

Loudest Comic Book in the Universe!! 32 Pages of meaningless, overblown violence, mayhem, and destruction! (Plus one Naughty Word)." "It wasn't so much a parody as an expulsion," said McCloud. "Because I knew that what was inside me was that same adolescent fanboy that was inside *all* artists. And I felt that almost all the artists in mainstream comics...were still playing 'king of the hill' with Jack Kirby. And they could never win!"

Gloriously drawn and funny, *Destroy!* said everything that needed to be said about the formulaic hollowness of superheroes, and about their eternal appeal. *Destroy!* didn't, however, have the intellectual weight and opportunities for fan self-congratulation that all those who either read superheroes or were reluctantly turning against them yearned for. It attracted less notice than it should have. No one, on the other hand, could fail to see *Watchmen* coming, even months in advance.

Before it came out, while *Swamp Thing* was still recovering from a rather sluggish year of tying into *Crisis*, DC sent Alan Moore to the San Diego Con. He set off a feeding frenzy among teenage and early-twenties fans like no one had seen even in the heyday of Claremont and Byrne. He was the comic book equivalent of the Beatles Invasion. Fans were showering gifts on him—one poor fifteen-year-old who'd read that Moore liked Laurie Anderson's *Oh Superman* gave him a boxed set of Anderson recordings that must have wiped his allowance out for a year—and following him everywhere, even to the stalls in the men's room, to demand his autograph. Moore swore he'd never come to another American convention (and so he hasn't), and people at DC apologized profusely. But surely they were secretly thrilled. They'd gambled, taking Moore and Dave Gibbons off the Charlton heroes, fearing that their apocalyptic reworking would make the characters unmarketable in the mainstream. The Charlton properties did indeed prove to be reasonably marketable. A standard superhero spin on *Captain Atom* sold solidly (Mar. 1987), and a light twist on *Blue Beetle* sold less well but won some fan affection for the

character (June 1986). Denny O'Neil's zen-and-liberalism reworking of Steve Ditko's *Question* scored critical acclaim, with Denys Cowan's moody art and some smooth scripts about urban corruption and individual integrity. They showed that O'Neil had learned as much from Miller as the other way around.

Moore and Gibbons were asked to turn their ideas into a series about heroes of their own. They called it *Watchmen*, as in the old Roman line, "Who watches the watchmen?" Their concept for Captain Atom become Dr. Metropolis, an atomic man who shifts endlessly and unpredictably along the time stream. Their Question became a sociopathic lunatic called Rorschach (his face a Rorschach inkblot, Ditko's de-

...but comments on the narrative devices of the medium as he goes. (Destroy!! #1, 1986.)

© 1986 Scott McCloud

No one had ever been as intricate or rigorous in visual storytelling as Alan Moore and Dave Gibbons. The "present" of the panel nine echoes the "past" of panel seven, both bookending the falling bottle in panel eight, a motif that runs through the issue and isn't revealed as an incident from the "future" until the very end. All twelve issues were like this. (*Watchmen* #9, May 1987.)

heroes (Sept. 1986–Feb 1987). Moore and Gibbons's exposure of the antisocial, fascist, and psychologically diseased implications of superheroes was chilling, especially to adult readers still fascinated by superheroes but no longer quite comfortable with the fascination. The storytelling itself was as relentless as any the medium had seen—tightly contained in nine-panel grids, lacking captions, and viewed through the cold and steady eye of a documentary film. The central story was offset by excerpts from an imagined book about the heroes' glorious past and by an apocalyptic pirate comic book, a Coleridgean meditation on the themes of violence and decay reflected by '80s comics.[2] Moore's arsenal of narrative tricks was fuller and more assured than anyone's, even Miller's.

Ultimately, twelve issues turned out to be over-long, and the resolution was anticlimactic: an alien invasion has been faked, and various Watchmen are being murdered by one of their own in order to unite mankind and teach it to overcome its own problems, an old Cold War science fiction cliché. For all of Moore's blinding technique and excruciating analysis of superheroic subtext, *Watchmen* turned out to be a bit emptier than its manner promised, less affecting than Moore's first several *Swamp Thing* stories. But long before the series ended, it had already been hailed as a revolution and a revelation. It had changed the way every young writer in the mainstream attacked his stories. Some of Moore's devices—like ending a scene on a shot of a distinctly shaped object, and then opening the next with a matching panel and a different, but topographically related object — became known as "Alan Moore transitions" or "Alan Moore flashbacks," but they were considered the common property of comicdom. Scarcely a caption would be seen in a DC comic, even the most mainstream, for years to come.

It was DC's year. Jim Shooter knew that his back was to the wall. Cadence Industries found a buyer for Marvel: New Line Pictures, Roger Corman's old studio, now looking to expand into animation and licensing. Nobody in the '80s bought a new company without making prominent person-

the disintegration of the self), and the others turned into various over-the-hill and mentally disturbed ex-heroes. Jenette Kahn, Dick Giordano, and company were left asking, Can a twelve-issue Baxter-paper miniseries about unknown heroes be sold on nothing but Moore's reputation and Gibbons's gorgeous but little-known art?

Yep. *Watchmen* didn't hit *Dark Knight* numbers, it never seemed to bring in many people from outside comics, and it didn't interest the preteen set. But no one connected to organized fandom dared miss an issue. For its first six issues, it systematically inverted everything fans had ever thought or felt about their

a new company without making prominent personnel changes, so Shooter knew the new owners would be watching closely.

Marvel hyped its New Universe to death. Shooter did, indeed, do the best writing of his career on *Star Brand*—and the most personal (Oct. 1986). The big, craggy, blue-collar mechanic who is granted cosmic power by a mysterious alien force had echoes of the young Jim Shooter, the Pittsburgh kid who was found by a couple of Legion fans and quickly thrust to the forefront of comic book power. There was a meanness in it too, though. An unstable young woman named Duck shows up at the hero's door, and when he tries to get rid of her she begs to stay. An hour later, we see him with a smug smile on his face, telling Duck that "that" ought to win her the "beak of the week award." Then the girl he really wants shows up, and he throws Duck out of his house. It was the new anger of Marvel brought down to a particularly painful and personal level.

Star Brand 1 didn't sell the million that Shooter had predicted. It sold about 150,000, and apparently a lot of those sat in the stores. Orders for later issues dropped sharply, and the news was worse for each subsequent New Universe release. The nastiness didn't let up. It even showed up in Archie Goodwin's *Justice*, a Spectre riff with good, gritty scripting but an edge of sadism reflecting Michael Fleisher. Then there was *Mark Hazzard: Merc*, the adventures of a mercenary, written by Peter David. One story was set in a fictional version of the Philippines, which was then going through the preamble to the fall of Marcos, and David played the Filipinos as idiots and lunatics, their women as weepy little love dolls, the Merc as a white god who could only sneer at this "weird country." It was shoddy, racist, smug, and as contemptuous of its audience as it was of its subject. The rest of the New Universe was all hack work. Kyle Baker, a very talented artist being developed by Marvel, worked with some other moonlighting artists in a cranked-out Kirby imitation under the name Jack Fury. It seemed that no one but Shooter had faith in the New

Universe, and that Marvel's morale and sense of team spirit were at an all-time low.

No, not all-time. Because then *The Village Voice* did a major article on the Kirby crusade. Everyone interviewed defended Jack. No one stuck up for Marvel, or Stan Lee, or Jim Shooter. Stan was crushed: the hip press that had always been so good to him was virtually calling him a fraud and a robber baron. He started lighting fires to get Kirby's art returned to him, and his new bosses joined in when some prospective licensing deals reportedly blew up in their faces after the bad publicity.

Then, in November, Michael Fleisher's suit against Groth and Ellison finally came to trial. Shooter began his testimony with businesslike reserve, but under cross-examination his defensive arrogance began to rise. Soon the phone lines of comicdom were buzzing—Shooter had said that Marvel never promoted its writers and artists because "we don't have to. We're Marvel Comics." He had declared Marvel to be "the author" of all its comics, no matter who scripted them. It was a legal point—under the standard work-for-hire contract, the owner of the property is the legal "author"—but the implications of Shooter saying it made freelancers shudder. Shooter was the enemy now, and nothing he did would ever change that.

It would have been a great time for DC to celebrate, but it had a war raging in its own halls. Its prize catches, Miller and Chaykin, had stirred up fears with their highly publicized "zex zex zex" and sexually predatory heroes. The Christian right was going after kids' entertainment then—*Pee Wee's Playhouse*, the Ralph Bakshi/John Kricfalusi *Mighty Mouse*—and all the "Holy Sex and Violence" hype only drew its attention to comics. If one wanted to find it, even DC's regular newsstand comics provided ammunition for a "do you know what your kids are watching?" crusade: the "teenage" Nightwing and Starfire evidently sleeping together in *Teen Titans*, Catwoman as whore in *Batman: Year One*, on sale next to Archie and Jughead.

2 This was a tribute to *Watchmen*'s editor, Joe Orlando, who had drawn pirate comics for EC in the '50s. It was Gibbons' idea; what kinds of comic books would be popular, he wondered, in a world in which superheroes were the province of the news instead of fantasy? It was a cute in-joke, but even in-jokes worked as part of the self-analysis and self-referentiality of this new way of looking at the medium.

Hot young writers and artists didn't give a damn about the Christian Right. They trusted the laissez-faire marketplace of '80s America and the hipness of the media to carry them through. Dick Giordano and Joe Orlando, however, couldn't be so cocky. They'd been rising young artists thirty years before, when a censorship campaign brought their whole industry crashing down and left them struggling for the next decade. In late 1986, to head off trouble, they decided on what seemed like a simple solution: a ratings system based on Hollywood's. They'd be willing to publish anything, but some comics would be for "adults only," some for "mature readers," and some for everybody.

The reaction stunned them. In the anticorporate mood stirred up by the Kirby conflict, anything that seemed repressive was viewed as a bid to take the creators' freedom and control away. Freelancers weren't just pressing for more freedom now, they were essentially pressing to take control of the industry. Alan Moore said he would never write for DC again, and he stuck to it. Len Wein, Marv Wolfman and Mike Barr quit the company (although it turned out they only gave up their editorial duties, and would continue to write scripts). Miller started making noise as if he was just as fed up with DC as he was with Marvel. The creators presented it as a free-speech issue, although there may have been baser motives as well. Surely people like Miller knew that most of their sales were coming from kids, and that a "mature readers" label on future *Dark Knight*-like projects would cut sharply into royalties. Principles and money make a potent mix, and it became another rallying point, another tempest in the *Journal*. This time, though, DC wouldn't play the "freelancer friendly" company. It stalled a little, but it wouldn't back down. The ratings themselves weren't as important as the basic matter of control. Another surrender to freelancers could have broken the publishers' power over what they saw as their own business.

The fissures were opening: publisher versus freelancer, superheroes versus "alternatives"—a more specific label had been needed to distinguish the commercial independents from the "artistic" ones. Between *Dark Knight, Destroy!,* and *Watchmen,* nearly every aspect of the superhero form had been exploited, exploded, and explored to its utmost. Scott McCloud said he saw no point in ever doing superheroes again. When *Zot!* returned, it proved to be far less about Zot's world and powers and far more about ours, about the conflict between Zot's naive worldview and Jennie's sad, adolescent accommodation to our ambiguous reality (*Zot!* #11, Jan.1987). McCloud said he was openly striving to keep up with the Hernandez brothers on their own turf. Los Bros were now totally dedicated to verisimilitude, and the toasts of the alternative scene. Gilbert, with stories like 1986's "Bullnecks and Bracelets," proved himself a powerful expressionist and an unflinching chronicler of human pain, and was being noticed by the progressive press of Europe and America.

Alan Moore asked rhetorically, "*how* do you follow *Watchmen*?" His next project, he said, would be a self-published, non-superhero story with Bill Sienkiewicz. Plenty of critics and thoughtful readers wondered if there was any point in *anyone* ever doing superheroes again. At the same time, those heroes had drawn so much attention that there was bound to be a new explosion in the genre in 1987, and anyone with an eye on royalties would be smart to get in on it. Another fissure: art versus commerce, elitist versus fanboy. Mark Waid had barely begun revamping *Amazing Heroes* when disagreements between him and Groth boiled over, and Groth canned him. Groth would choose meeker and more market-minded editors after that. The energy that held fandom together was allowed to dissipate.

Then a bombshell was dropped right in the middle of the field, not by a comic book publisher but by Pantheon Press. Art Spiegelman's *Maus* was in book form, and it was attracting attention. The New York intelligentsia were never indifferent to holocaust stories, and this one was so odd in its Aesopian casting of mice as Jews and cats as Germans, its use of a medium generally considered lightweight and its amazingly simple, focused telling that it made head-lines. No "Biff! Bam! Pow!" either. *Maus* was nom-inated for a National Book Critics Circle Award. At first comicdom seemed unsure what to do with it, whether to embrace it as one of its own or something related but odd. But *Journal* critics kept calling it the standard to aspire to, Harvey Pekar kept criticizing it for exploiting the experiences of camp survivors, and pretty soon Spiegelman was agreeing to appear at comic book conventions, to talk about the future of the medium on panels with people like Scott McCloud and *Beanworld*'s Larry Marder. He even came out publicly in support of Kirby. He was, for the moment, part of the community.

When Fantagraphics brought out *Anything Goes*, a benefit comic to cover its legal bills for the Fleisher lawsuit, among those who donated work were Frank Miller, Alan Moore, Neal Adams, George Pérez, Dave Sim, *Flaming Carrot*'s Bob Burden, the alternative cartoonist Sam Kieth, and the *Ninja Turtles* guys. Some ex-Fantagraphics employees said Groth spent all the money on a new sports car, but that didn't change the symbol-ism. All the fights and fissures were just part of the loudest and most exciting conversation the comic book world has ever known, a year-long conversa-tion, and no matter how much or how fast we talked that year, it seemed as though it could never all be said.

It was Frank's year, it was DC's year, it was the fans' year, it was the visionaries' year. It was Jack's year. It was 1986. It was everyone's favorite year.

CHAPTER 42

THE BIG PARTY

And then it was over. The February 1987 *Comics Journal* came wrapped in a magnificent Don Simpson cover showing Jim Shooter as a huge, Kirbyesque villain towering over fallen freelancers. The lead news item was that Michael Fleisher's lawsuit against the *Journal* and Harlan Ellison was over, and the court had ruled against the plaintiff. Groth crowed in victory. He organized a convention panel to discuss the case. Once the audience was in place, he gave a stentorian reading of the First Amendment, and then said simply, "That's all you need to know." Everyone knew he was declaring victory not just over Fleisher, who by then had faded almost completely from comic books, but over Jim Shooter.

There was more news. As suddenly as a Jack Kirby punch, Marvel's lawyers gave in. Kirby's art would be returned. Shooter and Stan Lee both claimed to have gotten it done, but some credit probably also goes to the new owners, who were free from the old screw-the-artist ethic of comics and accustomed to creator clout in Hollywood. Kirby gave in on a couple of issues. Marvel refused to concede him any creator credit, so that all Marvels still begin with the words, "Stan Lee Presents." It refused to declare that all missing, unreturnable artwork was legally Kirby's property, so he could never reclaim the art he saw for sale at comic conventions.[1] And, in fact, Jack got back only a little over 2,000 pages, not much over a tenth of what he'd produced for the company. Yet, to Jack, it was a victory. The entire comic book community had risen to his defense, and Marvel had backed down in full public view. Mark Evanier and Art Thibodeaux, one of Kirby's inkers, helped him unpack the pages, and found him in the best mood they'd seen him in years. "Hey, I got a good one!" he'd laugh when he'd find one of the few valuable pages. "How'd that happen?" Pretty soon he

was back to work again, drawing covers for Thibodeaux's self-published series, *The Last of the Viking Heroes.*

Everyone in comicdom knew that Jim Shooter's contract was up for renegotiation, and bets were being placed on where the chips would fall. On the day the negotiation period began, the Marvel staff noticed security guards appearing quietly in the halls. Shooter was asked to James Galton's office, where Galton and Mike Hobson were waiting for him. They told him that Marvel had decided not to renew his contract as editor-in-chief. They offered him alternatives, including an editor/writer deal of the kind Galton had forbidden for everyone else. But for Shooter it was command or nothing. He walked out. The security guards had been told to be ready for flying furniture, but there was none. Shooter went straight to the airport, took a red-eye to LA, and hit the headquarters of New World Pictures at opening time. He was going to talk Marvel's bosses into firing Galton and putting him in charge. No one would see him, and he sat in the waiting room all day. At last, rather quietly, he left. He would return to Marvel only to negotiate his severance package. Hobson, with a professionalism that only experience outside comic books could give, ordered the Marvel staff not to taunt or provoke him. Hobson's secretary prowled the halls, taking nasty anti-Shooter cartoons off the walls before each of Jim's visits. When the negotiating was done, Jim Shooter was gone. Back to Pittsburgh? Back to advertising? No one seemed to know.

The Marvel staff was almost giddy with relief. Shooter's successor, Tom DeFalco, was a different animal entirely, a Brooklyn "dese and dose" guy who'd put his feet on the desk and joke with freelancers wandering by. He saw his job as suggesting creative directions, cultivating hot artists, and meddling in the comics only when someone violated

[1] Some Marvel insiders have charged that the refusal grew from a fear that highly placed staffers would be prosecuted for stealing the art.

Marvel's standards of decency. Once Shooter was gone for sure, he allowed some childish crowing. Mark Gruenwald, who, for sheer love of Marvel Comics, had suffered the worst Shooter had to give, now inherited the moribund New Universe. He made a huge storyline out of "The Pitt," in which Pittsburgh gets blasted to a hole in the ground. John Byrne insisted on writing and drawing it.

What else could you do, after a year like 1986, except chuckle and play and bask in the afterglow?

Andy Helfer, Keith Giffen, and J.M. DeMatteis were doing it. Their new *Justice League* wasn't about *Dark Knight* passion or *Watchmen* ingenuity, it was just about hanging out and having fun (May 1987). They popped in whatever characters they wanted to play with, regardless of popularity: Batman, Captain Marvel, Guy Gardner, Blue Beetle, Martian Manhunter, Mr. Miracle. Gardner, who'd been a fairly standard hard-guy in *Green Lantern*, became an arrogant reactionary buffoon who was convinced he would be voted the League's leader. "*Dozens* of active GLs around and we get Rambo with a ring!" moans Black Canary. Plots were mixed in, but not enough to get in the way of the banter. Ten of the first issue's twenty-five pages are devoted to the League saving the United Nations, the other fifteen to them arguing among themselves. For three issues Guy Gardner rides the arrogant Batman, until he finally rips his ring off and says it's time to settle things once and for all. Batman bops him in the nose. No big Marvel fight. Batman bops him in the nose and he's out. "One punch!" howls Blue Beetle, grabbing his stomach with laughter. Black Canary enters. "Batman *belted* him—and I *missed* it?! Oh, God. I'm depressed." Giffen was great with the pacing, DeMatteis was good with the banter. Kevin Maguire, the penciler working over Giffen's layouts, handled the characters with humor and photographic clarity. Al Gordon's inks softened the stiffer lines gorgeously. All put together, it was the most simply endearing comic book to come out of the mainstream in a long, long time.

Giffen said *JL* was about "being with your coworkers." The heroes' antics were a little too insane for a work atmosphere, though. This was more about being with your buddies in the most entertaining high school ever, or being with your fellow fans at a never-ending convention where no one's too shy to act up. It was the answer to Alan Moore's question: "*How* do you follow *Watchmen?*" Obviously, by accepting the fact that superheroes can't go any further into art or realism, that they're just absurd fictional people we'd like to hang around on pizza night, to see who falls in love with who and to laugh at their pratfalls. The menaces they face might be seriously threatening—Giffen and company were smart about that in the early going, never letting the humor become the self-parody that fans always distrust—but nothing could feel so momentous as Guy Gardner getting bonked on the head and turning into a grinning sap who sings Carpenters' songs. *Justice League* was the affirmation of the society of fandom, a home for the lonely and a salve for the wounds of *Watchmen*. It was an immediate, gigantic hit in the direct market.

Helfer showed off his talent and twisted sensibility as a writer in the new *Shadow* series, which tossed

Keith Giffen had his humor beats down—and had Kevin Maguire's photographic immediacy and J.M. DeMatteis's smart-alec dialogue to sell the gags. Inks by Al Gordon. (*Justice League* #1, May 1987.)

313

the old pulp avenger into a surreal burlesque of the '80s (Aug. 1987). When Bill Sienkiewicz quit, he was replaced by an even more talented artist, Kyle Baker, another of Helfer's bright, cynical neurotics, interested in superheroes only to the degree that he could make fun of them. Alas, *The Shadow* would be canceled shy of twenty issues, and its few but fanatic followers would never find out whether the hero ever got his body back from the moon so he could get his head off that robot and reattach it. A series that probably would have been hailed as another breakthrough in 1986 passed largely unnoticed in the shadow of *Justice League*. Something was changing.

DeMatteis spun 180 degrees away from *Justice League*, deep into mournful character exploration, in a spin-off miniseries, *Martian Manhunter* (May 1988). Mark Badger's art was still ambitious beyond the reach of his craft, but it showed a cartoon visionary in the making. Unfortunately, the fanboys hated it. After the exhausting artistic challenges of '86, they wanted clarity and lightness. Older and more demanding fans were sensing that the artistic potential of superheroes had been exhausted, while the fans who still liked superheroes wanted them to be simply fun again.

DC was having better luck with George Pérez's *Wonder Woman* (Feb. 1987). It was clear and pretty, woven around sanitized Greek myths, and drew a genuine sweetness from its story of a naive amazon discovering the world of mankind with innocence and good will. The new *Flash* got off to a popular start with high-speed, stripped-down adventures of the former Kid Flash trying to take on the mantle of adulthood (June 1987). Mike Baron brought some of the bounciness of *Nexus* to the scripts, though none of *Nexus*'s oddity or darkness. He knew what fans were looking for, and was soon the hottest and most prolific writer in the mainstream.

In success or failure, everyone seemed to be having fun. It was the mood of the country, too. AIDS didn't look like it was going to exterminate mankind after all, Reagan hadn't gotten us into a nuclear war, Gorbachev was gladhanding New Yorkers, the stock market was booming. It was time to sit in a '50s diner and flip through the Sharper Image catalogue until Nick at Nite came on. The adolescent greed and competitiveness encouraged by our junk culture had been accepted as a norm, and free-spending young Americans aspired to die with the most toys and use the educations our parents had bought us in Trivial Pursuit. Comics, now the most adolescent and trivial of media, were finding their moment.

Fandom was growing. Wags noted that with every convention the "geek factor" went down and the "babe factor" went up, and it was true that the greater world was finding its way into comics. The number of new converts was still small enough to be absorbed into the subculture, but that couldn't last. A new breed of slick, pro-mainstream magazines about comics was appearing, and Mark Waid, lately fired from *Amazing Heroes*, was hired to create one by a group of young capitalists from outside fandom. Waid's *Comics Week* would have passed unnoticed but for the appearance of "It's Commentin' Time," by a teenage columnist named Sidney Mellon, who seemed to embody in one obnoxious little form everything that grown-up fans detested about fanboys. Sidney insisted that superheroes were the greatest myths of all time—"Could Ulysses fight off a super-scientific criminal with an exoskeleton of nigh limitless power?"—and that only superhero "myths" could claim to be "True Art." "Whereas *Maus* is about dead history," he wrote, "*New Mutants* is set against the titanic terrors of today.... You can see which one has the more realistic art. And look how much better the inking is...."

Comicdom's first reaction was outrage, but as Sidney's screeds became ever more ludicrous (he ascribed the quotes that led off his columns to "the great Bartlett") readers began to suspect that he wasn't a real boy at all, but a satire. "Who is Sidney Mellon?" became the great question of 1987. Now it was time for the mainstream to be outraged: Don Thompson, in *Comics Buyer's Guide*, assailed Sidney as a cruel hoax by "elitists" against the people who *really* support the comics industry. What only a few readers seemed to realize was that Sidney satirized the pretensions of older readers as much as the idiocies of Marvel Zombies.

Then Mark Waid got the call he'd been waiting his entire life for. DC was planning a creator-owned line and wanted him to interview for the editor's job. As it turned out, the job would go to a friend of Jenette Kahn's from the garment trade, Mark Nevelow, but Waid and another interviewee, Brian Augustyn, were hired as associate editors for the DC mainstream. (Sidney moved on to *Amazing Heroes*, which shot down the theory that Waid was the writer behind him.) Waid and Augustyn became instant soulmates—both silver age fans, both cocky and unintimidated by anybody, both used to being loud-mouthed outsiders, Waid through Fantagraphics and Augustyn through editing an independent humor comic called *Troll-Lords*. Augustyn, an ex-high school football player and printer's assistant from Chicago, was the direct type. His first day on the job, when an irritable editor referred to him as Mike Gold's "flunky," Augustyn grabbed him by the neck, lifted him to his tiptoes and said, "I've never been a flunky. Do you understand?" Dick Giordano was still laughing about it at the editorial meeting the next day. And just like in the comic books, Augustyn and the embarrassed editor went on to be friends.

Waid, on the other hand, specialized in ingenious subversion. He tried to slip stories into his pet title, *Secret Origins*, that undermined John Byrne's Superman continuity. He hired *normalman*'s Jim Valentino, *Stig's Inferno*'s Ty Templeton, a clever satirical cartoonist named Hilary Barta, and humor writer Gerard Jones to do their spins on superheroes. He called the Hernandez brothers to see if they wanted to crash the mainstream (and got a two-part answer: "No." Click.). He even gave a break to a struggling stand-up comic named Scott Lobdell, who smelled fame and money in comic books and hung around the DC offices trying to get someone to give him a shot. Waid and Augustyn were also among the last editors to give work to veterans who'd fallen out of favor in the slick-and-serious days: Curt Swan, Kurt Schaffenberger, Don Heck, and Carmine

INTRODUCTION BY MARK EVANIER!

#1 • $1.95
$2.95 Canada

Recommended For Mature Readers

THE TROUBLE WITH GiRLS

All The Sex And Twice The Violence!

Malibu

TM & © 1988 Will Jacobs and Gerard Jones. Artwork © 1988 Tim Hamilton

Infantino. After a couple of affectionate parodies of the old *Flash* and *Space Museum*, Infantino faded quietly into retirement.

Mark Nevelow, who got the job of creating Piranha Press, as he called the new line ("Comics with Teeth"), was another trouble maker: sarcastic, contemptuous of the mainstream, eager to offend everybody. The "creator-owned" line turned out not to be, since Warner Communications insisted on retaining trademarks and the right to continue a series even if the creators didn't like it, so Nevelow had to

By the late '80s it seemed like anyone could bring out a comic book—even the present authors. Jacobs and Jones's reluctant hero, Lester Girls, is drawn by Tim Hamilton (*The Trouble with Girls* #1, Aug. 1987.)

TM & © 1988 Will Jacobs and
Gerard Jones. Artwork ©
1988 Tim Hamilton

use all the pitching skills he'd learned selling rags to yuppies. Piranha, he said, would be the Virgin Records of comics, and he was looking for the next David Lynch, for the graphic equivalent of *Blue Velvet*. He had the whole industry hungry for his releases, and hating him personally.

This was a bold DC, willing to bring brawlers, smart-asses, and rebels under its roof. DC would never hire their like again.

The independents were becoming more "alternative" than ever. Everyone who'd been through the crash of '84 had predicted that the black-and-white glut would have to lead to a bust, and so it did—but at first only the obvious garbage, like all the *Turtles* imitations, took the brunt of it. Eclipse's Hamster, Koala, and Groundhog empire collapsed, but *Zot!* and the rest hung in. Then First Comics had a huge hit with a translation of Frank Miller's favorite Japanese comic, *Lone Wolf and Cub*. Eclipse set up a partnership with Viz Comics, a San Francisco subsidiary of Japan's Shogakukan, to bring out its own line of *manga*. Viz hired a talented crew to help with its translating and packaging: Toren Smith, writer and translator, whose Studio Proteus became America's most conscientious *manga*-translating firm; James Hudnall, becoming a respected mainstream writer; and a gifted cartoonist, Lea Hernandez. Viz/Eclipse scored with the charming *Mai, the Psychic Girl*, and announced plans to publish the great humorous

adventure comics of Rumiko Takahashi, the most commercially successful comic book creator in the world. A company called Now Comics popped up, adapting *Speed Racer* and other Japanese cartoons. Soon there were American imitations popping up, like *Ninja High School*. It seemed that a new revolution in comics, new aesthetics and whole new genres, might be coming to America from across the Pacific.

Dark Horse was going strong with *Concrete* and *The American*, eyeing Hollywood intently as more "comic book movies" like *Aliens* and *Predator* cleaned up at the box office. Comico was doing well with its heavy *Grendel* and its commercial licenses, well enough to hire a couple of well-respected veterans of retail and industry publishing, Diana Schutz and Bob Shreck, to oversee its growing line. Thanks to their wonky sensibilities, Comico gifted fandom with one of the most enchanting single comic books of all time: *Gumby's Summer Fun Special*, a dreamlike voyage through a world of space bears and magic whistles, via the odd mind of *Flaming Carrot*'s Bob Burden and the delicate cartooning of Art Adams. It was fantasy and adventure, but it quite pointedly wasn't about superheroes.

A little company called Eternity made a splash with *Pirate Corps*, a science-fiction humor romp by a wild cartoonist named Evan Dorkin. Jan Strnad's Mad Dog Graphics was having some luck with its charming *Keith Laumer's Retief*. Tom Mason did a fun humor comic, *Splat!*, for Strnad, then joined Dave Olbrich in creating Malibu Comics (from Scott Rosenberg's ill-gotten gains). Malibu released its first comics in the summer of 1987. Most were market-oriented grim-and-gritty stuff, like Mike Valerio's *Stealth Force* and R.A. Jones's *Darkwolf*. But it was a wide-open humor comic by Will Jacobs and Gerard Jones that won over the alternative comics crowd and kept going up in sales while the rest of the line was going down.

"We'd never planned to write comics," said Jones, "but when Mike Valerio told us Dave Olbrich was looking for ideas, we sent him part of an abandoned humor novel, *The Trouble with Girls*. We discovered that we could do anything in independent comics—*anything*—even things that made no sense narratively or commercially. Somehow with pictures, and with the self-referentiality and clubbishness of modern comics, they all worked. We had more fun on *Girls* than we've ever had on any project, and we did the best writing there that we've ever done, in any medium." The abandoned novel turned into one of the longest-running independent comics of its time, running to over fifty issues from three publishers, in color and black and white. There would be artistic contributions from Paul Gulacy, Walter Simonson, Bret Blevins, and others, but the vast bulk of the stories were drawn by Tim Hamilton, who started with a nice touch for facial expressions but little else, and matured in *Girls*'s pages into a solid artist who could combine farcical action and quiet naturalism like few other artists.

"Our hero is a Walter Mitty in reverse," Jacobs said. "A guy named Lester Girls, who just wants to live the quiet life with a mousy wife in a bungalow in a small town. But he's cursed to live the life of the American mass media dream—dames, action, Ferraris, caviar, 7.8 percent of the world's wealth. It started as a satire of cheesy commercial entertainment, but suddenly we were pouring into it everything we'd ever read or laughed at." Jacobs and Jones did riffs on Marvel excess, Mort Weisinger's Superman mythos, and Carl Barks's Donald Duck. Then they tackled William Faulkner, Philip K. Dick, and a jungle adventure that caused even the characters in the story to argue about whether it was a satire of Joseph Conrad or Francis Ford Coppola. "Nobody was doing independent comics for money then," said Jacobs, "so we were afraid of nothing. We went right after the hypersensitivity about sexism and racism that was starting to take over America in the late '80s." "*Girls* was labeled misogynistic by timid liberal goofballs," said Jones, "especially comic book guys who thought looking sensitive would get them laid. But real hardcore feminists got the satire and fell in love with it."

Among those who praised it was Angela Bocage, a cartoonist for *Wimmen's Comix* and creator of *Real Girl*: "Maxi Scoops, Lily Lee the Lizard Lady, even

the lively gang of lesbian pirates quoting Helen Reddy, succeed for me as Lynda Barry, Nicole Hollander, and many of my *Wimmen's* colleagues do, as insightful and finally very 'womanist' humor.... Jacobs and Jones craftily manage to embody the limitations of lives lived in subjection to our culture's straitjacketed ideals...with an egalitarian zeal and a fearless witness to such ideals' thoroughgoing absurdity." "Is it Art or Cuisinart?" asked a movie critic named D. Scott Apel. "Philosophically pure and hilariously puerile, 'Les' is indeed more; more than just a comic book, more than those artsy-fartsy 'commix'.... Is there anything more subversive than packaging [this] message of yearning

The many moods of Lester Girls, warmly cartooned by Tim Hamilton...

...and a peculiarly Jacobs-and-Jonesian paean to the lost glories of the consumer culture. (*The Trouble with Girls* #13, Nov. 1988.)

for lost values in the guise of an action-packed parody of contemporary society?" "We just thought we were being funny," said Jacobs.

"What we loved about *Girls* was what we loved about comics in those years," Jones has written. "It couldn't be pigeonholed, and it was constantly surprising everyone, even the creators. We couldn't imagine, then, the boundaries of comics could ever do anything but get wider and wider." Jones, still intoxicated by the field, started parlaying his new visibility into mainstream assignments, but found nothing that equalled the joy of writing about Lester Girls. Jacobs, sensing that the mainstream was going in directions he didn't like, stuck to Lester, his novels, and the used bookstore he was setting up. "Because of *The Comic Book Heroes*, everybody thought we'd be dying to write superheroes," Jacobs said. "But I didn't see anywhere to go with modern superheroes."

No one was getting rich on the independent market anymore, but that only served to make the people who stayed with it more dedicated than ever. With her husband, Harvey Pekar, established as an oddball sort of celebrity, Joyce Brabner organized some of the best in the business—Alan Moore, Stephen Bissette, John Totleben, Mark Badger, Mike Barr, Steve Leialoha, and more—for works of radical political comment. *Real War Stories* was counterpropaganda to the US military recruitment campaigns that followed the box office success of *Top Gun*. *Brought to Light* was a dramatization of the Christic Institute's discoveries about Reagan's Iran-Contra crimes. Warner Books planned to publish it, then lost its nerve and backed out. Eclipse got it into print. Alan Moore formed his own company, Mad Love, to publish *Aargh*, an anti-homophobia benefit book, and *Big Numbers*, a story about real life and real ethnicity in London, drawn by Bill Sienkiewicz. Cartoonists in the *Gay Comix* and *Wimmen's Comix* nexus brought out *StripAIDS USA*. Trina Robbins and a young feminist named Liz Schiller formed Angry Isis press to publish *Choices*, a benefit book for reproductive rights, with dozens of contributors.

Schiller was part of a new wave of young women

drawn to independent comics for their creative freedom and supportive community. Some—Angela Bocage, Mary Fleener, Carol Lay, and an army of others—became cartoonists in the neo-underground manner, articulating a new feminist aesthetic with their funky, funny, sexually-charged, artistically ambitious work. Fantagraphics and Kitchen Sink gave them prominent venues, helping some comic book boys to reconsider their ideas about women, gender, and sex. Other women, like Anina Bennett, were drawn more to the mainstream—but weren't the "geeks" of yore. Bennett was Oberlin-educated, poised, and attractive, and yet (and doesn't that "yet" say so much about comic book preconceptions?) she edited for First and Dark Horse, and wrote an offbeat action series, *Heartbreakers*, with artist Paul Guinan. Bennett, Schiller, and others like them formed an organization to make comics friendlier to females; they named it Friends of Lulu, after the greatest of all comic book girls, Little Lulu, whose adventures were sadly out of print except in hundred-dollar reprint collections. And like most fans of the alternatives, they had almost no interest in superheroes.

Organizing was in the air, as comicdom's leading citizens sought to sustain the electrifying unity of '86 in the aftermath of the Kirby uprising. Dave Sim, then almost a cult-leader to the self-publishing and small-press movements, pulled together a series of "creators' summits" to pound out an agenda for reforming the industry. Scott McCloud drafted a "Bill of Rights for Comics Creators," an elegantly simple statement of a creator's right to control his own material in every way. Frank Miller, Steve Grant, and some of their commercially-minded LA buddies created a newsletter called *WAP* ("Words and Pictures"), intended as a nexus for a freelancers' union. They filled it with hostile anti-corporate cartoons, inspirational articles (Dave Sim on self-publishing, Mike Barr on the DC writers' revolt of '67), and lots of bitchy gossip about Marvel and DC editors.

The priorities were different at Marvel. DeFalco let editors and freelancers run free and reinvent themselves, as long as they ran free in the direction of higher sales. The excitement was palpable, and the kids responded. In the wake of *Dark Knight* and its cartoony, Kirbyesque graphics, a look that only Frank Miller could have sold and gotten fans to accept as "serious," a new bigness was coming into Marvel art. Todd McFarlane, a favorite of conservative DC fans, jumped ship when he got a chance to take over *The Incredible Hulk* 330 (Apr. 1987). McFarlane was no Howard Chaykin. He was a blunt, rough-edged, guy from Eastern Canada. The joke went that he had a vocabulary of a hundred words, half of which were "fuck." But he knew people, he knew the world, he knew what he wanted and how to get there. The high-prestige projects were attracting all the best artists, but Todd wasn't into that kind of prestige, and he knew that the bread and butter of the industry was still the video-game set. He wanted to run his own life, which in comics meant commercial clout, which meant giving fourteen-year-old boys what they were craving. Power. Anger. Horror. Pyrotechnics. On *Infinity Inc.* Todd had done DC-style "class," but on *Hulk* he pushed the muscularity, the bigness—the Kirby. He'd even end up using Kirby's old collage technique. *Hulk* sales rose.

J.M. DeMatteis, with artist Mike Zeck, sold a lot of comics with his "Death of Kraven" arc in the Spider-Man titles, a canny blend of the *Watchmen* style with Marvel fights-and-angst (*Web of Spider-Man* 31, Oct. 1987). It proved that the brighter superhero fans liked fancy technique, but didn't want too much revisionism or deconstruction anymore. An even bigger success, at the same time, was the wedding of Peter "Spider-Man" Parker to Mary Jane, his girlfriend of fourteen years (in comic book time). No experimentation, just a pay-off for the dedicated fan (*ASM Annual* #21, Summer 1987).

When Archie Goodwin and his Epic line got a British team to do a revisionist take on superheroes in *Watchmen*'s wake, they got Kevin O'Neil and Pat Mills, from the violence-heavy *Judge Dredd*. Their *Marshal Law* (Oct. 1987) played superheroes as thugs and rapists serving a fascist state, and it made some fierce satirical comments on the genre with an unabashed leftism. But it also wallowed in its own violence and sexual titillation, and blurred the line between satire and serious superhero kicks with O'Neil's savagely energetic art. Under the guise of being anti-superheroic, it made itself fully salable to teenage fight-fans.

Carl Potts, having made his *Punisher* miniseries a success, followed with a regular series in the spring of '87. To pencil and ink it he turned to Frank Miller's regular inker, Klaus Janson, who brought to the Punisher a lighter, quick-reading version of the *Dark Knight* look. To write it he got Mike Baron, who let his ever-simmering anger run free in nonstop, brutal action, deftly sold with his most cynical humor. Even readers who complained about "gratuitous violence" found it impossible to put this *Punisher* down as the bodies piled up. Sales piled up even faster. Over the previous few years, DC had found a way to sell superheroes to older readers, and had briefly taken the lead in market share. But now Marvel had found a way to sell the highest-impact tricks of the DC style to its angry young men and action-loving boys. It rose back into first place, with a bullet.

As DC fought to keep up, things began to look a little ominous. It revived *The Doom Patrol* (Oct. 1987) and *The Spectre* (Apr. 1987) with a lot of Marvel-style darkness and angst. Mike Grell abandoned his low-key *Sable* for a DC Prestige-format miniseries called *Green Arrow: The Longbow Hunters*. Under the protection of DC's new "mature readers" advisory, it was one of the bloodiest and cruelest comics yet published, and twisted all the left-wing indignation of the superarcher into a vengeful, murderous rage against the slime who kidnapped and tortured his woman. It hit the stores in the summer of 1987, soon before the San Diego Con, and was a sobering event after the demanding, endearing, and funny DCs of the previous year. But it sold.

Soon Mike Baron would leave *Flash* to launch some bloody Prestige-format projects for DC: a new *Deadman*, with the powerful horror art of Kelly Jones, and *The Butcher*, about which nothing more need be said. Baron's *Nexus*, which had already lost

Steve Rude to assorted DC projects, lost most of its charm now, too, turning grimmer and darker. *Flash* would pass into the hands of William Messner-Loebs, the former Bill Loebs, who gave up his efforts to keep *Journey* alive and tried to bring his leisurely, humanistic style to commercial superheroes. It never worked, at least not the way *Journey* and *Jonny Quest* had worked.

The superhero genre and its impassioned fans and fans-turned-practitioners had done more than anything else to transform the comic book field. But the elevation of superheroes had reached a peak, and now there seemed to be nowhere else to go. When artists and writers did personal work, there were no capes or costumes to be seen. When they took on superheroes, it was with one eye on sales figures. No one knew where this business was going, and it wasn't time yet to think about it. For years the comics field had been looking forward, forward, forward. But in August of 1987, in the fading afterglow and the eternally balmy air of San Diego, it was time to look back.

The San Diego Con came around, as it always did, and Jack Kirby was there, as he always was. He wasn't just the creator of everyone's favorite heroes now, he was everyone's favorite hero in his own right. In a few weeks he'd be seventy years old, something that Kirby, typically, wasn't thinking about. Mark Evanier was thinking about it, as was Greg Theakston, an artist who was publishing anthologies of early Kirby work; they were organizing a surprise party. Evanier worked the convention floor, handing out invitations and asking for voluntary contributions to help defray the costs. "I have never experienced anything like it," Evanier later wrote for *Comics Buyer's Guide*. "For three and a half days, people at the convention—some of them total strangers to me; some of them people who couldn't even arrange to get to the party—were coming up to me and throwing money my way.... At one point Paul Levitz of DC...suggested that DC would gladly foot half the cost of the party or, if Marvel

wouldn't kick in the other half, the whole tariff. Carol Kalish quickly affirmed that Marvel would pay, match, or better any DC offer." But Evanier told them "that Jack's fans wanted this to be their party, not some company-sponsored thing." By the night of the party, Evanier had collected "thousands and thousands of dollars."

"I hope you were there that night," Evanier wrote. "Most of those who were have hailed it as a night they will never forget." It took some complex pretexts and some help from Roz Kirby, Sergio Aragonés, Richard Howell, and DC editor Bob Greenberger to drag Kirby to the closed door of a hotel ballroom, behind which waited hundreds of comic book artists, writers, editors, publishers, and critics. The Hernandez brothers, Marvel insiders, Piranha's Mark Nevelow. Len Wein and Marv Wolfman and other old vets who'd once been fanboys at Jack's feet. Matt Feazell, the king of stick-figure minicomics, leading a conversation on "Who's your favorite Kirby inker?" Then the word spread: "Kirby is coming."

"I slipped into the room," wrote Evanier, "and saw everyone standing there, quiet, smiling, waiting. I remember Frank Miller in the front of the pack, wearing a grin to make the Joker look like Buster Keaton. And then Jack came in, everyone started singing 'Happy Birthday,' and he got it." No one who was there can remember how long the party lasted. It rolled through a buzzing, yelling, teary, boozy night. Jack and Roz danced, and the crowd parted. Jack shook every hand that was shoved at him, listened to every "thank you for everything you've given me" that was gushed at him. "Thanks," he'd say back, "you're a real guy." He seemed to mean it every time, but no one in the room felt quite as real as Jack.

At last it ended, sometime early the next morning, and the makers of comic books shuffled on to their uncertain future. But for that one night, the comic book field wasn't such a tragic one after all.

CHAPTER 43

INVASION

The '80s had blown the gates off the village of comics and let it rush out into a bigger and richer world. What happens when a village does that, of course, is that the world also rushes in.

Tim Burton was having trouble making a story work for *Batman*. He was reportedly about to be bounced off the project when his *Beetlejuice* opened with a surprisingly strong box office. His black humor and feverish visual sense, it seemed, nailed young people at the end of the disenchanted '80s. Sam Hamm got himself hired to write Burton a coherent script (which he did, though one would never guess it by the post-rewriter, post-Burton result), and Warner Bros. green-lighted production. Hamm has said he didn't expect anything big, "just a fun little movie"—until Jack Nicholson agreed to play the Joker for a huge cut of the gross. Suddenly everyone in America knew *Batman* was coming, and in comics fandom it was Topic A for 1988. Bootleg comics for Hamm's script were passed around, then sold, and then finally advertised by some idiot in the *Buyer's Guide* before Warner took legal action. The *Buyer's Guide* letters pages were filled with arguments about who should play Batman—he needed that angular chin, that fierce nose. When Burton chose Michael Keaton, the arguments exploded into one long wail of dismay. That lumpy nose! That rolling chin! "The way they were going on about the chin and the nose," said DC's Brian Augustyn, "nobody would've satisfied them except Barbara Stanwyck."

Meanwhile, *Teenage Mutant Ninja Turtles* was exploding into the baffled American consciousness as the biggest cartoon-toy-and-licensing machine in the history of the consumer culture. Well into the '90s, there wasn't a parent of young children in America who'd never had a turtle-shaped bruise on the bottom of his foot. Kevin Eastman and Peter Laird had spent $1,200 to publish their first *Turtles*

comic and would end up as the masters of a two-billion-dollar industry. Archie Comics adapted the cartoon show—the only case anyone could recall of a comic book adaptation of an adaptation of a comic book—and made enough money for a ballyhooed revamp of the Riverdale gang. Peter Laird created the Xeric Foundation to support self-publishers, and Kevin Eastman formed Tundra Press to publish creator-owned, adult-oriented comics. Both Xeric and Tundra were explicitly shaped by the principles of Dave Sim's creator summits and Scott McCloud's Creator Bill of Rights. Unfortunately, neither had the impact that their founders hoped. Inexperienced management didn't help, but a bigger problem may have been the emerging truth about comics for adults. "I thought the market was a lot larger than it really was," Eastman would say. "I figured naturally people would grow up through *X-Men* and discover...*Dark Knight* and *Watchmen* and beyond. But every time you add another year to a comic reader's life...you automatically lose a certain percentage of that audience . . . Ninety percent of [adults] will not go into a comic book store." Eastman and Laird bought *Heavy Metal* magazine, hoping to make its readers more aware of "cutting-edge" comics, but the two audiences just didn't seem to mix.

Batman and *Turtles* were building so much heat in Hollywood that producers and studio execs started scanning the comics racks for likely properties and even possible writers. A syndicated *Superboy* TV show went into production, and would distract Andy Helfer, Mike Carlin, and other DC insiders from their comics by hiring them to write scripts. Sam Hamm was hired to write a *Watchmen* script. A cheap *Punisher* movie went into production. Frank Miller was hired to write a sequel to *Robocop*, an almost guaranteed screen credit. Howard Chaykin was juggling screenplay and teleplay offers. It wasn't just the hot stuff that was getting interest, either. Jeph Loeb and Matt Weissman, the *Commando* creators, put together a deal for *Reid Fleming, World's Toughest Milkman*, and then went after *The Trouble with Girls*. "We had three producers after *Girls*," said Will Jacobs, "when the comic was selling only six or seven thousand copies. We finally made a deal with 20th Century-Fox, not just for the option, but to write a screenplay." Even the Hernandez brothers were besieged by producers, although what *Love and Rockets* would be beyond the comics page was hard to imagine.

Joel Silver, who'd gone on from *48 Hours* to make *Lethal Weapon*, *Die Hard*, and *Predator*, was optioning comics by the dozen, and even put *Green Lantern* through a couple of rounds of script treatments. Mike Richardson at Dark Horse showed that he had not just the drive but the resources to be a player, putting a big chunk of that *Concrete* income into the license to adapt *Aliens* from 20th Century-Fox. He also had the brains to understand that the market for "comic book movies" wasn't just kids, so he targeted affluent older fans with good art, slick production, and heavy promotion. The first issue of the *Aliens* comic book sold more than 300,000 copies, almost unimaginable for an independent. He followed up quickly with *Predator*, with new stories about the murderous alien to be written by Mark Verheiden. In the course of working on it with Joel Silver, Verheiden pitched his *American*, got a deal out of it, and was soon Silver Pictures' hot new find. DC got the rights to do a "prequel" to Silver's next opus, *The Adventures of Ford Fairlane*, and gave the writing job to Gerard Jones, who was seen as an inexhaustible source of smart-ass dialogue. Based on the prequel, Jones was hired to write a screenplay for Silver. On the strength of *The Trouble with Girls*, a comic book that barely paid back its own expenses, Jones had two movie deals and more on the way. Yet, comics were exciting and lucrative enough that people like him and Verheiden didn't just drop them and run.

Jeph Loeb, meanwhile, couldn't get *Reid Fleming* into production and saw opportunities in the other direction. While schmoozing with Jenette Kahn

during one of her Hollywood tours, he pitched her an idea for a Chaykinesque revamp of *Challengers of the Unknown*. The idea of established screenwriters working for DC appealed to her, and Loeb and artist Tim Sale were soon working on it. Miguel Ferrer, who'd played the villain in *Robocop*, turned out to be a comics fan, and he and his friend Bill Mumy (who'd starred in TV's *Lost in Space*, which was stolen from *Space Family Robinson*) created a comic called *Comet Man* for Marvel. They became a fixture at the San Diego Con, along with their friend and fellow fan Mark Hamill, who had starred in *Star Wars*, which had been inspired by comics and then helped revive them. Ferrer and Mumy also played in a band, Seduction of the Innocent, at major comics conventions, along with Steve Leialoha, who'd inked the *Star Wars* comic book, and Max Allan Collins, who wrote *Ms. Tree* and whose mystery novels were starting to take off in the book trade. Mumy had also been in a band, Barnes and Barnes, which had been a favorite of the alternative comics scene before anyone knew that Mumy was in it or that Mumy was a comics fan. Then some British alt-rock song hit the airwaves with the lyric, "Alan Moore knows the score." And somewhere in there, a British writer named Neil Gaiman, already being stuck with the label "The Next Alan Moore," began hanging around with a young songwriter and singer named Tori Amos. The lines between comics and other media were getting awfully blurry.

DC hadn't known what to do with Batmania in '66 or Superfever in '78, but this time its Batsploitation would be relentless. Jim Starlin took over writing, but not drawing, *Batman* in late 1987, though he showed none of his old distinction and inventiveness. Frank Miller had established that the new Robin was dead in the "possible future" of *Dark Knight*, so now Starlin and Denny O'Neil made it their business to kill him. He'd been an obnoxious character from the start, but Starlin pushed that now with a mean-spiritedness and a love of sneering violence that he'd never approached even in the most brutal stretches of *Dreadstar* (and *Dreadstar* had long ago shed most of its characterization and philosophy in favor of formula combat). It was as if all the pain and anger that he'd once turned toward his heroes' crises of integration and self-transcendence were now being projected outward into sadistic villains and snarling, unthinking vigilantes. But hey, it was the '80s.

It all built to "A Death in the Family," a prolonged story line that teased readers with promises that it would—or wouldn't—kill Robin. O'Neil wanted to milk some PR out of the new 900 numbers that phone companies were pushing and saw a chance to kill that bird—and a Robin—with the same stone. He gave fans a highly publicized chance to kill Robin or save him. He expected all along that they'd vote to kill. And so they did.

There was a special cruelty to the death: Robin didn't die in heroic sacrifice, but because he defied Batman's orders and cockily charged in to "kick butt" when his surrogate father preached caution (*Batman* 428, 1988). The most vivid image of the whole thing was the Joker's glee at the act of killing. It was chilling but strangely satisfying to kids who saw parents as nothing but weaklings who couldn't hold them back while they rushed toward inevitable disaster.

The parents didn't like it. DC took tremendous mass-media flak for making children co-conspirators in the murder of a fictional child, further heated by the fact that most people assumed that this Robin was *the* Robin, the smiling lad they'd all grown up with. Sheltered within the strange world of violent fantasies and direct-market manipulations, otherwise decent people like Denny O'Neil had lost sight of how sickening it all was. The word came down from Warner never to do that again. The word came in from retailers, though, that the fans were gobbling it up, and new readers were actually coming into comic shops, made curious by all the hysteria. The collectibles market was responding, too. Speculators in pop culture ephemera, even from outside comics, were buying extra copies under the impression that this marked the end of Robin's fifty-year career. The smell of money was in the air. The trick to getting it,

obviously, was to come up with events that created an illusion of momentousness and collectability without angering grown-ups.

In the meantime, Starlin had proven that he might have abandoned everything that made him distinct and charming, that his scripting might be forcedly hard-edged and characterless, but he could structure a formula superhero story as well as anyone, hitting all the beats that made it feel compelling, butt-kicking, and cataclysmic enough to catch the attention of teenage fans from all the piles of overhyped superhero product. Starlin was becoming a name again, to a generation of fans who'd probably have had no interest in old cosmic fables. He got a Prestige miniseries—which freelancers were beginning to discover was the most lucrative format on the market—in *Batman: The Cult*, and his friend Berni Wrightson returned to the mainstream after a long absence to draw it. It was an even more mean-spirited story, another reactionary mythification of "urban scum," this one casting homeless people as a vast and violent horde threatening to descend upon cities and devour decent property owners. The story seemed poisoned by the greedy, competitive mood behind it, or by the shame around that mood, and the art didn't have a drop of the passion that Wrightson put into his illustration work. But it sold, and sold, and sold.

Next Starlin wrote a miniseries, *Cosmic Odyssey*, in which John Stewart, a Green Lantern, causes the death of a populous planet and then gets over it with just a bit of macho posturing. The art by Mike Mignola was powerful, but the story was pure manipulation, a far cry from Starlin's cosmic odysseys of the past.

Meanwhile, *Batman: The Killing Joke*, by Alan Moore and Brian Bolland, had finally hit print. It was a bit of an anticlimax, a complex story but a cold one, relying on a rather simplistic insanity metaphor and the narrative devices already familiar from *Watchmen*. It did sharpen fandom's hunger to see Batman and the Joker on the big screen, and sold steadily for long after the movie came out. Its greatest gift to the Batline of comics, however, was an injury gruesomely

[1] What he and the other hot new artists *didn't* take from Kirby was storytelling. They relied more and more on splash panels and "poster shots" of the heroes, undermining the narratives of their comics—but making their original art more far more salable at comic cons. The collectibles market was affecting comics through more than just circulation figures.

inflicted on Batgirl by the Joker, which enabled Denny O'Neil to stick her in a wheelchair in his regular series—joining the tradition of Denny's Carol Ferris and Heather. Paralysis and maiming would become ever more popular sales-gimmicks in DC comics, and O'Neil would later return to the back-breaking motif with very profitable results.

DC was learning the calculated pain and rage game, but Marvel had the edge, and soon the sales gap between the two companies started to widen again. *The Punisher* continued to build in popularity, even after Klaus Janson left, Mike Baron fell into "sausage making," and all the pickier fans drifted off. A second title, *Punisher War Journal*, soon joined it, (Nov. 1988) and more series and miniseries were in the works for when the *Punisher* movie came out. It appeared, in fact, that the Punisher was bringing in a new audience: boys and young men who were contemptuous of all the superpowers and masks of the real superheroes but found this guy with the gun adequately dignified. The stereotype that beckons here is "young white men," but they weren't necessarily. Black, Latino, and Asian males were feeling just as squeezed as white ones, if not in quite the same vice, and they were discovering comics and comic book movies now that they were no longer seen as geek turf—and now that more tough-guy comics were giving up preaching a middle-class liberal humanist ethos. From the Punisher, these new readers could be lured to Wolverine, and then to the X-Men, and then turned into a new and lucrative kind of Marvel Zombie who mixed their comics fandom with beach volleyball, action movies, and chasing cute chicks. And money. It didn't take long to learn that *X-Men* 94 had originally sold for forty cents and was now selling for three hundred dollars. A guy had to figure that if he got in on the next hot comic and stocked up on first issues, he could buy himself a Camaro.

Or he could *make* the next hot comic and buy a whole lot of Camaros. The artist on *Punisher War Journal* was Carl Potts's prize discovery, a young man from San Diego named Jim Lee. He was of Korean ancestry, not just one of the new, cool, good-looking young men finding their way into comics, but part of a new wave of California Asians, mixing those old family virtues of pragmatism and restraint with an aggressive sense of entitlement and capability. Several Asian-Americans were suddenly making impacts as comics artists—Whilce Portacio, Ron Lim—but Lee was the juggernaut. His draftsmanship was confident, his work ethic indefatigable, and month by month he steadily, relentlessly, made himself the master of everything that Marvel boys loved: monumental figures, facial torment, excruciating detail. His most distinctive invention was the Lee woman: elongated legs, plastic flesh, wasp waist, molded breasts, an icon of consumer-culture sexual symbols without a trace of sex, the *Sports Illustrated* swimsuit girl as action figure, collectible, superhero trophy.

He brought something more to his art, though, and it was that something that pushed him over the top. Lee was finding his style around 1985 and 1986, when Jack Kirby was in the air. It was the assimilation of Kirby's forward-thrusting composition, Kirby's blocky anatomy, Kirby's stripped-down content, and understanding of comics as iconography instead of illustration, that brought the force into Lee's art.[1] He and Potts worked well together. Both were graciously masculine, Californian, took worldly success as their due, and were fond of good food, Marvel heroes, and Jack Kirby. Neither displayed much open emotion, which in Lee's case showed in his characters' emotional contortions, never the wide-open explosions of Kirby or even the frenzy of Gil Kane, but the bottled-up angst, twisting without breaking free, that the new fans responded to. Potts and Lee would drink together, play all-night poker games together, and under Potts's craft-conscious editorial eye, Lee became the consummate comic book artist of his moment. He was too good for *The Punisher*, in fact. The action, the angst, the detail made him the perfect *X-Men* artist, the man Chris Claremont had been needing for years. So it seemed to Chris, at least, when he welcomed Lee aboard. Chris, alas, couldn't see his own future as clearly as

he could that of his mutants.

The X-franchise had already been educating Marvelites in flamboyantly surfaced, design-conscious art, and now it was Spider-Man's turn. Todd McFarlane had pushed his style toward the utmost intensity on *Hulk*, and when he moved to *Amazing Spider-Man* in 1988, he pushed further. He was still utterly controlled in his line work, intensely detailed, and driven by design more than movement or anatomy—all those things the video and computer generation still loved. But he wanted something utterly unique, something to make his Spider-Man quintessentially his own and quintessentially "Spidey," and he found it in Steve Ditko. He took Ditko's use of webbing as a design motif, his twisted anatomy, his organic lines, his evocation of the horror implicit in the concept of a "spider-man," and reworked it into an in-your-face, big-figured, high-violence, high-design style that sold to the modern audience.

"Marvel editor-in-chief Tom DeFalco once called me in the office and said, 'Quit drawing your spaghetti webbing,'" McFarlane recalled. "I said,

'Yes, sir.' 'Don't make the eyes so big. How come you put so much black in his costume?' I said, 'Oh, yes, sir. I'll change it back, sir.' Then the next issue I'd make the eyes twice as big, I'd make spaghetti webbing twice as long, and the sales would go up which would aggravate the editors even more." For Spidey's twenty-fifth anniversary (*ASM* 300, May 1988) he designed a horrific new villain named Venom—actually the black costume Spidey wore for a while after *Secret Wars*, but transformed by Todd's courageous grotesquerie into an animated embodiment of malice.

After years of solid "heroic realism" and slick sophistication, McFarlane's flamboyant cartooning, the sheer fun of his lines that stopped just shy of the adolescent threshold for tolerating humor, knocked the fourteen-year-olds flat. Older superhero junkies pooh-poohed it—"I miss that beautifully controlled work on *Infinity, Inc.*"—and DC editors dismissed it disgustedly as flash without substance. It was like the ghost of Sol Harrison whispering in the halls that Marvel's secret was "bad art." But that attitude was

Jim Lee was a punch in the face to young fans. The massiveness and forward thrust are from Kirby. The use of figures to the exclusion of setting, the exploding muscles, the plastic breasts, the grimaces—and all those Scott Williams ink lines—are straight from '80s America. (*The Uncanny X-Men* #275, Apr. 1991.)

325

killing DC with the kids. Marvel editors may not have understood Todd McFarlane's appeal, but the Marvel attitude was mercenary enough to make use of it. At DC, Dick Giordano and Joe Orlando set the visual tone of the company, and although they had once been almost radical in contrast to Sol Harrison, pushing for sophistication and nuance, now they were up against something more radical still, radical for its reductionism and bluntness. DC's old corporate culture—paternalism, loyalty, commitment to quality—lived on in new forms, reinforced by years as the "classy" company, the alternative to Marvel preferred by older fans. As Marvel became flashier and more successful, DC's artistic integrity seemed to translate into a determination to prove that the traditional ways were the right ways.

DC's stalwarts were conservative storytellers like Jerry Ordway and Dan Jurgens, or great traditional draftsmen like Eduardo Barreto and José Garciá-López, or young guys who worked hard to tell clear stories without calling too much attention to themselves, like Ron Randall and Mike Parobeck. Comics was showbiz, though, and attention was the whole game—and McFarlane showed he understood that when he moved to LA and started to hang out with Jim Lee.

It had always been wholesome DC against hip Marvel, except that in the late '80s wholesomeness meant the social and artistic conscience of Kahn, Levitz, and Giordano, and hipness meant the aggression of Shooter, DeFalco, and New World Pictures. When Brian Augustyn, a Chicago Democrat of the old school, pitched a short-term backup series about a liberal Mexican-American superhero named El Diablo, Jenette Kahn said no. It should be an ongoing series of its own, she said, "because it's the kind of thing we ought to do." It was a sincere act, and a brave one, which some commerce-minded staffers had little use for. Bruce Bristow in the marketing department was quoted by retailers as having told them, "Don't buy it, it's a stupid book." The lack of Latino creators was an obstacle, but Gerard Jones and Mike Parobeck did their best. The doggedly political

El Diablo sank like a rock, while Latino teenagers were buying Wolverine and Punisher.

To regain its momentum, DC went for another crossover. Crisis on Infinite Earths and Legends had shown that fans could be manipulated into buying comics they normally wouldn't through company-wide events, and now they were becoming annual expectations. DC kept its apocalyptic titles going with Millennium in late 1987. Marvel found that the trick could work even without a limited series to hang it on. The Fall of the Mutants story line sprawled through all the X-titles and a number of others in the summer of '88, tangling story lines, shedding blood, manipulating the "illusion of change," and boosting the sales of some middling series. In a separate gimmick, Mark Gruenwald, Marvel's "continuity cop," created a villain named Scourge to get rid of a bunch of minor villains with redundant powers that annoyed him, and sent him guest-starring across the line, slaughtering bad guys and upping the stakes for bloodshed in all future crossovers.

DC upped the commercial stakes in all future crossovers with Invasion, a three-issue miniseries that would completely dominate the continuity of two issues of every comic book in the DC Universe. Keith Giffen did the story, about an alien invasion of Earth that every DC hero has to fight in his or her own way. DC opened its purse strings to bring McFarlane back for the art (although he reined himself in a little more than on Spider-Man, as if restraint was just in the air at DC). It did well, but it wasn't the mammoth success DC wanted, partly because DC's continuity was rapidly being exposed as a horrendous mess. Crisis had sown more confusion than clarity, and now no one was following the post-Crisis rules: Superman had started over from scratch, Green Lantern just kept chugging through, and Batman jumped all over the place. Giffen, Andy Helfer, and J.M. DeMatteis were just going ahead doing their impudent thing on Justice League, knowing no one would mess with the company's hottest series, while other editors protected their characters' dignities by refusing to incorporate Giffen's "revisionist" ideas into their series. It could have been very liberating if more creators were allowed to run wild, but as Marvel soared and fear filled the air at DC, the mood of the company turned conservative. When Helfer and Giffen revamped Green Lantern in 1989, they added only a maudlin, alcoholic subplot to his origin and gave him gray temples. The new writer, Gerard Jones, wanted to start from scratch, but was told that the continuity of the old series would have to be wrapped up, and any change done slowly.

Marvel's crossovers invariably proved more successful, because the Marvel Universe could support them far more coherently. Even if the crossover itself was overlong, predictable, and messy, Marvel's continuity always seemed to gain in texture and coherence. DC's only got more confused. DC editors would argue about whether to be "more like Marvel" or to "find out what we do best and exploit that." The latter idea felt better, but no one could quite define what DC did best. There was no one to take command. Dick Giordano never really gave a damn about superheroes and continuity anyway, and he saw his job as encouraging creativity, not discouraging it with Shooter-like rules. He'd surrendered the reigns to Marv Wolfman on *Crisis*, and although Marv was gone now, he had no desire to pick them up again. Giordano started doing less editing and more inking, picking up some royalties by inking a lot of first issues and special projects, thinking about retiring before his job became nothing but crossover management.

Then *Batman* opened in May 1989 and became the biggest-grossing movie in history. A sequel was scheduled for 1992, a cartoon show began development, and a *Flash* primetime TV show was rushed to the screen.[2] DC was ready with a ton of product, and a lot of people made big royalties on Bat tie-ins.

Sales on *Batman* and *Detective* soared briefly, but the comics' tone, under Denny O'Neil, was somber and naturalistic, lacking Burton's kinkiness. A couple of Britons, Grant Morrison and Dave McKean, were hired for a follow-up to the Moore-Bolland *Killing Joke*: their *Arkham Asylum* was another Batman-Joker meditation on insanity, a big hit with older fans but

nearly incomprehensible to new readers. A new series, *Batman: Legends of the Dark Knight*, was timed to cash in on the movie, and showcased different writers and artists doing non-continuity takes on the hero (Oct. 1989). It was edited by Andy Helfer, which enabled Denny O'Neil to write the key story arcs—because DC, in another imitation of Marvel, had established a rule against writers editing themselves. O'Neil's opening arc, drawn by DC's in-house cover artist, Ed Hannigan, was just a solid riff on the arcana of Batman's origin. Next would come a moody but slow-paced Alan Moore-ish stint written by Grant Morrison. *Legends of the Dark Knight* would turn out to be aimed, not at potential new readers intrigued by the movie, but at those die-hard fans who'd been craving Batman "special events" since the '70s. Its biggest impact on comicdom was to anger freelancers who were getting tired of DC staffers being "assigned" to write and draw so many high-profile, monster-royalty first issues. Freelancers had accepted such doings as part of Marvel's venality ever since Shooter wrote *Secret Wars*—but DC doing the same felt like a confirmation that short-sighted profiteering had taken over the business.

The rest of the DC mainstream didn't benefit much. John Byrne had run out of gas on the Superman titles, and Andy Helfer had turned the editorship of the increasingly retrograde *Superman* and *Adventures of Superman* over to Mike Carlin. *Action Comics* went to Mike Gold, for a gimmick that he thought would do well with addicted fans: a weekly anthology of diverse heroes (including Green Lantern, whose title was canceled for the purpose). Marvel answered with a biweekly anthology, *Marvel Comics Presents*, headlined by Wolverine and other popular mutants. That turned into a hit, while DC's rushed-looking weekly staggered toward oblivion.

Then, shortly before *Batman* opened, John Byrne went back to the familiar characters and rising incentive payments of Marvel. There he lived up to his nickname, "Mr. Fixit," with relaunches of *Namor the Sub-Mariner*, *Avengers West Coast*, and *She-Hulk*. On *She-Hulk* he stole some of Helfer and Keith

[2] It flopped in its first season, but Howard Chaykin and his studio assistant, John Moore, were hired as story editors; it helped Chaykin move out of comics and gave Moore a cachet that helped him move in.

Giffen's thunder with self-referential fanboy humor of the brashest kind: on the cover of her first issue, the heroine tells readers that if they don't buy her comic, "I'm gonna come to your house and rip up all your *X-Men*" (May, 1989).

Suddenly bratty humor was working for Marvel, now that Burton had made angry self-mockery cool for comics fans. Chris Claremont was scoring with yet another mutant series, this one called *Excalibur*, combining fannish gags with an English setting dear to his heart. The artist, an Englishman of great grace and control named Alan Davis, was the sort of discovery DC would have made a few years earlier. Peter David, who'd won fans over with brisk action and *Hill Street Blues*-style subplots, turned the Hulk into wise-ass cynic who does troubleshooting in Vegas under the name, amusingly, of "Mr. Fixit." David's *Hulk* would be a solid seller with a hardcore following deep into the '90s, and would win him Best Writer honors in the *Comics Buyer's Guide* fan poll year after year. When Fabian Nicieza, who hustled his way out of Marvel's manufacturing department into an editorial post, launched *Wonder Man*, he hired an Alan Davis fan named Jeff Johnson to draw it and the gag-minded Gerard Jones to write it. It wasn't a big success, but Fabian's attitude raised his profile—pretty soon he was writing a lighthearted *Captain America* miniseries, drawn by Kevin Maguire, who'd left DC's *Justice League*. When the X-Men-related annuals needed some snappy dialogue, Fabian got the nod. Meanwhile, a very hip and witty new writer, Dwayne McDuffie, had drawn some notice with his *Damage Control*, about a company that cleans up rubble after superhero fights. With the punchy art of Ernie Colón, it was the freshest superhero self-commentary since Andy Helfer launched *Justice League*.

As for *JL* itself, its fans were still devoted, but it was falling prey to perfunctory gags and farcical plots. When Helfer and Giffen spun off a sequel, *Justice League Europe*, they tried to go for more straight superheroics. The artist, Bart Sears, tried to combine McFarlane's grotesquerie with Kevin Maguire's character bits, but he didn't seem to bring

over any Marvel readers. Giffen spun off two new series in 1989: a retooled *Legion of Super-Heroes* and a twentieth-century-based spinoff, *L.E.G.I.O.N. '89*. The former (written with Tom and Mary Bierbaum, two stars of *Legion* fandom) was intricate and esoteric, aimed at hardcore fans of the old series. It would spend the '90s in a perpetual state of revamp. *L.E.G.I.O.N.* was more Marvelish, with the bold art of Barry Kitson and the smart-ass dialogue of Alan Grant. It was a decent success, mainly because of one character: Lobo, a minor Wolverine imitation here turned into an amoral, wisecracking, bigger-than-reality, genocidal mercenary. Sixteen-year-old boys loved him, but DC had nothing of remotely comparable crassness to offer them. DC made money during the new Batmania, but Marvel kept its lead in market share. It was 1966 all over again.

They were flush times for Marvel. In 1989 New World Pictures sold the company to a holding firm, MacAndrews and Forbes, which in 1990 made the first public stock offering of the Marvel Entertainment Group. Shares opened at eighteen dollars. Within a couple of years they'd soared to sixty, and then split. The principal owner would end up being Ron Perlman, chief owner of Revlon Cosmetics, a boom-and-bust corporate raider of the rampant '80s breed. In 1990, James Galton became chairman of the board, and the presidency went to Terry Stewart. Stewart had never seen the lean days of comics, had never known Jim Shooter, and saw his job as managing an invincible empire, expanding into toys, trading cards, theme parks, and other new frontiers. Tom DeFalco, for his part, joked that whenever a freelancer came in complaining about Marvel, he would just hand him a fin and say, "So get a cab to DC." He called Marvel "an unstoppable juggernaut," and so it seemed to be.

DeFalco's strategy was to build series around familiar characters, juice them up in the old Stan-and-Jack style, and give them big, splashy art. The "back to basics" that had worked for Byrne's *Fantastic Four* and Simonson's *Thor* (and for Simonson's *Fantastic Four*, since he'd taken it over for some fun

Kirbyesque adventures) was becoming a house style. Roy Thomas had even come back, leaving his editorial post at DC to become a freelance writer of old-time heroes for both companies. *The Silver Surfer, Nick Fury, Agent of S.H.I.E.L.D., Ghost Rider, Dr. Strange,* and *Moon Knight* got series again, and this time, with the growing hordes of Marvel Zombies who bought the whole line, they'd stick around. Wolverine got his own title, written by Chris Claremont in the manner of the miniseries he'd done with Miller, and it was an instant hit.

DC was trying to catch up, but inconsistently, even reluctantly. It hired Tim Truman, of *Grimjack* and *Scout,* to do a dark, mean version of the Hawkman mythos with *Hawkworld,* but it was too isolated from the mainstream to affect much. Mike Grell continued *Green Arrow* in the vein of *Longbow Hunters,* with a "mature readers" label that limited its market. DC hooked one hot new artist and then lost him. Rob Liefeld was the poster-boy of a new generation, aggressive young guys who saw comics as a way to make big money, not as a calling. The industry's success and visibility had finally caught up to it. The new kids saw instantly that Lee and McFarlane were the guys to follow, and that the directness of their styles made them easy to mimic. Liefeld was a pug-nosed surfer type from Southern California, who looked fresh out of high school but was afraid of nothing and felt the lack of nothing in himself. His Hawk and Dove miniseries for DC put him on the map, but then Marvel snagged him, letting him take over *New Mutants.* He hung out with McFarlane and Lee, had been accepted by them as promising enough to spend time with, and knew that they were where he wanted to be. Addressing a convention panel, he explained why he wanted to get into comics: "Todd McFarlane lives on the beach in Malibu." Then, as if taking the audience's silence for incomprehension, he stressed again: "He lives right—on—the—*beach*!" Rob was young, but he knew the game.

Todd knew the game, too. He insisted on writing his own comics, stripping down the plots and words and making them a pageant of poster shots, which he

knew the fourteen-year-olds would pay for. Editor Danny Fingeroth was resistant; he'd always like the verboseness and complexity of Spidey, and he wanted to keep *Amazing Spider-Man* in that vein. But Marvel couldn't lose Todd. It was suggested that McFarlane could take over one of the other, "lesser" series, the sluggish *Web of Spider-Man.* Todd had a better idea: cancel *Web* and give him a new first issue, a guaranteed collectible, a guaranteed royalty boon for him. So he created *Spider-Man* 1. It didn't have

Kids went nuts for Todd McFarlane's ornate webbing and visual impact. Investors went nuts for what the kids went nuts for, and the rush was on. (*Spider-Man* #1, Aug. 1990.)

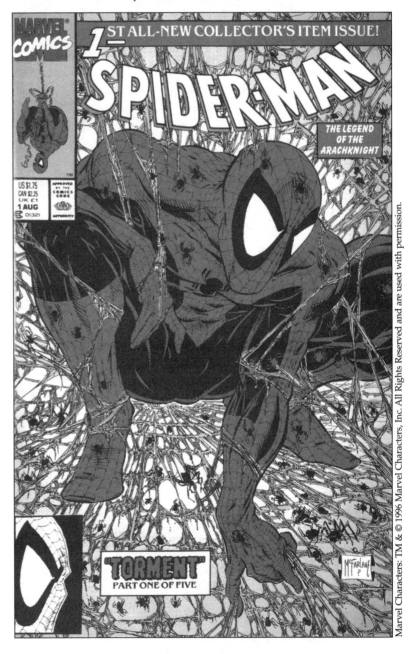

much plot, basically just showed off a monstrous version of the Lizard, with some great effects, the boldest McFarlane Spider-Man pinups yet, some big sound effects, and hammer-over-the head narrative tricks. It also had an editorial by Todd asserting belligerently that nobody needs writers in comics. Marvel played with every gimmick it could think of to promote collectors' interest, including editions in bags (even better than mint if the bag was never opened), different colored covers, everything. Dealers were excited. Speculators, the ones who'd puffed up and then ruined the black-and-white market, were excited. A whole new wave of speculators, moving their money over from the slumping baseball card field, was noticing, and getting excited. Marvel began to realize that this could be more than a hit, that it could do more than the three or four hundred thousand copies of the X-books, that it could be the biggest comic book in a decade. This thing could sell a million.

It sold three million. This was a whole new ball game.

CHAPTER 44

RETREAT

A hundred stories could show the shift in the comic book world, but this is one we happen to know. In the excitement of 1986, Dan Vado, of Slave Labor Graphics, created *Hero Sandwich* with a cartoonist friend named Chuck Austen. *Hero Sandwich* was a sweet, humane riff on superheroes in their daily lives, and Austen's art was more animated and cheerful than anything on the stands. Slave Labor's small circulation made it hard for Austen to pay his bills, however, so when Mark Waid offered him DC's *Phantom Lady*, he jumped at it. Phantom Lady was a near-naked heroine from the late '40's, when the adolescent audience for crime and gore comics had created a small boom in "good girl" art, or cheesecake. Austen's gift for rendering voluptuous female flesh without sacrificing humor or humanity seemed perfect for a warmer spin on the character. As the project neared, however, Waid felt the pressure of DC's increasing nervousness, and told Austen to make his art more "hard-edged" and "gritty." It was the last thing anyone should have asked of Chuck Austen, and it annoyed him into giving up on mainstream comics. When a brief boom in sex comics followed the success of *Omaha the Cat Dancer*, he created a couple of erotic soap operas: *Strips* for Last Gasp and *Hard Ball* for Malibu. The insecurities of the black-and-white market wore him down, though. He moved to the video game industry, and comics lost one of the most appealing cartoonists of the '80s.

Waid's conversion to grittiness had come too late. He was fired by DC for too many in-print jokes and insubordinations. He'd have to fight his way back into comics as a freelancer writer. His friend Brian Augustyn had learned to play the commercial game better, and when he took over *The Flash* he assigned Waid to write it. When Waid and Gerard Jones collaborated on a '60s-style *Flash-Green Lantern* team-up, DC management came down on them in a rage

(*Flash* 69-70 and *GL* 30-31, Sept. 1992). From that point on, Jones began losing interest in commercial superheroes, but Waid focused on cloaking his silver age tastes in a darker, more continuity-driven style. Soon he was emerging as a hot writer.

Dan Vado made his contribution to hard-edged comics by publishing *Sidney Mellon's Thunderskull!*, the "epic masterwork" of the eternally pubescent critic, and a broad satire of the violence and pretension afflicting superheroes (1989). Chuck Austen and his friend Norman Felchle happily did the art. That was Sidney's final statement, and he faded from a comic book scene that was becoming too much a satire of itself. Vado and Felchle went on to create *The Griffin*, a meditative series about a hero returning to earth after a long voyage among the stars. Jenette Kahn liked its warmth and humanity, and picked it up as a six-issue DC Prestige series. Unfortunately, it got lost among all the darker and louder comics on the stands. Vado was eventually hired by Brian Augustyn to write *Justice League America*, where he did his best to jam anger and violence into his work. After a few years of frustration, he quit to devote himself to Slave Labor and the organizing of the Alternative Press Exposition.

So the '80s became the '90s.

Darkness and revisionism were in at DC. Near the end of his *Swamp Thing* tenure, Alan Moore had taken his protagonist to the planet Rann, where he revealed that Adam Strange was not a champion brought to the planet by chance—he was merely a breeding stud for the lovely Alanna, and all those wonderful Gardner Fox menaces were hoaxes concocted by Alanna's manipulative scientist father. Richard Bruning and Andy Kubert followed with the *Adam Strange* miniseries, in which Rann is decimated, Alanna is killed, and Adam picks up a girlfriend from Earth (1990). Moore had mourned the loss of Superman's "world of imagination," but now he'd helped undermine everything charming and unique in DC's great space-romance. Superman was just another muscleman, Adam Strange was just another angry tough-guy. The fans who'd been so encouraged in the early '80s by DC's return to lightness, imagination, and respect for the past now asked themselves, "What's the point?"

Grim reductionism found an audience, though: literate fans in their late teens and early twenties who wanted to see comics advance in sophistication and "seriousness"—or at least in the esteem of cute girls and the hipper quarters of the mass media. The depressive soul-deadness of twenty-somethings in a screwed-up world was becoming hip, as evidenced by the wailings of alt-rock singers and pseudoliterary hokum like Brett Easton Ellis's *Less Than Zero.* The college—and college drop-out—crowd was particularly impressed if it was sold with overeducated irony and a touch of gruesome shock value, as in gothic rock and in horror fantasy of the Clive Barker mold. In comics, it would prove to be British writers, following the model of Alan Moore, who mastered the mood.

The nexus was Karen Berger, a lovely and cultured lass who'd first stumbled into comicdom as a DC editorial assistant. Gradually the job of editing *Swamp Thing* fell upon her, and in Alan Moore's sensibility she found a raft she could cling to in the sea of comic book testosterone. She networked through Moore, made regular missions to the UK Comic Arts Convention, and eventually became DC's official English liaison. Under her editorship, a friend of Moore's called Jamie Delano [1] spun a character from *Swamp Thing* into the hip horror of *Hellblazer* (Jan. 1988). It was dark, funny, overwritten, unpredictable, and intriguingly foreign. It bore a "mature readers" advisory, which enabled it not only to be violent and sexual, but to have the characters talk the way real young people talked, and even to play with the questions of sexual orientation and gender identity that were very much on the minds of urbane youth but were religiously closeted in superhero comics. Bisexual girls lounging in black camisoles, teenage

male hookers in men's rooms—they'd become staples of what DC started calling "sophisticated suspense." The ratings system that Frank Miller and others had assailed as an attack on their freedom set writers like Delano free to create comics that felt authentic to readers in their twenties.

Another Berger contact was a former journalist named Neil Gaiman, who had become a comic book writer thanks largely to having interviewed Alan Moore. He showed a reporter's touch for dialogue and for the low-key vignette revealing a character's quirks and vulnerabilities. His themes were childhood trauma and the compulsions of art, both of them well-suited to his moment and his literate young readers. He made his reputation in England with *Violent Cases*, a disturbing fantasy interweaving stories of organized crime and child abuse. His artistic collaborator was Dave McKean, an experimenter in moody obscurantism, mixed media, and Pop collage. Gaiman was Moore's chosen successor on *Marvelman/Miracleman*, where he plunged deeply—and frighteningly—into exploring the idea that power and violence lead to insanity (*Miracleman* 17, Jan. 1990). For Berger, Gaiman and McKean did a *Black Orchid* miniseries, a cocky jumble of narrative tricks, comments on the superhero form, and shattered hunks of pop culture ephemera (Winter 1988). "I wanted to do a pacifist fable," Gaiman said later, "in which acts of violence did occur but were unpleasant—in which meditation and beauty played a very important part. *Black Orchid* was sort of a look at all the things I *didn't* like in comics...." The fable never gelled, perhaps because of its didactic intentions, but its literary and artistic ambitions thrilled one stratum of fans.

McKean had already moved on to *Arkham Asylum*, DC's most-hyped product of 1989. It was the most commercially ambitious project a comics publisher had ever undertaken: a twenty-five-dollar, fully-painted, hardback Batman story. McKean's images were nebulous, his visual storytelling intentionally difficult, and his Batman only an oblique shadow, a fantasy rather than a man. He and Grant

Morrison played with the implications of homosexuality in the Batman-Robin relationship and sexual repression as the core of Batman's obsessive vigilantism. Their Joker was sadistic, sexually aggressive, and philosophical—an extension of Frank Miller's sex-equals-evil motif into a trendy riff on DeSade and Foucault. They jammed their story full of shock-value violence and glib notes on the physical manifestations of psychic pain. Batman masochistically—and pointlessly—shoved a glass shard through his hand in a bit of psychodrama that validated the introverted bloodlust of Morrison and McKean's fans.

Fueled by the *Batman* movie and the growing curiosity about these British revisionists, *Arkham Asylum* was an immediate hit. Paul Levitz found himself signing quarter-million-dollar royalty checks to McKean and writer Grant Morrison, and shaking his head at how the comics industry had changed. Along with Marvel's *Havok and Wolverine: Meltdown*—in which Jon J. Muth and Kent Williams used painterly panache in service to straight mutant adventure (Mar. 1989)—it turned painted comics into a craze. Superhero pencilers started teaching themselves to handle a brush. (A few of them, like Dan Brereton, were genuinely good at combining superheroic excitement with the moodiness of the painterly surface. Most of them, though, only laid overwrought surfaces on top of vague storytelling and awkward figures, until they turned the craze into a bust.)

Morrison's *Arkham Asylum* script had already won him a regular series under Karen Berger, a revision of another obscure DC trademark, *Animal Man* (Sept. 1988). It began with rather conventional superheroics, overlaid with Morrison's passionate vegetarianism and support for animal rights. Gradually, however, a series of cruel traumas and bizarre events afflict the increasingly helpless hero, leading to the series' big revelation: that Animal Man is at the mercy, not of villains, but of a capricious creator, Grant Morrison himself (*Animal Man* 26, Oct. 1990). This was the same kind of self-reference that John Byrne was doing for laughs in *She-Hulk*, but Morrison

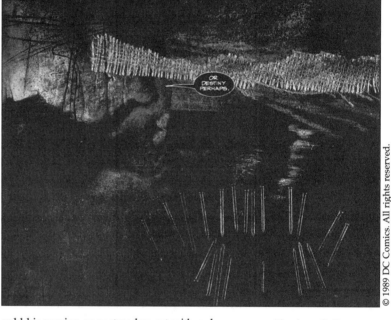

sold his version as postmodern art with a slow pace, sad irony, and a self-pitying soliloquy by Grant about his lonely childhood—solitary walks on the moors, pathetic fantasies about friendly foxes who knew that he was the one human who would understand him. Morrison knew his audience: its hypersensitivity to pain and perverse fascination with cruelty, its alienation from human society and sentimental projections onto animals, its romantic Anglophilia and belief that expository self-examination is superior to action. To a fragile Lit student with notebooks full of amorphous short stories and hair full of black dye, Morrison was a validating and unchallenging role model. And there were tens of thousands of those students, or readers

The roles are finally completely reversed: the artist doesn't serve the superhero icon, the superhero icon serves the artist. Dave McKean saw Batman as a platform for visual experimentation, and the power of paint overwhelms the power of the original design and concept. Script by Grant Morrison. (*Arkham Asylum*, 1989.)

like them, clinging to comics or glancing at comics or open to reading the comics that their cooler friends showed them.

Next Morrison took over *Doom Patrol* (19, Apr. 1989), which had been faltering under the more conventional Paul Kupperberg—especially since artist Erik Larsen had jumped to the Spider-Man stable to get rich emulating Todd McFarlane. DC's chiefs figured that if they couldn't compete with Marvel for the kids, they could at least expand its audience of twenty-year-olds. In the letters page, Morrison told his readers that his goal was to create "a superhero team for the '90s," and to supplant the dominant Claremont-Byrne model. He said he would employ automatic writing, images from his dreams, and obscure literature of the fantastic and the surreal (he even included a bibliography). He took the Doom Patrol's original label, "the world's strangest heroes," quite literally. He added a member with Multiple Personality Disorder to the team (with different superpowers for each personality). He pitted the team against the Scissormen, taken from one of the most hideous of cautionary ninteenth Century children's books, *Struwwelpeter* (in which kids who suck their thumbs have them cut off by the Scissor Man). He created villains called the Brotherhood of Dada, an assortment of graphic ciphers and found-art assemblages with absurd motives and garbled speech patterns. All of this he did with character-bits and continuity tricks in the '80s superhero style, but with an ironic voice that told readers it was all a romp. The art, by Richard Case, was smart and solid, with an easy mainstream accessibility.

Then, gradually, Morrison let his stories drift away from superheroics and into a new sort of fantasy melodrama: rambling tales of losers and drifters in various hip and seedy milieus, into which would erupt elements of the supernatural or surreal. Morrison had more in common with Chris Claremont than he'd have wanted to admit—his endless, talky subplots and unresolved set-ups eventually made *Doom Patrol* inaccessible for new readers and frustrating for old ones, just like *X-Men*—but he'd taken

the techniques of Claremont and the other ambitious superhero creators of the early '80s into a new genre.

That genre, the intersection of horror, fantasy, and the quotidian misadventures of emotionally damaged outsiders, was becoming the hallmark of the Berger stable. It reached its apex with Neil Gaiman's *Sandman* (Jan. 1989). The name came from a couple of ancient DC superheroes, but this was pointedly not a superhero comic. Gaiman's Sandman was Morpheus, pale and scrawny as a junkie, lord of the land of dreams and brother of Death, whose intervention in the slumber of tormented souls could lead them to peace. The concept owed something to the old *Phantom Stranger*, but Gaiman's stage was vast, his long story arcs sprawling through hell and Earth, through an *Arabian Nights* Baghdad and the London of Shakespeare and Marlowe. His stories were slow, sometimes as oddly structured as dreams, and intentionally anticlimactic in a way that left fanboys baffled but left all those Lit students convinced they'd read something of a higher order of art and truth. He could be self-aggrandizing and twee, but he could also be witty, touching, and genuinely disturbing. He set one story at a serial killers' convention—modeled cleverly on a comic con—and took us into the dreams of a child-killer (*Sandman* 8, Sept. 1989).

Sandman sold poorly at first, but word of mouth spread through fandom and beyond. Soon it was Berger's biggest hit, selling a steady 80,000, and when DC collected the early issues into book form it discovered a solid market for it in the bookstores. Gaiman got his friend Tori Amos to write an introduction—another seal of hipness for Brit-writ comics, to go with Alan Moore's musical connections and Hellblazer's overt resemblance to Sting. Goth-rockers went nuts for *Sandman*, and young people who'd never read comics before were showing up at cons, dressed as Morpheus or Death. Gaiman hired a publicist, worked the cons intelligently in his trademark shades and unsmiling countenance, and was soon winning every Best Writer award the industry had to offer. Sometimes he even beat Peter David in the very mainstream *Comics Buyer's Guide* fan poll.

He attracted great artists: Sam Kieth, who had the cartoony power of a McFarlane but a more twisted and original sensibility; Kelley Jones, comics' best horror artist; P. Craig Russell at his loveliest. Gaiman pushed DC into reviewing its contracts and allowing co-ownership. And when he announced that he'd eventually want to end the series, DC broke all precedent by agreeing to cancel it upon his departure.

Sandman used all the tricks of superhero comics: a "new Sandman" took the "powers" and "costume" of the original; the hero died; crossovers linked it with other DC horror series; cover gimmicks reminiscent of McFarlane's *Spider-Man* 1 called attention to special issues; and McFarlane even contributed a pin-up. Its readers would become quite irate at any suggestion that it was one of those lowly superhero comics—but as superhero fans lost interest in that genre, *Sandman* gave them a comfortable place to retreat to.

More "sophisticated suspense" series tumbled out, most using forgotten superhero titles in the service of horror and fantasy: *Shade the Changing Man*, *Kid Eternity*, even reworkings of Joe Simon's Geek and Prez. An art-style developed for them, with pale coloring, heavy on brown for a look of soiled reality, and craggy inks to set them apart from the mainstream. The covers were quasi-abstractions in photo-collage and paint—'90s versions of the "these aren't funnybooks, these are literature" packaging of '60s Gold Keys. Setting the tone, and running it all with a transatlantic *hauteur*, like a Victoria Regina of an Anglophile Empire, was Karen Berger. Neil Gaiman called her "the perfect editor, because I tell her what I want to do and she says okay." But some American artists who worked with her called her one of the pickiest, most hands-on, most frustrating editors they knew. She let her Englishmen do what they would, but kept superheroes and superhero creators at bay, to make sure that her readers could safely return to the Brit-strips each month without fearing contamination from the noisy, masculine, better-selling mainstream that they so disdained.

DC was going for class. It put its "mature" series and other direct-market only comics in a pricey "New

Format." It gradually took the coloring of its comics away from old production-department hands and turned them over to innovative artists like Steve Oliff and Lovern Kindzierski. It encouraged experimentation with computer coloring, and even tried a hardbound Batman graphic novel, *Digital Justice* (1990), drawn entirely on computer by Pepe Moreno. Marvel had started collecting its early comics into its gaudy, hardbound Marvel Masterworks, but now DC put those to shame with its sleek, annotated Archive Editions. It turned its graphic novels and reprint collections into a sub-industry, and made some headway into bookstores. Some books, with reprintings, would hit the half-million sales mark—the first time in the history of quick-turnover, mainstream comics that a publisher's backlist was becoming a significant

A villain who amuses the intellect instead of speeding the pulse. In a sense we've returned to the dawn of the silver age—Richard Case's visualizations of the Brotherhood of Dada are as conceptual, as design-based, and as lacking in visceral menace as Carmine Infantino's Mirror Master. The big difference is in the age of the intended readers. Script by Grant Morrison, inks by Stan Woch. (*Doom Patrol* #51, Feb. 1992.)

335

source of income and stability. DC's sales force—which had become a joke in the industry for coasting on the security of the direct market—was beefed up with a new crew of marketers, recruited from outside comicdom and sparked by the diminutive but indefatigable Patty Jeres.

DC hired away the man who'd made Epic Comics Marvel's one class act: Archie Goodwin. At first it looked as though he'd been hired to develop off-beat new properties, but instead he was handed bigger and bigger chunks of the DC mainstream. When he wrote for DC, it was for superheroes, in the new smart 'n' dark style—most profitably with *Night Cries*, a hardbound, fully painted Batman graphic novel with a child-abuse hook (1992). DC published high-end, out-of-continuity superhero miniseries, like Dave Gibbons and Steve Rude's gorgeous *World's Finest* (1990). Brian Augustyn and Mike Mignola did a Batman "imaginary story" called *Gotham by Gaslight* (1989), which kicked off a whole line of "Elseworlds" projects, starring superheroes in various impossible settings. DC even tackled *The Ring of the Nibelung*, by Roy Thomas and Gil Kane (1989-1990), and even if the creators did manage to make Wagner's opera read like a long *Conan* story, it was still satisfying to see an old rebel like Kane get one more shot at broadening the frontiers of commercial comics. Very quietly, Paul Levitz and company seemed to be opting out of the market-share game, conceding the fanboys and speculators to Marvel, and seeking slower but steadier income elsewhere.

DC even tried to be crass with class. Denny O'Neil put Peter Milligan and another, more superhero-oriented British writer, Alan Grant, on the Batman line. They knew how to play the fanboy game. When Time-Warner, the conglomerate into which DC had been merged, demanded yet another new Robin, O'Neil and his writers delivered a standard late-adolescent tough guy, essentially independent of Batman (and in long pants), of exactly the type the market demanded. But the Brits did add a touch of clever cruelty—like the story in which the Riddler forces Batman to perform a tracheotomy on

a toddler.

Dan Raspler—another bright editor, like Andy Helfer, who was easily bored with superheroes and needed to find odd twists to keep himself awake—turned to Alan Grant to revive Jack Kirby's Demon (July 1990), which Alan Moore had reintroduced to DC consciousness in *Swamp Thing*. The character leant himself to violence and subversion, and Grant wrote all his dialogue in rhyme, which made for some amusing, if not always very substantial, writerly strutting. Grant was also Keith Giffen's dialogue man for a series of miniseries starring the amoral Lobo. Every one of them was among the most violent, vulgar, cynical—and screwy—comics ever made. The star-hopping, beer-drinking, cigar-puffing, wall-pissing mercenary was likely to do anything: murder Santa Claus, turn half-female, try to assassinate God, break his fourth grade teacher's neck (in gruesome close-up), or win a murderous spelling bee. The art, in the best stories, was by another Englishman, a ferocious cartoonist named Simon Bisley, with a touch of Ralph Steadman and a nose for the tastes of eighteen-year-old fanboys. He delivered superhero action without ever failing to expose the nastiness and absurdity of it, and so did Giffen and Grant. Fans lined up to buy Lobo, artists lined up to draw pin-ups of him, and editors lined up to borrow him for guest-appearances. *Lobo* and *The Demon* were satires, admissions to slightly-too-savvy fanboys that the idea of artful or meaningful superhero stories was becoming a joke. But at the same time they gave those fanboys their monthly dose of cynicism and male rage. They suggested that DC might actually be able to hook those young guys who found Marvel a little too heavy, a little too cornball—unless something even louder and more cynical came along.

For all that, the British writers could still inspire some American superhero creators to reach higher. In 1991, under Andy Helfer's aegis, Gerard Jones began exhaustively developing *Green Lantern: Mosaic*, the ambitious, optimistic, sometimes goofy story of a black Green Lantern trying to keep peace in a cosmic melting pot. Jones jammed it with cultural references, threw out superhero convention, and had the hero address the readers like an actor on a stage. He and the artist, the intelligent and design-conscious Cully Hamner, thought they were going to build a bridge between the Green Lantern mythos and the Morrison-Gaiman school, over which superheroes might march to the future. They were in for a rude surprise.

Some of the bright lights of the '80s weren't going to make it long in the '90s. Mark Nevelow tried to make his Piranha Press imprint a haven for comics without superheroes or even superhero narrative conventions. He had a few triumphs: Kyle Baker's deft satire of love and isolation among screwed-up New Yorkers, *Why I Hate Saturn*; William Messner-Loebs and Sam Kieth's voluptuous spoof of Greek mythology and philosophy, *Epicurus the Sage*; and *Gregory*, Marc Hempel's cartoon riff on modern psychosis. But Nevelow had more disappointments than triumphs—especially commercial disappointments. Fandom didn't seem interested in being challenged any more, and both DC and retailers had too much hot new product to distract them. Piranha couldn't keep any top talent, not without a real creator-ownership contract or royalties to compete with the booming mainstream. Kyle Baker said, "The only people who like my comics are the ones who get them free," and then left comics for a development gig with Fox TV. Sam Kieth found the lure of Marvel incentives irresistible. DC had branded him "too cartoony" for anything but Piranha, but in the wake of Todd McFarlane, his fluid and violent cartooning was suddenly in demand for *Wolverine*.

After a series of conflicts with DC, Nevelow quit. Andy Helfer, rapidly losing interest in superheroes, left the mainstream to take over Piranha. He renamed it Paradox Press, and reoriented it toward the mainstream bookstore trade. He would lead with gimmick books—*The Big Book of Urban Legends, The Big Book of Conspiracy Theories*—and follow with a line of genre crime novels in comics form. Classy and professional, like the new DC, but without much bravura or daring.

Mike Gold, meanwhile, was having comparably bad luck at developing new approaches to the DC mainstream. His last major effort was the Impact imprint, an attempt to create "entry level" comics for kids. He assembled a crew of humane writers and artists with clean, cartoony lines, well-intentioned people like William Messner-Loebs, Len Strazewski, Mike Parobeck, and David Antoine Williams. Unfortunately, they seemed to pick the worst of every world: the slow plots and endless melodramas of the '80s, with the politeness and insubstantiality of the '60s comics that Gold and his colleagues had read as kids. It didn't help that the titles chosen for Impact were the tired Archie hero-line, which DC had licensed: *The Fly*, *The Jaguar*, *Steel Sterling*, and the rest of them. *X-Men* and *Spider-Man* were the entry level comics of the '90s. Impact didn't stand a chance. Pretty soon Mike Gold was working as a consultant for a retail firm.

The middle ground of comics—between male wrath and epicene melancholy, between the devourers and the despisers of superheroes—was falling apart. The independents had been losing ground steadily. Japanese comics didn't save First or Eclipse; most American fans retreated to familiar ground, leaving about 30,000 *manga* maniacs to support the field. Eclipse dug deep to pay Marv Wolfman to write *Total Eclipse*, a *Crisis*-like crossover for all its superheroish series (May 1988). It was a flop, the final blow to Eclipse as a comic book publisher. Cat Yronwode and Dean Mullaney would hang in as book publishers for a while, until their business, and their marriage, dissolved. First Comics jumped on the crossover bandwagon with Crossroads (July 1988), and then took an expensive risk by buying the *Classics Illustrated* rights (Feb. 1990). It hired the most respected artists in the business to adapt the best-known books in the public domain, but all it succeeded in doing was emphasizing what a gulf had opened between the comic book elite and the American mainstream. How many comics fans wanted to read *Moby Dick*? How many parents or teachers wanted to subject their kids to the graphic challenges of Bill Sienkiewicz? First was dead. Comico tried an ambitious expansion in

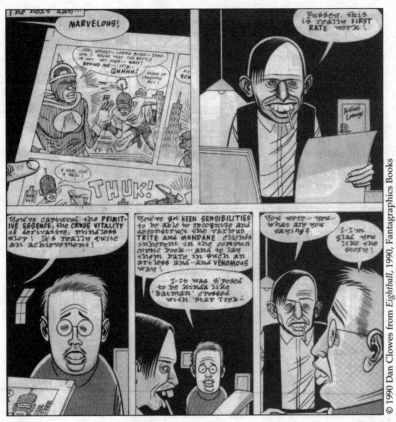

© 1990 Dan Clowes from *Eightball*, 1990, Fantagraphics Books

Young Dan Pussey, Dan Clowes's personification of the superhero artist, just plain doesn't get it when he's thrown in with caricatures of Art Spiegelman...

1989, overextended itself, and went broke. Its guiding lights, Diana Schutz and Bob Shreck, would end up at Dark Horse, which hung in thanks to its Hollywood connections. Dark Horse was even putting together Hollywood producing deals for *Dr. Giggles* and *The Mask*. Some said it was starting to view its comics as a research-and-development department.

Whatever hope the independents had was destroyed by the glut of Bat-product in 1989 and the *Spider-Man* 1 phenomenon of early 1990. Low-budget publishers like Fantagraphics were the only survivors, and they did it by publishing comics that offered a total alternative to the mainstream. To *Love and Rockets* had been added another steady success, Peter Bagge's creepy and hilarious slacker soap opera, *Hate*. Bagge openly loathed all superhero and action-adventure comics, and so did most of his readers. Another Fantagraphics cartoonist, Daniel Clowes, put the relationship of the mainstream and the alternatives in fierce perspective in his *Eightball* (1989). Clowes was the most intelligent cartoonist of his generation, generally concerned with surreal tales and odd glimpses of

modern life, but he paused occasionally to tell stories of Young Dan Pussey, an aspiring superhero artist. Pussey is a geek and a moron, incapable of living life, contacting his own emotions, or drawing anything that hasn't been reduced to formula by hundreds of superhero artists before him. When he encounters the likes of Gary Groth and Art Spiegelman, he understands vaguely that he's being insulted but doesn't understand why. Pussey was sometimes compared to Sidney Mellon, but he took a step further: Sidney was aware enough of alternative comics to want to drag them into the mainstream, but Pussey was in another world entirely. Clowes still presumed that his readers knew both worlds, but he was announcing that those worlds could only spin further apart.

Fantagraphics could no longer be a nexus for the assorted sects of fandom. Gary Groth, having lost Jim Shooter as a target and the Kirby crusade as a rallying point, was fighting countless little brush-wars against people like the *Ms. Tree* team and the *Buyer's Guide* staff. Then, always seeking sacred cows to slaughter, he decided to expose what he considered to be an overblown cult of worship for Will Eisner. Eisner had become a father figure to comicdom, and although his work was losing its force and was falling prey to sentimentality, he remained a teacher, a gentleman, an inspiration to young artists, a supporter of independent publishing, and a key to Kitchen Sink's success. Groth's article was an attack, nasty and smarmy in tone, impugning Eisner's ethics and reading his sentimentality as an obfuscation of Eisner's own participation in the bloodsucking corporate world. It drew nothing but counterattacks for months, and cost Gary all but his most fervent allies. The *Journal* thereafter drifted into covering little but the "new undergrounds," foreign comics, and newspaper strips. *Amazing Heroes* was losing readers as its coalition of superhero fans who wanted something better dissolved. New, slicker, and crasser magazines like *Wizard* and *Hero* appeared, glorifying the red-hot Marvels and the collectibles market. When *Amazing Heroes* was canceled, Fantagraphics became a village unto itself.

The fights that had held the comics world together in 1986 now blew it apart. Frank Miller and Steve Grant had intended their *WAP!* newsletter partly as a nexus for a freelancers' union, but that never happened. Gary Groth called Miller and Grant mercenaries and fascists, they called him a poseur, and pretty soon *WAP* and the *Journal* were in a full-fledged feud. *WAP* pretty much killed itself when it passed on gossip that Groth was supposedly not only cheating the Hernandez brothers of their royalties but had conned them into painting his garage. It exposed a nasty, condescending, vaguely racist streak in the tough-guy stars of comics, and cost the *WAP* gang any credibility they may have had as leaders.

Dave Sim, tired of taking flack for his extremism in believing that all comics creators should publish themselves, withdrew from the creator summits—and from all public appearances and discussions—in 1989. *Cerebus* drew deeper into its long and esoteric plotlines. Even within *The Frying Pan*, Scott McCloud and Larry Marder's "apa" for artistically dedicated creators, hostilities were breaking out. Chester Brown, a cartoonist whose satirical and autobiographical *Yummy Fur* was making him a star of the alternative scene, attacked comic book writers as a class: "What are you guys doing in this business, anyway? Looking for a Kirby or Ditko you can ride to fame and fortune?"

The great mavericks of the mainstream were withdrawing as fans went crazy for the Lees and Liefelds and McFarlanes. Howard Chaykin tried to continue as DC's boundary-pusher, but with diminishing returns. His work was still clever, but it was bitter, and had lost the whimsy and affection for his characters that had made *Flagg!* work. His *Blackhawk* was so sexually crass that retailers screamed, DC had to agree to take returns, and it lost money (Mar. 1988). He wrote a couple of miniseries for DC—including *Twilight* (1990), a dark, gruesome revision of all of Julie Schwartz and Jack Schiff's charming old science fiction heroes—but they died. He jumped on the sex-comics craze with a riff on nuns, prostitution and garter belts called *Black Kiss*

for Vortex. Readers screamed that it was flimsy and overpriced. Chaykin was more interested in pursuing his Hollywood career, bringing little but his natural charisma to comics.

Frank Miller was back, but he'd left his superheroes behind. *Give Me Liberty* and *Hard Boiled*, for Dark Horse, were both near-future action stories, nicely crafted but without his old intensity. Both were beautifully drawn—by Dave Gibbons and Geoff Darrow—but not by Frank himself. He cranked out a graphic novel for Marvel, *Elektra Lives Again*, and it sold well, but it felt perfunctory. When Miller finally got sick of Hollywood and returned to drawing his own heartfelt work, it would be for Dark Horse again, with the film noir pastiche of *Sin City*—a very closed and very private world (*Dark Horse Presents Fifth Anniversary Special*, Apr. 1991).

Stephen Bissette, of *Swamp Thing*, switched to publishing his own intellectual horror anthology, *Taboo*. Among its prize catches was Alan Moore's new series, *From Hell*, a meticulous and introverted

...and Gary Groth.

(*Eightball* #3, June 1990.)

exploration of the Jack the Ripper legend. The artist was Eddie Campbell, a minimalistic and naturalistic cartoonist who'd never ventured near the mainstream.

Marvel flirted with the "mature" market, but it would prove to be only a flirtation. Epic, in Archie Goodwin's last days, had begun beautiful translations of the best of Jean "Moebius" Giraud. Moebius even teamed up with Stan Lee for a very pretty but insubstantial *Silver Surfer* miniseries (Dec. 1988). But when Goodwin was replaced by Carl Potts, Epic shifted toward more mainstream heroic adventure. Marvel tried to crash the British horror market with *Clive Barker's Hellraiser*, by assorted creators (1989), but that was one piece of turf that couldn't be wrested from DC. Carol Kalish, in the direct sales department, tried some off-beat projects, including the commercial humor of *Yuppies from Hell* and a science fiction series under Kurt Busiek's editorship, *Open Space*. None of it worked out well.[2] When Kalish died suddenly, prematurely, of heart trouble, Marvel's focus shifted more and more to its superheroes at the exclusion of all else.

A few personal works found safety in the neglected corners of the mainstream. Peter David kept his *Hulk* on its quirky course. Ann Nocenti wrote a strange and astonishing run on *Daredevil* (254-291, May 1988-May 1991), including a story in which the blind crimefighter journeys to a heavenly realm of "billboard beauties," a consumer-culture version of Plato's world of ideals, where women lose their souls to gain plastic perfection. Nocenti had already proven that a comic book woman could be talented and physically beautiful. Now she proved that she could use the superhero genre to comment, with poignance and scathing satire, on the genre's own exploitative tendencies, the medium's weird physical ideals, and Nocenti's own place in the junk culture in which she labored. She was joined by artist John Romita Jr., who left behind the pyrotechnics—and the big money—of his *X-Men* assignments to turn in the most sensitive art of his career. This was one of the few mainstream comics ever to grapple with issues

vital to adolescent girls and young women—and fandom mostly ignored it. Nocenti moved on to write outré series for Karen Berger, Romita returned to his big, jagged mutant work, and *Daredevil* was put through a violent transformation under D.G. Chichester, a male writer.

As the subtler talents of the field retreated from superheroes, Marvel's hotshots retreated just as quickly from the world at large. The Lee-McFarlane-Liefeld look—along with the busy but hypercontrolled ink surfaces of Scott Williams, Lee's studio mate and favorite inker—was dubbed the West Coast style, and became the model for a generation. The layouts, poses, lines, and minimal story elements of Marvel superheroes became a set of stock gestures, all copied and distilled from earlier comics, as cold and self-important as the art of the French Academy after all the real artists quit to be Impressionists. All artists learn from earlier artists, but as recently as the Chaykin-Simonson-Starlin generation, comics artists had been incorporating reality, non-comics art, and the deeper recesses of the artistic self into their work. Now comics artists learned exclusively by copying the comics that were hot when they were teenagers, often with no formal training or life-drawing practice. Older artists had complained of the syndrome in Byrne and Pérez, but those guys looked like Monet and Manet compared to Lee and McFarlane, who in turn looked like the real thing next to Liefeld—and now kids were popping up in print *imitating Rob Liefeld!*

"I used to look at Nick Fury, the way Steranko drew him," said Eddie Campbell, "and I noticed the trim and immaculately tailored suits he used to wear. And I used to think, 'One day I am going to get me one of those three-piece suits!' Now I pick up a new comic from Marvel, such as . . . *X-Factor*, and you know that in the entire comic there were only two ordinary, everyday people in suits! One of them was Nick Fury, and the other was the president of the United States! And the suits were horrendously drawn! . . . Our generation of artists . . . can draw muscles upon muscles, but we can't draw a simple collar on a suit!"

Muscles upon muscles and basketballs upon female chests. The exaggeration of gender traits was reaching a new extreme among the hot young male artists, an extreme that shrieked with the panic and defensiveness of confused pubescent boys (and puberty in America seemed to be going on longer all the time). Male characters, with their pin-heads and boulder-muscles and steroid-veins, were drawn with a deadly earnestness, and with none of the charm of caricature. Females, perpetually bending over, arching their backs, and heaving their anti-gravity breasts into readers' faces, defied all the laws of physics. They ran the gamut of character from A to B: Angel (dewy, pliable, non-threatening) to Bitch (pouty-lipped, slit-eyed, dripping with sensual rivulets of blood). The Victoria's Secret catalogue became the bible of every superhero artist, an endless source of stilted poses ripe for swiping by boys who wanted their fantasies of women far removed from any human reality. The twin models of female sexuality were MTV chicks and the campy girlie-girls of Alberto Vargas and other artists of the postwar men's magazines. In the '80s, the superhero crowd had gone crazy for the posters of Nagel, which reduced fashion-mag women to cold graphic design. In the '90s, fanboys lost interest even in that degree of sophistication, flocking to the Bettie Page cult and the plasticizing technique of "good girl" painters like Olivia. It was a retreat to a fantasied prefeminist Eden, when men were unchained and women were inflatable.

Such stuff worked well for a new genre slipping out of the back alleys of fandom. These were the days, not only of smart horror like *Hellblazer* and *Taboo*, but of the "slasher" movie fad, which spilled over into comics geekdom. In 1988, R.A. Jones created *Scimidar* for Malibu Comics, part Elektra imitation and part vampiric orgy—one cover showed the heroine licking blood off a sword and making eyes at the reader in a pose familiar to any reader of hardcore porn. About the same time, a young artist and comic shop clerk named James O'Barr started drawing *The Crow* (Feb. 1989). He wove in the storytelling structures and design tricks of superheroes, along with

some bloody vigilante fantasies—his protagonist rose from the dead to slaughter the "inner city" gang responsible for murdering him and his fiancée. The owner of the store where he worked formed Caliber Press to publish it, and it rose from nowhere to become a cult hit.

Then came David Quinn and Tim Vigil's *Faust*, immortalized in the *Overstreet Price Guide* for its "decapitation covers" (1989). Malibu struck again in 1991 with Brian Pulido's *Evil Ernie*, ripe with rotting flesh and dismemberments, all amateurish but explicit (Dec. 1991). It introduced a character who instantly hooked a male audience of her own: Lady Death, who combined the naked excess of an inflatable superheroine with a macabre viciousness. Pulido broke from Malibu to form Chaos! Comics, and soon had a whole stable of "bad girls" like Chastity and Purgatori, bubble-breasted bloodsuckers out of a horny misogynist's nightmares. Harris Publications, a cheesy magazine firm, tentatively brought back the old Warren Publishing properties, now written by Kurt Busiek, Peter David, and other superhero creators. Then came *Vampirella* 1 with a cover by Adam Hughes (Nov. 1992). Hughes was the star of a group of Southern artists called Gaijin Studio, which produced slick, designy comics favored by older fanboys. Hughes became a fan fave with a stint on *Justice League*, where his cute, curvy superheroines seemed plucked straight from an auto-parts calendar from 1949. *Vampirella* was a hit, and Harris Comics was in business.

Soon "bad girls" were even becoming a fixture at conventions, as these new publishers starting hustling their wares with spokesmodels, just like vendors at an auto show. Most of the spandexed models were buxom fan-girls or battered-looking ex-strippers, but Harris lucked into the services of a terribly sweet young woman named Cathy Christian, who combined a swimsuit model's sleekness with the big-eyed cuteness of a freshman cheerleader, and a seemingly inexhaustible ability to smile at sweaty geeks. Cathy, in her lint-speck of a Vampirella suit, became the passion of every comic-con boy from fifteen to thirty-

THE COMIC BOOK HEROES

[3] The old series had had its official title changed to *Uncanny X-Men*.

five, and the status of comics as cheap male fantasy was confirmed.

Harris and other publishers had tumbled to the fact that the way to prosper as an independent now wasn't by selling more heartfelt alternatives to superheroes but by selling the same fantasies in even less demanding forms. The market for those fantasies seemed bottomless, now that collectors and speculators were laying down the bucks. *Spider-Man* 1 had turned into a huge boon for Marvel, and for retailers, and so *New Mutants* was canceled and relaunched as a new series, *X-Force*, with plots and art by Rob Liefeld and dialogue by Fabian Nicieza (Aug. 1991). This time Marvel shipped it in a plastic bag with assorted trading cards; the rubes had to buy five copies to get them all, plus a sixth with metallic ink but no card. It was another hit, and Jim Lee and Chris Claremont followed immediately with a new *X-Men* 1 (Oct. 1991).[3] Marvel used multiple covers again, hoping they'd help this one do as well as *Spider-Man* had. It did better than twice as well, selling eight million copies, more than any comic in history.

Superhero universes were still selling better than anything, and finally one independent publisher had the resources and savvy to create its own. Jim Shooter had not, it turned out, gone back to Pittsburgh or the real world after his firing from Marvel. He joined a music-industry lawyer named Steve Massarsky to form a new company, Voyager Communications, which picked up assorted licensed properties—Nintendo games, the World Wrestling Federation—for comics publication. They got the rights to some of the old Western/Gold Key heroes and brought out two new series, *Magnus, Robot Fighter* (May, 1991) and *Solar, Man of the Atom* (Sept. 1991), under the imprint Valiant Comics. They had that solid Shooter storytelling, a lot of his scripting, and some good art by Bob Layton, Art Nichols, and others. For readers who found the Marvel mainstream too hysterical, the DC mainstream too dispirited, and the new stuff either too gory or too esoteric, they were a pleasant read. They started to build a following. When Massarsky struck up a relationship with Jim Lee, Shooter said he'd only interested if Lee would tell stories "my way." Shooter told his associates that he was going to knock Marvel off the stands, was going to prove that that solid, old-style comics were what the fans really wanted.

CHAPTER 45

IMAGE IS EVERYTHING

The hot artists were feeling unappreciated. They'd made a lot of money on *Spider-Man*, *X-Men*, and *X-Force*, and Marvel thought they should be grateful for that, but they knew they'd made a lot more money for Marvel than they had for themselves. *X-Men* had become a cartoon now, a hugely popular one, generating still more money that the comic books' writers and artists never got any direct piece of. By now they were a clique, all in Southern California, close to each other and far from Marvel: Todd McFarlane, Jim Lee, Rob Liefeld, Erik Larsen, and another rising hotshot on *X-Men*, Marc Silvestri. And there was Jim Valentino. The man who'd done *normalman* had spent years trying to break into Marvel and DC, networking aggressively. As Marvel expanded insanely, there was suddenly room for almost anyone to get a series there, and Valentino worked his way into writing and drawing a revived *Guardians of the Galaxy*. It was vapid stuff, but it hit all the notes of the West Coast style, and soon he was part of the gang. If he didn't share the others' talent, he shared their cockiness and determination to make money off Marvel Zombies.

It was Liefeld, the youngest and cutest of the six, who first strayed from Marvel. Hollywood was noticing him after the success of *X-Force*. Rob was a dream discovery, a kid just like his consumers, without the grown-up esoterica of a Frank Miller or a Howard Chaykin. He appeared in a Levi's 501 commercial with Spike Lee that ran on MTV—a sort of harmonic convergence of commercial hip, two corporations and two artists selling flash and the appearance of daring without a lot of substance to clutter things up. The fact that he had hardly any original ideas or story sense, that his success was based entirely on a cartooning style that couldn't be transferred to the screen, didn't register. Hot was hot. Rob, however, knew that he could never fully profit from Hollywood's attention unless he owned something he could sell. So, in 1991, he started his own one-shot comic book.

It was called *Youngblood*, and it was about a superteam remarkably like X-Force. It wasn't something Marvel should know much about, so Rob went shopping for independent publishers. The best deal came from right in his own back yard. Malibu Comics had been clinging to life with reprints of old comic strips and adaptations of minor cartoon shows, like *Macross*. Now its publisher, Dave Olbrich, made a desperation offer. He'd push *Youngblood* with all his distribution connections and marketing resources—Malibu's only real assets—in exchange for only 10 percent of the take.

When word reached Marvel, the grumbling and veiled threats began. As maverick a spirit as Fabian Nicieza, who dialogued *X-Force*, said, "Rob's behaving very unprofessionally." But *Youngblood* orders broke 400,000—and 90 percent of that was more money than Liefeld could make on millions of Marvels. Rob's friend McFarlane, sick of battling with anal-retentive Marvel editors, told him that if he wanted to jump ship, "I'm on board, too." Rob and Todd knew the value of the Marvel Universe, and saw that Valiant was doing well with its universe.

Tundra, meanwhile, was attracting a lot of attention from older fans with Rick Veitch's Heroica Universe, which he called "slightly more demented that anything anyone else is doing." He'd been around the creative edges of comics for twenty years—undergrounds, the Kubert School's first graduating class, an Alan Moore-ish effort at superhero revisionism called *The One* for Epic (July 1985)—and had taken over *Swamp Thing* from Moore and Steve Bissette, only to quit in disgust when Jenette Kahn forbade him from using Jesus in one of his stories. In 1990 he released *Bratpack*, satirizing all the perverse implications of teen sidekicks, and soon announced more Heroica miniseries, *The Maximortal* and *Hellhead*. Few fans were lining up for such superhero revisionism anymore, but the gimmick of a creator-owned universe had people curious.

So McFarlane and Lee recruited Larsen, Silvestri, and Valentino to launch a line of artist-owned but interconnected heroes. Malibu was their ace in the hole, but their ideal was a creator-ownership deal with Marvel—if Marvel would be smart enough to outbid Dave Olbrich. They were a powerful group, but they felt they were missing one element: the man McFarlane called "Marvel's golden boy," Jim Lee.

The whole comic book industry had just discovered what a powerful force Lee was at Marvel. Chris Claremont had always used a lot of input from his artists, but Lee had stronger ideas about what the X-Men should be than any artist since John Byrne. He felt Claremont had slid too far into character work and too far from action, so he'd replot the stories, turning in pages that bore no relation to what Chris was expecting. Claremont complained to his editor, Bob Harras, expecting to be supported as Chris Claremont was always supported. But Harras didn't think that was his job. Harras was an ambitious editor, like his friend Fabian Nicieza, less interested in protecting the toys of his childhood than in figuring out what '90s kids wanted and climbing the ladder of success by delivering it. He and Fabian had started in the Shooter days, but had been unable to rise while Shooter rewarded loyalty more than ambition. Now, in the laissez-faire DeFalco age, they were exploding. Harras was more of a Marvel formula guy—his writing stint on *Avengers* was a very Shooteresque and satisfying run—while Fabian was a little edgier, glib

with tough-guy lines ("I'm about to make your dentist a very rich man") and quirky character twists. They made a good team when Fabian wrote X-comics, and knew they had more to offer the core readership than Claremont did.

Fans had been griping for a few years that Claremont had burned out and gotten boring, but as Lee took over, they started saying that ol' Chris had woken up. The stories underwent a fundamental shift, as the mutants became active instead of reactive, charging out to kick butt to advance the cause of mutant rights instead of sitting around their mansion until some mutant hater attacked them. This was a new series, not the geek-hit of 1980, but the young man's companion to Operation Desert Storm. Jim Lee was the reason *X-Men* was red hot again, and Harras knew it. As the Lee-Claremont disputes heated up, Harras backed Lee. After sixteen years of ruling the mutant-verse, after more than a decade looming over the mainstream, Chris Claremont found himself with no control of his stories. He even found himself sharing plot credits with an artist, an artist who probably wasn't even old enough to rent a car. Chris Claremont was being reduced to a mere dialoguer. When he protested, he was treated like just an old nuisance. It was too much. The ground shook a little under comicdom's feet when Claremont stomped away from Marvel in 1991. He predicted that the mutant empire would collapse. But it only got bigger.

Now, how far backward would Marvel bend to keep Jim Lee? Lee agreed to join McFarlane and company in a meeting with Marvel's president, Terry Stewart, but McFarlane knew that prying Lee away from Marvel would be hard. Lee, like his mentor Carl Potts, was a company man, and only some significant executive arrogance or stupidity could possibly alienate him. "God love Terry Stewart!" said McFarlane later. "He said the wrong things at the right time.... You see, Terry likes to count his pennies, and he was saying things like, 'Well, we're not going to give you this extra benefit, and we're not going to fly your wife to this or that meeting.... You want to rent a car, you pay for it.'" McFarlane called comics "one of those weird businesses where being successful is a hindrance.... Comics is an entertainment business, and in most entertainment businesses, the one who sells the most...gets shmoozed the most, you know? But Jim Lee wasn't getting shmoozed...it wasn't the money, it was the principle of the thing.... So he said, 'Fuck it! If I was Mickey Mantle, you don't think they'd fly Mickey Mantle's wife around with him if he asked them to?'"

And that was it. In one stroke, Marvel had lost its five hottest artists, and Jim Valentino. Marvel stock prices plunged. To *The New York Times*, Terry Stewart shrugged that freelancers come, they go, and they come back again. Nothing could hurt Marvel.

As for the West Coast gang, what else could they call themselves but Image Studios? This wasn't just the triumph of art over writing and flash over substance, but of reputation over proven commodities— because these comics were best-sellers before anyone even knew what they were like. Malibu resolicited *Youngblood*, now that it was part of a new universe, and this time the orders broke a million (Apr. 1992). All the other first issues were in the same ballpark, even Valentino's. McFarlane's *Spawn* 1 (May 1992) sold 1.7 million, more than quadruple the highest sales for any independent prior to the spring of 1992. And these guys knew what their fans would want to see. Lee's *WildC.A.T.S.* featured equivalents of the X-Men, but stripped of mutanthood and turned into government agents (Aug. 1992). Larsen's monster-hero in *Savage Dragon* (July 1992), Silvestri's trendy supergroup, *Cyberforce* (Oct. 1992), and Valentino's dully gritty *Shadowhawk* (Aug. 1992) were just what Marvel kids had been trained to want. The only one who shifted away from what he'd been doing at Marvel was McFarlane, whose *Spawn* was like a combination of Dr. Strange and the Spectre with a touch of Faust. The visuals, however, were pure Todd, the mystical milieu a chance for him to open his Ditko-cum-'90s visuals even wider than on *Spider-Man*.

Even after first-issue fever burned off, most of the series held steady at astounding levels: a half-mil-

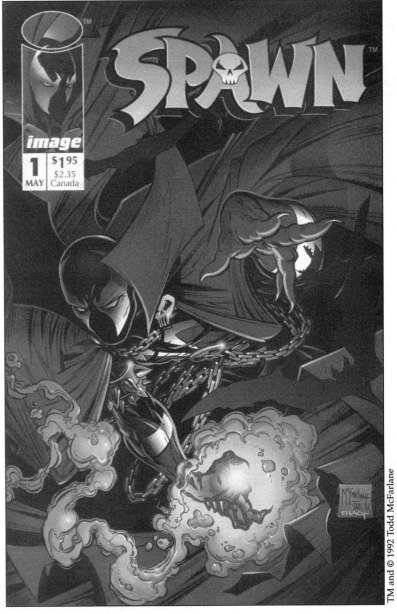

TM and © 1992 Todd McFarlane

No one outdid the Image guys for '90s flash. Black-and-white can only hint at the vividness of Todd McFarlane's art, as computer-colored by Steve Oliff's Olyoptics. (*Spawn* #1, May 1992.)

lion and more, at $1.95 each. Other pros tried to calculate how much money the Image guys were making off their 90 percent, but they stopped counting when the dollars went over a million. The comic book world had barely gotten used to the idea that Chris Claremont had bought his mom a private plane when suddenly it had to face the fact that the Image guys owned a company that could claim to be the third of a Big Three.

Everyone wanted to be with Image, and it seemed that everyone was. Dan Jurgens, Jerry Ordway, Kevin Maguire, Al Gordon, and every other hot artist was either moving to Image or flirting with it. Nearly all of them brought in loud, gory, cynically adolescent fantasies—"think puberty" was Al Gordon's advice. But there was power and a sense of liberation in the work, for even those who hated the Image aesthetic were hailing this as a triumph of creators over corporations, a staggeringly successful implementation of Dave Sim's self-publishing principles.

With some prominent exceptions. Dark Horse had released *John Byrne's Next Men* to solid but unspectacular sales just a few months earlier (Jan. 1992). Now Byrne's personal X-riff was being shredded underfoot in a stampede of fanboys desperate for the flashier X-riffs of Liefeld and Lee. Byrne fired cranky letters to the *Buyer's Guide* and filled online comics forums with pompous denunciations of the Image guys—they never created *one, single original thing* roared the man who'd made a fortune revamping the X-Men, the Fantastic Four, and Superman. As the number of Byrne's fans at comic cons shrank, he was noted to be growing ruder and more arrogant to those who remained. His old buddy Claremont treated his ever-fewer fans with scarcely more humility. He huffed and puffed at cons that it was he alone who'd saved comics in the '70s. He'd made Marvel profitable, he declared on one panel, and now his *Sovereign Seven* was "going to do the same for DC." It took forever for his new team-comic to see print, and when it did, it proved to be almost unreadable. It was no substitute for Image's X-Men substitutes.

Peter David, in his column in the *Buyer's Guide*, went after Image too, partly out of loyalty to Marvel and partly because the Image guys weren't hiring any real writers. They were either writing everything themselves or handing the scripting over to assistants and teenage groupies whom they figured could dress up their pictures with words good enough for comics. "Artists don't need writers," McFarlane had written, and all the Image money was going for pencilers, inkers, and colorists. Artists who'd been thrilled to get a hundred and fifty dollars a page at Marvel or DC were being offered three hundred, even four hundred at Image. Steve Oliff, king of the computer col-

orists, was suddenly the head of Olyoptics, a booming company giving Image its high-gloss "visual effects." It was like rock and roll, running on "stupid money," as some old hands were calling it. The Image moguls were setting young stud artists up in L.A. houses, throwing money at them and making them feel like geniuses for learning how to ape the Lee-Liefeld look before they'd learned how to draw a straight line. The studs would draw a splash page, play some pick-up basketball, buy a car or two, cruise the babes in Venice, draw a two-page spread. And when a whole comic book had finally been slapped together out of splashes, spreads, and giant panels that made no narrative sense, Lee or Liefeld would slap the big Image "I" on it and it would sell a half-million copies.

The studs weren't necessarily getting some other things: rights to their work, royalties, and all those other little extras that men like Neal Adams, Steve Gerber, Jack Kirby, and Frank Miller had fought for. The Image guys were turning into '90s versions of Jack Liebowitz, outbidding the competition in up-front money and stroking the vanities of artists by telling them that they were "hot enough for Image," but skimming all the long-term money and ownership rights. There was more than a little Martin Goodman in them, too, because they were pumping out solicitations for new comics as fast as retailers could process them, even when the comics themselves wouldn't be finished for months. And most of those solicitations were for first issues, where the big money was. Only McFarlane focused on one series, keeping *Spawn* fans fed once a month. Liefeld was particularly addicted to new titles, nearly all in the same mold as *X-Force*. Even Lee, who'd been the model of consistency at Marvel, took nearly a year and a half to bring out five issues of *WildC.A.T.S.* That first-issue money was too big to pass up.

The mystery was, where was the money coming from? Part of it was a new readership. Comics had been rising in the nation's junior-high-school consciousness since the *Batman* movie and now, with the sequel coming out, with the *Batman* cartoon being promoted—and even from the previews it looked like the coolest adventure cartoon in TV history—and all the Marvel hype of the past couple of years, they exploded into a genuine craze. The stardom of the Image artists fueled the fire. A twelve-year-old who discovered *Youngblood* in 1992, and then went to a convention or a store signing and saw young, cute, confident Rob Liefeld, with one of his beautiful girl-friends in tow, looking just like he did in the *People Magazine* feature, would have a very different impression of comics than a twelve-year-old in 1980, getting into *X-Men* or *Titans* and seeing (and we hope the gentlemen will forgive us this) Chris Claremont, John Byrne, Marv Wolfman, or George Pérez. When word got out that Liefeld had walked into Steven Spielberg's office and sold a concept called *Doom's IV* for a huge development fee, young fans could see in the Image guys not just entertainers but role models. And when older fans complained that *Doom's IV* was just a blatant rip-off of *Fantastic Four*, one millimeter shy of lawsuit territory, the kids just shrugged. It was a rip-off world, and the Image guys just knew how to use it. When the Image guys brought out an impudent self-parody, *Splitting Image* (Mar. 1993), making fun of their own crassness and greed, they only confirmed the magnitude of their success and their testicles. So yes, part of it was a new readership. Preteens, teens, and twenty-somethings without pretensions to taste were trooping to comic shops in a number and a cross-section that comics had never seen before.

Another part of it, though, and it would turn out to be a huge part of it, was speculator money. The collectibles market was slumping after a boom in the '80s, responding to the general slowdown of the American economy, and people who'd built up fortunes in sports memorabilia, toys, trading cards, and other ephemera were looking for a new place to put their money. Shops popped up everywhere carrying "comics, cards, 'n' more." Comic shops had always prided themselves on carrying full lines of comics, on being fan resources and parts of a subculture, but these new shops might carry nothing

but Image, mutants, Spider-Man, and Batman. If it didn't turn over fast and in huge volume, they weren't interested.

Like most small-time American speculators, they could be shockingly stupid. They'd stockpile copies of *X-Men* 1 and imagine that someday, even though eight million existed and fewer than half a million people were reading the series, there'd be a demand for them. And publishers were happy to take advantage of them. When multiple covers became old hat, Marvel tried holograms, glow-in-the-dark ink, and foil covers. DC answered with pull-tabs that made

It seems that nearly every issue of Spawn tries to top the last in savagery, gore, or gruesome twists—as with nearly every Image and Image-style comic, it's a competition with itself that can't be won. The price of sensationalism. (*Spawn* #1, May 1992.)

TM and© 1992 Todd McFarlane

347

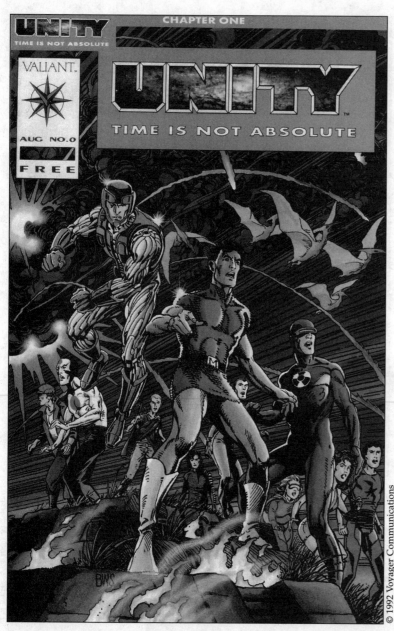

Jim Shooter's Valiant Comics caught fans' eyes with a flashy '90s look, but kept them coming back with late-'70s fundamentals. Script by Jim Shooter, pencils by Barry Windsor-Smith, and inks by Bob Layton. (*Unity* 0, 1992.)

telling stories anymore, it was about manipulating a collectibles market. Writers and artists who still felt they had something to say started to feel as though they may as well be painting Elvis on plates.

There were shrewder speculators, too. They were perfectly willing to sell Image Comics to the rubes and kids to keep their cash flowing going, but they knew the big killings were to be made in back issues. That market kept roaring. *Action Comics* 1, which had made the news a little more than a decade before for breaking the $10,000 barrier, was now listing at over $100,000. *Fantastic Four* 1 was going for $15,000, and the first *Teenage Mutant Ninja Turtles* could bring a few hundred. The trick for speculators was to find comics that had started with small print runs, and there was a perfect case right in front of them: Valiant.

Sales on the line had been rising as older fans spread the word that Magnus and Shooter were both back. Then mainstream fans starting spreading the word that Barry Windsor-Smith was contributing some art (*Solar* 1-2, Sept.-Oct. 1991). Windsor-Smith had been popping up in comics since royalties had become more impressive. He brought his considerable skill to simulating the West Coast style, adding bigness and cragginess to his old grace and mood. He was good with violence too, as he'd always been, but now with a penchant for agony and severed heads, the way '90s kids liked it. When he wrote and drew an especially brutal *Wolverine* series for *Marvel Comics Presents*, he became Marvel's flavor of the month (*MCP* 72-84, Aug. 1991-Feb. 1992). Shooter knew how to take advantage of that. He cut Windsor-Smith a great deal to tease readers with the *Solar* art and then to draw the first issue of a new Bob Layton creation, *X-O Manowar* (Feb. 1992). Sales were good, and collectors went scouring for the early *Solars*, and then for the early issues of *Magnus* as they got hooked on the Valiant universe. When Image hit soon after, and the numbers of kids looking for hot new comics swelled, Valiant sales jumped and prices on its first few issues jumped again. Speculators snatched up early Valiants, word got out that Valiant was hot, it all mixed in with Bat-fever and X-fever, and another rush was on.

cover illustrations wiggle. No longer restricted to first issues, "enhancements" were slapped on hundredth-issue "specials," twenty-fifth issues, and even the beginnings of story arcs. They made the shoddiest comics sell for three or four bucks and retailers raged against them, but even as they raged, they kept ordering them. Ten-year-olds, baffled by the oceans of identical, lurid comics filling the racks, grabbed at them because they stood out. So did neophyte collectors, as attracted to shiny things as magpies. And the retailers themselves stashed them in their back rooms as investments. Making comic books wasn't about

The San Diego Con of 1992 was expected to be "the Image convention," and so it was. Lee, McFarlane, and company commanded four-hour-long lines of kids willing to pay five bucks for an autograph. The Image display tables were mob scenes. Sneering Liefeld flunkies climbed on the tables and tossed limited edition first issues into the crowd just to watch twelve-year-olds dive to the floor and claw each other like starving rats. All freelancers could talk about was, How do you get in with Image? Unexpectedly, however, it was also the Valiant convention. Image announced August as "Image Month," solicited tons of product—and got nothing out on time. Desperate retailers pushed Valiant. Lines for autographs from Bob Layton and others caught everyone by surprise, and Valiants only a year old were selling for a hundred dollars. Valiant started hinting at a major expansion.

Everyone, in fact, was hinting at a major expansion. Image was signing up so many hot artists that it seemed to be planning on thirty or forty titles for 1993. Dark Horse grouped Byrne, Frank Miller, Mike Mignola, and some others into a "Legends" imprint of creator-owned comics, and hinted at a possible superhero line. Malibu, knowing that the Image guys wouldn't want to keep forking over 10 percent now that they were established, threw some minor superheroes together in its Genesis line and began actively recruiting freelancers for a new, upscale universe. A group of prominent black creators—Denys Cowan, Dwayne McDuffie, Michael Davis—entered into a deal with DC for a line of nonwhite, urban superheroes. And of course there were self-publishers and small companies popping up everywhere, most of them selling latex-fleshed, blood-smeared superheroines and female assassins, to cover the Jim Lee and the Lady Death bases at once. 1993 looked to be a superhero boom to outdo 1966, to rival 1940.

No publisher was expanding more aggressively, more insanely, than Marvel. Joey Cavalieri, who'd very quietly established a reputation as one of the most professional editors in the business, was given his chance to shine on a line telling the adventures of Marvel's heroes in the future. The line drew some publicity with the news that it would include Stan Lee's first monthly series in more than twenty years, *Ravage 2099* (Dec. 1992). It was the success of Peter David and Rick Leonardi's *Spider-Man 2099* (Nov. 1992), however, that sent Marvel plunging into futuristic versions of Ghost Rider, the X-Men, and a few dozen others. Carl Potts announced an Epic sub-imprint called Heavy Hitters for early 1993. It would include a couple of off-beat projects—Joe Kubert's *Tor* and Jacobs and Jones's *The Trouble with Girls*, with art by Bret Blevins—but it featured mainly tough-guy action series by established names like Peter David, George Pérez, Ron Lim, and Howard Chaykin. After that would come the Razorline, a whole set of superhero-tinged horror titles conceived by Clive Barker.

Oversize quarterly companion-titles were launched for nearly every prominent Marvel title. The Spider-Man family was expanded with miniseries and specials. The X-family would expand most of all. Marvel had been aggressive about keeping as much artistic talent as it could—Joe Kubert's sons, Andy and Adam, were reportedly guaranteed a combined annual salary of at least $576,000 to remain on *X-Men* instead of defecting to Valiant—and it was keeping mutant sales as high as before the defections of Lee and Liefeld. This market had room for so much product that it appeared that Terry Stewart's nonchalance was justified.

The one company that responded with dread and queasiness rather than greed and aggression was DC. It had seemed unconcerned with market share after a few years mired in second place, but now a chill filled its halls: Malibu/Image briefly slipped into second place, and Valiant wasn't far behind. DC had been able to count on a steady 30 to 40 percent of the market in the late '80s, but now, in some months, it fell below 20. *Batman Returns* had done stunning box office, but it hadn't generated the licensing bonanza of the first movie. Sequels never do, but the DC people hadn't really planned on that. With the comics talent pool stretched so thin by Marvel and Image, the Batman line offered little that was spectacular. DC editors were telling their inkers to copy Scott Williams, telling their pencilers to copy Lee or McFarlane or somebody, and in some cases even telling their writers to "write Image-style." That was good for a chuckle or two in the DC freelancer pool, since the one thing everyone could agree on was that nothing much like writing had yet been discovered in an Image comic. It was a chuckle for the gallows, though.

Dick Giordano had been easing toward retirement for a while. Suddenly, in the early summer of 1992, with the aid of a golden parachute and perhaps a gentle shove, he was gone. Instead of choosing a new executive editor, Jenette Kahn and Paul Levitz decided to get more involved in editorial themselves, and promoted five editors to "group editor" status: Andy Helfer, Karen Berger, Denny O'Neil, Mike Carlin, and Archie Goodwin. Their first group decision was that the DC line needed to be rationalized, divided, and then unified into sections. Helfer was already off in his own corner, with Paradox. Berger now moved her "sophisticated suspense" stable away from the mainstream and gave it its own imprint, Vertigo. Some Vertigo titles—*Animal Man, Doom Patrol*—would still have their roots in superheroes. Some new ones would revamp old superhero trademarks—like *Sandman Mystery Theater*, in which Matt Wagner used his compelling narrative gifts to remake DC's original 1940s Sandman into a vehicle for mystery stories against a prewar backdrop (Jan. 1993). Essentially, though, the Berger stable, along with many of its fans and its most prominent creators, left superheroes behind.

That left Carlin, O'Neil, and Goodwin—the Holy Trinity, the Tribunal, or, in Carlin's own words, the Three Stooges—to share the DC Universe, and there was no question that Carlin was the first among equals. Goodwin liked his offbeat projects, taking the Justice League stable and his other mainstream properties as the price to pay. O'Neil wanted to run his Batman group and be left alone, with an occasional glance at the Green Lantern stable he'd inherited from Helfer (for, despite his avowed disinterest in the

character, those thirteen issues of *Green Lantern/Green Arrow* he'd done with Neal Adams twenty years before had forever cursed him to be involved with the tired emerald gladiator). Carlin was the one who cared about superheroes, who took a Shooteresque interest—and even a Shooteresque approach—in tightening and standardizing the line. The others would always defer to the Carlin dynamo.

Their first act was to cancel three titles that didn't fit the new, tight, Marvelized DC Universe. Len Strazewski and Mike Parobeck had just revived the golden age heroes of *Justice Society of America* to good sales, but Carlin and company said it gave DC a musty look (the line going around the DC offices was that kids were saying, "Image is our comics, Marvel is our parents' comics, and DC is our grandparents' comics"). *Aquaman* harked back to a gentler generation of fantasy comics under Sean McLaughlin and the decorative art of Ken Hooper—too gentle, it seemed. And *Green Lantern: Mosaic*, Gerard Jones's ménage of John Broome, Grant Morrison, and Shelby Steele was, in Carlin's words, "Just too weird!" The cancellation of *Mosaic* in the face of solid sales was an important signal to DC's readers and creators. Its loyal fans screamed that it should be turned into a Vertigo title but Carlin and crew felt that the Green Lantern reality had to be kept intact, and that nothing could straddle the line between Vertigo and the DC Universe. Fans had to be able to pick up a "DCU" comic and know what they were going to get. Everyone knew in an instant that the Giordano days were done.

It was time to get commercial. The days of the superhero as a catalyst for artistic advancement were done. The days of the superhero as cash cow were back, and the money-madness was madder than ever. Even in the World War II boom there'd been a few people like Whitney Ellsworth, trying to make superheroes a little more respectable, and Sheldon Mayer, trying to make them a little more artful. Now everybody was getting a hunk of the money, and money had become the whole game. The new wave of artists had already figured that out, and even the staff of staid DC was getting it. Now there were writerly equivalents of the Image artists hustling their way into comics. Jim Starlin wrote a series of formulaic cosmic crossovers for Marvel, working with West Coast style artists like Ron Lim. Starlin groomed a sort of assistant writer, Ron Marz, who took off on his own with minimal plots that stressed big panels, non-stop action, and minimal stories, just like Image.

Scott Lobdell became the heir apparent to Chris Claremont with no talents more evident than those for shmoozing and seizing opportunities. After Mark Waid gave him some legitimacy with a *Secret Origins* story, Lobdell devoted his life to hanging out in editors' offices, writing proposals on his laptop computer, and using the glibness he'd developed as a stand-up comic to get himself noticed. After some scattered assignments, he was called on to save Bob Harras from a deadline crisis by dialoguing an entire issue overnight. He did it, with a flair for fanboy wisecracks and Claremont pastiche, and before anyone realized what was happening, he was taking Chris's place on *Uncanny X-Men.* His was a Hollywood soul, a Sammy Glick soul, focused every moment on pleasing his superiors, keeping underlings off-balance, assessing the value of new acquaintances, and frustrating rivals. Soon he'd become the head writer for the whole sprawling mutant stable. He worked best with another Hollywood soul, one actually trained in the movie game. Jeph Loeb, the cocreator of *Commando,* saw a shot at X-royalties and used his movie-producer

aggression to pick up the assignments that Lobdell couldn't fit into his schedule.

Other writers passed through the mutant world too, but they'd entered comics as fans and writers when it was a collaborative, collegial world. None could submit for long to the stable's deadline nightmares, Harras's relentless commercial demands, and Lobdell's will to dominate. John Moore was a master of adopting different styles, and seemed a good match with the stable. But he'd left the TV industry because he wanted to be a *writer*, and now he quit *Excalibur* for the same reason. J.M. DeMatteis and Peter David passed briefly through the Harras office. Even Fabian Nicieza, an experienced corporate warrior, finally threw in the towel.

Mark Waid, who'd impressed most of his peers and critics as the best writer in the superhero genre with his *Flash* and *Captain America*, looked like the rising star of the X-titles when Harras recruited him. After Waid declined Lobdell's offers to mentor him in mutant-writing, however, hostilities broke out. Eventually, Waid gave up an estimated $120,000 a year rather than continue the war. He explained that he quit because he and Lobdell simply didn't get along. Lobdell, on the other hand, told *Wizard* magazine that "I couldn't be any happier," and said of Mark Waid, "He is one of the least talented, fattest fucking people in comics today." It was just about the crudest, stupidest thing any comics professional had ever said for publication, but it showed just how crude and stupid the business had become.

CHAPTER 46

DEATH AND REMEMBRANCE

They called him the Great Carlini, and he earned the nickname with comics' greatest magic act—making Superman readers appear from nowhere. Mike Carlin marked a return to the editors of yore. He built a team of conservative storytellers: Dan Jurgens and Jerry Ordway, the quintessential DC-style artist/writers; Roger Stern and Louise Simonson, who, like Carlin, had worked under Shooter at Marvel; Karl Kesel, a solid inker who methodically trained himself to be an equally solid scripter; and clear, modestly dynamic artists like Jon Bogdanove. Carlin called frequent editorial summits with his crew and involved himself deeply in coplotting. He laid down a formula structure, which ran plots and subplots through all four Superman titles—*Superman, Action, Adventures of Superman*, and the new *Superman, the Man of Steel*—as a ceaseless weekly comic book. The issues were numbered not just by title but by year and chapter: the first *Superman* of 1992 was labeled 1992-1, the first *Action* 1992-2, and so on. It worked, not at setting fandom on fire, but at winning a solid hundred thousand or so readers who wanted dependable, pro-establishment superheroics. It was a pat on the back instead of a slap in the face, the sort of thing Marvel had offered in the early Shooter years, before anger, chaos, and hysteria had taken over.

Superman's greatest sins, in fandom's mind, were being ancient and stodgy, but Carlin figured out how to use them to his advantage. The Byrne revamp had attracted tremendous media attention, and it happened again when, in early 1992, Carlin had Superman and Lois Lane finally become engaged. Apparently a big chunk of the American public, a mostly female chunk, had a romantic investment in the myth of Superman and Lois, of the innocent hero and the career girl needing rescue from her own life. Those women didn't read the comics, and indeed they wouldn't have found much to satisfy them had they done so, but they remembered the romance scenes from the first couple of Superman movies, and they smiled when Dan Rather announced the engagement. It all helped heat up interest in a TV show, *Lois and Clark*, which had been in development for a few years and was finally scheduled for a fall '93 premiere. Carlin had intended a wedding issue earlier, but waiting until the show premiered seemed like a smart idea. Not wanting to lose momentum, he figured he needed another event, one to plug into *Superman* 75 (Jan. 1993). He decided to fall back on that old standby, the hero's death.

Comics fans knew how it worked—the apparent death, the world in mourning, the villain triumphant, the miraculous return at the last moment—but they'd usually tune in to play along with the drama and see how it was handled. Plus, it might make for a little real-world publicity, even though surely no one would take it seriously. Image hit in the meantime, so Carlin and staff decided that Superman's "death" should occur in a big, brainless fist fight with a big, ugly monster called Doomsday. Dan Jurgens wrote and drew the story in a cynical, pseudo-Image style, with a full issue of overblown splash pages—unabashed shlock for a shlock market.

Then DC's publicity whiz, Martha Thomases, started promoting. Thomases was an interesting mix of elements: political radical, mom, published writer and editor, Norman Mailer's assistant on *The*

Executioner's Song. But she was also a comic book fan and the creator of a female adventure hero for Marvel named Dakota North. She had a unique ability to see what was going on in a comic book and then see how that could be made interesting to a public that really didn't give a damn about comics. It was Thomases who had turned the engagement issue into a media event, and now she had the death of a hero to play with, a chance to spin it in a more positive way than the death of Robin four years before. Not that she thought anyone would take it seriously. Surely no one would believe that DC would actually get rid of Superman—would they?

A few years before they probably wouldn't have. But so many things that had defined public life for most of the century were suddenly gone. The Iron Curtain vanished and the Soviet Union dissolved. After twenty years of fearing "another Vietnam," we'd finally had the long-dreaded Middle East War, and it had ended in days, with scarcely a hundred American dead. George Bush had put himself forward as the leader of a "New World Order," and had promptly been swept from office, ending twelve years of Republican hegemony. The computer revolution had finally struck completely home, with incessant news chatter of an Information Superhighway that was going to transform the texture of our lives, making paper, the work place, and even cities obsolete. The census had driven home how huge the immigration wave of the '80s had been, how thoroughly America had become a part of a non-white, non-English-speaking planet. There were gays and cross-dressers in the mass media, and the President Elect was speaking out for tolerance. Postmodernists were insisting that Western culture was passing through a massive "paradigm shift" in our perception of self and body. A book called *Listening to Prozac* hit the best-seller list, suggesting that psychopharmacology might not just cure depression, but might change our entire concept of the individual personality.

It was the last decade of the millennium, and it was feeling like it. Why shouldn't Superman, that

embodiment of a white male America, that veteran of the Depression and World War II, die for real? No one in the mass media knew that Superman comics were still selling. His last couple of movies had bombed, and those nihilistic, sexually ambivalent, narratively chaotic *Batman* movies had supplanted them. And so it hit the news in the fall of 1992: an era was ending, the last issue of *Superman* would be hitting comics shops on November 18, and you'd better grab it while you can.

The armies of speculators already throwing their money at Image and Valiant were joined by a horde of amateur collectors and investors who were convinced that the Death of Superman was a major cultural event. And in the consumer culture, a major cultural event must be bought. *Superman* 75, which

The punch that "killed" Superman. DC tried to out-Image Image with a big, dumb fist fight shown in nothing but splash panels. The results are obvious: ugly composition, graceless figures, lack of drama, and words straining to do what the pictures should but don't. The fruits of a speculator-driven field. Words and pictures by Dan Jurgens, inks by Brett Breeding. (*Superman* #75, Jan. 1993.)

353

[1] Ditko, as ever, used the work to fund his more private projects, including a ferocious excoriation of the venality of modern comics publishing called The Ditko Public Service Package.

[2] The name seems slightly less dopey when one considers that Dark Horse had adopted the campy slogan, "World's Greatest Comics." As we say—slightly.

every comics fan in America knew was just a stunt, ended up selling six million copies. Countless signed and special editions were hawked through cable shopping networks and collectibles catalogues. Carlin's cleverly choreographed follow-ups, with months of mourning and of ersatz "new Supermen" (one black, one adolescent, one metal, one evil) jockeying for the job, kept his stable selling at close to *X-Men* levels.

The death of the hero may not have been real, but from that moment the very real death of the speculator market was foreordained. No sooner had *Superman* 76 come out than all those investors from beyond comicdom began to suspect that they'd been rooked. About the same time, the kids who were stocking up on new Valiant and Image issues were beginning to realize that their investments weren't going up in value. The explosive comics market of the past few years had trained collectors to expect instant payoff, and that meant instant disillusionment.

This was a new Valiant, too. When the company needed a financial bailout in mid-1992, on the verge of the boom, Jim Shooter insisted that any new capitalization must give him unilateral control. Steve Massarsky and the new backers bounced him—just in time for the gift of "Image Month." Massarsky's strategy was to "ride the market." He put Bob Layton in charge, and together they dumped the conservative Shooter style, pushed for an Image look, and started pumping out the product with an ever-thinner talent pool.

Everyone was getting excited—and getting scared—about the coming flood of heroes. Milestone, the DC-allied company spearheaded by Denys Cowan and Dwayne McDuffie, kicked it off with *Hardware* (Apr. 1993), *Blood Syndicate* (Apr. 1993), *Icon* (May 1993), and *Static* (June 1993). Most of the series fell into the traps and tropes familiar from Image and Marvel, but they were well-textured by Cowan's punchy superhero designs—done about the same time he was designing the hero for TV's *M.A.N.T.I.S.*—and McDuffie's fast, funny,

slang-rich writing. The characters were uncommonly human and the stories were wrapped in slick bits of comic book self-reference (like Icon's teen sidekick, "Rocket, the Unwed Mother"). But sales were only decent. "Too specific a market," said industry insiders, trying to convince themselves that conditions were fundamentally sound.

The Topps trading card company was on the bandwagon, too. It had some success in licensed properties like *Jurassic Park*, and in a comics version of its own *Mars Attacks* cards (with some input from Len Brown, who'd cocreated the cards with Wally Wood and was now a Topps executive). Then it hired Jim Salicrup, a Marvel editor from the Shooter era, to assemble a superhero line. He hired his boyhood favorites, battered warhorses like Roy Thomas, Gerry Conway, Don Heck, and Steve Ditko.[1] For concepts and cover designs he turned to Jack Kirby. Kirby could hardly draw anymore, but how could the man who'd never gotten enough credit resist the chance to launch series called *Jack Kirby's Secret City Saga* (Apr. 1993), *Jack Kirby's Teenagents* (Aug. 1993), and *Jack Kirby's Silver Star* (Oct. 1993)? Sales weren't good, though. "Too old-fashioned," said industry insiders, desperate to believe that the market would support new products if they were the right products.

Everybody had a gimmick. Malibu's was a "writer-driven universe" to counter the "artist-driven" Image that so many fans found vapid. It gathered three respected veterans—Steve Englehart, Steve Gerber, and Mike Barr—and three current mainstreamers known for smarter-than-average stuff—James Hudnall, Len Strazewski, and Gerard Jones—and sent them to a resort in Scottsdale, Arizona, to create an "Ultraverse." They responded with a creative joy that none of them had felt in years, and delivered ideas that were both odd and good.

Dark Horse's editors were creating a new superhero universe with a slight surreal twist, "Comics' Greatest World." [2] They set different odd heroes—X, Ghost, Monster, The Machine (and Barb Wire, to pick up that "bad girl" cash)—in fictional cities with distinct aesthetic tones. After a launch by in-house staff, the series would be farmed out to an off-beat crew ranging from Eddie Campbell to Adam Hughes to Tim Hamilton.

Jim Shooter was hustling capital to get his own company going. He called it Defiant Comics, and chose a medieval tower as its symbol. For its main selling point he chose Jim Shooter, casting himself as an angry Old Testament God. Its most frequent ad slogan was, "And on the seventh day he rested."

It would be a glut, but insiders could still fantasize that the burgeoning direct market could support it all. There were estimated to be 10,000 comics retailers nationwide. Gary Colabuono, of the Moondog's comic shops, was now executive officer of Classics International Entertainment, a chain of fourteen stores, a big mail order business, and owner of the *Classics Illustrated* rights. Capital City Distributing had twenty-five warehouses. The San Diego Comic Con was drawing 30,000 visitors. Movie studios were shipping young male faves like Jean-Claude Van Damme to cons to promote their wares. DC, Marvel, and even some smaller publishers were building towering convention displays with giant TV screens and deafening sound systems. Publishers and retailers were spending millions flying creators around the country for autograph sessions. Companies were formed just to buy thousands of copies of special issues and pay the creators to sign them—up to five dollars per signature—even though autographed comics had never proven themselves as a collectible. Top freelancers were making more money off signatures than off royalties, and those royalties were staggering.

Batman was a huge hit as a cartoon, even with grown-ups, and millions of kids were still watching *X-Men*. Nearly every Image comic was in development as a cartoon show or a movie, or both. Todd McFarlane formed his own toy company. Marvel had new cartoons in the works, and moviemakers from James Cameron to Oliver Stone were attached to development deals for Marvel superheroes. One producer spent over a million dollars on an unreleased

Fantastic Four movie just to retain the rights for a later huge-budget version. Marvel was cranking out comics by assistant editors and rookie artists who couldn't have found a fill-in job in the '80s—and retailers kept ordering them. Marvel's stocks, having hit sixty dollars per share and split once, now mounted into the high fifties and split again. It bought a toy company, Toy Biz, and a card company, Fleer, and was scaring the hell out of retailers with plans to open its own chain of Marvel stores.

Industry veterans remembered how the black-and-white glut had shaken retailers, and knew that a superhero glut could do far more than shake them. But everyone had to try for the next big hit—publishers, distributors, retailers, speculators, and fans alike—even though all of them knew that sinking too much money into comics that didn't go anywhere could leave them bankrupt. It was a gamble, but who can leave the table when the dice are hot?

The first tremors came in the spring of 1993. Epic's Heavy Hitters line sank like a stone. Image sales were slowing as it kept pumping out new series. Some distributors got hurt when they overordered Sam Kieth's *The Maxx* (Mar. 1993), anticipating big reorders, and found themselves with cartons full of unsold copies. While most Image recruits kept to the styles that had made them hot at Marvel, Kieth was emboldened by the surging cartoonist testosterone of McFarlane and the boys to drop all his accommodations to commerciality and turn in the broadest, funniest cartooning that anyone had seen in mainstream comics since the '40s. He was tapping into adolescent fantasies, but they were the heartfelt fantasies of kids trapped in screwed-up lives and dreaming of release—and they were made funny and sweet with the help of dialogue by William Messner-Loebs. The protective monster called the Maxx was taken to heart by sensitive preteens and alienated teenagers, and would go on to be a cult hit and a cartoon on MTV. But he didn't grab the lemming-like hordes of Image zealots. Fights were reported between the Image guys, as the more market-minded partners screamed that prestige projects like *The Maxx* and

355

The violence and forcefulness of Image art opened the door to a new cartooniness and weirdness in reconsidering the superhero symbol. Sam Kieth is always brash and conscious of his adolescent audience, but always heartfelt. Dialogue by William Messner-Loebs. (*The Maxx* 1, Mar. 1993.)

[3] "Writers Are the Best Enhancement," read one of its ad slogans, in the ultimate reduction of creativity into market terms.

crates of pulp suitable only for recycling.

Malibu looked like the one sure winner among the new lines. It spent hundreds of thousands on promotion, and even put commercials on MTV. It pushed the Ultraverse as a line with substance instead of gimmicks.[2] Barry Windsor-Smith and a rising English scripter, James Robinson, agreed to launch new series for it, and SF writer Larry Niven contributed ideas. DC's design director, Jim Chadwick, defected to it, saying that Malibu was the only publisher "doing everything right." There weren't a lot of major artists left on the market, but Malibu hooked Norm Breyfogle, a hot *Batman* artist, to kick off Len Strazewski and Gerard Jones's *Prime*. Aaron LoPresti was seduced away from Marvel for *Sludge*, which would also feature Steve Gerber's sharpest writing in years. Promising young artists—Jeff Johnson, Darick Robertson, Cully Hamner, Gene Ha, Ben Herrera—were climbing on board.

Alan Moore's new *1963* were blowing the company's reputation with its preteen audience—although its reputation had really been far more damaged by too many promised comics that never came out, too many cover "enhancements," too many lousy scripts, and substitute artists.

The bubble popped when retailers ordered over a million copies of Valiant's new title, *Turok, Dinosaur Hunter* (June 1993). The kids just didn't want to read about an American Indian fighting dinosaurs, and they didn't believe it would be worth anything in a year. An estimated three quarters of the copies didn't sell. Retailers had sunk nearly a million dollars into

The market was getting nervous, though, and that nervousness spread to the Malibu staff. They'd planned to release three titles in October, followed gradually by more, so as not to overtax the staff or the customers. But then Dark Horse announced that its quickie universe would premier in June, and everything changed. Malibu rushed three titles out in June and two more in July. By its original start-date, it was juggling eleven monthly series. Its production was error-prone, its coloring was often witless, and its artists were rushed into monthly series before they'd developed anything like work-habits. James Hudnall's *Hardcase* was saddled with a different artist nearly every issue. Every series but *Prime* and Steve Englehart's *Strangers* was devastated by late-ships. Despite that, and despite the fact that giant crossovers had been growing steadily more unpopular with fans since *Crisis on Infinite Earths*, editor-in-chief Chris Ulm pushed immediately for a crossover drawn by George Pérez. It only infuriated readers, screwed up storylines, and called attention to late-ships.

Gerard Jones had been looking forward to getting *Prime* settled, and then moving on to his solo projects after he got his Marvel and DC work wrapped up. But he suddenly found himself doing *Prime, Freex*, and *Solitaire* all at once, plus three Marvel and DC series. If he'd had any sense, he'd have said no to the quick launches of *Freex* and *Solitaire*, but he was caught up in the greed and fear of the moment—do it now before it all crashes. His first issue scripts were great, because they'd been percolating in his mind for months. From there it was straight downhill.

Retailers were nervous, too. Ulm had predicted that all the Ultraverse titles would sell steadily above 150,000 copies, but after the first issues, sales dropped immediately to about 100,000. By the time the mess of the crossover had cleared, they were plunging toward 50,000. Panic set in. The gimmicks that supposedly wouldn't happen started happening. The first issue of *Solitaire* was published in an opaque black bag, hiding the most commercially attractive cover Malibu had yet produced (evidently neither Marvel nor DC had tried the opaque black bag trick yet). Mike Barr's *Mantra* had a great concept—a male warrior reincarnated in a female body—but the editors decided it was "making people nervous" and pushed for naked female flesh with no psychological kinks. The editors started writing their own comics, just like Marvel editors. And then there was the team-up series, *Ultraforce*, which finally put the lie to the "writer-driven universe" and was only created because Dic, the shoddiest animation compa-

ny in the business, had said it would develop a show with such a title and concept. When the show hit the air, sales hit the basement.

Dark Horse was holding steadier under the editorial guidance of Diana Schutz and Bob Shreck, and it scored some successes with its creator-owned Legend imprint—but that set off another frantic wave of imitation. Malibu spent huge sums of money to publish the Bravura line, featuring stars of the '80s and before—Howard Chaykin, Jim Starlin, Marv Wolfman, Gil Kane, Walt Simonson, Peter David, and Ernie Colón—plus Dan Brereton, a master of the moody, painted style that was losing favor with fans.

The post-Image boom could be liberating. Norm Breyfogle was a good Batman artist, but he came into his own with his explosive, organically rich work for the goopiest new hero in comics, Prime. The series won a Parents' Choice Award for its portrayal of teenage life and moral questions. Script by Gerard Jones and Len Strazewski. (*Prime* 2, July 1993.)

357

[4] The name of the humorless, controlling, creativity-hating villain from *The Prankster* of O'Neil's long-ago youth. Consciously or not, the writer's mind will have its little jokes.

Simonson brought back his *Starslammers* from the early '80s, Chaykin satirized superheroes with his familiar cleverness and kink, Starlin did muscles and blood. They still had fan bases, but age, attrition, and the disgust of older fans with the new market had taken their toll. Bravura was a gigantic money-loser.

Malibu was the most thorough example of what was going wrong, and the one that these writers know best, but it was only one. The heavily hyped Image-Valiant crossover was incoherent thanks to Image's inability to get its comics out on time, and in any case would have been too long and too sloppy even for the Image audience. Defiant launched in October and disappeared in the deluge. Marvel was drowning in a sea of its own swill, caught with something like 150 comics on the market—far more than even the most compulsive Marvel Zombie could afford, hardly any of them worth reading—just when the market contracted sharply. Marvel's greatest selling card, the one thing that had guaranteed decent sales for almost any superhero series it released, was that thousands of Marvelites could be counted on to want to keep up with its whole universe. Now that was financially impossible, and the betrayed and exploited Zombies were learning to be picky—or just throwing up their hands in disgust and finding another hobby. Marvel started canceling like mad, laying off editors and staffers, but sales kept hemorrhaging. Its stock prices were sagging to the low twenties, and then to the teens.

DC fared better, thanks to the death of Superman and Paul Levitz's faith in the big continuity event. Denny O'Neil had built an interlocking Batman stable in emulation of Carlin's Superman line, with creators—Chuck Dixon, Doug Moench, Barry Kitson, Bret Blevins, and others—who could reliably produce straight DC stuff with a little more mood and grit than the wholesome Super-crew. It was as if DC had turned full circle to the days of Jack Schiff and Mort Weisinger, though for an audience of twenty-year-olds instead of eight-year-olds. As soon as the news of Superman's death started driving up Carlin's sales, O'Neil hit with an arc called Knightfall that would sprawl through ten titles and seventy-one

issues (beginning *Batman* 492, Apr. 1993). Batman didn't die, but he did suffer the time-honored O'Neil fate: he had his back broken by a big, ugly, Image-style killer named Bane.[4] He was replaced for a year by a crazed, homicidal, ersatz Batman called Azrael, which infuriated most DC Zombies but kept them tuning in. In the end, Batman got his job back, O'Neil got a deal to write a novelization that would hit the best-seller list, Azrael got his own series, and DC got a steady franchise.

The next hero in line for trauma, announced Paul Levitz, was Green Lantern. When the series' regular writer proved unwilling to produce an idea shocking enough, Levitz stepped in personally. He assigned O'Neil, Goodwin, and Carlin to plot a new direction in one night. They did it. Hal Jordan goes insane, becomes a villain, and slaughters his loyal friends and his godlike bosses, every member of the Green Lantern Corps and the Guardians of the Universe. The last, dying Guardian gives a power ring to the first being he comes across—who, luckily for DC's marketing department, proves to be a twenty-year-old white American male with a babe girlfriend fated to be killed so he can go savagely angry (*GL* 48-50, Feb.-Apr. 1994). The old writer, Gerard Jones, was replaced by Jim Starlin's cosmic-action protégé, Ron Marz. The art was given to diverse, but generally Image-like, hands. A sophisticated colorist, Steve Mattsson, was brought in to give the whole thing some West Coast sleekness. Sales jumped, at least for a while. Levitz, O'Neil, Goodwin, and Carlin had almost a century of commercial comics experience between them, and all but Carlin had been there since the birth of the direct market. They were proving that they were the best in the business at manipulating the collector's market and the continuity zombies—and that was what the business of comics had become.

The key to survival in this market glutted with superheroes has not been uniqueness but dreary sameness. Superman had once been unique for being part of a community of expatriate survivors. Batman had been unusual for being a surrogate father, and Robin for being a boy hero. Green Lantern had been unique for having Corps-mates and metaphysical bosses. Superman and Batman had once seemed to be in their late thirties, Robin had been about ten, and other heroes covered the range in between. Now Superman is a lone strong man in his late twenties, Batman a lone tough guy in his late twenties, Robin a lone tough guy in his late teens, and Green Lantern a lone strong man of about twenty.

They are more than just tedious, though. They are also dangerously narrow symbols of maleness and heroism. As the twentieth century comes to a close, it becomes increasingly clear that our unchecked consumer culture has been destroying symbols of community and maturity, teaching us all to behave like adolescents in competition with a world of peers. Robert Bly, who's done his share of thinking about the heroic narratives of childhood, has called ours a "sibling society," and called our lives "horizontal"— allowing for neither transcendence nor descent into shadow, valuing neither authority nor compassion. There can be no sadder symbols of that than today's superheroes. John Broome's Guardians of the Universe were authoritarian figures, but they also functioned as cartoon symbols of transcendent wisdom. Beginning in 1970, they were systematically trivialized, and in 1993 were finally destroyed. Some superheroes do acknowledge the psychological shadow, for Green Lantern can go insane and Batman can be replaced by a murderous look-alike. But that shadow is always reduced to simple rage, and it serves only as an excuse for carnage. Superman, Batman, Green Lantern, Spider-Man, and the members of Youngblood, for all their slight variations in tone and personality, are all the same figure. They are all perpetual adolescents, alone and self-absorbed in an atomized world, with nothing to inspire us toward, except victory in fist fights.

As sales kept sliding, publishers and marketers persisted in blaming stupid retailers and speculators who encouraged a glut that would just require "readjustment." It was, indeed, an overloaded market. By the end of 1993, there were more than 900 comics on the racks that a year before had held

about 600. When the direct market had looked stable in the mid-'80s, there'd been about 300. But there were signs, too, of a much bigger problem. The kids were losing interest. A couple of new fads hit big in 1994: *Magic*, a collectible fantasy card game, and pogs.[5] Retailers found that they had to jump on them or die. Convention attendance began to drop after more than thirty years of constant growth. Store signings were dying.

And why not? Comicdom had done hardly anything to bring in new readers or to hang onto the ones who'd dropped by out of curiosity. This was the fatal flaw of the direct market, of the self-sustaining comic book subculture. The emphasis on vast continuities, endlessly prolonged story lines, crossovers that made kids feel they had to buy twenty titles, gimmicks that drove up prices, and increasingly esoteric art and narrative tricks, had scored big with fandom but had raised towering obstacles to new readers who didn't know the code. And for those who didn't wish to wallow in the brutal fantasies of frightened boys or the collegiate nausea of the Vertigo crowd, there was precious little to make cracking the code worthwhile.

Even the Image guys, who had briefly turned comics into a genuine fad, were unable to escape their utter immersion in the subculture that had made them rich and glamorous and arrogant. They hired Larry Marder, veteran of advertising and self-publishing, to bring some sanity to their publishing plan, but he couldn't control their content. They did stories like the one in which two superheroes meet on a rooftop, decide to see which one is stronger, just for fun, and fight for twenty pages with absolutely nothing at stake. Such stuff drew appreciative snorts from young superhero addicts who could appreciate the cynicism and the mocking self-contempt—not to mention the endless variations on fight-poses that they savored the way pottery collectors did the numberless flowers and leaves of Roseville and Van Briggle. But what could it possibly mean to a kid who actually wanted a story? How could the issues of *Savage Dragon* devoted to Johnny Redbeard, Erik Larsen's caricature of John Byrne, captivate a kid who knew nothing of comic-

[5] Based on a Hawaiian kids' game which originally used the cardboard lids from the Haleakulani Dairy's passion-orange-guava ("p-o-g") juice. On the mainland, the game became just another contrived collecting fad, but one that competed with comics. Pogs finally drove home to the more dedicated comics creators that in eight years they—*we*—had gone from inventing a new art form to manufacturing collectibles. Elvis on plates, indeed.

dom's schoolyard spats? Rob Liefeld scored a collector's market hit by hiring *Vampirella* spokesmodel Cathy Christian as the model and cocreator for *Avengelyne*, in which she appeared snarling and murdering and dripping with viscous rivulets of blood (Sept. 1995). Con-geeks gobbled it up for the chance to gape at the real Cathy's cleavage, and visualize those viscous rivulets, as she signed copies of it. But what made it unique to boys who didn't go to cons? How could any of these comics compete for kids' attention with a TV show or a CD-ROM? One can almost see Mort Weisinger rising from the grave, ranting that "market conditions" were just a cop-out for creators who wouldn't face the *real* reasons sales on typical Image titles dropped from 700,000 in 1992 to 200,000 in 1994.

The kids of the early '90s liked humor and bright graphics and appealing characters to latch onto. *The Simpsons* and Nickelodeon proved that. And despite all the talk of "postliterate" culture, they liked narrative. The astonishing success of R.L. Stine's *Fear Street* and *Goosebumps* series of juvenile horror stories proved that. These kids had grown from toddlerhood to school age loving the Ninja Turtles and the Muppets. They'd been raised in a commercialized, competitive time, but generally by parents more serious about their duties than parents of the late '60s and '70s. Most kids of the middle class, at least, had been given a relatively optimistic and structured world. What could the superhero subculture, with its bizarre combination of vicious violence, hard-boiled posing, whiny melodrama, and geeky pretension, say to them?

The disgust of creators weaned on earlier comics was beginning to show. Back in 1984, Marv Wolfman had married Wonder Girl to Terry Long with sweet humor and affectionate mawkishness. Nine years later, he brought Starfire and Dick Grayson to the brink of matrimony, only to have a demonically possessed Raven invade the ceremony, blow the minister to shreds, and then rape and impregnate the bride—her friend and teammate—with a blast of demonic "seed" equally evocative of semen and vomit (*New Titans* 100, July 1993). Marv

couldn't have found a more vivid expression of creative sickness and pain. He left comics soon after, preferring the cuteness of a TV cartoon of his own devising, *Pocket Dragons*.

Will Jacobs, a writer capable of good genre fiction and good absurdist humor, was utterly stumped by brief stints on DC's *Guy Gardner* and *Justice League Europe*. "The contrived 'darkness' and 'realism' of modern comics is ridiculous," he'd say. "I felt a 'real' hero who had unlimited power like Guy Gardner should be doing something astounding, so I pitched a storyline in which he'd go searching for the edge of the universe. But instead he was supposed to fight thugs and monsters on a 'realistic' Earth. The DC Earth is constantly being invaded by aliens and is full of guys with superpowers and super-devices, so 'realism' should mean dealing with the effects of that. What DC editors mean by it, though, is just a prime-time TV version of '90s New York. Back when superhero stories didn't aspire to be anything but fantasy, the stories and the milieu worked together. Now they require a suspension of disbelief that only an addict could force on himself."

His frequent collaborator, Gerard Jones, owed a prosperous DC career to an ability to slip into the schizoid aesthetic of the genre, but he ultimately found it impossible to go on. "Every script I wrote turned into another combination of the same half-dozen genre elements," he said. "Then I'd look back at John Broome and Otto Binder stories and realize that they were fresher than they'd been thirty or fifty years ago. The commercial restrictions on superheroes were narrower than they'd ever been. Even the '70s were starting to look good." Jones did a final miniseries for Dark Horse: *Oktane*, with artist Gene Ha, a satire about an antiquated cyborg in a future America full of stupid conflict, who destroys a glitzy entertainment mecca and then trudges off into the California desert (Aug. 1995). Then he trudged off into screenwriting and book writing.

The past was looking good to greater comic book talents, too. "After *Watchmen* and *Miracleman* I had become pretty thoroughly sick of superheroes," said

Alan Moore. "I had become particularly sick of the postmodern superheroes that followed in their wake.... Now everywhere I turn there're these psychotic vigilantes dealing out death mercilessly! With none of the irony that I hoped I brought to my characters.... It seemed I had unknowingly ushered in a new dark age of comic books...where there was none of the delight, freshness, and charm that I remembered of the comics of my own youth. It struck me as a terrible shame." Moore responded with *1963*, a miniseries created "Marvel method" with Stephen Bissette and Rick Veitch (Apr. 1993). "It would be fun," he said, "to attempt to recreate a more innocent age of comics...to try and create a line of imaginary comics—as they would have been in 1963! With all that innocence, and all that naïveté intact." Its innocence would prove to be more pose than reality, for what Moore wrote was a parody and an ironic reexamination of early Marvel. It was too esoteric for kids, but it was charming to old Marvelites.

Later in 1993 came James Robinson's *The Golden Age*, an Elseworlds miniseries about the autumn years of DC's first generation of heroes. It was clearly modeled on *Watchmen*, but pulled its heroes out of the darkness and irony with a fervid romanticism and a fannish devotion to the minutiae of its subjects. It led to *Starman* (Oct. 1994), an ongoing series about the son of a golden age hero in the present, in which Robinson uses the tricks of modern comics narrative to meditate on the link between present and past, hope and disillusion. It's been embraced by older fans who've drifted toward the Vertigo style but have never quite been able to leave their superheroes behind.

The real torch bearers of the old superheroes, however, the twin favorites of adult fandom, have been those two slow-rising and late-blooming scholars from '70s fandom, Mark Waid and Kurt Busiek. They're bookends: smart and garrulous, round and funny, more passionate about superhero comics than life itself, easily mocked as fanboys but amusedly impervious to the mockery. They're opposites, too: Waid the yearning romantic who built a Phantom

Zone projector to escape from the limbo of American adolescence, Busiek the analyst who joined Carol Kalish's sales force when his writing career wasn't taking off. Between them they give form to all the dreams of those fans who endure all the trends and booms and busts and remain loyal to their heroes.

When Waid took over *Flash*, he put his whole melancholy heart and ingenious brain into it. It was a modern comic book in many ways, with long, complex story arcs full of reality-warps, cliffhangers, and soap opera. But it was also full of superspeed gimmicks straight out of John Broome, sentimentality for

The new cartooning has even penetrated weary old Marvel and DC, but only with a few favored artists. Here Mike Wieringo restores some of the vivacity and lightness of Carmine Infantino to the Flash, though with a very '90s look. Inks by Jose Marzan Jr., script by Mark Waid. (*Flash* 80, Sept. 1993.)

the lost father-figure of Barry Allen, and a constant reaffirmation of the sense of heroic duty that underlay '60s comics—now stated in far more earnest than ever in Broome's stories, for Waid was defying the dominant culture where Broome had been toying with it. When Mike Wieringo, an artist with a heavily cartooned style reminiscent of Todd McFarlane's but without the terror and twisted torment, joined Waid in 1993, word began to spread that something refreshing—something *fun*—was going on in *Flash*. It didn't steal many kids from Image, but for middle-aged readers it recovered some of the excitement they remembered from the silver age, and slightly younger fans found it to be a step forward from relentless adolescent grimacing. Sales rose slowly but surely, and Waid rose in the fan-polls until he was unseating even Peter David and Neil Gaiman.

Waid and the charming cartoonist Humberto Ramos soon spun off *Impulse*, a breezily funny series about a teenage speedster from the far future stuck in an Alabama high school (Apr. 1995). In the figure of the outcast but imperturbable Impulse, being mentored by Flash and another older speedster, Waid created the perfect fantasy version of the old-time comic book geek, learning from silver age superheroes how to endure adolescent idiocy and prepare for a better future. Waid would give up higher-profile and higher-paying jobs like *X-Men*, would even take on Brian Augustyn as a cowriter on *Flash*, but nothing could pry him from *Impulse*.

While Waid was hooking up with Wieringo, Busiek was hooking up with a painter named Alex Ross. He was a blossoming superhero artist with a Buscema-like monumentality, who mastered painting just as the fad for painted art was burning out. Luckily for him, his style—heavily dependent on photo reference, using the light and surface techniques of the hyperrealism that grew out of Pop Art, hewing to mainstream comics narrative—proved to be just what superhero fans were hungry for. Ross brought in the veracity of photography without photography's tendency to deromanticize, glorifying the heroes and making them feel real at the same time.

Busiek had never shown an explosive imagination, but he had a passion for analyzing comics that went back to his endless conversations with Scott McCloud in high school, and he knew just what to do with Ross's gifts.

When *Marvels* was announced in mid-'93, it hit the fanboys and the retailers like a lightning bolt. That promotional shot—a worm's eye view of Giant-Man looming over traffic in a classic Kirby pose—was every old Marvelite's childhood fantasies made as palpable as a *Newsweek* cover. The story was just what all those old fans had been craving for years without realizing it: a photojournalist covers the rise of the superheroes, giving us a street-level view of all the major Marvel events from *Fantastic Four* 1 onward. He meditates on the nature of heroism, and comes to some conclusions that would have fit perfectly into a Lee-Ditko *Spider-Man*. Fittingly, it ends with the death of Gwen Stacy, the emotional endpoint of Marvel's silver age. It's the final stroke that makes Busiek's protagonist realize the heroic dream isn't turning out to be what he hoped it would be. He gives up on his heroes and moves on. For fans who'd clung to the love of superheroes not because they liked what was coming out but because they kept hoping to recover what they'd found in childhood, it was a chilling moment—and a validating one. Yes, it said, there had been a silver age, and it was better than what the present offered. Superhero comics could never do better than to revisit it.

That silver age, it turned out, was symbolic as much as actual. Readers too young to have read '60s comics, but feeling the same yearning for lost fantasies, the sense that there had once been something more fulfilling, were drawn to *Marvels* too. It was the one great success of early 1994, when everything else was skidding downhill.

Its timing was almost too perfect. On February 6, 1994, just about the time the sad conclusion of *Marvels* hit the stands, the bad news was buzzing through the industry: Jack Kirby was dead. He had gotten out of bed, picked up the morning paper, and suffered a heart attack. Within hours, every phone in comicdom was ringing. Comic book people had always been good at maudlin and perfunctory farewells to their dead, but this was different. This was Kirby. Barely a month before, Image had brought out an unpublished Kirby project called *Phantom Force*—and Lee, McFarlane, Liefeld, and the rest of them had teamed up to do the inking. It turned out to be Jack's last series. Dozens of artists and writers have echoed what Scott Kolins, a penciler then in his early twenties, said about the day Jack died. As a kid, Kolins had hardly known about Kirby. He'd never met him. And yet, Kirby had become his greatest inspiration, almost a mentor in absentia. He even named his dog after him. When he heard the news, he couldn't keep working. He put down his pencil and took his dog for a walk. He said, "It felt like something huge had ended."

It was as if Jack were taking comic books with him. The market went from a slump to a free fall. In February 1994, the whole industry was praying for the "summer rebound" to save it. By April, everyone knew the rebound wasn't going to happen. Retailers ordered the inevitable new releases—which were even crasser and more imitative than the previous year's—but the mullet weren't biting. Shops were going broke across the country. Smaller distributors started folding. Valiant, overextended and deeply in debt, sold out to the Acclaim video game company. The new owners allowed the editors to spend a fortune luring in artists like Dan Jurgens, Paul Gulacy, and Norm Breyfogle. Sales didn't even come close to meeting the costs. Malibu still defensively claimed to be the winner of the new-universe sweepstakes, but when winning meant sales of 20,000 instead of the competition's 15,000, it wasn't much of a win. Debts mounted until Malibu's owner, Scott Rosenberg, sold out to Marvel and vanished from comics with a big hunk of cash. Marvel would fire all the founding writers and artists, dump nearly the whole Malibu staff, and let the Ultraverse wither. Well before it was over, 1994 was being declared the worst year in the direct market's history, the scariest time in comics in twenty years. But then, no one had seen 1995.

Total comic book sales dropped by a third from 1994 to 1995. In early 1996, they fell to half what they'd been at the same time in 1995. By then, the number of comics retailers had dropped from 10,000 to about 4,000. Capital City had fallen from twenty-five warehouses to one. Gary Colabuono resigned from Classics International Entertainment after its holdings were reduced to two stores and no publishing plans. Small conventions were folding. Marvel, which had always rented twenty or thirty booth spaces at Chicago Con, rented only three in 1996, less than the average back-issue dealer.

Media interest in superheroes continued, but no longer with much heat. The *X-Men* and *Batman* cartoons passed their peaks and began to lose ratings. A new flurry of Marvel cartoons went nowhere. Marvel ended up selling seven-year exclusive TV rights for all its characters to Fox—obviously, a buyer's market. The announcement of a new *Superman* cartoon didn't set off great waves. The Image cartoons were already gone. *Lois and Clark* built itself into a modest primetime success, then began to age. *Batman Forever* did well at the box office, but other comic book movies—*Judge Dredd, Tankgirl*—had died ugly. Hollywood buzz was that James Cameron's *X-Men* and the other hot comics properties in development had cooled, and probably wouldn't happen. Dark Horse was becoming a successful production company, but only with properties like *Timecop* and *The Mask*, which the world didn't associate with comic books.

Marvel tried to act boldly in the face of others' insecurity. Copying the death of Superman and the crippling of Batman, it revealed in 1994 that the Spider-Man whom readers had been following for years was in fact a *clone* of Spider-Man, and that twenty years of continuity hadn't been "real." Readers reacted with outrage. Marvel Zombies called for boycotts of their once-beloved company. Sales fell so drastically that the news made the front page of *The Wall Street Journal*. Danny Fingeroth, the long-time editor of all the Spider-titles, was soon out of a job. New gimmicks—a Midnight Sons imprint gathering Marvel's horror heroes, a Marvel Edge imprint for even darker and grittier takes on its heroes than usual—all failed.

In early 1995, Marvel bought out a distributing company, Hero's World, and coerced retailers into buying Marvels only from it. It was a disaster. Hero's World was far too small to handle the job. Retailers protested. Some boycotted all but the top-selling X-titles. DC responded with an exclusive deal with Diamond Distributing, and Image and Dark Horse followed suit. The whole distribution infrastructure began to crack. Marvel sales plummeted further. Terry Stewart was transferred into another part of the company, away from the comics. His job was given to a tough New York lawyer named Jerry Calabrese—he had "hatchet man" written all over his face. Massive cancellations were ordered, including stalwarts like *The Punisher*, *Daredevil*, and *Conan*. The editor-in-chief position was eliminated, and Tom DeFalco was sent packing. In a clumsy imitation of DC's editorial-group system, five editors were put in charge of the company—Carl Potts, Mark Gruenwald, Bob Harras, Bob Budiansky, and Bobbi Chase—but that was another disaster. Chaos reigned.

Ron Perlman put the company on the market. Some high profile investors looked at it, including LucasFilm and Dreamworks SKG, which might actually have known what to do with Marvel's properties. They saw a loser and backed off. Marvel's stock prices dropped to nine. In January 1996, Marvel laid off 275 employees, nearly half its staff. Two of those laid off were senior editors, Budiansky and Potts. After thirteen years of loyal service and vocal defense, Carl Potts, who'd believed that if you just gave yourself to your corporation and worked hard, then everything would work out, was out of a job, out of an industry.

As if to mock Marvel's idiocy, DC abandoned the group-editor system, making Mike Carlin executive editor of the DC Universe and hired one of Marvel's fired editors, Joey Cavalieri, to take over the Superman line. Marvel promptly recreated its editor-in-chief position, giving it to Bob Harras. But

no one expected miracles. Harras's *X-Men* stable was back at the top of the sales charts, but only because it was losing sales more slowly than everything else. Gene Ha, an immensely talented young artist, took on a miniseries called *Askani Son,* written by Scott Lobdell and tied into *X-Men* continuity. It looked like a sure bet to make him enough in royalties to buy time for personal, nonsuperhero work. It didn't make him nearly enough. He, like a lot of artists in comics, began to look into self-publishing and the small press, realizing that the big companies offered no sure bets any longer.

Nearly all the new superhero lines were gone, or sliding steadily into oblivion. Valiant bought off its expensive artist contracts, slashed its production, and hired Fabian Nicieza as editor-in-chief to bring it some of that '80s Marvel magic. Few were optimistic. New publishers, mostly from other media and naive about the comics market, kept jumping in. Tekno Comics made a huge push in 1994, bought concepts from creators who thrilled fandom—from Leonard Nimoy to Neil Gaiman—but within a year was having trouble meeting its payroll. Jim Shooter found new employers, Broadway Video, but the launch of Broadway Comics in 1996 didn't stir much interest.

Image was still chugging, but at sales levels that DC would have found normal a couple of years before. Jim Lee announced that he'd be launching a new line of creator-owned alternative comics, but consisting only of small-press and self-published series that had already built up followings. One had to wonder if he was more interested in advancing the medium or in picking up a source of modest but stable income. At the same time, he and Rob Liefeld signed a deal to take over production of some of Marvel's most venerable titles: *Fantastic Four, Captain America, Avengers, Hulk, Iron Man*, and *Thor*. Both sides played it as a victory. "They tried to leave but they came back," went the Marvel implication. "We not only beat them, we're taking over their Universe," went the Image one. But the impression it left was of two drowning sailors grabbing for the same piece of flotsam. Early orders on the Lee titles were solid but nothing more, on the Liefelds, not even that.

DC weathered the storm best of all, but it couldn't reverse the downward spiral. Its big event of 1994 was *Zero Hour*, a *Crisis on Infinite Earths* redux, which made DC continuity more confusing in the name of clarifying post-*Crisis* problems. It gave every series a brief boost in sales, but it alienated more old readers than it lured in new ones, and sales soon dropped lower than they had been. In late 1995, DC teamed up with Marvel for a series of gimmicky crossovers, but sales were disappointing. DC, like the rest of the mainstream, was stuck. Nothing sold well in the direct market unless it was aimed at die-hard fans, but fanboy gimmicks drove away borderline readers and kept potential new ones at bay. The torturous conflict showed through in a DC editorial from mid-1996, in which Archie Goodwin described the company's spirit as "a combination of diversity and attitude, with a strong desire to work with like-minded creators and functioning as a unified team." Only the contradictions of comicdom could have brought an intelligent writer like Goodwin to claim that a "unified team" of "like-minded creators" can produce "diversity." About the same time, in a more candid moment, Denny O'Neil lamented, "I'm afraid we're only to selling the same, shrinking market."

As the industry kept falling, Kurt Busiek and Mark Waid kept rising. *Marvels* had made Busiek, in his own words, "a hot writer after eleven years in the business." He was immediately offered *Marvels II*, but he turned it down, foregoing a lot of likely royalty money, because he just didn't want to tell the story of the Marvel Universe in the age of angst and blood. He turned instead to *Untold Tales of Spider-Man*, a revisitation of the Ditko days (Sept. 1995), and to the project he'd been daydreaming about forever, *Kurt Busiek's Astro City* (Aug. 1995). This was his own superhero universe, with representatives of all the archetypes of the genre. Its execution, as ever with

Busiek, would be analytical rather than visceral, but its careful detail was so pleasing to superhero fans that it found a home with Image.

When Rob Liefeld asked him what he thought the next big thing in comics was going to be, Kurt answered, "The return of the John Broome hero." As Busiek interprets that icon, there is little of the humorous subtext that the writers of this book value so much in Broome's work. Busiek's Broomian hero is an earnest man of the old school who "just does what needs to be done." Like Broome's silver age creations, however, Busiek's hero is a kind of self-commentary on the superhero per se. The heroes of Astro City are memories of a childhood adulation that is no longer supported by the heroes of the present.

Alex Ross, meanwhile, moved on to *Kingdom Come* with Mark Waid. DC intended it as an exploitation of the *Marvels* audience, but Waid and Ross made it still more millenialist and more hopelessly nostalgic. It's an Elseworlds story of a near future in which a middle-aged Superman has retired because Image-style superheroes have won the world's affection. The point of division between old heroes and new is that the old ones won't kill and the new ones will. But the savagery of the new heroes causes a holocaust in the Midwest, and Superman gathers his old Justice League cohorts to restore the old order. It's a story by a fan, for fans, about the state of the superhero business. It's full of obscure DC references, woven together with Waid's infernal fanboy ingenuity. Yet its tone is of heartrending wistfulness. "Superman and Batman and Wonder Woman have stood the test of time," Waid said, "without armor, without bazookas, without veined biceps the size of cannons. They have survived— they are important—because they are a reflection of our dreams, not our nightmares. Super-heroes were created to represent the best in all of us. *Kingdom Come*...is the story of good men and good women who willingly put their lives on the line to wring order from chaos."

Kingdom Come was profoundly conservative, devoted to order and old codes, fearing chaos and

Whence come we, whither go we? As the century wanes, some of comicdom's best reflect on the heroes of their childhoods from an adult perspective. Alex Ross paints DC's heroes as ancient, august, and not at all pleased. (*Kingdom Come* #2, June 1996.)

upheaval. Ross redesigned the heroes with medieval armor and faces of stone, all uplit and glorified like something off a poster for Wagner's *Ring*—or a fascist rally. When DC scrolled his painting of Green Lantern in medieval armor across its giant TV screen at the San Diego Con, with a Wagnerian soundtrack

booming ponderously through the hall, it was impossible not to think of the monumental paintings of Hitler as a knight. It was equally impossible not to understand the power of the fantasy, the yearning for great parent figures to descend from the sky—or from the past—to save us from chaos.

Yet, there was no air of menace in *Kingdom Come*. It was a sweet but sad story, affirming the old ethics of kids' entertainment even while it acknowledged that the heroes who come to save us from savagery are themselves visitors from the past, not leaders for the future. When it debuted in May 1996, its first issue sold over 200,000 copies, making it the hot comic in a cold market. It even broke out of the comic book ghetto to pick up some national media attention and some sales to ex-fans and casual readers. But whenever Waid did a radio interview, he did so as a comic book trivia expert, a novelty act who could tell people that Captain Marvel was modeled after Fred MacMurray. Waid even admitted, as the promotional flurry for *Kingdom Come* died down, that he had no idea where to go next.

DC touted it as the next *Dark Knight*, the next *Watchmen*. But Mark Waid knew better than anyone that *Kingdom Come* wasn't the next great breakthrough for superheroes. Like *1963*, *The Golden Age*, *Astro City*, and the most touching of Waid's own *Flash* stories, it was a last visit, a toast, a sigh of resignation. It was goodbye.

CHAPTER 47

TO BE CONTINUED...?

Akid looking for exciting comics in 1996 would have had a weird time. If he liked funny animals, he could find a few good Disney comics, including Carl Barks's first story in thirty years. A little searching could unearth Archie and his deathless pals and gals. There were still a few comics licensed from TV hits and toys, even after Marvel's sinking sucked most of them under the water. If a kid wanted *heroes*—well, there were enough to boggle his mind with their sheer profusion. But if he wanted anything that stood out, any story that demanded to be *read*, he might have found nothing at all. He'd have seen row upon row of covers, all slickly produced and luridly colored, all plastered with angry steroid cases in furious battle with salivating foes, all viscerally exciting but hardly any giving a clue to narrative or character. Hardly any suggesting a mystery, a drama, or just a *situation*. And very possibly none suggesting any connection to the kid's own life.

One of yours truly was privileged to attend the 1996 San Diego convention with almost-nine-year-old Jeff Filice. Jeff, like his father and his father's peers, was a child of pop culture. His great passions were Indiana Jones, the Cartoon Network, and *Goosebumps*. He had a good time at the con, buying trading cards and action figures, getting his picture taken with Scooby-Doo. He looked at some Spider-Man comics, because he knew the character from old cartoons and computer games. But he found no comics he wanted to read, not one.

An adolescent boy would have found more to interest him at the con, at least if he had a big appetite for musclemen and bubble-women. But unless he took a long time to resolve some developmental

issues, unless he wanted to end up like the furry dudes hawking *Double Impact*—bopping to a heavy-metal boom box while aging porno starlets autographed posters of blood-dripping naked babes—he'd get quickly bored.

An adult or late adolescent would have had a better time, especially if he or she were already into the medium and understood its narrative codes. With the collapse of the superheroes, alternative comics were fighting their way back toward the spotlight. High-end venues were limited—Epic and Tundra hadn't survived the crash and Dark Horse had curtailed its line—but stubborn survivors like Dan Vado's Slave Labor Graphics were getting more attention from fans and industry insiders than they had in years. Kitchen Sink and Fantagraphics were still kicking. Caliber had gone beyond publishing *The Crow* to establish itself as a haven for creator-owned projects that tested the boundaries of the action-adventure mainstream. Matt Groening, the alternative cartoonist whose *Simpsons* had turned him into a mogul, had started his own line of Bongo Comics. Under the imprint Zongo he published works by Mary Fleener and other comic-book oddballs, giving back to the cartoon community from which he'd come. Reprint books kept the cream of comics' first hundred years in print. Japanese *manga*, thanks to Viz and Studio Proteus, reached a growing audience. Sleazy porno and splatter comics abounded, but so did smart, humane sex and horror stories.

Dave Sim quietly hit issue 200 of *Cerebus*, and more young cartoonists seemed to be following his lead into self-publishing than ever before. Jeff Smith's cartoony adventure series *Bone* had become

AS COMICS GROWS INTO THE NEXT CENTURY, CREATORS WILL ASPIRE TO MANY HIGHER GOALS THAN APPEALING TO THE "LOWEST COMMON DENOMINATOR."

IGNORANCE AND SHORT-SIGHTED BUSINESS PRACTICES WILL NO DOUBT OBSCURE THE POSSIBILITIES OF COMICS FROM TIME TO TIME AS THEY ALWAYS HAVE.

BUT THE TRUTH ABOUT COMICS CAN'T STAY HIDDEN FROM VIEW FOREVER AND SOONER OR LATER--

--THE TRUTH WILL SHINE THROUGH!

© 1993 Scott McCloud

Scott McCloud, former superhero fan, superhero artist, and superhero satirist, transcends his genre to give the comics field its first wholly original work of criticism . . .

science fiction writers and comic book creators; Verité let Vertigo creators bring their aesthetic to more reality-based stories. Larry Marder, *Beanworld* visionary and Image executive, was making a mission of bringing in properties that would appeal to female readers. He had a rich field to choose from: many of the most impressive talents to emerge in the '90s were women, from the underground-based Roberta Gregory to the more mainstream Anina Bennett. The Friends of Lulu party was pronounced *the* social event of the San Diego Con.

But less than two weeks after the convention, the field was shaken by more bad news: Diamond, the exclusive distributor for DC, Image, and Dark Horse, had bought Capital, the last powerful friend of the alternative press. Capital's accounts payable were frozen, not forever but long enough to destroy many a small publisher. Diamond, the master manipulator of the direct market, was the last major survivor of the distribution wars.

The bad news continued. In January, during the Marvel layoffs, veteran artist Jack Abel had died of heart failure in the Marvel bullpen. On the eve of the San Diego Con, a heart attack killed Mike Parobeck, an artist still in his thirties. Mike had been one of very few artists who tried to bring buoyancy and humor to mainstream comics—for which editors dismissed him as "too cartoony." By the end, his only regular venue was *Batman Adventures*, a comic book allowed to be vibrant, fun, and accessible only because it was spun off from a popular cartoon series. Mike had a number of physical problems, but all were worsened by work-related frustrations.

Then, less than a month later, heart failure took another life: Mark Gruenwald, Marvel's senior editor and continuity maven, its last major link to early fandom and the last officer of the company whom everyone agreed to like and trust. He was forty-two years old, in good health, with no history of heart disease. But no one felt the disappointment and confusion of the '90s more than Mark—because Mark loved the characters and the comics, not the money. "Mark was the weathervane," said Lia Pelosi, a former Marvel

a bona fide self-publishing success story, outselling every other black-and-white and most mainstream color comics; now it had a distribution deal with Image. Dave Lapham's self-published *Stray Bullets* was bringing Alex Toth's influence back to comics and advancing the cause of character-driven crime stories. Movements were afoot to create distribution and publishing collectives for the mutual support of self-publishers. Mentoring everybody in the ideals and realities of publishing was Will Eisner.

DC unveiled two new imprints aimed at more general readers: Helix brought together established

staffer, now out of comics. "If he was bopping around, we knew that things were going well. If he wasn't, we worried. In the end, I think comics just broke his heart."

Not everyone was prepared to pronounce comics doomed in 1996. Optimists agreed that the crash had bottomed out, and that overall sales were no worse than they'd been a decade before, when comics had been a small but rather stable pond. Some '80s veterans, those who'd managed to stay employed, were glad of it. "Too many people got into comics for the wrong reasons," they were heard to say. The ones who'd gotten in for money instead of the love of the medium were leaving now, and the fanboys and fangirls were pleased to have their playground back. The people who'd yearned for the world's recognition and acceptance ten years before had learned a bit about what the world was really like, and were more than happy to be left alone again.

In some ways, too, their long-ago yearnings have been fulfilled. Comic books are more a part of mainstream media consciousness than ever before. Comic book novelizations are standard book-industry fodder, anthologies of stories by comics writers popping up, and nearly every hot comics writer—Peter David, Neil Gaiman, Chris Claremont, Denny O'Neil—has novels in print. Art Spiegelman, on the strength of *Maus* and *Raw*, became art director of the revamped *New Yorker*, where he continues to show a gift for attracting media attention. Avon Books has experimented with a line of graphic novels under the imprint Neon Lit, beginning with an adaptation of Paul Auster's *City of Glass* by erstwhile superhero artist David Mazzucchelli. Comics industry news is reported on the business pages of newspapers. The city and news media of San Diego have helped turned the con there—now called Comic Con International—into a major tourist draw, with banners lining the streets and features filling the air waves and newsprint.

When we wrote the first edition of this book eleven years ago, no one on the publishing staff knew anything of comics except that somebody, some-

where, bought the things. This time around, our editor, the aquisitions editor, the managing editor, and several other staffers have turned out to be serious fans, with opinions of Rob Liefeld and *Kingdom Come* even stronger than our own. When we tried to describe our book to non-comics fans in 1985, many of them weren't quite sure what "superhero" referred to. Now everyone we meet seems to have at least some kind of opinion on the way superheroes reflect our society. The superhero genre may be fading as a fad, but it's been established as a staple of movies, cartoons, and toys. Manly action stars, who have traditionally awaited the chance to "do a love story" or "do a comedy," now also want to "do a superhero." Despite Sylvester Stallone's embarrassment in *Judge Dredd*, actors from Tom Cruise to Wesley Snipes have superhero projects in development. Seemingly every young producer and development executive in show biz is a fanboy, and comic books litter the offices of Hollywood. Fabian Nicieza, turning his considerable energy toward making Valiant Comics a Hollywood player, has set up several deals for 1997.

...and, as only Scott can, he gives us hope. (*Understanding Comics*, Tundra Press/Viking Press, 1993.)

© 1993 Scott McCloud

MEANWHILE...

THE TRUTH ABOUT EVERYTHING AND ALL THE REST!

HEY, FRANK, HOW YA DOIN', BUDDY?

WH-WHAH THAH— SKINNY?

FRANK'S RECENT EXPERIENCE CERTAINLY SEEMS TO HAVE HAD AN EFFECT.

THAT'S ALL HE'LL SAY. I'M WORRIED.

HE SEEMS TO BE IN A WORLD ALL HIS OWN.

© 1996 Mike Allred

Can Mike Allred's brain-battered hero be speaking for the whole superhero icon here? (*Madman Comics* #11, 1996.)

cially of the magic that happens between the panels—came as a revelation. His passion for the medium and his unshakable faith in its limitless potential came as an emotional liferaft for comics creators sinking in the despair of 1994 and 1995.

That *Understanding Comics* immediately became a must-read for everyone serious about creating comics wasn't surprising. The surprise came when Viking Press picked it up for bookstore republication and found a solid market for it outside comicdom. McCloud found himself invited to symposia of commercial illustrators and designers, found his book discussed seriously in the fine arts press. McCloud drew hardly a line for two years, as promoting *Understanding Comics* turned into a full-time job. Evidently a lot of grown-ups thought comics were important enough to understand.

Perhaps the superheroes had done their work. Other forces had helped transform the medium, of course: the undergrounds, *Maus*, and the increasingly adult comic strips of the newspapers. But the underground legacy might not have survived without the comic shops made possible by superhero collectors. Spiegelman might not have made it through the lean, early years of *Raw* without readers and critics who'd come of age in the intellectually ambitious superhero fandom of the 1970s. And readers of newspaper strips who became curious about comic books might have found none to hold their interest—maybe none at all—without the alternative comics created by all those ex-superhero fans in the '80s.

With that work done, the superheroes may have no artistic frontiers left. Most of them survive now by the grace of those fans who are still attached to the recycled icons of the genre. When Alan Moore needs cash to support *From Hell* and other projects, he bangs out scripts for *Spawn* and other Image series. But there's no art, no daring in them. Scott McCloud is writing some Superman stories, but only to pay his bills while he prepares his new project, *The Further Adventures of Abraham Lincoln*. No superhero project stirred up any excitement in comicdom in 1996, except the symbolic leave-taking of *Kingdom Come*.

In 1993, while most of the comic book industry was keeping its eye on the sales figures of new superhero universes, Tundra released the book that had been keeping Scott McCloud busy and invisible for two years. *Understanding Comics* was the first serious effort to create a critical vocabulary unique to the medium—and, with that genius for inventing the obvious thing that everyone else has overlooked, Scott executed it entirely in comics form. Along the way, he attempted a new vision of the relationship between words and pictures in fine art and literature. He overreached himself a bit there, and missed the boat on some of his cultural history, but his explication of the tools of comic book storytelling—espe-

And yet, the whole history of superheroes shows that every time they look finished, something happens. The one alternative-press superhero hit of the '90s, Michael Allred's *Madman*, reads like a commentary on the fatigue and emptiness of the genre—and yet somehow Allred keeps spinning out new stories, exploring the absurd and surreal possibilities of an unheroic superman in a world somewhat like our own. And with every jump he makes, from self-publishing to Tundra to Dark Horse's Legends imprint to Hollywood, he finds more fans. Maybe this is what the new heroes of our tired and overstimulated culture will look like: aware of their soul-sickness, unable to control their world, but somehow finding a path by affirming absurdity.

On the opposite end of the cultural spectrum are young cartoonists like Ben Herrera and David Antoine Williams, who have become devout Christians and believe they can use superheroes to tell stories of genuine moral and spiritual force. Williams's *Spectrum* has found a home with Tapestry, Caliber's new imprint for kid-friendly projects. Meanwhile, Scott Kolins plans to play with the Christian mythos less devoutly but with equal moral conviction in his *Adam*. Kolins's hero, Jack Kirby, often drew on the Bible for inspiration, and Kolins hopes that in spinning a heroic legend out of Genesis he'll rediscover the lost roots of the heroes.

And then there are the women. While most comics women fled superheroes as the Todd McFarlanes and Jim Lees took over, some new female creators have been drawn to the genre by phenomena like the *Batman* movies and cartoon. Devin Kalile Grayson and Julie Huffman, two Bay Area writers who move easily through diverse worlds—mainstream, alternative, straight, and queer—are reexam-

Bix the Trumpet-Playing Dog, the most popular new hero of Gerard Jones and Mark Badger's Wonderland, which is drawn completely electronically and posted—free to all customers—on the World Wide Web at http://www.interactive.net/~thehop/lemon_custard. Anything is possible in Wonderland—as it may be in comics.

ining the superheroic icon with emotional daring, humor, and reverence. Neither of them read comics as a kid or was aware of comics fandom prior to 1989. By 1996, they'd made their first incursions into the comics industry (Grayson on *Batman Chronicles*, Huffman on *Solitaire*), and whoever has seen their work has noticed it. They may open the door to a whole new way of using superheroes to explore questions of gender, community, and responsibility.

But what of the industry itself, as attrition winnows the ranks of fans who climbed aboard in the '80s and early '90s? If the new generation of little kids isn't discovering comics, and if the speculator market isn't lucrative enough to tempt teenagers into the hobby, will there be enough readers in five or ten years to sustain the comic shops? One way to get comics to new readers—badly neglected because it fails to excite the imagination of fans and fans-turned-pros—is non-fiction. Larry Gonick's *Cartoon History* books are selling better than ever, as are the similar *For Beginners* books. DC's Paradox Press has done well with *The Big Book of Urban Legends* and its sequels. Valiant will launch new Classics and Young Readers lines for bookstore distribution in 1997. Robert Crumb, more in the public consciousness than ever after a former cartoonist and comic shop owner named Terry Zwigoff made him the subject of a documentary, has told the story of Frank Kafka in graphic form. Joyce Brabner and Harvey Pekar weave their autobiographical and political work tighter and tighter together with projects like *Our Cancer Year*. Schools and public services groups are using comics to disseminate information to kids and people unaccustomed to reading books. Mark Badger, who tried to make it as a superhero artist in the heady mid-'80s but refused to adjust to the Image era, has broken new ground with comics on inner-city activism, Cambodian refugees, and pesticide contamination of farm workers. In 1996, he created *Marks and Angles* for Caliber Press to bring his artistic, political, and humorous explorations together in a regular forum.

Now Badger finds himself pioneering a new frontier, one that many people see as the medium's best hope. In early 1995, his *Batman: Jazz* miniseries announced his emergence as the master of drawing and painting comics completely on computer. His computer renderings of postwar Gotham, in fact, drew far more attention than Gerard Jones's story of Batman meeting Charlie Parker. Badger and Jones then created their own comics universe, *Wonderland*, for the World Wide Web (http://www.interactive.net/~thehop/lemon_custard)— the first comics created completely on computer, and specifically for online distribution, by established creators. *Wonderland* is free of charge, existing solely for the rejuvenation of its creators and the expansion of its medium. It embraces some oddball riffs on superheroes—the Human Ideal and the Haunted Man—but throws them together with a socialist dancing skeleton named Delores and the jazz-king of Voodoo Island, Orpheus Black.

In 1996, America Online contracted with Marvel for a *Spider-Man* series, the first major commercial attempt at online comics, and hired Badger to translate the material into computer terms. Badger's visual effects were stunning, and would be impossible on the printed page, but the stories and art were standard Marvel stuff. Many in the industry predict that the "information superhighway" is the future—and in some ways comics, with their combination of text and pictures, are perfect for computers—but so far that future seems far off. The time required to download comics files makes for an inconvenient and expensive way to get a small chunk of visual narrative. There's no way to make online comics collectible, which makes them uninteresting to most superhero hobbyists, and yet so far nearly all of them are targeted at those very hobbyists. Breakthroughs—not just technological but conceptual—are needed for comics to survive electronically.

For the comic book to survive in any form, it may have to break from the community that's evolved around it over the past four decades. It may have to become like text, music, and video: part of the greater culture, more global, more atomized, and far less esoteric. That might create more room for idiosyncratic visions—or less. It might also create more opportunities for huge commercial success—but if so, that success will have to come by creating comics compelling to millions of people, not by manipulating a collectibles market.

And yet, if such a break is to happen, that same community may have to play a crucial role. If creators and fans can direct their immense love and knowledge of the medium away from their sheltered world and outward to unimagined fields, they might be able to bring the comic book back to life yet again. The crash of '94 and '95 could prove to be the beginning of the end, or it could prove to be a blessing in disguise. Not since the 1950s have there been so many unemployed and marginally employed comics professionals, freed of the luxury and the obligation to keep the industry's gears turning, forced to reinvent themselves and their work.

Whether or not the citizens of comicdom prove to be up to that challenge, there's no disputing that they, like the superheroes, did their work. They saved the medium during the crisis of the 1970s, when every force of economics, culture, and the industry's own shoddiness seemed to be pushing it toward destruction. They gave it the artistic and commercial tools to escape the spin-racks and dare to be a vital participant in American culture. Even when, in their secret hearts, they could never see themselves except as timid teenage geeks, they dared to play with the big boys. And the community goes on. In the long run, the medium's greatest resource may prove to be simply comicdom's ability to endure success and failure alike, to ride out fads and discouragements, and still remain comicdom. For that reason alone, the comic book field may never again be the tragic field it once was.

When Gerard Jones bumped into Paul Levitz among the back-issue dealers at a convention and announced that he'd burned out on comics and was leaving them for other media, Levitz nodded and said, "Good idea. Take a rest and then come back." Jones was about to protest that this *wasn't* a rest, that he was *really leaving*, damn it—and then he thought of the bag full of old *Little Archies* and *Strange Adventures* in his hand, thought of the six hundred dollars he'd just dropped on Dick Sprang's new Batman lithographs, thought of the Jack Kirby Memorial Tribute he'd just attended. And he knew that comicdom was like the Catholic Church and the CIA. No one ever *really* leaves.

That evening, Jones took a seat in the hotel bar and watched the parade of conventioneers. Will Eisner held court at a table surrounded by Scott McCloud, Dave Olbrich, Jeff Smith, and assorted retailers, giving a mini-seminar in self-publishing. Larry Marder zipped by with Rob Liefeld and Cathy Christian. Heidi MacDonald, now a weary Disney editor, plopped down with Mike Baron and Anina Bennett. Denny O'Neil was being interviewed by a newspaper reporter. Gil Kane—frail from a bout with cancer but still magnificent in navy blazer, white tie, and silver hair—entered with Gary Groth. Groth was in his forties now, but still boyish, still wary. When Kane headed toward the corner where Julie Schwartz sat, Groth drifted off.

Schwartz was eighty-one but ageless, fresh from yet another Strange Schwartz Stories panel but still scanning the room for someone to swap anecdotes with. No sooner had Kane joined him than Jim Shooter emerged from the shadows in his three-piece suit, the picture of the indestructible executive. The three fell into conversation as if they'd been together for hours, or as if they were continuing some conversation from another convention, another year. Telling Mort Weisinger stories? Remembering the script for *Captain Action* that a teenage Shooter had once sold to a fiftyish Schwartz for a ballsy Kane-at-midlife to draw? Then Schwartz gave the chipmunk grin that always signaled a wisecrack, and the laughter of Shooter and Kane carried across the bar.

Had it really been only forty years since *Showcase* number 4?

A

Aardvark-Vanaheim, 275, 278

Aargh, 318

Abel, Jack, 368

Abruzzo, Tony, 57

Academy of Arts and Sciences, 64-65

Acclaim video game company, 363

Action Comics, 6, 14, 15, 27, 81, 138, 183, 196, 232, 260-261, 302, 328, 352

Adam, 371

Adam Link stories, 171171

Adams, Art, 316

Adams, Neal, 121, 122, 123, 132, 133, 136, 138, 142, 146, 148, 151, 162, 165, 172, 178, 180, 181, 188, 194, 196, 207, 210, 213, 220, 222, 244, 246, 251, 252, 253, 262, 266, 275, 311

Adam Strange, 20-23, 27, 78, 331-332

Adkins, Dan, 109, 114, 133, 135, 153, 215

Adler, Jack, 98, 184

Adolescent Radioactive Black Belt Hamsters, 303

Adventure Comics, 14, 80, 81, 138, 174
    Superboy, 85

Adventures into the Unknown, 46

The Adventures of Ford Fairlane, 322

Adventures of Jerry Lewis, 75

Adventures of Jesus, 118

Adventures of Rex the Wonder Dog, 8

Adventures of Superman, 302, 328, 352

The Adventures of the Fly, 41

The Adventures of Young Dr. Masters, 41

African-Americans. *See* Black characters

AIDS, 29

Airboy, 277

Albano, John, 177

Alcala, Alfredo, 170, 186, 253

Alien Legion, 263

Aliens, 316, 322

Alien Worlds, 252

All-American Comics, 6

All American Men of War, 56

Allen, Irwin, 44

Alley Awards, 67

All in Color for a Dime (Lupoff & Thompson), 143

Allred, Mike, 370

All-Star Comics, 195, 213

All Star Squadron, 261, 294

All Star Western, 8

All the President's Men, 207

Alpha Flight, 269

Alter-Ego, 64

Amazing Adult Fantasy, 59

Amazing Adventures, 137, 165

Amazing Heroes, 254, 299, 305-306, 310, 314, 338

Amazing High Adventure, 293

Amazing Spider-Man, 329

The Amazing World of DC, 209

Ambush Bug, 286

Amendola, Sal, 179, 285

The American, 304, 316, 322

American Comics Group, 40, 45-46

American Flagg!, 273-274, 277, 282, 303

American Graffiti, 187

American News Company, 5, 8
    Western Printing and Lithography and, 42

American Splendor, 218, 279, 297

America Online, 372

Americomics, 275

Amethyst, Princess of Gemworld, 264

Amos, Tori, 322, 334

Anderson, Brent, 246, 252

Anderson, Laurie, 307

Anderson, Murphy, 11, 19, 23, 24, 34, 35, 38, 97, 121, 144, 150, 152, 182, 196, 285
    and *Adam Strange,* 21
    The Atom, 65
    at New York Con, 1965, 67

Andrews, Julie, 222

Andru, Ross, 56, 57, 141, 154, 185, 191, 193, 196, 240, 250

Angry Isis Press, 318

Animal Man, 333, 350

Annenberg, Max, 5

Annenberg, Moe, 5

Anthro, 129, 170

Ant-Man (Tales to Astonish), 69

Anything Goes, 311

Apa 5, 212

Aparo, Jim, 13, 111, 112, 126, 127, 142, 174, 179

Apel, D. Scott, 317

Aquaman, 29-30, 127, 138, 205, 221, 350

Aragonés, Sergio, 127, 187, 253, 256, 320

Arak, 262

Archie, 140

Archie Comics, 33, 40, 95, 128, 194, 321
    Comics Code and, 10
    in 1950s, 41

Argosy Magazine, 4

Arkham Asylum, 327, 332-333